Truth

A Contemporary Reader

Also available from Bloomsbury

Skepticism: From Antiquity to the Present edited by Diego Machuca and Baron Reed

The Philosophy of Death Reader edited by Markar Melkonian

The Philosophy of Knowledge: A History edited by Stephen Hetherington, Nicholas D. Smith, Henrik Lagerlund, Stephen Gaukroger and Markos Valaris

Truth

A Contemporary Reader

Edited by
Douglas Edwards

B L O O M S B U R Y
NEW DELHI • LONDON • OXFORD • NEW YORK • SYDNEY

BLOOMSBURY INDIA
Bloomsbury Publishing India Pvt. Ltd
Second Floor, LSC Building No. 4, DDA Complex, Pocket C-6&7,
Vasant Kunj, New Delhi 110070

BLOOMSBURY, BLOOMSBURY ACADEMIC INDIA and the Diana logo are
trademarks of Bloomsbury Publishing Plc

First published in India 2025
First published in Great Britain 2019

Cover design: Avni Patel
Cover Image © Steve Stringer Photography / Getty Images

This edition published with permission from Bloomsbury Publishing Plc,
50 Bedford Square, London, WC1B3DP, UK

A catalogue record for this book is available from the British Library.
A catalog record for this book is available from the Library of Congress.

ISBN: 978-93-61317-54-5

Typeset by Deanta Global Publishing Services, Chennai, India
Printed in India by Manipal Technologies Limited, Manipal

To find out more about our authors and books
visit www.bloomsbury.com and sign up for our newsletters

Contents

Preface

What is truth? To what extent does truth depend on the world, and to what extent does it depend on us? Can we know what is true? Why – if at all – should we care about truth? This reader brings together some key readings in the contemporary study of truth that offer answers to these central philosophical questions about the nature and value of truth, and the connections between them. These connections provide an important reminder that much of the seemingly abstract philosophical work on the nature of truth has very real implications for the way that we think of truth in our ordinary lives, and the significance that we give to truth both personally and culturally.

The reader is aimed at those interested in teaching or studying the contemporary landscape of work on truth in analytic philosophy. Accordingly, I have tried to balance the need to give the reader a sense of current work on the topics with the need to give an understanding of the historical background. I hope that the balance has been well struck, and I have given detailed accounts in the introductions to the chapters to bring the reader up to speed on any historically relevant views, and included references in the further readings sections to direct those who are interested in the historical background to the appropriate sources.

In order to keep the reader at a reasonable length, I also had to be selective about the number of pieces included in each section. I aim to have provided enough readings to give a broad account of each theory or issue considered without overwhelming the reader with too much material. My hope is that teachers who want to use some, but not all, of the papers, are able to do so without too much surplus, and those who want to use more are able to use the further reading suggestions to structure additional content.

The reader is structured in such a way as to be useful as a basis for constructing a class on the nature and value of truth. It starts with debates between the 'traditional' theories of truth – correspondence theory, coherence theory, and pragmatism – in the first two sections, before moving on to the deflationary, primitivist, and pluralist views that became prominent in the late twentieth and early twenty-first centuries. These views all – in their own way – question the underlying assumptions behind the 'traditional' debates about truth, and pose interesting questions about philosophical methodology and the goals of philosophical analysis in general. Whilst these discussions tend to be framed in terms of topics in the nature of truth, in many papers these issues are intertwined with key issues concerning the value and normativity of truth. The value and normativity of truth is also explicitly addressed in the final section. The material in the book can be used on its own, or to provide a basis for teachers to develop in their own way if they choose, with some suggestions to do so included in the further reading sections.

Each section begins with an introduction written by me, and I also provide a general introduction to the study of truth at the beginning. These introductions are based on my experience teaching work on truth to students in the past ten years or so, and are informed by the parts of the views that students typically find tricky. They are intended to provide a background to the topics and readings discussed, and I hope they prove useful. I have aimed to be as neutral as possible in these introductions, but anyone interested in more details on my own views about the subject can find them in my paper in the volume (Ch. 17), and in my recent monograph *The Metaphysics of Truth* (Oxford University Press, 2018).

Acknowledgements

This project has been a few years in the making, and there are a number of people I am grateful to for helping to bring it to fruition. I'd first like to thank Colleen Coalter at Bloomsbury, who worked with me on the project from the beginning, whose advice and guidance was invaluable throughout. One of the main challenges in doing the reader was working out how to get a useful text at a reasonable price given the high costs of permissions to reproduce material, and Colleen's help to balance these needs was vital to the project, as was her work to negotiate fees with the various publishers involved. I am also grateful to Andrew Wardell for his help on these matters, and to Becky Holland, Giles Herman, and Rennie Alphonsa for their assistance during the production process.

I would also like to thank all the authors who I had contact with about including their papers in this volume. All were very helpful and attentive to the issues faced when putting together a reader such as this, and I am very grateful for their help. Many provided me with formatted files of their papers, and all were very understanding and willing to help keep the costs of using the material low whenever they could. Thank you very much to all.

I am grateful to Utica College for offering additional financial assistance to put towards the costs of permissions, and to my colleagues in the philosophy department, Chris Riddle and Leonore Fleming, for their help and encouragement.

The idea for this reader first came from teaching a class on the nature of truth at University College Dublin in 2009. The text I used then was Michael Lynch's *The Nature of Truth* (MIT Press, 2001). While excellent, I felt there was room for a more streamlined and updated alternative. I subsequently taught versions of the class at the University of Aberdeen, Hamilton College, and Utica College, which enabled me to further develop ideas for the reader, particularly the idea of including focus on the value of truth. I am very grateful to the excellent students I have been fortunate to have the opportunity to teach in these classes, who were no small part of my motivation to work on the project. I would also like to thank my teachers, particularly Crispin Wright, Michael Lynch and Patrick Greenough, who cultivated my interest in truth, and whose work has helped shape the contemporary debates about truth discussed in this volume. Thanks also to Nikolaj Pedersen, Cory Wright, Aaron Cotnoir, Filippo Ferrari, Jeremy Wyatt, Will Gamester, Sebastiano Moruzzi, and Nathan Kellen for many interesting conversations about both researching and teaching truth over the years.

Finally, and most significantly, as always I would like to thank my family, particularly my wife Alex, who has been a constant source of support, and my son Theo, who has been a constant source of amusement.

The original publication details for the articles in this reader are as follows.

1. Bertrand Russell, 'Truth and Falsehood', was originally published in Russell's *Problems of Philosophy*, Williams and Holgate, 1912. It is in the public domain.

2. Marian David, 'Truth-Making and Correspondence', was originally published in E. J. Lowe (ed.), *Truth and Truth-Making*. Acumen Press, 2009. Reprinted with permission of the author and Taylor and Francis.

3. Hartry Field, 'Tarski's Theory of Truth', was originally published in *The Journal of Philosophy* 69 (13), 1972. Reprinted with permission of the author and The Journal of Philosophy.

4. Dorothy Grover, 'Truth and Language – World Connections', was originally published in *The Journal of Philosophy* 87 (12), 1990. Reprinted with permission of the author and *The Journal of Philosophy*.

5. F.H. Bradley, 'On Truth and Copying', was originally published in *Mind*, 16 (62), 1907. It is in the public domain.

6. Paul Thagard, 'Coherence, Truth, and the Development of Scientific Knowledge', was originally published in *Philosophy of Science*, 74 (1), 2007. Reprinted with permission of the author and The University of Chicago Press.

7. Charles S. Peirce, 'How to Make Our Ideas Clear', was originally published in *Popular Science Monthly* 12, 1878. It is in the public domain.

8. William James, 'Pragmatism's Conception of Truth', was originally published in *The Journal of Philosophy* 4, 1907. It is in the public domain.

9. Cheryl Misak, 'Pragmatism on Solidarity, Bullshit, and Other Deformities of Truth' was originally published in *Midwest Studies in Philosophy* 32 (1), 2008. Reprinted with permission of the author and Wiley-Blackwell.

10. Paul Horwich, 'A Defense of Minimalism', was originally published in *Synthese* 126 (1), 2001. Reprinted with permission of the author and Springer. Paul Horwich also provided new additions to the article for this volume.

11. Hartry Field, 'Deflationist Views of Meaning and Content', was originally published in *Mind* 103 (411), 1994. Reprinted with permission of the author and Oxford University Press.

12. Dorothy Grover, 'On Two Deflationary Truth Theories', was originally published in J. Dunn and A. Gupta (eds.), *Truth or Consequences*, Kluwer Academic Publishers, 1990. Reprinted with permission of the author and Springer. Dorothy Grover also provided new additions to the paper for this volume.

13. Matti Eklund, 'What is Deflationism about Truth?', was originally published in *Synthese*, online first, 2017. It is an open access publication, and is reprinted with permission of the author.

14. Donald Davidson, 'The Folly of Trying to Define Truth', was originally published in *The Journal of Philosophy* 93 (6), 1996. Reprinted with permission of The Journal of Philosophy.

15. Trenton Merricks, 'Truth as a Primitive', was originally published in Merricks's *Truth and Ontology*, Oxford University Press, 2007. Reprinted with permission of the author and Oxford University Press.

16. Crispin Wright, 'Truth: A Traditional Debate Reviewed', was originally published in *Canadian Journal of Philosophy* 28, Supplement 1, 1998. Reprinted with permission of the author and Taylor and Francis.

17. Douglas Edwards, 'Simplifying Alethic Pluralism', was originally published in *The Southern Journal of Philosophy*, 49 (1), 2011. Reprinted with permission of the author and Wiley-Blackwell. I lightly edited the paper for this volume.

18. Gila Sher, 'In Search of a Substantive Theory of Truth', was originally published in *The Journal of Philosophy* 101 (1), 2004. Reprinted with permission of the author and *The Journal of Philosophy*.

19. Linda Zagzebski, 'Intellectual Motivation and the Good of Truth', was originally published in L. Zagzebski and M. DePaul (eds.), *Intellectual Virtue: Perspectives From Ethics and Epistemology*. Oxford University Press, 2003. Reprinted with permission of the author and Oxford University Press.

20. Michael P. Lynch, 'Minimalism and the Value of Truth', was originally published in *The Philosophical Quarterly*, 54 (217), 2004. Reprinted with permission of the author and Oxford University Press.

21. Huw Price, 'Truth as Convenient Friction', was originally published in *The Journal of Philosophy* 100 (4), 2003. Reprinted with permission of the author and *The Journal of Philosophy*.

22. Catherine Z. Elgin, 'True Enough', was originally published in *Philosophical Issues* 14 (1), 2004. Reprinted with permission of the author and Wiley-Blackwell.

Aside from the three cases noted above of the papers by Horwich, Grover, and myself, I have endeavoured to present each of these works in their original form, and have only engaged in minor editing to some of the references in some of the chapters in order to make the reader easier to navigate. Any editorial interjections are clearly indicated. I chose to retain the original formatting and language of the papers in order to most accurately reproduce the original texts. As some authors wrote in UK English, and some in US English, this means that there is some variation in use of certain punctuation marks, such as quotation marks, across different chapters. I have also retained the original referencing formats, though footnotes have been changed to endnotes. I trust that this will not cause undue confusion, and mention it here just make the reader aware.

General introduction

1 Truth: An introduction

Truth plays a familiar, and often significant, role in our lives. From a young age we are told to tell the truth, and we get in trouble if we don't. We all know the oath taken in court to tell the truth, the whole truth and nothing but the truth. Many of us spend a lot of our time pursuing truth, whether it be the pursuit of the profound, such as a biologist aiming to discover the truth about what cures cancer, or the everyday, such as you trying to work out the truth about where your wallet is. Perhaps because of this familiarity, philosophical inquiry into truth is as old as the subject itself, with the question of what separates the true from the false being one of the major philosophical questions. As with many topics in philosophy, this interest in the subject has led to a rich and fascinating array of discussions about what truth is, and why we should care about it. The chapters in this volume represent the work of some of the most significant philosophical figures in the last couple of centuries on truth, and you will see that there are many different proposals about what the nature of truth is, and indeed, whether we should take truth to have a nature at all.

2 Some preliminaries

Suppose you are on a jury in an important trial. A key witness enters the courtroom. What are they expected to do? Familiarly, they are expected to tell the truth, the whole truth and nothing but the truth. By implication, they are also expected to *not* do something else: state falsehoods, or tell lies. This is a very specific task which is given to the witness, and one that can help us understand the project of trying to uncover the nature of truth. There is a whole host of things that the witness could say, and of all the possible things they could say, they are being asked to select some very specific things to say: the true things. The witness is expected to state all and only those relevant things that are true.

Let's compare an analogous case. Suppose I work in a hardware store, and you come in looking for some screws, some metal screws, in particular. You don't know what size you'll need, so you ask me to bring you all the metal screws I have. This sets me a very specific task: out of all the screws in the store, which holds metal and plastic screws, I am to bring you just the metal screws. This requires me to single out the screws that are metal; and separate them from the screws that are plastic. Note that there are two things that are important for me to be able to fulfil my task here: (1) there must be something that *being metal* consists in, which makes it in principle possible for me to separate the metal screws from the plastic ones, and (2) I must have some way of telling the metal from the non-metal screws. Condition (1) suggests that there is some essence, or nature, to metallicness, and (2) suggests that it is possible for me to grasp that essence, or nature. In the hardware store case, we can suppose that both of these conditions are fulfilled: there is some nature to metallicness, which marks the metal screws out from the plastic screws, and this nature gives rise to features which makes me able to discern the metal from the non-metal.

With this in mind, let's now return to the case of the witness expected to tell the truth. It seems as though the two conditions we noted for metallicness need to also hold for truth. For the witness to live up to her oath, it seems as though (1) there needs to be some nature to truth, which makes it possible in principle to separate the true things that could be said from the false ones; and (2) the witness must have some way of telling the true things from the false things. If (1) fails, and there is no nature of truth, then the witness's task seems impossible: you cannot give someone something that isn't there, just as the hardware store clerk cannot give you metal screws if there is no such thing as metal. If there is no nature of truth, how is she to tell the truth? If (2) fails, then she is also faced with an impossible task, as, even if we suppose that there *is* a nature of truth, and also that there are true things she could say which differ from the false things she could say, her inability to discern one from the other makes her unable to communicate truths as opposed to falsehoods.

Now, while they are closely connected, (1) and (2) are different things. Condition (1) is what we find when we think about the nature of truth, and this is what a number of the chapters in this collection focus on: What is it, precisely, that truths have that falsehoods lack? Projects that engage with (1) take it that truth is a real feature of the world, and that some things that are said or believed have that feature, others lack it, and it is a central job of philosophy to discern what that feature is. This is what we might call, the *alethic* question: it focuses just on the nature of truth. Condition (2), on the other hand, is more concerned with how (if at all) we can *know* the truth. This is what we might call the *epistemic* question: suppose that there is a batch of truths available, how is it possible for us to know what they are? Different philosophers take different stances on the relations between the alethic and epistemic questions. Some see that a key job of a theory of truth is to provide answers to *both*: it should explain what truth is, and how truth is knowable, and any theory that, for example, answers the alethic question at the expense of the epistemic question is lacking. Others think that the two are independent: a theory of truth must answer the alethic question, but it is a job for another branch of philosophy, the theory of knowledge, to answer the second. As we will see as we progress through the readings, both of these stances are represented throughout the truth debate. One thing we can perhaps say at this stage is that the alethic question is the primary question when it comes to considering the nature of truth per se, and that then different theories take different views on the importance of the epistemic question.

3 Predicates, concepts, properties

It is worth at this point briefly pausing to note some distinctions which are important in the truth literature, particularly when we talk about the nature of truth. These distinctions are between the truth predicate, the truth concept and the truth property. The truth *predicate*, typically taking the form 'is true' is the linguistic entity appended to certain sentences, as in '"snow is white" is true'. One who competently uses the words 'true' and 'truth' can be said to possess the concept of truth, and an analysis of the concept of truth will aim to uncover what those conditions of competent use consist in. The *property* of being true is what is ascribed by the truth predicate.

To get clearer on these distinctions, consider the following analogy with water (this analogy is originally due to Alston (2002)). We have the predicate 'is water', which we use to say of a certain substance that it is water (e.g. 'the liquid in the bottle is water'). We also have the concept of water, that any competent user of the term 'water' understands (e.g. that water is a clear, colourless, tasteless liquid, that it comes out of taps, and runs through rivers and streams). We also have the *property* of being water, which is what the stuff that corresponds to the concept, and is referred to by the predicate, *consists in*. Scientific discoveries have deemed the property of water to be identical to the property of being H_2O, and this tells us what the nature of water is. In the water case, then, the system works as follows. We have the water predicate, which is used to ascribe a particular property – being water – to particular substances. Competent users of the water predicate will be said to possess the concept of water, and this concept demarcates a kind of worldly substance. The property of water captures the essence of this worldly substance (H_2O). Note also that it is not a condition on competent users of the concept that they be aware of the nature of the property (as indeed was not the case before the discovery of water as H_2O): possessing the concept does not necessarily require possessing knowledge of the essence of the property.

Most of the investigations into the *nature* of truth concern the essence of the truth property. However, as we will see, in the story of truth, the concept of truth and the truth predicate have important roles to play.

4 The nature of truth: An overview

Given our distinctions above, we can conceive of debates about the nature of truth as debates about the property of being true. Historically speaking, the three 'traditional' theories of truth – correspondence theory, coherence theory and pragmatism – take three different views on what the nature of this property is. In the twentieth and twenty-first centuries, however, a significant trend emerged which questioned a key presupposition of this project: that there is a substantial nature of truth to be uncovered. So-called 'deflationary' positions emerged which held that the three traditional theories had it all wrong: they were looking for a nature of truth that was not there at all. As we will discuss in the deflationism section, whether this means that deflationists think that there is no property of being true is a complex matter, but let us for now content ourselves with the idea that the claim is that there is no interesting, or substantial, nature to truth which is worthy of philosophical investigation. The reaction to deflationism has consisted not only in the re-assertion of the traditional views but also in the development of new directions, namely primitivism, which holds that there is a nature of truth but that it is unanalysable; and pluralism, which holds that the nature of truth may not be uniform across different subject-matters.

We can represent the broad structure of these positions in the following flow chart:

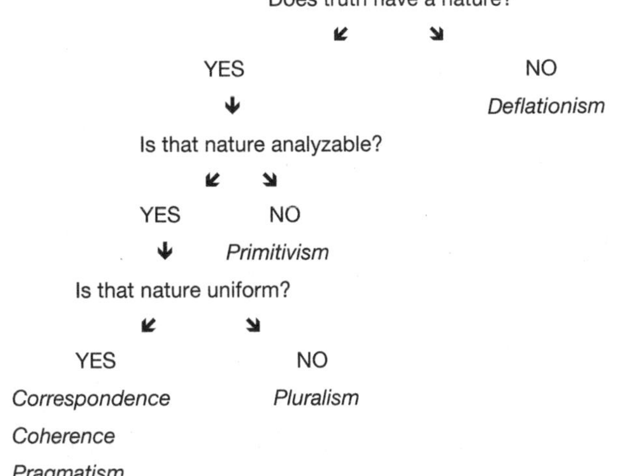

We will delve into some of the complexities of each of the positions below and in subsequent section introductions, but this should give you an idea of how each of the views relate to each other.

4.1 Correspondence, coherence, pragmatism

It is interesting to note that the three 'traditional' views about truth which are standardly opposed to one another each end up on the same terminal node of the flow chart. This is because these three views, despite taking very different stances on what the nature of truth *is*, share the key assumptions that (a) there is a nature of truth; (b) it is analysable; and (c) it is uniform. These assumptions are not unusual; indeed, they tend to be the default assumptions driving most projects of analysis of key philosophical concepts. The assumption tends to be that there is a nature of *F*, whether *F* is truth, knowledge, goodness, beauty; that this nature is analysable in terms of a single set of necessary and sufficient conditions that yield a biconditional of the form *x* is *F* if and only if … . This understanding of philosophical analysis which stems from Plato's *Euthyphro* is the standard understanding of philosophical method, so it is unsurprising that this approach is represented in the truth debate.

So, these three views all hold that there is a nature of truth – an interesting property of being true – which is analysable by the standard method of philosophical analysis, and that is uniform in the sense that there is only one correct analysis of this property. What they differ on is the form that this analysis should take. *Correspondence theories* typically think of truth as reflecting reality: true propositions represent reality as it really is. On this view, truth is held to be a relation between a proposition and the non-propositional world. The idea is that we see the world and our attempts to represent the world as entirely separate, just like we might think of a map and the terrain it aims to represent as entirely separate. Propositions are like maps attempting to represent terrain, and they are true just when they do accurately represent how things are, just as a map is a good map just in case it accurately represents the terrain it purports to.

Coherence theories of truth take a different tack. They are sceptical of the correspondence theorist's ability to separate *the world* from our abilities to represent it. Also, returning to our distinctions between (1) and (2) above, they are concerned that such an approach makes it impossible for us to ever know what propositions are true, for to do so would require us to 'see' reality as it really is, outside of any means we have of representing it, which seems on the face of it to be impossible. Accordingly, they think that what makes a proposition true is its coherence with other propositions as part of a coherent system. Different coherence theories cash this idea out differently, but the broad idea is that, when considering the truth of a proposition, we do not look for it to match the non-propositional world; instead, we look to see how it fits with other propositions taken to be true.

Pragmatist theories share the coherence theorist's concerns about correspondence theory, but look in slightly different places to understand truth. Pragmatists are concerned with the practical value of having true beliefs, and think that true beliefs must play a particular practical role in order to qualify as being true. Different pragmatists theories develop this idea differently, but all pragmatist views give a key role to the notion of verification: true beliefs are those that we can verify to be true. This also ties truth to the notion of justification, as true beliefs must be beliefs that we are justified in believing, through a process of verification. Whether this verification is something that can take place now, or at some idealized point of inquiry is a matter which different pragmatist theories disagree upon.

4.2 Deflationism

Deflationist theories are arguably the most radical of all those we will discuss. They think that the three traditional views just discussed are all engaged in a fool's errand: they are looking for something that is not there. Deflationists take a keen interest in truth predicate 'is true', and argue that it does not behave like a normal predicate. Once we see how it behaves, they think we will see that it is not correct to think that the predicate ascribes some interesting property to propositions. One way to look at this is to think that the predicate 'is true' is used as a way to endorse a proposition. For example, if you say, 'boiled eggs are gross' and I say, 'that's true', one way to look at this is just me saying that I agree with what you have said. This does not imply that any interesting property of being true is ascribed to the claim that boiled eggs are gross; rather, I am just using the word 'true' to express agreement. Obviously, there is more to the story than this, and we will examine this carefully in the deflationism section, but the consequences of such a view are significant. If we have been wrong in thinking that the predicate 'is true' ascribes an interesting property to propositions, then the whole project of investigating the nature of truth makes little sense, for there is no nature to uncover. This can have a liberating effect, if correct, as it would effectively remove a significant philosophical problem from the books. However, it would also come at some costs, as are explored throughout the volume.

4.3 Primitivism

We can see *primitivist* theories of truth as emerging from dissatisfaction with both of the lines discussed so far. Primitivists are sceptical of the idea that truth can be analysed, though not for quite the same reasons as deflationists. It is no secret that the standard project of philosophical analysis described above has not yielded many positive results, and some primitivists take this to show that there is something mistaken about it. They are also sceptical, not just about the method but also about trying to apply the method to truth. The method usually involves breaking one concept down into other concepts which are more basic than the target concept. But, primitivists think, what could be more basic than truth? Surely it is a mistake to think that something so fundamental to our thought and practice could be broken down into more basic components. Primitivists are not deflationists, though, and dismiss the idea that there is no nature to truth. Indeed, holding that truth is a fundamental, unanalysable, property seems very antithetical to deflationism, as it gives truth a significant theoretical position: it can be the basic property that is used to explain a whole range of phenomena, which seems very far from saying that it does not exist.

4.4 Pluralism

Pluralism, unlike deflationism, accepts that truth has a nature, and, unlike primitivism, accepts that truth is analysable. Where it parts company with the traditional views is on the idea that this nature is uniform. Pluralists think that the mistake of the traditional views is that they all think that the truth of a proposition has to always and everywhere be determined by the same thing. They invite us to think about the differences between the kinds of subject-matter that we think and talk about, such as the physical world, mathematics, ethics, aesthetics, to name just a few, and recommend that we consider the idea that the way that propositions about these subjects are made true needs to be considered differently in these cases. Pluralists thus recommend the view that the nature of truth is not uniform; not the same for all true propositions. Different kinds of propositions about different kinds of subjects will be true in different ways.

5 The value of truth: An overview

We noted at the beginning that we tend to assign some positive value to truth. We teach children to tell the truth, and generally prefer honest people to liars. We also expect people to tell the truth in significant situations, such as in court or on official documents. But what is the source of this value, and, indeed, are we right to think that truth has this value at all?

In terms of the first question, one key issue to consider is whether truth is something that is good for instrumental reasons, or whether it has some deeper value. Something is valuable instrumentally if its value is entirely sourced from the effects it brings. For example, if I value your friendship solely because being friends with you means I can play on your new games console, I value your friendship entirely instrumentally: I value being friends with you just because your friendship gets me something else that I want. If you were to lose your games console, then the value I assign to your friendship would disappear. Things that have more than instrumental value, on the other hand, are good not just because of the things that they might bring with them, but because they are good in themselves. For example, you might think that happiness is something that is more than instrumentally good: many things you do you do because they make you happy, but the state of being happy is something you value in itself, and not because it brings about some further end.

In terms of truth, most agree that having true beliefs is instrumentally good. For one thing, having true beliefs seems to enable one to navigate the world properly. If you did not have true beliefs about what side of the road cars drove on in your country, or what items you can eat and which you can't, you probably would not live for very long. Insofar as living is something that you want, true beliefs help you do this, and, in this sense, they are instrumentally valuable. However, we can note that there may be cases where having true beliefs leads to significant pain and suffering, such as if one discovers that one has a rapidly advancing terminal illness, or that one's partner is having an affair.

Whether truth is more than instrumentally valuable is a trickier matter. One way to think about this question is to consider why we think lying is bad: Is it bad because telling a lie might have bad effects, or is it bad because failing to tell the truth is something wrong in itself? If there is some non-instrumental value to truth, it seems as though we always have reason not to lie, regardless of the consequences, whereas if truth is just instrumentally valuable, then perhaps lying is bad only when something bad happens as a result of giving the person false information. We can ask these questions in relation to belief too. I have a false belief, is this something that is bad in itself, even if that false belief does not lead to any negative effects? In other words, is believing the truth something that has intrinsic value?

These issues about the value of truth are connected with what is often called the *normativity* of truth, and the connection between this and the notions of belief and assertion. There are a very wide range of things that we can believe, and also a very wide number of things we can say, or assert. One question that arises is which of all the possible alternatives of things we could believe or say are the things that we should believe, or say. This calls out for a rule, or 'norm', to guide us in working out what we should believe or say. One answer to this question is to consider *truth* the norm of belief and assertion: we should believe what is true, and we should assert what is true. This marks out a significant role for truth in determining the things we ought to believe and say, and this issue is the subject of significant debate in terms of (a) whether truth can provide such a norm; and (b) whether it is truth and not some other epistemic value, such as knowledge, which is better suited to the role.

6 The nature and value of truth: An overview

There are significant connections between these issues in the value of truth and the aforementioned debates about the nature of truth. First, notice that much of the thoughts about the value of truth seem to imply that a belief being true is something significant: a belief having a certain feature – truth – makes it good to believe in certain situations. This has implications for the first question asked in the flow chart above, namely, does truth have a nature? If these thoughts about the value of truth are correct, it seems as though truth *must* have a nature, or else they don't seem to make sense. On the face of it, this would seem to put the deflationary position in jeopardy, as this is a view which denies that there is a nature of truth. However, deflationists try to take this in their stride and show that their view is capable of squaring these thoughts about the value of truth with the idea that truth has no nature. The ingenious moves made here, and questions about their success, occupy much current debate about truth, and are represented in this volume.

A second issue concerns the connections made earlier between the nature of truth and our ability to recognize truth. If we think that having true beliefs is valuable, and something we ought to aim at, then the distinction between issues (1) and (2) becomes important. If we ought to strive to have true beliefs, then it is important that having true beliefs is something that we are capable of. Moreover, if the value of truth is to have any significance in terms of guiding how we ought to accordingly act, it seems as though we should be able to recognize when our beliefs are true, otherwise the principle has no real practical application. This may suggest a narrowing of the distinction between (1) and (2), in that, if a theory of the nature of truth is to be compatible with these thoughts about the value of truth, it must be able to show how – in principle – we are able to tell if our beliefs are true or not. This suggests that epistemological issues concerning how we are able to know if a belief is true are not so separate from the metaphysical issues about the nature of truth after all.

7 Truth bearers

Finally, it is worth noting an important issue which crops up throughout debates about truth – the issue of what the things are that bear truth. Truth bearers, as the name suggests, are things that can be true or false. Three key examples of truth bearers are: beliefs, utterances of sentences and propositions. Of these three things, it is perhaps propositions that are the most controversial. This is because the formation of beliefs and the utterances of sentences are typically thought of as being capable of being recorded as physical events, taking place at particular points in space and time. Propositions, though, do not seem to take this form.

Why would one think that we need propositions, in addition to beliefs and/or sentences? Some philosophers think that we need them to explain how beliefs and sentences have *meaning* or *content*. Consider the following examples. Suppose Gill utters the sentence 'I am hungry,' and Barry also utters the sentence 'I am hungry.' It looks, on the face of it, as though Gill and Barry have said the very same thing: they have both uttered the same string of words, making the same sounds, using – it seems – the same sentence. But, even though it looks as though they have used the same sentence, they mean different things: what Gill says is true just in case *Gill* is hungry, and what Barry says is true just in case *Barry* is hungry. But if what they mean is just captured by the sentences they uttered, then we seem to have a problem, as they uttered the very same sentence. One way to get around this problem is to say that they both used the same sentence to express different meanings or different *propositions*. Gill used the sentence 'I am hungry' to express the proposition that Gill is hungry at 2.28pm on 21 January 2019. Barry used the sentence 'Barry is hungry' to express the proposition that Barry is hungry at 2.28pm on 21 January 2019. Once we cash out the propositions that they each expressed with their uses of the same sentence, we can see that they actually meant different things with what they said, in virtue of expressing different propositions. This cuts the other way as well. Suppose I say, 'snow is white', a sentence of English, and you say 'eira yn wyn', a sentence of Welsh. These are different sentences: they are made up of different sequences of letters; they sound different; and they belong to different languages. However, there is a significant sense in which we have both *said the same thing* with our utterances, for 'eira yn wyn', in Welsh, means what 'snow is white' means in English. We can use propositions to capture this. We want to say that 'snow is white' and 'eira yn wyn' mean the same thing, even though they are different sentences. The way to do this using propositions is to say that they both have the *same meaning*; they both express *the same proposition*.

Propositions can be used in relation to beliefs as well. Let's suppose that your beliefs are contained in your head, and mine are contained in my head. Now, there are many things that it's plausible to think we both believe: that the Earth is a sphere, for example. But how do we explain this commonality in belief? Your belief is contained in your head, and my belief is contained in my head. They are separately existing things, existing in different places. Once again propositions can come to the rescue. We can say that, while our beliefs are located in different places, what they have in common is that they are both beliefs in *the same proposition*: the proposition that the Earth is round. Just as sentences can be said to express propositions, beliefs can be said to be beliefs *about* propositions.

Propositions, then, are quite useful when it comes to explaining the content of sentences and beliefs, and, as such, are useful in explaining how sentences and beliefs are able to express truths and falsehoods. Indeed, some philosophers see propositions as the primary bearers of truth, with sentences and beliefs only being true *derivatively*, in virtue of expressing true propositions. On this account, the sentence 'snow is white' is not *itself* true, but rather the proposition that snow is white is true, and the sentence can be said to be true in virtue of expressing that proposition. However, despite the utility of propositions, some philosophers prefer not to get involved with them. This is because they are often thought of as *abstract* objects, and some philosophers prefer not to posit the existence of such things.

To get a grip on this idea we can consider propositions in relation to sentences and beliefs. Utterances of sentences are particular physical actions: they happen at a particular time, and they are the sorts of things that can be heard or seen (if written down). We might think similar things about beliefs: running with the idea that beliefs are in our heads, we might be able to pinpoint where my beliefs are, and where your beliefs are, and track when the particular time was that a belief was formed. These things suggest that utterances of sentences and beliefs exist in space and time; they are parts of the physical world around (and inside) us. Propositions, on the other hand, seem to exhibit none of these features. Propositions are not uttered at specific times, even though they might be *expressed* at particular times. They are not formed at particular times, even if beliefs *about them* might be formed at particular times. They also do not seem to be located at any particular point. While we can locate the utterance of the sentence 'snow is white' at a particular point, or locate my belief that snow is white inside my head, where can we locate the *proposition* that snow is white? As we have noted earlier, it is separate from any particular expression of the proposition, so we cannot locate it with any expression of it, but if it cannot be located with any expression, where can we locate it? The answer seems to be nowhere, at least nowhere in space and time.

Thus propositions are often thought to be abstract objects, existing outside of space and time, in much the same way as numbers are thought to exist, if they are thought to exist at all. The existence of abstract objects in general is a controversial issue in philosophy, and whether or not one wants to countenance the existence of propositions may well depend on whether or not one wants to countenance the existence of abstract objects in general.

Further reading

There are a number of good introductory books on truth which explore these issues further. Particularly recommended in the context of this volume are Wrenn (2015) and Engel (2002), which discuss both the nature and value of truth. For those who wish for more technical introductions, which concern the nature of truth and connections to the logic of truth, Künne (2003) and Burgess and Burgess (2011) are recommended. In terms of internet resources, readers may want to consult Glanzberg (2014) and Dowden and Swartz (IEP).

References

Alston, W. P. 2002. Truth: Concept and Property. In R. Schantz (ed.), *What is Truth?* Berlin and New York: Walter de Gruyter, 11–26.

Burgess, P. and Burgess, A. 2011. *Truth*. Princeton: Princeton University Press.

Dowden, B. and Swartz, N. IEP. Truth. In J. Fieser and B. Dowden (eds), *Internet Encyclopedia of Philosophy*, URL = http://www.iep.utm.edu/truth

Engel, P. 2002. *Truth*. Chesham: Acumen Press.

Glanzberg, M. Fall 2014 Edition. Truth. In Edward N. Zalta (ed.), *The Stanford Encyclopedia of Philosophy*, URL = http://plato.stanford.edu/archives/fall2014/entries/truth/

Künne, W. 2003. *Conceptions of Truth*. Oxford: Oxford University Press.

Wrenn, C. 2015. *Truth*. Cambridge: Polity Press.

Section 1 Correspondence theories of truth

Editor's introduction

DOUGLAS EDWARDS

We begin with correspondence theories of truth, which represent the most famous approach to truth. Correspondence theories of truth claim that the truth of a proposition is a matter of the relations between that proposition and reality. Beyond this, there are a number of different ways of spelling out the view, the central proposals of which are represented in the chapters in this section.

Correspondence to fact

The first approach is perhaps most famously expressed by Bertrand Russell, in his article 'Truth and Falsehood'. Russell takes the view that true beliefs correspond to the facts, and that each true belief corresponds to some specific fact. On this view, we see the world as constituted of facts, with true beliefs being the beliefs that match these facts. A key aspect of Russell's view is the idea that there are structural similarities between propositions and facts: the correspondence between them is due to their sharing a similar shape, as it were.

For example, take the belief that snow is white. This belief, in Russell's terms, 'knits' together an object – snow – with a property – being white. This gives a certain structure to the belief, which relates an object to a property in a certain way. This belief is true, on Russell's theory, just in case there is a fact in the world which exhibits the same structure as this belief, namely, just in case there is a fact which has the structure of snow instantiating the property of being white. Think of this in terms of Cinderella's glass slipper. The belief in this analogy is the glass slipper, which has a certain shape and structure such that it can only fit some entity – a foot, in this case – which has the same sort of dimensions as it has. Cinderella's foot is the equivalent of the worldly fact which fits exactly into the slipper due to its specific dimensions and shape. A true belief fitting a fact on Russell's view is very much like the glass slipper fitting Cinderella's foot. It fits the fact due to a similarity in structure between the belief and the fact, just as Cinderella's foot fits the glass slipper due to a similarity in structure between them.

One concern with the correspondence theory of truth as presented by Russell is that there needs to be a specific fact to make each proposition true, and that fact needs to exhibit the same sort of structure as a proposition in order to make it true. In terms of the shared structure aspect, some philosophers have wondered whether it makes sense for beliefs and facts to be so structured as Russell thought, and others were concerned that the need for them to exhibit *the same* structure would lead not to the idea that true propositions *correspond* to facts but to the idea that true propositions *are* facts. This is because it seems plausible that two things that share exactly the same structure are identical, but if true propositions are identical to facts, then we seem to lose the original idea of the correspondence theory that there is a separation between propositions and the representation-independent world. In terms of the claim that each proposition is made true by a uniquely structured fact, others have been concerned that there seem to be some distinct propositions that are made true by the same fact. For example, take the fact that Socrates exists. This makes true the proposition that Socrates exists, but it also makes true the proposition that some thing exists. These two propositions are distinct in structure, so it seems that they cannot both correspond to the same fact on Russell's view. But yet, they are both seemingly made true by the same fact, so how do we explain this?

Problems like these have led those tempted by the correspondence theory of truth to look elsewhere.

Truthmaking

One alternative proposal, developed in the paper by Marian David, considers the idea that facts make propositions true, but not in virtue of any structural similarity between fact and true proposition, but because the very existence of the fact *necessitates* the truth of the proposition. This is the idea behind the theory of *truthmaking*. On this view, we retain the basic components of the correspondence theory of truth, namely that the world is constituted of facts, which are distinct from propositions, but true propositions do not correspond to facts in virtue of any shared structural similarity, rather the very existence of the relevant facts makes certain propositions true. This view also avoids a commitment to the idea that there has to be a unique fact for each true proposition, as one fact might necessitate the truth of more than one proposition. To return to our example above, the fact that Socrates exists would necessitate both the truth of the proposition that Socrates exists and the truth of the proposition that some thing exists.

A key question for truthmaker theories is the exact nature of the relation between a fact and a true proposition, and how exactly specific facts make specific propositions true. This is particularly problematic as we are dealing with a relation between two different kinds of things: propositions and facts. We find more familiar relations between items of the same kind, such as entailment between propositions, and (perhaps) causation between facts, but truthmaking seems to require a whole new kind of relation. A further issue is that the truthmaking theory retains a commitment to the existence of facts from Russell's view, which some find unpalatable.

Truth and reference

An alternative version of the correspondence theory of truth denies that there exist such things as facts, but maintains the connection between true propositions and reality in virtue of the relations of reference and satisfaction. The first systematic version of this approach was given by Hartry Field, who developed some ideas from the Polish logician and philosopher Alfred Tarski. While Field himself does an excellent job at summarizing the key themes from Tarski he is interested in, I will briefly summarize them here. Tarksi's work on truth was very varied, taking on a number of different issues that take us further afield than the issues under consideration in this volume, such as the construction of formal languages and the liar paradox, among others. Here we will focus just on the issues that are relevant for Field's development of the view.

Some background: Tarski

Tarski begins his influential (1944) paper 'The Semantic Conception of Truth and the Foundation of Semantics' by discussing what he calls 'the classical conception of truth', the intuitions behind which he initially attempts to express in three different ways:

- **(i)** To say of what is that it is not, or of what is not that it is, is false, while to say of what is that it is, and what is not that it is not, is true. (from Aristotle's *Metaphysics*, 1011b25)
- **(ii)** The truth of a sentence consists in its agreement with (or correspondence to) reality.
- **(iii)** A sentence is true if it designates an existing state of affairs. (Tarski 1944: 343)

Tarski rejects these as unsatisfactory expressions of the classical view, and looks for something which is, in his terms, "more precise" (Tarski 1944: 343). He goes on to say:

> Let us start with a concrete example. Consider the sentence "*snow is white*". We ask the question under what conditions this sentence is true or false. It seems clear that if we base ourselves on the classical conception of truth, we shall say that the sentence is true if snow is white, and false if snow is not white. Thus, if the definition is to conform to our conception, it must imply the following equivalence:
>
> The sentence "snow is white" is true if, and only if, snow is white. (Tarski 1944: 343)

He then goes on to offer the generalized schema:

> (T) X is true iff *p* (Tarski 1944: 344).[1]

This passage gives us perhaps Tarski's most famous contribution to debates about truth – the 'T-schema' – along with its canonical instance:

> 'Snow is white' is true if and only if snow is white

Let's explain how this works. You will see that the sentence 'snow is white' appears twice. On the left-hand side of the biconditional it appears as the *name* of the sentence 'snow is white', and on the right-hand side it is the sentence itself which appears. One way to put this difference is in terms of the use/mention distinction in the philosophy of language. On the left-hand side the sentence is mentioned, as the sentence is the thing that is being talked about. Just as we talk about the sentence 'snow is white' when we say that 'snow is white' is composed of three words of English, we are talking about the sentence 'snow is white' when we say that the sentence is true. In order to talk about something, Tarski claimed, we need a name to refer to it by, so 'snow is white', in quotation marks, is the name of the sentence. On the right-hand side, however, we are not talking about the sentence, we are simply using it, just as I use the sentence if we are disputing the colour of snow and I say to you, 'look, snow is white'. In that context, the sentence 'snow is white' is used to say something, and it is not part of what is said that anything is said about that sentence. Tarski generalized this formula by saying that we can take any sentence, *p*, and construct a name for that sentence, X. Using these stand-ins for particular sentences, we can say:

X is true if and only if p.

Tarski took this schema, and its instances, to be non-negotiable aspects of truth that any theory of truth must accommodate. However, he did not think that they gave us the end of the story about truth, and, indeed, he thought that they themselves were capable of being explained by some further things. In particular, he thought that the notions of reference and satisfaction were key to understanding what is going on the right-hand side of each of the T instances. This is evidenced by his ideas that truth is a 'semantic concept':

> I should like to propose the name "*the semantic conception of truth*" for the conception of truth which has just been discussed.
>
> *Semantics* is a discipline which, speaking loosely, *deals with certain relations between expressions of a language and the objects* (or "states of affairs") *"referred to" by those expressions.* (Tarski 1944: 345)

He goes on to say:

> It turns out that the simplest and the most natural way of obtaining an exact definition of truth is one which involves the use of other semantic notions, e.g., the notion of satisfaction. (Tarski 1944: 345)

Tarksi thus proposed understanding the T instances as follows. In the case of a simple subject-predicate sentence such as 'snow is white', the idea is that

> 'snow is white' is true if and only if the object referred to by 'snow' satisfies the predicate 'is white'.

This lays down explicit conditions under which the sentence 'snow is white' is true, and also underwrites the relevant T instance. What Tarski does is note that the right-hand side of the T instance involves the use of a sentence, and that the use of that sentence requires explanation. In particular, he claims that what the sentence does is claim that a particular object – snow – satisfies a particular predicate – 'is white'. If snow does satisfy this predicate, then the sentence is true, and if it does not then the sentence is false. Equipped with this, we can explain the relevant T instance, as, if the stuff referred to by 'snow' does satisfy the predicate 'is white', then the sentence 'snow is white' is true, which is the right-to-left conditional of the biconditional. Conversely, we can hold that, if the sentence 'snow is white' is true, then the stuff referred to by 'snow' satisfies the predicate 'is white'. If we take it – as Tarski did – that whether or not an object or substance satisfies a particular predicate is a worldly, as opposed to a linguistic, matter, then we have our connection between language and the world that is intended to characterize truth on a correspondence view.

Field and Grover

Tarski's correspondence theory uses the notions of reference and satisfaction to give an account of truth. However, the theory is incomplete until we say more about reference and satisfaction. If the connection between language and the world is to be understood in terms of reference and satisfaction, then we need to understand more about these notions in order to understand precisely what this connection is supposed to be. An influential development of Tarksi's view in this direction is given by Hartry Field, in his paper 'Tarski's Theory of Truth', originally published in 1972. In this paper Field proposes a causal theory of reference to serve as a companion to Tarski's theory, thus positing that the connection between language and world is a causal one, seemingly making truth respectable from the point of view of those who wish to see truth as part of the regular, causal, physical, non-mysterious world. Dorothy Grover, in her 'Truth and Language-World Connections', considers the various ways a correspondence theory of truth can be formulated before analysing Field's view in detail.

Note

1. As noted, here 'X' stands for the name of a sentence, and *p* stands for the sentence itself. This section on Tarski draws on Edwards (2018: 43).

Further reading

A good overview of the various formulations of correspondence theory is given by David (2015). For more on the classical correspondence theory, alternative formulations which are worth examining are found in Wittgenstein (1921), David (1994) and Vision (2004). See also the influential exchange between Austin (1950) and Strawson (1950). For more on the role of causal role of correspondence truth, see Kitcher (2002). For Tarskian approaches, a key paper of Tarski's is Tarski (1944). More on Field's development of Tarski can be found in Sher (1999), and the approach is connected with representation in cognitive science by Lynch (2009, Ch. 1). In terms of introductory volumes on truth, discussion of the correspondence theory can be found in Künne (2003, Ch. 3), Engel (2002, Ch. 1), Wrenn (2015, Ch. 5) and Burgess and Burgess (2011, Chs. 2 and 5).

References

Austin, J. L. 1950. Truth. *Proceedings of the Aristotelian Society* 24: 111–28.

Burgess, P. and Burgess, A. 2011. *Truth*. Princeton: Princeton University Press.

David, M. 1994. *Correspondence and Disquotation: An Essay on the Nature of Truth*. Oxford: Oxford University Press.

David, M. Fall 2015 Edition. The Correspondence Theory of Truth. *The Stanford Encyclopedia of Philosophy*, Edward N. Zalta (ed.), URL = http://plato.stanford.edu/archives/fall2015/entries/truth-correspondence/

Edwards, D. 2018. *The Metaphysics of Truth.* Oxford: Oxford University Press.

Engel, P. 2002. *Truth*. Chesham: Acumen Press.

Kitcher, P. 2002. On the Explanatory Role of Correspondence Truth. *Philosophy and Phenomenological Research* 64 (2): 346–64.

Künne, W. 2003. *Conceptions of Truth*. Oxford: Oxford University Press.

Lynch, M. P. 2009. *Truth as One and Many*. Oxford: Oxford University Press.

Sher, G. 1999. What is Tarski's Theory of Truth? *Topoi* 18: 149–66.

Strawson, P. 1950. Truth. *Proceedings of the Aristotelian Society* 24: 129–56.

Tarski, A. 1944. The Semantic Conception of Truth and the Foundation of Semantics. *Philosophy and Phenomenological Research* 4: 341–76.

Vision, G. 2004. *Veritas: The Correspondence Theory and Its Critics*. Cambridge: MIT Press.

Wittgenstein, L. 1921. *Tractatus Logico-Philosophicus*. English translation by D. F. Pears and B. F. McGuinness. London and Henley: Routledge and Kegan Paul.

Wrenn, C. 2015. *Truth*. Cambridge: Polity Press.

1 Truth and falsehood

BERTRAND RUSSELL

Our knowledge of truths, unlike our knowledge of things, has an opposite, namely *error.* So far as things are concerned, we may know them or not know them, but there is no positive state of mind which can be described as erroneous knowledge of things, so long, at any rate, as we confine ourselves to knowledge by acquaintance. Whatever we are acquainted with must be something; we may draw wrong inferences from our acquaintance, but the acquaintance itself cannot be deceptive. Thus there is no dualism as regards acquaintance. But as regards knowledge of truths, there is a dualism. We may believe what is false as well as what is true. We know that on very many subjects different people hold different and incompatible opinions: hence some beliefs must be erroneous. Since erroneous beliefs are often held just as strongly as true beliefs, it becomes a difficult question how they are to be distinguished from true beliefs. How are we to know, in a given case, that our belief is not erroneous? This is a question of the very greatest difficulty, to which no completely satisfactory answer is possible. There is, however, a preliminary question which is rather less difficult, and that is: What do we *mean* by truth and falsehood? It is this preliminary question which is to be considered in this chapter.

In this chapter we are not asking how we can know whether a belief is true or false: we are asking what is meant by the question whether a belief is true or false. It is to be hoped that a clear answer to this question may help us to obtain an answer to the question what beliefs are true, but for the present we ask only 'What is truth?' and 'What is falsehood?' not 'What beliefs are true?' and 'What beliefs are false?' It is very important to keep these different questions entirely separate, since any confusion between them is sure to produce an answer which is not really applicable to either.

There are three points to observe in the attempt to discover the nature of truth, three requisites which any theory must fulfil.

1. Our theory of truth must be such as to admit of its opposite, falsehood. A good many philosophers have failed adequately to satisfy this condition: they have constructed theories according to which all our thinking ought to have been true, and have then had the greatest difficulty in finding a place for falsehood. In this respect our theory of belief must differ from our theory of acquaintance, since in the case of acquaintance it was not necessary to take account of any opposite.
2. It seems fairly evident that if there were no beliefs there could be no falsehood, and no truth either, in the sense in which truth is correlative to falsehood. If we imagine a world of mere matter, there would be no room for falsehood in such a world,

and although it would contain what may be called 'facts', it would not contain any truths, in the sense in which truths are things of the same kind as falsehoods. In fact, truth and falsehood are properties of beliefs and statements: hence a world of mere matter, since it would contain no beliefs or statements, would also contain no truth or falsehood.

3 But, as against what we have just said, it is to be observed that the truth or falsehood of a belief always depends upon something which lies outside the belief itself. If I believe that Charles I died on the scaffold, I believe truly, not because of any intrinsic quality of my belief, which could be discovered by merely examining the belief, but because of an historical event which happened two and a half centuries ago. If I believe that Charles I died in his bed, I believe falsely: no degree of vividness in my belief, or of care in arriving at it, prevents it from being false, again because of what happened long ago, and not because of any intrinsic property of my belief. Hence, although truth and falsehood are properties of beliefs, they are properties dependent upon the relations of the beliefs to other things, not upon any internal quality of the beliefs.

The third of the above requisites leads us to adopt the view—which has on the whole been commonest among philosophers – that truth consists in some form of correspondence between belief and fact. It is, however, by no means an easy matter to discover a form of correspondence to which there are no irrefutable objections. By this partly – and partly by the feeling that, if truth consists in a correspondence of thought with something outside thought, thought can never know when truth has been attained – many philosophers have been led to try to find some definition of truth which shall not consist in relation to something wholly outside belief. The most important attempt at a definition of this sort is the theory that truth consists in *coherence.* It is said that the mark of falsehood is failure to cohere in the body of our beliefs, and that it is the essence of a truth to form part of the completely rounded system which is The Truth.

There is, however, a great difficulty in this view, or rather two great difficulties. The first is that there is no reason to suppose that only *one* coherent body of beliefs is possible. It may be that, with sufficient imagination, a novelist might invent a past for the world that would perfectly fit on to what we know, and yet be quite different from the real past. In more scientific matters, it is certain that there are often two or more hypotheses which account for all the known facts on some subject, and although, in such cases, men of science endeavour to find facts which will rule out all the hypotheses except one, there is no reason why they should always succeed.

In philosophy, again, it seems not uncommon for two rival hypotheses to be both able to account for all the facts. Thus, for example, it is possible that life is one long dream, and that the outer world has only that degree of reality that the objects of dreams have; but although such a view does not seem inconsistent with known facts, there is no reason to prefer it to the common-sense view, according to which other people and things do really exist. Thus coherence as the definition of truth fails because there is no proof that there can be only one coherent system.

The other objection to this definition of truth is that it assumes the meaning of 'coherence' known, whereas, in fact, 'coherence' presupposes the truth of the laws of logic.

Two propositions are coherent when both may be true, and are incoherent when one at least must be false. Now in order to know whether two propositions can both be true, we must know such truths as the law of contradiction. For example, the two propositions, 'this tree is a beech' and 'this tree is not a beech', are not coherent, because of the law of contradiction. But if the law of contradiction itself were subjected to the test of coherence, we should find that, if we choose to suppose it false, nothing will any longer be incoherent with anything else. Thus the laws of logic supply the skeleton or framework within which the test of coherence applies, and they themselves cannot be established by this test.

For the above two reasons, coherence cannot be accepted as giving the *meaning* of truth, though it is often a most important *test* of truth after a certain amount of truth has become known.

Hence we are driven back to *correspondence with fact* as constituting the nature of truth. It remains to define precisely what we mean by 'fact', and what is the nature of the correspondence which must subsist between belief and fact, in order that belief may be true.

In accordance with our three requisites, we have to seek a theory of truth which (l) allows truth to have an opposite, namely falsehood, (2) makes truth a property of beliefs, but (3) makes it a property wholly dependent upon the relation of the beliefs to outside things.

The necessity of allowing for falsehood makes it impossible to regard belief as a relation of the mind to a single object, which could be said to be what is believed. If belief were so regarded, we should find that, like acquaintance, it would not admit of the opposition of truth and falsehood, but would have to be always true. This may be made clear by examples. Othello believes falsely that Desdemona loves Cassio. We cannot say that this belief consists in a relation to a single object, 'Desdemona's love for Cassio', for if there were such an object, the belief would be true. There is in fact no such object, and therefore Othello cannot have any relation to such an object. Hence his belief cannot possibly consist in a relation to this object.

It might be said that his belief is a relation to a different object, namely 'that Desdemona loves Cassio'; but it is almost as difficult to suppose that there is such an object as this, when Desdemona does not love Cassio, as it was to suppose that there is 'Desdemona's love for Cassio'. Hence it will be better to seek for a theory of belief which does not make it consist in a relation of the mind to a single object.

It is common to think of relations as though they always held between *two* terms, but in fact this is not always the case. Some relations demand three terms, some four, and so on. Take, for instance, the relation 'between'. So long as only two terms come in, the relation 'between' is impossible: three terms are the smallest number that render it possible. York is between London and Edinburgh; but if London and Edinburgh were the only places in the world, there could be nothing which was between one place and another. Similarly *jealousy* requires three people: there can be no such relation that does not involve three at least. Such a proposition as '*A* wishes *B* to promote *C*'s marriage with *D*' involves a relation of four terms; that is to say, *A* and *B* and *C* and *D* all come in, and the relation involved cannot be expressed otherwise than in a form involving all four. Instances might be multiplied indefinitely, but enough has been said to show that there are relations which require more than two terms before they can occur.

The relation involved in *judging* or *believing* must, if falsehood is to be duly allowed for, be taken to be a relation between several terms, not between two. When Othello believes that Desdemona loves Cassio, he must not have before his mind a single object, 'Desdemona's love for Cassio', or 'that Desdemona loves Cassio', for that would require that there should be objective falsehoods, which subsist independently of any minds; and this, though not logically refutable, is a theory to be avoided if possible. Thus it is easier to account for falsehood if we take judgement to be a relation in which the mind and the various objects concerned all occur severally; that is to say, Desdemona and loving and Cassio must all be terms in the relation which subsists when Othello believes that Desdemona loves Cassio. This relation, therefore, is a relation of four terms, since Othello also is one of the terms of the relation. When we say that it is a relation of four terms, we do not mean that Othello has a certain relation to Desdemona, and has the same relation to loving and also to Cassio. This may be true of some other relation than believing; but believing, plainly, is not a relation which Othello has to *each* of the three terms concerned, but to *all* of them together: there is only one example of the relation of believing involved, but this one example knits together four terms. Thus the actual occurrence, at the moment when Othello is entertaining his belief, is that the relation called 'believing' is knitting together into one complex whole the four terms Othello, Desdemona, loving, and Cassio. What is called belief or judgement, is nothing but this relation of believing or judging, which relates a mind to several things other than itself. An *act* of belief or of judgement is the occurrence between certain terms at some particular time, of the relation of believing or judging.

We are now in a position to understand what it is that distinguishes a true judgement from a false one. For this purpose we will adopt certain definitions. In every act of judgement there is a mind which judges, and there are terms concerning which it judges. We will call the mind the *subject* in the judgement, and the remaining terms the *objects.* Thus, when Othello judges that Desdemona loves Cassio, Othello is the subject, while the objects are Desdemona and loving and Cassio. The subject and the objects together are called the *constituents* of the judgement. It will be observed that the relation of judging has what is called a 'sense' or 'direction'. We may say, metaphorically, that it puts its objects in a certain *order,* which we may indicate by means of the order of the words in the sentence. (In an inflected language, the same thing will be indicated by inflections, e.g. by the difference between nominative and accusative.) Othello's judgement that Cassio loves Desdemona differs from his judgement that Desdemona loves Cassio, in spite of the fact that it consists of the same constituents, because the relation of judging places the constituents in a different order in the two cases. Similarly, if Cassio judges that Desdemona loves Othello, the constituents of the judgement are still the same, but their order is different. This property of having a 'sense' or 'direction' is one which the relation of judging shares with all other relations. The 'sense' of relations is the ultimate source of order and series and a host of mathematical concepts; but we need not concern ourselves further with this aspect.

We spoke of the relation called 'judging' or 'believing' as knitting together into one complex whole the subject and the objects. In this respect, judging is exactly like every other relation. Whenever a relation holds between two or more terms, it unites the terms into a complex whole. If Othello loves Desdemona, there is such a complex whole as 'Othello's love for Desdemona'. The terms united by the relation may be themselves complex, or may be simple, but the whole which results from their being united must be complex. Wherever there is a relation which relates certain terms, there is a complex object formed of the union of those terms; and conversely, wherever there is a complex object, there is a relation which relates its constituents. When an act of believing occurs, there is a complex, in which 'believing' is the uniting relation, and subject and objects are arranged in a certain order by the 'sense' of the relation of believing. Among the objects, as we saw in considering 'Othello believes that Desdemona loves Cassio', one must be a relation—in this instance, the relation 'loving'. But this relation, as it occurs in the act of believing, is not the relation which creates the unity of the complex whole consisting of the subject and the objects. The relation 'loving', as it occurs in the act of believing, is one of the objects—it is a brick in the structure, not the cement. The cement is the relation 'believing'. When the belief is *true,* there is another complex unity, in which the relation which was one of the objects of the belief relates the other objects. Thus, e.g., if Othello believes *truly* that Desdemona loves Cassio, then there is a complex unity, 'Desdemona's love for Cassio', which is composed exclusively of the *objects* of the belief, in the same order as they had in the belief, with the relation which was one of the objects occurring now as the cement that binds together the other objects of the belief. On the other hand, when a belief is *false,* there is no such complex unity composed only of the objects of the belief. If Othello believes *falsely* that Desdemona loves Cassio, then there is no such complex unity as 'Desdemona's love for Cassio'.

Thus a belief is *true* when it *corresponds* to a certain associated complex, and *false* when it does not. Assuming, for the sake of definiteness, that the objects of the belief are two terms and a relation, the terms being put in a certain order by the 'sense' of the believing, then if the two terms in that order are united by the relation into a complex, the belief is true; if not, it is false. This constitutes the definition of truth and falsehood that we were in search of. Judging or believing is a certain complex unity of which a mind is a constituent; if the remaining constituents, taken in the order which they have in the belief, form a complex unity, then the belief is true; if not, it is false.

Thus although truth and falsehood are properties of beliefs, yet they are in a sense extrinsic properties, for the condition of the truth of a belief is something not involving beliefs, or (in general) any mind at all, but only the *objects* of the belief. A mind, which believes, believes truly when there is a *corresponding* complex not involving the mind, but only its objects. This correspondence ensures truth, and its absence entails falsehood. Hence we account simultaneously for the two facts that beliefs (a) depend on minds for their *existence*, (b) do not depend on minds for their, *truth.*

We may restate our theory as follows: If we take such a belief as 'Othello believes that Desdemona loves Cassio', we will call Desdemona and Cassio the *object-terms,* and loving the *object-relation.* If there is a complex unity 'Desdemona's love for Cassio', consisting of the object terms related by the object-relation in the same order as they have in the belief, then this complex unity is called the *fact corresponding to the belief.* Thus a belief is true when there is a corresponding fact, and is false when there is no corresponding fact.

It will be seen that minds do not *create* truth or falsehood. They create beliefs, but when once the beliefs are created, the mind cannot make them true or false, except in the special case where they concern future things which are within the power of the person believing, such as catching trains. What makes a belief true is a *fact,* and this fact does not (except in exceptional cases) in any way involve the mind of the person who has the belief.

Having now decided what we *mean* by truth and falsehood, we have next to consider what ways there are of knowing whether this or that belief is true or false. This consideration will occupy the next chapter.[1]

Note

1. [Editor's note: the 'next chapter' Russell refers to here is the next chapter of his book *Problems of Philosophy*, not the next chapter of this volume.]

2 Truth-making and correspondence

MARIAN DAVID

The *truth-maker principle* says that for every truth there is something that makes it true, that every truth has a truth-maker. A *correspondence theory of truth* aims to account for truth in terms of correspondence with reality, or rather with appropriate chunks of reality, typically said to be facts. One feels that there is a natural kinship between the two. D. M. Armstrong puts it like this: "Anybody who is attracted to the Correspondence theory of truth should be drawn to the truth-maker. Correspondence demands a correspondent, and a correspondent for a truth is a truthmaker" (Armstrong 1997: 14).

On the other hand, it is only kinship. Armstrong also maintains (*ibid.:* ch. 8.5) that the correspondence theory is too ambitious in certain crucial respects and that the truth-maker principle improves on it by being more modest while at the same time capturing what is right about the correspondence theory. Michael Dummett, rather less sympathetic to the correspondence theory, had said earlier that "we have nowadays abandoned the correspondence theory of truth"; but he added that it nevertheless "expresses one important feature of the concept of truth...: that a statement is true only if there is something in the world in virtue of which it is true" (Dummett 1959: 14). Alex Oliver has put this more starkly: "The truth-maker principle is a sanitised version of a correspondence theory of truth" (Oliver 1996: 69).

The view seems to be that a correspondence theory of truth is committed to the truth-maker principle, but not the other way round, so that one can keep the latter while abandoning the former, as some say we must. Because of this relationship between the two, friends of the truth-maker principle maintain that it captures something (important) that is right in the correspondence theory; and those not sympathetic towards the correspondence theory would add that it captures *all* that is right in the correspondence theory, which is not very much. In this paper, I want to take a closer look at how the relationship between a correspondence theory and the truth-maker principle is to be conceived, especially considering that correspondence appears to be a symmetric relation while truth-making appears to be, or is supposed to be, an asymmetric relation.

1 From truth-making to correspondence and back

The truth-maker principle occurs in various formulations. The following three are always treated as interchangeable variants of each other. I state them assuming that the role of truth-bearers (i.e. truth-or-falsehood-bearers) is played by *propositions*; this is fairly common practice in discussions of the truth-maker principle:

(TM) Every true proposition is made true by something.
For every true proposition there is something that makes it true.
Every true proposition has a truth-maker.

The first two formulations emphasize the *truth-making relation* and remind us that we can express it in the active and the passive voice. The third formulation de-emphasizes the relation for the sake of the neat term 'truth-maker', which goes so nicely with the term 'truth-bearer'. Although this third formulation gives the truth-maker principle its name, it appears less fundamental. The term 'truth-maker' is intended merely as a label for whatever items stand in the relation of truth-making to a truth. It is the truth-making relation that is crucial. It would have been just as well to refer to the truth-*maker* principle as the truth-*making* principle.

How does this principle relate to a correspondence theory? Say one regards (TM) as expressing a basic intuition about truth. Let us see how one might arrive at a correspondence theory, taking (TM) as one's starting-point. (TM) is the most *generic* truth-maker principle. It does not say anything at all about what sorts of items are truth-makers or whether they must satisfy any further conditions. It is maximally modest on this score. It is also not very informative. One might then want to embrace a further truth-maker principle, one that is more ambitious because more specific than (TM):

(TMF) Every true proposition is made true by a fact.

This is a *special truth-maker principle.* Note that it does not involve a repudiation of the generic principle. On the contrary, it implies the generic principle. It is an attempt to add to the generic principle, to be more informative. Evidently, this is only one of many possible special truth-maker principles. Here is a still more special special truth-maker principle:

(TMC) Every true proposition is made true by a fact it corresponds with.

This principle might be what friends of truth-making have in mind when they say or imply that a correspondence theory is committed to the truth-maker principle, but not the other way round: (TMC) obviously implies (TM), but (TM) does not imply (TMC). On this way of looking at things, a correspondence theory would be a species, or rather a subspecies, of a truth-maker theory.

So far, our correspondence "theory" is a very small theory: a one-liner minitheory. We would normally expect a bit more, some account that tells us about the nature of facts and especially about the nature of correspondence. Concerning the latter, George Pitcher (1964:9–14) makes a helpful distinction. He points out that there are two separable aspects to the notion of correspondence. The first he calls *correspondence-as-correlation,* familiar from mathematical contexts, where one finds talk of correspondence in the sense of a correlation between the members of two sets in accordance with some rule or function. Pertaining to this aspect, our correspondence theorists might want to add further claims to (TMC), claims that commit them to one or both of the following:

Correlation:

(a) If a proposition corresponds with a fact, then there is no other fact the proposition corresponds with.

(b) If a proposition corresponds with a fact, then there is no other proposition that corresponds with that fact.

Taken together, (a) and (b) say that correspondence is a one-one relation: each true proposition corresponds with exactly one fact; and different true propositions always correspond with different facts. I said correspondence theorists *might* want to commit themselves to both parts of Correlation. In fact, it is not easy to find any who are clearly committed to part (b), which, by my lights, goes beyond what even a rather enthusiastic champion of the correspondence approach needs to maintain.[1] Explicit commitment to part (a) is equally rare. However, one does find real-life correspondence theorists moving comfortably from talk about a given true proposition to talk about *the* fact it corresponds with: a move that signals commitment to part (a) of Correlation.

The second aspect of correspondence Pitcher calls *correspondence-as-congruity.* Unlike correspondence-as-correlation, which does not imply anything about the inner nature of the corresponding items, correspondence-as-congruity involves that the corresponding items are similar in certain relevant respects, which in turn requires that they have the same or sufficiently similar *structure.* This aspect of correspondence, which is more prominent (and more notorious) than the previous one, is also much more difficult to make precise. Let us say, rather roughly, that our correspondence theorists might want to add claims to (TMC) that commit them to something like the following:

Structure:
If a proposition corresponds with a fact, then they have the same or sufficiently similar structure: the overall correspondence between a proposition and a fact is a matter of part-wise correspondence, of their having corresponding constituents in corresponding places in the same structure, or in sufficiently similar structures.

Take the proposition that Ludwig is hungry. Assume it is true. A correspondence theorist is likely to say that it corresponds with the fact that Ludwig is hungry; and one who is also committed to (a strong version of) Structure might add: the proposition and the fact have constituents arranged in a certain way. The constituents of the proposition are the Ludwig-concept and the hungry-concept; the constituents of the fact are Ludwig and the property of being hungry. The Ludwig-concept corresponds with Ludwig, and the hungry-concept corresponds with the property of being hungry. Proposition and fact have the same structure and have corresponding constituents in the same structure. What is this shared structure? Well, it does not have a very good name but one could say, albeit somewhat misleadingly, that it is the subject-predicate structure, meaning that it is the sort of structure that shows itself, by way of a linguistic symptom, in the grammatical subject-predicate structure of the single sentence that can be used to perspicuously describe both the proposition that Ludwig is happy and the fact that Ludwig is happy.

Correlation and Structure reflect distinct aspects of the notion of correspondence: one might want to advocate one without the other.[2] However, it is unlikely that they are entirely independent. Correlation, it seems, requires further explanation: what is the function by which true propositions are correlated with facts? It is not easy to see how an answer to this question could ultimately avoid talking about the structure and constituents of the correlated propositions and facts – especially if the correlation is supposed to be one-one. The road from Structure to Correlation is even more straightforward. The more one pushes Structure, that is, the closer the required match between true propositions and facts, the more likely that the resulting account will be committed to Correlation, although it seems to me that one might reasonably try to avoid part (b) of Correlation: different true propositions might reasonably be said to correspond to (have sufficiently similar constituent-structure as) the same fact as long as they are not too different.[3]

Here we have a model of what a correspondence theory of truth might look like. Various alternative versions could be generated from the generic truth-maker principle, (TM), by producing alternatives to the specific truth-maker principles. Our model makes it easy to see, on the one hand, why friends of truth-making who reject our sample correspondence theory nevertheless find some good in it. Its characteristic claim, (TMC), implies the generic truth-maker principle (TM): our correspondence theorists are truth-maker theorists, so they are at least in the right ballpark. One can also see why, on the other hand, our correspondence theory will meet strong resistance from many friends of truth-making. They will maintain that this attempt to fill in the generic truth-maker principle, to say something more informative than what is said by (TM), has failed; that our correspondence theorists are way too ambitious; that they end up with a whole zoo of funny facts that are not needed and are not well motivated by the basic truth-maker intuition.

This criticism should be fleshed out a bit. Friends of truth-making who reject our correspondence theory may raise objections against each of its ingredients. I shall only give a few examples, beginning with objections to Structure (the most contentious ingredient), working backwards until only the generic truth-maker principle is left standing. Many additional examples, and more argumentative support, can be found in, for example, Mulligan *et al.* (1984), Russell (1918), Fox (1987), Bigelow (1988) and Armstrong (1989, 1997, 2004). The objections usually rely on a methodological background principle – a truth-maker version of Ockham's razor: do not postulate a relatively more complex truth-maker for a truth where a simpler truth-maker will suffice.

- *Against Structure:* Take the disjunctive proposition that Ludwig is happy or Ludwig is hungry. There is no need for a disjunctive fact. The proposition can be made true by the fact that Ludwig is happy. Even on a very loose interpretation of Structure, this fact does not have the same complexity, does not have the same constituent-structure, as the proposition it makes true.
- *Against Correlation (b):* Take the following two disjunctive propositions: the proposition that Ludwig is happy or Ludwig is hungry, and the proposition that Ludwig is happy or Ludwig is thirsty. Again, there is no need for disjunctive facts. Both propositions can be made true by the fact that Ludwig is happy: two different propositions can have the same fact as truth-maker.[4]
- *Against Correlation (a):* Take the proposition that there are some happy dogs. There is no need to postulate an existentially generalized fact. The proposition can be made true by the fact that Ludwig is happy, and also by the fact that Lassie is happy, and also by the fact that Fido is happy, and so on. So, one proposition can be made true by many different facts.
- *Against (TMC):* Once Structure, Correlation (b) and Correlation (a) have been rejected, the claim that all true propositions are made true by *corresponding* facts has to go

too, at least on any reasonably substantive interpretation of 'corresponding', one that gives some additional content to this term and does not eviscerate it to such an extent that (TMC) is nothing more than a verbose notational variant of (TMF), the claim that all true propositions are made true by facts.[5]

- *Against (TMF):* Take the proposition that Ludwig is a dog. Assuming that Ludwig is essentially a dog, Ludwig by himself suffices to make true the proposition that Ludwig is a dog. There is no need to postulate the fact that Ludwig is a dog. Also, take the proposition that Ludwig exists. It too is made true just by Ludwig himself. And the proposition that Ludwig is identical with Josef, if true, is also made true just by Ludwig, that is, by Josef. There is no need to postulate, in addition, the fact that Ludwig exists or the fact that Ludwig is identical with Josef.

From this point on, there is considerable divergence. Some truth-maker theorists maintain that facts are not needed as truth-makers at all. For example, Kevin Mulligan *et al.* (1984) are strongly inclined to hold that facts are not even needed as truth-makers for singular contingent propositions, such as the proposition that Ludwig is happy. According to them, such propositions are made true by individual substances and/or individual accidents, also known as particularized qualities, moments, tropes or modes. Armstrong (1989a, 1997), on the other hand, maintains that facts are needed as truth-makers for propositions that attribute contingent properties (or relations) to individual substances, provided the properties (or relations) in question are genuine universals. He even holds that the most basic propositions of this sort, atomic propositions, when true, are made true by *corresponding* atomic facts – so that a version of the correspondence theory, albeit restricted to contingent atomic propositions, survives at the core of his truth-maker theory. This is why Armstrong always speaks quite favourably of the correspondence theory.[6]

Others, those who speak unfavourably of the correspondence theory, reject it not only because of its ontological dimension; they deny, in addition, the intelligibility of the idea of a proposition corresponding with a slice of reality. They hold that the very notion of correspondence, as employed by the correspondence theory, is bankrupt, and that the theory should not be allowed to survive at all, not even when restricted to atomic propositions. They would maintain, like Dummett (1959: 14), that the truth-maker principle captures *all* that is good in the correspondence theory, which is not a whole lot. This is why Alex Oliver (1996: 69) says that the truth-maker principle is "a sanitised version of the correspondence theory", although, seeing that our correspondence theory is a species of the truth-maker principle, the insult might be better put by saying that the correspondence theory is a polluted, or insane, version of the truth-maker principle.

Advocates of truth-making who are opposed to correspondence theories hold that the latter's attempts to provide more than the generic truth-maker principle, (TM), are much too ambitious. However, some do not rest content just with (TM). They too want to provide more, although they tend to be less interested in truth and the truth-making relation, and to focus more on ontological questions.[7] They want to employ the generic truth-maker principle as a guide to doing ontology, asking the question: items of what ontological categories are needed as truth-makers for the propositions we are committed to accept as true? This enterprise can be understood as trying to provide a number of special truth-maker principles of the form 'Every true proposition of type *K* is made true by items of ontological category *C*', and as aiming to eventually replace the generic truth-maker principle with one that is more informative along the ontological dimension:

(TM⁺) If *y* is a true proposition, then *y* is made true by some item from category C1 or by some item from category C2 or by some item from category C3 or by ...; and there is nothing else that makes any true proposition true.

The final version of this principle, if it can be completed, would be the ideal grand finale of truth-maker-driven ontology. One hopes that it would be fairly succinct. But even if it ends up being rather longwinded, it will still be more informative than the generic truth-maker principle, as long as there is a closure clause ('and there is nothing else that makes any true proposition true'). Moreover, one hopes that it will be accompanied by many special truth-maker principles, telling us in much more detail which types of propositions can be made true by items of which ontological categories.

2 Truth-making and a more realistic correspondence theory

In the previous section, I presented a model correspondence theory whose relation to the generic truth-maker principle, (TM), is quite perspicuous. It is easy to see why friends of truth-making might want to reject this theory on the grounds that it is overwrought along various dimensions, while at the same time applauding it, if maybe only mildly, on the grounds that it has at least a good core: its characteristic principle, (TMC), obviously implies the generic truth-maker principle, (TM). But this simple and somewhat pleasing story is not realistic. One of its main characters, the central principle of our model correspondence theory,

(TMC) Every true proposition is made true by a fact it corresponds with

is fictitious: there is no real-life correspondence theory whose central principle takes the form of (TMC).[8] The sort of correspondence principles that one can find at the centre of some real-life correspondence theories will look much more like this (modulo variations in terminology):

(C) A proposition is true if and only if it corresponds with a fact,

which may again be thought of as accompanied by, or embedded in, a version of Structure or Correlation or both.[9]

(C) is a (generalized) biconditional: it offers a sufficient as well as a necessary condition for a proposition's being true. (TMC), on the other hand, is only a (generalized) one-way conditional: it offers only a necessary condition. By itself, this difference would be trivial because any truth-maker principle is easily converted into a biconditional, for the simple reason that '*x* makes *y* true' trivially implies '*y* is true'. There is, however, a deeper reason for this seemingly superficial difference. Advocates of (C) want to answer the question: what is truth? They intend (C) to be understood with sufficient strength so that the biconditional can be upgraded to a property identity, telling us that truth *is* correspondence with a fact, that the property *being true* is the general relational property *corresponding with some fact.* They intend to provide a *definition* of truth, in one sense of this term.[10]

(C) does not contain the phrase 'is made true by' or the phrase 'makes true'. Its intended role as a definition also explains this second difference between (C) and (TMC): the definition provided by (C) would become circular if it did contain these phrases.

Advocates of truth-maker principles regard their favourite principle as stating an important necessary truth about truth. But they do not typically intend it as a definition, which is one reason why truth-maker principles are formulated as mere one-way conditionals even though they are trivially convertible into biconditionals: to signal that they are not intended as definitions. I take it that the fear of circularity is the main reason why truth-maker principles, although trivially convertible into biconditionals, are not typically put forth as definitions.

How serious the threat of circularity actually is at this point is somewhat less clear-cut than it might seem. It is not entirely obvious that a definition of truth using the phrase '*x* makes *y* true' is circular. After all, the phrase does *not* decompose into '*x* makes *y* and *y* is true', which would yield an explicitly and undeniably circular definition. One might suggest that 'makes true' functions like 'is a father of' and propose that a definition of truth in terms of 'makes true', or rather 'is made true by something', can be understood along the lines of a definition of fatherhood in terms of 'is a father of someone': maybe not very informative, but not entirely uninformative either – at least it tells us that what on the linguistic surface looks like an absolute property should be understood as a general relational property. On the other hand, friends of the truth-maker principle usually hold that the following states a crucial necessary condition on truth-making: if *x* makes *y* true, then, necessarily, if *x* exists then *y* is true. If this condition is intended as partly definitional of truth-making, as it seems to be, then a definition of truth in terms of 'makes true' would turn out to be (indirectly) circular after all. Although this whole issue is somewhat tricky, I will assume that the threat of circularity is serious and a major reason why truth-maker principles are typically not put forth as definitions of truth.[11]

3 Bridge-principles

Our earlier correspondence theory obviously implies the generic truth-maker principle, (TM), because the central claim of that theory, (TMC), already contains the notion of truth-making. But that theory is a fiction. Our present correspondence theory, whose central characteristic principle is (C), is not a fiction. But it does not obviously imply (TM). So what is the relation between our non-fictitious correspondence theory and (TM), the generic truth-maker principle?

Let us try a simple suggestion. They are connected by *bridge-principles.* I use this term deliberately because it is reminiscent of treatments of theory reduction in the philosophy of science. An example (no doubt vastly oversimplified) will illustrate the basic idea (cf. Hempel 1966). Say fundamental chemistry contains theoretical terms like 'H' and 'O', but does not, strictly speaking, contain common-sense terms like 'water'. One nevertheless wants to say that the theory underwrites (vindicates, is implicitly committed to) some of our ordinary beliefs about water, our *folk-theory* of water, at least the parts of it that are not false. Although the scientific theory, not containing the term 'water', does not by itself imply any principles of our folk-theory of water, one can still say that it underwrites it to the extent that laws of our folk-theory can be deduced from the conjunction of the laws of the scientific theory together with bridge-laws, such as 'Water is constituted by H_2O'. The bridge-laws themselves do not, strictly speaking, belong to the scientific theory; they serve to connect the scientific theory with our folk-theory.

Let us apply a version of this to our correspondence theory of truth (by which I do not mean to suggest that such a "theory" has anything like the sort of respectability of a serious scientific theory). Our improved model correspondence theory, whose central claim is (C), underwrites (is committed to) the generic truth-maker principle, (TM), in the sense that (TM) can be derived from the conjunction of the official theory together with at least one bridge-principle, which connects the notion of truth-making to the official terminology of the theory, but which does not, and should not, be understood as belonging to the official theory, because adding it would raise a serious threat of circularity.

The friends of truth-making, even the ones that are hostile to the correspondence theory, should take an interest in such a bridge-principle. For they will want to maintain that (TM) captures something (or everything) that is good in our improved, more realistic, (C)-based correspondence theory. It is hard to see how this claim could be upheld without a bridge-principle. Note that the overall picture fits rather well with the idea, frequently voiced by friends of truth-making, that the generic truth-maker principle, (TM), expresses a *basic intuition* about truth: the friends of truth-making, we may observe, are telling us that (TM) is part of our folk-theory of truth.

Our correspondence theorists should also take some interest in such a bridge-principle, for they will want to hold that their theory is committed to (TM). The present picture fits well with the actual practice of real-life correspondence theorists. Reading their works, one finds that they too employ the notion of truth-making – some of them quite frequently – but only, as it were, in the surrounding text. When it comes to stating the official formulation (or summary) of their theory or definition, they keep the notion of truth-making at bay so as to avoid worries about circularity. This practice suggests that they too take the notion of truth-making, and the truth-maker principle, (TM), to be parts of our folk-theory of truth, and that they conceive of their official correspondence theory as underwriting this folk-theory by way of a (typically unstated) bridge-principle.[12]

So, let us look for a bridge-principle that, in conjunction with our improved model correspondence theory whose central claim is

(C) A proposition is true if and only if it corresponds with a fact,

allows us to derive the generic truth-maker principle:

(TM) Every true proposition is made true by something.

Our correspondence theorists will aim for a strong bridge-principle, preferably a biconditional, which can be upgraded to a property identity, allowing them to say that truth-making just *is* …, where '…' contains only vocabulary from their official theory. With such a strong principle, that is, a (real) definition of truthmaking, they could maintain that their theory already contains, albeit implicitly, an account of the truth-making relation and that much of our folk-theory of truth, at least in so far as it concerns truth and truth-making, can be reduced to the correspondence theory. The simplest proposal that would support such a claim would be the biconditional: '*x* makes *y* true if and only if *y* corresponds with *x*', which, if defensible, could be upgraded to the thesis that truth-making just is correspondence. Evidently, this is overly simplistic. For even the weaker, one-sided bridge-principle,

(B1) If *y* corresponds with *x*, then *x* makes *y* true,

which obviously would have to hold for the above proposal to be defensible, already looks quite untenable.[13]

Correspondence, it seems hard to deny, is a *symmetric* relation: necessarily, for any *x* and *y*, if *y* corresponds with *x*, then *x* corresponds with *y*. It is also a *reflexive* relation: necessarily, for any *x* and *y*, if *y* corresponds with *x*, then *y* corresponds with *y*. Truth-making, on the other hand, appears to be neither reflexive nor symmetric. (In fact, it is widely assumed, I think, that truth-making is *asymmetric,* which may well be a mistake, as we shall see below.) Assume a proposition *p* corresponds with a fact *f*. By (B1), it would follow that *f* makes *p* true. But by the symmetry of the correspondence relation, it also follows that *f* corresponds with *p:* from which it would follow, by (B1), that *p* makes *f* true. In general, according to (B1), any proposition that corresponds with a fact would not only be made true by that fact but also make it true. (B1) is not a viable bridge-principle. Hence the truth-making relation cannot just *be* the correspondence relation.

What bridge-principle could we put in place of (B1), so that (TM) is still derivable from (C) plus that principle? Leading up to another fairly simple but more tenable suggestion, let us take a closer look at the central correspondence principle, this time spelled out in slightly more formal terms. Using 'F' for 'fact', 'C' for 'corresponds with', 'P' for 'proposition', '∃' for 'there is a', and 'T' for 'true':

(C) For every *y*: T*y* if and only if (∃*x*)(P*y* & *y*C*x* & F*x*)

We can observe that our correspondence theorist does not actually define truth (for propositions) just as correspondence, but by way of the complex expression 'P*y* & *y*C*x* & F*x*'. What does this expression stand for? It stands for a relation; if the linguistic representation can be trusted, it stands for a complex, composite relation. (Admittedly, it may be somewhat unusual to refer to what is depicted by such an expression as a relation, but it is hard to see why it would not deserve that name.) Now note that, although the correspondence relation itself

*y*C*x*

is symmetric, the complex, composite relation

P*y* & *y*C*x* & F*x*

is asymmetric, provided the following principle – let us call it *Non-identity* – holds: necessarily, no proposition is identical with a fact; that is, necessarily, for any *x* and *y*, if P*y* & F*x*, then $y \neq x$.

Given Non-identity, the complex relation is obviously, if somewhat boringly, asymmetric. Take any pair, *p* and *f*, such that 'P*p* & *p*C*f* & F*f*' holds, the result of switching '*p*' and '*f*' throughout the whole expression is automatically false just because nothing is both a proposition and a fact. What, then, about Non-identity? It does not contain the notion of truth-making, so our correspondence theorists can and will regard it as a fundamental metaphysical principle, belonging to the official part of their theory, together with some version of Structure and/ or Correlation. Non-identity, by the way, is common ground, embraced by the friends of truth-making as well.[14]

The suggestion now is to replace the overly simplistic bridge-principle (B1) with the slightly more sophisticated

(B2) If P*y* & *y*C*x* & F*x*, then *x*MT*y*,

where 'MT' is short for 'makes true'. The conjunction of (C) with (B2) will obviously enable us to derive the generic truth-maker principle (TM).[15]

You might complain that (B2) seems a bit shallow and that not much progress has been made. You might even suggest that an advocate of (B1) would, as it were, already have intended it in the sense of (B2). Fair enough. However, there is a temptation, when thinking about correspondence theories of truth, to conceive of correspondence as somehow already "applied" to propositions and facts. Taking Non-identity for granted, "the correspondence relation" may then be conceived of as an asymmetric relation. But on reflection one will still find oneself judging that it is a symmetric relation; after all, the correspondence relation itself is symmetric. The difference between (B1) and (B2) at least sorts out this possible confusion.

The conjunction of (C) with (B2) allows our correspondence theorists to derive the generic truth-maker principle (TM); in addition, it also allows them to derive the special truth-maker principles mentioned earlier, (TMF) and (TMC):

(TM) Every true proposition is made true by something.
(TMF) Every true proposition is made true by a fact.
(TMC) Every true proposition is made true by a fact it corresponds with.[16]

At this point you might find yourself worried by the following thought: how can (B2), which states after all only a sufficient condition for truth-making, yield the result that facts, even corresponding facts, must be the truth-makers of true propositions? But note that this worry reads too much into (TMF) and (TMC). They do not imply that facts, or corresponding facts, are *the,* that is, *the only,* truth-makers of true propositions. Focus for the moment just on (TMF). It says that for every true proposition there is a fact that makes it true, which allows that some, even all, true propositions are also made true by items other than facts. The inclination to read more than this into (TMF) arises, I think, because (TMF) feels redundant when taken literally, so that one naturally takes it to say something stronger than it literally says. This, in turn, has to do with another principle that has been operating in the background all along, namely the *Converse* of the generic truth-maker principle:

Converse Every proposition that is made true by something is true.

This principle is not much discussed by friends of truth-making because it is presupposed by their use of the phrase 'makes true'. It functions as a meaning postulate for this phrase and is, consequently, even more basic than (TM) is taken to be by the friends of truth-making. One who denies Converse or, rather, one who rejects the sentence written above, next to the label 'Converse', must be using the words 'makes true' and 'is made true by' in a way that differs significantly from the way in which the friends of truth-making use them when stating the generic truth-maker principle (TM). On such a divergent (technical) use of these phrases, there would be no reason for saying that (TM), or rather, the sentence above, next to the label '(TM)', expresses a basic intuition about truth, which is of course what the friends of truth-making are saying.

Consider (TM). It is formulated as a necessary condition for truth. But, because of Converse, the condition (TM) states, *being made true by something,* is already sufficient for truth. What, then, is the point of (TMF) adding what looks like a "further" necessary condition? Is that not redundant? Well, assume *x* makes a proposition *y* true; according to (TMF), either *x* is already a fact or, if *x* is a non-fact, then *x*'s making true *y* entails that there is also a fact *z* such that *z* makes true *y.* In other words, (TMF) tells us that a proposition is made true by a non-fact, only if it is also made true by a fact, so that such a proposition will have at least two truth-makers. Similarly for (TMC); it tells us that a proposition is made true by an item that is not a corresponding fact, only if it is also made true by a corresponding fact, so that such a proposition will have at least two truth-makers.[17] So (TMF) and (TMC) are indeed implied by the conjunction of (C) with (B2), but they are weaker than one might take them to be at first glance. (TMF) does not imply that true propositions are made true only by facts; (TMC) does not imply that true propositions are made true only by corresponding facts.

These stronger claims will be derivable from (C) in conjunction with a second bridge-principle our correspondence theorists will want to advocate. Let us turn to this now. (B2) will suggest to our correspondence theorists that the folk-notion of truth-making picks out a complex relation composed of the properties of being a proposition, being a fact, and the relation of correspondence. But (B2) is not strong enough to bear out this suggestion. This will require, in addition, a bridge-principle like (B2) but running in the opposite direction:

(B3) If *x*MT*y*, then P*y* & *y*C*x* & F*x*.

In conjunction with (C), this bridge-principle entails that true propositions are made true only by facts, and that true propositions are made true only by corresponding facts. One naturally expects our correspondence theorists to be committed to these stronger claims, going beyond (TMF) and (TMC), because of their advocacy of (C) as their central principle about truth, especially because they understand (C) as providing a definition of truth. It would be wrongheaded to maintain that truth *is* correspondence with a fact while allowing that some, or even all, true propositions are made true by non-facts as long as that entails that they are also made true by corresponding facts. (B3) rules out truth-makers that are non-facts and rules out truth-makers that are facts but fail to correspond with the propositions they make true.

Note also that (B3) is needed for deriving Converse. However trivial or analytic Converse might be, since it contains the notion of truth-making, it is not part of the official correspondence theory, and it cannot be derived from a bridge-principle like (B2), which has truth-making in its consequent: for deriving Converse, our correspondence theorists need a bridge-principle with truth-making in the antecedent rather than the consequent. It seems to me that the ability to derive Converse is crucial, and that it is crucial just because Converse is trivial, self-evident, analytic, platitudinous, a meaning-principle, constitutive of the very notion of truth-making (etc.). Imagine our correspondence theorists could not derive Converse. One would then have strong grounds to question whether their claim that their theory underwrites at least a significant part of our folk-theory of truth and truth-making is adequately supported. One should even worry about their derivation of (TM) from (C) & (B2). If they were not committed to Converse, why think that what our correspondence theorists call "(TM)" is the genuine article, the principle that actually involves the notion of truth-making?

Let us take stock. Our correspondence theorists advocate (C) together with some version of Structure or Correlation or both. This is their official correspondence theory. By way of connecting this theory with our folk-theory of truth and truth-making, they also advocate the bridge-principles (B3) and (B2), which together with (C) imply Converse, (TM), (TMF), (TMC), and a still stronger principle saying that true propositions are made true only by corresponding facts. Finally, since (B3) and (B2) combined make for a biconditional, they will take this to support their claim that their official theory already contains, albeit implicitly, an account of the folk-notion of truth-making in terms of the properties of being a proposition, being a fact and the relation of correspondence.

Friends of truth-making reject most of this – the friends of truth-making, that is, who reject our correspondence theory. But note that they do accept (B2); they too embrace the conditional: *if a* proposition corresponds with a fact, then it is made true by that fact. Since the conjunction (C) & (B2) implies (TM), they applaud the correspondence theory for being committed to (TM) and maintain that (TM) captures something important that is good in the correspondence theory. But the conjunction (C) & (B2) also implies (TMF) and implies (TMC). Champions of truth-making reject (TMC), hence they reject (C); contemporary champions of truth-making reject both (TMC) and (TMF); some of their ancestors, for example Russell ([1918] 1985), reject only (TMC): either way, they reject (C). Note that their attitude towards (B3) differs significantly from their attitude towards (B2). They accept (B2) but reject (B3). Obviously, (B3) cannot be an acceptable principle by their lights: correspondence with a fact, they say, is not necessary for being made true. Along with (B3), they reject the stronger versions of (TMF) and (TMC), that is, the claim that all true propositions are made true only by (corresponding) facts.[18]

Viewed from the theory/folk-theory perspective, the debate between the two parties can be understood along the following lines. Our correspondence theorists maintain that their theory underwrites, in a relatively strong sense, our folk-theory of truth, at least in so far as it involves principles (intuitions) about truth-making. The friends of truth-making who oppose our correspondence theory – I will simply call them "the Truth-makers" from now on – object that, although this theory is to be applauded for being committed to the very important folk-theory principle (TM), it nevertheless has to be rejected because its additional commitments are in conflict with our folk-theory of truth, especially with intuitions against funny facts (logically complex facts). To this our correspondence theorists will respond with a two-pronged strategy: (a) the alleged intuitions reported by their opponents are not really there or are not very strong or central; and/or (b) to the extent that they are there, they are wrong and deserve to be corrected by the correspondence theory of truth – after all, folk-theoretical principles may well be wrong and in need of correction by theory. To this the Truth-makers will respond that the relevant recalcitrant intuitions are really there and are central and strong (and, maybe, supported by considerations independent from questions about truth), so that, on the contrary, these intuitions must be seen as refuting the correspondence theory rather than deserving correction by that theory.

I will not try to enter into this debate. Instead, I want to emphasize a point that I adumbrated earlier, suggesting that the picture I have drawn here of the relationship between our correspondence theory and the truth-maker principle has some aspects to it that are a bit murky.

Let us look at the situation from the point of view of the Truth-makers. As long as we focus exclusively on the truth-maker principle, (TM), the picture seems fairly clear. The Truth-makers themselves accept (B2). By their lights, the correspondence theory is *in fact* committed to (TM) – whether its advocates believe it or not, care for (TM) or not – because (TM) follows from (B2) plus (C). The Truth-makers can reason like this: "If (B2) then, if (C) then (TM); (B2) is true; hence: if (C) then (TM), that is, (C) is committed to (TM) in the straightforward sense that (C) holds only if (TM) holds."

When Converse is added to this picture it becomes less clear. The Truth-makers do of course embrace Converse wholeheartedly. But they do not accept (B3), which is used by the correspondence theorist to derive Converse from (C). So, according to them, the correspondence theory itself is not in fact committed to Converse; remember that (B3), being a bridge-principle, is not part of the official correspondence theory. It is just that the advocates of the correspondence theory believe (B3) and so *believe* that they are in fact committed to Converse: they are subjectively committed to it but not objectively, not according to the Truth-makers.[19]

But does this consideration not tend to undermine the Truth-makers' seemingly straightforward reason for thinking that the correspondence theory is committed to (TM) via (B2)? Converse surely is very fundamental to the Truth-makers: it is a meaning-principle or – if you do not like that language – a platitude, constitutive of the very notion of truth-making. Without objective commitment to Converse, it should be at least dubious, by the lights of the Truth-makers, whether the correspondence theory can really be said to be committed to (TM), involving as it does the notion of truth-making, or merely to an impostor, labelled '(TM)', which involves some other notion labelled 'truth-making'. Of course, the correspondence theorists assent to what looks like (B2) and, consequently, to what looks like (TM). They also believe they are committed to Converse but, according to the Truth-makers, they do so based on the false (B3). Can this be enough, by the lights of the Truth-makers, to count as genuine commitment to (TM)?

4 Is truth-making asymmetric?

In this last section I want to address a point I mentioned parenthetically in the previous section. It is quite natural to think that truth-making is an asymmetric relation, and it is, I think, widely assumed that truth-making is asymmetric. Related to this, it is also quite natural to think, maybe even more so, that truth-making is irreflexive, that is, that nothing can make itself true, and this too seems to be typically taken for granted. One may note that there is a logical connection between asymmetry and irreflexivity: an asymmetric relation must be irreflexive: any case of *aRa* will yield a *reductio* of the assumption that R is asymmetric.[20]

The natural assumption that truth-making is asymmetric (hence irreflexive), seems to play a considerable role in people's attitudes towards the truth-maker principle *vis-à-vis* the correspondence theory. Indeed, it seems that the perceived asymmetry of the truth-making relation is part of the appeal of the truth-maker principle. The truth-maker principle, one is inclined to say, is importantly right in trying to characterize truth by way of an asymmetric relation; on this point the correspondence theory leaves something to be desired because it tries to account for truth by way of a symmetric and reflexive relation.

I have already suggested earlier that the second part of this thought, the one about the correspondence theory, may to some extent derive from a tendency to confuse the symmetric correspondence relation, *yCx,* on the one hand, with the complex asymmetric relation P*y* & *yCx* & F*x*, on the other. Our correspondence theory says that for *y* to be true is for it to be related to some *x* by way of that complex asymmetric relation. Admittedly, this may not be quite satisfying, because the complex relation owes its asymmetry entirely to the fact that nothing can be both a proposition and a fact. One may well feel that the correspondence theory would be more satisfying if the genuinely relational component of the complex relation, *yCx*, were itself asymmetric; the account that is being offered of the truth-making relation by way of the complex relation P*y* & *yCx* & F*x* may strike one as somewhat shallow for the same reason.

But what about the perceived asymmetry of truth-making? Is the truth-making relation really asymmetric?

Consider the proposition that Ludwig is a dog. On the face of it, it seems quite plausible to think that this proposition is made true by Ludwig himself because Ludwig is essentially a dog: Ludwig, being essentially a dog, is necessarily such that, if he exists, then the proposition that he is a dog is true – which suggests that Ludwig is sufficient as a truth-maker for any proposition that correctly attributes one of his essential properties to him. Based on this, one will hold, accordingly, that the general existential proposition that there is at least one dog is also made true by Ludwig himself and, in addition, by each and every dog: each dog is a truth-maker for the proposition that there is a dog. Now consider the general existential proposition *that there is at least one proposition.* Assuming that every proposition is essentially a proposition, which seems plausible, it follows by the same line of reasoning that the proposition that there is at least one proposition is made true by each and every proposition, including itself: it is among its own truth-makers. So here we have a case where something makes itself true, which generates a counter-example to the natural assumption that truth-making is asymmetric, via being a counter-example to the natural assumption that truth-making is irreflexive: truth-making, it seems, is merely non-symmetric.[21]

The crucial ingredient of the reasoning leading to the counter-example is its starting-point: the assumption or intuition that Ludwig, being essentially a dog, suffices to make true the proposition that Ludwig is a dog. This assumption seems quite plausible and quite a few of the Truth-makers will think that it belongs to, or can be extracted from, our folk-theory of truth and truth-making. However, our intuitions to the effect that truth-making is asymmetric and irreflexive seem at least equally strong. They too are plausibly regarded as belonging to our folk-theory, or rather, as being extractable from our folk-theory (one would not typically expect to find them there couched in these technical terms). The reasoning above shows that there is a conflict here.[22]

How will our Truth-makers react to this? Some may want to respond that the alleged intuitions to the effect that truth-making is asymmetric and irreflexive were never really part of our folk-theory to begin with. Others may want to say the same thing about alleged intuitions to the effect that propositions correctly attributing essential properties to objects are made true just by those objects. Others may want to argue that all these intuitions do belong to our folk-theory of truth and that this theory is implicitly inconsistent, which is by no means unheard of when it comes to folk-theories (and our folk-theory of truth, in particular, is likely to be implicitly inconsistent anyway because of the intuitions that give rise to the liar paradox). This third response may then lead into a debate about which of our intuitions are mistaken and in need of correction, a debate that in many instances will be indistinguishable from the debate between advocates of the first two responses.

I will not enter into this debate. Instead, I want to end by briefly considering whether this issue bears on the relationship between our correspondence theory and the truth-maker principle, as seen from the point of view of those Truth-makers who hold that truth-making is *not* asymmetric, that is, those who accept the starting-point of the above line of reasoning and its conclusion.[23]

Based on bridge-principles (B2) and (B3), our correspondence theorists maintain that truth-making is the complex relation that holds between x and y if and only if Py & yCx & Fx. According to the Truth-makers presently under consideration, this is yet another reason for rejecting this position. More specifically, it is yet another reason for rejecting bridge-principle (B3), which is the one that is directly relevant here because it says: if $xMTy$, then Py & yCx & Fx. If truth-making is not asymmetric, this cannot be correct. The complex relation that appears in the consequent of this conditional is asymmetric, and the holding of a relation that is not asymmetric cannot be sufficient for the holding of a relation that is asymmetric.

Our correspondence theorists will not be much moved by this point. By their lights, it does not really insert a fresh consideration into the debate. The reasoning that resulted in the counter-example to the asymmetry assumption started from the Truth-makers' intuition that Ludwig himself, because he is essentially a dog, makes true the proposition that Ludwig is a dog. Our correspondence theorists are already firmly committed to the view that, since truth *is* correspondence with a fact, only facts can make true propositions true. They hold that intuitions to the contrary, if genuinely present, are in need of correction by the correspondence theory. Tire truth-maker relation, they say, is asymmetric.

Looking at the situation from the point of view of the Truth-makers, on the other hand, underscores the worry I raised at the end of the previous section. By their lights, the truth-making relation is neither symmetric nor asymmetric, which must surely be a fundamental fact about the nature of this relation. The Truth-makers are initially inclined to think that they and the correspondence theorists share a core insight, because it looks as if they are both committed, objectively committed, to:

(B2) If y is a proposition that corresponds with a fact x, then x makes y true,

which appears to build a bridge between the official correspondence theory and the generic truth-maker principle, (TM). (B2), unlike (B3), does not imply that truth-making is asymmetric. But the correspondence theorists do hold that it is; or rather, they hold that the relation expressed by the words 'makes true' is an asymmetric relation, which is quite wrong according to the Truth-makers. It seems that this should further undermine the Truth-makers' confidence in their initial view that the correspondence theorists are really committed to truth-making and not merely to "truth-making".[24]

Notes

1. G. E. Moore is the only one I am aware of who explicitly advocates both (a) and (b), although at later places in the same work he mentions only (a); cf. Moore (1953: 256, 276–7).

2. J. L. Austin ([1950] 1979) advocates correspondence with Correlation but without Structure, although he does not tell us whether he wants both parts of Correlation or only part (a).
3. Some critics find Structure an obviously ludicrous idea, but they tend to think of *truth-bearers* as *linguistic* items. Austin, for example, a prominent critic of Structure, takes the truth-bearers to be what he calls *statements,* that is, sentences as used on a certain occasion; cf. Austin ([1950] 1979:119). It does indeed seem ludicrous to maintain that all the details of grammatical structure exhibited by our (true) sentences have their analogues in correspondingly structured facts. This is why correspondence theorists who advocate Structure will typically emphasize the gap between the sentences of ordinary language, on the one hand, and propositions, on the other hand: sentences with significantly different grammatical structures, they will say, can express the same proposition – the wider the gap one finds between sentences and expressed propositions, the closer the match one can advocate between (true) propositions and corresponding facts. This is also why correspondence theorists tend to promote *ideal languages,* designed to cut through the idiosyncrasies of ordinary language. The sentences (formulas) of an ideal language are intended to mirror perfectly the structure of the propositions they express. In this way they are supposed to provide – via the correspondence between true propositions and facts – a better representation of the real structure of facts.
4. Disjunctive facts are regarded as funny facts *par excellence* by the friends of truth-making. One of the main sources for this is Russell: "I do not suppose that there is in the world a single disjunctive fact corresponding to '*p* or *q*'. It does not look plausible that in the actual objective world there are facts going about which you could describe as '*p* or *q*'" (1956: 209); and also: "You must not look about the real world for an object which you can call 'or', and say 'Now, look at this. This is "or"'" (*ibid.:* 209ff.). A generalized version of the second point appears in Wittgenstein's *Tractatus,* another important influence on advocates of truth-making: "My fundamental idea is that the 'logical constants' are not representatives; that there can be no representatives of the *logic* of facts" (1921: 4.0312).
5. Russell (1956), a very important influence on contemporary advocates of truth-making, would stop at this point: he wants to keep (TMF); cf. e.g. Russell (1956: 183).
6. This is the overall picture presented in Armstrong (1989a, 1997), and in parts of his *Truth and Truthmakers* (2004:48-50). However, in other parts of *Truth and Truthmakers,* Armstrong seems to take seriously an argument to the effect that particulars have all their properties necessarily. Since facts are not needed as truth-makers for propositions that attribute necessary properties to particulars, this would seem to do away with the need for facts entirely. In Russell's *The Philosophy of Logical Atomism* ([1918] 1985), a restricted version of the correspondence theory also survives at the core; but he differs significantly from Armstrong (1989, 1997) on the range of the restriction and on the question whether facts are the only truth-makers.
7. See e.g. Mulligan *et al.* (1984), Fox (1987), Bigelow (1988), Armstrong (1989, 1997, 2004), and the papers in Beebee & Dodd (2005).
8. There is an exception. My *Random House Unabridged Dictionary* (2nd edn) contains the following entry: "correspondence theory, *Philos,* the theory of truth that a statement is rendered true by the existence of a fact with corresponding elements and similar structure". This is very close to (TMC), applied to statements and enriched with a bit of Structure.
9. In the twentieth century, the formula 'truth is correspondence with a fact' came to be used as representative of the whole family of now so-called correspondence theories. It derives from

Russell (1912: ch. 12) [This volume, Ch. 1 – Ed.], and Moore (1953: chs 14–15) (the latter publishes lectures given in 1910–11).

10. At least a "real definition". This does not commit them to the claim that (C) provides a definition in the sense of giving a synonym for the term 'true'. Nowadays, most correspondence theorists would consider it implausibly and unnecessarily bold to maintain that 'true' *means the same as* 'corresponds with a fact'. Interestingly, the *Oxford English Dictionary* would nevertheless seem to lend some mild support even to this bold claim, for it contains the entry: "Truth n. Conformity with fact; agreement with reality; accuracy, correctness, verity (of statement or thought)".
11. What is wrong with circular definitions? It does not seem right to respond that they are all entirely uninformative. In any case, that's a methodological or epistemological issue. What is wrong with them metaphysically speaking? With respect to definitions that are intended as real definitions, the answer must be something like this. A real definition is supposed to describe the constituent-structure of a property or relation. A circular real definition would entail that the defined property or relation contains itself as a proper constituent: but nothing can possibly contain itself as a proper constituent.
12. In *Some Main Problems of Philosophy,* Moore employs the notion of truth-making early on (1953: 254); it then falls away and does not show up in any of his official attempts at defining truth (*ibid.:* 256, 267, and esp. 277). Russell lays out and summarizes his account of truth without the notion of truth-making; he only uses this notion afterwards to drive home the point that truths are not made true by our minds or beliefs (1912: 129) [This volume, Ch. 1, p. 8 – Ed.]. Austin says: "When a statement is true, there is, *of course,* a state of affairs which makes it true..." ([1950] 1979: 123); but again, the official formulation of his definition does not contain the notion of truth-making. Austin's definition, by the way, does not fit very neatly into the simple straitjacket of (C); cf. *ibid.,* 121–2.
13. Note that (Bl), being a correspondence-to-truth-making conditional, is clearly relevant here: if it did hold, one could quickly derive (TM) from (C) plus (B1).
14. Compare this with the *identity theory of truth,* according to which a proposition is true iff it is identical with a fact; cf. Dodd (2000); David (2001). This theory is a natural enemy of both correspondence and truth-maker theorists. The identity theory, they point out, leads to the unacceptable claim that every true proposition makes itself true (via a bridge-principle saying that every proposition that is identical with a fact is made true by that fact, that is, by itself).
15. The two bolder proposals midway between (B1) and (B2),

    If P*x* & *y*C*x,* then *x*MT*y*,
    If *y*C*x* & F*x*, then *x*MT*y*,

    are not viable. Since every proposition corresponds with itself, the first has the unacceptable consequence that every proposition makes itself true. Since every fact corresponds with itself, the second has the unacceptable consequence that every fact makes itself true.
16. (TMF) and (TMC) follow from (C) & (B2) because, if (B2) holds, then so must the conditionals that are just like (B2) except that their consequents are expanded to '*x*MT*y* & F*x*' and '*x*MT*y* & F*x* & *y*C*x*'.
17. Many friends of truth-making hold, for example, that Ludwig himself makes true the proposition that Ludwig exists. (TMF) and (TMC) allow for this, but they add the following. Necessarily,

if Ludwig makes true the proposition that Ludwig exists, then there is a (corresponding) fact that makes true the proposition that Ludwig exists. Given Structure, that would be the fact that Ludwig exists. According to (TMF) and (TMC), if there were no such (corresponding) fact as the fact that Ludwig exists, making true the proposition that Ludwig exists, then Ludwig would not make the proposition true either (he would not exist).

18. Russell (1956) is an interesting case. His overall strategy can be understood along the following lines. He wants to replace (C) with its restriction to *atomic* propositions:

    (CA) If *y* is atomic, then *y* is true iff *y* corresponds with a fact.

    He then wants to account for the truth-values of molecular propositions by way of laws detailing the logical relations between propositions – what we would now call *recursive clauses* – such as: a disjunctive proposition is true iff at least one of its disjunctive is true. He was not, however, entirely clear about the consequences of this strategy; compare, for example, his remark that "the correspondence of a molecular proposition with facts *is of a different sort* from the correspondence of an atomic proposition with a fact" (1956: 210, emphasis added). He should not have talked about "correspondence" here at all, for he held that there are no disjunctive facts for true disjunctive propositions to correspond with (hence, that the correspondence theory is false). He should have said instead that the truth or falsehood of every proposition can be explained in terms of (derived from) the logical relations between propositions, that is, the recursive clauses, together with (CA), that is, the correspondence or non-correspondence of atomic propositions with facts. This recursive approach to truth can be pursued with the aim to *reject* (TM) by way of the claim that not all truths have truth-makers, only atomic truths have truth-makers. But it can also be pursued – and this seems to have been Russell's intention at the time – with the aim to *secure* (TM) even though the correspondence theory has been rejected: not every truth corresponds with a fact, only atomic truths do, but every truth is made true by something (a fact, in Russell's case), where the recursive clauses are supposed to show how truth-making without correspondence, but grounded in correspondence, comes about. Unfortunately, Russell was a bit cavalier about this last part of his programme.

19. The bridge-principles, being *bridge*-principles, function somewhat like inference rules. So compare the following scenario. Say a philosopher, advocating a theory *T*, which you do not accept, derives 'There are possible worlds' from *T* by way of an inference rule that you do not accept either. Would you say that *she* is ontologically committed to possible worlds? Yes. Would you say that *her theory* is ontologically committed to possible worlds? No, she just believes, wrongly, that it is.

20. For truth-making to be an *asymmetric* relation, the following has to hold. Necessarily, for any *x* and *y*, if *x*MT*y*, then not *y*MT*x*. For truth-making to be *irreflexive,* the following has to hold. Necessarily, if *x*MT*y*, then $x \neq y$. I assume throughout that relations have such properties as being symmetric, asymmetric, reflexive (etc.) necessarily, if they have them at all. In mathematical logic one typically treats such properties as *relativized* to certain sets, so that one relation, *R,* can consistently be said to be asymmetric *in* a set *A* but not asymmetric *in* another set *B*. Both our correspondence theorists and the Truth-makers, will regard such talk as not to be taken quite literally, holding that it does not, strictly speaking, apply to *R* itself, but to different "restrictions" of *R*. For better or for worse, they want to know about the nature of the relation *R* itself, whether it is, for example, asymmetric (period).

21. Which is consistent with saying that it "typically behaves" like an asymmetric relation, meaning, roughly, that in the vast majority of cases where something *x* makes a proposition *y* true, *y* does not, and cannot possibly, make *x* true.
22. Actually, additional assumptions are involved: (a) an existential generalization is made true by anything that makes any of its instances true; (b) propositions are essentially propositions; and (c) propositions are truth-bearers. It is hard to see how a Truth-maker could object to any of them.
23. A number of contemporary Truth-makers are committed or strongly' drawn to the view' that propositions correctly attributing essential properties to objects are made true just by those objects (no facts need apply); cf. Mulligan *et al.* (1984); Fox (1987: 190); Bigelow (1988a: 128); and also Armstrong (2004). Armstrong's attitude towards this view in A *World of States of Affairs* is a bit complicated, because he is inclined to reject essential properties to begin with (1997: 124). His favourite argument in that book is the "truth-maker argument". Assume the proposition that *a* is *F* is true. Armstrong asks: what is its truth-maker? It cannot be *a*, because *a* can exist without the proposition being true. It cannot be the universal *being F*, for that can exist and be instantiated in the absence of *a*. It cannot be the pair of the particular and the universal, because the universal might be instantiated in some particular other than *a*. It must be the fact that *a* is *F* (cf. *ibid.*: 115). Note that this argument, which is supposed to establish the need for facts as truth-makers, does not establish such a need with respect to true propositions attributing essential properties to *a*, for which the first step of the argument fails: if *a* is essentially' *F*, then *a* cannot exist without the proposition that *a* is *F* being true – nothing more than *a* seems needed in this case.
24. Thanks to Adolf Rami and Ted Warfield.

References

Armstrong, David. M.: 1989. *A Combinatorial Theory of Possibility*. Cambridge: Cambridge University Press.

Armstrong, David. M.: 1997. *A World of States of Affairs*. Cambridge: Cambridge University Press.

Armstrong, David. M.: 2004. *Truth and Truthmakers*. Cambridge: Cambridge University Press.

Austin, John. L.: 1950. Truth. Reprinted in *Philosophical Papers*, 3rd ed., edited by J.O. Urmson and G.J. Warnock. Oxford: Oxford University Press 1979: 117–133.

Beebee, H. and Dodd, J., eds.: 2005. *Truthmakers: The Contemporary Debate*, Oxford: Clarendon Press.

Bigelow, John: 1988. *The Reality of Numbers: A Physicalist's Philosophy of Mathematics*. Oxford: Oxford University Press.

David, Marian: 2001. Truth as Identity and Truth as Correspondence. In M. Lynch, ed., *The Nature of Truth*. Cambridge,Mass.: The MIT Press: 683–704.

Dodd, Julian: 2000. *An Identity Theory of Truth*. New York: St. Martin's Press.

Dummett, Michael: 1959. Truth. Reprinted in Truth and Other Enigmas. Cambridge, Mass.: Harvard University Press: 1–28.

Fox, John F.: 1987. Truthmaker. *Australasian Journal of Philosophy* 65: 188–207.

Hempel, Carl G.: 1966. *Philosophy of Natural Science*. Englewood Cliffs, N.J.: Prentice Hall.

Moore, G. E.: 1953. *Some Main Problems of Philosophy*. London: George Allen & Unwin. (Lectures given in 1910–11.)

Mulligan, Kevin, Simons, Peter, and Smith, Barry: 1984. Truth-Makers. *Philosophy and Phenomenological Research* 44: 287–321

Oliver, Alex: 1996. The Metaphysics of Properties. *Mind* 105: 1–80.
Pitcher, George: 1964. Introduction. In G. Pitcher, ed., *Truth*. Englewood Cliffs, N.J.: Prentice Hall: 1-15.
Russell, Bertrand: 1912. *The Problems of Philosophy*. Reprinted at Oxford: Oxford University Press 1971.
Russell, Bertrand: 1918. The Philosophy of Logical Atomism. In *Logic and Knowledge*, edited by R. C. Marsh. New York: Capricorn Books 1956: 176–281.
Russell, Bertrand: 1956. *Logic and Knowledge: Essays, 1901–1950*. London: George Allen and Unwin.
Wittgenstein, Ludwig: 1921. *Tractatus Logico-Philosophicus*. In *Annalen der Naturphilosophie*. English translation by D. Pears and B. F. McGuinnes. London: Routledge & Kegan Paul 1961.

3 Tarski's theory of truth

HARTRY FIELD

In the early 1930s there was prevalent, among scientifically minded philosophers, the view that semantic notions such as the notions of truth and denotation were illegitimate: that they could or should not be incorporated into a scientific conception of the world. But when Tarski's work on truth became known, all this changed. Popper wrote: 'As a result of Tarski's teaching, I no longer hesitate to speak of "truth" and "falsity"' (1959: 274); and Popper's reaction was widely shared.[1]

A philosopher who shared Popper's reaction to Tarski's discoveries would presumably argue as follows. 'What Tarski did was to define the term "true", using in his definitions only terms that are clearly acceptable. In particular, he did not employ any undefined semantic terms in his definitions. So Tarski's work should make the term "true" acceptable even to someone who is initially suspicious of semantic terms.'

This contention has an initial plausibility, but I will argue that it is radically wrong. My contrary claim will be that Tarski succeeded in reducing the notion of truth *to certain other semantic notions*; but that he did not in any way explicate these other notions, so that his results ought to make the word 'true' acceptable only to someone who already regarded these other semantic notions as acceptable.

By claiming that Tarski merely reduced truth to other semantic notions, I don't mean to suggest that his results on truth are trivial. On the contrary, I think that they are extremely important, and have applications not only to mathematics but also to linguistics and to more directly philosophical problems about realism and objectivity. I think, however, that the real value of Tarski's discoveries for linguistics and philosophy is widely misunderstood, and I hope to eradicate the most central misunderstandings by clarifying and defending the claim that Tarski merely reduced truth to other semantic notions.

I

I believe that Tarski presented his semantic theory in a very misleading way, one that has encouraged the misinterpretations just alluded to. In this section I will present Tarski's theory as I think he should have presented it. However, I do not expect instant agreement that this new way is better than the old, and so I will use the name 'Tarski*' for a logician who gave the sort of semantic theory I will now sketch. Later in the chapter I will compare Tarski*s semantics to the semantics that the real Tarski actually gave; by doing this I will cast light on the issues raised in my introductory paragraphs.

In sketching Tarski*s theory, I will focus my attention on a particular object language L. The language L that I choose will be a quantificational language with names ('c_1', 'c_2', ...), one-place function symbols ('f_1', 'f_2',...), and one-place predicates ('p_1', 'p_2', ...). The language of course cannot be viewed as an 'uninterpreted' language, i.e., just as a bunch of strings of meaningless marks, for then there would be no truth to worry about. Instead, the language should be regarded as something that people actually speak or write; and it is because the speakers speak or write the way they do that the words of the language have the meaning they have.[2]

Initially I will follow Tarski in supposing that in L 'the sense of every expression is unambiguously determined by its form' (Tarski 1956*a*: 166), i.e., that whenever two speakers use the same name (or one speaker uses it on two occasions) they are referring to the same thing, that whenever two speakers use the same sentence either both are saying something true or neither is, etc. In these circumstances it makes sense to speak of the names of the language denoting things (a name denotes whatever the users of the name refer to) and the sentences being true or false (true when speakers who use it say something true by so doing). The more general situation, in which there are expressions whose 'sense' is not determined wholly by their form, will be dealt with later. (We'll see that it is one of the advantages of Tarski*s semantics that it can easily handle this more general situation.)

The syntax of L can be given by two recursive definitions: first we define the *singular terms* by saying that all names and variables are singular terms, and a function symbol followed by a singular term is a singular term; then we define the *formulas* by saying that a predicate followed by a singular term is a formula, as is the negation of a formula, the conjunction of two formulas, and the universal quantification of a formula with any variable. The *sentences, or closed formulas,* are then singled out in the usual way.

Now we can proceed to Tarski*s semantics. Rather than characterize truth directly, we characterize it relative to some assignment of objects to the variables, say s_k to 'x_k'. The idea is going to be to treat the variables, or at least the free variables, as sort of 'temporary names' for the objects assigned to them. So we proceed by fixing a sequence $s = \langle s_1, s_2 \ldots\rangle$ of objects, to be assigned to 'x_1', 'x_2',..., respectively; and we want to say what it is for a formula to be true$_s$, i.e., true relative to the assignment *s*. As a preliminary we say what it is for a term to denote$_s$ an object, i.e., to denote it relative to the assignment s. The denotation of 'x_k' relative to *s* is evidently s_k, for this is the object assigned to 'x_k'. But what is the denotation relative to *s* of 'c_k'? Evidently what objects are assigned to the variables here is irrelevant, and the denotation$_s$ of 'c_k' is some fixed object that users of the language refer to when they use the name 'c_k'. Just what this object is depends on facts we have not yet been given about the use of 'c_k'. Similarly there are facts we have not yet been given about the use of 'p_k' and 'f_k' which we need in order to fix the truth value of sentences containing them. For 'p_k' the relevant facts concern the extension of the predicate—what objects the predicate *applies to*—for it is this which affects the truth value of all utterances containing 'p_k', For 'f_k', the relevant facts concern what pairs of objects *fulfill* that function symbol—in the sense that the pair (John Adams, John Quincy Adams) and every other father-son pair fulfill the. function symbol 'father of'.

With these points in mind it is now easy to give an inductive characterization of denotation$_s$:

T1 (A) 1. 'x_k' denotes$_s$ s_k
2. 'c_k' denotes$_s$ what it denotes

3. $\ulcorner f_k(e)\urcorner$ denotes$_s$ an object a if and only if
(i) there is an object b that e denotes$_s$
and (ii) 'f_k' is fulfilled by $\langle a,b\rangle$.

(Here 'e' is a variable ranging over expressions of L.) Similarly we define 'true$_s$' for formulas—what Tarski calls satisfaction of a formula by s:

(B) 1. $\ulcorner p_k(e)\urcorner$ is true$_s$ if and only if
(i) there is an object a that e denotes$_s$
and (ii) 'p_k' applies to a
2. $\ulcorner{\sim}e\urcorner$ is true$_s$ if and only if e is not true$_s$
3. $\ulcorner e_1 \wedge e_2\urcorner$ is true$_s$ if and only if e_1 is true$_s$ and so is e_2
4. $\ulcorner \forall x_k(e)\urcorner$ is true$_s$ if and only if for each sequence s^* that differs from s at the kth place at most, e is true$_{s^*}$.

This completes the characterization of truth relative to an assignment of objects to the variables. In the case of sentences it is easily seen that we get the same results whatever such assignment we pick; we can say

(C) A sentence is true if and only if it is true$_s$ for some (or all) s.

This completes my elaboration of Tarski*s 'truth definition' T1 for L—or his *truth characterization* (TC), as I prefer to call it. What is its philosophical significance? The obvious answer, and the correct one, I think, is that the TC reduces one semantic notion to three others. It explains what it is for a sentence to be true in terms of certain semantic features of the primitive components of the sentence: in terms of what it is for a name to denote something, what it is for a predicate to apply to something, and what it is for a function symbol to be fulfilled by some pair of things. It is convenient to introduce the expression 'primitively denotes' as follows: every name *primitively denotes* what it denotes; every predicate and every function symbol *primitively denotes* what it applies to or is fulfilled by; and no complex expression primitively denotes anything. In this terminology, what T1 does is to explain truth in terms of primitive denotation. Similarly we can explain denotation for arbitrary closed singular terms (such as '$f_1(c_1)$') in terms of primitive denotation, i.e., in terms of the semantic features of the names and function symbols from which the complex singular term is composed—we merely say that a closed singular term denotes an object a if it denotes$_s$ a for some (or all) s, where denotation$_s$ is defined as before. We see then that *Tarski*s semantics explains the semantic properties of complex expressions* (e.g., truth value for sentences, denotation for complex singular terms) *in terms of semantic properties of their primitive components.*

To explain truth in terms of primitive denotation is, I think, an important task. It certainly doesn't answer *every* question that anyone would ever want answered about truth, but for many purposes it is precisely what we need. For instance, in model theory we are interested in such questions as: given a set Γ of sentences, is there any way to choose the denotations of the primitives of the language so that every sentence of Γ will come out true given the usual semantics for the logical connectives?[3] For questions such as this, what we need to know is how the truth value of a whole sentence depends on the denotations of its primitive nonlogical parts, and that is precisely what T1 tells us. So *at least for model-theoretic purposes,* Tarski*s TC is precisely the kind of explication of truth we need.

I want now to return to a point I mentioned earlier, about Tarski's restriction to languages in which 'the sense of every expression is unambiguously determined by its form.' Natural languages are full of expressions that do not meet this requirement. For instance, different tokens of 'John takes grass' can differ in 'sense'—e.g., one token may be uttered in saying that John Smith smokes marijuana, and another may be uttered in saying that John Jones steals lawn material, and these differences may give rise to differences of truth value in the tokens. (I say that a complete[4] token of a sentence is true if the person who spoke or wrote that token said something true by so doing; I also say that a name token denotes an object if the person who spoke or wrote the token referred to the object by so doing.) The prevalence of such examples in natural languages raises the question of whether Tarski's type of semantic theory is applicable to languages in which the sense is *not* determined by the form; for if the answer is no, then Davidson's very worthwhile project (Davidson 1967) of giving truth characterizations for natural languages seems doomed from the start.

It seems clear that if we stick to the kind of TC that Tarski actually gave (see next section), there is no remotely palatable way of extending TC's to sentences like 'John takes grass'. But if we use TC's like T1 there is no difficulty at all. The only point about languages containing 'John' or 'grass' or 'I' or 'you' is that for such languages 'true', 'denotes', and other semantic terms make no clear sense as applied to expression types; they make sense only as applied to tokens. For this reason we have to interpret clause (B)2 of T1 as meaning

A token of $\ulcorner{\sim}e\urcorner$ is true_s if and only if the token of e that it contains is not true_s,

and similarly for the other clauses. Once we interpret our TC in this way in terms of tokens, i.e., individual occasions of utterance, that TC works perfectly: someone who utters 'John is sick' (or 'I am sick') says something true if and only if his token of 'sick' applies to the person he refers to by 'John' (or by 'I'); and the fact that other speakers (or this speaker on other occasions) sometimes refer to different things when they use 'John' (or 'I') is beside the point.

This analysis leaves entirely out of account the ways in which 'I' and 'John' differ: it leaves out of account, for instance, the fact that a token of 'I' always denotes the speaker who produced it. But that is no objection to the analysis, for the analysis purports merely to explain truth in terms of primitive denotation; it does not purport to say anything about primitive denotation, and the differences between 'I' and 'John' (or their analogues in a language like L) are purely differences of how they denote. (The word 'I' denotes according to the simple rule mentioned two sentences back; 'John' denotes according to much more complex rules that I have no idea how to formulate.)

Of course, the fact that a theory of denotation for a word like 'I' is so simple and obvious, makes it possible to alter the TC so that the theory of denotation for such a word is built into the TC itself—such a course is adopted, for instance, at the end of Davidson 1967. I myself prefer to preserve the analogies of the word 'I' to. words that function less systematically, e.g., 'we', 'she', and 'John'. How one treats 'I' is more or less a matter of taste; but the less systematic words I've just mentioned cannot be handled in the say that Davidson handles 'I', and the only reasonable way I can see to handle them is the way I have suggested: use a truth characterization like T1 (except stated in terms of tokens rather than types), and leave it to a separate theory of primitive denotation to explain the relevant differences between tokens of 'John' that denote John Adams and tokens of 'John' that denote John Lennon, and between tokens of 'bank' that apply to things along rivers and tokens of 'bank' that apply to the Chase Manhattan.[5]

There are other advantages to T1 besides its ability to handle ambiguous sentences, i.e., sentences for which the sense is not determined by the form. For instance, Tarski required that the vocabulary of the language be fixed once and for all; but if we decide to give truth characterizations of type T1, this is unnecessary: all that is required is that the general structure of the language be fixed, e.g., that the semantic categories[6] (name, one-place predicate, etc.) be held constant. In other words, if a language already contained proper names, the invention of a new name to baptize an object will not invalidate the old TC; though introduction of a name into a hitherto nameless language will.

To show this, we have merely to reformulate the given TC so that it does not rely on the actual vocabulary that the language contains at a given time, but works also for sentences containing new names, one-place predicates, etc., that speakers of the language might later introduce. To do this is trivial: we define denotation$_s$ by

1. The *k*th variable denotes$_s$ s_k
2. If e_1 is a name, it denotes$_s$ what it denotes
3. If e_1 is a singular term and e_2 is a function symbol, then $\ulcorner e_2(e_1)\urcorner$ denotes$_s$ *a* if and only if

    (i) as before

    and (ii) e_2 is fulfilled by $\langle a, b\rangle$

and we can generalize the definition of truth$_s$ in a similar manner.[7] This shows that, in giving a TC, there is no need to utilize the particular vocabulary used at one temporal stage of a language, for we can instead give a more general TC which can be incorporated into a diachronic theory of the language (and can also be applied directly to other languages of a similar structure). *If,* that is, we accept the modification of Tarski proposed in this section.

II

The kind of truth characterization advocated in the previous section differs from the kind of TC Tarski offered in one important respect. Tarski stated the policy 'I shall not make use of any semantical concept if I am not able previously to reduce it to other concepts' (1956*a*: 152-3), and this policy is flagrantly violated by T1: T1 utilizes unreduced notions of proper names denoting things, predicates applying to things, and function symbols being fulfilled by things.

Tarski's truth characterizations, unlike T1, accorded with his stated policy: they did not contain any semantic terms like 'applies to' or 'denotes'. How did Tarski achieve this result? Very simply: first, he translated every name, predicate, and function symbol of L into English; then he utilized these translations in order to reformulate clauses 2 and 3(ii) of part (A) of the definition and clause 1(ii) of part (B). For simplicity, let's use '$\overline{c_1}$', '$\overline{c_2}$', etc. as abbreviations for the English expressions that are the translations of the words 'c_1', 'c_2',... of L: e.g.: if L is simplified German and 'c_1' is 'Deutschland', then '$\overline{c_1}$' is an abbreviation for 'Germany'. Similarly, let '$\overline{f_1}$' abbreviate the translation into English of the word 'f_1' of L, and let

'$\bar{p}_1$' abbreviate the translation of 'p_1' into English. Then Tarski's reformulated truth definition will read as follows:

T2 (A) 1. as before
2. 'c_k' denotes$_s$ $\bar{c}_k$
3. ⌜$f_k(e)$⌝ denotes$_s$ a if and only if
(i) as before
(ii) a is $\bar{f}_k(b)$
(B) 1. ⌜$p_k(e)$⌝ is true$_s$ if and only if
(i) as before
(ii) $\bar{p}_k(a)$
2–4. as before
(C) as before

What T2 is like depends of course on the precise character of the translations of the primitives that are utilized. For instance, if we translate 'c_1' as 'the denotation of "c_1"', translate 'p_1' as 'is something that "p_1" applies to', etc., then T2 becomes identical with T1. This of course is *not* what Tarski intended. What Tarski intended is that T2 not contain unexplicated semantic terms, and if we are to get this result we must not employ any semantic terms in our translations.[8]

But other restrictions on translations are also necessary: if we were to translate 'Deutschland' as 'Bertrand Russell', a truth characterization T2 that was based on this translation would grossly misrepresent L. In order to state the matter more generally, I introduce the term 'coreferential': two singular terms are coreferential if they denote the same thing; two predicative expressions are coreferential if they have the same extension, i.e., if they apply to the same things; and two functional expressions are coreferential if they are fulfilled by the same pairs. It is then easily seen that any departure from coreferentiality in translation will bring errors into T2. For instance, suppose we translate the foreign predicate 'glub' as 'yellow', and suppose 'glub' and yellow are not *precisely* coreferential; then clause $(B)_1$ will say falsely that 'glub (x)' is true of just those objects which are yellow.

Let us say, then, that

(1) An adequate translation of a primitive e_1 of L into English is an expression e_2 of English such that

(i) e_1 and e_2 are coreferential, and

(ii) e_2 contains no semantic terms.

This notion of an adequate translation is of course a semantic notion that Tarski did not reduce to nonsemantic terms. But that is no objection to his characterization T2 (at least, it isn't obviously an objection), for the notion of an adequate translation is never built into the truth characterization and is not, properly speaking, part of a theory of truth. On Tarski's view we need to adequately translate the object language into the metalanguage in order to give an adequate theory of truth for the object language; this means that the notion of an adequate translation is employed in the methodology of giving truth theories, but it is not employed in the truth theories themselves.

In what follows I shall assume that the language L with which we are dealing is so related to English that all its primitives *can* be adequately translated into English, according to the standards of adequacy set forth in (1). (This is another restriction that we avoid if we give TC's of the type T1; quite a significant restriction, I think.) If we then suppose that the translation given ('$\bar{c}_1$' for 'c_1', etc.) is one of the adequate translations, then T2, like T1, is a correct recursive characterization of truth for the language L. There is, of course, a simple procedure for transforming recursive characterizations such as these into explicit characterizations. To carry the procedure through in these cases would be pretty complicated, but it could be done; so we could regard T1 (or T2) as implicitly specifying a metalinguistic formula '$A_1(e)$' (or '$A_2(e)$'), and saying that an utterance *e* of L is true if and only if $A_1(e)$ (or $A_2(e)$). If we regard T1 and T2 as written in this form, then the key difference between them is that '$A_1(e)$' *contains semantic terms* and '$A_2(e)$' *does not.* The question then arises: is the fact that '$A_2(e)$' does not contain semantic terms an advantage of T2 over T1? If so, then *why* is it an advantage?

In order to discuss the possible advantages of T2 over T1, I think we have to go beyond mathematical considerations and focus instead on linguistic and other philosophical matters. It is not enough to say that T2 *defines* truth without utilizing semantic terms, whereas T1 defines it only in other semantic terms: this is not enough until we say something more about the purpose of definition. If the purpose of giving a 'definition' of truth is to enable you to do model theory, then the elimination of semantic terms from T1 gives no advantage. For what purpose do we want definitions for which the elimination of semantic terms is useful?

One purpose to which definitions are sometimes put is in explaining the meaning of a word. This of course is very vague, but I think it is clear enough to enable us to recognize that neither T1 nor T2 has very much to do with explaining the meaning of the word 'true'. This is especially obvious for T2: a T2-type truth definition works for a single language only, and so if it 'explains the meaning of' the word 'true' as applied to that language, then for *any* two languages L_1 and L_2, the word 'true' means something different when applied to utterances of L_1 than it means when applied to utterances of L_2! I make this point not in criticism of T2, but in criticism of the idea that the significance of T2 can be explained by saying that it 'gives the meaning of' the word 'true'.

We still need to know what purpose a truth characterization like T1 or T2 could serve that would give someone reason to think that are without unexplicated semantic terms would be better than a TC with unexplicated semantic terms. Tarski hints at such a purpose in one place in his writings, where he is discussing the importance of being able to define the word 'true', as opposed to merely introducing axioms to establish the basic properties of truth. If a definition of semantic notions such as truth could not be given, Tarski writes,

> it would then be difficult to bring [semantics] into harmony with the postulates of the unity of science and of physicalism (since the concepts of semantics would be neither logical nor physical concepts), [1956*b*: 406]

This remark seems to me to be of utmost importance in evaluating the philosophical significance of Tarski's work, and so I will now say something about the general philosophical issues it raises. When this is done we will be in a better position to understand Tarski's choice of T2 over T1.

III

In the early 1930s many philosophers believed that the notion of truth could not be incorporated into a scientific conception of the world. I think that the main rationale for this view is hinted at in the remark of Tarski's that I quoted at the end of the last section, and what I want to do now is to elaborate a bit on Tarski's last hint.

In the remark I have quoted, Tarski puts a heavy stress on the doctrine of physicalism: the doctrine that chemical facts, biological facts, psychological facts, and semantical facts, are all explicable (in principle) in terms of physical facts. The doctrine of physicalism functions as a high-level empirical hypothesis, a hypothesis that no small number of experiments can force us to give up. It functions, in other words, in much the same way as the doctrine of mechanism (that all facts are explicable in terms of *mechanical* facts) once functioned: this latter doctrine has now been universally rejected, but it was given up only by the development of a well-accepted theory (Maxwell's) which described phenomena (electromagnetic radiation and the electromagnetic field) that were very difficult to account for mechanically, and by amassing a great deal of experiment and theory that together made it quite conclusive that mechanical explanations of these phenomena (e.g., by positing 'the ether') would never get off the ground. Mechanism has been empirically refuted; its heir is physicalism, which allows as 'basic' not only facts about mechanics, but facts about other branches of physics as well.[9] I believe that physicists a hundred years ago were justified in accepting mechanism, and that, similarly, physicalism should be accepted until we have convincing evidence that there is a realm of phenomena it leaves out of account. Even if there *does* turn out to be such a realm of phenomena, the only way we'll ever come to know that there is, is by repeated efforts and repeated failures to explain these phenomena in physical terms.

That's my view, anyway, but there are philosophers who think that it is in order to reject physicalism now. One way of rejecting physicalism is called 'vitalism': it is the view that there are irreducibly biological facts, i.e., biological facts that aren't explicable in nonbiological terms (and hence, not in physical terms). Physicalism and vitalism are incompatible, and it is because of this incompatibility that the doctrine of physicalism has the methodological importance it has for biology. Suppose, for instance, that a certain woman has two sons, one hemophilic and one not. Then, according to standard genetic accounts of hemophilia, the ovum from which one of these sons was produced must have contained a gene for hemophilia, and the ovum from which the other son was produced must not have contained such a gene. But now the doctrine of physicalism tells us that there must have been a *physical* difference between the two ova that explains why the first son had hemophilia and the second one didn't, if the standard genetic account is to be accepted. We should not rest content with a special biological predicate 'has-a-hemophilic-gene'—rather, we should look for nonbiological facts (chemical facts; and ultimately, physical facts) that underlie the correct application of this predicate. That at least is what the principle of physicalism tells us, and it can hardly be doubted that this principle has motivated a great deal of very profitable research into the chemical foundations of genetics.

So much for vitalism; now let us turn to other irreducibility doctrines that are opposed to physicalism. One such irreducibility doctrine is Cartesianism: it is the doctrine that there are irreducibly mental facts. Another irreducibility doctrine has received much less attention than either vitalism or Cartesianism, but it is central to our present concerns: this doctrine, which might be called 'semanticalism', is the doctrine that there are irreducibly semantic facts. The semanticalist claims, in other words, that semantic phenomena (such as the fact that 'Schnee' refers to snow) must be accepted as primitive, in precisely the way that electromagnetic phenomena are accepted as primitive (by those who accept Maxwell's equations and reject the ether); and in precisely the way that biological phenomena and mental phenomena are accepted as primitive by vitalists and Cartesians. Semanticalism, like Cartesianism and vitalism, posits nonphysical primitives, and as a physicalist I believe that all three doctrines must be rejected.

There are two general sorts of strategy that can be taken in rejecting semanticalism, or Cartesianism, or vitalism. One strategy, illustrated two paragraphs back in discussing vitalism, is to try to explicate the terms of a biological theory in nonbiological terms. But there is another possible strategy, which is to argue that the biological terms are illegitimate. The second strategy seems reasonable to adopt in dealing with the following predicate of (reincarnationist) biology: '*x* has the same soul as *y*'. A physicalist would never try to find physical or chemical facts that underlie reincarnation; rather, he would reject reincarnation as a myth.

Since biological theory is as well developed as it is, we usually have a pretty good idea which biological terms require explication and which require elimination. When we turn to psychology and semantics, however, it is often not so obvious which strategy is the more promising. Thus in semantics, physicalists agree that all *legitimate* semantic terms must be explicable nonsemantically—they think in other words that there are no irreducibly semantic facts—but they disagree as to which semantic terms are legitimate. That disagreement has become fairly clear in recent years in the theory of meaning, with the work of Quine: the disagreement is between those physicalists who would look for a nonsemantic basis for terms in the theory of meaning, and those who would follow Quine in simply throwing out those terms. Our concern, however, is not with the theory of meaning, but with the theory of reference, and here the disagreement has been less clear, since there haven't been many physicalists who openly advocate getting rid of terms like 'true' and 'denotes'. There were such physicalists in the early 1930s; part of the importance of Tarski's work was to persuade them that they were on the wrong track, to persuade them that we should explicate notions in the theory of reference nonsemantically rather than simply get rid of them.

The view that we should just stop using semantic terms (here and in the rest of this paper, I mean terms in the theory of reference, such as 'true' and 'denotes' and 'applies to') draws its plausibility from the apparent difficulty of explicating these terms nonsemantically. People utter the sounds 'Electrons have rest mass but photons don't', or 'Schnee ist weiss und Gras ist grün', and we apply the word 'true' to their utterances. We don't want to say that it is a primitive and inexplicable fact about these utterances that they are true, a fact that cannot be explicated in nonsemantic terms; this is as unattractive to a physicalist as supposing that it is a primitive and inexplicable fact about an organism at a certain time that it is in pain. But how could we ever explicate in nonsemantic terms the alleged fact that these utterances are true? *Part* of the explication of the truth of 'Schnee ist weiss und Gras ist grün', presumably, would be that snow is white and grass is green. But this would only be part of the explanation, for still missing is the connection between snow being white and grass being green on the one hand, and the German utterance being true on the other hand. It is this connection that seems so difficult to explicate in a way that would satisfy a physicalist, i.e., in a way that does not involve the use of semantic terms.

If, in face of these difficulties, we were ever to conclude that it was *impossible* to explicate the notions of truth and denotation in nonsemantic terms, we would have either to give up these semantic terms or else to reject physicalism. It seems to me that that is essentially what Tarski is saying in the quotation at the end of the last section, and I have tried to make it plausible by sketching analogies to areas other than semantics. Tarski's view, however, was that, for certain languages at least, semantic terms *are* explicable nonsemantically, and that truth definitions like T2 provide the required explication. It is understandable that as far *as philosophical* purposes go Tarski should think that T1 leaves something to be desired: after all, it merely explicates truth in terms of other semantic concepts; but what good does that do if those other concepts can't be explicated nonsemantically? T2, then, has a strong prima facie advantage over T1. In the next section I will show that it is not a genuine advantage.

IV

The apparent advantage of T2 over T1, I have stressed, is that it appears to reduce truth to nonsemantic terms; and I *think* this is why Tarski wanted to give a truth definition like T2 rather than like T1. This interpretation makes sense of Tarski's remark about physicalism, and it also explains why someone who was certainly not interested in 'meaning analysis' as that is usually conceived would have wanted to give 'definitions' of truth and would emphasize that, in these 'definitions,' 'I will not make use of any semantical concept if I am not able previously to reduce it to other concepts.' In any case, the problem of reducing truth is a very important problem, one which T1 and T2 provide a partial solution to, and one which T2 *might* be thought to provide a full solution to; and it is not at all clear what *other* interesting problems T2 could be thought to solve better than T1.

In his own exposition of his theory of truth, Tarski put very little stress on the problem of reduction or on any other problem with a clear philosophical or mathematical motivation; instead, he set up a formal criterion of adequacy for theories of truth without any serious discussion of whether or why this formal criterion is reasonable. Roughly, the criterion was this:[10]

(M) Any Condition of the form

(2) $(\forall e)[e \text{ is true} \equiv B(e)]$

should be accepted as an adequate definition of truth if and only if it is correct and *'B(e)'* is a well-formed formula containing no semantic terms. (The quantifiers are to be taken as ranging over expressions of one particular language only.)

The 'only if' part of condition M is not something I will contest. It rules out the possibility of T1 *by itself* being an adequate truth definition; and it is right to do so, if the task of a truth definition is to reduce truth to nonsemantic terms, for T1 provides only a *partial* reduction. (To complete the reduction we need to reduce primitive denotation to nonsemantic terms.) T2, on the other hand, meets condition M; so either T2 is superior to T1 as a reduction, or else condition M is too weak and the 'if' part of it must be rejected. My own diagnosis is the latter, but the other possibility seems initially reasonable. After all, how could condition M be strengthened? We might try requiring that '*B* (*e*)' be not only *extensionally* equivalent to '*e* is true', but *intentionally* equivalent to it; but this clearly won't do, for even if we grant that there is an intelligible notion of intensional equivalence, our concern is not with analyzing the meaning of the word 'true' but with performing a reduction. A clear and useful standard of equivalence that is stronger than extensional equivalence but not so strong as to rule out acceptable, reductions is unknown at the present time, so I know no way to improve on condition M. My view is that we have a rough but useful concept of reduction which we are unable to formulate precisely; but I must admit that the alternative view, that extensional equivalence is adequate, has an initial appeal.

A closer look, however, will reveal quite conclusively that extensional equivalence is not a sufficient standard of reduction. This can be seen by looking at the concept of valence. The valence of a chemical element is an integer that is associated with that element, which represents the sort of chemical combinations that the element will enter into. What I mean by the last phrase is that it is possible—roughly, at least—to characterize which elements will combine with which others, and in what proportions they will combine, merely in terms of their valences. Because of this fact, the concept of valence is a physically important concept, and so if physicalism is correct it ought to be possible to explicate this concept in physical terms—e.g., it ought to be possible to find structural properties of the atoms of each element that determine what the valence of that element will be. Early in the twentieth century (long after the notion of valence had proved its value in enabling chemists to predict what chemical combinations there would be) this reduction of the concept of valence to the physical properties of atoms was established; the notion of valence was thus shown to be a physicalistically acceptable notion.

Now, it would have been easy for a chemist, late in the last century, to have given a 'valence definition' of the following form;

(3) $(\forall E)\ (\forall n)$ (*E* has valence $n \equiv E$ is potassium and n is $+1$, or ... or E is sulphur and n is -2)

where in the blanks go a list of similar clauses, one for each element. But, though this is an extensionally correct definition of valence, it would not have been an acceptable reduction; and had it turned out that nothing else was possible—had all efforts to explain valence in terms of the structural properties of atoms proved futile—scientists would have eventually had to decide either (a) to give up valence theory, or else (b) to replace the hypothesis of physicalism by another hypothesis (chemicalism?). It is part of scientific methodology to resist doing (b); and I also think it is part of scientific methodology to resist doing (a) as long as the notion of valence is serving the purposes for which it was designed (i.e., as long as it is proving useful in helping us characterize chemical compounds in terms of their valences). But the methodology is not to resist (a) and (b) by giving lists like (3); the methodology is to look for a real reduction. This is a methodology that has proved extremely fruitful in science, and I think we'd be crazy to give it up in linguistics. *And I think we are giving up this fruitful methodology, unless we realize that we need to add theories of primitive reference to* T1 *or* T2 *if we are to establish the notion of truth as a physicalistically acceptable notion.*

I certainly haven't yet given much argument for this last claim. I *have* argued that the standard of extensional equivalence doesn't guarantee an acceptable reduction; but T2 is obviously not trivial to the extent that (3) is. What *is* true, however, is roughly that T2 minus T1 is as trivial as (3) is. One way in which this last claim can be made more precise is by remembering that really we often apply the term 'valence' not only to elements, but also to configurations of elements (at least to stable configurations that are not compounds, i.e., to radicals). Thus, if we abstract from certain physical limitations on the size of possible configurations of elements (as, in linguistics, we usually abstract from the limitations that memory, etc., impose on the lengths of possible utterances), there is an infinite number of entities to which the term 'valence' is applied. But it is an important fact about valence that the valence of a configuration of elements is determined from the valences of the elements that make it up, and from the way they're put together. Because of this, we might try to give a recursive characterization of valence. First of all, we would try to characterize all the different *structures* that configurations of elements can have (much as we try to characterize all the different grammatical structures before we give a truth definition like T1 or T2). We would then try to find rules that would enable us to determine what the valence of a complicated configuration would be, given the valences of certain less complicated configurations that make it up and the way they're put together. If we had enough such rules, we could determine the valence of a given configuration given only its structure and the valences of the elements that make it up. And if we like, we can transform our recursive characterization of valence into an explicit characterization, getting

V1 $(\forall c)(\forall n)$ (c has valence $n \equiv B\ (c,n)$)

The formula '$B\ (c,n)$' here employed will still contain the term 'valence', but it will contain that term only as applied to elements, not as applied to configurations. Thus our 'valence definition' V1 would characterize the valence of the complex *in terms of the valences of the simple.*

It would now be possible to eliminate the term 'valence' from '$B\ (c,n)$', in either of two ways. One way would be to employ a genuine reduction of the notion of valence for elements to the structural properties of atoms. The other way would be to employ the pseudo-reduction (3). It is clear that we could use (3) to give a trivial reformulation V2 of V1, which would have precisely the 'advantages' as a reduction that T2 has over T1. (V2, incidentally, would also have one of the disadvantages over V1 that T2 has over T1: V1 does not need to be overhauled when you discover or synthesize new elements, whereas V2 does.)

That is a sketch of one way that the remark I made two paragraphs back about 'T2 minus T1' could be made more precise. But it is somewhat more fruitful to develop the point slightly differently: doing this will enable me to make clearer that there is unlikely to be *any* purpose that T2 serves better than T1 (not merely that T2 is no better at reduction).

To get this result I'll go back to my original use of the term 'valence', where it applies to elements only and not to configurations. And what I will do is compare (3) not to Tarski's theory of *truth,* but to Tarski's theory of *denotation* for names; the effect of this on his theory of truth will then be considered. Tarski states his theory of denotation for names in a footnote, as follows:

> To say that the name *x* denotes a given object *a* is the same as to stipulate that the object *a* ... satisfies a sentential function of a particular type. In colloquial language it would be a function which consists of three parts in the following order: a variable, the word 'is' and the given name *x* (1956*a:* 194).

This is actually only part of the theory, the part that defines denotation in terms of satisfaction; to see what the theory looks like when all semantic terms are eliminated, we must see how satisfaction is defined. The definition is given by the (A) and (B) clauses of T2, for, as I've remarked, 'satisfaction' is Tarski's name for what I've called 'truth$_s$'. What Tarski's definition of satisfaction tells us is this: for any name *N,* an object *a* satisfies the sentential function ⌜x_1 is *N*⌝ if and only if *a* is France and *N* is 'France' or ... or *a* is Germany and *N* is 'Germany'. Combining this definition of satisfaction (for sentential functions of form ⌜x_1 is *N*⌝) with the earlier account of denotation in terms of satisfaction, we get:

(DE): To say that the name *N* denotes a given object *a* is the same as to stipulate that either *a* is France and *N* is 'France', or ... or *a* is Germany and *N* is 'Germany'.

This is Tarski's account of denotation for English proper names. For foreign proper names, the definition of denotation in terms of satisfaction needs no modification (except that the 'is' must be replaced by a name of a foreign word, say 'ist' for German). Combining this with the definition (again given by T2) of satisfaction for foreign sentential functions like ⌜x_1 is *N*⌝, we get:

(DG): To say that the name *N* denotes a given object *a* is the same as to stipulate that either *a* is France and *N* is 'Frankreich', or ... or *a* is Germany and *N* is 'Deutschland'.

DE and DG have not received much attention in commentaries on Tarski, but in fact they play a key role in his semantic theory; and it was no aberration on Tarski's part that he offered them as theories of denotation for English and German names, for *they satisfy criteria of adequacy exactly analogous to the criteria of adequacy that Tarski accepted for theories of truth.*[11] Nevertheless, it seems clear that DE and DG do not really reduce denotation to nonsemantic terms, any more than (3) reduces valence to nonchemical terms. What would a real explication of denotation in nonsemantic terms be like? The 'classical' answer to this question (Russell's) is that a name like 'Cicero' is 'analytically linked' to a certain description (such as 'the denouncer of Catiline'); so to explain how the name 'Cicero' denotes what it does you merely have to explain

(i) the process by which it is linked to the description (presumably you bring in facts about how it was learned by its user, or facts about what is going on in the user's brain at the time of the using);

and (ii) how the description refers to what it does.

Because of (ii), of course, the project threatens circularity: the project is to explain how names refer in terms of how descriptions refer; but the natural way to explain how descriptions refer is in terms of how they're built up from their significant parts,[12] and how those significant parts refer (or apply, or are fulfilled), and those significant parts will usually include names. But Russell recognized this threat of circularity, and carefully avoided it: he assumed that the primitives of the language were to be partially ordered by a relation of 'basicness', and that each name except a most basic ('logically proper') name was to be analytically linked to a formula containing only primitives more basic than it. The most basic primitives were to be linked to the world without the intervention of other words, by the relation of acquaintance.

This classical view of how names (and other primitives) latch onto their denotations is extremely implausible in many ways (e.g., it says you can refer only to things that are definable from 'logically proper' primitives; it requires that there be certain statements, such as 'If Cicero existed then Cicero denounced Catiline', which are analytic in the sense that they are guaranteed by linguistic rules and are immune to revision by future discoveries). I conjecture that it is because of the difficulties with this classical theory, which was the only theory available at the time that Tarski wrote, that Tarski's pseudotheories DE and DG seemed reasonable—they weren't exciting, but if you wanted something exciting you got logically proper names. The diagnosis that any attempt to explain the relation between words and things they are about must inevitably lead to either a wildly implausible theory (like Russell's) or a trivial theory (like Tarski's) seems to be widely accepted still; but I think that the diagnosis has become less plausible in recent years through the development of *causal* theories of denotation by Saul Kripke[13] and others. According to such theories, the facts that 'Cicero' denotes Cicero and that 'muon' applies to muons are to be explained in terms of certain kinds of causal networks between Cicero (muons) and our uses of 'Cicero' ('muon'): causal connections both of a social sort (the passing of the word 'Cicero' down to us from the original users of the name, or the passing of the word 'muon' to laymen from physicists) and of other sorts (the evidential causal connections that gave the original users of the name 'access' to Cicero and give physicists 'access' to muons). I don't think that Kripke or anyone else thinks that *purely* causal theories of primitive denotation can be developed (even for proper names of past physical objects and for natural-kind predicates); this however should not blind us to the fact that he has suggested a kind of factor involved in denotation that gives new hope to the idea of explaining the connection between language and the things it is about. It seems to me that the possibility of *some such* theory of denotation (to be deliberately very vague) is essential to the joint acceptability of physicalism and the semantic term 'denotes', and that denotation definitions like DE and DG merely obscure the need for this.

It might be objected that the purpose of DE and DG was not reduction; but what was their purpose? One answer might be that (DE) and (DG) enable us to eliminate the word 'denote' whenever it occurs. ('To explain is to show how to eliminate.') For instance,

(4) No German name now in use denotes something that does not yet exist.

would become

(4') For any name *N* now in use, if *N* is 'Frankreich' then France already exists, and ..., and if *N* is 'Deutschland' then Germany already exists.

provided that (DG) is a correct and complete list of the denotations of all those German proper names that have denotations. It seems reasonably clear that we could specify a detailed procedure for transforming sentences like (4) into materially equivalent sentences like (4'). A similar claim could be made for the 'valence definition' (3). Such a valence definition makes it possible to eliminate the word 'valence' from a large class of sentences containing it, and in a uniform way. For instance,

(5) For any elements *A* and *B*, if one atom of *A* combines with two of *B*, then the valence of *A* is −2 times that of *B*.

is materially equivalent to

(5′) For any elements *A* and *B*, if one atom of *A* combines with two of *B*, then either *A* is sodium and *B* is sodium and +1 = −2 (+1), or…, or *A* is sulphur and *B* is sodium and −2 = −2 (+1), or …

provided that (3) is a correct and complete list of valences. So if anyone ever wants to eliminate the word 'denote' or the word 'valence' from a large class of English sentences by a uniform procedure, denotation definitions and valence definitions are just the thing he needs. There are, however, sentences from which these words are not eliminable by the sketched procedure. For instance, in semantics and possibly in chemistry there are problems with counterfactuals, e.g., 'If "Germany" had been used to denote France, then … Moreover, there are special problems affecting the case of semantics, arising from the facts

(i) that the elimination procedure works only for languages in which nothing is denoted that cannot be denoted (without using semantic terms) in one's own language,

(ii) that it works only for languages that contain no ambiguous names,

and

(iii) that the denotation definitions provide no procedure for eliminating 'denote' from sentences where it is applied to more than one language; e.g., it gives no way of handling sentences like '"Glub" denotes different things in different languages.'

But, subject to these three qualifications (plus perhaps that involving counterfactuals), the elimination procedure for 'denote' is every bit as good as that for 'valence'.

What value did Tarski attach to such transformations? Unfortunately he did not discuss the one about valences, but he did discuss the one that transforms 'Smith used a proper name to denote Germany' into something logically equivalent to 'Smith uttered "Deutschland".' And it is clear that to this definition he attached great philosophical importance. After defining semantics as 'the totality of considerations concerning those concepts which, roughly speaking, express certain connexions between the expressions of a language and the objects and states of affairs referred to by those expressions' (1956*b*: 401), he says that with his definitions, 'the problem of establishing semantics on a scientific basis is completely solved' (1956*b*: 407). In other places his claims are almost as extravagant. For instance, the remark about physicalism that I quoted at the end of section II is intended to apply to denotation as well as to truth: if definitions of denotation like DE and DG could not be given, 'it would … be impossible to bring [semantics] into harmony with … physicalism' (1956*b*: 406); but because of these definitions, the compatibility of the semantic concept of denotation with physicalism is established. By similar standards of reduction, one might prove that witchcraft is compatible with physicalism, as long as witches cast only a finite number of spells: for then 'cast a spell' can be defined without use of any of the terms of witchcraft theory, merely by listing all the witch-and-victim pairs.

In other places Tarski makes quite different claims for the value of his denotation definitions. For example:

> We desire semantic terms (referring to the object language) to be introduced into the meta-language only by definition. For, if this postulate is satisfied, the definition of

truth, or of any other semantic concept [including denotation, which Tarski had already specifically mentioned to be definable], will fulfill what we intuitively expect from every definition; that is, it will explain the meaning of the term being defined in terms whose meaning appears to be completely clear and unequivocal. (1944: 351)

But it is no more plausible that DE 'explains the meaning of' 'denote' as applied to English, or that DG 'explains the meaning of' 'denote' as applied to German, than that (3) 'explains the meaning of' 'valence'—considerably *less* so in fact, since for 'valence' there is no analogue to the conclusions that 'denote' means something different when applied to English than it means when applied to German. In fact, it seems pretty clear that denotation definitions like DE and DG have no philosophical interest whatever. But what conclusions can we draw from this about Tarski's *truth* definitions like T2? I think the conclusion to draw is that *T2 has no philosophical interest whatever that is not shared by T1.* How this follows I will now explain.

We have seen that Taiski advocated theories of denotation for names that had the form of mere lists: examples of his denotation definitions were DE and DG, and for language L his denotation definition would take the following form:

D2 $(\forall e)$ $(\forall a)$ [e is a name that denotes $a \equiv$ (e is 'c_1' and a is $\bar{c}_1$) or (e is 'c_2' and a is $\bar{c}_2$) or…]

where into the dots go analogous clauses for every name of L. Similarly, we can come up with definitions of application and fulfillment which are acceptable according to Tarski's standards, and which also have the form of mere lists. The definition of application runs:

A2 $(\forall e)$ $(\forall a)$ [e is a predicate that applies to $a \equiv$ (e is 'p_1' and $p_1(a)$) or (e is 'p_2' and $\bar{p}_2(a)$) … or].

Similarly, we can formulate a list-list characterization F2 of fulfillment for the function symbols. Clearly neither A2 nor F2 is of any more theoretical interest than D2.

Tarski, I have stressed, accepted D2 as part of his semantic theory, and would also have accepted A2 and F2; and this fact is quite important since D2, A2, and F2 together with T2 imply T1. In other words, T1 is simply a weaker version of Tarski's semantic theory; it is a logical consequence of Tarski's theory. Now, an interesting question is what you have to add to T1 to get the rest of Tarski's semantic theory. Suppose we can find a formula R that we can argue to be of no interest whatever, such that Tarski's semantic theory (T2 $\wedge$ D2 $\wedge$ A2 $\wedge$ F2) is logically equivalent to T1 $\wedge$ R. It will then follow that the whole interest of Tarski's semantic theory' lies in T1—the rest of his semantic theory results simply by adding to it the formula R, which (I have assumed) has no interest whatever. And if there is nothing of interest in the conjunction T2 $\wedge$ D2 $\wedge$ A2 $\wedge$ F2 beyond T1, certainly there can be nothing of interest in T2 alone beyond T1.

An example of such a formula R is D2 $\wedge$ A2 $\wedge$ F2: it is obvious that Tarski's semantic theory is logically equivalent to T1 $\wedge$ D2 $\wedge$ A2 $\wedge$ F2. Because of this, *any interest in Tarski's semantic theory over* T1 *must be due to an interest in* D2 *or* A2 *or* F2 (*or to confusion*): *in this sense* D2 $\wedge$ A2 $\wedge$ F2 is 'T2 *minus* T1'. But I've already argued that D2, A2, and F2 have no theoretical interest whatever, and so that establishes that T2 has no theoretical interest whatever that is not shared by T1.

V

Much of what I've said in this paper gains plausibility by being put in a wider perspective, and so I now want to say a little bit about why we want a notion of truth. The notion of truth serves a great many purposes, but I suspect that its original purpose—the purpose for which it was first developed—was to aid us in utilizing the utterances of others in drawing conclusions about the world. To take an extremely simple example, suppose that a friend reports that he's just come back from Alabama and that there was a foot of snow on the ground there. Were it not for his report we would have considered it extremely unlikely that there was a foot of snow on the ground in Alabama—but the friend knows snow when he sees it and is not prone to telling us lies for no apparent reason, and so after brief deliberation we conclude that probably there *was* a foot of snow in Alabama. What we did here was first to use our evidence about the person and his situation to decide that he probably said something true when he made a certain utterance, and then to draw a conclusion from the truth of his utterance to the existence of snow in Alabama. In order to make such inferences, we have to have a pretty good grasp of (i) the circumstances under which what another says is likely to be true, and (ii) how to get from a belief in the truth of what he says to a belief about the extralinguistic world.

If this idea is right, then two features of truth that are intimately bound up with the purposes to which the notion of truth are put are (I) the role that the attempt to tell the truth and the success in doing so play in social institutions, and (II) the fact that normally one is in a position to assert of a sentence that it is true in just those cases where one is in a position to assert the sentence or a paraphrase of it. It would then be natural to expect that what is involved in communicating the meaning of the word 'true' to a child or to a philosopher is getting across to him the sorts of facts listed under (I) and (II); for those are the facts that it is essential for him to have an awareness of if he is to put the notion of truth to its primary use (child) or if he is to get a clear grasp of what its primary use is (philosopher).

I think that this natural expectation is correct, and that it gives more insight than was given in sections II and IV into why it is that neither T1 nor T2 can reasonably be said to explain the meaning of the term 'true'—even when a theory of primitive reference is added to them. First consider (I). The need of understanding the sort of thing alluded to in (I), if we are to grasp the notion of truth, has been presented quite forcefully in Dummett 1959, in his analogy between speaking the truth and winning at a game. It is obvious that T1 and T2 don't explain anything like this (and in fact Dummett's fourth paragraph, on Frege-style truth definitions, can be carried over directly to T1 and T2).

The matter might perhaps be expressed in terms of assertibility conditions that one learns in learning to use the word 'true': part of what we learn, in learning to use this word, is that in cases like that involving the friend from Alabama there is some prima facie weight to be attached to the claim that the other person is saying something true. But there are also *other* assertibility conditions that one learns in learning the word 'true', assertibility conditions which have received considerable attention in the philosophical literature on truth. To begin with, let's note one obvious fact about how the word 'true' is standardly learned: we learn how to apply it to utterances of our own language first, and when we later learn to apply it to other languages it is by conceiving the utterances of another language more or less on the model of utterances of our own language. The obvious model of the first stage of this process is that we learn to accept all instances of the schema

(T) *X* is true if and only if *p*.

where '*X*' is replaced by a quotation-mark name of an English sentence *S* and '*p*' is replaced by *S*. This must be complicated to deal with ambiguous and truth-value-less sentences, but let's ignore them. Also let's ignore the fact that certain pathological instances of (T)—the Epimenides-type paradoxical sentences—are logically refutable. Then there is a sense in which the instances of (T) that we've learned to assert determine a unique extension for the predicate 'true' as applied to sentences of our own language (cf. Quine 1953: 136). Our views about what English sentences belong to this unique extension may be altered, but as long as we stick to the instances of (T) they cannot consistently be altered without also altering our beliefs in what those sentences express. This fact is extremely important to the functions that the word 'true' serves (as the Alabama example illustrates).

In stressing the assertibility conditions for simple sentences containing the word 'true', I have followed Quine (1953: 138); for, like him, I believe that such assertibility conditions are enough to make the term 'true' reasonably clear. But now it might be asked, 'Then why do we need causal (etc.) theories of reference? The words "true" and "denotes" are made perfectly clear by schemas like (T). To ask for more than these schemas—to ask for causal theories of reference to nail language to reality—is to fail to recognize that we are at sea on Neurath's boat: we have to work *within* our conceptual scheme, we can't glue it to reality from the outside.'

I suspect that this would be Quine's diagnosis—it is strongly suggested by §6 of Quine 1960, especially when that is taken in conjunction with some of Quine's remarks about the inscrutability of reference and truth value, the underdetermination of theories, and the relativity of ontology. It seems to me, however, that the diagnosis is quite wrong. In looking for a theory of truth and a theory of primitive reference we *are* trying to explain the connection between language and (extralinguistic) reality, but we are *not* trying to step outside of our theories of the world in order to do so. Our accounts of primitive reference and of truth are not to be thought of as something that could be given by philosophical reflection prior to scientific information—on the contrary, it seems likely that such things as psychological models of human beings and investigations of neurophysiology will be very relevant to discovering the mechanisms involved in reference. *The reason why accounts of truth and primitive reference are needed is not to tack our conceptual scheme onto reality from the outside; the reason, rather, is that without such accounts our conceptual scheme breaks down from the inside.* On our theory of the world it would be extremely surprising if there were some nonphysical connection between words and things. Thus if we could argue from our theory of the world that the notion of an utterer's saying something true, or referring to a particular thing, cannot be made sense of in physicalist terms (say, by arguing that any semantic notion that makes physicalistic sense *can* be explicated in Skinnerian terms, and that the notions of truth and reference *can't* be explicated in Skinnerian terms), then to the extent that such an argument is convincing we ought to be led to conclude that, if we are to remain physicalists, the notions of truth and reference must be abandoned. No amount of pointing out the clarity of these terms helps enable us to escape this conclusion: 'valence' and 'gene' were perfectly clear long before anyone succeeded in reducing them, but it was their reducibility and not their clarity before reduction that showed them to be compatible with physicalism.

The clarity of 'valence' and 'gene' before reduction—and even more, their *utility* before reduction—did provide physicalists with substantial reason to think that a reduction of these terms was possible, and, as I remarked earlier a great deal of fruitful work in physical chemistry and chemical genetics was motivated by the fact. Similarly, insofar as semantic notions like 'true' are useful, we have every reason to suspect that they will be reducible to nonsemantic terms, and it is likely that progress in linguistic theory will come by looking for such reductions. (In fact, the fruitfulness of Tarski's work in aiding us to understand language is already some sign of this, even though it represents only a partial reduction.) Of course, this sort of argument for the prospects of reducing semantic notions is only as powerful as our arguments for the utility of semantic terms; and it is clear that the question of the utility of the term 'true'—the purposes it serves, and the extent to which those purposes could be served by less pretentious notions such as warranted assertibility—needs much closer investigation.

All these remarks require one important qualification. The notion of valence, it must be admitted, is *not* reducible to nonchemical terms on the *strictest* standards of reduction, but is only *approximately* reducible; yet, in spite of this, we don't want to get rid of the notion, since it is still extremely useful in those contexts where its approximate character isn't too likely to get in the way and where if we did not approximate we'd get into quantum-mechanical problems far too complex for anyone to solve. (Moreover, considerations about the purposes of the notion of valence were sufficient to show that the notion of valence would only be approximately reducible: for the utility of the notion of valence is that it aids us in approximately characterizing which elements will combine with which and in what proportions; yet it is obvious that no *precise* such characterization is possible.)

Similarly, it may well be that a detailed investigation into the purposes of the notion of truth might show that these purposes require only an approximate reduction of the notion of truth. Still, to require an approximate reduction is to require quite a bit; after all, 'is a reincarnation of' isn't even approximately reducible to respectable biology, and 'electromagnetic field' is not approximately reducible to mechanics. Obviously the notion of approximate reduction needs to be made more precise (as in fact does the notion of strict, or nonapproximate, reduction); but even without making it so, I think we can see that T2 is no more of an approximate reduction than is V2, since D2 ∧ A2 ∧ F2 is no more of an approximate reduction than is (3). In other words, the main point of the paper survives when we replace the ideal of strict reduction by the ideal of approximate reduction.

It should be kept carefully in mind that the Quinean view that all we need do is clarify the term 'true', in the sense that this term is clarified by schema T (or by schema T plus a theory of translation to handle foreign languages; or by schema T plus the sort of thing alluded to in connection with Dummett), is *not* Tarski's view. Tarski's view is that we have to provide a truth characterization like T2 (which, when we choose as our object language L a 'nice' fragment of our own language, can be shown correct merely by assuming that all instances of schema T are valid—cf. fn. 10, pp.14–15); and such a truth characterization does much more than schema T does. It does not do everything that Tarski ever claimed for it, for Tarski attached much too much importance to the pseudo-theories D2, A2, and F2; but even when we 'subtract' such trivialities from his truth characterization T2, we still get the very interesting and important truth characterization T1, T1, I believe, adequately represents Tarski's real contribution to the theory of truth, and in doing this it has a number of positive advantages over T2 (in addition to the important negative advantage I've been stressing, of preventing extravagant claims based on the fact that T2 contains no semantic terms). First of all, T1, unlike T2, is applicable to languages that contain ambiguities and languages that contain terms not adequately translatable into English. Second, T1, unlike T2, can be used in diachronic linguistics: it doesn't need overhauling as you add new words to the language, provided those new words belong to the same semantic category as words already in the language. Third, I think that the reason why Tarski's theory of truth T2 has seemed so uninteresting to so many people is that it contains the vacuous semantic theories D2, A2, and F2 for the primitives of the language. By expressing the really important features of Tarski's results on truth, and leaving out the inessential and uninteresting 'theories' of the semantics of the primitives, T1 should make the philosophical importance of Tarski's work more universally recognized.[14]

Notes

1. Cf. Carnap 1963: 61.
2. It is sometimes claimed that Tarski was interested in languages considered in abstraction from all speakers and writers of the language; that the languages he was dealing with are abstract entities to be specified by giving their rules. This seems incorrect: Tarski was interested in giving the semantics of languages that mathematicians had been writing for years; and only as a result of Tarski's work was it then possible for philosophers like Carnap to propose that the clauses of a Tarski-type truth definition for such languages be called rules of the languages and be used in defining the languages as abstract entities.
3. Actually in model theory we are interested in allowing a slightly unusual semantics for the quantifiers: we are willing to allow that the quantifier not range over everything. We could build this generalization into our truth definition, by stipulating that in addition to the denotations of the nonlogical symbols we specify a universe U, and then reformulating clause (B)4 by requiring that the *k*th member of *s** belong to U. If we did this, then it would be the range of the quantifiers as well as the denotations of the nonlogical primitives that we would have explained truth in terms of.
4. An *incomplete* sentence token is a sentence token which [like the occurrence of '2 + 2 = 4' inside '~(2 + 2 = 4)'] is part of a larger sentence token.
5. Note that the claims I've been making are intended to apply only to cases where different tokens have different semantic features; they are not intended to apply to cases of indeterminacy, i.e., to cases where a particular name token or predicate token has no determinate denotation or extension. To deal with indeterminacy requires more complex devices than I employ in this paper.
6. The notion of a semantic category is Tarski's (1956*a*: 215).
7. To do so in the obvious way requires that we introduce semantic categories of negation symbol, conjunction symbol, and universal-quantification symbol; though by utilizing some ideas of Frege it could be shown that there is really no need of a separate semantic category for each logical operator. The use of semantic categories in the generalized truth characterization raises important problems which I have had to suppress for lack of space in this paper.
8. For simplicity, I have assumed that L itself contains no semantic terms.

9. This, of course, is very vague, but most attempts to explicate the doctrine of physicalism more precisely result in doctrines that are very hard to take seriously (e.g., the doctrine that for every acceptable predicate '$P(x)$' there is a formula '$B(x)$' containing only terminology horn physics, such that '$\forall x(P(x) = B(x))$' is true). Physicalism should be understood as the doctrine (however precisely it is to be characterized) that guides science in the way I describe.
10. Tarski actually gives a different formulation, the famous Convention T, evidently because he does not think that the word 'correct' ought to be employed in stating a criterion of adequacy. First of all Tarski writes

   > ... we shall accept as valid every sentence of the form
   >
   > [T] the sentence *x* is true if and only *p*
   >
   > where '*p*' is to be replaced by any sentence of the language under investigation and '*x*' by any individual name of that sentence provided this name occurs in the metalanguage (1956*b*: 404).

   Is Tarski's policy of accepting these sentences as 'valid' (i.e., true) legitimate? It seems to me that it is, in a certain special case. The special case is where

   I. The object language is a proper part of the metalanguage (here, English).

   II. The object language contains no paradoxical or ambiguous or truth-value-less sentences.

   In this special case—and it was the case that Tarski was primarily concerned with—I think it will be generally agreed that all instances of Schema T hold. From this, together with the fact that only grammatical sentences are true, we can argue that, if a necessary and sufficient condition of form (2) has the following consequences:

   (a) Every instance of Schema T

   (b) The sentence '$(\forall x)$ (x is true $\supset s(x)$)', where '$S(x)$' formulates (correct) conditions for an utterance of L to be a sentence

   then that necessary and sufficient condition is correct. Let's say that a 'truth definition' for L (a necessary and sufficient condition of truth in L) *satisfies Convention* T if it has all the consequences listed under (a) and (b). Then, restating: when L is a language for which I and II hold, then any truth definition satisfying Convention T is correct; and since only quite uncontroversial assumptions about truth are used in getting this result, anyone will admit to the correctness of a truth characterization satisfying Convention T. If we use the term 'formally correct definition' for a sentence of form (2) in which '$B(e)$' contains no semantic terms, this means that a formally correct definition that satisfies Convention T is bound to satisfy Condition *M* (when the language L satisfies I and II). As far as I can see, this is the only motivation for Convention T; if so, we can discredit Convention T by discrediting Convention M.

   Tarski sometimes states a more general form of Convention T, which applies to languages that do not meet restriction I: it is what results when one allows as instances of Schema T the results of replacing '*p*' by a *correct translation* of the sentence that the name substituted for '*x*' denotes (in some sense of 'correct translation' in which correctness requires preservation of truth value). But then the advantage of the ungeneralized form of Convention T (viz., that anything satisfying it wears its correctness on its face, or more accurately, on the faces of its logical consequences) is lost.

11. A sentence of the form '(∀N) (∀x) [N denotes x = B (N, x)]' *satisfies convention D* if it has as consequences every instance of the schema *'y denotes z'*, in which 'y' is to be replaced by a quotationmark name for a name *N*, and *'z'* is to be replaced by (an adequate translation of *N* into English, i.e.) a singular term of English that contains no semantic terms and that denotes the same thing that *N* denotes. Clearly DE and DG are not only extensionally correct, they also satisfy Convention D. Presumably philosophers who are especially impressed with Convention T will be equally impressed with this fact, but they owe us a reason why satisfying Convention D is of any interest.
12. For example, by extending our definition of denotation_s to descriptions by:

    ⌜$x_k(e)$⌝ denotes_s *a* if and only if [for each sequence *s** which differs from *s* at the *k*th place at most, *e* is $\text{true}_s{}^*$ if and only if the *k*th member of *s** is *a*].

    and then defining denotation in terms of denotation_s by stipulating that a closed term denotes an object if and only if it denotes_s that object for some (or all) *s*.
13. Some of Kripke's work on names will appear as Kripke 1972. What I've said about Russell's view is influenced by some of Kripke's lectures on which his paper there is based.
14. This paper grew out of a talk I gave at Princeton in the fall of 1970, where I defended T1 over T2. Donald Davidson and Gilbert Harman—and later, in private conversation, John Wallace—all came to the defense of T2, and their remarks have all been of help to me in writing the paper. I have also benefited from advice given by Michael Devitt, Paul Benacerraf, and especially David Hills.

References

Carnap, Rudolf. (1963). 'Autobiography'. In *The Philosophy of Rudolph Carnap*, ed. Paul Scfall pp. La Salle: Open Court, 3–84.

Davidson, D. (1967). 'Truth and Meaning', *Synthese 17*, 304–23.

Dummett, M (1959). 'Truth', *Proceedings of the Aristotelian Society* 19, 141–62.

Kripke, Saul. (1972). 'Naming and necessity'. In D. Davidson and G. Harman (eds.), *The Semantics of Natural Language*. Dordrecht: Reldel, 253–355.

Popper, K. (1959). *The Logic of Scientific Discovery*. New York: Basic Books.

Quine, W.V. (1953). 'Notes on the theory of reference'. In his *From a Logical Point of View.* New York: Harper, 130–8.

Quine, W.V. (1960). *Word and Object*. Cambridge, Mass.: MIT Press.

Tarski, A. (1944). The Semantic Conception of Truth and the Foundations of Semantics', *Philosophy and Phenomenological Research* 4, 341–76.

Tarski, A. (1956a). 'The concept of truth in formalized languages'. In his *Logic, Semantics, Metamathematics.* Oxford: Clarendon Press, 152–278.

Tarski, A. (1956b). 'The establishment of scientific semantics'. In his *Logic, Semantics, Metamathematics.* Oxford: Clarendon Press, 401–8.

4 Truth and language-world connections

DOROTHY GROVER

Philosophers have notoriously had little success in their search for a satisfactory, substantive correspondence theory of truth.[1] According to the early Bertrand Russell, true beliefs correspond to facts: the fact that snow is white makes the belief that snow is white true. The difficulties such fact theories face are well known. For example, none of the explanations of falsehood is close to being satisfactory. One suggestion is that beliefs are false because there are no facts to which they correspond. This kind of theory easily degenerates into the *existence* theory (A. N. Prior's terminology, *op. cit.*) of truth. In the *Theaetetus,* Plato wrestles with the dilemma posed by the existence theory: if sentences are false when there is nothing to which they correspond, then false sentences would appear to be about nothing. Part of the solution to the difficulty, offered in the *Sophist,* is to recognize that sentences have both subjects and predicates; for then a sentence can be about something (Theaetetus), and yet false (Theaetetus flies). This does not leave us within reach of a theory of truth and falsity, however.

Alternative proposals for falsehood have encountered other difficulties. Russell[2] suggests that false beliefs (false sentences, or false propositions) might correspond to objective falsehoods; or, alternatively, that belief is a relation between the believer and an indefinite number of objects. Then later Russell[3] proposes that a true sentence corresponds in one way to a fact and a false sentence corresponds in a different way to the same fact. What are facts, and what are objective falsehoods? What kinds of language-world connections are there that might provide the assumed correspondence?

The picture theory of the *Tractatus* might be viewed as offering a natural explanation of correspondence—for one is supposed just to *see* what a picture pictures. But it is pretty obvious we do not just see what a picture pictures, for different people with different backgrounds see many different things.[4] Furthermore, how can a mere configuration of natural linguistic objects (or names) be propositional? To the extent that a picture theory more satisfactorily addresses this question, the picture analogy seems undermined. Relations (of implication, for example) that obtain between sentences do not obtain between pictures. If we loosen up on the picture analogy, what explanation do we have of the connections between language and reality?

Faced with problems such as these, many philosophers have abandoned the idea that the correspondence-to-facts framework will lead to an acceptable theory of truth (or meaning). Indeed, alternatives to a substantive correspondence truth theory have been offered. There is Alfred Tarski's theory, according to which truth definitions that are formally correct and materially adequate capture all that is to be captured in the notion of "correspondence"; there are the disquotational theories,[5] and the prosentential theory of truth.[6]

Those seeking a substantive truth theory—usually because they think truth has a causal explanatory role—think, however, that none of these "deflationary" alternatives provides adequate explanations of truth as a needed language-world relational property. Hartry Field[7] is one such philosopher. Convinced that truth has an explanatory role, Field offers a suggestion as to the form a substantive correspondence theory might take. His suggestion is that something along the lines of the causal-historical theories of reference should be employed to provide an account of truth as a substantive relational property connecting language with the world. Because we need a better understanding of the possible points of contact between *truth* and *language-world connections,* it will be useful to examine this provocative suggestion of Field's. Field's paper is important because of the deep issues it raises; for that reason, it has also been controversial.[8] Despite this attention by philosophers expressing widely divergent views, an interesting feature of Field's suggestion seems to have gone unnoticed: it does not accomplish what I believe Field (and, I presume, many readers) thought it would accomplish—it does not lead us to a theory in which truth would have a *distinctive* substantive role in connecting language to the world.

My main goal is to highlight, in section IV, this curious feature of a correspondence theory of truth that incorporates as its substantive language-world connections the language-world connections of the causal-historical theory of reference. As a step toward this end, I first outline, in section I, Field's assessment of Tarski's truth definition. In section II, taking up Field's suggestions, I sketch a few of the details of how the causal-historical theory of reference connections might be incorporated in a Tarskian theory of truth. In Section III, I briefly reflect on a criticism of Field's program which is pertinent to the issue I pursue. Then in Section IV, after defining falsity, I show that true sentences are not uniquely connected to the world on Field's proposal. In the remainder of the paper, I argue that language-world connections, like those of the causal-historical theory of reference, fail to provide truth itself with the explanatory role Field speculates truth has. I conclude with the suggestion that it seems we can, and perhaps should, treat the issues of language-world connections, and truth and falsity, separately.

I Field's program

In his 1972 paper criticizing Tarski's truth definition, Field proposed that Tarski's theory needs to be supplemented because truth has an explanatory role. For according to Field, Tarski's definition does not accomplish the goal Tarski set himself—a definition that would satisfy the demands of a physicalist who believes in the unity of science. He says, further, that Tarski's definition is only language-specific. Field argues that, if Tarski's definition of truth were modified so that truth for arbitrary languages would be defined, then 'denotes' and 'applies' would appear in Tarski's base clauses; so truth is, in effect, explained by Tarski only with the help of other semantic terms. Field proposes eliminating these terms in a way that would satisfy physicalists.

Thus, the recursive clauses of Tarski's truth definition provide (only) the first important step of Field's definition. For Field's Tarskian base clauses for primitive terms and atomic sentences contain the semantic terms 'denotes' and 'applies'. Field suggests that the causal-historical theory of reference (or something similar) be used to explain 'denotes' and 'applies'. Let us take a close look at the suggestion that the causal-historical theory of reference might yield the kind of truth theory Field seeks. First, 'true' would be eliminated in favor of 'denotes' and 'applies'; then 'denotes' and 'applies', in their turn, are to be eliminated with the help of recent causal-historical theories of reference.

This discussion will move more smoothly if I assume, as Field would need to, that causal-historical theories provide an analysis of reference that would satisfy physicalists. And, despite my preference for another theory of truth, I shall also for the moment follow Field in assuming that truth is a relational property, and in particular, a property of sentence tokens.

II Field's truth definition

As a first step toward a truth definition which will be applicable to all languages, and from which all semantic terms can eventually be eliminated, Field offers the following base clauses for selected primitive terms and atomic sentences. (I ignore his function symbols. As Tarski's recursive clauses are not in dispute, I ignore those also.) I follow Field in using '...is true on *s*' for a given sequence *s*, rather than '*s* satisfies ...'.

For a given sequence *s*,

A. (i) the *k*th variable denotes the *k*th member of *s*;
   (ii) the *k*th constant denotes what it denotes.

B. For a given predicate '*F*' and term *e*, '*Fe*' is true if and only if
   (i) there is a (unique?) object *x* that '*e*' denotes; and
   (ii) '*F*' applies to *x*.

These clauses provide only a first step toward a definition; for 'denotes' and 'applies' have yet to be eliminated. Beyond directing us to Kripke's causal-historical account of reference, Field does not give us details as to how the elimination is to be achieved.[9] Also, note that the above definition yields a truth definition for sentence types rather than tokens. As I mentioned above, Field intends a definition for sentence tokens, in part because he says he wants to provide a definition that will cope with ambiguity. I shall usually ignore this detail.

According to causal-historical theories of reference, tokens of singular terms are causally[10] connected to objects, and tokens of predicates like count nouns, natural-kind terms, etc., are causally connected to the members of sets of objects. Unfortunately, these details do not suggest unique ways of eliminating 'denotes' from Field's base clauses, even in outline. So I shall provide only schematic elimination clauses.

For a given sequence *s*, 'denotes' can be eliminated from the A-clauses and B(i) by means of

D. A token *x denotes y* iff *x* is appropriately causally connected to *y*.

The situation for predicates [which is what we must look to in unpacking 'applies' in B(ii)] is more complicated.[11] Whereas for a singular-term token only one extralinguistic object is usually assumed involved, for a predicate "baptisms" typically involve a set of sample objects, a subset of which are paradigmatic samples of the predicate's extension. Bits of junk are likely to be included along with the paradigmatic samples in the initial baptismal sets. In the case of 'water' and 'gold', for example, the samples may include dirty or salty water, and fool's gold. "Experts" in the society shoulder the responsibility of doing some sorting out here, for facts about the world determine extension; and the experts are supposed to know about the world. They must sort out which or what among baptismal samples are paradigmatic to a determination of extension, as well as the complete extension of the predicate. I cannot offer ways of handling (B) [or (A)] which will do justice to the details of causal-historical theories of reference. Appropriate eliminations must presumably rely, however, on something like the following elimination schema, for a given sequence *s*,

AP. A token '*F*' *applies* to *x* iff

(a) there is a (possibly empty) paradigmatic set of objects *f′* included in a baptismal set of sample objects; and the members of *f′* are appropriately causally connected to the token '*F*';[12] and

(b) there is a (possibly empty) set *f*—the extension of the token of '*F*'—such that the members of *f* are similar in appropriate respects to the members of *f′*.

Tarski allows primitive predicates with empty extensions. As Field does not comment on this point, I assume he also allows empty extensions for predicates. I do not know how he would do this. Nevertheless, I have allowed that the set of paradigmatic samples, *f′*, included in the baptismal set, could be empty; and I have allowed that the extension of the token of '*F*' could be empty. [Perhaps definite descriptions are used to pick out the members of the initial *f′* when *f* (and *f′*) are empty; and sometimes nothing satisfies the definite description. Or perhaps *f′* could be empty in another way: if causal connections are involved, the baptismal set will have to be nonempty; however, *f′* would be empty if the baptismal set contained no objects that can be counted as paradigmatic.]

AP(a) and (b) do not alone suffice to eliminate 'applies', of course. They ensure only that the terms in a token of *Fe* have *extensions.* Given the syntactic structure of *Fx*, I complete AP with

(c) *x* is a member of *f*.

Note that I could just as easily have used '*x* is *F*' in place of '*x* is a member of *f*'. Either would give the right extension for 'true', *providing* the other clauses do their job. For we usually explain set membership to those new to set theory by means of more commonplace predicates, e.g., we explain 'Adam is a member of the set of fathers' by means of 'Adam is a father'.[13]

This concludes my schematic development of Field's proposal for a causal-historical truth definition.

III Criticism of field's proposal

Field's proposal for a substantive correspondence theory seems, in some respects, an advance on earlier proposals for a substantive theory. For Field does not assume that there is a correspondence without making some attempt at identifying the "correspondence"; and, following Tarski, he does not appear to assume connections with facts.

Despite these positive features, there have been criticisms of Field's proposal, as I mentioned above. Pertinent to the point I want to make is an issue that relates to a criticism John McDowell raises. McDowell questions Field's location of language-world connections at the level of primitive reference. Field says that language-world connections at the level of sentences are to be explained or derived from language-world connections at the level of the primitive terms of the language—via Tarski's recursive clauses. The language-world connections at the level of primitive terms on which I am focusing are those of causal-historical theories of reference. Let us consider, then, the task of drawing on the details of causal-historical theory of reference as we try to fill in the gaps in the schematic elimination clauses D and AP for 'denotes' and 'applies'.

We have been told that referential chains are determined by complex social linguistic factors. Saul Kripke and Hilary Putnam[14] give us some of these details. For example, scientific experts have a role in the determination of reference, etc. Charles Chastain[15] provides other kinds of details; for example, he illustrates some of the ways in which proper names can be introduced into a discourse:

> D14. A man named Fred Schultz runs a liquor store around the corner from here. He was held up yesterday, and …
>
> D15. A man known to the underworld as Joe the Snake was found dead in a vacant lot this morning. Police spokesmen stated …
>
> D17. A certain bookie I know whom I'll just call "Harry" told me that…
>
> D18. Stella Houston (a fictitious name) underwent a sex-change operation six months ago. "She" told this reporter that … (*ibid.,* pp. 216–7).

Of these Chastain says:

> Sometimes it appears that a proper name is introduced *de novo* into a context, in such a way that it is not referentially linked to another occurrence of the same name in another context. This is indicated explicitly in DI7 by the phrase 'whom I'll just call "Harry" '; the pseudonym is introduced simply in order to have a name *in that context* for the person whom the speaker is referring to by another singular term ('a certain bookie I know'), and previous occurrences of the name in other contexts are irrelevant. … Sometimes the situation is just the opposite: the first occurrence of the name in the context harks back to previous occurrences in other contexts, as in … D14, D15 … (*ibid.*).

The causal-historical explanation of reference portrays a situation where complex human linguistic behavior is causally or historically linked to extralinguistic reality. Our D and AP clauses must take account of the fact, for example, that both the immediate discourse, and earlier discourses—as well as the expertise, intentions, and theories of speakers of the language—have a role in determining reference. In particular, our elimination clauses must take account of the fact that initial baptisms typically involve sentences, not just terms. Putnam and Kripke illustrate this aspect of their theories with examples like 'This (liquid) is water', 'Gold is the substance instantiated by the items over there, or at any rate, by almost all of them'. Whole sentences (not just terms) also typically appear at later stages of referential chains, as in D14 and D15, for example.

These excerpts serve to illustrate partially the criticism that the causal-historical theory of reference does not provide Field with what his program would need. For the causal-historical theory does not have language-world connections occurring first at the level of primitive terms, and then only derivatively at the level of sentences—as Field's project seems to assume. Field needs to do some sorting out here.[16]

The point I want to draw attention to in all of this is that causal-historical theories do not assume *true* sentences have a unique role in causal-historical chains—false sentences, as well as true sentences, appear in the chains.

This observation raises an initial question concerning Field's program. Correspondence theorists usually assume that the language-world connections of true sentences should be different from the language-world connections of false sentences. Since true sentences do not appear to have a unique role in causal-historical theories of reference, one wonders whether a truth theory of the kind Field proposes will yield different language-world connections for true and false sentences. This is the issue I am chasing.

IV Falsehood

Field's definition yields extensions for only 'true' and, by implication, 'not true'. 'False' is left to us. A question arises when we think about how we should handle the existential quantifiers in the above clauses. Both Field's A-clauses and his overall discussion suggest that he follows Tarski in assuming that the languages under consideration contain only denoting singular terms. As this is the simplest assumption to accommodate, I shall proceed on that assumption in defining falsity. So the base clauses, A(i) and A(ii), will be the same for falsity as for truth.

It remains to define 'A token of *Fe* is false'. For this, I shall construct C-clauses, following as closely as possible the above B-clauses. C-clause can be the same as B-clause up to the end of (i), since we continue with the assumption that singular terms denote. As I am defining falsity and not 'not true', I cannot simply add '*F* does not apply to *x*', since I assume Field would hold that all predicates appearing in the primitive sentences of his languages have extensions—though possibly empty. For this reason, C(ii) will be more complex than B(ii). The following should suffice.

For a given sequence *s*,

C. A token of '*Fe*' is *false* on *s* if and only if
   - (i) There is a (unique?) object *x* that the token '*e*' denotes; and
   - (ii) (a) The given token of '*F*' has a (possibly empty) extension; and
     - (b) '*F*' does not apply to *x*.

D and AP, above, can be used to eliminate 'denotes' and 'applies'. That leaves 'has an extension', which for a given predicate is assumed to be causal-historically determined. Note that AP(a) and (b) contain all we need for an elimination clause. Rewritten, in the form of a (schematic) definition we get for a given *s*,

E. A token of '*F*' has an *extension* iff
   - **(i)** There is a (possibly empty) paradigmatic set of objects *f′* included in a baptismal set of sample objects; and the members of *f′* are appropriately causally connected to the token of *F;* and
   - **(ii)** There is a (possibly empty) set *f* such that the members of *f* are similar in appropriate respects (as identified by the experts) to the members of *f′*.

Providing the details could be filled out, this would yield a definition of falsity from which all semantic terms would be eliminated. In general, '*F*' does not apply to *x* if any of AP(a), (b), or (c) were denied. On the assumption that '*F*' has an extension [i.e., C(ii) (a) obtains], however, '*Fe*' will be false only if *x* is not a member of *f.*

In summary, we have:

> '*Fe' is true,* on *s,* just in case,
>
> *e* is appropriately causally connected to *x* (its denotation); '*F*' is appropriately causally connected to certain members (the objects in *f′*) of *f* ('*F*'s extension); and *x* is a member of *f*;
>
> '*Fe' is false,* on *s*, just in case,
>
> *e* is appropriately causally connected to *x* (its denotation); '*F*' is appropriately causally connected to certain members (the objects in *f′*) of *f* ('*F*'s extension); and *x* is not a member of *f*.

With the base clauses of the definition set out in this fairly tidy way, we can see immediately where the causal-historical theory establishes substantive causal-historical connections between sentences and the world. The connections are between some of the parts of a sentence and extralinguistic objects. We also see that, since a sentence contains the same words whether or not it is true or false, these causal-historical connections are the same for a sentence whether or not it is true or false.

It is only in the final clauses of the definitions for "'*Fe*' is true" and "'*Fe*' is false" that there is a difference. In the case where *'Fe'* is true, it is required that *x* (the object which is causally connected to *e)* belong to *f* (the causally determined extension of '*F*'); in the case where *'Fe'* is false, it is required that *x* not belong to *f.* This is a difference that has nothing to do with the causal historical language-world relations, however.[17] It concerns only extralinguistic reality—if one is a realist. Indeed, this difference between true and false sentences is one that deflationists recognize. Consider Tarski's requirement of material adequacy, according to which a theory of truth should have among its theorems T-sentences like "'Snow is white' is true if and only if snow is white."

And so my point can now be made:

> The causal-historical connections between language and the world—which have been incorporated in this proposed definition of truth—are the same for a sentence whether or not the sentence is true or false.[18]

This feature of Field's language-world connections is perhaps not surprising, when one considers that the language-world connections Field utilizes come from causal-historical theories of reference. According to these theories, the same kind of story is to be told about 'this ring' and 'gold', for example, whether or not tokens of these terms appear in declaratives like 'This ring is gold' and 'This ring is not gold', or in questions like 'Where is the gold ring?' and 'Whose is this ring?', or in commands like 'Give me that ring!'. No presently proposed theory (to my knowledge) suggests that different kinds of causal-historical referential connections obtain depending on whether a term occurs in a question, a command, or a declarative— or in a true declarative or a false declarative.

It is true that Field is cautious in suggesting that the causal-historical theory of reference provides correspondence theorists with exactly what is needed.

> [Kripke] has suggested a kind of factor involved in denotation that gives new hope to explaining the connection between language and the things it is about. It seems to me that the possibility of *some such* theory of denotation (to be deliberately very vague) is essential to the joint acceptability of physicalism and the semantic term 'denotes' ... (*op. cit.*, p. 367).

The vagueness makes it hard to tell, however, what 'some such theory' includes. If Field includes theories that are motivated by issues that we traditionally associate with "meaning," then we should be aware that the same substantive language-world relations might emerge for a sentence, whether it is true or false.

Consider for a moment, and more generally, some of the factors that can influence the selection of language-world connections in a theory that seeks a replacement for, or an account of, denotation. If we suppose that there are certain language-world connections that determine (or partly determine) the significance of a word in a sentence, these language-world connections must presumably be the same whenever the significance of the word remains the same. Given, further, that the contribution the component words make to a sentence is usually more or less fixed, we assume that a sentence has roughly the same meaning, whether it is true or false.[19] (I ignore the interesting complications that indexicals and vagueness introduce.) Accordingly, we can expect that the kinds of language-world connections to which Field directs us might be the same, whether the sentences in question are true or false.[20]

There are a number of reasons for thinking Field may have hoped for different language-world connections for true and false sentences, however. One reason is that he believes truth has an explanatory role. I discuss this issue in the next section. There is also the following.

> . . . *Part* of the explanation of the truth of 'Schnee ist weiss und Gras ist grun', presumably, would be that snow is white and grass is green. But this would only be part of the explanation, for still missing is the connection between snow being white and grass being green on the one hand, and the German utterance being true on the other hand (*op. cit.* pp. 359–360).

In this passage, Field tells us what he is looking for by way of substantive language-world connections. Part of the requirement is captured in AP(c)—the deflationary Tarski part. Beyond that, he seeks a connection between the sentence and 'snow being white and grass being green'. Field's way of stating this requirement unfortunately brings to mind the problems the earlier fact theories encountered. For consider the sentence, 'The cat is on the mat', when the cat is up the tree. Is the sentence connected to the cats not being on the mat (a negative fact), or the dogs being on the mat, or the cats being up the tree?[21] What we do know is that 'The cat is on the mat', if false, cannot be connected to the cats being on the mat, because there is no such thing—the language-world connections must presumably be different for true and false sentences, if we approach language-world connections from this direction.

I believe, however, that Field's talk of 'snow being white', etc., is only a manner of speaking that we should not take seriously. Let us back off a bit. The crucial test for Field's theory will come in those places where he claims truth has an explanatory role. Does Field *need* a theory of truth according to which there are different language-world connections for true sentences and false sentences?

V A causal explanatory role for truth

A reason Field gives for advocating a substantive correspondence theory of truth is that he thinks truth has a causal explanatory role, otherwise he seems to think a disquotational theory of truth would do. His most recent defense of these claims appears in "The Deflationary Conception of Truth."[22] In that paper, Field speculates that certain kinds of systematic reliability, T-reliability, can only be explained with a "full-blooded" correspondence theory. The task is

> . . . the matter of explaining T-reliability (as opposed to using T-reliability in explanations). If, under a given interpretation J, an agent's states are highly T-reliable and converse T-reliable—i.e. for certain sorts of p, when the agent has a belief whose truth-conditions under J are that p, then generally p; and conversely when p then the agent has a belief whose truth-conditions under J are that p—then this fact is a striking regularity that calls for some sort of explanation. Just what the explanation will be like will of course vary greatly from case to case, depending on the interpretation J and the nature of the class of p for which the agent is T-reliable (and converse T-reliable) under J. Suppose we have a successful social activist, whose success is explained in part by her extensive knowledge of social movements of the past. The interpretation useful in explaining her success will make her T-reliable (and converse T-reliable) about such events as the Kronstadt rebellion; and we will need an explanation of the striking correlation between her belief-states and the events involving the Kronstadt sailors. It seems likely the explanation would have to involve something like causal networks of information . . .
>
> A familiar proposal for giving a correspondence theory of truth (perhaps most explicit in Field, 1972 [This volume, Ch. 3 – Ed.]) is to explain the truth conditions of sentences in terms of reference or reference-like relations for the basic parts of the sentence, and then to give explanations of the reference-like relations for the parts; and it is often assumed that something like causal networks of information of the sort just alluded to will play a role in the theories of reference for the parts. Abstracting from the details of the proposal, it seems that a central feature of the proposal is to build into the theoretical explication of correspondence truth just the sort of thing that is needed to *explain* the striking T-reliability and converse T-reliability that agents have (about some matters), under the interpretations that we find useful in explaining their success. . . . And perhaps it is not surprising that the explanation of such a systematic T-reliability would have to involve the systematic elements required of an explication of the notion of truth conditions (*ibid.,* p. 104).

Let us suppose Field is right when he suggests that causal connections will be a "central feature" of explanations of T-reliability. Has Field built into his "theoretical explication of correspondence truth just the sort of thing that is needed to explain . . . T-reliability"?

I assume one thing we should require of a good explanation of T-reliability is that it provide an explanation of why some people are T-reliable and why others are not T-reliable. So it would seem to follow that, if certain kinds of causal connections between language or an observer and the world are what is needed to explain T-reliability, then the causal connections that obtain when a person is T-reliable will not obtain when a person is not T-reliable. Otherwise, the presence of the causal connections will contribute little (if anything) to an explanation of the differences between being T-reliable and failing to be T-reliable.

If we continue assuming the causal-historical connections of current theories of reference, then the utterances of articulate coherent speakers will tend to be appropriately causally connected to the objects about which they talk. Articulate coherent speakers can have false beliefs, however, and so fail to be T-reliable. Indeed, the presence of referential causal-historical connections—though they may have a role in explaining articulateness—seem to have little to do with a person's T-reliability or lack of T-reliability. For reasons such as these, I conclude that the language-world connections Field suggests we consider incorporating in his truth theory are unlikely to help us distinguish between those articulate persons who are T-reliable and those articulate persons who are not T-reliable.[23]

A good explanation of T-reliability, along the lines Field seeks, would seem to call for different language-world connections for true and false beliefs.[24] As Field's proposal for a theory of truth does not provide the kind of truth property he needs, we face a problem.

What can be salvaged? We have considered the possibility of incorporating in a theory of truth the language-world connections of reference. If truth is to have a causal explanatory role, however, then it seems there must be different causal connections with the world for true and false sentences. And this, we have seen, seems to make the causal connections of reference unsuitable for the task. If truth has an explanatory role we need to look somewhere else for the required language-world connections.

What are our options if truth does not have an explanatory role? While I am inclined to drop the idea of incorporating language-world in our analysis of truth, many philosophers find the spirit of Field's project appealing.[25] Would there be any harm in incorporating something like the language-world connections of reference in an account of truth?

One such approach might proceed as follows. We are free to stipulate how we will use 'true', 'false', 'truth', and 'falsity'; and so, as it pleases us, it seems we could use these terms to designate an identifiable set of causal relations. The causal-historical connections of theories of reference seem relevant to an explanation of linguistic activity. They seem pertinent, for example, to an explanation of meaning, or to an explanation of the fact that a given sequence of sounds is a token of a sentence in a given language. Incorporation of referential connections in an analysis of truth would then seem an option, since harmless. In the particular case we are considering, if referential causal-historical connections have an explanatory role (in explaining meaning, perhaps) then truth would also—though admittedly this would not give truth and falsity explanatory roles of their own.

Those who endorse deflationists' accounts of the utility of the truth predicate[26] have reasons for not endorsing the above supposedly harmless suggestion.[27] I shall explain briefly.

According to some who advocate either a disquotational or prosentential theory, 'true' and 'false' are only useful words; since they only provide us with a way of generalizing with respect to sentences, a way of achieving linguistic ascent and descent, etc. That is, truth and falsity, and 'true' and 'false', rather than provide or contain answers to questions regarding such issues as language-world connections, T-reliability, meaning, and realism, provide only the expressibility that we need to say some of the things we want to say, and to ask some of the questions we want to ask about these and other issues. For example,

(i) Is there a causal relation that obtains between a sentence and the world when it is true, but does not obtain when it is false?

(ii) What justifies us in claiming that statements about theoretical entities are true?

These questions do not need to be interpreted as giving truth a property-ascribing role. On the prosentential theory, (i) and (ii) have instances like

(i') Is there a causal relation that holds between 'Reagan cannot remember' and the world, when Reagan cannot remember, which does not hold between the sentence and the world, when Reagan remembers?

(ii') What justifies us in claiming that electrons have mass?

If the expressibility offered by 'true' and 'false' can be separated off from these more substantial issues, then there would seem to be advantages in reflecting this fact in our theories. We are not then faced with the difficulty that there seems no clear intuition as to what more there is to truth. And if we separate the issues, we are less likely to confuse them.

There is, I believe, another reason for not incorporating the language-world connections of reference in a prosentential analyses of truth.[28] Incorporation of language-world connections would presumably give 'true' a property-ascribing role. If we accept the prosentential explanation of the expressibility with which 'true' and 'false' provide us, then the cost of adding to this prosentential role, a property-ascribing role, is inconsistency. Construed only as a modified prosentence, 'This is false' lacks content because it is ungrounded; whereas if 'false' has a property-ascribing role in addition to its prosentence-forming role, 'This is false' embodies an inconsistency.[29]

I have shown that, in his stimulating papers, Field has presented a confused picture as to the kind of truth theory he thinks we need, since, on the one hand, he has proposed a substantive correspondence truth theory according to which true and false sentences are connected by the same kinds of causal connections to reality. On the other hand, his suggestion that truth has an explanatory role shows we would need different (if any) language-world connections for true and false sentences. The question arises whether we might consider incorporating causal language-world connections of denotation in a truth theory, nevertheless. If 'true' and 'false' provide expressibility of the kind disquotational and prosentential theorists have proposed—and truth itself does not have an explanatory role—I believe there are reasons for not doing so.[30]

Notes

1. See, for example, A. N. Prior's survey of the correspondence theory in "Correspondence Theory of Truth," in *Encyclopedia of Philosophy,* Paul Edwards, ed. (New York: Macmillan, 1967). By a *substantive correspondence theory of truth* I mean a theory that construes truth as a substantive relational property connecting language or thought with an extralinguistic reality. I include the correspondence theories of Russell, and I shall include Hartry Field's.

   Some philosophers (e.g., Prior) follow Alfred Tarski in claiming that a formally correct definition that has as consequences, so-called T-sentences, like

   'Snow is white' is true iff snow is white.

   captures all there is to capture in correspondence theories of truth. On this view, nothing further needs to be said about truth "relating" language to the world. Theories like this, and others, have been called *deflationary*. It is expected that deflationists assume truth does not have a causal explanatory role.

2. "On the Nature of Truth and Falsehood" (first published in 1910), in *Philosophical Essays* (New York: Simon & Schuster, 1966).
3. "The Philosophy of Logical Atomism," reprinted in *The Philosophy of Logical Atomism,* David Pears, ed. (LaSalle: Open Court, 1985).
4. See Nelson Goodman, "The Way the World is," in *Problems and Projects* (New York: Bobbs-Merrill, 1972). Another problem: it has been claimed that pictures picture what they picture in virtue of certain conventions. Can an account be given of the conventions governing verbal "pictures" without assuming language already understood?
5. See W. V. Quine, *The Philosophy of Logic* (Englewood Cliffs, NJ: Prentice- Hall, 1970), pp. 10–13; Steven Leeds, "Theories of Reference and Truth," *Erkenntnis,* XIII (1978): 111–129; Paul Horwich, "Three Forms of Realism," *Synthese,* LI (1982): 181–201; and Scott Soames "What is a Theory of Truth?" *The Journal of Philosophy*, LXXXI, 8 (August 1984): 411–429.
6. See Grover, Joe Camp, and Nuel Belnap, "A Prosentential Theory of Truth," *Philosophical Studies,* XXVII (1975): 72–124; my "Inheritors and Paradox," *The Journal of Philosophy*, LXXIV, 10 (October 1977): 590–604; my "Truth: Do We Need It?" *Philosophical Studies,* XL (1981): 69–103; and my "On Two Deflationary Theories of Truth," in *Truth and Consequences,* M. Dunn and A. Gupta, eds. (Boston: Kluwer, forthcoming); R. Brandom, "Reference Explained Away," *The Journal of Philosophy*, LXXXI, 9 (September 1984): 469–492; and K. Wilson, "Some Reflections on the Prosentential Theory of Truth," in *Truth and Consequences.*
7. "Tarski's Theory of Truth," *The Journal of Philosophy*, LXIX, 13 (July 13, 1972): 347–375.
8. For example, Devitt [*Designation* (New York: Columbia, 1981), and *Realism and Truth* (Princeton: University Press, 1984)] and Michael Friedman ["Truth and Confirmation," *The Journal of Philosophy*, LXXVI, 7 (July 1979): 361–382] have endorsed Field's claim that something like causal-historical explanations of reference may constitute a crucial element of a theory of truth; whereas Donald Davidson ["Reality without Reference," *Dialectica,* XXXI (1977): 247–258, Hilary Putnam [*Reason, Truth and History* (New York: Cambridge, 1981), ch. 2], John McDowell ["Physicalism and Primitive Denotation: Field on Tarski," *Erkenntnis,* XIII (1978): 131–152], Leeds *(op. cit.),* Robert Stalnaker [*Inquiry* (Cambridge: MIT, 1984), ch. 2], and Soames *(op. cit.)* have raised some doubts.
9. This is not surprising, for Saul Kripke's "Naming and Necessity" [in *Semantics of Natural Language,* D. Davidson & G. Harman, eds. (Boston: Reidel, 1972), pp. 253–355] had not at that time appeared in print.
10. I shall often speak of 'causal connections' rather than the longer 'causal-historical connections'.
11. Field refers us to Kripke, *op. cit.* It happens that all of Kripke's examples involving 'water', 'gold', etc., have these terms occurring in subject place. I do not know whether this is deliberate. I shall follow Field in assuming Kripke intended his account of reference to apply also when such terms occur in predicate position.
12. I assume the causal connection is not with the set *f*', but with its members.
13. Given our lack of understanding of the set-theoretic paradoxes, it is doubtful we should view '*x* is a member of *f*'' as contributing to a better explanation than '*x* is an *F*' would.
14. "The Meaning of 'Meaning'," in *Language, Mind, and Knowledge,* K. Gunderson, ed. (Minneapolis: Minnesota UP, 1975), pp. 131–193.
15. "Reference and Context," in *Language, Mind, and Knowledge,* pp. 194–269.

16. Devitt thinks there are optional strategies here; e.g., along the lines suggested in *Designation,* pp. 113–124; and in *Realism and Truth,* ch. 10.
17. Field's use of 'applies' makes it easy for us to overlook this point.
18. Like the early theorists, Field begins with an idea that sounds appealing initially—when one thinks only about truth. As soon as one tries to complete the theory with an account of falsity, however, the theory appears to raise more (important) questions than it answers.
19. We make this assumption when we judge that sentences of the form '*S* & not *S*' are contradictory.
20. I have shown, in sect. III, that true sentences do not have a special role in the version of the causal-historical theory of reference I considered. From this, I cannot conclude there is no theory of denotation according to which some true sentences (and no false sentences) are uniquely connected to the world. For what it is worth, however, I am almost certain there are no interesting causal connections that obtain between all and only true-sentence tokens and extralinguistic reality.
21. These questions are taken from Peter Strawson, "Truth," *Proceedings of the Aristotelian Society,* Supp. Vol. xxiv (1950): 129–156.
22. In *Fact, Science, and Morality: Essays on A. J. Ayer's Language, Truth, and Logic,* G. MacDonald & C. Wright eds. (New York: Blackwell, 1986), pp. 55–117.
23. Friedman, *op. cit.,* argues that a truth theory like Field's is needed to justify scientific methods of confirmation. I believe that such a truth theory is ill-suited to that task also.
24. I suspect connections like those often associated with justified belief are more likely to be relevant.
25. I believe a reason the incorporation of language-world connections is initially attractive—whether or not one has a view on explanatory role—is that this move addresses a problem for truth *created* by correspondence theorists. Their move to a metalinguistic truth predicate, as in " 'Snow is white' is true," leads one to ask how it is that the sequence of marks on paper which constitute the inscription 'Snow is white' come to be used to say what we say when using it. If we think, instead, of 'true' as functioning at the level of the object language—as 'she' and 'he' do—this question does not arise in connection with truth and falsity. Of course, it does arise when we start thinking about language, no matter what theory of the truth predicate we adopt.
26. I do not have space to give more details of either the disquotational or prosentential theories. For that, the reader is referred to the references given in footnotes 5 and 6. [See also Chs. 12 and 13 of this volume – Ed.]
27. Although Field grants that 'true' and 'false' are used in the way disquotationalists have suggested, I do not know whether he would endorse one of the deflationary theories if truth had no explanatory role.
28. I continue to assume there are no substantive language-world connections that obtain between only true sentences and the world. The whole situation changes if this assumption is false.
29. See my "Inheritors and Paradox" for details. The need for Tarski-style truth models does not thereby vanish, if we adopt the prosentential theory; Tarski-style truth models are needed so that we can track the logic of prosentences, modified prosentences, and ungrounded prosentences.
30. I thank Michael Devitt, Anil Gupta, and Jerry Kapus for their comments on earlier drafts. I am afraid I have probably not adequately addressed all of Devitt's doubts. Thanks also to the philosophers at Victoria University/Wellington, for their helpful comments.

Section 2 Epistemic theories of truth

Editor's introduction

DOUGLAS EDWARDS

Traditionally speaking, the correspondence theory of truth is opposed to the theories that are developed and discussed in this section. They each, in various ways, offer so-called 'anti-realist' alternatives to the realist position advocated by the correspondence theory of truth. The realist aspect of the correspondence theory holds that reality is completely separate from our ways of thinking and talking about it, and, consequently, that whether or not a belief is true is a completely separate matter from the reasons we might have for believing it to be true. The views in this section are all sceptical of this realist move. They doubt that any sense can be made of the idea that true beliefs match reality, and take issue with the fact that, on the realist view, we cannot ever know for sure if our beliefs *are* true. This is because we would need access to both the belief and the world in order to check whether a belief is true, but this seems to be an impossible thing to do, for we can only check reality through the sensory apparatus we have. This means that all of our access to reality is mediated by beliefs, and, consequently, we can never step outside of our beliefs to check if they match reality. Accordingly, epistemic theories of truth do not look to some separate reality to explain truth; rather they look to give an account of truth in terms of materials more readily available to hand, such as the reasons for which we are justified in holding certain beliefs.

The coherence theory

The coherence theory of truth, most famously expounded by F. H. Bradley, holds that truth is not a relation between a belief and reality, but rather a relation between a belief and a system of beliefs. The coherence theory was traditionally associated with the metaphysical picture of *idealism*, where reality is considered to be somehow constituted by beliefs or perceptions.

If we think of reality as just being constituted by beliefs, then the idea of beliefs matching an independent reality does not seem to make sense. Accordingly, truth was thought of instead as a matter of coherence between beliefs: what matters is the sustenance of a coherent system. On the face of it, however, there are reasons to think that there is an association between truth and coherence independently of this metaphysical thesis. When assessing a set of beliefs for truth one thing that we often check is whether the beliefs are consistent with one another. For example, consider the following set of beliefs:

(1) My keys are in my jacket.

(2) My jacket is in the closet.

(3) My keys are in the car.

A significant problem with holding all of these beliefs at once is that holding any two entails the negation of the third. As a consequence, if one holds all of these beliefs at once, one's belief system entails a contradiction, which is a sign that all the beliefs one holds cannot be true. Consistency is thus an important factor in determining truth, and the coherence theory of truth takes consistency as a key aspect of what makes beliefs true. What is wanted on the coherence theory is a system of beliefs that cohere with one another partly in virtue of the set of beliefs held being consistent. However, consistency is not thought to be the only feature of a coherence theory of truth. Coherence theorists tend to argue that coherence is not simply consistency, but rather a range of different, but related, features, including that the components of the system not only are consistent, but also provide mutual explanatory support.

One famous objection to the coherence theory is due to Bertrand Russell (see Russell, this volume, Ch. 1, and also Wright, this volume, Ch. 16). Russell thought that mere consistency would not suffice to make a belief true. This is because it is possible that there are a number of coherent systems, and a belief will, in theory, cohere with one of the possible coherent systems. As a consequence, the coherence theory makes it too easy for a belief to be true, for we can be sure that, for any belief, there will be a system with which it coheres. The typical way to respond to this concern is to say that truth is not coherence with any old system, but that there is a single privileged system, the *maximally coherent system*, which is the system that beliefs must cohere with if they are to be true. Of course, this raises a new question, namely what the maximally coherent system is, and how we can know whether our current beliefs cohere with this system. Some are concerned that this re-introduces the sorts of sceptical concerns which were pressed against the correspondence theory of truth, and points us towards two competing demands on epistemic theories of truth: the need to make truth accessible, on the one hand, and the need to make truth objective, to some degree, on the other. Whether these key demands can be met is a key issue for all epistemic theories of truth.

Russell also objected to the idea that consistency can be used as a suitable definition of truth, on the grounds that consistency itself depends on a prior notion of truth in order to explain it. For example, the most natural way to explain the problem with (1)–(3) above is that the *truth* of any two entails the falsity of the third; and thus that (1), (2) and (3) cannot *all* be *true*. This is what makes for the inconsistency: an inconsistent system is one in which all of the components cannot all be true. However, Russell argued, if this is the case, then consistency is defined in terms of truth, which means that we cannot use consistency in our efforts to explain what truths is, as that would be a circular definition. At most, according to Russell, consistency can be used as a test for truth, but not as an analysis of truth itself.

An interesting contemporary discussion of coherence theory is given by Paul Thagard in his paper 'Coherence, Truth, and the Development of Scientific Knowledge'. Thagard considers the relationship between coherence and truth, and argues that, while the connections traditional coherence theories take may be mistaken, there are ways for coherence to be an important tool in scientific understanding.

Pragmatism

Pragmatist theories of truth offer another key line of opposition to the correspondence theory. They take issue with the idea that reality is simply out there, waiting to be discovered, and that our beliefs are aiming to map this static world of facts. Truth is a much more dynamic process for pragmatists, tied closely to the reasons we have for believing things. Pragmatists reject the simple bifurcated mind/world picture of reality given to us by the correspondence theorists, and see human minds and actions as fully integrated into reality, as opposed to being separate from it, looking on. Truths are not simply there to be found; rather, they are *made*, by our processes of belief formation and interaction with the world. This is because pragmatists think that every concept we have must have a particular function, or purpose, otherwise we would not have it at all. Truth's purpose, for pragmatists, is to serve as 'the good of belief', as William James puts it. To call something true is to designate it as having a particular positive mark, and one that marks that thing out as something worthy of believing. This ties truth closely with our practices of belief formation, and immediately causes conflict with the correspondence approach. The correspondence theory of truth, as we have seen, severs any necessary ties between truth and what is believed: because truth is determined by mind-independent reality, it is conceivable that we do not believe anything true at all. This conception of truth is incompatible with the pragmatist's views on the utility of truth, for truth could not work as a standard for belief if we had no way of knowing whether any of our beliefs were true: this would be like trying to fire arrows at a target in the dark.

Accordingly, for pragmatists, truth is closely tied to reasons for belief. Exactly how we understand truth in this context is accounted for slightly differently by different pragmatists. C. S. Peirce's influential suggestion is that truth is 'what is fated to be believed at the end of inquiry'. Peirce recognizes that there is a catch in holding that truth is simply what we have reason to believe, for there are cases where we are mistaken in believing what we have reason to believe. For example, at one time the best evidence we had gave us reason to believe that the sun circled the earth, but this was subsequently shown to be mistaken. Peirce, in an effort to take this into account, holds that truth is not what is believed at some particular stage of inquiry, but is instead what would be believed at some ideal limit of inquiry. The ideal limit of inquiry would be the point at which we are in possession of all the possible information on an issue, and thus the reasons we had for believing something would be in no danger of being overturned. This seems to address the concern about the possibility of error at a particular time: in the case of the sun and the earth we would not have to say that the belief that the sun circled the earth was true at one time but false at a later time, for it would not have met the standard of being something we had reason to believe at the limit of inquiry, and hence would always have been false.

However, while the view seems to be able to respond to this objection, its way of resolving the problem introduces a new concern. Recall that the pragmatist's objection to the correspondence theory of truth involved the idea that truth cannot have the practical purpose it has if it is impossible to know whether our beliefs are true. The worry is that this can now be turned back against Peirce's view, for how are we to know what we would have reason to believe at the ideal limit of inquiry? It seems obvious that we are not at such a limit now, so how are we to know whether the things we think are true now *are* true? While Peirce's view maintains a connection between truth and belief, one might think it shares the same sorts of problems as the correspondence theory does, from the pragmatist's point of view.

A different sort of proposal is put forward by William James. James's view is hard to pin down as he expresses a number of different proposals in his article, and not all of them seem consistent. Nonetheless, with careful reading a range of significant proposals can be outlined. James first floats the idea that what is true is what is useful to believe. This is the most explicit connection of truth to the pragmatist's idea of utility that we will find: the true beliefs are the beliefs that help us get things done. For instance, in science we might think that the truth of a theory is determined by how useful it is: if it enables us to build planes that successfully fly through the air, then this is as good a mark as any that the theory is true. However, this aspect of James's view has been met with stern opposition. Many think that it simply cannot hold as an analysis of truth, for, the objection goes, there are many examples of things that it may be useful to believe that are not true. For example, it may be useful for me to believe each week that I am going to win the lottery, because it will make me happier to do so. But, of course, that doesn't make it true that I will win the lottery each week.

A simple analysis of truth in terms of utility thus does not look encouraging. However, James moves on from talk of utility to talk of *verification*, suggesting that what is true is what is verified. He offers a number of different processes of verification beyond simple perceptual verification of beliefs, which in time influence the pluralist theories of truth of Section 5. We return here to the idea that truths are *made*, as opposed to simply being there. James's proposal is that a belief becomes true when it is verified to be true, and that there are different processes of verification appropriate to different sorts of beliefs. James is sensitive to the sorts of concerns that moved Peirce to posit an ideal limit of inquiry, but is a little less concerned about them than Peirce was. James places a higher value on the utility of truth, and hence is less concerned about truth in terms of what we would have reason to believe at the ideal limit of inquiry, and is more concerned about truth in terms of what we have most reason to believe *now*. Accordingly, he is more prepared to think of truth in terms of what we have best reason to believe at a time, even if the content of what we have most reason to believe changes at a later time. Whether this is a better direction to go than Peirce for a pragmatist remains open to debate. For a useful comparison of James's view and coherence theory, see the note at the end of Bradley's Ch. 5.

Cheryl Misak's paper 'Pragmatism on Solidarity, Bullshit, and Other Deformities of Truth' provides a very useful discussion of different forms of pragmatism, particularly the views of Peirce and James. It also focuses directly on the connection that pragmatists make between truth and what is good to believe, focusing on cases of lying and bullshitting. She addresses the concern that pragmatist theories of truth, in making the connection that they do between what is true and what is useful, have a hard time saying what is wrong with lying and bullshitting if they have useful or positive results. Misak argues that the pragmatist is misunderstood here, and that a proper understanding of their position shows them not to be as permissive as they first seem. In doing so, Misak offers some very useful clarifications and developments of the pragmatist position, particularly in terms of the development of James's view.

Further reading

For coherence theory, an alternative development can be found in Blanshard (1939), and a detailed study is given in Walker (1989). An alternative interpretation of Bradley's view is given in Candlish (1989). Coherence theory has also recently been applied in ethics by Dorsey (2006). For more on Peircean developments of pragmatism, see Putnam (1981), Misak (2004) and Wright (2000). For a very influential discussion of the connections between pragmatism and verificationism, see Dummett (1978). One influential development of the Peircean strategy is Wright's notion of 'superassertibility', which is discussed in Chapter 16 of this volume, and in Wright (1992). Another influential pragmatist worth investigating is Richard Rorty, such as Rorty (1979). In terms of introductory volumes on truth, discussion of epistemic theories can be found in Künne (2003, Ch. 7), Engel (2002, Ch. 1), Wrenn (2015, Ch. 4) and Burgess and Burgess (2011, Ch. 6).

References

Blanshard, B. 1939. *The Nature of Thought*. London: George Allen & Unwin.

Burgess, P. and Burgess, A. 2011. *Truth*. Princeton: Princeton University Press.

Candlish, S. 1989. The Truth about F. H. Bradley. *Mind* 98 (391): 331–48.

Dorsey, D. 2006. A Coherence Theory of Truth in Ethics. *Philosophical Studies* 127: 493–523.

Dummett, M. 1978. Truth. In his *Truth and Other Enigmas*. Oxford: Oxford University Press.

Engel, P. 2002. *Truth*. Chesham: Acumen Press.

Künne, W. 2003. *Conceptions of Truth*. Oxford: Oxford University Press.

Misak, C. 2004. *Truth and the End of Inquiry*. Oxford: Oxford University Press.

Putnam, H. 1981. *Reason, Truth, and History*. New York: Cambridge University Press.

Rorty, R. 1979. *Philosophy and the Mirror of Nature*. Princeton: Princeton University Press.

Walker, R. C. S. 1989. *The Coherence Theory of Truth: Realism, Anti-realism, Idealism*. London and New York: Routledge.

Wrenn, C. 2015. *Truth*. Cambridge: Polity Press.

Wright, C. J. G. 1992. *Truth and Objectivity*. Cambridge: Harvard University Press.

Wright, C. J. G. 2000. Truth as a Sort of Epistemic: Putnam's Peregrinations. *Journal of Philosophy* 97 (6): 335–64.

Further reading

References

5 On truth and copying

F.H. BRADLEY

Mr. Joachim in his interesting work on *The Nature of Truth* did, I think, well to discuss once more that view for which truth consists in copying reality. It is a view which for myself I have been accustomed to treat as exploded, but it is a natural way of taking things, and, I suppose, can never cease to be popular. And, since from time to time a discussion of this topic is likely to be useful, I will venture to offer some remarks on it here.

The idea that truth consists in mere copying is suggested from many sides. A man through language and ideas has to convey fact to other men, and how can he do this unless his ideas copy fact so far as the purpose requires? And, in dealing practically with the present or the future situation, unless I have mirrored in my mind the main features of that situation, how can I hope to succeed? And in recalling the past we are bound above all things not to alter it, and how can we avoid this unless in some way, however indirect, we produce a copy? Finally truth implies agreement amongst the ideas of separate individuals. And, since this agreement is not made by one or another individual, and so not by all of them, it therefore seems due to all of them following one original fact. But unless they mentally repeat this fact, how, it will be asked, can they follow it?

The above view is natural, but, even as it stands, seems hardly consistent with itself, for how the past or future can be copied is at least not evident. And it is soon in trouble, as is well known, with regard to the sensible properties of things. But, not to dwell on this, the whole theory goes to wreck in principle and at once on a fatal objection. Truth has to copy facts, but on the other side the facts to be copied show already in their nature the work of truth-making. The merely given facts are in other words the imaginary creatures of false theory. They are manufactured by a mind which abstracts one aspect of the concrete known whole, and sets this abstracted aspect out by itself as a real thing. If on the other side we exaggerate when we maintain that all facts are inferences, yet undeniably much of given fact is inferential. And if we cannot demonstrate that every possible piece of fact is modified by apperception, the outstanding residue may at least perhaps be called insignificant.[1] Or (to put it from the other side) if there really is any datum, outward or inward, which, if you remove the work of the mind, would in its nature remain the same, yet at least there seems no way of our getting certainly to know of this. And, if truth is to copy fact, then truth at least seems to be in fact unattainable.

If the above objection cannot be met, and I do not know how it can be met, the theory in principle is ruined. In the end truth is not copying, but it is possible, while admitting this, to attempt to save the theory in a modified form. We may draw a distinction between perceptional and reflective thinking. As to what is perceived we may allow that we cannot argue that this is copied, but in any case, we may go on to urge, our ideas must copy our perceptions. And thus, after all, our secondary and reflective truth must seek to mirror reality. The position taken here is founded on a distinction which in itself is important, but for the purpose in hand seems wholly ineffectual. And apart from such difficulties as might once more be raised as to given facts which are past and future, we have only to apply this view in order to find it break down in our hands.

Disjunctive, negative, and hypothetical judgments cannot be taken as all false, and yet cannot fairly be made to conform to our one type of truth. And in general the moment we leave perceived facts and seek explanation—which after all is implied in the desire for truth—we find that we are moving away from the given. Universal and abstract truths are not given facts, nor do they merely reproduce the given, nor are they even confined to the limits of actual perception. And in the end when we come to general truth about the Universe, it seems impossible to regard this as transcribed from the given Universe. Our truths in short can all of them in some sense be verified in fact, but, if you ask if they all are copied from fact, the answer must be different. And we are driven to admit that, at least when we pass from individual truths, our truth no longer represents fact but merely 'holds' or 'is valid'. And, asking what these phrases mean, we are forced to perceive that both truth and reality go beyond the perceived facts. The given facts in other words are not the whole of reality, while truth cannot be understood except in reference to this whole.[2]

We saw in the first place that given facts are even themselves not merely given, but already even in themselves contain truth. And secondly we have seen that, even if the perceived facts were given, truth cannot merely transcribe them. And, since truth goes beyond the given, it is impossible to understand how truth can copy reality. For, before the reality has been reached, there is no original to copy, and, when the reality has been attained, that attainment already is truth, and you cannot gain truth by transcribing it.

I will now break off the consideration of that view for which truth consists in copying fact, and will endeavour briefly to indicate a better way of resolving the problem. But I must begin by pointing out the main error which, if left unremoved, makes the problem insoluble. This error consists in the division of truth from knowledge and of knowledge from reality. The moment that truth, knowledge, and reality are taken as separate, there is no way in which consistently they can come or be forced together. And since on the other hand truth implies that they are somehow united, we have forthwith on our hands a contradiction in principle. And, according to the side from which the subject is approached, this contradiction works itself out into a fatal dilemma.

This defect in principle has been illustrated by the view we have been, examining, and it may repay us to notice in a different case the result of the self-same error. An attempt is sometimes made to escape from difficulty by insisting that truth is merely what 'holds' or is what merely 'serves' or merely 'works'. But since these phrases are relative and, I presume, relative to something which is known, we have at once a division of truth from knowledge. On the one side is known reality, and on the other side is mere truth, and in short we have repeated the error of that view which took truth as a copy. And the fatal result of our proceeding soon becomes manifest.[3] Truth is merely to be that which subserves something else, and I am to know that this is so, and that this is so is true. But, if so, this truth about truth seems itself to go beyond truth, and our theory is dissolved in self-contradiction.

Let us consider this more in detail. We are, it seems, to take an end, such say as the abstraction of practical success or of felt pleasure, and we are to understand truth as a means, an external means, to this end. And what, we may hear, can be more plain and intelligible than this? It is, I agree, almost as clear as the former view for which truth merely copied things, and perhaps this suggestion may be an omen. But first let us ask as to our end, is this known or unknown? If it is unknown, how, do we know that it is an end served by means? And, if it is known, then what are we going to say of *this* knowledge? Is it true? Can we discuss it? Have we got a truth about our end, and, if so, does 'about' mean no more than merely subserving? I do not myself know how these particular questions should be answered, but in general I cannot see how to defend truth which is external to knowledge or knowledge which is external to: reality, and with this I must pass to another difficulty which attaches to the present view. Truth has been taken as being *merely* the means to an end, and we naturally understand this, to say that truth is *really* the means. But here at once arises a well-known puzzle. The end, we all agree, in a sense dictates the means, but on the other hand the end, we are accustomed to think, must choose those means which are really possible. We are hence, given the end, in the habit of discussing the means. We have to consider in short about suggested means whether they are means really and in truth. But, with this, we seem to have knowledge and truth and reality, certainly all in relation with the one real end, but on the other side all external to it and apparently more or less independent of it. We started in other words by saying 'Truth is nothing beyond that which subserves,' and we have ended in explaining that 'Truth is that which in fact and in truth subserves'. And when in a given case a question is raised as to this fact and truth, it is answered apparently by appealing to something other than the end. Any such appeal obviously is inadmissible, but when we reject it, we seem now to have excluded all truth about our means, just as before we seemed to have no knowledge or any truth about our end.[4]

And a prescribed remedy, if I rightly understand, is to throw overboard all preconceived ideas as to truth and reality. Truth is merely the ideas which are felt in a certain way, and are felt to dominate in a mind or in a set of minds, and any further question as to their truth is senseless. You may indeed ask psychologically, if you please, how they have come to dominate, but, however they have come to dominate, their truth is the same. If you and I disagree we both so far have truth, and if you argue with me and persuade me, that is one way of agreement. But, if you prefer to knock me on the head, that, so far as truth goes, is the same thing, except that now there is truth not in two heads but one. And as to there being any other truth *about* all this state of things, or in short any truth at all beyond mere prevalence, the whole notion is ridiculous. And, if you deny this, you do but confirm it, since your denial (though of course true) must also be false, since it is true only because in fact it has prevailed. And if you want further proof, you can perhaps demonstrate all this by a downward deduction. For either this or the copy-theory must be the truth about truth, and as the copy-theory will not work, this by inevitable consequence remains as true. But there is no one, I think, who is ready apart from some reserve to accept the above result.

It would be easy, passing on, to point out how the same main error, appearing in other forms, works itself out from other sides into conflicting dilemmas. But the limits of this article compel me to proceed. The division of reality from knowledge and of knowledge from truth must in any form be abandoned. And the only way of exit from the maze is to accept the remaining alternative. Our one hope lies in taking courage to embrace the result that reality is not outside truth. The identity of truth knowledge and reality, whatever difficulty that may bring, must be taken as necessary and fundamental. Or at least we have been driven to choose between this and nothing.

Any such conclusion, I know, will on many sides be rejected as monstrous. The last thing to which truth pretends, I shall hear, is actually to be or even bodily to possess, the real. But though this question, I know, might well be argued at length, the issue in my judgment can be raised and can be settled briefly. Truth, it is contended, is not to be the same as reality. Well, if so, I presume that there is a difference between them. And this difference, I understand, is not to be contained in the truth. But, if this is so, then clearly to my mind the truth must so far be defective. How, I ask, is the truth about reality to be less or more than reality without so far ceasing to be the truth? The only answer, so far as I see, is this, that reality has something which is not a possible content of truth. But here arises forthwith the dilemma which ruined us before. If such an outstanding element is known, then so far we have knowledge and truth, while, if it is not known, then I do not know of it, and to me it is nothing. On the one hand to divide truth from knowledge seems impossible, and on the other hand to go beyond knowledge seems meaningless.

And, if we are to advance, we must accept once for all the identification of truth with reality. I do not say that we are to conclude that there is to be in no sense any difference between them. But we must, without raising doubts and without looking backwards, follow the guidance of our new principle. We must, that is, accept the claim of truth not to be judged from the outside. We must unhesitatingly assert that truth, if it were satisfied itself, and if for itself it were perfect, would be itself in the fullest sense the entire and absolute Universe. And agreeing to the uttermost in this claim made by truth, we must attempt, truth and ourselves together, to judge truth from its own standard.

I will endeavour first to point out briefly in what this standard consists. The end of truth is to be and to possess reality in an ideal form. This means first that truth must include without residue the entirety of what is in any sense given, and it means next that truth is bound to include this intelligibly. Truth is not satisfied until we have all the facts, and until we understand perfectly what we have. And we do not understand perfectly the given material until we have it all together harmoniously, in such a way, that is, that we are not impelled to strive for another and a better way of holding it together. Truth is not satisfied, in other words, until it is all-containing and one. We are not obliged here, I think, to inquire further how these aspects of the idea of system are related, and whether, and in what sense, they have their root in a single principle. It is sufficient here to insist that both aspects[5] are essential to truth, and that any theory which ends in dividing them is certainly false.

But, when we judge truth by its own standard, truth evidently fails. And it fails in two ways, the connexion between which I will not here discuss. (i.) In the first place its contents cannot be made intelligible throughout and entirely. A doubt may indeed be raised whether even in any part they are able wholly to satisfy, but this again is a question on which here it is unnecessary to enter. For in any case obviously a large mass of the facts remains in the end inexplicable. You have perpetually to repeat that things are so, though you do not fully understand how or why, and when on the other hand you cannot perceive that no how or why is wanted. You are left in short with brute conjunctions where you seek for connexions, and where this need for connexions seems part of your nature. (ii.) And, failing thus, truth fails again to include all the given facts, and any such complete inclusion seems even to be in principle unattainable. (*a*) On the one hand the moment's felt immediacy remains for ever outstanding, and, if we feel this nowhere else, we realise at each moment the difference between the knower and his truth. (*b*) And on the other hand the facts before us in space and time remain always incomplete. How is it possible for truth to embrace the whole sensible past and future? Truth might understand them (do you say?) and so include them *ideally.* Well but, if truth could do as much as this, which I myself think not possible, truth after all would not include these facts *bodily.* The ideal fact after all and the sensible fact will still differ, and this difference left outside condemns truth even as ideal. And in short we are entangled once more in our old dilemma. We have an element given which in no way we can get inside the truth, while on the other side, if we leave it out, truth becomes defective. For there seems really no sense in endeavouring to maintain that what remains outside is irrelevant.

With this at first sight we have ended in bankruptcy, but perhaps we may find that the case is otherwise and that our failure has carried us to success. For we were looking for the connexion between truth and reality, and we discovered first that no external connexion is possible. We then resolved to take truth as being the same with reality, and we found that, taken so, truth came short of its end. But in this very point of failure, after all, lies the way to success. Truth came short because, and so far as, it could not become that which it desired to be and made sure that it was. Truth claimed identity with an individual and all-inclusive whole. But such a whole, when we examine it, we find itself to be the Universe and all reality. And when we had to see how truth fails, as truth, in attaining its own end, we were being shown the very features of difference between truth and reality. And in passing over into reality and in thus ceasing to be mere truth, truth does not pass beyond its own end nor does, it fail to realise itself. Hence being the same as reality, and at the same time different from reality, truth is thus able itself to apprehend its identity and difference. But, if this is so, we seem to have reached the solution of our problem.[6]

Truth is the whole Universe realising itself in one aspect. This way of realisation is one-sided, and it is a way not in the end satisfying even its own demands but felt itself to be incomplete. On the other hand the completion of truth itself is seen to lead to an all-inclusive reality, which reality is not outside truth. For it is the whole Universe which, immanent throughout, realises and seeks itself in truth. This is the end to which truth leads and points and without which it is not satisfied. And those aspects in which truth for itself is defective; are precisely those which make the difference between truth and reality. Here, I would urge, is the one road of exit from disastrous circles and from interminable dilemmas. For on the one side we have a difference between truth and reality, while on the other side this difference only carries out truth. It consists in no more than that which truth seeks itself internally to be and to possess.

Truth, we thus can say, at once is and is not reality, and we have found that the difference is not external to truth. For truth would be satisfied in its own self-sought completion, and that completion would be reality. And if you ask how truth after all stands to reality, and whether after all truth is not a copy, the answer is obvious. Apart from its aspect of truth the reality would not be the reality, and there surely is no meaning in a copy which makes its original. In truth and in other aspects of the Universe we find onesidedness and defect, and we may go on to see that everywhere the remedy for defect lies in the inclusion of other aspects more or less left out. But as for comparing the Universe, as it is apart from one aspect, with the Universe as complete, such a comparison is out; of our power. And it is even, when we reflect, ridiculous to seek to discover by thinking what the Universe would be like without thought. You cannot take reality to pieces and then see how once more it can be combined to make reality. And thus, if we are asked for the relation of truth to reality, we must reply that in the end there is no relation, since in the end there are no separate terms. All that we can say is that, in order for truth to complete itself into reality, such and such defects in truth itself would have to be rectified.

That there are difficulties in the way of this solution I readily admit,[7] but difficulties and impossibilities, I urge, are not the same thing. And any other exit from our maze is, I submit, closed impassably. On the one hand we must not use words that have no positive sense, and, with this, all reality that falls outside experience and knowledge is, to my mind, excluded. On the other hand we cannot rest in that which, when you try to think it, conflicts with itself internally, and is dissolved in dilemmas. But, in order to know that the Universe is a whole with such and such a general nature, it is not necessary to perceive and to understand how such a Universe is possible, and how its various aspects are held apart and together. We desire to know this, I agree, but I fail myself to see how we can, and I think that with less than this we can gain positive knowledge enough to save us from mere scepticism.[8]

If we now return to that view for which truth is a mere copy of things, we have seen that in the end no such doctrine is admissible. But from a lower point of view it may be convenient to speak of truth as corresponding with reality and as even reproducing facts. In the first place the individual in truth-seeking must subject himself. He must (I cannot attempt to explain this here) suppress ideas, wishes and fancies, and anything else in his nature which is irrelevant to and interferes with the process of truth-seeking. And hence in a sense the individuals can have something in common, correspondence to which is essential for truth. Secondly in truth-seeking the individual (once again I cannot try to explain this) must follow the object. Our understanding has to co-operate in the ideal development of reality, and it has not, like will, to turn ideas into existences. And thus following the object the ideas of the individual in a sense must conform to it.[9] In the third place reflexion, as we have seen, must take up sensible qualities as given matter, and it must accept also more or less brute conjunctions of fact. Intelligence of itself does not recreate the given past nor does it procreate entirely the given present or future. And it may be said to wait on and to follow a course of events which it is powerless to make. And finally to some extent language and truth must seek even to copy perceived facts, and, as we saw, to convey them faithfully, though of course in a partial manner. In the above senses truth may be spoken of as corresponding to facts, and it is right and proper as against one-sided theories to insist on this correspondence.[10] But, as we have seen, such a way of speaking is not permissible in the end.

I will ask finally how what we may call the copy-theory of truth is affected by the connexion between thought and volition. That in some sense thought depends on desire and will is even obvious, and it is a doctrine in which most of us, perhaps, have, we may say, been brought up. But it is a doctrine on the other hand which can be interpreted in various ways. If in the first place truth is made wholly to depend in its essence on the individual's desire, then in this case, naturally, since truth itself goes, the copy-theory of truth goes also, together with every other sane theory of truth. But otherwise, if you simply take truth to be copying, the desire for truth will be a desire for copying, and by laying emphasis on the aspect of desire I do not see that you add anything.

Further if you adopt a one-sided intellectual view, and maintain that reality is an original system of thought which you try to rethink, or a world of ideal essences whose presence you desire—it seems useless in such a case to speak about copying, since copying is excluded. There may be an original here, but, whatever else you are doing, you do not copy that original, since obviously you have no original before you to copy. The realisation in detail of a general end is clearly in itself not repetition, and on the other side, as clearly, repetition and reproduction cannot all be called copying. Hence to ask here why we should desire to copy, is obviously irrelevant. The rational question to ask is about our desire for reproduction and repetition or for the presence in or to our minds of a self-existent reality.

But, if we adopt a more concrete view, all such questions become idle. On such a view my desire and my will to have truth is the will and the desire of the world to become truth in me. Truth is a mode of the self-realisation of myself and of the Universe in one. And if you ask why the full reality cares to spill itself into gratuitous vessels, or whence and why to me comes this mania for turning myself into a superfluous receptacle or instance—the answer is ready. Such inquiries are based on and betray a most stupendous misconception. The Universe is nowhere but in the lives of the individuals, and, whether as truth or otherwise, the Universe realises itself not at all except in their differences. And on the other side the individuals, if they are to realise themselves personally, must specialise this common life of which truth is one aspect. And to suppose that the individuals can seek their end and their reality somehow apart (say in the abstraction of mere practice or of private pleasure) is in the end really meaningless. Thus truth, the same in all, is from the other side not wholly the same, since difference to it is vital and it gains difference in each. The personal diversity of the individuals is hence not superfluous but essential. For viewed from one side this diversity brings with it fresh quality, and from the other side, even so far as truth is common to the individuals, it must be taken none the less as modified in each case by its fresh context. But I must hasten here to add that no such general doctrine can be verified in detail.

The process of knowledge is, on any view like this, not something – apart and by itself. It is one aspect of the life of the undivided Universe outside of which life there is no truth or reality. And to speak here of copying as in a mirror, we may once more repeat, is absurd. If you like to add that the absurdity is heightened when we remember that life in general, and knowledge in particular, imply will and desire, to this naturally I make no objection. But for myself I have always been contented to know that the whole suggestion of copying is here ridiculously irrelevant. Still as according to some critics my destiny is to illustrate what they call "intellectualism," this article, if I could understand it, is doubtless a blind flutter against the limits of my cage.

Note to page 77.—Compare here Mind, N.S., No. 51, p. 323, and again Höffding, *Problems of Philosophy,* pp. 79 foll. (Eng. trans.), a passage the force of which, it seems to me, Prof. James fails to appreciate. I may perhaps use this opportunity to say something with regard to points really or apparently at issue between Prof. James and myself. [Editor's note: you may wish to read James's Ch. 7 of this volume for comparison.] I cannot undertake to criticise Prof. James's ultimate view as to truth knowledge and reality, because that is accessible nowhere, I believe, except in more or less occasional and fragmentary articles, and I do not think that justice can be done to it until it is put out in a more complete and systematic form. But it has been a relief to me to see that, as I understand him, Prof. James rejects the idea that the essence of truth consists in nothing but its mere practical results. In accepting the standard of clearness and inclusiveness and self-consistency (MIND, N.S., No. 52), Prof. James apparently adopts the view in which I at least was brought up, a view for which of course the notion of any external standard of truth was an exploded fallacy. This explanation on the part of Prof. James seems to me to have removed wholly one supposed point of disagreement.

Next as to "working," I of course agree that in proportion as a truth is idle it is less true, and I again agree that in the end no truth can be wholly idle. A truth that makes no difference to truth is to my mind an impossibility. But I cannot agree that, wherever we fail to see this further difference, it is non-existent, and the alleged truth therefore not true at all. It is one thing to say that, so far as we perceive, such or such a truth has no importance, and to act accordingly, and it is surely another thing to insist that such a truth has no truth whatever. And I seem in passing to remember that Hegel, rightly or wrongly, incurred censure for an attitude more or less of this kind towards some facts or truths of natural science. Next I agree that in the end all truth has practical and again aesthetic consequences. I believe in a word in the implication of all aspects of reality with one another. But once more I cannot believe that we can see this implication in detail, so as everywhere to use the consequence (whatever consequence it is) as a criterion. And to my mind it would be senseless to allege that the several aspects of the whole are each nothing but their consequences. Further I have no objection to identifying reality with goodness or satisfaction, so long as it is clear that this does not mean mere practical or any other one-sided satisfaction. Again I agree that any idea which in any way "works," has in some sense truth. Only to my mind it has not on this account ultimate truth. It need not be a way of expression which gives a theoretical satisfaction in which we can rest. In the sciences we use working ideas and convenient mythology, and, while not admitting that these have ultimate truth, I should think it, absurd to deny to them truth altogether. And surely so it may be again with morality and religion. The ideas that are really here required, most certainly, I should say, must be true. But to conclude from this that they have ultimate truth for metaphysics is to my mind irrational. And if you ask what I am to say then when these truths are contradicted by metaphysics, I reply that in my opinion they are not so contradicted, though certainly in my opinion metaphysics must understand them otherwise. If however any one believes in this contradiction, he should in my judgment on no account sacrifice or subordinate his practical truths, though as certainly he should not offer them as the sole and final truth about the Universe. But nothing, I fear, that I can say is likely to shake the pernicious prejudice that what is wanted, for working purposes is the last theoretical truth about things (see my *Appearance,* p. 451 and elsewhere). This prejudice, tends everywhere to result in one-sided attempts at consistency. In our moral practice, for instance, there evidently in fact is involved some element of uncertainty as to the issue. Hence on this point the Christian religion, clinging to the concrete whole, on one side maintains this element of moral struggle, but on the other side completes it (inconsistently no doubt) with an assurance of final victory. And here from both sides comes a protest, and a one-sided cry for clearness and consequence. Unless really, and as an ultimate fact, there is an uncertain future, morality, we hear, is destroyed. God therefore, to save morality, must be made sufficiently ignorant and sufficiently weak for the future really to be doubtful. And apparently it is not seen that, with this, there is an end logically of all that is meant (and much is meant) by "the peace of God". Again, on the same principle but from the other side, some fanatic from time to time insists on the utter supremacy of Good. And hence he concludes in the older style that morality is irrelevant and worthless, or to-day in a newer mode that the individual, as such, is perfect, and that there is no toothache but ignorance. But for practical purposes surely there is something higher than theoretical consistency, even if such consistency in practice were actually attainable. Hence, unless ultimate theoretical truth itself may be inconsistent, it is better for practice surely not to identify our working ideas with ultimate truth. For practice you want ideas which keep hold of all sides of the main substance, and to sacrifice any part of that substance to theoretical consistency is practical error. But on the other hand the reader must be warned that to agree with us here is to incur the peril, whatever that is, of being called an "Intellectualist".

To come now to that which Prof. James would call "humanism," I am reminded forthwith that an accusation of mere humanism was one of the charges long ago brought against German Idealism. And since (if I may speak for myself) I do not believe in any reality outside of and apart from the totality of finite mind, and since there is certainly nothing original in my disbeliefs or beliefs, once more here I fail to perceive the chasm which separates the new " humanism " from what went before. And I am again relieved to find that on the whole Prof. James himself takes this view, and regrets an attitude of hostile criticism on our side as due largely to mistake. Prof. James doubtless here does not remember that on our side nothing was said until we found ourselves judged and sentenced. The philosophic world, ostensibly in Prof. James's behalf, was divided into sheep and goats, and the trumpet was blown, and Plato and Aristotle summoned from the dead to witness the triumph of the one philosopher and the confusion of the sophists. But for my part I have no wish to recall such extravagances, if Prof. James will not forget that it was his fortune, however ill-merited, to inspire them. And if I can do anything to remove or to throw light on any issue between Prof. James and those who cannot follow him, it will be a pleasure to me to attempt this.

(1) In the first place as to "pragmatism," we want to hear definitely from Prof. James whether the practical side of our nature is to be made supreme, or whether there is anything else which has value and rights of its own. Even now I ask myself in what sense, or whether at all, mutilation is advocated. I still do not know if I am called on to enter into life halt and maimed, to say nothing of being blind of one eye. And a reassuring statement in general terms is, I think, not sufficient. But if Prof. James would explain to us how in the end he understands the human Good, and how its elements are related to one another, this point perhaps would become clear. We might at last know whether we all should or should not call ourselves Pragmatists. (2) Next as to "humanism," surely we should be informed, first, whether "finite mind" is to stand merely for some of the inhabitants of a single planet, or is to have a far wider meaning, and, if the latter, we, should be told what that meaning is. This is not a new question (it might even be called an old and familiar one), and in some aspects the difference here between various views may be really enormous. It seems to myself at least imperative that such a point should not be left in darkness. And (3) in the process of Humanity (however Humanity is understood) we have to inquire how the individuals stand to the whole. Have both sides of the process equal reality, or, if this is not so, what is the alternative? If the individuals are the final realities, what in the end are we to say of the "together" and of the whole process? These are well-known problems, and they surely call

for systematic treatment. (4) Then, to say nothing of questions about knowledge—a subject with which Prof. James has in some degree dealt—what in the end is the meaning of and the truth about Progress? Endless progress as an ideal is itself hardly above criticism, but is there in the end any meaning in progress at all? Is mere prevalence and survival to be the same as progress, and, if not that, then what else is progress to mean? And is the temporal process of the Universe (which process is apparently the one reality) to be taken as a progress, and if so, on what grounds? We have once more here an old problem which calls for solution. (5) Finally I need perhaps say nothing as to the difficulty with regard to "a condition" outside of finite minds, except to point out that any obscurity on this head must naturally affect the entire view.

The above questions, and others, can 'hardly be answered satisfactorily unless they are dealt with all together and as connected parts of one inquiry. Prof. James's answer to them, when it comes, will not altogether, I imagine, meet all our difficulties, but most assuredly it will be welcome. Even at Oxford we have not yet been so deafened by periodical manifestoes and by prophetic outcries as to be incapable of hearing. And there, as indeed everywhere else, Prof. James may count upon willing and respectful attention.

Notes

1. I am not assuming here that we have no feelings so elementary as to be unmodified by apperception. I am pointing out that any assumption on the other side seems hazardous and could at any rate not extend far.
2. This is the main conclusion which was urged in my *Principles of Logic* (Oxford: Oxford University Press, 1883). It did not occur to me that I should be taken there or anywhere else to be advocating the copy-theory of truth.
3. *Cf.* the note at the end of the article.
4. One is, I presume, naturally led to avoid this difficulty by maintaining that our knowledge in the end is intuitive. We have, that is to say, an experience in which reality, truth, and knowledge are one. But, with this, there is an end at once and in principle of the view that truth is an external means to something else. And on our new ground the problem of Error, the question how we can hold for true what is false, obviously threatens to become pressing.
5. We may use a variety of phrases here. We may speak, for instance, of homogeneity and specification, or again of integration and differentiation. The main point is this that trutit must leave nothing outside, and, with regard to what it contains, must not have to ask for further explanation as to how one part stands to another part.
6. On the whole question see my *Appearance and Reality* (London: George Allen & Unwin, 1893). From this basis we can deal with the difficulty as to truth's being able consistently to pronounce itself imperfect. The dilemma, that arises here, was noticed by me (p. 513) and solved by a distinction (pp. 544–547). On this a sceptical critic (in MIND, NO. 11, p. 336), seizing his opportunity, urged against me this dilemma which I had noticed, forgetting to mention that 1 had noticed it, and omitting the fact that, having noticed it, I had offered a solution. This opportunity for criticism I confess that I had not observed, but in the second edition of my book, desiring always, so far as I can, to be of use to all the world, I called attention to this opening, more or less by way, if I may say so, of invitation (p. 620). And this standing invitation, I was going to add, has been lately accepted by Captain Knox, in MIND, No. 54, p. 212. But in view of this writer's

extensive ignorance of the work which he came forward to criticise (see MIND, No. 55), I can hardly suppose that such an assertion would be justified. Still, if I cannot credit myself here with a successful invitation, I think that at least I may lay claim to a true prophecy.

7. On this whole matter see my *Appearance and Reality.* One difficulty, on which stress has been rightly laid, is that we have no direct experience of any total experience which comprises in itself finite centres. I do not however myself see that this is more than a difficulty.
8. By scepticism I of course do not mean any positive view as to knowledge in general, and still less any kind of conclusion supported by proof. I mean by it denial or doubt with regard to the existence *de facto* for me, – of that which satisfies intellectually. This denial or doubt rests certainly on a positive basis, but, so long as the basis is not made explicit and the denial remains particular, the basis itself is not denied, and the position remains consistent. On the other hand the scepticism which itself poses as a doctrine, which deals in general truth, and in a word claims to be *de jure,* to my mind does not understand itself. No consistent scepticism can, in my opinion, offer a reasoned proof of itself, nor can a consistent scepticism maintain any general positive doctrine, or indeed any universal thesis of any kind whatever.
9. So far as concerns "the suppression of the subjective," as it is sometimes called, that of course belongs alike to everything serious in life. In this general respect there is no difference between the pursuits of truth beauty and moral goodness. When, in order to create a work of art, a man has to keep down (so far as is necessary) what is merely particular to himself, that does not mean either that the work of art makes itself without him, or that it is not different because he in particular has made it. So also in the process of the will for good. When that is called "objective," the meaning is not that the individual's will makes no difference. The meaning is that whatever in him is irrelevant to the issue, is suppressed as *merely* "subjective". So again in truthseeking. The ideal development of the object itself, which I follow, does not make itself. In the first place apart from individual minds there is no object anywhere. In the second place, so far as I in particular am concerned, the process of truth demands my personal self-realisation. If you took that away, the objective process would not exist in me at all, and, more than that, its nature would to some extent be modified by my personal failure. On the other side the "objective" development cannot possibly take up into itself then and there everything that is at the moment psychically present in myself when I seek truth. It calls therefore for the suppression, so far as is required, of whatever in me falls outside of and is irrelevant to this special development.

   Any reader who wishes not to criticise but to understand, must try to bear in mind two things, (i.) The suppression of "the subjective " takes place in regard to truth beauty and goodness alike, and not more in regard to one than the others. (ii.) The merely "subjective" does not mean what is personal. It means that which for the special purpose in hand is irrelevant and in this sense is *merely* personal (see *Appearance and Reality*, p. 237). On the other hand the reader who wishes simply to criticise will, I think, find no difficulty so long as the above points are ignored.
10. This I myself did in MIND, N. S., No. 51. I did not refer here to the fact that I had written elsewhere on the nature of truth, but I took care to warn the reader (p. 311) that I could not in that article attempt to point out the meaning of truth and falsehood. Notwithstanding this my article has literally been taken as a statement of my view as to the ultimate nature of truth.

6 Coherence, truth, and the development of scientific knowledge

PAUL THAGARD[1]

What is the relation between coherence and truth? This paper rejects numerous answers to this question, including the following: truth is coherence; coherence is irrelevant to truth; coherence always leads to truth; coherence leads to probability, which leads to truth. I will argue that coherence of the right kind leads to at least approximate truth. The right kind is explanatory coherence, where explanation consists in describing mechanisms. We can judge that a scientific theory is progressively approximating the truth if it is increasing its explanatory coherence in two key respects: broadening by explaining more phenomena and deepening by investigating layers of mechanisms. I sketch an explanation of why deepening is a good epistemic strategy and discuss the prospect of deepening knowledge in the social sciences and everyday life.

1 Introduction

The problem of the relation between coherence and truth is important for philosophy of science and for epistemology in general. Many epistemologists maintain that epistemic claims are justified, not by a priori or empirical foundations, but by assessing whether they are part of the most coherent account (see, e.g., Bonjour 1985; Harman 1986; Lehrer 1990). A major issue for coherentist epistemology concerns whether we are ever warranted in concluding that the most coherent account is true. In the philosophy of science, the problem of coherence and truth is part of the ongoing controversy about scientific realism, the view that science aims at and to some extent succeeds in achieving true theories. The history of science is replete with highly coherent theories that have turned out to be false, which may suggest that coherence with empirical evidence is a poor guide to truth.

This paper argues for a more optimistic conclusion, that coherence of the right kind leads to approximate truth. The right kind is explanatory coherence that involves theories that progressively broaden and deepen over time, where broadening is explanation of new facts and deepening is explanation of why the theory works. First, however, I will consider alternative accounts of the relation between coherence and truth, including the claims that coherence is truth, that coherence is irrelevant to truth, and that probability theory provides the link between coherence and truth.

I take coherence to be a relation among mental representations, including sentence-like propositions and also word-like concepts and picture-like images. Coherence is a global relation among a whole set of representations but arises from relations of coherence and incoherence between pairs of representations. Section 3 describes how this works in detail for explanatory coherence. As a preliminary account of truth, let me offer the following, adapted from Goldman (1999, 59): a representation such as a proposition is true if and only if it purports to describe reality and its content fits reality.

The theory I will develop about the relation of coherence and truth is naturalistic in two respects. First, my theory of coherence is psychologistic in that it employs a model of how human minds make inferences based on coherence considerations. Second, my main conclusion about how coherence can lead to truth is based on examples from the history of science, under the assumption that natural science is the major source of human knowledge. This paper is not *about* naturalistic epistemology, but is an instance of it.

2 The relation between coherence and truth

Before developing my own proposal for when coherence leads to truth, I shall deal very briefly with several other accounts about the relation of coherence to truth. The most audacious of these is the coherence theory of truth, according to which the truth of a representation consists of its coherence with other representations, not of its correspondence to a nonmental world; advocates include Blanshard (1939) and Rescher (1973). There are many standard objections to the coherence theory of truth (Young 2001), but here I mention only a novel one. Coherence with scientific evidence strongly suggests that the universe is more than 10 billion years old, but that representations constructed by humans have existed for less than a million. Thus we can infer that there was a world existing independent of any human representation for billions of years. This inference does not in itself show that truth cannot consist in a relation only among representations, because a proponent of the coherence theory could simply maintain that there were no representations and hence no true representations until intelligent beings evolved. But if there is a world independent of representation of it, as historical evidence suggests, then the aim of representation should be to describe the world, not just to relate to other representations. My argument does not refute the coherence theory, but shows that it implausibly gives minds too large a place in constituting truth.

Hence truth must consist of some sort of relation between the representations that occur in human minds or artifacts and the world. Truth is not a purely mental matter, because our best evidence suggests that minds and their representations have not been around all that long. The advocate of the coherence theory of truth could desperately contend that truth is coherence in the mind of God, but this supposes that the most coherent view includes belief in the existence of God, a supposition that I have challenged (Thagard 2000, Chapter 4). There are of course intensely skeptical challenges that can be made to this use of scientific evidence, but I will hold off addressing these until Section 10.

A different way of trying to protect the coherence theory of truth against my argument would be to say that the bearers of truth are not mental representations but eternal abstract entities. In this view, propositions are not mental structures, but platonic objects constituting the meanings of sentences irrespective of whether there are any sentences. The problem with this platonic reply is that we have no evidence that such abstract entities exist. In contrast, there is ample evidence from contemporary psychology and neuroscience that people employ mental representations, which therefore qualify as potential bearers of truth. Of course, the fact that, as far as we know, there were no mental representations 10 billion years ago does not undermine the correspondence theory of truth, because we can consider the fit, or lack of fit, between current representations and the state of reality at that time. The key point against the coherence theory of truth is that coherence with currently available evidence supports the view that reality is independent of representation of it.

At the other extreme from the coherence theory of truth, there is the view that coherence is simply irrelevant to truth. In epistemology, coherentist theories of knowledge are contrasted with foundational theories, which contend that knowledge is based, not on a group of representations fitting with each other, but on a ground of indubitable truths. Rationalist foundationalists maintain that this ground consists of a set of truths known a priori, whereas empiricist foundationalists maintain that the ground is truths arising from sense experience. Unfortunately, both kinds of foundationalism have been dramatically unsuccessful in establishing a solid basis for knowledge. If there are any a priori truths, they are relatively trivial, such as Hilary Putnam's (1983) principle that not every statement is both true and false. No one has succeeded in constructing a priori principles that receive general agreement and enable the derivation of substantial knowledge.

Similarly, the empiricist project of deriving knowledge from sense experience foundered because of the noncertain nature of sense experience and the nonderivability of scientific knowledge from experience alone. Our greatest epistemic achievements are scientific theories such as relativity theory, quantum theory, the atomic theory of matter, evolution by natural selection, genetics, and the germ theory of disease. None of these reduces to rationalist or empiricist foundations, so some kind of coherence theory of knowledge must be on the right track. (I am assuming that contextualism is a variety of coherentism; but see Henderson [1994].) Rejection of a connection between coherence and truth is therefore tantamount to adopting general skepticism about the attainability of scientific knowledge. In Section 4, I will discuss skepticism arising from doubts about whether science really does attain truth.

I must also mention another prominent approach to relating coherence and truth that uses probability theory (e.g., Shogenji 1999; Olsson 2002). In this view, it should be possible to establish a connection between coherence and truth by means of an intermediary connection between coherence and probability. If we could show that propositions with greater coherence have higher probability, then we could judge that they are more likely to be true. This is a laudable project, but I see three insurmountable problems with it: interpretation, realization, and implementation.

The interpretation problem for probabilistic epistemology is the need to choose what meaning to assign to probabilities, which may be taken as either frequencies or degrees of belief. The frequency interpretation of probability clearly applies well to scientific areas in which data have been collected, but it does not apply at all to scientific theories. The probability of drawing a spade from a deck of cards is .25, meaning that in the long run the ratio of spades to cards drawn will approximate .25. But there are no comparable ratios applicable to scientific theories. On the other hand, viewing probabilities as degrees of belief is complicated by substantial evidence that human thinking does not naturally conform to Bayesian standards (Kahneman, Slovic, and Tversky 1982; Gilovich, Griffin, and Kahneman 2002). Normatively, one might insist that it should, but there would still be the gap between subjective degrees of belief and objective truth. Using probability as the connection between coherence and truth presupposes that there are links between (1) coherence and probability and (2) probability and truth. The frequentist interpretation of probability fails in making the first link, whereas the degree-of-belief interpretation fails in making the second link.

By the realization problem I mean the difficulty of analyzing coherence in such a way that these links can be made. Ingenious analyses of coherence in terms of probability have been made by Shogenji (1999) and Olsson (2002), but on their own terms they have been unsuccessful in connecting coherence and truth, independent of the problem of interpreting probability. A third problem, less commonly discussed in the philosophical literature, concerns the difficulty of implementing probabilistic reasoning computationally. Splendid computational tools have been developed for making inferences with probabilities (e.g., Pearl 1988). But applying them to realistic cases of causal inference such as those involved in scientific or legal reasoning requires the concoction of large numbers of conditional probabilities that no reasoner would have available. For further discussion of the interpretation and implementation problems in the context of legal inference, see Thagard (2004).

Hence probability will not provide the needed connection between coherence and truth. Adherents of probabilistic epistemology would probably react by saying: so much the worse for coherence. But the intractability of the interpretation and implementation problems suggests a different response: so much the worse for probability, whose epistemological use is limited to areas such as statistical inference, where the frequency interpretation applies. In the rest of this paper, I will pursue a nonprobabilistic approach to the connection between coherence and truth.

3 Explanatory coherence

This pursuit requires much greater specification of what coherence is, and for that purpose I will employ my theory of explanatory coherence (Thagard 1989, 1992, 2000). The theory consists of the following principles:

Principle E1. *Symmetry.* Explanatory coherence is a symmetric relation, unlike, say, conditional probability. That is, two propositions *p* and *q* cohere with each other equally.

Principle E2. *Explanation*. (a) A hypothesis coheres with what it explains, which can be either evidence or another hypothesis; (b) hypotheses that together explain some other proposition cohere with each other; and (c) the more hypotheses it takes to explain something, the lower the degree of coherence.

Principle E3. *Analogy*. Similar hypotheses that explain similar pieces of evidence cohere.

Principle E4. *Data priority*. Propositions that describe the results of observations have a degree of acceptability on their own.

Principle E5. *Contradiction*. Contradictory propositions are incoherent with each other.

Principle E6. *Competition*. If *P* and *Q* both explain a proposition and if *P* and *Q* are not explanatorily connected, then *P* and *Q* are incoherent with each other. (*P* and *Q* are explanatorily connected if one explains the other or if together they explain something.)

Principle E7. *Acceptance*. The acceptability of a proposition in a system of propositions depends on its coherence with them.

These principles do not fully specify how to determine coherence-based acceptance, but algorithms are available that can compute acceptance and rejection of propositions on the basis of coherence relations. The most psychologically natural algorithms use artificial neural networks that represent propositions by artificial neurons or "units" and represent coherence and incoherence relations by excitatory and inhibitory links between the units that represent the propositions. Acceptance or rejection of a proposition is represented by the degree of activation of the unit. The program ECHO spreads activation among all units in a network until some units are activated and others are inactivated, in a way that maximizes the coherence of all the propositions represented by the units. ECHO has been applied to many cases of scientific and legal reasoning, without the implementation and interpretation problems that afflict probabilistic models of causal reasoning. The theory of explanatory coherence depends on the notion of explanation, which Section 7 discusses in terms of causal mechanisms.

The question now arises: Do we have any reason to believe that a set of hypotheses that are accepted because they maximize explanatory coherence are at least approximately true? In ordinary life, counterexamples abound. For example, the theological and political beliefs of Osama bin Laden constitute a highly coherent set for him and his followers, but we would not want to acknowledge the truth of many of them. All of us have had the experience of making an inference to the best explanation about the behavior of a friend or the breakdown of a piece of machinery, only to learn that our inference was erroneous. Such everyday cases are often deficient, however, in considering the full range of evidence and alternative hypotheses; so perhaps if explanatory coherence had been assessed properly, the erroneous inference might have been avoided. But the history of science contains many cases in which theories high in explanatory coherence have turned out to be false.

4 The pessimistic induction

Newton-Smith (1981, 14) named as the "pessimistic induction" the inference that any scientific theory will eventually be discovered to be false. Laudan (1981) compiled a long list of theories from the history of science that support this induction, including

- the crystalline spheres of ancient and medieval astronomy
- the humoral theory of medicine
- catastrophist geology
- the phlogiston theory of chemistry
- the caloric theory of heat
- the vital force theory of physiology
- the ether theories of electromagnetism and optics
- theories of spontaneous generation.

The phlogiston theory, for example, had very substantial explanatory coherence, providing explanations of phenomena such as combustion and rusting that dominated chemistry for most of the eighteenth century. It was clearly the best explanation of the evidence until it was supplanted by Lavoisier's oxygen theory in the 1780s (Thagard 1992, Chapters 3–4). The pessimistic induction does not require that we know about the falsehood of previous theories by virtue of the truth of the theories that replaced them, which would make the induction incoherent. All it requires is noticing that many theories accepted as true were later rejected as false.

The pessimistic induction suggests that, since a great many theories in the history of science have turned out to be false, we should expect our current theories to turn out to be false as well. There may not be strong alternatives now for our most coherent theories such as relativity and evolution, but we should expect that eventually they will be superseded by theories with more explanatory coherence. Hence we should not associate the maximization of explanatory coherence with truth. The history of science thus suggests that coherence, even explanatory coherence along the lines I have suggested, is a poor guide to truth.

Various responses are available to the pessimistic induction (Psillos 1999). It is noteworthy that Laudan's examples are all from before the twentieth century, and one could argue that recent science has been more successful in achieving true theories. After all, the personal and material resources of science have increased steadily over the past 100 years. However, the temporal induction that recent theories will turn out to be true seems rather shaky, because there just might not have been enough time for superior theories to come along and demonstrate the weaknesses of current theories. Smolin (2001) suggests that problems in making quantum theory and relativity theory compatible with each other may lead to the replacement of both by a quantum theory of gravity. We need a more epistemologically satisfying induction that can tell us when we can take a coherent theory to be true.

5 Whewell's overoptimistic induction

William Whewell, the great nineteenth-century historian and philosopher of science, identified a feature of theories that he thought identified ones that are true. He used the term "consilience of inductions" to describe the support for a hypothesis that comes when it enables us to explain cases of a kind different from those that were contemplated in its formation (Whewell 1968, 153). Whewell had a comprehensive knowledge of the history of science to the midnineteenth century, and he generalized as follows: "No example can be pointed out, in the whole history of science, so far as I am aware, in which this Consilience of Inductions has given testimony in favour of an hypothesis afterwards discovered to be false" (154–155). Consilience requires a hypothesis to increase its explanatory coherence, not merely by explaining a new fact, but by explaining a kind of fact different from ones previously explained. If Whewell were right, then we would have the basis for an optimistic induction about the relation of coherence and truth: Theories that become more coherent over time by explaining new kinds of facts turn out to be true.

Whewell's favorite examples of consilience were Newton's theory of universal gravitation and the undulatory (wave) theory of light. A century and a half after Whewell's generalization, these examples appear rather unfortunate. Newton's theory of gravitation was never able to explain the perihelion of Mercury, but Einstein showed in 1915 that his theory of general relativity yielded more accurate predictions of it than Newton did (Gondhalekar 2001). Thus it appears that, contrary to Whewell's optimistic induction about a particular kind of coherence signaling truth, we have yet another instance of the pessimistic induction. Einstein rejected Newton's assumption that gravitational force is a function only of mass and distance, along with his assumptions of absolute space and time. Similarly, the wave theory of light has been superseded by the quantum theory that views light as consisting of particle-like photons that have wave-like properties.

An even more damning counterexample to Whewell's optimistic induction is the phlogiston theory, which was originally developed to explain combustion by Johann Becher, who called the principle of inflammability *terra pinguis*. Becher and Georg Stahl, who renamed this substance "phlogiston," applied it also to explain calcination (rusting) and respiration. Since rusting and breathing appear very different from burning, extension of the phlogiston theory to calcination seems to constitute an instance of the consilience of inductions; but already by Whewell's time the falsity of the phlogiston theory had been recognized (Partington 1961).

Thus Whewell was overoptimistic about the epistemic power of the consilience of inductions. Still, I think he was on the right track in looking for temporal properties of developing theories that might mark them as good candidates for truth. At least we can say that the theory of universal gravitation and the wave theory of light are not so totally false as the theories of crystalline spheres, phlogiston, and caloric turned out to be. Below I will try to identify a sense in which Newtonian gravitation is partly true, but first I want to discuss a truth-related mark of coherent theories that is more promising than consilience.

6 Deepening and the cautiously optimistic induction

There are two main ways in which a hypothesis can increase its explanatory coherence over time. The first is to explain new facts, which I will call "broadening." Whewell's consilience is a special kind of broadening in which the new facts explained are of a kind different from those already explained. The consilience of Wilson (1998) is an even more special kind of broadening involving the interlocking of causal explanations across disciplines.

The second way in which a hypothesis can increase its explanatory coherence is to be explained by another hypothesis, which I will call "deepening." The process of a hypothesis being explained is most easily understood by legal examples in which questions of motive arise. The hypothesis that an accused is responsible for killing a victim gets its main explanatory coherence from its ability to explain a range of evidence, for example, that the accused's fingerprints are on the murder weapon. This hypothesis can be broadened by finding new evidence that it explains, for example, that one of the victim's hairs was found on the accused's clothes. Homicide detectives also want to know about possible motives of the accused in order to provide an explanation of why the accused committed the murder. For example, the case that O. J. Simpson killed his ex-wife was based mainly on the evidence that he did so, but also on his having the motive of jealousy for attacking her and her boyfriend. We then get a deeper explanation of the crime, because the motive explains the killing, which explains the evidence. In the normal practice of the law, the explanation draws on folk rather than on scientific psychology, attributing the behavior of the accused to ordinary beliefs, desires, and emotions rather than on richer structures and processes for which there is experimental evidence.

Normally, the deeper hypothesis is not adduced merely for the purpose of explaining the basic one, but has independent evidence supporting it. Figure 6.1 shows the structure of a hypothesis A that has broadened by explaining pieces of evidence 2 and 3 in addition to evidence 1, and deepened by being explained by hypothesis B.

In science, deepening occurs when an explanation provides an underlying causal basis for a causal hypothesis. For example, consider the germ theory of disease, which says that contagious diseases are caused by microorganisms such as bacteria, viruses, and fungi. (To modern ears, this might sound like a tautology, but contagion was recognized long before the pathological effects of germs.) A particular instantiation of the germ theory identifies a specific disease that is caused by a specific microbe; for example, influenza is caused by viruses of the family *Orthomyxoviridae*. This theory has been deepened over the years by microbiological accounts that explain how viruses infect cells, replicate themselves, and disrupt the functions of cells and organs. For many viruses, biologists have identified all their genes and the functions they perform. Thus we know not only that myxoviruses cause different types of influenza, but how they do so by their mechanisms of attachment, infection, and reproduction. Some other examples of deepening in recent history of science include the use of microbiology to explain how genetic transmission works and the use of the quantum-mechanical theory of molecular bonding to explain how atoms combine into molecules, which explains molecular theories of chemical reactions.

Now let me venture my own version of an optimistic induction about the relation between coherence and truth, which I call the "deepening maxim":

> Explanatory coherence leads to truth when a theory not only is the best explanation of the evidence, but also broadens its evidence base over time and is deepened by explanations of why the theory works.

I am unaware of any broadened and deepened theory that turned out to be mostly false but am aware that counterexamples may arise; so let me call this the "cautiously" optimistic induction. Actually, we do not need a universal generalization here: it would be enough if we could show from a survey of the history of science that broadened and deepened theories rarely turn out to be false. It is remarkable that none of the theories that I discussed in connection with the pessimistic induction that theories turn out to be false were ever deepened. That is, no underlying mechanisms were identified for how entities such as phlogiston and caloric worked. The deepening maxim is a generalization not only about

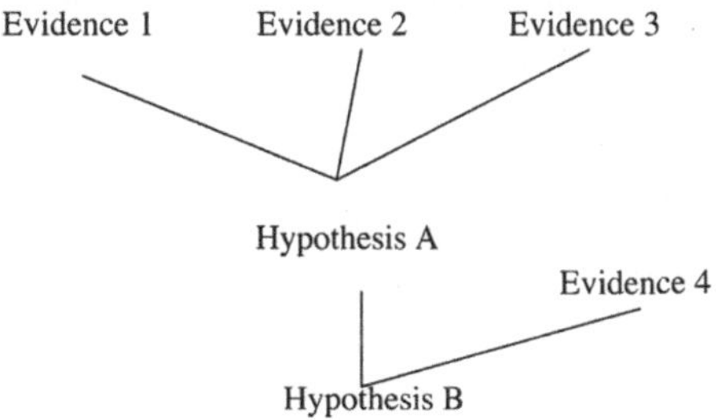

Fig. 6.1 Hypothesis A is broadened by explaining new kinds of evidence and deepened by being explained by hypothesis B, which explains additional evidence.

past theories but about future ones, predicting that future theories that are broadened and deepened will tend to be true.

My response to the pessimistic induction is very different from one recently criticized by Stanford (2003). He argues that scientific realism is undermined rather than supported by attempts to show that discarded theories such as phlogiston and caloric were at least partially successful with respect to the reference of central terms, core causal descriptions, partial truth, select preservation, and/or historical continuity. Instead of trying to defeat the pessimistic induction by arguing that the discarded theories are at least partly true, my strategy is to admit their falsehood and look for features that mark current theories as promising candidates to avoid joining phlogiston and caloric in the dustbin of history. The combination of broadening and deepening seems to be such a feature, but more needs to be said about how mechanistic explanations are deepened.

The importance of broadening and deepening is entailed by the theory of explanatory coherence discussed in Section 3. It follows from Principle E2, explanation, that the more a hypothesis explains, the more coherent it is, other things being equal. Hence finding a new fact that is explained by a theory increases its explanatory coherence. Principle E2 also implies that a hypothesis explained by another hypothesis is more coherent, other things being equal. However, the theory of explanatory coherence by itself is neutral about the nature of explanation, but fits well with the view that explanations are based on causal mechanisms.

7 Mechanisms and explanation

To explicate the deepening maxim further, I need to say much more about how a theory can receive a deeper explanation. This requires an account of the nature of explanation, which can be provided by attention to the nature of mechanisms. It then becomes possible to characterize the nature of approximate truth in terms of the ontology of mechanisms.

In accord with much recent work in the philosophy of science, I hold that to explain a phenomenon is to describe a mechanism that produces it (Salmon 1984; Bechtel and Richardson 1993; Glennan 1996; Machamer, Darden, and Craver 2000; Thagard 2003; Bechtel and Abrahamsen 2005). A mechanism is a system of parts whose properties and relations produce regular changes in those properties and relations. For example, we explain how brains work by specifying their parts, which are neurons organized into neuronal groups and functional areas. Neurons have properties such as their electric potentials and relations such as their links to other neurons via excitatory and inhibitory synapses. We can use mathematical equations and computer models to infer the behavior of groups of neurons from their properties and relations, including inputs from an external environment.

If explanation is mechanism-based, we can develop an account of deepening in terms of parts. A deeper explanation for an explanatory mechanism M1 is a more fundamental mechanism M2 that explains how and why M1 works. M1 consists of parts, and M2 describes parts of those parts whose properties and relations change in ways that generate the changes in the properties and relations of the parts in M1. For example, neural mechanisms are deepened by noting that neurons consist of parts: proteins, and other molecules that are organized into functional areas such as the nucleus, mitochondria, axons, dendrites, and synapses. Chemical reactions involving these proteins enable nerve cells to carry out their basic functions, including taking inputs from presynaptic neurons, building up electric charges, spiking, and sending signals to postsynaptic neurons. Thus neuroscience is deepened by molecular biochemistry, which explains how neurons work. This is a special case of how cell biology is deepened by molecular biochemistry, as has progressively happened over the past half century. Similarly, medical theories such as the germ theory of disease have been deepened by finding lower-level mechanisms for the operations of cells and their microbial invaders. As I mentioned in the last section, medicine knows enough about the parts of bacteria, viruses, and fungi to be able to explain how they invade and disrupt the normal function of bodily cells.

Deepening is also pervasive in modern chemistry and physics. We explain the chemical behavior of elements and compounds by the atoms that compose them. In turn, contrary to the original ancient and nineteenth-century atomic theories, the behavior of atoms can be explained by describing their parts, right down to the level of quarks and possibly superstrings. I am not assuming the traditional philosophical view of reductionism, according to which the deeper theory serves to deductively predict what goes on at the higher level: the complexity and sensitivity to chaos of higher- and lower-level systems may make such predictions impossible to achieve. But we gain much understanding nevertheless by noting that the mechanism at the upper level works as it does because of the operations of the parts at the lower level. The deepening maxim obviously does not apply to the most fundamental level in subatomic physics, but still has ample room for application in other areas of physics as well as chemistry, biology, and the social sciences. The instances claimed to support the pessimistic induction in Section 4 are not at the fundamental level to which deepening cannot apply.

Thus in important areas of medicine, biology, chemistry, and physics, we commonly get deepening by theoretical mechanisms that show how the parts, properties, relations, and changes at the higher level decompose into parts at the lower level. Evidence for the lower-level mechanism is not just that it explains the higher-level one. For example, there is ample molecular and chemical evidence for the structure and operations of neurons and the operations of microbes, so molecular biochemistry provides support for the acceptability of the neuronal theory of brain operation and for the germ theory of disease. The deepening maxim can then be specified as the induction that theories can be judged to be true if they have been deepened by having the mechanisms they describe decomposed into more fundamental mechanisms for which there is independent evidence. As we have seen, inductive support for the deepening maxim includes the germ theory of disease, the neuronal theory of brains, molecular cell biology, molecular genetics, and the atomic theory of matter. Attention to mechanistic explanation serves to spell out and support my cautiously optimistic induction about the connection between coherence and truth.

8 Approximate truth

However, there are some cases from the history of science that may constitute challenges to the deepening maxim and require weakening it to conjecture a connection only between coherence and approximate rather than absolute truth. Consider, for example, the atomic theory of matter. I used this as an example of deepening, because we can now explain how atoms undergo changes such as forming molecules by using quantum mechanical theories about their parts. But I also noted that this deepening required abandonment of the previously definitional truth that atoms do not have parts. So strictly speaking, the atomic theory was not deepened, but rendered false. It would be a mistake, however, to treat a theory as merely a conjunction of hypotheses that is false if any one of them is false. Instead, we should spell out what the theory claims about mechanisms consisting of parts, properties, relations, and resulting changes and identify how many of these claims turn out to be wrong. We can then maintain that the atomic theory of matter has survived because most of its claims about the constituents of things are still taken to be true: elements and compounds have properties, relations, and changes that result from the atoms of which they consist.

Newtonian mechanics is another difficult case. I used it to challenge as overoptimistic Whewell's induction about consilience. But it is also a possible challenge to my deepening maxim, because it might be argued that general relativity deepens Newtonian theory by providing an explanation in terms of the curvature of space-time of how Newton's force of gravity works. Then Newton's theory of gravitation seems like a counterexample to the deepening maxim, in that it has been deepened but is acknowledged to be false by virtue of its failed predictions and rejected assumptions such as that mass is independent of energy.

However, to say that general relativity totally replaced Newtonian gravitation would be as much of a mistake as saying that it fully incorporates it (see Thagard [1992, 214–215] for the details). Newton's three laws and the principle of gravitation are good approximations to what general relativity predicts as long as velocities and masses are small. Although Newtonian mechanics does not accurately predict the perihelion of Mercury, its degree of inaccuracy was only 8%: 43 arc seconds per century (Gondhalekar 2001, 162). So it is reasonable to maintain that Newtonian mechanics is approximately true in the sense that its major claims are quantitatively close to those supported by evidence and the theory that replaced it. I take a theory to be approximately true if it is partly true, that is, if most of its claims are nearly true in achieving quantitative closeness to accepted values. Assessment of approximate truth does not simply involve counting sentences, but needs to qualitatively consider the central mechanistic claims that the theory makes about parts, properties, relations, and resulting changes. For further discussion of approximate truth, also known as verisimilitude and truth-likeness, see Psillos (1999), Kuipers (2000), and Thagard (2000).

My cautiously optimistic induction is thus cautious in two respects. First, it allows for the possibility that a major instance of a deepened theory could turn out to be false. I do not expect fields such as molecular medicine, genetics, and atomic theory to be radically overthrown, but it could happen. Second, it allows for the possibility, which seems to have happened in both the atomic theory of matter and Newtonian mechanics, that deepening by virtue of a more fundamental mechanism may lead to some revisions in the original theory, with recognition that it is only approximately (partly and nearly) true. Accordingly, here is my final version of the deepening maxim: If a theory not only maximizes explanatory coherence, but also broadens its evidence base over time and is deepened by explanations of why the theory's proposed mechanism works, then we can reasonably conclude that the theory is at least approximately true. This induction is the strongest relation available between coherence and truth.

If a theory is broadened and deepened, is it still the same theory? As in the discussion of approximate truth, it is useful to think of a theory not just as a set of sentences but rather as a representation of parts, properties, relations, and changes. Broadening a theory by finding a new explanatory application of it and deepening it by identifying an underlying mechanism clearly do not generate a new theory, as long as the original hypotheses about parts, properties, relations, and changes remain substantially the same.

9 Deepening the deepening maxim

The deepening maxim gains credibility from the numerous theories in the history of science, such as the germ theory of disease and the atomic theory of matter, that have both undergone deepening and avoided the dustbin of rejected theories. But it would gain increased credibility if we could say why it is true that deepened theories tend to hold up well to empirical investigation and therefore appear to be approximately true. Deepening is not a necessary condition of the acceptability of a scientific or philosophical claim, because knowledge about underlying mechanisms may simply not be available at a given time. The germ theory of disease, the theory of evolution by natural selection, and atomic theory were all credible before microbiology, genetics, and subatomic physics were developed. Nevertheless, they gained additional credibility when underlying mechanisms became understood.

Hence it is useful to ask why deepened theories tend to avoid becoming instances that support the pessimistic induction. One superficial explanation might be that deepened theories tend to survive because scientists simply prefer deepened theories as part of their overall strategy of maximizing explanatory coherence. Deepened theories survive not because they are good candidates for approximate truth, but merely because they are popular with scientists. The flaw in this explanation is that it ought also to apply to broad theories: broad theories survive just because they are what scientists like, not because they have anything to do with truth. But we have seen abundant examples of broad theories that were superseded by broader theories, as oxygen superseded phlogiston and thermodynamics replaced caloric. Even theories that underwent broadening—Whewell's examples of Newtonian mechanics and the wave theory of light—have given way to successors.

Following a suggestion of Peter Railton's (personal communication), I think that the most plausible explanation of why deepened theories survive and thrive is that they are at least approximately true. The success of theories for which underlying mechanisms are found is not the result of scientific fashion, but rather the result of a strategy that fits well with the structure of the world that science investigates. Different kinds of experiments and instruments enable science to study the structure of the world at different levels, and these levels fit together naturally. For example, when a health researcher can transfer illness from one animal to another, the tools of bacteriology and virology explain why this is so. In turn, the tools of molecular biology enable an explanation of how viruses and bacteria infect cells by means of molecular signals. In turn, the tools of physical chemistry enable an explanation of how atoms form molecules and how chemical reactions occur. Here the deepening strategy works because the world is in fact organized in terms of parts, from organisms down to subatomic particles, and layers of mechanisms, from viral infection down to chemical bonding. Hence the best explanation of the great success of deepened theories is that they are finding out about the world at multiple levels. Scientific realism should not consider individual theories in isolation from each other, but should notice how well the most successful of them manage to nest vertically with each other as well as to fit with experimental observations. This nesting, accomplished by instruments and experiments and theorizing that operate at multiple interacting levels, is the key to a deep account of the relation between coherence, deepening, and truth.

The argument in this section is a special case of the general abductive argument for scientific realism, which has the following form:

1 Science is successful with respect to predictions, technological applications, cumulation of knowledge, and agreement among practitioners.
2 The best explanation of this success is that scientific theories are at least approximately true.
3 Therefore, scientific theories are at least approximately true.

This is not the place to discuss or defend the general argument (see Thagard 1988, Chapter 8; Kitcher 2002). I am presenting a more specific argument:

4 Deepening maxim: Theories that have undergone deepening by lower-level mechanisms have survived empirical investigation.
5 The best explanation of this survival is that scientific theories about layers of mechanisms are at least approximately true.
6 Therefore, scientific theories about layers of mechanisms are at least approximately true.

Notice that point 6 follows deductively from point 3, so that the general support for scientific realism supports scientific realism about mechanisms, which then supports the deepening maxim. The support is mutual, as is generally the case in explanatory coherence: When a hypothesis explains evidence or another hypothesis, both the explainer and the explained support one another. In the current context, the crucial point is that the deepening maxim has been deepened by a hypothesis about the approximate truth of theories about layers of mechanisms.

Levin (1984) challenged scientific realists to give mechanistic explanations of how truth produces success, which would require at least a sketch of the mechanisms by which the truth of theories about layers of mechanisms produces the success described by the deepening maxim. This task is daunting but should be doable for particular cases such as my medical example relating infectious diseases to underlying mechanisms. The relevant mechanisms include use of instruments that detect features of the world at different levels of detail, ranging from stethoscopes to magnetic resonance imaging machines to optical and electron microscopes. Defending the reliability of these instruments provides further support for scientific realism, in accord with the "Galilean strategy" of Kitcher (2001). Additional relevant mechanisms include physical and social processes by which experiments are carried out and cognitive mechanisms by which human minds collect and interpret data.

Thus filling out the explanation in point 5 that links approximate truth with deepening is very complex, but there is reason to believe that it could be done mechanistically.

10 Conclusion

I have argued that many of the standard claims about the relation of coherence to truth—that coherence is truth, that coherence is irrelevant to truth, and that coherence leads to probability, which leads to truth—are implausible. Instead, I have built on my theory of explanatory coherence and the mechanism-based theory of explanation deepening to produce a cautiously optimistic induction about when coherence usually leads to truth in natural science. This induction constitutes a response to doubts whether coherence connects to truth. (Millgram [2000] raises the question of whether approximation to coherence of the sort performed by available algorithms leads to truth; for a response, see Thagard [n.d.].)

To conclude, I will discuss the implications of this view of the relation between coherence and truth for social science, everyday life, and philosophical deliberation about the nature of knowledge. Social science has not witnessed the extent of deepening found in the natural sciences, but there are some good prospects. Cognitive psychology is now heavily enmeshed with neuroscience, and cognitive theories, which were previously couched only in terms of representations and computations, are increasingly being fleshed out in terms of neural structures and processes. The neurological turn in cognitive psychology, and to a lesser extent in other areas of psychology such as social, developmental, and clinical, opens the possibility of the field being deepened by neuroscience, just as neuroscience is being progressively deepened by neurochemistry. Another promising trend is that economics, which formerly dealt with highly idealized models of human rationality that had little to do with human psychology, is increasingly tied to cognitive psychology and neuroscience, through the development of the field of behavioral economics. I am not raising the prospect of reducing economics to psychology and psychology to neuroscience, but rather pointing to the salutary trend of economics enriching its theories by information about psychological mechanisms, and psychology enriching its understanding by information about neurological mechanisms, which in turn are deepened by biochemical mechanisms. Hence there is a reasonable prospect that my cautiously optimistic induction may eventually apply to social science as well as natural science.

What about everyday life? Most epistemologists have worried about people's ordinary knowledge, such as what we are purported to know about the external world and other people. Although the deepening maxim does not apply to most beliefs of most people, this does not mean that they are grossly unwarranted. The deepening maxim specifies conditions under which coherence very reliably leads to truth, but it does not imply that there is no truth without deepening. Broad explanatory theories in everyday life may well turn out to be often true, for example, our common, everyday beliefs about physical objects and the behavior of other people.

More important, if we step outside everyday beliefs and detect their origins in psychophysical processes, we can deepen everyday explanations considerably. For example, beliefs about physical objects that arise from sense perception can be understood more deeply by going beyond ordinary people's knowledge about seeing, through appreciation of the physical and neurological processes that connect objects and our perception of them by photons of light, retinal stimulation, and neural processing. Physics and neuroscience then provide mechanisms explaining why people have experiences and beliefs about the external world, thereby deepening their knowledge about it. Similarly, scientific psychology and neuroscience provide a basis for explaining why folk psychology is sometimes right about why people think and behave the ways they do and sometimes wrong.

Whereas commonsense perception and cognition are open to deepening by physical and neurological mechanisms, skeptical theories are not. Skeptics have suggested that our experiences may arise, not from veridical psychological processes, but by the machinations of a deceptive god, evil genius, or matrix of brains in vats. These alternative theories are inherently shallow, in that there are no evidence-supported mechanisms that explain how we could be so systematically deceived. To consider only the most recent example, the hypothesis from the *Matrix* movies, that human experiences arise by illusory inputs from intelligent machines, fails to take into account the physical and computational implausibility of generating the complexity and rapidity of such experiences. It takes years to produce an animated movie such as *Finding Nemo,* so there is no plausible technology that could produce the multiple streams of interconnected experiences portrayed in the *Matrix*. Thus commonsense epistemology is open to deepening by reasonable extensions of current physics, psychology, and neuroscience, whereas skeptical epistemologies float flimsily in the air. Hence developments in the cognitive sciences should eventually have the result that the everyday hypothesis that our perceptions arise largely as the result of interactions with an external world will fall within the scope of the cautiously optimistic induction. Then naturalistic epistemology will mesh with the philosophy of science to provide a deep justification of everyday as well as scientific knowledge.

Note

1. For helpful suggestions, I am grateful to Josh Brown, Dave DeVidi, Eric Lormand, Elijah Millgram, Eric Olsson, Peter Railton, and anonymous referees.

References

Bechtel, W., and A. A. Abrahamsen (2005), "Explanation: A Mechanistic Alternative," *Studies in History and Philosophy of Biology and Biomedical Sciences* 36: 421–441.

Bechtel, W., and R. C. Richardson (1993), *Discovering Complexity*. Princeton, NJ: Princeton University Press.

Blanshard, B. (1939), *The Nature of Thought*, vol. 2. London: Allen and Unwin.

BonJour, L. (1985), *The Structure of Empirical Knowledge*. Cambridge, MA: Harvard University Press.

Gilovich, T., D. Griffin, and D. Kahneman, eds. (2002), *Heuristics and Biases: The Psychology of Intuitive Judgment*. Cambridge: Cambridge University Press.

Glennan, S. (1996), "Mechanisms and the Nature of Causation," *Erkenntnis* 44: 49–71.

Goldman, A. (1999), *Knowledge in a Social World*. Oxford: Oxford University Press.

Gondhalekar, P. (2001), *The Grip of Gravity: The Quest to Understand the Laws of Motion and Gravitation*. Cambridge: Cambridge University Press.

Harman, G. (1986), *Change in View: Principles of Reasoning*. Cambridge, MA: MIT Press/Bradford Books.
Henderson, D. K. (1994), "Epistemic Competence and Contextualist Epistemology: Why Contextualism Is Not Just the Poor Man's Coherentism," *Journal of Philosophy* 91: 627–649.
Kahneman, D., P. Slovic, and A. Tversky (1982), *Judgment under Uncertainty: Heuristics and Biases*. New York: Cambridge University Press.
Kitcher, P. (2001), "Real Realism: The Galilean Strategy," *Philosophical Review* 110: 151–197.
Kitcher, P. (2002), "On the Explanatory Role of Correspondence Truth," *Philosophy and Phenomenological Research* 64: 346–364.
Kuipers, T. (2000), *From Instrumentalism to Constructive Realism*. Dordrecht: Kluwer.
Laudan, L. (1981), "A Confutation of Convergent Realism," *Philosophy of Science* 48: 19–49.
Lehrer, K. (1990), *Theory of Knowledge*. Boulder, CO: Westview.
Levin, M. (1984), "What Kind of Explanation Is Truth?" in J. Leplin (ed.), *Scientific Realism*. Berkeley: University of California Press, 124–139.
Machamer, P., L. Darden, and C. F. Craver (2000), "Thinking about Mechanisms," *Philosophy of Science* 67: 1–25.
Millgram, E. (2000), "Coherence: The Price of the Ticket," *Journal of Philosophy* 97: 82–93.
Newton-Smith, W. H. (1981), *The Rationality of Science*. London: Routledge and Kegan Paul.
Olsson, E. J. (2002), "What Is the Problem of Coherence and Truth?" *Journal of Philosophy* 99: 246–272.
Partington, J. (1961), *A History of Chemistry*. London: Macmillan.
Pearl, J. (1988), *Probabilistic Reasoning in Intelligent Systems*. San Mateo, CA: Morgan Kaufman.
Psillos, S. (1999), *Scientific Realism: How Science Tracks the Truth*. London: Routledge.
Putnam, H. (1983), "There Is at Least One *a Priori* Truth," in H. Putnam (ed.), *Realism and Reason: Philosophical Papers*, vol. 3. Cambridge: Cambridge University Press, 98–114.
Rescher, N. (1973), *The Coherence Theory of Truth*. Oxford: Clarendon.
Salmon, W. (1984), *Scientific Explanation and the Causal Structure of the World*. Princeton, NJ: Princeton University Press.
Shogenji, T. (1999), "Is Coherence Truth-Conducive?" *Analysis* 61: 338–345.
Smolin, L. (2001), *Three Roads to Quantum Gravity*. New York: Basic Books.
Stanford, K. S. (2003), "Pyrrhic Victories for Scientific Realism," *Journal of Philosophy* 100: 553–573.
Thagard, P. (1988), *Computational Philosophy of Science*. Cambridge, MA: MIT Press/Bradford Books.
Thagard, P. (1989), "Explanatory Coherence," *Behavioral and Brain Sciences* 12: 435–467.
Thagard, P. (1992), *Conceptual Revolutions*. Princeton, NJ: Princeton University Press.
Thagard, P. (2000), *Coherence in Thought and Action*. Cambridge, MA: MIT Press.
Thagard, P. (2003), "Pathways to Biomedical Discovery," *Philosophy of Science* 70: 235–254.
Thagard, P. (2004), "Causal Inference in Legal Decision Making: Explanatory Coherence vs. Bayesian Networks," *Applied Artificial Intelligence* 18: 231–249.
Thagard, P. (n.d.), "Coherence: The Price Is Right," http://cogsci.uwaterloo.ca/Articles/Pages/coh.price.html.
Whewell, W. (1968), *William Whewell's Theory of Scientific Method*. Pittsburgh: University of Pittsburgh Press.
Wilson, E. O. (1998), *Consilience: The Unity of Knowledge*. New York: Vantage.
Young, J. O. (2001), "The Coherence Theory of Truth," in Edward N. Zalta (ed.), *The Stanford Encyclopedia of Philosophy*. http://plato.stanford.edu/archives/sum2001/entries/truth-coherence/.

7 How to make our ideas clear

CHARLES S. PEIRCE

I

Whoever has looked into a modern treatise on logic of the common sort, will doubtless remember the two distinctions between *clear* and *obscure* conceptions, and between *distinct* and *confused* conceptions. They have lain in the books now for nigh two centuries, unimproved and unmodified, and are generally reckoned by logicians as among the gems of their doctrine.

A clear idea is defined as one which is so apprehended that it will be recognized wherever it is met with, and so that no other will be mistaken for it. If it fails of this clearness, it is said to be obscure.

This is rather a neat bit of philosophical terminology; yet, since it is clearness that they were defining, I wish the logicians had made their definition a little more plain. Never to fail to recognize an idea, and under no circumstances to mistake another for it, let it come in how recondite a form it may, would indeed imply such prodigious force and clearness of intellect as is seldom met with in this world. On the other hand, merely to have such an acquaintance with the idea as to have become familiar with it, and to have lost all hesitancy in recognizing it in ordinary cases, hardly seems to deserve the name of clearness of apprehension, since after all it only amounts to a subjective feeling of mastery which may be entirely mistaken. I take it, however, that when the logicians speak of "clearness," they mean nothing more than such a familiarity with an idea, since they regard the quality as but a small merit, which needs to be supplemented by another, which they call *distinctness.*

A distinct idea is defined as one which contains nothing which is not clear. This is technical language; by the *contents* of an idea logicians understand whatever is contained in its definition. So that an idea is *distinctly* apprehended, according to them, when we can give a precise definition of it, in abstract terms. Here the professional logicians leave the subject; and I would not have troubled the reader with what they have to say, if it were not such a striking example of how they have been slumbering through ages of intellectual activity, listlessly disregarding the enginery of modern thought, and never dreaming of applying its lessons to the improvement of logic. It is easy to show that the doctrine that familiar use and abstract distinctness make the perfection of apprehension has its only true place in philosophies which have long been extinct; and it is now time to formulate the method of attaining to a more perfect clearness of thought, such as we see and admire in the thinkers of our own time.

When Descartes set about the reconstruction of philosophy, his first step was to (theoretically) permit skepticism and to discard the practice of the schoolmen of looking to authority as the ultimate source of truth. That done, he sought a more natural fountain of true principles, and professed to find it in the human mind; thus passing, in the directest way, from the method of authority to that of apriority, as described in my first paper.[1] Self-consciousness was to furnish us with our fundamental truths, and to decide what was agreeable to reason. But since, evidently, not all ideas are true, he was led to note, as the first condition of infallibility, that they must be clear. The distinction between an idea *seeming* clear and really being so, never occurred to him. Trusting to introspection, as he did, even a knowledge of external things, why should he question its testimony in respect to the contents of our own minds? But then, I suppose, seeing men, who seemed to be quite clear and positive, holding opposite opinions upon fundamental principles, he was further led to say that clearness of ideas is not sufficient, but that they need also to be distinct, i.e., to have nothing unclear about them. What he probably meant by this (for he did not explain himself with precision) was, that they must sustain the test of dialectical examination; that they must not only seem clear at the outset, but that discussion must never be able to bring to light points of obscurity connected with them.

Such was the distinction of Descartes, and one sees that it was precisely on the level of his philosophy. It was somewhat developed by Leibnitz. This great and singular genius was as remarkable for what he failed to see as for what he saw. That a piece of mechanism could not do work perpetually without being fed with power in some form, was a thing perfectly apparent to him; yet he did not understand that the machinery of the mind can only transform knowledge, but never originate it, unless it be fed with facts of observation. He thus missed the most essential point of the Cartesian philosophy, which is, that to accept propositions which seem perfectly evident to us is a thing which, whether it be logical or illogical, we cannot help doing. Instead of regarding the matter in this way, he sought to reduce the first principles of science to formulas which cannot be denied without self-contradiction, and was apparently unaware of the great difference between his position and that of Descartes. So he reverted to the old formalities of logic, and, above all, abstract definitions played a great part in his philosophy. It was quite natural, therefore, that on observing that the method of Descartes labored under the difficulty that we may seem to ourselves to have clear apprehensions of ideas which in truth are very hazy, no better remedy occurred to him than to require an abstract definition of every important term. Accordingly, in adopting the distinction of *clear* and *distinct* notions, he described the latter quality as the clear apprehension of everything contained in the definition; and the books have ever since copied his words. There is no danger that his chimerical scheme will ever again be overvalued. Nothing new can ever be learned by analyzing definitions. Nevertheless, our existing beliefs can be set in order by this process, and order is an essential element of intellectual economy, as of every other. It may be acknowledged, therefore, that the books are right in making familiarity with a notion the first step toward clearness of apprehension, and the defining of it the second. But in omitting all mention of any higher perspicuity of thought, they simply mirror a philosophy which was exploded a hundred years ago. That much-admired "ornament of logic"—the doctrine of clearness and distinctness—may be pretty enough, but it is high time to relegate to our cabinet of curiosities the antique *bijou,* and to wear about us something better adapted to modern uses.

The very first lesson that we have a right to demand that logic shall teach us is, how to make our ideas clear; and a most important one it is, depreciated only by minds who stand in need of it. To know what we think, to be masters of our own meaning, will make a solid foundation for great and weighty thought. It is most easily learned by those whose ideas are meagre and restricted; and far happier they than those such as wallow helplessly in a rich mud of conceptions. A nation, it is true, may, in the course of generations, overcome the disadvantage of an excessive wealth of language and its natural concomitant, a vast, unfathomable deep of ideas. We may see it in history, slowly perfecting its literary forms, sloughing at length its metaphysics, and, by virtue of the untirable patience which is often a compensation, attaining great excellence in every branch of mental acquirement. The page of history is not yet unrolled which is to tell us whether such a people will or will not in the long-run prevail over one whose ideas (like the words of their language) are few, but which possesses a wonderful mastery over those which it has. For an individual, however, there can be no question that a few clear ideas are worth more than many confused ones. A young man would hardly be persuaded to sacrifice the greater part of his thoughts to save the rest; and the muddled head is the least apt to see the necessity of such a sacrifice. Him we can usually only commiserate, as a person with a congenital defect. Time will help him, but intellectual maturity with regard to clearness comes rather late, an unfortunate arrangement of Nature, inasmuch as clearness is of less use to a man settled in life, whose errors have in great measure had their effect, than it would be to one whose path lies before him. It is terrible to see how a single unclear idea, a single formula without meaning, lurking in a young man's head, will sometimes act like an obstruction of inert matter in an artery, hindering the nutrition of the brain, and condemning its victim to pine away in the fullness of his intellectual vigor and in the midst of intellectual plenty. Many a man has cherished for years as his hobby some vague shadow of an idea, too meaningless to be positively false; he has, nevertheless, passionately loved it, has made it his companion by day and by night, and has given to it his strength and his life, leaving all other occupations for its sake, and in short has lived with it and for it, until it has become, as it were, flesh of his flesh and bone of his bone; and then he has waked up some bright morning to find it gone, clean vanished away like the beautiful Melusina of the fable, and the essence of his life gone with it. I have myself known such a man; and who can tell how many histories of circle-squarers, metaphysicians, astrologers, and what not, may not be told in the old German story?

II

The principles set forth in the first of these papers lead, at once, to a method of reaching a clearness of thought of a far higher grade than the "distinctness" of the logicians. We have there found that the action of thought is excited by the irritation of doubt, and ceases when belief is attained; so that the production of belief is the sole function of thought. All these words, however, are too strong for my purpose. It is as if I had described the phenomena as they appear under a mental microscope. Doubt and Belief, as the words are commonly employed, relate to religious or other grave discussions. But here I use them to designate the starting of any question, no matter how small or how great, and the resolution of it. If, for instance, in a horse-car, I pull out my purse and find a five-cent nickel and five coppers, I decide, while my hand is going to the purse, in which way I will pay my fare. To call such a question Doubt, and my decision Belief, is certainly to use words very disproportionate to the occasion. To speak of such a doubt as causing an irritation which needs to be appeased, suggests a temper which is uncomfortable to the verge of insanity. Yet, looking at the matter minutely, it must be admitted that, if there is the least hesitation as to whether I shall pay the five coppers or the nickel (as there will be sure to be, unless I act from some previously contracted habit in the matter), though irritation is too strong a word, yet I am excited to such small mental activities as may be necessary to deciding how I shall act. Most frequently doubts arise from some indecision, however momentary, in our action. Sometimes it is not so. I have, for example, to wait in a railway station, and to pass the time I read the advertisements on the walls, I compare the advantages of different trains and different routes which I never expect to take, merely fancying myself to be in a state of hesitancy, because I am bored with having nothing to trouble me. Feigned hesitancy, whether feigned for mere amusement or with a lofty purpose, plays a great part in the production of scientific inquiry. However the doubt may originate, it stimulates the mind to an activity which may be slight or energetic, calm or turbulent. Images pass rapidly through consciousness, one incessantly melting into another, until at last, when all is over—it may be in a fraction of a second, in an hour, or after long years—we find ourselves decided as to how we should act under such circumstances as those which occasioned our hesitation. In other words, we have attained belief.

In this process we observe two sorts of elements of consciousness, the distinction between which may best be made clear by means of an illustration. In a piece of music there are the separate notes, and there is the air. A single tone may be prolonged for an hour or a day, and it exists as perfectly in each second of that time as in the whole taken together; so that, as long as it is sounding, it might be present to a sense from which everything in the past was as completely absent as the future itself. But it is different with the air, the performance of which occupies a certain time, during the portions of which only portions of it are played. It consists in an orderliness in the succession of sounds which strike the ear at different times; and to perceive it there must be some continuity of consciousness which makes the events of a lapse of time present to us. We certainly only perceive the air by hearing the separate notes; yet we cannot be said to directly hear it, for we hear only what is present at the instant, and an orderliness of succession cannot exist in an instant. These two sorts of objects, what we are *immediately* conscious of and what we are *mediately* conscious of, are found in all consciousness. Some elements (the sensations) are completely present at every instant so long as they last, while others (like thought) are actions having beginning, middle, and end, and consist in a congruence in the succession of sensations which flow through the mind. They cannot be immediately present to us, but must cover some portion of the past or future. Thought is a thread of melody running through the succession of our sensations.

We may add that just as a piece of music may be written in parts, each part having its own air, so various systems of relationship of succession subsist together between the same sensations. These different systems are distinguished by having different motives, ideas, or functions. Thought is only one such system, for its sole motive, idea, and function, is to produce belief, and whatever does not concern that purpose belongs to some other system of relations. The action of thinking may incidentally have other results; it may serve to amuse us, for example, and among *dilettanti* it is not rare to find those who have so perverted thought to the purposes of pleasure that it seems to vex them to think that the questions upon which they delight to exercise it may ever get finally settled; and a positive discovery which takes a favorite subject out of the arena of literary debate is met with ill-concealed dislike. This disposition is the very debauchery of thought. But the soul and meaning of thought, abstracted from the other elements which accompany it, though it may be voluntarily thwarted, can never be made to direct itself toward anything but the production of belief. Thought in action has for its only possible motive the attainment of thought at rest; and whatever does not refer to belief is no part of the thought itself.

And what, then, is belief? It is the demi-cadence which closes a musical phrase in the symphony of our intellectual life. We have seen that it has just three properties: First, it is something that we are aware of; second, it appeases the irritation of doubt; and, third, it involves the establishment in our nature of a rule of action, or, say for short, a *habit*. As it appeases the irritation of doubt, which is the motive for thinking, thought relaxes, and comes to rest for a moment when belief is reached. But, since belief is a rule for action, the application of which involves further doubt and further thought, at the same time that it is a stopping-place, it is also a new starting place for thought. That is why I have permitted myself to call it thought at rest, although thought is essentially an action. The *final* upshot of thinking is the exercise of volition, and of this thought no longer forms a part; but belief is only a stadium of mental action, an effect upon our nature due to thought, which will influence future thinking.

The essence of belief is the establishment of a habit, and different beliefs are distinguished by the different modes of action to which they give rise. If beliefs do not differ in this respect, if they appease the same doubt by producing the same rule of action, then no mere differences in the manner of consciousness of them can make them different beliefs, any more than playing a tune in different keys is playing different tunes. Imaginary distinctions are often drawn between beliefs which differ only in their mode of expression;—the wrangling which ensues is real enough, however. To believe that any objects are arranged as in Figure 7.1, and to believe that they are arranged in Figure 7.2, are one and the same belief; yet it is conceivable that a man should assert one proposition and deny the other.

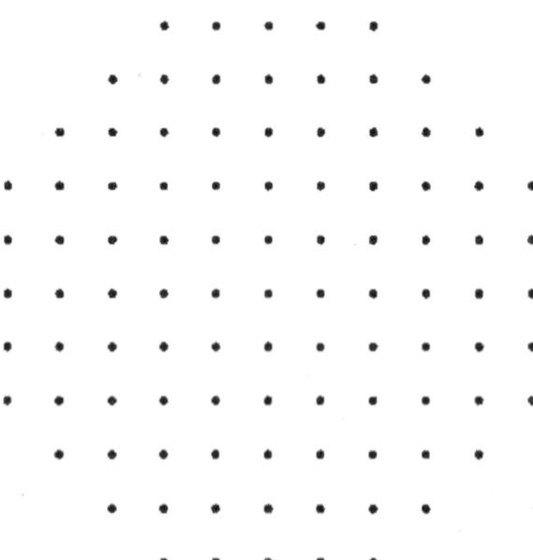

Fig. 7.1

Fig. 7.2

Such false distinctions do as much harm as the confusion of beliefs really different, and are among the pitfalls of which we ought constantly to beware, especially when we are upon metaphysical ground. One singular deception of this sort, which often occurs, is to mistake the sensation produced by our own unclearness of thought for a character of the object we are thinking. Instead of perceiving that the obscurity is purely subjective, we fancy that we contemplate a quality of the object which is essentially mysterious; and if our conception be afterward presented to us in a clear form we do not recognize it as the same, owing to the absence of the feeling of unintelligibility. So long as this deception lasts, it obviously puts an impassable barrier in the way of perspicuous thinking; so that it equally interests the opponents of rational thought to perpetuate it, and its adherents to guard against it.

Another such deception is to mistake a mere difference in the grammatical construction of two words for a distinction between the ideas they express. In this pedantic age, when the general mob of writers attend so much more to words than to things, this error is common enough. When I just said that thought is an action, and that it consists in a relation, although a person performs an action but not a relation, which can only be the result of an action, yet there was no inconsistency in what I said, but only a grammatical vagueness.

From all these sophisms we shall be perfectly safe so long as we reflect that the whole function of thought is to produce habits of action; and that whatever there is connected with a thought, but irrelevant to its purpose, is an accretion to it, but no part of it. If there be a unity among our sensations which has no reference to how we shall act on a given occasion, as when we listen to a piece of music, why we do not call that thinking. To develop its meaning, we have, therefore, simply to determine what habits it produces, for what a thing means is simply what habits it involves. Now, the identity of a habit depends on how it might lead us to act, not merely under such circumstances as are likely to arise, but under such as might possibly occur, no matter how improbable they may be. What the habit is depends on when and *how* it causes us to act. As for the *when,* every stimulus to action is derived from perception; as for the *how,* every purpose of action is to produce some sensible result. Thus, we come down to what is tangible and practical, as the root of every real distinction of thought, no matter how subtile it may be; and there is no distinction of meaning so fine as to consist in anything but a possible difference of practice.

To see what this principle leads to, consider in the light of it such a doctrine as that of transubstantiation. The Protestant churches generally hold that the elements of the sacrament are flesh and blood only in a tropical sense; they nourish our souls as meat and the juice of it would our bodies. But the Catholics maintain that they are literally just that; although they possess all the sensible qualities of wafer-cakes and diluted wine. But we can have no conception of wine except what may enter into a belief, either—

1 That this, that, or the other, is wine; or,
2 That wine possesses certain properties.

Such beliefs are nothing but self-notifications that we should, upon occasion, act in regard to such things as we believe to be wine according to the qualities which we believe wine to possess. The occasion of such action would be some sensible perception, the motive of it to produce some sensible result. Thus our action has exclusive reference to what affects the senses, our habit has the same bearing as our action, our belief the same as our habit, our conception the same as our belief; and we can consequently mean nothing by wine but what has certain effects, direct or indirect, upon our senses; and to talk of something as having all the sensible characters of wine, yet being in reality blood, is senseless jargon. Now, it is not my object to pursue the theological question; and having used it as a logical example I drop it, without caring to anticipate the theologian's reply. I only desire to point out how impossible it is that we should have an idea in our minds which relates to anything but conceived sensible effects of things. Our idea of anything is our idea of its sensible effects; and if we fancy that we have any other we deceive ourselves, and mistake a mere sensation accompanying the thought for a part of the thought itself. It is absurd to say that thought has any meaning unrelated to its only function. It is foolish for Catholics and Protestants to fancy themselves in disagreement about the elements of the sacrament, if they agree in regard to all their sensible effects, here or hereafter.

It appears, then, that the rule for attaining the third grade of clearness of apprehension is as follows: Consider what effects, which might conceivably have practical bearings, we conceive the object of our conception to have. Then, our conception of these effects is the whole of our conception of the object.

III

Let us illustrate this rule by some examples; and, to begin with the simplest one possible, let us ask what we mean by calling a thing *hard*. Evidently that it will not be scratched by many other substances. The whole conception of this quality, as of every other, lies in its conceived effects. There is absolutely no difference between a hard thing and a soft thing so long as they are not brought to the test. Suppose, then, that a diamond could be crystallized in the midst of a cushion of soft cotton, and should remain there until it was finally burned up. Would it be false to say that that diamond was soft? This seems a foolish question, and would be so, in fact, except in the realm of logic. There such questions are often of the greatest utility as serving to bring logical principles into sharper relief than real discussions ever could. In studying logic we must not put them aside with hasty answers, but must consider them with attentive care, in order to make out the principles involved. We may, in the present ease, modify our question, and ask what prevents us from saying that all hard bodies remain perfectly soft until they are touched, when their hardness increases with the pressure until they are scratched. Reflection will show that the reply is this: there would be no *falsity* in such modes of speech. They would involve a modification of our present usage of speech with regard to the words hard and soft, but not of their meanings. For they represent no fact to be different from what it is; only they involve arrangements of facts which would be exceedingly maladroit. This leads us to remark that the question of what would occur under circumstances which do not actually arise is not a question of fact, but only of the most perspicuous arrangement of them. For example, the question of free-will and fate in its simplest form, stripped of verbiage, is something like this: I have done something of which I am ashamed; could I, by an effort of the will, have resisted the temptation, and done otherwise? The philosophical reply is, that this is not a question of fact, but only of the arrangement of facts. Arranging them so as to exhibit what is particularly pertinent to my question—namely, that I ought to blame myself for having done wrong—it is perfectly true to say that, if I had willed to do otherwise than I did, I should have done otherwise. On the other hand, arranging the facts so as to exhibit another important consideration, it is equally true that, when a temptation has once been allowed to work, it will, if it has a certain force, produce its effect, let me struggle how I may. There is no objection to a contradiction in what would result from a false supposition. The *reductio ad absurdum* consists in showing that contradictory results would follow from a hypothesis which is consequently judged to be false. Many questions are involved in the free-will discussion, and I am far from desiring to say that both sides are equally right. On the contrary, I am of opinion that one side denies important facts, and that the other does not. But what I do say is, that the above single question was the origin of the whole doubt; that, had it not been for this question, the controversy would never have arisen; and that this question is perfectly solved in the manner which I have indicated....[2]

IV

Let us now approach the subject of logic, and consider a conception which particularly concerns it, that of *reality.* Taking clearness in the sense of familiarity, no idea could be clearer than this. Every child uses it with perfect confidence, never dreaming that he does not understand it. As for clearness in its second grade, however, it would probably puzzle most men, even among those of a reflective turn of mind, to give an abstract definition of the real. Yet such a definition may perhaps be reached by considering the points of difference between reality and its opposite, fiction. A figment is a product of somebody's imagination; it has such characters as his thought impresses upon it. That those characters are independent of how you or I think is an external reality. There are, however, phenomena within our own minds, dependent upon our thought, which are at the same time real in the sense that we really think them. But though their characters depend on how we think, they do not depend on what we think those characters to be. Thus, a dream has a real existence as a mental phenomenon, if somebody has really dreamt it; that he dreamt so and so, does not depend on what anybody thinks was dreamt, but is completely independent of all opinion on the subject. On the other hand, considering, not the fact of dreaming, but the thing dreamt, it retains its peculiarities by virtue of no other fact than that it was dreamt to possess them. Thus we may define the real as that whose characters are independent of what anybody may think them to be.

But, however satisfactory such a definition may be found, it would be a great mistake to suppose that it makes the idea of reality perfectly clear. Here, then, let us apply our rules. According to them, reality, like every other quality, consists in the peculiar sensible effects which things partaking of it produce. The only effect which real things have is to cause belief, for all the sensations which they excite emerge into consciousness in the form of beliefs. The question therefore is, how is true belief (or belief in the real) distinguished from false belief (or belief in fiction). Now, as we have seen in the former paper, the ideas of truth and falsehood, in their full development, appertain exclusively to the scientific method of settling opinion. A person who arbitrarily chooses the propositions which he will adopt can use the word truth only to emphasize the expression of his determination to hold on to his choice. Of course, the method of tenacity never prevailed exclusively; reason is too natural to men for that. But in the literature of the dark ages we find some fine examples of it. When Scotus Erigena is commenting upon a poetical passage in which hellebore is spoken of as having caused the death of Socrates, he does not hesitate to inform the inquiring reader that Helleborus and Socrates were two eminent Greek philosophers, and that the latter having been overcome in argument by the former took the matter to heart and died of it! What sort of an idea of truth could a man have who could adopt and teach, without the qualification of a perhaps, and opinion taken so entirely at random? The real spirit of Socrates, who I hope would have been delighted to have been "overcome in argument," because he would have learned something by it, is in curious contrast with the naive idea of the glossist, for whom discussion would seem to have been simply a struggle. When philosophy began to awake from its long slumber, and before theology completely dominated it, the practice seems to have been for each professor to seize upon any philosophical position he found unoccupied and which seemed a strong one, to intrench himself in it, and to sally forth from time to time to give battle to the others. Thus, even the scanty records we possess of those disputes enable us to make out a dozen or more opinions held by different teachers at one time concerning the question of nominalism and realism. Read the opening part of the "Historia Calamitatum" of Abelard, who was certainly as philosophical as any of his contemporaries, and see the spirit of combat which it breathes. For him, the truth is simply his particular stronghold. When the method of authority prevailed, the truth meant little more than the Catholic faith. All the efforts of the scholastic doctors are directed toward harmonizing their faith in Aristotle and their faith in the Church, and one may search their ponderous folios through without finding an argument which goes any further. It is noticeable that where different faiths flourish side by side, renegades are looked upon with contempt even by the party whose belief they adopt; so completely has the idea of loyalty replaced that of truth-seeking. Since the time of Descartes, the defect in the conception of truth has been less apparent. Still, it will sometimes strike a scientific man that the philosophers have been less intent on finding out what the facts are, than on inquiring what belief is most in harmony with their system. It is hard to convince a follower of the *a priori* method by adducing facts; but show him that an opinion he is defending is inconsistent with what he has laid down elsewhere, and he will be very apt to retract it. These minds do not seem to believe that disputation is ever to cease; they seem to think that the opinion which is natural for one man is not so for another, and that belief will, consequently, never be settled. In contenting themselves with fixing their own opinions by a method which would lead another man to a different result, they betray their feeble hold of the conception of what truth is.

On the other hand, all the followers of science are fully persuaded that the processes of investigation, if only pushed far enough, will give one certain solution to every question to which they can be applied. One man may investigate the velocity of light by studying the transits of Venus and the aberration of the stars; another by the oppositions of Mars and the eclipses of Jupiter's satellites; a third by the method of Fizeau; a fourth by that of Foucault; a fifth by the motions of the curves of Lissajoux; a sixth, a seventh, an eighth, and a ninth, may follow the different methods of comparing the measures of statical and dynamical electricity. They may at first obtain different results, but, as each perfects his method and his processes, the results will move steadily together toward a destined centre. So with all scientific research. Different minds may set out with the most antagonistic views, but the progress of investigation carries them by a force outside of themselves to one and the same conclusion. This activity of thought by which we are carried, not where we wish, but to a foreordained goal, is like the operation of destiny. No modification of the point of view taken, no selection of other facts for study, no natural bent of mind even, can enable a man to escape the predestinate opinion. This great law is embodied in the conception of truth and reality. The opinion which is fated[3] to be ultimately agreed to by all who investigate, is what we mean by the truth, and the object represented in this opinion is the real. That is the way I would explain reality.

But it may be said that this view is directly opposed to the abstract definition which we have given of reality, inasmuch as it makes the characters of the real to depend on what is ultimately thought about them. But the answer to this is that, on the one hand, reality is independent, not necessarily of thought in general, but only of what you or I or any finite number of men may think about it; and that, on the other hand, though the object of the final opinion depends on what that opinion is, yet what that opinion is does not depend on what you or I or any man thinks. Our perversity and that of others may indefinitely postpone the settlement of opinion; it might even conceivably cause an arbitrary proposition to be universally accepted as long as the human race should last. Yet even that would not change the nature of the belief, which alone could be the result of investigation carried sufficiently far; and if, after the extinction of our race, another should arise with faculties and disposition for investigation, that true opinion must be the one which they would ultimately come to. "Truth crushed to earth shall rise again," and the opinion which would finally result from investigation does not depend on how anybody may actually think. But the reality of that which is real does depend on the real fact that investigation is destined to lead, at last, if continued long enough, to a belief in it.

But I may be asked what I have to say to all the minute facts of history, forgotten never to be recovered, to the lost books of the ancients, to the buried secrets.

Full many a gem of purest ray serene
  The dark, unfathomed caves of ocean bear;
Full many a flower is born to blush unseen,
  And waste its sweetness on the desert air.

Do these things not really exist because they are hopelessly beyond the reach of our knowledge? And then, after the universe is dead (according to the prediction of some scientists), and all life has ceased forever, will not the shock of atoms continue though there will be no mind to know it? To this I reply that, though in no possible state of knowledge can any number be great enough to express the relation between the amount of what rests unknown to the amount of the known, yet it is unphilosophical to suppose that, with regard to any given question (which has any clear meaning), investigation would not bring forth a solution of it, if it were carried far enough. Who would have said, a few years ago, that we could ever know of what substances stars are made whose light may have been longer in reaching us than the human race has existed? Who can be sure of what we shall not know in a few hundred years? Who can guess what would be the result of continuing the pursuit of science for ten thousand years, with the activity of the last hundred? And if it were to go on for a million, or a billion, or any number of years you please, how is it possible to say that there is any question which might not ultimately be solved?

But it may be objected, "Why make so much of these remote considerations, especially when it is your principle that only practical distinctions have a meaning?" Well, I must confess that it makes very little difference whether we say that a stone on the bottom of the ocean, in complete darkness, is brilliant or not—that is to say, that it *probably* makes no difference, remembering always that that stone *may* be fished up to-morrow. But that there are gems at the bottom of the sea, flowers in the untraveled desert, etc., are propositions which, like that about a diamond being hard when it is not pressed, concern much more the arrangement of our language than they do the meaning of our ideas.

It seems to me, however, that we have, by the application of our rule, reached so clear an apprehension of what we mean by reality, and of the fact which the idea rests on, that we should not, perhaps, be making a pretension so presumptuous as it would be singular, if we were to offer a metaphysical theory of existence for universal acceptance among those who employ the scientific method of fixing belief. However, as metaphysics is a subject much more curious than useful, the knowledge of which, like that of a sunken reef, serves chiefly to enable us to keep clear of it, I will not trouble the reader with any more Ontology at this moment. I have already been led much further into that path than I should have desired; and I have given the reader such a dose of mathematics, psychology, and all that is most abstruse, that I fear he may already have left me, and that what I am now writing is for the compositor and proof-reader exclusively. I trusted to the importance of the subject. There is no royal road to logic, and really valuable ideas can only be had at the price of close attention. But I know that in the matter of ideas the public prefer the cheap and nasty; and in my next paper I am going to return to the easily intelligible, and not wander from it again. The reader who has been at the pains of wading through this month's paper, shall be rewarded in the next one by seeing how beautifully what has been developed in this tedious way can be applied to the ascertainment of the rules of scientific reasoning.

We have, hitherto, not crossed the threshold of scientific logic. It is certainly important to know how to make our ideas clear, but they may be ever so clear without being true. How to make them so, we have next to study. How to give birth to those vital and procreative ideas which multiply into a thousand forms and diffuse themselves everywhere, advancing civilization and making the dignity of man, is an art not yet reduced to rules, but of the secret of which the history of science affords some hints.

Notes

1. [Editor's note: here Peirce is referring to his 1877 paper, "The Fixation of Belief" in *Popular Science Monthly*.]
2. [Editor's note: omitted here is Peirce's extensive discussion of weight and force, which is somewhat technical, and tangential to our purposes here.]
3. Fate means merely that which is sure to come true, and can nohow be avoided. It is a superstition to suppose that a certain sort of events are ever fated, and it is another to suppose that the word fate can never be freed from its superstitious taint. We are all fated to die.

8 Pragmatism's conception of truth

WILLIAM JAMES

When Clerk-Maxwell was a child it is written that he had a mania for having everything explained to him, and that when people put him off with vague verbal accounts of any phenomenon he would interrupt them impatiently by saying, 'Yes; but I want you to tell me the *particular go* of it!' Had his question been about truth, only a pragmatist could have told him the particular go of it. I believe that our contemporary pragmatists, especially Messrs. Schiller and Dewey, have given the only tenable account of this subject. It is a very ticklish subject, sending subtle rootlets into all kinds of crannies, and hard to treat in the sketchy way that alone befits a public lecture. But the Schiller-Dewey view of truth has been so ferociously attacked by rationalistic philosophers, and so abominably misunderstood, that here, if anywhere, is the point where a clear and simple statement should be made.

I fully expect to see the pragmatist view of truth run through the classic stages of a theory's career. First, you know, a new theory is attacked as absurd; then it is admitted to be true, but obvious and insignificant; finally it is seen to be so important that its adversaries claim that they themselves discovered it. Our doctrine of truth is at present in the first of these three stages, with symptoms of the second stage having begun in certain quarters. I wish that this lecture might help it beyond the first stage in the eyes of many of you.

Truth, as any dictionary will tell you, is a property of certain of our ideas. It means their 'agreement', as falsity means their disagreement, with 'reality'. Pragmatists and intellectualists both accept this definition as a matter of course. They begin to quarrel only after the question is raised as to what may precisely be meant by the term 'agreement', and what by the term 'reality', when reality is taken as something for our ideas to agree with.

In answering these questions the pragmatists are more analytic and painstaking, the intellectualists more offhand and irreflective. The popular notion is that a true idea must copy its reality. Like other popular views, this one follows the analogy of the most usual experience. Our true ideas of sensible things do indeed copy them. Shut your eyes and think of yonder clock on the wall, and you get just such a true picture or copy of its dial. But your idea of its 'works' (unless you are a clockmaker) is much less of a copy, yet it passes muster, for it in no way clashes with the reality. Even though it should shrink to the mere word 'works', that word still serves you truly; and when you speak of the 'time-keeping function' of the clock, or of its spring's 'elasticity', it is hard to see exactly what your ideas can copy.

You perceive that there is a problem here. Where our ideas cannot copy definitely their object, what does agreement with that object mean? Some idealists seem to say that they are true whenever they are what God means that we ought to think about that object. Others hold the copy-view all through, and speak as if our ideas possessed truth just in proportion as they approach to being copies of the Absolute's eternal way of thinking.

These views, you see, invite pragmatistic discussion. But the great assumption of the intellectualists is that truth means essentially an inert static relation. When you've got your true idea of anything, there's an end of the matter. You're in possession; you *know;* you have fulfilled your thinking destiny. You are where you ought to be mentally; you have obeyed your categorical imperative; and nothing more need follow on that climax of your rational destiny. Epistemologically you are in stable equilibrium.

Pragmatism, on the other hand, asks its usual question. 'Grant an idea or belief to be true,' it says, 'what concrete difference will its being true make in any one's actual life? How will the truth be realized? What experiences will be different from those which would obtain if the belief were false? What, in short, is the truth's cash-value in experiential terms?'

The moment pragmatism asks this question, it sees the answer: *True ideas are those that we can assimilate, validate, corroborate and verify. False ideas are those that we can not.* That is the practical difference it makes to us to have true ideas; that, therefore, is the meaning of truth, for it is all that truth is known-as.

This thesis is what I have to defend. The truth of an idea is not a stagnant property inherent in it. Truth *happens* to an idea. It *becomes* true, is *made* true by events. Its verity *is* in fact an event, a process: the process namely of its verifying itself, its veri-*fication.* Its validity is the process of its valid-*ation*.

But what do the words verification and validation themselves pragmatically mean? They again signify certain practical consequences of the verified and validated idea. It is hard to find any one phrase that characterizes these consequences better than the ordinary agreement-formula—just such consequences being what we have in mind whenever we say that our ideas 'agree' with reality. They lead us, namely, through the acts and other ideas which they instigate, into or up to, or towards, other parts of experience with which we feel all the while—such feeling being among our potentialities—that the original ideas remain in agreement. The connexions and transitions come to us from point to point as being progressive, harmonious, satisfactory. This function of agreeable leading is what we mean by an idea's verification. Such an account is vague and it sounds at first quite trivial, but it has results which it will take the rest of my hour to explain.

Let me begin by reminding you of the fact that the possession of true thoughts means everywhere the possession of invaluable instruments of action; and that our duty to gain truth, so far from being a blank command from out of the blue, or a 'stunt' self-imposed by our intellect, can account for itself by excellent practical reasons.

The importance to human life of having true beliefs about matters of fact is a thing too notorious. We live in a world of realities that can be infinitely useful or infinitely harmful. Ideas that tell us which of them to expect count as the true ideas in all this primary sphere of verification, and the pursuit of such ideas is a primary human duty. The possession of truth, so far from being here an end in itself, is only a preliminary means towards other vital satisfactions. If I am lost in the woods and starved, and find what looks like a cow-path, it is of the utmost importance that I should think of a human habitation at the end of it, for if I do so and follow it, I save myself. The true thought is useful here because the house which is its object is useful. The practical value of true ideas is thus primarily derived from the practical importance of their objects to us. Their objects are, indeed, not important at all times. I may on another occasion have no use for the house; and then my idea of it, however verifiable, will be practically irrelevant, and had better remain latent. Yet since almost any object may some day become temporarily important, the advantage of having a general stock of *extra* truths, of ideas that shall be true of merely possible situations, is obvious. We store such extra truths away in our memories, and with the overflow we fill our books of reference. Whenever such and extra truth becomes practically relevant to one of our emergencies, it passes from cold-storage to do work in the world and our belief in it grows active. You can say of it then either that 'it is useful because it is true' or that 'it is true because it is useful'. Both these phrases mean exactly the same thing, namely that here is an idea that gets fulfilled and can be verified. True is the name for whatever idea starts the verification-process, useful is the name for its completed function in experience. True ideas would never have been singled out as such, would never have acquired a class-name, least of all a name suggesting value, unless they had been useful from the outset in this way.

From this simple cue pragmatism gets her general notion of truth as something essentially bound up with the way in which one moment in our experience may lead us towards other moments which it will be worth while to have been led to. Primarily, and on the common-sense level, the truth of a state of mind means this function of a *leading that is worth while.* When a moment in our experience, of any kind whatever, inspires us with a thought that is true, that means that sooner or later we dip by that thought's guidance into the particulars of experience again and make advantageous connexion with them. This is a vague enough statement, but I beg you to retain it, for it is essential.

Our experience meanwhile is all shot through with regularities. One bit of it can warn us to get ready for another bit, can 'intend' or be 'significant of' that remoter object. The object's advent is the significance's verification. Truth, in these cases, meaning nothing but eventual verification, is manifestly incompatible with waywardness on our part. Woe to him whose beliefs play fast and loose with the order which realities follow in his experience; they will lead him nowhere or else make false connexions.

By 'realities' or 'objects' here, we mean either things of common sense, sensibly present, or else common-sense relations, such as dates, places, distances, kinds, activities. Following our mental image of a house along the cow-path, we actually come to see the house; we get the image's full verification. *Such simply and fully verified leadings are certainly the originals and prototypes of the truth-process.* Experience offers indeed other forms of truth-process, but they are all conceivable as being primary verifications arrested, multiplied or substituted one for another.

Take, for instance, yonder object on the wall. You and I consider it to be a 'clock', although no one of us has seen the hidden works that make it one. We let our notion pass for true without attempting to verify. If truths mean verification-process essentially, ought we then to call such unverified truths as this abortive? No, for they form the overwhelmingly large number of the truths we live by. Indirect as well as direct verifications pass muster. Where circumstantial evidence is sufficient, we can go without eyewitnessing. Just as we here assume Japan to exist without ever having been there, because it *works* to do so, everything we know conspiring with the belief, and nothing interfering, so we assume that thing to be a clock. We *use* it as a clock, regulating the length of our lecture by it. The verification of the assumption here means its leading to no frustration or contradiction. Verifi*ability* of wheels and weights and pendulum is as good as verification. For one truth-process completed there are a million in our lives that function in this state of nascency. They turn us *towards* direct verification; lead us into the *surroundings* of the objects they envisage; and then, if everything runs on harmoniously, we are so sure that verification is possible that we omit it, and are usually justified by all that happens.

Truth lives, in fact, for the most part on a credit system. Our thoughts and beliefs 'pass', so long as nothing challenges them, just as banknotes pass so long as nobody refuses them. But this all points to direct face-to-face verifications somewhere, without which the fabric of truth collapses like a financial system with no cash-basis whatever. You accept my verification of one thing, I yours of another. We trade on each other's truth. But beliefs verified concretely by *somebody* are the posts of the whole superstructure.

Another great reason—beside economy of time—for waiving complete verification in the usual business of life is that all things exist in kinds and not singly. Our world is found once for all to have that peculiarity. So that when we have once directly verified our ideas about one specimen of a kind, we consider ourselves free to apply them to other specimens without verification. A mind that habitually discerns the kind of thing before it, and acts by the law of the kind immediately, without pausing to verify, will be a 'true' mind in ninety-nine out of a hundred emergencies, proved so by its conduct fitting everything it meets, and getting no refutation.

Indirectly or only potentially verifying processes may thus be true as well as full verification-processes. They work as true processes would work, give us the same advantages, and claim our recognition for the same reasons. All this on the common-sense level of matters of fact, which we are alone considering.

But matters of fact are not our only stock in trade. *Relations among purely mental ideas* form another sphere where true and false beliefs obtain, and here the beliefs are absolute, or unconditional. When they are true they bear the name either of definitions or of principles. It is either a principle or a definition that 1 and 1 make 2, that 2 and 1 make 3, and so on; that white differs less from grey than it does from black; that when the cause begins to act the effect also commences. Such propositions hold of all possible 'ones', of all conceivable 'whites' and 'greys' and 'causes'. The objects here are mental objects. Their relations are perceptually obvious at a glance, and no sense-verification is necessary. Moreover, once true, always true, of those same mental objects. Truth here has an 'eternal' character. If you can find a concrete thing anywhere that is 'one' or 'white' or 'grey' or an 'effect,' then your principles will everlastingly apply to it. It is but a case of ascertaining the kind, and then applying the law of its kind to the particular object. You are sure to get truth if you can but name the kind rightly, for your mental relations hold good of everything of that kind without exception. If you then, nevertheless, failed to get truth concretely, you would say that you had classed your real objects wrongly.

In this realm of mental relations, truth again is an affair of leading. We relate one abstract idea with another, framing in the end great systems of logical and mathematical truth, under the respective terms of which the sensible facts of experience eventually arrange themselves, so that our eternal truths hold good of realities also. This marriage of fact and theory is endlessly fertile. What we say is here already true in advance of special verification, *if we have subsumed our objects rightly.* Our ready-made ideal framework for all sorts of possible objects follows from the very structure of our thinking. We can no more play fast and loose with these abstract relations than we can do so with our sense-experiences. They coerce us; we must treat them consistently, whether or not we like the results. The rules of addition apply to our debts as rigorously as to our assets. The hundredth decimal of π the ratio of the circumference to its diameter, is predetermined ideally now, though no one may have computed it. If we should ever need the figure in our dealings with an actual circle we should need to have it given rightly, calculated by the usual rules; for it is the same kind of truth that those rules elsewhere calculate.

Between the coercions of the sensible order and those of the ideal order, our mind is thus wedged tightly. Our ideas must agree with realities, be such realities concrete or abstract, be they facts or be they principles, under penalty of endless inconsistency and frustration.

So far, intellectualists can raise no protest. They can only say that we have barely touched the skin of the matter.

Realities mean, then, either concrete facts, or abstract kinds of thing and relations perceived intuitively between them. They furthermore and thirdly mean, as things that new ideas of ours must no less take account of, the whole body of other truths already in our possession. But what now does 'agreement' with such threefold realities mean?—to use again the definition that is current.

Here it is that pragmatism and intellectualism begin to part company. Primarily, no doubt, to agree means to copy, but we saw that the mere word 'clock' would do instead of a mental picture of its works, and that of many realities our ideas can only be symbols and not copies. 'Past time', 'power', 'spontaneity'—how can our mind copy such realities?

To 'agree' in the widest sense with a reality *can only mean to be guided either straight up to it or into its surroundings, or to be put into such working touch with it as to handle either it or something connected with it better than if we disagreed.* Better either intellectually or practically! And often agreement will only mean the negative fact that nothing contradictory from the quarter of that reality comes to interfere with the way in which our ideas guide us elsewhere. To copy a reality is, indeed, one very important way of agreeing with it, but it is far from being essential. The essential thing is the process of being guided. Any idea that helps us to *deal,* whether practically or intellectually, with either the reality or its belongings, that doesn't entangle our progress in frustrations, that *fits,* in fact, and adapts our life to the reality's whole setting, will agree sufficiently to meet the requirement. It will hold true of that reality.

Thus, *names* are just as 'true' or 'false' as definite mental pictures are. They set up similar verification-processes, and lead to fully equivalent practical results.

All human thinking gets discursified; we exchange ideas; we lend and borrow verifications, get them from one another by means of social intercourse. All truth thus gets verbally built out, stored up, and made available for every one. Hence, we must *talk* consistently just as we must *think* consistently: for both in talk and thought we deal with kinds. Names are arbitrary, but once understood they must be kept to. We mustn't now call Abel 'Cain' or Cain 'Abel'. If we do, we ungear ourselves from the whole book of Genesis, and from all its connexions with the universe of speech and fact down to the present time. We throw ourselves out of whatever truth that entire system of speech and fact may embody.

The overwhelming majority of our true ideas admit of no direct or face-to-face verification—those of past history, for example, as of Cain and Abel. The stream of time can be remounted only verbally, or verified indirectly by the present prolongations or effects of what the past harbored. Yet if they agree with these verbalities and effects, we can know that our ideas of the past are true. As *true as past time itself was,* so true was Julius Cæsar, so true were antediluvian monsters, all in their proper dates and settings. That past time itself was, is guaranteed by its coherence with everything that's present. True as the present *is*, the past *was* also.

Agreement thus turns out to be essentially an affair of leading—leading that is useful because it is into quarters that contain objects that are important. True ideas lead us into useful verbal and conceptual quarters as well as directly up to useful sensible termini. They lead to consistency, stability and flowing human intercourse. They lead away from eccentricity and isolation, from foiled and barren thinking. The untrammelled flowing of the leading-process, its general freedom from clash and contradiction, passes for its indirect verification; but all roads lead to Rome, and in the end and eventually, all true processes must lead to the face of directly verifying sensible experiences *somewhere,* which somebody's ideas have copied.

Such is the large loose way in which the pragmatist interprets the word agreement. He treats it altogether practically. He lets it cover any process of conduction from a present idea to a future terminus, provided only it run prosperously. It is only thus that 'scientific' ideas, flying as they do beyond common sense, can be said to agree with their realities. It is, as I have already said, *as if* reality were made of ether, atoms or electrons, but we mustn't think so literally. The term 'energy' doesn't even pretend to stand for anything 'objective'. It is only a way of measuring the surface of phenomena so as to string their changes on a simple formula.

Yet in the choice of these man-made formulas we can not be capricious with impunity any more than we can be capricious on the common-sense practical level. We must find a theory that will *work;* and that means something extremely difficult; for our theory must mediate between all previous truths and certain new experiences. It must derange common sense and previous belief as little as possible, and it must lead to some sensible terminus or other that can be verified exactly. To 'work' means both these things; and the squeeze is so tight that there is little loose play for any hypothesis. Our theories are wedged and controlled as nothing else is. Yet sometimes alternative theoretic formulas are equally compatible with all the truths we know, and then we choose between them for subjective reasons. We choose the kind of theory to which we are already partial; we follow 'elegance' or 'economy'. Clerk-Maxwell somewhere says it would be 'poor scientific taste' to choose the more complicated of two equally well-evidenced conceptions; and you will all agree with him. Truth in science is what gives us the maximum possible sum of satisfactions, taste included, but consistency both with previous truth and with novel fact is always the most imperious claimant.

I have led you through a very sandy desert. But now, if I may be allowed so vulgar an expression, we begin to taste the milk in the coconut. Our rationalist critics here discharge their batteries upon us, and to reply to them will take us out from all this dryness into full sight of a momentous philosophical alternative.

Our account of truth is an account of truths in the plural, of processes of leading, realized *in rebus,* and having only this quality in common, that they *pay*. They pay by guiding us into or towards some part of a system that dips at numerous points into sense-percepts, which we may copy mentally or not, but with which at any rate we are now in the kind of commerce vaguely designated as verification. Truth for us is simply a collective name for verification-processes, just as health, wealth, strength, etc., are names for other processes connected with life, and also pursued because it pays to pursue them. Truth is *made,* just as health, wealth, and strength are made, in the course of experience.

Here rationalism is instantaneously up in arms against us. I can imagine a rationalist to talk as follows:

'Truth is not made,' he will say; 'it absolutely obtains, being a unique relation that does not wait upon any process, but shoots straight over the head of experience, and hits its reality every time. Our belief that yon thing on the wall is a clock is true already, although no one in the whole history of the world should verify it. The bare quality of standing in that transcendent relation is what makes any thought true that possesses it, whether or not there be verification. You pragmatists put the cart before the horse in making truth's being reside in verification-processes. These are merely signs of its being, merely our lame ways of ascertaining after the fact, which of our ideas already has possessed the wondrous quality. The quality itself is timeless, like all essences and natures. Thoughts partake of it directly, as they partake of falsity or of irrelevancy. It can't be analysed away into pragmatic consequences.'

The whole plausibility of this rationalist tirade is due to the fact to which we have already paid so much attention. In our world, namely, abounding as it does in things of similar kinds and similarly associated, one verification serves for others of its kind, and one great use of knowing things is to be led not so much to them as to their associates, especially to human talk about them. The quality of truth, obtaining *ante rem,* pragmatically means, then, the fact that in such a world innumerable ideas work better by their indirect or possible than by their direct and actual verification. Truth *ante rem* means only verifiability, then; or else it is a case of the stock rationalist trick of treating the *name* of a concrete phenomenal reality as an independent prior entity, and placing it behind the reality as its explanation. Professor Mach quotes somewhere an epigram of Lessing's:

Says Hänschen Schlau to cousin Fritz,
'How come, cousin Fritzen,
That's the richest in the world,
Own the most money?[1]

Hänschen Schlau here treats the principle 'wealth' as something distinct from the facts denoted by the man's being rich. It antedates them; the facts become only a sort of secondary coincidence with the rich man's essential nature.

In the case of 'wealth' we all see the fallacy. We know that wealth is but a name for concrete processes that certain men's lives play a part in, and not a natural excellence found in Messrs. Rockefeller and Carnegie, but not in the rest of us.

Like wealth, health also lives *in rebus.* It is a name for processes, and digestion, circulation, sleep, etc., that go on happily, though in this instance we are more inclined to think of it as a principle and to say the man digests and sleeps so well *because* he is so healthy.

With 'strength' we are, I think, more rationalistic still, and decidedly inclined to treat it as an excellence pre-existing in the man and explanatory of the herculean performances of his muscles.

With 'truth' most people go over the border entirely, and treat the rationalistic account as self-evident. But really all these words in *th* are exactly similar. Truth exists *ante rem* just as much and as little as the other things do.

The scholastics, following Aristotle, made much of the distinction between habit and act. Health *in actu* means, among other things, good sleeping and digesting. But a healthy man need not always be sleeping, or always digesting, any more than a wealthy man need be always handing money, or a strong man always lifting weights. All such qualities sink to the status of 'habits' between their times of exercise; and similarly truth becomes a habit of certain of our ideas and beliefs in their intervals of rest from their verifying activities. But those activities are the root of the whole matter, and the condition of there being any habit to exist in the intervals.

'The true', to put it very briefly, is only the expedient in the way of our thinking, just as 'the right' is only the expedient in the way of our behaving. Expedient in almost any fashion; and expedient in the long run and on the whole of course; for what meets expediently all the experience in sight won't necessarily meet all farther experiences equally satisfactorily. Experience, as we know, has ways of *boiling over,* and making us correct our present formulas.

The 'absolutely' true, meaning what no further experience will ever alter, is that ideal vanishing-point towards which we imagine that all our temporary truths will some day converge. It runs on all fours with the perfectly wise man, and with the absolutely complete experience; and, if these ideals are ever realized, they will all be realized together. Meanwhile we have to live today by what truth we can get today, and be ready tomorrow to call it falsehood. Ptolemaic astronomy, Euclidean space, Aristotelian logic, scholastic metaphysics, were expedient for centuries, but human experience has boiled over those limits, and we now call these things only relatively true, or true within those borders of experience. 'Absolutely' they are false; for we know that those limits were casual, and might have been transcended by past theorists just as they are by present thinkers.

When new experiences lead to retrospective judgements, using the past tense, what these judgements utter *was* true, even though no past thinker had been led there. We live forwards, a Danish thinker has said, but we understand backwards. The present sheds a backward light on the world's previous processes. They may have been truth-processes for the actors in them. They are not so for one who knows the later revelations of the story.

This regulative notion of a potential better truth to be established later, possibly to be established some day absolutely, and having powers of retroactive legislation, turns its face, like all pragmatist notions, towards concreteness of fact, and towards the future. Like the half-truths, the absolute truth will have to be *made,* made as a relation incidental to the growth of a mass of verification-experience, to which the half-true ideas are all along contributing their quota.

I have already insisted on the fact that truth is made largely out of previous truths. Men's beliefs at any time are so much experience *funded.* But the beliefs are themselves parts of the sum total of the world's experience, and become matter, therefore, for the next day's funding operations. So far as reality means experienceable reality, both it and the truths men gain about it are everlastingly in process of mutation—mutation towards a definite goal, it may be—but still mutation.

Mathematicians can solve problems with two variables. On the Newtonian theory, for instance, acceleration varies with distance, but distance also varies with acceleration. In the realm of truth-processes facts come independently and determine our beliefs provisionally. But these beliefs make us act, and as fast as they do so, they bring into sight or into existence new facts which redetermine the beliefs accordingly. So the whole coil and ball of truth, as it rolls up, is the product of a double influence. Truths emerge from facts; but they dip forward into facts again and add to them; which facts again create or reveal new truth (the word is indifferent) and so on indefinitely. The 'facts' themselves meanwhile are not *true.* They simply *are*. Truth is the function of the beliefs that start and terminate among them.

The case is like a snowball's growth, due as it is to the distribution of the snow on the one hand, and to the successive pushes of the boys on the other, with these factors co-determining each other incessantly.

The most fateful point of difference between being a rationalist and being a pragmatist is now fully in sight. Experience is in mutation, and our psychological ascertainments of truth are in mutation—so much rationalism will allow; but never that either reality itself or truth itself is mutable. Reality stands complete and ready-made from all eternity, rationalism insists, and the agreement of our ideas with it is that unique unanalyzable virtue in them of which she has already told us. As that intrinsic excellence, their truth has nothing to do with our experiences. It adds nothing to the content of experience. It makes no difference to reality itself; it is supervenient, inert, static, a reflexion merely. It doesn't *exist,* it *holds* or *obtains,* it belongs to another dimension from that of either facts or fact-relations, belongs, in short, to the epistemological dimension—and with that big word rationalism closes the discussion.

Thus, just as pragmatism faces forward to the future, so does rationalism here again face backward to a past eternity. True to her inveterate habit, rationalism reverts to 'principles', and thinks that when an abstraction once is named, we own an oracular solution.

The tremendous pregnancy in the way of consequences for life of this radical difference of outlook will only become apparent in my later lectures. I wish meanwhile to close this lecture by showing that rationalism's sublimity does not save it from inanity.

When, namely, you ask rationalists, instead of accusing pragmatism of desecrating the notion of truth, to define it themselves by saying exactly what *they* understand by it, the only positive attempts I can think of are these two:

1. 'Truth is the system of propositions which have an unconditional claim to be recognized as valid.'[2]
2. Truth is a name for all those judgements which we find ourselves under obligation to make by a kind of imperative duty.[3]

The first thing that strikes one in such definitions is their unutterable triviality. They are absolutely true, of course, but absolutely insignificant until you handle them pragmatically. What do you mean by 'claim' here, and what do you mean by 'duty'? As summary names for the concrete reasons why thinking in true ways is overwhelmingly expedient and good for mortal men, it is all right to talk of claims on reality's part to be agreed with, and of obligations on our part to agree. We feel both the claims and the obligations, and we feel them for just those reasons.

But the rationalists who talk of claim and obligation *expressly say that they have nothing to do with our practical interests or personal reasons.* Our reasons for agreeing are psychological facts, they say, relative to each thinker, and to the accidents of his life. They are his evidence merely, they are no part of the life of truth itself. That life transacts itself in a purely logical or epistemological, as distinguished from a psychological, dimension, and its claims antedate and exceed all personal motivations whatsoever. Though neither man nor God should ever ascertain truth, the word would still have to be defined as that which *ought* to be ascertained and recognized.

There never was a more exquisite example of an idea abstracted from the concretes of experience and then used to oppose and negate what it was abstracted from.

Philosophy and common life abound in similar instances. The 'sentimentalist fallacy' is to shed tears over abstract justice and generosity, beauty, etc., and never to know these qualities when you meet them in the street, because the circumstances make them vulgar. Thus I read in the privately printed biography of an eminently rationalistic mind: 'It was strange that with such admiration for beauty in the abstract, my brother had no enthusiasm for fine architecture, for beautiful painting, or for flowers.' And in almost the last philosophic work I have read, I find such passages as the following: 'Justice is ideal, solely ideal. Reason conceives that it ought to exist, but experience shows that it can not.... Truth, which ought to be, can not be.... Reason is deformed by experience. As soon as reason enters experience it becomes contrary to reason.'

The rationalist's fallacy here is exactly like the sentimentalist's. Both extract a quality from the muddy particulars of experience, and find it so pure when extracted that they contrast it with each and all its muddy instances as an opposite and higher nature. All the while it is *their* nature. It is the nature of truths to be validated, verified. It pays for our ideas to be validated. Our obligation to seek truth is part of our general obligation to do what pays. They payments true ideas bring are the sole why of our duty to follow them. Identical whys exist in the case of wealth and health.

Truth makes no other kind of claim and imposes no other kind of ought than health and wealth do. All these claims are conditional; the concrete benefits we gain are what we mean by calling the pursuit a duty. In the case of truth, untrue beliefs work as perniciously in the long run as true beliefs work beneficially. Talking abstractly, the quality 'true' may thus be said to grow absolutely precious and the quality 'untrue' absolutely damnable: the one may be called good, the other bad, unconditionally. We ought to think the true, we ought to shun the false, imperatively.

But if we treat all this abstraction literally and oppose it to its mother soil in experience, see what a preposterous position we work ourselves into.

We cannot then take a step forward in our actual thinking. When shall I acknowledge this truth and when that? Shall the acknowledgment be loud?—or silent? If sometimes loud, sometimes silent, which *now?* When may a truth go into cold-storage in the encyclopedia? and when shall it come out for battle? Must I constantly be repeating the truth 'twice two are four' because of its eternal claim on recognition? or is it sometimes irrelevant? Must my thoughts dwell night and day on my personal sins and blemishes, because I truly have them?—or may I sink and ignore them in order to be a decent social unit, and not a mass of morbid melancholy and apology?

It is quite evident that our obligation to acknowledge truth, so far from being unconditional, is tremendously conditioned. Truth with a big T, and in the singular, claims abstractly to be recognized, of course; but concrete truths in the plural need be recognized only when their recognition is expedient. A truth must always be preferred to a falsehood when both relate to the situation; but when neither does, truth is as little of a duty as falsehood. If you ask me what o'clock it is and I tell you that I live at 95 Irving Street, my answer may indeed be true, but you don't see why it is my duty to give it. A false address would be as much to the purpose.

With this admission that there are conditions that limit the application of the abstract imperative, *the pragmatistic treatment of truth sweeps back upon us in its fulness.* Our duty to agree with reality is seen to be grounded in a perfect jungle of concrete expediencies.

When Berkeley had explained what people meant by matter, people thought that he denied matter's existence. When Messrs. Schiller and Dewey now explain what people mean by truth, they are accused of denying *its* existence. These pragmatists destroy all objective standards, critics say, and put foolishness and wisdom on one level. A favourite formula for describing Mr Schiller's doctrines and mine is that we are persons who think that by saying whatever you find it pleasant to say and calling it truth you fulfil every pragmatistic requirement.

I leave it to you to judge whether this be not an impudent slander. Pent in, as the pragmatist more than anyone else sees himself to be, between the whole body of funded truths squeezed from the past and the coercions of the world of sense about him, who so well as he feels the immense pressure of objective control under which our minds perform their operations? If anyone imagines that this law is lax, let him keep its commandment one day, says Emerson. We have heard much of late of the uses of the imagination in science. It is high time to urge the use of a little imagination in philosophy. The unwillingness of some of our critics to read any but the silliest of possible meanings into our statements is as discreditable to their imaginations as anything I know in recent philosophic history. Schiller says the true is that which 'works'. Thereupon he is treated as one who limits verification to the lowest material utilities. Dewey says truth is what gives 'satisfaction'. He is treated as one who believes in calling everything true which, if it were true, would be pleasant.

Our critics certainly need more imagination of realities. I have honestly tried to stretch my own imagination and to read the best possible meaning into the rationalist conception, but I have to confess that it still completely baffles me. The notion of a reality calling on us to 'agree' with it, and that for no reasons, but simply because its claim is 'unconditional' or 'transcendent', is one that I can make neither head nor tail of. I try to imagine myself as the sole reality in the world, and then to imagine what more I would 'claim' if I were allowed to. If you suggest the possibility of my claiming that a mind should come into being from out of the void inane and stand and *copy* me, I can indeed imagine what the copying might mean, but I can conjure up no motive. What good it would do me to be copied, or what good it would do that mind to copy me, if further consequences are expressly and in principle ruled out as motives for the claim (as they are by our rationalist authorities) I can not fathom. When the Irishman's admirers ran him along to the place of banquet in a sedan chair with no bottom, he said, 'Faith, if it wasn't for the honour of the thing, I might as well have come on foot.' So here: but for the honour of the thing, I might as well have remained uncopied. Copying is one genuine mode of knowing (which for some strange reason our contemporary transcendentalists seem to be tumbling over each other to repudiate); but when we get beyond copying, and fall back on unnamed forms of agreeing that are expressly denied to be either copyings or leadings or fittings, or any other processes pragmatically definable, the *what* of the 'agreement' claimed becomes as unintelligible as the why of it. Neither content nor motive can be imagined for it. It is an absolutely meaningless abstraction.[4]

Surely in this field of truth it is the pragmatists and not the rationalists who are the more genuine defenders of the universe's rationality.

Notes

1. [Editor's note: James's original text contains the epigram in German, but I have included an English translation in the main text here instead. The original German text is:

   Sagt Hänschen Schlau zu Vetter Fritz,
   'Wie kommt es, Vetter Fritzen,
   Dass grad' die Reichsten in der Welt,
   Das meiste Geld besitzen?'.]

2. A. E. Taylor, *Philosophical Review,* 14: 288.
3. H. Rickert, *Der Gegenstand der Erkenntniss: Einfuhrung in die tranzenden-tale philosophie* (Tübingen, 1904), ch. on 'Die Urtheilsnothwendigkeit'.
4. I am not forgetting that Professor Rickert long ago gave up the whole notion of truth being founded on agreement with reality. Reality according to him, is whatever agrees with truth, and truth is founded solely on our primal duty. This fantastic flight, together with Mr Joachim's candid confession of failure in his book *The Nature of Truth* (Oxford, 1906), seems to me to mark the bankruptcy of rationalism when dealing with this subject. Rickert deals with part of the pragmatistic position under the head of what he calls 'Relativismus'. I cannot discuss his text here. Suffice it to say that his argumentation in that chapter is so feeble as to seem almost incredible in so generally able a writer.

9 Pragmatism on solidarity, bullshit, and other deformities of truth

CHERYL MISAK

1 Introduction

The pragmatist offers an account of truth on which truth is linked to human inquiry. The received view in analytic philosophy is that it fails quite dismally. The received view is that pragmatism fails to latch on to the concept of truth, speaking rather of some deformed version of it. The pragmatist, that is, delivers not an account of truth, but an account of warranted assertibility, agreement within a community, rational belief, or some such thing. While these phenomena might be of great interest to epistemologists and to ordinary human beings, they are not of much interest to analytic truth theorists.

The received view is nicely captured by Paul Horwich. He thinks that "truth has a certain purity." Hence, our understanding of it must be kept independent of the ideas of verification, success, and the like (1990, 12). His deflationist view has it that there is nothing more to the notion of truth than the infinite instances of the schema: "'*p*' is true if and only if *p*." Since the whole point of pragmatism is to link the concept of truth to human inquiry (to verification, success, and the like), the pragmatist and the analytic truth theorist would seem to be in permanent and irreconcilable tension.

In what follows, I shall suggest that this is not the most helpful way of understanding the relationship between contemporary deflationist views of truth and pragmatism. The founder of pragmatism, Charles Sanders Peirce, was a resolutely analytic philosopher, who never tired of chiding his good friend William James and the other Harvard philosophers about their poor training in formal logic and their lack of rigorous thinking. It might well be that the theories of truth offered by James and his follower Richard Rorty[1] are best described as theories not of truth but of something else. But when we look at Peirce's theory of truth, we shall see that he was sensitive to the kind of point that Horwich makes about the purity of the concept of truth. And we shall see that he offered the makings of an argument about how to close the gap between the deflationism and pragmatism.

Once I show how pragmatism need not offer a theory of a deformity of truth, I will shift my focus to the question of how the pragmatist might think about some phenomena that become prominent when one thinks about the deformities of truth – lying and the recently popular topic of bullshitting. We will see that in managing the issues that arise here, Peircean pragmatism again has distinct advantages over Jamesian/Rortyian pragmatism.

2 The Jamesian/Rortyian pragmatist account of truth

A debate has raged within pragmatism, from its very inception in the mid-1880s through to today, about how best to conceive of truth.[2] On one side of the divide we have William James, John Dewey, and Richard Rorty who take truth to be connected to the products of actual human inquiry. These pragmatists think of truth as roughly what works for us (James); what it is found to be warranted (Dewey); or what is agreed upon among members of our community (Rorty). Here is James:

> Any idea upon which we can ride ... any idea that will carry us prosperously from any one part of our experience to any other part, linking things satisfactorily, working securely, simplifying, saving labor, is ... true *instrumentally*. (1907/1949, 58)

"Satisfactorily," for James, "means more satisfactorily to ourselves, and individuals will emphasize their points of satisfaction differently. To a certain degree, therefore, everything here is plastic" (1907/1949, 61).

James tends to put forward this view as a view of truth itself—as what we would now call a reductive definition of truth. Truth *is* an idea upon which we can ride; it *is* what satisfies us.

Horwich's kind of argument about the purity of truth arose very early in the history of pragmatism. Paul Carus in his 1911 *Truth on Trial* argues that James replaces

> the belief in the stability of truth, in its persistence and eternality with a more elastic kind of truth which can change with the fashions and makes it possible that we need no longer trouble about inconsistencies; for what is true to one need no longer be true to others, and the truth of to-day may the real now, and yet it may become the error of the to-morrow. (1911, 110)

The point, of course, is that this more elastic kind of truth is not truth at all.

G. E. Moore and Bertrand Russell[3] leveled similar objections against James. It is an anathema, they point out, to think that truth, like usefulness, is a property that may come and go. It is an anathema to think that a belief, which might be held at many different times, may be true at some of those times and false at others. Whatever property James is identifying, it is not the property of truth.

These are good objections. And they have stuck to pragmatism ever since they were made, despite the fact that James may be the lone pragmatist who *identifies* truth with what works.[4]

At times Rorty can be found saying with James that truth just *is* solidarity or what is agreed upon in the community. His more considered view is that we need to abandon the idea of truth; that is, more often than not, he takes a non-Jamesian approach to what it is that he is identifying. He holds that the account on offer from the pragmatist is not an account of truth at all, since an account of truth, as it is usually conceived, is not possible. We need to cease thinking of the mind as a great mirror which holds representations of the world. Once we abandon this account of truth, we will want to focus on beliefs that serve us well. What we aim at is not truth, but solidarity or what our peers will let us get away with saying (1979, 176).

That is, in the gap left when one gives up on a theory of truth, Rorty offers an account of the best we human inquirers can do. We cannot get the truth, but we can get what works for us, what is warranted, or what we agree upon. We can get solidarity.

The way that Rorty gets to this conclusion is by examining our practices of inquiry. What he finds is that the concept of what he calls Capital-T Truth plays no role in inquiry whatsoever. He concludes that philosophers should stop trying to think about the idea of truth: Truth is "not the sort of thing one should expect to have an interesting philosophical theory about" (1982, xiii). The yearning for an unconditional, impossible, indefinable, sublime thing like truth comes at the price of "irrelevance to practice" (2000, 2). Inquirers simply do not aim at that sort of thing. Since there is no practical difference between aiming to hold True beliefs and aiming to hold beliefs that will stand up in our community, it makes no sense to speak of Truth as a goal of inquiry. The inquirer can not try to compare her beliefs with reality—she can only try to live up to her epistemic responsibilities or the standards of her epistemic community.

Rorty, that is, seems to agree with the purity theorist that pragmatism is not a theory of truth, but a theory of something else. Indeed, Rorty eventually came to the view that the purity theorist was right in thinking that the deflationary theory was uninteresting enough and that it captured all that we could say about truth. But not many deflationists have gone on to agree with him that once the deflationary view is accepted, we must see our inquiry and deliberations aiming only at agreement with our peers. That continues to strike a wrong note for the analytic truth theorist.

3 The Peircean account of truth

On the other side of the debate over the heart and soul of pragmatism, we have the founder of pragmatism, Charles Peirce and his contemporary followers.[5] This kind of pragmatist rejects theories of truth which unlink truth from inquiry, but is nonetheless committed to doing justice to the very idea of truth and to the objective dimension of human inquiry. The focus is on the fact that those engaged in deliberation and investigation take themselves to be aiming at the truth—at getting things right, at avoiding mistakes, and at improving their beliefs and theories. Truth is not linked to the actual products of human inquiry, but rather, to the products of human inquiry, were they to be the best they could be, opening up some distance between what is justified now and what would really be justified.

Peirce argues that a true belief would be "indefeasible"; or would not be improved upon; or would never lead to disappointment; or would stand up to all the evidence and argument, no matter how far we were to pursue our inquiries. Although he is often taken to have held that a true belief is one that is fated to be believed at the end of inquiry, he on the whole tries to stay away from the unhelpful idea of the final end of inquiry and he never goes anywhere near the unhelpful ideas of perfect evidence and ideal inquiry.

He starts off with the thought that we must look to the consequences of a concept like truth in order to fully understand it:

> We must not begin by talking of pure ideas—vagabond thoughts that tramp the public roads without any human habitation—but must begin with men and their conversation. (CP 8.112[6])

This is the pragmatic maxim. It asserts that in order to have a complete grasp of a concept, we must connect it to that with which we have "dealings" (CP 5.416).

It is critical to see that in Peirce's hands, the pragmatic maxim is not a semantic principle about the very meaning of our concepts. That is, it is not designed to capture a full account of meaning. He argued that the maxim captures an important aspect of what it is to understand something. Not only does one have to know how to give an analytic definition of a concept and know how to pick out instances of it, but one has to know what to expect if beliefs involving the concept are true or false. If a belief has no consequences—if there is nothing we would expect would be different if it were true or false—then it lacks a dimension we would have had to get right were we to fully understand it. Without that dimension, it is empty or useless for inquiry and deliberation.

So Peirce thought that the pragmatic aspect of understanding is a rather important one, while being very clear that it is not the be-all-and-end-all. He says, with respect to the difference between analytic definition and pragmatism:

> I believe I made my own opinion quite clear to any attentive Reader, that the pragmaticistic grade of clearness could no more supersede the Definitiary or Analytic grade than this latter grade could supersede the first. That is to say, if the Maxim of Pragmaticism be acknowledged, although Definition can no longer be regarded as the supreme mode of clear Apprehension; yet it retains all the *absolute* importance it ever had, still remaining indispensable to all Exact Reasoning. (MS 647, p. 2)

This is in 1910, after he has decided that others (mostly James) have abused his "bantling 'pragmatism'" so severely that he is going to kiss it goodbye and introduce "the word 'pragmaticism,' which is ugly enough to be safe from kidnappers" (CP 5.414).

When the pragmatic maxim is turned on the concept of truth, the upshot is an aversion to "transcendental" accounts of truth, such as the correspondence theory, on which a true belief is one that corresponds to, or gets right, or mirrors the believer-independent world (CP 5.572). Such accounts of truth are examples of those "vagabond thoughts." They make truth the subject of empty metaphysics. The very idea of the believer-independent world, and the items within it to which beliefs or sentences might correspond, seem graspable only if we could somehow step outside of our corpus of belief, our practices, or that with which we have dealings.

That is, this concept of truth is missing the dimension that makes it suitable for practice and inquiry. Peirce is perfectly happy with it as a "nominal" or "formal" definition, useful only to those who have never encountered the word before.[7] If we want a more robust or full account of truth, we need to have an account of the role the concept plays in practical endeavors. We need to provide a pragmatic elucidation of the concept of truth as well as an analytic definition of it.[8]

So, anticipating recent moves in debates about truth, Peirce was very careful to stay away from a reductive definition of truth: He did not want to *define* truth as that which satisfies our aims in inquiry. A dispute about definition, he says, is usually a "profitless discussion" (CP 8.100) or a "folly" as Donald Davidson (1996) has said. David Wiggins sees Peirce's point perfectly:[9]

> To elucidate truth in its relations with the notion of inquiry, for instance, as the pragmatist does, need not ... represent any concession at all to the idea that truth is *itself* an "epistemic notion." (2002, 318)

When a concept is, as Wiggins (2002, 316) puts it, "already fundamental to human thought and long since possessed of an autonomous interest," it is pointless to try to define it. Rather, we ought to attempt to get leverage on the concept, or a fix on it, by exploring its connections with practice. This is the insight at the very heart of pragmatism.

So the Peircean pragmatist is committed to thinking that our concept of truth can be illuminated by looking at the practices which are bound up with the concept of truth—inquiry, belief, assertion, and the like. Once we see, for instance, that truth and assertion are intimately connected—once we see that to assert that *p* is true is to assert *p*—we can look to our practices of assertion to see what commitments they entail.

What Peirce finds when he looks at the linkages between truth and our practices of assertion is that the concept of truth is bound up with the concepts of reasons, evidence, experience, and inquiry. As Wiggins (2004) again so nicely puts it, hard on the heels of the thought that truth is internally related to assertion comes the thought that truth is also internally related to inquiry, reasons, evidence, and standards of good belief. If we unpack the commitments we incur when we assert, we find that we have imported all these notions. When we assert that *p*, we assert that *p* does and would continue to stand up to the reasons and evidence.

Hence, when Peirce engages in the task that led to Rorty's abandoning the concept of truth, he gets a very different result. When Peirce tries to get leverage on the concept of truth by examining its role in inquiry, he finds first that inquirers do indeed aim at truth. Inquirers aim at getting things right or at something that goes beyond the best that they can do here and now.

Peirce and Rorty certainly agree about the correspondence theory of truth. Peirce takes one of the most pressing problems for the correspondence theorist to be that he fails to make the aim of inquiry "readily comprehensible" (CP 1.578). How could anyone aim for a truth that goes beyond experience or beyond the best that inquiry could do? How could an inquirer adopt a method that might achieve that aim? The correspondence theory makes truth "a useless word" and "having no use for this meaning of the word 'truth,' we had better use the word in another sense" (CP 5.553). What distinguishes the Peirce from the Rorty is that the former thinks that there is another perfectly good sense of the word "truth."

Today we might put his thought like this. In all domains of inquiry and deliberation, we distinguish between thinking we are right and being right, we criticize the beliefs and actions of others, and we think that we can improve our judgments, learn from our mistakes, etc. These distinctions and practices are quite literally dependent on the notion of truth—we can understand them only by supposing that we aim at the truth. Peirce's argument against Rorty would be that he has an impoverished view of practice. As Jeffrey Stout puts it, "getting something right ... turns out to be among the human interests that need to be taken into account" (2007, 18).

It may already be clear that pragmatism, as expressed by Peirce, and deflationism, as expressed by some of the purity theorists, have much in common. They share the naturalist thought that there is an unseverable connection between making an assertion and claiming that it is true. What we do when we offer a justification of "*p* is true" is to offer a justification for the claim that *p*. If we want to know whether it is true that Toronto is north of Buffalo, there is nothing additional to check on ("a fact," "a state of affairs")—nothing over and above our consulting maps, driving or walking north from Buffalo to see whether we get to

Toronto, etc. Inquiring about the truth of the statement does not involve anything more than investigating the matter in our usual ways. Pragmatism and deflationism share, that is, an aversion to empty metaphysics.

The difference between the two positions is that Peirce would think that the purist's quest to keep truth away from the ideas of verification, success, and the like is bound to result in an empty and useless account. The way to deflate truth—the way to make it less metaphysical—it is link truth to these down-to-earth notions, not to claim independence from them. The difference between Peirce's view and the purist's view is precisely the difference between Crispin Wright's view and the purist's view. Both think that although the deflationist offers a fine nominal definition of truth, more needs to be said. And both think, in Wright's words, that what needs to be said is that truth is a special kind of warranted assertion:

> A statement is superassertible ... if and only if it is, or can be, warranted and some warrant for it would survive arbitrarily close scrutiny of its pedigree and arbitrarily extensive increments to or other forms of improvement of our information. (1992, 48)

The pragmatist (at least the pragmatist of the Peircean variety) and the analytic truth theorist are not as far apart as they first seemed to be.

4 Genuine belief and deformed belief

There is a long-standing interest among truth theorists in some phenomena associated with the concept of truth. Much of that interest has been in the phenomenon of lying, mostly due to issues involving the liar paradox. But recently there has been some attention paid to a related kind of speech—bullshitting—thanks to the reissue of Harry Frankfurt's *On Bullshit* (2005).

The liar, Frankfurt thinks, is more closely involved in the truth business than is the bullshitter. Of course, the liar has an aim other than truth—he aims to mislead the hearer of his utterance so that he can satisfy some end. But in order to do this, the liar is "inescapably concerned with truth-values" (Frankfurt 2005, 51). He must respond to the truth or pay close attention to it, for he believes that what he is saying is not true and he intends to utter those untruths. The concept of lying is thus very much parasitic on the concept of truth.

The bullshitter, Frankfurt argues, ought to be distinguished from the liar. The bullshitter does not know that he is uttering falsehoods, with the intention to mislead. For the bullshitter does not care whether what he is saying is true or false—he is indifferent to how things really are (Frankfurt 2005, 34). "He does not care whether the things he says describe reality correctly. He just picks them out, or makes them up, to suit his purpose" (2005, 56). Like the liar, the bullshitter has strategic ends and it is those other ends that matter. Perhaps he wants others to think that he is clever or interesting. Perhaps he wants to impress by speaking colorfully or vivaciously (Frankfurt 2005, 31).

So bullshitters and liars, with a strategic end explicitly or implicitly in view, represent themselves falsely as endeavoring to communicate the truth (2005, 54). It is just that one of them has to pay attention to what is true, whereas the other does not.

Frankfurt distinguishes another kind of speech act—that found in a "bull session" or in "shooting the bull." Here "participants try out various thoughts and attitudes in order to see how it feels to hear themselves saying such things and in order to discover how others respond, without its being assumed that they are committed to what they say" (2005, 36). The purpose is not to communicate beliefs, but to take an experimental approach to a subject matter.

Participating in these bull sessions is not so bad, by Frankfurt's lights, for there is no pretense at trying to communicate the truth. That is what he is dismayed by: those who do not respect the truth or who hold the truth in contempt. And here the liar comes out looking better than the bullshitter. At least the liar "assumes that there are indeed facts that are in some way both determinate and knowable" (2005, 61). The liar knows that there is a difference between getting things wrong and getting things right.

One reason there is so much bullshit around these days, Frankfurt suggests, is that there is a rampant skepticism about our ability to have any access to reality. No doubt Frankfurt would place pragmatism among these dangerous "anti-realist doctrines."

Let's take it for granted that Frankfurt's main concern is legitimate—that bullshitting is a common and unwelcome phenomenon and that bullshitters are encouraged by anti-realist views of truth. The more interesting question for the epistemologist, I think, is whether there are epistemological, as well as moral, grounds for criticizing someone who discards the aim of truth. Why should we value truth for its own sake, rather than value it for some strategic end?

Here a sharp query is indeed raised for the Jamesian/Rortyian pragmatist, who seems to say that it does not make sense to talk about "truth for its own sake." We value truths insofar as they contribute to the satisfaction of our aims. The question is how this kind of pragmatist can possibly distinguish between the strategic ends of the liar and bullshitter, on the one hand, and the presumably better ends of the scientist and honest deliberator on the other. How can the pragmatist maintain that the aims of understanding the world, predicting the future course of experience, and the like are better than the aims of getting agreement in the community, making me feel comfortable, or even making me look clever and interesting?

James and Rorty seem determined to turn their backs on this question. James infamously argues in "The Will to Believe" (1897/1979) that if the belief in God makes a satisfactory impact on my life, then I can take it to be true. For James, non-epistemic criteria, such as making one more comfortable or making one's life more harmonious, seem to be relevant to belief acceptance and to truth. The Jamesian pragmatist seems to be exactly the sort of person Frankfurt has in his sights on—someone who is not concerned about whether or not his belief is true in the sense of really getting things right.

Indeed, as soon as James started publishing on the issues, this was the charge laid against him. Here is J. B. Pratt in 1909, taking on James view that religious hypotheses can be believed to be true if so believing would be good for one:

> Pragmatism ... seeks to prove the truth of religion by its good and satisfactory consequences. Here, however, a distinction must be made; namely between the "good," harmonious, and logically confirmatory consequences of religious concepts as such, and the good and pleasant consequences which come from believing these concepts. It is one thing to say a belief is true because the logical consequences that flow from it fit in harmoniously with our otherwise grounded knowledge; and quite another to call it true because it is pleasant to believe. (1909, 186–87)

The difference between the views of Peirce and James can be nicely summarized by Pratt's distinction. Peirce, with two important caveats, holds that "a belief is true because the logical consequences that flow from it fit in harmoniously with our otherwise grounded knowledge" and James seems to hold that a belief is true "because it is pleasant to believe" (1897/1979) One of the caveats with respect to Peirce's view is that, as we have seen, he insisted that he was not giving a reductive definition of truth. The other is that he insisted on a subjunctive formulation: A true belief is such that the logical consequences *would* fit harmoniously with our otherwise grounded knowledge, were we to pursue our investigations as far as they could fruitfully go.

Peirce did not shy away from the kind of question prompted by Frankfurt's analysis of bullshit. He argued that the pragmatist can justify the aims of understanding the world, predicting the future course of experience, and the like over the aims of getting agreement in the community, making one feel comfortable, and making one look clever and interesting. He was one of those who reacted strenuously to James' view: "I thought your *Will to Believe* was a very exaggerated utterance, such as injures a serious man very much."[10]

The aims of science, Peirce thought, clearly trump the aims that James put forward. In a nutshell, his argument is that we have no choice but to pay attention to the course of experience, which gives us indexical connection to the real world. Experience impinges upon us, forcing us to take it seriously. And when we do take it seriously, we find that it tends not to lead us astray.[11] Hence, the method of science, which has experience and observation at its core, is the method we ought to adopt. These are epistemic reasons for discriminating between the different aims we might have. These are epistemic reasons for preferring the aims of the scientist or the honest inquirer over those of the liar or bullshitter.

The Peircean pragmatist, that is, is not the "anti-realist" Frankfurt is set against. The Peircean pragmatist thinks that in engaging in the practices of believing, asserting, and acting in the world, we presume that there is a way the world is and that we are trying to articulate how it is. We cannot hope to get this exactly right, as if we could have access to the way the world is independently of our ways of trying to find out about it. But that does not toss us into a sea of conflicting aims and values, with no way of adjudicating which are better than others.

Notes

1. Rorty says that his narratives about pragmatism "tend to center around James's version (or, at least, certain selected versions out of the many that James casually tossed off) of the pragmatic theory of truth" (Rorty 1995, 71).
2. What follows is a potted history. For a more nuanced, supported, and careful account, see Misak (in press) and Misak (forthcoming). Were I to bring Dewey fully into this picture, I would align him with Rorty, in linking not truth, but its stand-in (warranted assertibility) to the actual products of inquiry. [See also Chs. 7 and 8 in this volume – Ed.]
3. See Russell and Moore in Olin (1992).
4. Even here one will find many James scholars and James himself arguing that he did not intend to make this identification. See, for instance, James (1909/1914: xv, 180).
5. See Putnam (1981), Stout (2007), Fine (2007), and Misak (1991/2004).

6. References to Peirce's *Collected Papers* are in standard form: volume number, followed by paragraph number. MSx refers to the Peirce Papers, with X being the manuscript number. For full textual evidence that the following account of the pragmatic maxim is indeed Peirce's view, see Misak (1991/2004): chap. 1.
7. MS 283, p. 39.
8. Of course, the issue will be whether Peirce's pragmatic elucidation is compatible with his analytic definition. But since Peirce thinks that the latter has such limited use (it is useful only to those who need an introduction to the concept), it is clear that he will argue that the pragmatic elucidation is the thing we should be concerned with.
9. Sellars (1962, 29) seems to have seen it as well.
10. Quoted in Perry (1948, 291).
11. For the sustained argument, see Misak (1991/2004), chap. 2.

References

Carus, Paul. 1911. *Truth on Trial: An Exposition of the Nature of Truth*. Chicago: Open Court. Reprinted in *Early Critics of Pragmatism*, vol. 3, ed. John Shook, 1–143. Bristol, England: Thoemmes Press, 2001.

Davidson, Donald. 1996. "The Folly of Trying to Define Truth." *Journal of Philosophy* 87: 263–78.

Fine, Arthur. 2007. "Relativism, Pragmatism, and the Practice of Science." In *New Pragmatists*, ed. Cheryl Misak, 50–68. Oxford: Oxford University Press.

Frankfurt, Harry. 2005. *On Bullshit*. Princeton, NJ: Princeton University Press.

Horwich, Paul. 1990. *Truth*. Oxford: Basil Blackwell.

James, William. 1897/1979. *The Will to Believe and Other Essays in Popular Philosophy*. In *The Works of William James*, vol. 6, ed. Frederick H. Burkhardt, Fredson Bowers, and Ignas K. Skrupskelis. Cambridge, MA: Harvard University Press.

James, William. 1907/1949. *Pragmatism: A New Name for Some Old Ways of Thinking*. New York: Longmans Green and Co.

James, William. 1909/1914. *The Meaning of Truth: A Sequel to Pragmatism*. New York: Longmans Green and Co.

Misak, Cheryl. 1991/2004. *Truth and the End of Inquiry: A Peircean Account of Truth*, 2nd ed. Oxford: Oxford University Press, 2004.

Misak, Cheryl. In press. "The Reception of Early American Pragmatism." In *The Oxford Handbook of American Philosophy*, ed. Cheryl Misak. Oxford: Oxford University Press.

Misak, Cheryl. Forthcoming. *The American Pragmatists*. Oxford: Oxford University Press.

Moore, G. E. 1992. "Professor James's Pragmatism." In *William James's Pragmatism In Focus*, ed. Doris Olin, 161–96. London: Routledge.

Olin, Doris, ed. 1992. *William James' Pragmatism in Focus*. London: Routledge.

Peirce, Charles Sanders. 1931–35, 1958. *Collected Papers of Charles Sanders Peirce*, i–iv, ed. C. Hartshorne and P. Weiss, 1931–35; vii–viii, ed. A. Burks, 1958. Cambridge, MA: Belknap Press.

Peirce, Charles Sanders. Unpublished. *Charles S. Peirce Papers*. Houghton Library, Harvard University.

Perry, Ralph Barton. 1948. *The Thought and Character of William James*. Cambridge, MA: Harvard University Press.

Pratt, James B. 1909. *What is Pragmatism?* Reprinted in *Early Critics of Pragmatism*, vol. 1, ed. John Shook, 1–269. Bristol, England: Thoemmes Press, 2001.

Putnam, Hilary. 1981. *Reason, Truth and History*. Cambridge, England: Cambridge University Press.

Russell, Bertrand. 1992. "William James's Conception of Truth." in *William James's Pragmatism In Focus*, ed. Doris Olin, 196–212. London: Routledge.

Rorty, Richard. 1979. *Philosophy and the Mirror of Nature*. Princeton, NJ: Princeton University Press.

Rorty, Richard. 1982. *Consequences of Pragmatism (Essays 1972–80)*. Minneapolis: University of Minnesota Press.

Rorty, Richard. 1995. "Response to Richard Bernstein." In *Rorty and Pragmatism: The Philosopher Responds to his Critics*, ed. H.J. Saakamp, 68–72. Nashville, TN: Vanderbilt University Press.

Rorty, Richard. 2000. "Universality and Truth." In *Rorty and his Critics*, ed. Robert Brandom, 1–30. Oxford: Oxford University Press.

Sellars, Wilfrid. 1962. "Truth and Correspondence." *Journal of Philosophy*, 59: 29–56.

Stout, Jeffrey. 2007. "On Our Interest in Getting Things Right: Pragmatism without Narcissism." In *New Pragmatists*, ed. Cheryl Misak, 7–32. Oxford: Oxford University Press.

Wiggins, David. 2002. "An Indefinibilist cum Normative View of Truth and the Marks of Truth." In *What Is Truth?* ed. R. Shantz, 316–33. Berlin: DeGruyter.

Wiggins, David. 2004. "Reflections on Inquiry and Truth arising from Peirce's Method for the Fixation of Belief." In *The Cambridge Companion to Peirce*, ed. Cheryl Misak, 87–126. Cambridge, England: Cambridge University Press.

Wright, Crispin. 1992. *Truth and Objectivity*. Cambridge, MA: Harvard University Press.

Section 3 Deflationary theories of truth

Editor's introduction

DOUGLAS EDWARDS

Deflationary theories of truth occupy an unusual position in debates about the nature of truth. Unlike the other views under consideration, which presuppose that there is a nature of truth, deflationists deny that there is any nature of truth, and thus the entire project of attempting to discover it is a fool's errand. This is a radical and controversial view, but it has grown considerably in support in recent years, to the extent that it is certainly a – if not the – main player in contemporary discussions of truth.

The term 'deflationism' is a blanket term that covers a range of different views, but they all tend to subscribe to the following central theses:

(1) The word 'true' exists solely to serve some logical and expressive needs.

(2) All occurrences of the word 'true' are explainable in terms of the instances of the basic T schema, being (ES), '<p> is true iff p', for propositions, and (DS), '"p" is true iff p', for sentences. (The angled brackets < > stand for 'the proposition that'.)

(3) There is no 'substantial' property of truth referred to by 'true', and, as a consequence, truth plays no significant explanatory role.

(4) There is an explanatory purity to the word 'true', in the sense that it can be understood alone, without reference to any other notions, such as reference or satisfaction.

Deflationism in the twentieth and twenty-first centuries grew out of what is often called the 'redundancy' theory of truth, often attributed (mistakenly) to F. P. Ramsey (1927). The most extreme form of the redundancy theory would be the view that we do not need the word 'true' in our language at all. This is because it can be eliminated without loss of meaning whenever it occurs. For example, if I say, 'it is true that grass is green', I could equally well have said the very same thing if I had just said 'grass is green'. The extreme redundancy view holds that the statement 'grass is green' has the exact same meaning as 'it is true that grass is green', which shows that the words 'it is true that' have no meaning of their own, and can be discarded. This apparently simple observation of the equivalence between truth-involving and non-truth-involving statements on the face of it demystifies the nature of truth: there is none! This word 'true' which has been the focus of so much discussion and debate is meaningless, and there is no such thing as truth!

While the ideas involved in the expression of this extreme redundancy theory have retained importance, few endorse its strong conclusion that the word 'true' is meaningless. Some, taking influence from Strawson (1950), see the addition of 'it is true that' as adding some performative rhetorical flourish to an assertion, allowing one to make a statement with additional force. This view still limits the scope for investigation into truth, of course, as there is still the denial that there is any interesting nature of truth to uncover beyond the facts about the expressive ways the word is used. Contemporary forms of deflationism, building on the work of Quine (1990), see the equivalences between truth-involving and non-truth-involving statements to be of central importance, but they disagree with the extreme redundancy theorists that the word 'true' can be eliminated without loss from a language. On the contrary, they see the word 'true' as essential to performing certain expressive and logical needs, so not as a redundant predicate at all. However, they do agree that these expressive and logical needs are the only reason we have the word 'true' in our language, and they subsequently deny that there is any deep nature of truth that a substantial philosophical theory is needed to uncover.

To see why deflationists think the word 'true' is useful, we can imagine a language which did not have the word in it, and see some problems that would emerge with a person's ability to express certain thoughts in that language. Suppose I want to endorse a particular thing that somebody said, but I don't know exactly what they said. For example, suppose you are at a dinner party and the guests are discussing the wine. Your friend Sarah, who is knowledgeable about wine, remarks on it, but due to the general hubbub you don't manage to hear what she says. Someone then asks for your opinion, and, not being knowledgeable about wine, you simply want to endorse whatever Sarah just said, as you trust her opinion. Without the word 'true' in your repertoire, this is very difficult, if not impossible. Because you don't know what Sarah said, you have to consider all the possible things she could have said, and essentially say something like the following:

If what Sarah just said is that the wine is fresh, then the wine is fresh, and
If what Sarah just said is that the wine is fruity, then the wine is fruity, and
If what Sarah just said is the wine is corked, then the wine is corked, and ...

Evidently, there are many possible things that Sarah could have said about the wine, perhaps even an infinite number, which makes it nigh on impossible for you to endorse what she said to your interlocutor. The addition of the word 'true', though, governed by (ES), comes to your rescue. We can take one of the lines above, such as:

If what Sarah just said is that the wine is fruity, then the wine is fruity.

Using (ES) we can transform this into:

If what Sarah just said is that the wine is fruity, then it is true that the wine is fruity.

We can then replace the singular terms with variables and bind them with a quantifier to get:

(∀x) (If *x* is what Sarah just said, then *x* is true)

This means that, for all things, if what Sarah said is that thing, then that thing is true, which is a more formal way of putting the phrase 'What Sarah just said is true'. This is a much easier way of endorsing what Sarah said than listing all the possible things she could have said. One simply says that, whatever it is that Sarah said, that thing is true. Once again, the word 'true' is involved, but simply as a useful device through the (ES) schema.[1]

This, according to deflationists, is the central reason why we have a word 'true' in our language. They deny that these uses rest on there being some deep metaphysical nature to truth, and thus deny that there is a deep metaphysical nature of truth to be uncovered. Whether this means that they deny that there is a property of being true at all is a matter for debate, and is explored later. We can also note that these uses of 'true' do not require there to be any essential connections between truth and other philosophical concepts, which lends support to the deflationary idea that truth can be understood independently from all other things.

With these in mind, let us turn to discuss the three main forms of deflationism represented here: Horwich's minimalism, Field's disquotationalism and Grover's prosententialism.

Minimalism

Horwich begins with the instances of what he calls the 'Equivalence Schema' (ES), one example of which is:

<snow is white> is true iff snow is white.

The similarities between the instances of ES and the T instances we looked at in relation to Tarski should be evident, but they differ in that the ES instances use propositions as the primary truthbearers, and the T instances use sentences. Horwich argues that the ES instances comprise the essential things that one needs to know about truth. Having a grasp of the concept of truth, for Horwich, is just being disposed to accept all the ES instances. Moreover, unlike Tarski, who thought that the T instances were in need of some explanation, Horwich holds that they are 'epistemologically basic', and, as such, are incapable of any further explanation. For Horwich, we have a brute disposition to accept such instances, and no substantive explanation for them can be given: they capture a basic fact about our use of the word 'true'.

It is important to note that Horwich does not think that we can give a general schema for the instances of ES in the way that Tarski thought we could give a general schema for T. Horwich's minimalist theory of truth does not provide a general principle which is applicable to all true propositions, rather it is just comprised of the (perhaps infinite) list of the particular instances of ES. The best Horwich can offer by way of generalization of ES is that all propositions that have the form

<<p> is true iff p>

are guaranteed to be true. We will explore the reasons for this later when comparing minimalism with disquotationalism.

Horwich's claim is that truth is deceptively simple. The concept of truth is given by just the list of ES equivalences, and possessing the concept of truth is to have the disposition to accept any such instance. One we have the instances up and running, the truth predicate is able to perform the important linguistic functions we discerned earlier, and, according to Horwich, this is all we need from truth.

There is no substantial property of being true that all true propositions have for Horwich, and at most all true propositions have the 'lightweight' property of falling under the concept of truth. Having outlined his view, Horwich spends the majority of his paper defending the view from a battery of objections, and, in doing so, clarifies the content of the position further. Many of the objections Horwich responds to can be found in other chapters in this volume, and it is worth familiarizing yourself with the objections in these chapters as you read Horwich's defences.

Disquotationalism

You may remember Harty Field from Section 1, where we saw that he outlined a development of Tarski's theory of truth in the spirit of the correspondence theory. Field later changed his mind about truth, however, and advocated a form of deflationism known as 'disquotationalism'. This view was developed by Quine (1990), and is similar to minimalism in many of its key ideas, but differs in that it takes utterances of sentences to be the primary bearers of truth, not propositions. This is a relevant difference if you are the sort of philosopher who distrusts propositions, as discussed in the introductory section on truth bearers. Accordingly, the central schema of disquotationalism is the 'disquotational scheme' (DS):

(DS): 'p' is true if and only if p.

The central use of the predicate 'is true' in DS is to remove the quotation marks around 'p', and, in the process, allow one to move from a context in which the sentence is *mentioned* to a context in which the sentence is *used*. This use/mention distinction is important in the philosophy of language, and allows us to distinguish between cases where we are talking about bits of language, such as '"snow is white" is composed of three words', as opposed to talking about the world, such as 'snow is white'. In the former case the sentence 'snow is white' is *mentioned*, as it is the subject of a larger sentence in which it is talked about, and in the latter case the sentence is *used* as it is used to say something about the world, namely that snow is white. It is useful for us to be able to move between these cases, as it allows us to move from talk about the world to talk about language, and back again. The predicate 'is true', according to the disquotationalist, allows us to do precisely this: it takes us directly from a case where we are mentioning a sentence – when we say it is true – to a case where the sentence is used. In doing so we can move from claims about pieces of language (that they are true) to direct claims about the world.

This linguistic function is the central reason why we have a truth predicate in our language for the disquotationalist. Indeed, it is what enables the important functions of the word 'true' discussed earlier. 'True' does not mark some significant property of our sentences, it is merely a device used to allow us to move between talk of language to talk of the world. Field is very explicit about the 'inversion' of thought here in comparison to the Tarski-inspired correspondence theory of truth. He fully acknowledges that, on the disquotationalist view, truth cannot be explained in terms of reference, and that disquotational truth is incompatible with a theory of meaning which uses truth as an explanatory resource. In fact, Field sees these features as assets of the view, which plays a central role in 'dethroning' the influential idea that the meaning of a sentence is given by the conditions under which it is true.

One key difference between minimalism and disquotationalism is the generalizability of their core schema. As we saw above, the minimalist cannot give a general statement of ES, with the most they can say being that all propositions that have the form <<p> is true iff p> are true. This means that the minimalist theory is made up of not a single principle but the infinite list of instances of ES. Field, on the other hand, holds that there is a general statement of DS available to the disquotationalist. This is because Field accepts *substitutional quantification*, which allows quantification over sentences and not just objects. Field's generalized version of DS is as follows:

Πp ('p' is true if and only if p)

The symbol Π is the universal substitutional quantifier, and ranges over all sentences. The principle holds that the sentence in the brackets will be true for any candidate sentence, p, that one chooses to plug into it. This allows the disquotational theory to be expressed as a single principle, as opposed to a long list of instances. The reason for this difference is that Horwich rejects substitutional quantification in this context, as he holds that it can only be understood in terms of truth, and hence is not a suitable thing to be used to generate an axiom of a theory of truth.

Prosententialism

Suppose you say, 'snow is white', and I say, 'that's true'. On one way of looking at this, what has happened is that I have taken something you have said – 'snow is white' – and attributed a particular property – being true – to that sentence. On a second way of looking at the situation, I have just simply said the same thing you said, but in different words.

This second interpretation is the idea behind the *prosentential theory of truth*, advocated by Dorothy Grover. Grover sees the word 'true' not as a predicate, which is the way all the other theories of truth see it, but rather as what she calls a 'prosentence'. We can explain prosentences by reference to pronouns. We often use pronouns as shorthand to help us say things more easily and quickly. For example, if you say, 'Did you see the game last night?', and I say, 'Yes, it was crazy', then I have used the word 'it' as a pronoun rather than saying in response, 'Yes, the game was crazy', which would seem like an unusual thing to say given that you have already made clear what we are talking about. Likewise if I say, 'Kane hit the bar, and then he hit the post', I use the word 'he' as a pronoun, which is used as shorthand to enable me to avoid having to repeat the name twice given that I have made clear who I am talking about. Words like 'he', 'she', and 'it' are pro*nouns* as they stand in for proper nouns in sentences once it is clear what or who is being talked about. Pro*sentences* work in a similar way: once it is clear what sentence is being discussed, a prosentence can be used in place of the original sentence. So, in our original example, when you say, 'snow is white', and I say, 'that's true', I'm using the phrase 'that's true' as a prosentence: it is something that stands in for the sentence 'snow is white', and it allows me to express my agreement with you without simply repeating what you have said, which would seem conversationally awkward. This allows for expediency in other cases as well, such as in the expression of arguments. Suppose you say, 'snow is cold', it is easier for me to then say, 'if that's true, we should bring coats to Alaska' than to rather robotically say in response, 'if snow is cold, we should bring coats to Alaska'.

The idea of the prosentential theory of truth is that this is the primary function of the word 'true' in our language: to serve as a prosentence. This marks a divergence from all the other theories of truth available, as all other theories take 'is true' to be a *predicate*, not a prosentence. This feature frees the prosentential theory from having to think of truth as a *property*, in any sense, as we only need to think of truth as a property if we take 'is true' to be a predicate. This is particularly useful from a deflationary perspective, as now tricky issues about truth's status as a lightweight or insignificant property are removed altogether.

However, you may have noticed that the examples given to drive the prosentential theory are all contexts of a specific sort: they are cases where one person wants to re-assert something another person has said. What about cases where this does not happen, such as if I simply assert 'it is true that snow is white', without any reference to what has been said by anyone else (or myself) beforehand? In cases like these the prosentential theory holds that the attribution of truth is redundant, and can simply be removed without loss of meaning. That is, it holds that the words 'it is true that' can be removed, and my assertion just considered to be the assertion of the sentence 'snow is white'. This is where the DS scheme is used by the prosentential theory, as it can be seen as providing, for specific truth ascriptions, a procedure for eliminating the ascription of truth. For example, if we take the ascription of truth to 'snow is white', we can use the relevant instance of DS to show how we can replace that truth ascription with the equivalent sentence of 'snow is white':

'snow is white' is true iff snow is white

What the prosententialist is able to do is simply substitute the left-hand side of the biconditional for the right-hand side, and thus eliminate the occurrence of 'is true' from the truth ascription. Cases like direct truth ascriptions, the prosententialist thinks, do not call for any analysis of truth, as the word 'true' can be removed without loss of meaning. What this gives us is a view where the word 'true' can either be deleted without loss of meaning, as it is in straightforward truth ascriptions, or, in cases where it cannot be, as it does not make grammatical sense to do so, such as in cases like 'that's true', the word serves as a prosentence, not a predicate.[2]

Grover's paper contrasts the prosentential theory of truth with disquotationalism, and argues that the prosentential theory is the better view. One key area of dispute involves the idea that the word 'true' performs the disquotationalist's key linguistic function of allowing movement between talk of language and talk of the world. Think back to our two interpretations at the start of this section of the exchange where you say, 'snow is white', and I say, 'that's true'. There is an important difference between the two interpretations we gave: in the first case the word 'true' is used to ascribe a particular property – truth – to a linguistic entity – a sentence; whereas in the second case the word 'true' is used to directly say something about the world, namely that snow is white. This is because in the second case the idea is that saying 'that's true' simply re-asserts the initial sentence, which was attributing whiteness to snow, and says nothing about the properties of any linguistic entity. This is one distinctive aspect of the prosentential view: unlike the disquotational theory, it does not see 'true' as a predicate of sentences; instead, it sees it as a way to say just what sentences themselves say. In this way, truth ascriptions are always about the world, so to speak, and are never about sentences. Thus the word 'true' cannot be used to move between talk of language and talk of the world, as it is always and only used to talk about the world.

Clarifications

As you will have seen, there are a number of different interpretations of what deflationary theories of truth are. A useful overview and exploration is given in Matti Eklund's paper 'What is deflationism about truth?', where he considers some issues key to the formulation of the view, such as the concept/property distinction, and the idea that truth does not have an explanatory role.

Critiques of deflationism in this volume

Perhaps due to its radical nature, deflationism has prompted a wide array of critical discussion. Many of the key objections to deflationism are contained in papers in other sections of this volume. I will list the relevant papers, and page numbers within those papers if necessary, for each of the references. I also recommend consulting the corresponding section introductions for more details on the arguments.

Ch. 14, Donald Davidson, 'The Folly of Trying to Define Truth', pp. 231–235
Ch. 16, Crispin Wright, 'Truth: A Traditional Debate Reviewed', pp. 257–263
Ch. 18, Gila Sher, 'In Search of a Substantive Theory of Truth', pp. 302–307
Ch. 20, Michael Lynch, 'Minimalism and the Value of Truth'
Ch. 21, Huw Price, 'Truth as Convenient Friction'

Notes

1. This discussion in section draws upon Edwards (2018: 23–4).
2. Ibid., 12–13.

Further reading

The literature on deflationism is large, and a useful overview is given by Stoljar and Damnjanovic (2010). For Horwich's minimalism, the classic book is Horwich (1998a), and his position is expanded in Horwich (1998b, 2010). For disquotationalism, Quine (1990) and Leeds (1978) are recommended. For prosententialism, Brandom (1994) develops the view further, and see also Beebe (IEP). A useful resource for a number of additional texts on deflationism is Armour-Garb and Beall (2005), which is a volume dedicated to deflationism. Additional influential critiques of deflationism are given by Gupta (1993) and Bar-On and Simmons (2007). See also Wright (1992), Lynch (2009), and Edwards (2018) for extended critiques. In terms of introductory volumes on truth, discussion of deflationism can be found in Künne (2003, Chs. 2.2.4, 4, and 6), Engel (2002, Ch. 2), Wrenn (2015, Chs. 6 and 8) and Burgess and Burgess (2011, Ch. 3).

References

Armour-Garb, B. and Beall, J. C. (eds) 2005. *Deflationary Truth*. Chicago: Open Court.

Bar-On, D. and Simmons, K. 2007. The Use of Force Against Deflationism. In D. Greimann and G. Siegwart (eds), *Truth and Speech Acts: Studies in the Philosophy of Language*. New York: Routledge, 61–87.

Beebe, J. IEP. Prosentential Theory of Truth. In J. Fieser and B. Dowden (eds), *Internet Encyclopedia of Philosophy*, URL = http://www.iep.utm.edu/truthpro/

Brandom, R. 1994. *Making It Explicit*. Cambridge: Harvard University Press.

Burgess, P. and Burgess, A. 2011. *Truth*. Princeton: Princeton University Press.

Edwards, D. 2018. *The Metaphysics of Truth*. Oxford: Oxford University Press.

Engel, P. 2002. *Truth*. Chesham: Acumen Press.

Gupta, A. 1993. A Critique of Deflationism. *Philosophical Topics* 21 (2): 57–81.

Horwich, P. 1998a. *Truth: Second Edition*. Oxford: Oxford University Press.

Horwich, P. 1998b. *Meaning*. Oxford: Oxford University Press.

Horwich, P. 2010. *Truth-Meaning-Reality*. Oxford: Oxford University Press.

Künne, W. 2003. *Conceptions of Truth*. Oxford: Oxford University Press.

Leeds, S. 1978. *Erkenntnis* 13: 111–29.

Lynch, M. P. 2009. *Truth as One and Many*. Oxford: Oxford University Press.

Quine, W. V. 1990. *Pursuit of Truth*. Cambridge: Harvard University Press.

Ramsey, F. P. 1927. Facts and Propositions. *Proceedings of the Aristotelian Society*, 7 (1): 153–70.

Stoljar, D. and Damnjanovic, N. 2010. The Deflationary Theory of Truth, *Stanford Encyclopedia of Philosophy*, (Fall 2014 Edition), Edward N. Zalta (ed.), URL = http://plato.stanford.edu/archives/fall2014/entries/truth-deflationary

Strawson, P. 1950. Truth. *Proceedings of the Aristotelian Society* XXIV: 111–28.

Wrenn, C. 2015. *Truth*. Cambridge: Polity Press.

Wright, C. J. G. 1992. *Truth and Objectivity*. Cambridge: Harvard University Press.

10 A defense of minimalism

PAUL HORWICH

My aim in this paper is to clarify and defend a certain 'minimalist' thesis about truth: roughly, that the meaning of the truth predicate is fixed by the schema, 'The proposition *that p* is true if and only if p'.[1] The several criticisms of this idea to which I wish to respond are to be found in the work of Davidson, Field, Gupta, Richard, and Soames, and in a classic paper of Dummett's. But before addressing these criticisms let me begin by saying something more about the thesis itself.

Consider biconditionals like

<snow is white> is true ↔ snow is white

and

<lying is wrong> is true ↔ lying is wrong[2]

– that is, instances of the *equivalence schema*

<p> is true ↔ p

It can be argued that such biconditionals are *epistemologically fundamental* – *we* do not arrive at them, or seek to justify our acceptance of them, on the basis of anything more obvious or more immediately known. It can be argued, in addition, that our underived inclination to accept these biconditionals is the source of *everything else* we do with the truth predicate. For example, from the premises

What he said is that he was abducted

and

What he said is true

we are prepared to infer

He was abducted

This particular use of the word "true" is explained by supposing that we first employ Leibniz's Law to get from our pair of premises to

<He was abducted> is true

and then invoke the relevant instance of the equivalence schema. And, more generally, it can be made plausible that no further fact about the truth predicate – nothing beyond our allegiance to the equivalence schema – is needed to explain *any* of our ways of using it. It is for this reason that we are entitled to conclude that the meaning of "true" is determined by that schema. For, plausibly, the property of a word that constitutes its having the particular meaning that it has should be identified with the property that best coheres with our strongest pre-theoretical convictions about meaning – in particular, that a word's meaning what it does helps explain when sentences containing it are accepted, and is recognized (via inference to the best explanation) on the basis of the observation of such facts of use.[3] Thus my minimalist thesis is the product of two prior claims: first, that our underived endorsement of the equivalence schema is explanatorily fundamental with respect to the overall use of the truth predicate; and second, that a word's meaning what it does is engendered by the fact about it that explains its overall use.

This line of thought can be challenged at various points and no doubt stands in need of considerable further support.[4] But my main aim here is not to defend my *route* to the minimalist conclusion, but rather to defend that conclusion itself: namely, that the meaning of "true" stems from the equivalence schema. For most of the recent objections to this thesis do not target any particular rationale for it, but purport to demonstrate that the thesis itself cannot be correct. However, before addressing these objections, let me help to prepare the ground for my replies to them by saying a little more to clarify just what the proposal is, and is not, intended to encompass.

Several different kinds of theory, with very different explanatory objectives, might appropriately be labeled "theories of truth". So it is important to be clear about what sort of theoretical work the minimalist proposal is not meant to do and should not be blamed for failing to do. In the first place, it is not intended to provide an *explicit definition* of the word "true", neither descriptive nor stipulative; it does not offer a way of re-articulating the contents of sentences containing the word; indeed, it implies that no such reformulations are possible.[5] In the second place, the proposal does not amount to a substantive *reductive theory* of the property of being true – something in the style of 'water is H_2O' – which would tell us how truth is constituted at some underlying level. Again, it suggests that the search for such a theory would be misguided. And in the third place, it is not a 'theory of truth' in the sense of a set of fundamental theoretical postulates on the basis of which all other facts about truth can be explained.[6] Its immediate concern is with the *word* "true" rather than with truth itself. It purports to specify which particular non-semantic property of that word is responsible for its meaning what it does; and the property it so specifies is, roughly speaking, the role of that word in the equivalence schema.

Now let me turn to an array of objections. I will look at one difficulty raised by Hartry Field, three devised by Anil Gupta, one due to Mark Richard, a couple that I put to myself, an old but still influential objection of Michael Dummett's, and two posed by Donald Davidson. My discussion of each of these problems will be brief – merely indicating the lines along which I think the response should be given, rather than giving it in full. In some cases these responses will be somewhat concessive – involving certain significant adjustments of the minimalist thesis.

Objection 1: The minimalist proposal would leave it mysterious how we are able to attribute meanings to sentences that predicate truth of *untranslatable* foreign statements. If an utterance V is known to mean (say) *that dogs bark,* then (according to the proposal) the sentence "V is true" (or "V expresses a truth") might be interpreted as saying roughly *that dogs bark.* However, given an utterance, U, that cannot be translated into our language, the proposal enables us to attach no meaning at all to "U is true" – even though it surely *would* be meaningful. So the minimalist proposal is defective.

(Field[7])

But, as I stressed from the outset, the minimalist form of deflationism does not offer an explicit or contextual definition of "true": it does not purport to provide a way of reformulating or re-articulating the content of each sentence containing the word "true". On the contrary, it insists that no such a thing is possible. So one cannot reasonably complain that the minimalist proposal fails to yield a conceptual analysis of "U is true".

One certainly *could* complain if the proposal implied that this sentence lacked meaning – but it has no such implication. It aims to specify the underlying use-property in virtue of which the truth predicate means what it does. To that end, it identifies certain deployments of that predicate as explanatorily fundamental and hence meaning-constituting – namely, those that appear in instances of the equivalence schema. But other tokens of the word may perfectly well have the very same meaning, as long as their deployment is partially explained by the fundamental ones. Thus if a person reasons inductively to "U expresses something true" on the basis of the fact that the other assertions of the speaker – those that *can* be translated – have turned out to be true (where those 'turnings out' depend on applying the equivalence schema), then that person uses the truth predicate with a constant meaning, one that is engendered by the schema.

Objection 2: The equivalence schema is not strong enough to identify the meaning of the truth predicate, because exactly parallel schemata are satisfied by predicates that do not mean the same as "true". For example, instances of the schema, '<p> is true-and-not-red ↔ p', are just as obviously correct as instances of the equivalence schema (since, obviously, no proposition is red). But "is true and not red" is not a strict *synonym* of the truth predicate. More generally, the schema, '<p> is f ↔ p', will be endorsed relative to a variety of predicates, "f", that possess somewhat different meanings from one another; therefore, for no given "f", can it be that our acceptance of instances of '<p> is f ↔ p' is what fixes "f"'s meaning.

(Gupta[8])

Indeed. However, what qualifies some property of a word (e.g. some particular way of deploying it) to be the *meaning* of that word is, of course, not merely the word's *possession* of that property, but also that this possession plays a fundamental role in explaining the word's overall use. And in the case of the truth predicate that, quite plausibly, is what's done by our tendency to accept instances of the equivalence schema. This is the basic law of use for "true" that governs all of the word's occurrences. Certainly there are parallel schemata, constructed with other predicates in place of "true" that are no less acceptable. However, in any such case our commitment to the parallel schema is not an underived explainer of the predicate's overall deployment; rather, that commitment is itself explained in part by the truth-predicate's meaning-constituting use.

For example, our acceptance of instances of '<p> is glub ↔ p' – where "glub" abbreviates "true and not red" – is a consequence of three more basic commitments: (i) our endorsing the equivalence schema for "true", (ii) our accepting "No proposition is red", and (iii) our accepting "x is glub ↔ x is true and not red". The meaning of "glub" is given by (iii), rather than by the 'glub'-schema. Only in the case of the *truth* predicate does the schema capture what is explanatorily basic in our usage of the predicate. So only in *that* case is the schema meaning-constituting.

> Objection 3: The minimalist proposal implies *either* that the word "true" will never be fully understood *or* that the meaning of each person's truth predicate depends on, and varies with, whatever else is in his vocabulary. For the proposal is tantamount to the definition:
>
> x is true = [x = <dogs bark> & dogs bark; or
> x = <pigs fly> & pigs fly; or
> ... and so on]
>
> Therefore, if the "and so on" is intended to cover *all* propositions, then – since some of them must involve concepts that no-one possesses – the meaning of "true" will not be fully known to anyone. And if, alternatively, the definition of each person's truth predicate is supposed to cover only those propositions he himself can currently grasp, then, as new concepts are deployed and new terms coined, his definition of "true" will change. But neither of these alternative implications of minimalism is acceptable. Surely our understanding of the truth predicate is both complete and constant.
>
> (Gupta[9])

Agreed. But my proposal is perfectly consonant with such intuitions, because it is not at all equivalent to the above alleged definition. As already emphasized, the minimalist thesis does not offer anything like an explicit definition. Rather it purports to specify the fact of usage that provides the truth predicate with its meaning. That fact of usage, it claims, is the explanatory role of our inclination to accept instances of the equivalence schema – a fact that remains fixed as the rest of our language evolves. So, for example, at the moment that the term, "tachyon", enters our language, we become inclined to accept

<tachyons go backwards in time> is true ↔ tachyons go backwards in time

But this is merely one more application of a single and invariable regularity – our inclination to accept any instance of the schema that we understand. That inclination preceded the introduction of the term "tachyon" and was in no way altered by it. Thus the minimalist thesis implies neither that the meaning of the word "true" can't be fully grasped, nor that it changes with expansions of our vocabulary.[10]

> Objection 4: Our reliance on the equivalence schema will not suffice to explain our commitment to *general* facts about truth. Consider, for example, "All propositions of the form, <p → p>, are true". No doubt our *particular* logical convictions of that form, together with our acceptance of the equivalence schema, can explain, *for any single proposition,* why we take it to be true that this proposition implies itself. Thus we can explain, given our logical commitment to "dogs bark → dogs bark", why we also accept "The proposition *that dogs bark → dogs bark* is true". But we have not

> thereby explained how the above *generalization* is reached. Therefore our allegiance to the equivalence schema does not really suffice to account for *all* uses of the truth predicate. So that practice does not fix the meaning of "true", contrary to what the minimalist maintains.
>
> (Gupta, Soames[11])

Granted, if all uses of "true" are to be accounted for, it will not be enough *merely* to cite our allegiance to the equivalence schema. Further explanatory premises will be needed. But this is an obvious and familiar point. Note, for example, the reference above to our acceptance of "dogs bark + dogs bark" in explaining why we accept "The proposition *that dogs bark + dogs bark* is true". That is perfectly consistent with minimalism because the further explanatory factor makes no mention of the word "true". So perhaps the present objection can be defused in the same way?

In other words, it remains to be seen whether or not the extra factors needed to account for our acceptance of *generalizations* explicitly concern the word "true". Only if they do can one conclude that the explanatorily adequate regularities of use governing "true" must go beyond our underived acceptance of "<p> is true ↔ p" – so that minimalism is defective. But we have been given no reason to think that this is so. On the contrary, there is good reason to suspect that it isn't so.

Suppose it were the case that whenever anyone is disposed to hold, concerning each F, that it is G, then he comes, on that basis, to believe that every F is G. Our disposition to accept, for each proposition of a certain form, that it is true would then suffice to explain our acceptance of the generalization, "Every proposition of that form is true".

Now this particular response to the objection can't be right as it stands, because the proposed extra explanatory premise is glaringly incorrect. It is *not* always the case that having shown, for each F, that it is G, one will inevitably come to the belief that all Fs are G. After all, such demonstrations may well coincide with the mistaken conviction that not all the Fs have been considered. Imagine, for example, that someone mistakenly suspects that there are mountains higher than Everest. He might nevertheless be able to show, of every actual mountain, that it is no higher than Everest; but he does not believe the generalization that all mountains have that property.

However, a modified version of this strategy is much more promising. Let us restrict the proposed extra premise to kinds of entity, F, and properties, G, that satisfy the following condition:

> We cannot conceive of there being additional Fs – beyond those Fs we are disposed to believe are G – which we would not have the same sort of reason to believe are G.

This restriction is satisfied when (a) it is essential to our conception of the Fs to maintain that all Fs result from the application of certain operations to certain basic Fs (– thus Fs might be propositions, numbers, or sets); and (b) given any such F, there is a uniform way of proving it to be G.

Thus a more plausible version of our extra premise would run along the following lines:

> Whenever someone is disposed to accept, for any proposition of structural type F, that it is G (and to do so for uniform reasons) then he will be disposed to accept that every F-proposition is G.

And this will do the trick. We are indeed disposed to accept, for any proposition of the form, <p → p> , that it is true. Moreover, the rules that account for these acceptances are the same no matter which proposition of that form is under consideration. Therefore it is now possible to infer that we accept that all such propositions are true, and hence to *explain* why we do so.

Thus we have a sound explanatory premise which, in conjunction with our commitment to '<p> is true ↔ p', will enable us to explain our acceptance of generalizations about truth. And since that premise does not mention the word, "true", the need for it does nothing to suggest that the basic (hence, meaning-constituting) use of it must exceed the bounds set by minimalism.[12]

> Objection 5: Certain people (mostly philosophers) do *not* in fact have a completely general inclination to endorse the equivalence schema. Some hold that ethical pronouncements fail to yield acceptable instances. Others take that view of contingent statements about the future, or of applications of vague predicates to borderline cases, or of sentences containing empty names. But all these people nevertheless mean the same thing as we do by the word "true". After all, we might argue with them about "Whether ethical pronouncements can be true?" – yet each of us expresses the issue in just that way. Consequently, it cannot be that to understand the English truth predicate one must have an inclination to accept *every* instance of the schema. (Richard[13])

Notice that the present objection is not that certain instances of the equivalence schema actually *are* incorrect, or that some of them are unhesitatingly rejected by everyone. The point rather is that even if someone – perhaps, mistakenly – has no inclination to *accept* a certain class of instances, he might nonetheless *understand* them exactly as we do. And so we have to conclude, it would seem, that an endorsement of the *general* schema is *not* what provides the word "true" with its meaning.

But this conclusion is unwarranted. For we can invoke *social externalism* in order to reconcile our minimalist thesis with the facts under consideration. The rough idea is that a word is a social entity with a certain public meaning, and each member of the linguistic community will (unless he has decided otherwise) deploy the word with that meaning – even if his own usage of it diverges radically from everyone else's. What fixes that shared meaning is the basic use that *predominates* within the community (or, in the case of a technical term, within the sub-community in which it is deployed). After all, it is such 'predominant basic use' that translation mappings are attempting to preserve.

Now, our word "true" is not a merely technical term. And most people's use of it is unaffected by philosophical fretting, so tends to be governed by the *full* equivalence schema. Therefore, its shared meaning derives from that characteristic. And even those few who are inclined to reject certain instances of it are nonetheless using the truth predicate with that shared meaning.

> Objection 6: But what about the notorious *paradox*-inducing instances of the schema – e.g. the one that results from applying it to the statement *that this very statement is not true?* It is easy to prove that such instances lead to contradiction. *As* a consequence, many of us have learned not to accept them. Indeed, most people, *were they* to grasp *the* relevant proofs, *would* agree that those instances are unacceptable. Thus our

meaning what we do by "true" does not require us (or most of us, or the 'experts' among us) to have a disposition to accept *every* instance of the equivalence schema.

It seems to me that this point is correct, but not devastating. One way of accommodating it is to concede that the meaning of "true" does not derive from an *entirely* unrestricted equivalence schema. Rather, it might be said, the basic meaning-constituting practice is merely to accept patently non-paradoxical instances-instances concerning propositions, like <snow is white> and <lying is wrong>, that make no mention of truth. Given these, we are then tempted to generalize and to accept *all* instances of the schema. But when this conclusion is found to lead into contradiction, the retreat back to a more constrained schema need involve no revision of the meaning-constituting use of "true".

However, there's an alternative strategy – one that strikes me as preferable. Instead of linking the meaning of "true" with the disposition to wholeheartedly accept a certain restricted class of instances, we might link it with the *defeasible inclination* to accept *any* instance. We might suppose that, in paradoxical cases, this inclination is over-ridden; but that it nonetheless continues to exist – sustaining the sense of paradox.

Objection 7: Mightn't there be a foreign linguistic community in which the very existence of truth is widely debated – in which *some* people are disposed to accept some (or all) instances of their equivalence schema – '<p> is schmoo ↔ p' – but some reject it altogether, and most are simply not sure? And isn't it natural to report them (as I just did) as disagreeing about the reality of *truth?* Wouldn't their word "schmoo" mean exactly the same as our "true"?

If so, then the social externalism of meaning will not suffice to rescue minimalism. The moral will be, rather, that there must be some way of using "true" that (a) is implicit in, but *weaker* than, an endorsement of the equivalence schema, (b) is displayed by the community of truth-debaters (but with "schmoo" in place of "true") and by ourselves, and (c) constitutes what both communities mean by their words. And this conclusion would seem to be at odds with minimalism.

However, there is a natural minimalist way to implement it. We must appreciate that even the truth-sceptics are prepared sometimes to *suppose for the sake of argument* (what they do not actually believe) that certain things are "schmoo". And when they do this, they will proceed within the context of this supposition to 'accept' their equivalence schema. In addition, when they suppose, again merely for the sake of argument, that *some* schema of the form, '<p> is Φ ↔ p', holds, they *will* be prepared to infer (relative to that supposition) instances of '<p> is schmoo ↔ p'. Moreover, we non-skeptics also follow these rules – but using "true" instead of "schmoo".[14] Thus we have here a way of deploying the equivalence schema that is shared by skeptics and non-skeptics alike, and this is what we can take to provide a truth predicate with its meaning.

Objection 8: Truth is valuable: we ought to pursue it and we ought to avoid false belief. But these normative sentiments are not contained in (nor can they be extracted from) instances of '<p> is true ↔ p', which merely tell us *when* beliefs possess the property of being true, and are completely silent on the question of whether its possession is desirable. Consequently, our concept of truth is not fully captured by the equivalence schema; so the minimalist proposal is false.

(Dummett[15])

On the contrary, there is no tension at all between recognizing the value of truth and the minimalist view that our use of "true" is adequately explained by the equivalence schema. To see this, consider proposition-specific norms of belief such as

It is desirable that (one believe *that wombats fly* ↔ wombats fly)

Clearly our commitments to norms like this one have nothing to do with the concept of truth; for that concept is completely absent from their articulation. Nor is there any reason to suppose that the concept of truth will need to be deployed in explaining *why* we accept them.

Let us then imagine that all such specific normative commitments are somehow explained.[16] Suppose, that is, we can account for our attachment to all norms of the form

It is desirable that (one believe *that p* ↔ p)

Given our a priori knowledge of the equivalence schema, we will then be able to explain our attachment to every norm of the form

It is desirable that (one believe <p> ↔ <p> is true)

that is, to every norm of the form

It is desirable that (one believe x ↔ x is true)

But this engenders (via the mechanism discussed in the response to Objection 4) a commitment to the generalization

(x) [It is desirable that (one believe x ↔ x is true)]

– or, in English, to the principle

It is desirable to believe what is true and only what is true.

Thus our view about what we should want regarding the truth of our beliefs has two sources: first, our disposition to commit ourselves to anything of the form, "It is desirable *that one believe that p* ↔ *p*"; and second, our use of "true" to package all of those commitments together – which we are able to do thanks to the equivalence schema.

Objection 9: The minimalist proposal implies that the meaning of the word, "true", depends on the meaning of the expressions, "the proposition that ...". For someone's acceptance of, for example, "The proposition *that Hesperus rotates* is true if and only if Hesperus rotates" manifests a standard understanding of the truth predicate only to the extent that its component, "The proposition that ...", is being understood in the standard way. Thus minimalism implies that one must *already* understand "that"-clauses – i.e. one must understand sentences of the form "u expresses the proposition *that p*" – in order to be in a position to acquire the concept of truth. But this surely gets things the wrong way round! Surely the intimately related notions of meaning and proposition must be analysed in terms of truth (or better, perhaps, must be *replaced* by truth-conditional notions). More specifically, we must suppose that, insofar as there are any facts of the form

u means (says, expresses the proposition) *that p*

their presence must be inferred from facts of the form

u is true (i.e. expresses a truth) if and only if p

> Thus truth is conceptually prior to meaning, contrary to what is required by the minimalist proposal.
>
> (Davidson[17])

Davidson gives three reasons for thinking that TRUTH is a more basic concept than MEANING.

First and foremost there's his signature idea: namely that our capacity to understand the complex expressions of a language requires that their meanings be derivable from the meanings of the component words, and that this possibility (this so-called *compositionality of meaning*) requires that the meanings of sentences be inferred from their truth conditions which are themselves logically deduced (a la Tarski) from reference-theoretic articulations of the meanings of words.

But this perspective may well be resisted. For, in the first place, it's far from obvious that Davidsonian truth-theories can be found for *natural* languages, (a) because so many natural language sentences defy formalization in logical terms, and (b) because the step Davidson needs to take from the deduced truth condition of a *logical* sentence to the truth condition of the sentence it formalizes depends on a notion of meaning-equivalence that's beyond his resources. And, in the second place, there's a simple alternative to Davidson's way of arriving at sentence-meanings from word-meanings – a way that's not at all truth-theoretic, that's free of the above difficulties, and that was successfully deployed well before Davidson came along. The natural way of translating a certain foreign sentence is by finding a sentence of our own that has the same structure and whose words have the same meanings as the corresponding foreign words. We can pursue interpretation simply *assuming* that meaning is compositional, and without feeling the need to explain how it can be.

Davidson's second reason for thinking that TRUTH is a more basic concept than MEANING is that there are sentences (such as "That is red") whose meaning-constituting, acceptability conditions are to accept those sentences only when they are *true.*

But the inference from this fact to Davidson's conclusion involves several mistakes:

(1) It neglects the fact that, for each specific sentence, p, of that special sort, its acceptability condition takes the form, 'One should accept "p" only *if* p' – in which *the concept of truth is not deployed.* This concept is needed only by the theoretician who wishes to make the *general* point that there are sentences of that kind (i.e. to be accepted only when true). It isn't needed to formulate any *particular* acceptability condition.

(2) His rationale wrongly presupposes that meaning-constituting regularities or rules of use are *explicitly* known by the speakers of a language. Even if the truth-predicate *were* to be needed in order to articulate the fact about a person that underlies her understanding of some word (e.g. her respect for a certain acceptability condition), we could not conclude that she herself would have to possess the concept of truth.

(3) Davidson confuses the conditions for understanding particular non-semantic sentences, like "That is red", with the real issue here – namely, the conditions

> for understanding 'that'-clauses, i.e. for grasping the concept of 'proposition'. Remember that his thesis was that one cannot have the concept of meaning without possessing the concept of truth. Thus the issue is *not* whether one can have various non-semantic concepts – such as 'red' – without the concept of truth.

Davidson's third stated reason for thinking that TRUTH is conceptually prior to MEANING is that *someone's affirmation of a sentence can be justified only if he believes that the sentence is true.* Thus it would seem that the concept of ACCEPTABILITY CONDITION – i.e. of when one is justified in assenting to a sentence – presupposes the concept of truth. And, in that case, (or so he argues), one could not agree with a deflationary order of explanation: which would go from acceptability conditions, to meanings, to truth.

But, in fact, this deflationist-friendly sequence of conceptual dependencies coheres perfectly well with the normative constraint on public affirmation, to which Davidson calls attention. For note first that S's believing *that "p" is true* is equivalent to S's accepting the sentence, ""p" is true", which, given deflationism, correlates with S's accepting "p". In addition – and this is the basic norm here – S *should* assent publicly to "p" only if he privately accepts it. It then follows, as Davidson says, that S should assent to "p" only if and only if he believes it to be true. However, the just-given account of why this norm holds does not preclude that the meanings of terms be constituted by the conditions in which sentences containing them are (or should be) accepted.

It might be protested that what we call "accepting" a sentence is simply a matter, as Davidson would say, of "holding it true". So, relative to the deflationist's 'acceptance-conditions' account of meaning, it may appear that the notion of truth is, after all, prior to the notion of proposition. But this use of the term, "holding true", is a somewhat misleading one, given that the intended commitment –'holding' – is to a sentence that does not contain the truth predicate. The notion needed here is simply that of *relying on* a sentence as a premise in inference (both theoretical and practical), and that psychological role may be explicated without bringing in the notion of truth.[18,19]

> Objection 10: 'That'-clauses cannot be regarded as referring expressions, because there is no way of seeing how their referents would be determined by the referents of their component words. Therefore, sentences like "The proposition *that Hesperus rotates* is true", insofar as they are construed as predicating truth of the entities to which 'that'-clauses refer, are in fact unintelligible. But if such truth ascriptions (so construed) are unintelligible, then the minimalist proposal cannot be correct.
>
> (Davidson[20])

Davidson's basis for maintaining that the alleged referents of 'that'-clauses would not be determinable by the referents of the parts of these clauses is that – as Frege observed – substitution of co-referential terms (e.g. putting "Phosphorus" in place of "Hesperus") within a 'that'-clause occurring in some sentence (e.g. "Mary believes that Hesperus rotates") will not always preserve the sentence's truth value. From which it appears to follow that if the two 'that'-clauses were referring expressions they would have to refer to different things – but inexplicably so, since the referents of their component words are the same. But why doesn't Davidson reject this inference, as Frege does, concluding rather that an expression within a 'that'-clause does not have its *standard* referent, but instead refers to the usual *meaning* (i.e. sense) of that expression? Why not identify the referent of "that Hesperus rotates" with the meaning of "Hesperus rotates" and identify the referents (in that context) of the contained words "Hesperus" and "rotates" with *their* usual meanings?

The reason given is that the meanings of words in 'that'- clauses are obviously just their normal meanings. After all, we understand "The proposition that Hesperus rotates" only if we understand the isolated sentence "Hesperus rotates". And in the biconditional, "The proposition *that Hesperus rotates* is true ↔ Hesperus rotates", the two occurrences of "Hesperus rotates" are clearly supposed to be understood in the same way. But in that case – since meaning determines reference – how could words in 'that'-clauses fail to have their standard referents? And if they do have their standard referents then 'that'-clauses cannot refer, since what would be determined by those standard referents would be the *wrong* thing (e.g. "that Hesperus rotates" would acquire the same referent as "that Phosphorus rotates").

However, there's a pretty obvious response to this anti-Fregean story. We can simply deny that meaning *all by itself* determines reference. We can allow – and this, of course, is completely uncontroversial – that the referent of a term is fixed in part by the *context* in which it occurs. More specifically, we might say that the admittedly uniform meaning of "Hesperus" yields one referent (the planet) for standard (non-opaque) occurrences of the word, and that it yields a different referent (the meaning, or sense, of "Hesperus") for occurrences of the word within the context of a 'that'-clause.

It's worth emphasizing that although our Fregean response is far from problem-free, it is not being introduced ad hoc, merely for the sake of a certain theory of truth. After all, ordinary language is full of 'that'-clauses (e.g. in attributions of belief). And there is no available strategy for dealing with them that is evidently less problematic than Frege's – which is to suppose that they designate entities (nowadays called "propositions"), and that each of our 'attitude' attributions asserts that a certain psychological relation (of believing, or conjecturing, or stating, etc.) holds between a person and one of these entities (so designated).

Finally, the question arises, if one *were* to prefer a non-Fregean semantics for 'that'-clauses, why it could not be deployed by minimalists? Consider, for example, an approach suggested by Davidson's 'paratactic' analysis of 'S says that p'.[21]

We might interpret

The proposition *that Hesperus rotates* is true

as

The proposition expressed by *this* – Hesperus rotates – is true

– where "Hesperus rotates" is uttered as an aside. Thus the equivalence schema would become:

The proposition expressed by *this* (- p -) is true ↔ p

Or, along similar lines, we might reformulate it as:

The proposition expressed by the *immediately following* sentence-token is true ↔ p[22]

Therefore, even if Davidson's squeamishness about Fregean 'that'-clauses were correct – and my first response argued that it is not – the minimalist proposal can be salvaged. For its truth schema may be articulated in one of the two ways just-mentioned.

The *full* minimalist picture of truth includes considerably more than the thesis I have been defending in this paper. It involves, besides the present claim about how the meaning of "true" is constituted, an affiliated view about the *function* of the truth predicate (namely – as illustrated in response to Objection 8 – that it is merely a device of generalization), an affiliated view about the *underlying nature* of truth (namely, that there is no such thing), and an affiliated view about the general shape of the basic theory that will best explain all the facts about truth (namely, that its postulates are instances of the equivalence schema). I have not attempted to elaborate or establish these further minimalist doctrines. However, since what I have been concerned with here is the central component of minimalism, my defense of that thesis, if successful, provides important support for the view as a whole.[23]

Notes

1. For a thorough discussion of the relationship between *deflationism* and *minimalism* about truth, see "Varieties of Deflationism" – Ch. 2 of my *Truth-Meaning-Reality*, Oxford University Press, 2010. But here, for convenience, is a summary. Deflationism is the somewhat vague idea that truth is not a 'substantive' property, that no reductive theory of it should be anticipated, and that our grasp of the truth predicate comes from our appreciation of the trivial way that each statement specifies its own condition for being true. But philosophers who sympathize with this general point of view disagree amongst themselves about how best to elaborate it. Minimalism is one such strategy – the one defended here and previously articulated in my *Truth* (2nd edn., Oxford University Press, 1998). Besides minimalism, the main alternative forms of deflationism about truth are: (l) *disquotationalism,* according to which sentences (rather than propositions) should be regarded as the bearers of truth, and the schema, "p" is true ↔ p, will be the core of what defines the truth predicate; (2) *prosententialism,* which denies that "true" is a genuine (logical) predicate, and which stresses instead the analogy between a pronoun and "That is true" (insofar as both inherit their content from some other contextually salient expression); (3) *the redundancy theory,* whereby "The proposition *that* p is true" means exactly the same as "p"; (4) *the sentence-variable analysis,* which analyses truth-talk in terms of quantification into sentence positions – 'x is true' means '(∃p)(x = <p> & p)'; and (5) *Tarski's theory,* which explains the truth of each sentence of a language in terms of the referential properties of its components (characterized disquotationally) and the logical structure in which they are embedded. The relative advantages of the minimalist version of deflationism are elaborated in the above-cited "Varieties of Deflationism". In a nutshell, its merits are that (a) it deals with our *actual* concept of truth, rather than some allegedly superior one; (b) it does not attempt to explain truth in terms of notions that should themselves be explained in terms of truth (e.g. substitutional quantification); (c) it recognizes that there is no call for an *explicit* definition of truth; (d) it can countenance the attribution of truth to propositions whose logical forms we do not know; and (e) it does justice to the role of truth as a device of generalization.
2. "<p>" abbreviates "the proposition that p"; and "↔" is the *material* biconditional.
3. This view of how meaning-constituting properties of words are to be identified is an instance of the general idea that an underlying property U constitutes a relatively superficial property S

when U's being co-extensive with S explains why S has the characteristics that it does. My speaking of S as being *constituted* by U in those circumstances, rather than as being *identical* to U, requires a fine-grained conception of 'property' whereby two predicates stand for the same property only when they have the same meaning. This way of speaking does not preclude also deploying a more coarse-grained conception whereby, if fine-grained property U constitutes fine-grained property S, then each of them is associated with a single coarse-grained property.

4. For justification of the claim that the equivalence schema is explanatorily fundamental, see *Truth,* pp. 50–1. For justification of the use theory of meaning, see my *Meaning* (Oxford: Clarendon Press, 1998, Ch. 3), *Reflections on Meaning* (Oxford: Oxford University Press, 2004, Ch.2), and "Regularities, Rules, Meanings, Truth Conditions, and Epistemic Norms"-ch. 7 of *Truth-Meaning-Reality*.
5. To claim that "x is true ↔ x is F" is the explicit definition of the truth predicate (where "F" might be replaced with "in correspondence with reality", "verifiable", "useful", etc.) is to claim that our acceptance of such a principle is explanatorily fundamental with respect to our overall use of that predicate. But such a claim is incompatible with the minimalist thesis according to which it is rather our endorsement of the equivalence schema that is explanatorily basic.
6. There is, however, a plausible theory of truth itself that is closely affiliated with the minimalist account of the meaning of the word, "true". Arguably, the axioms of the fundamental theory of truth itself– those that will provides the best explanation (i.e. simplest derivation) of all facts about truth – are instances of '<p> is true ↔ p'. For (a) such axioms would appear to suffice (in conjunction with theories of other matters) to explain every other fact about truth; and (b) it is hard to imagine a simpler body of principles on the basis of which those instances could themselves be explained. For further discussion see *Truth,* pp. 25–31, 50–1.
7. Field, H. "Critical Notice: Paul Horwich's *Truth", Philosophy of Science* 59 (1992) 321–30. The importance of being able to attribute truth to untranslatable statements has been emphasized by Stewart Shapiro. See his "The Guru, the Logician, and the Deflationist", *Nous* 37 (2003), 113–32.
8. This objection was put to me by Gupta in October 1992, and appears in n. 17 of his "Deflationism, the Problem of Representation, and Horwich's Use Theory of Meaning", *Philosophy and Phenomenological Research* 67, (Nov. 2003), 654–66.
9. Gupta, A. "A Critique of Deflationism", *Philosophical Topics* 21 (1993) 57–81; and his "Minimalism", *Philosophical Perspectives* 7 (1993) 359–69.
10. A further objection of Anil Gupta's – one that I *do* think is correct – is that our underived endorsement of the equivalence schema will not explain our refusal to apply truth to things such as Julius Caesar (i.e. it won't explain our confident acceptance of sentences like "Julius Caesar was not true"). To accommodate this point we can suppose that the explanatorily-basic, meaning-constituting facts about "true" include, not merely allegiance to the equivalence schema, but also our underived acceptance of the principle, "Only propositions are true".
11. Gupta, A. "Minimalism". This objection has also been forcefully articulated by Scott Soames in his "The Truth About Deflationism", E. Villanova (ed.) *Philosophical Issues* 8, Atascadero, Cal., Ridgeview Publishing Company, 1997. See also "Some Remarks on Deflationism" (unpublished) by Paolo Casalegno (University of Milan). A version of the problem was raised by Tarski in sect. 5 of "The Concept of Truth in Formalized Languages", *Logic, Semantics, Metamathematics: Papers from 1923 to 1938,* (Oxford: Oxford University Press, 1958).

12. For an extended response to the above 'generalization' problem, see "A Minimalist Critique of Tarski" – Ch. 5 of *Truth-Meaning-Reality*.
13. Richard, M. "Deflating Truth", E. Villanova (ed.), *Philosophical Issues* 8, op. cit. See his book, *When Truth Gives Out,* (Oxford University Press, 2008), for further elaboration of his anti-minimalistic perspective.
14. *This* idea (generalized from TRUTH to other concepts) is elaborated in "Ungrounded Reason", section 5: Ch. 10 of *Truth-Meaning-Reality*. Another way of putting the basic idea here (due to Russell, Carnap, and David Lewis) is that although our acceptance of our fundamental theory of f-ness, "T(f)", suffices to fix the meaning of predicate "f", all that's really necessary for us to give the word that meaning is that we accept the conditional, "If there is a unique property, with the characteristics specified by "T_", then that property is f-ness". Or, in logical terms, "$(\exists!\Phi)\ [T(\Phi)] \rightarrow T(f)$".
15. Dummett, M. "Truth", *Proceedings of the Aristotelian* Society (1959), 141–62. [See also the discussion in Lynch's Ch. 20 of this volume – Ed.] Arguably, a more accurate formulation of our value-of-truth norm will not imply that true belief is *always* worth pursuing. But my response to the present objection will apply no matter which such belief-truth principles are taken to be correct.
16. I would argue that the explanatory basis for our commitment to these specific norms is both *pragmatic* (*insofar* as we are more likely to get what we want if we abide by them) and *moral* (*the* value of truth for its own sake). For more, see my "Belief-Truth Norms" in T. Chan (ed.) *The Aim of Belief*, Oxford University Press, 2013, 17–31.
17. Davidson, D. "The Folly of Trying to Define Truth", *Journal of Philosophy* 87 (1996) 267–78). [This volume, Ch. 14 – Ed.] More accurately, his view is that the meaning-claim is to be inferred from the discovery that: a theorem of the agreement-maximizing truth-theory for the language of u is 'u is true if and only if p'.
18. See my *Meaning,* pp. 84–6, for a sketch of how this can be done.
19. For elaboration of these responses to Davidson see my "Deflating Compositionality", (chapter 8 of *Reflections on Meaning*, Oxford University Press, 2005) and my "Davidson's Wittgensteinian View of Meaning" (in C. Verheggen (ed.) *Wittgenstein and Davidson on Thought, Language, and Action*, Cambridge University Press, 2017).
20. Davidson, D. "The Folly of Trying to Define Truth", *op. cit*. [This volume, Ch. 14 – Ed.]
21. He proposes that "S says that dogs bark" be construed as "S's utterance same-says *that.* Dogs bark." – where the demonstrative in the speaker's supposed first sentence refers to the subsequent utterance of "Dogs bark". See Davidson's "Saying that", collected in his *Essays on Truth and Interpretation.*
22. Clearly these formulations still trade in *propositions*! However, Davidson is careful to emphasize that his complaint about minimalism is *not* its commitment to such things. His point, rather, is that *if* they exist, then the logical form of what designates them must be "The proposition expressed by u" (instead of "The proposition that p"). Perhaps he would be prepared to analyze this along the lines of "The class of utterances that *same-say* u".

    In addition to *Davidson's* critique of minimalism, which focuses on the way that propositions are *designated,* there are several objections to the very *existence* of propositions – objections that a minimalist must be able to rebut. The main ones are (1) that propositions lack satisfactory identity conditions; (2) that *false* propositions do not exist (because any actual combination of objects and properties would amount to a *fact*); (3) that propositions are ontologically weird and explanatorily unnecessary. For discussion of some of these issues, see the end of "Varieties of Deflationism", op. cit. For a more complete discussion see *Truth,* pp, 86–97, 106.

23. I am most grateful to Hartry Field and Michael Lynch for their feedback on the material here.

    The present paper is a somewhat improved version of what appeared under the same title as chapter 3 of my *Truth-Meaning-Reality.* That chapter was in turn a considerably revised version of a paper published, under the same title, in *The Nature of Truth,* ed. M. Lynch (Cambridge, Mass.: MIT Press, 2001). And this was itself a revision of an earlier paper, written for the conference on Truth that took place in Leuwen in 2000, and published with the other conference papers in *Synthese* (vol. 126, Special Issue on Truth, eds. Volker Halbach and Leon Horsten, (2001) pp. 149–165.

11 Deflationist views of meaning and content

HARTRY FIELD

1 Two views of meaning and content

I see the philosophy of language, and the part of philosophy of mind concerned with intentional states like believing and desiring and intending and the like, as pretty much bifurcated into two traditions. The traditions differ over the role that the notion of truth conditions plays in the theory of meaning and in the theory of the content of intentional states.

One of the traditions, whose early advocates include Frege, Russell, the early Wittgenstein, and Ramsey, has it that truth conditions play an extremely central role in semantics and the theory of mind; a theory of meaning or content is at least in large part a theory of truth conditions. A strong prima facie reason for the attractiveness of this position is that the way we standardly ascribe meanings and contents is via "that" clauses, and the ascription of "that" clauses is in effect the ascription of truth conditions: to describe an utterance as meaning that snow is white, or a belief state as a state of believing that snow is white, is in effect to say that the utterance or belief state has the truth conditions that snow is white. Since "that" clauses and hence truth conditions play such a central role in our *ascriptions* of meaning and content, it would seem as if they ought to play a central role in the *theory* of meaning and content. However, it isn't easy to say precisely what this central role is that truth conditions allegedly play; that I think is a main motivation for the alternative tradition.

As a crude paradigm of the other tradition, consider the verifiability theory of meaning. Here the main concept is not truth conditions but verification conditions. The verification conditions of a type of utterance might be given by the class of sensory stimulations that would or should lead to the acceptance of an utterance in that class. Notice that if the verification conditions of a type of utterance are given in this way, then they are given without a "that" clause; and indeed, there is no immediately clear way in which to obtain a "that" clause from them. It is because of this that an advocate of the Frege-Russell-Ramsey-*Tractatus* tradition is likely to react to a verification theory of meaning as leaving out what is central to semantics: a theory of meaning according to which you can fully describe the "meaning" of an utterance without saying that it means *that snow is white* (or that something else) has left out the central element of meaning. That central element is truth conditions.

Some advocates of the Frege-Russell tradition might prefer to describe what has been left out as not truth conditions but *propositional content*. There is a way of understanding this that makes it unobjectionable, but it could be misleading. For a verificationist is likely to simply deny the charge that he has left out propositional content (or even, the charge that he has demoted it from a central place in his theory). A proposition, he can say, is simply a class of verification conditions; for an utterance or belief state to express the proposition is for it to have verification conditions in that class. So propositions in the verificationist's sense needn't be described by "that" clauses: the most direct way to specify a proposition in the verificationist's sense is directly in terms of verification conditions. No one can deny that propositions *so understood* play a central role in the verificationist's theory. An advocate of the Frege-Russell tradition is likely to say that these "propositions" aren't what *she* means by propositions, and that is doubtless so; that is because propositions as she conceives them must *encapsulate truth conditions*. (They may encapsulate more than truth conditions, but they encapsulate at least this much.) So it seems to me that to describe the difference between the two traditions in terms of truth conditions rather than in terms of propositional content brings to the forefront what is really central.

I do not mean to suggest that a verificationist is precluded from speaking of truth or truth conditions; he can do so in either of two ways. One way, which seems to me a very bad idea, is to introduce some epistemic notion of truth conditions: that is, to define truth in terms of verification (e.g. "would be verified in the long run"), so that truth conditions are derivatively defined in terms of verification conditions. I won't discuss this line here. The other way is to make use of what has been called a *deflationary* conception of truth. I take this to have several variants, but the variant I will primarily focus on is called *pure disquotational* truth. As a rough heuristic, we could say that for a person to call an utterance true in this pure disquotational sense is to say that it is true-as-he understands-it. (This is *not* intended to provide a *definition* of pure disquotational truth in terms of some other notion of truth plus a notion of understanding; it is intended only as a heuristic, to motivate the features of pure disquotational truth I now proceed to enumerate.) As the heuristic suggests, a person can meaningfully apply "true" in the pure disquotational sense only to utterances that he has some understanding of; and for such an utterance u, the claim that u is true (true-as-he-understands-it) is cognitively equivalent (for the person) to u itself (as he-understands it).[1] A qualification is needed, since the claim that u is true involves an existential commitment to the utterance u, whereas u itself doesn't; this keeps the two from being fully cognitively equivalent. The qualified version is that the claim that u is true is cognitively equivalent to u *relative to the existence of the utterance u*; just as "Thatcher is such that she is self-identical and snow is white" is cognitively equivalent to "Snow is white" *relative to the existence of Thatcher*. (To say that A is cognitively equivalent to B relative to C means that the conjunction of A and C is cognitively equivalent to the conjunction of B and C; so that as long as C is presupposed we can treat A and B as equivalent.) Having made this qualification, I will generally leave it tacit, and simply say that in the purely disquotational sense of "true", the claim that u is true (where u is an utterance I understand) is cognitively equivalent for me to u itself (as I understand it).[2]

There are both oddities and attractive features to this as a reading of "true"; I will discuss these later on, starting in Section 5. But odd or not, the cognitive equivalence of the claim that u is disquotationally true to u itself provides a way to understand disquotational truth independent of any nondisquotational concept of truth or truth conditions (and independent of any concept of proposition). That is: if I understand "Snow is white", and if I also understand a notion of disquotational truth as explained above, then I will understand "'Snow is white' is true", since it will be equivalent to "Snow is white". This will hold on any view of understanding, even a crude verificationist view according to which understanding it is simply a matter of having verification conditions for it: for the verification conditions of "'Snow is white' is true" will be precisely those of "Snow is white". Certainly there is no need to presuppose that understanding an utterance involves correlating a proposition or truth condition with it, as propositions and truth conditions are understood in the Frege-Russell tradition. Because of this, there can be little doubt that the notion of pure disquotational truth is a notion which a verificationist is entitled to—and which other opponents of the Frege-Russell tradition who have a more sophisticated alternative than verificationism are entitled to as well. (Adherents of the Frege-Russell tradition are entitled to it too, though not all want it.)

And using this notion of truth, even a crude verificationist can grant the legitimacy of talk of truth *conditions* of his own utterances. For the cognitive equivalence of "'Snow is white' is true" and "Snow is white" will lead to the (more or less indefeasible) acceptance of the biconditional "'Snow is white' is true iff snow is white"; and a natural way to put this (more or less indefeasible) acceptance is to say "'Snow is white' has the truth conditions that snow is white". A pure disquotational notion of truth gives rise to a purely disquotational way of talking about truth conditions.

An opponent of the Frege-Russell tradition can try to use this purely disquotational way of talking about truth conditions, or some variant or extension of it, to allow the legitimacy of talk of the truth conditions of utterances and mental states without giving truth conditions the central role that they play in the Frege-Russell tradition. For instance, if one of our mental states can be described as an attitude of believing or accepting the sentence "Snow is white", then it can be described both as a state of believing that snow is white and as a state with the truth conditions that snow is white. The connection of "that" clauses to truth conditions noted in the second paragraph thus remains, but the initial impression that it leads inevitably to the Frege-Russell view is at least lessened. It may not be obvious that all legitimate talk of the truth conditions of mental states can be handled in this way or by an extension of it, but that is what the opponent of the Frege-Russell tradition contends. (This may involve disallowing as illegitimate certain uses of truth conditional talk that an advocate of the Frege-Russell view would allow.)[3] Such a view might naturally be called a *deflationist view of meaning and content*; or more accurately, a deflationist view of *meaning that* and *having the content that*, or a deflationist view about *the role of truth conditions in meaning or content*. The first of the three labels (which I have used in the title for brevity) could be misleading, since some versions of the view are in a sense quite undeflationist about meanings: for instance, the crude verificationism I described is not in the least deflationist about verification conditions; and it identifies them with meanings. What it is deflationist about is truth conditions; or, the locutions "means *that*" and "has the content *that*". From now on I'll simply use the label "deflationist". So that my labels not be thought as prejudging the merits of the views, I'll call the Frege-Russell tradition "inflationist".

The division between the inflationist and deflationist positions is in some ways the most fundamental division within the theory of content and meaning (though as with many fundamental divisions in philosophy, the line between the two views is not absolutely sharp). I myself strongly feel the attractions of each position, though I have come to favor deflationism. In this paper I will formulate a fairly radical version of deflationism,[4] say a few things to try to motivate it, and try to defend it against some obvious objections. I will also mention some deeper lines of objection that I cannot deal with here; these seem to me the places where the battle between deflationism and inflationism must ultimately be fought.

2 More on the deflationist/inflationist distinction

The version of deflationism I outlined in my opening remarks was built around a crude verificationism. It hardly needs arguing that such a version of deflationism isn't satisfactory. But the main idea behind deflationism doesn't require verificationism, it requires only that what plays a central role in meaning and content not include truth conditions (or relations to propositions, where propositions are conceived as encapsulating truth conditions).

I must admit at the start that the question of whether truth conditions (or propositions encapsulating truth conditions) play a central role in meaning and content is not a very clear one, for three reasons. First, the notions of meaning and content aren't clear as they stand. Some ways of clarifying them involve legislating truth conditions into or out of meaning and content, which would make the issue of deflationism totally uninteresting. My way of resolving this unclarity will be to interpret "meaning" and "content" as broadly as possible short of explicitly legislating truth conditions into meaning or content. Second, the idea of a *central* role isn't initially clear either. My goal is to clarify this as I go along, by making explicit the limited role that I think the deflationist can give to truth conditions, and identifying kinds of role that deflationism cannot allow truth conditions to have. Unfortunately I cannot complete the job in this paper: to keep the paper to a manageable size I have had to leave to another occasion discussion of the crucial subject of the role of truth conditions in psychological explanation.

There is also a third source of unclarity to the question, one which I think makes a complete sharpening impossible. If deflationism is to be at all interesting, it must claim not merely that what plays a central role in meaning and content not include truth conditions *under that description*, but that it not include *anything that could plausibly constitute a reduction of* truth conditions to other more physicalistic terms. And it is well known that there is no sharp line between reduction and elimination, so that this crucial tenet of deflationism is not an altogether precise one. In other words, a theory of content and meaning might end up not employing the notion of truth conditions directly (in a central role), but employing (in that role) certain physicalistic relations that *could* be regarded as reducing the relation "S has the truth conditions p", but could *only* be so regarded on a rather loose conception of reduction. Such a theory of content and meaning would occupy the borderline between a deflationist and inflationist theory: it would be rather a matter of taste which way we describe it. I'll have a bit more to say about this possibility later.

I remarked earlier that a deflationist need not be a verificationist. What elements instead of or in addition to verification conditions does he have available for inclusion in meaning or content? One element that can certainly be included in content is conceptual or computational role: role in a (perhaps idealized) computational psychology that describes how the agent's beliefs, desires, etc. evolve over time (partly in response to sensory stimulations).[5] The conceptual role of a belief state includes its verification conditions, but includes much more besides. (It includes a wider variety of evidential relations;[6] it includes the conceptual consequences of having the belief; etc.) But conceptual role isn't enough: it is both "internalist" and "individualist", and a plausible deflationism is going to have to give to content both "externalist" and "social" aspects.

In describing these further aspects of content, it will help if I make what I hope is a harmless assumption. The assumption is that we can speak of a language-user as believing and desiring sentences of his or her own language—or at least, as believing and desiring internal analogs of them in which some or all of the ambiguities may have been removed—and that this relation can be made sense of without a prior notion of content for the belief or desire states or of meaning for the sentences. In other words, this relation is one that a deflationist can perfectly well appeal to. There is a good bit that needs to be said about just what this assumption comes to, but let me simply say that I think that when it is unpacked it is pretty unobjectionable.[7]

Now let's get back to the aspects of content that go beyond conceptual role. The most obvious "externalist" element that a deflationist can put into content is indication relations. It is a fact about me that I am a pretty good barometer of whether there is rain falling on my head at that moment: when there is rain falling on my head, I tend to believe "There is rain falling on my head"; conversely, when I do believe this sentence, usually there is rain falling on my head. This is simply a correlation, there to be observed; and a deflationist is as free to take note of it as is anyone else, and as free as anyone else to deem it an ingredient of what he calls content. The correlation of people's belief states to the world outside presumably extends past the directly observed; the beliefs of astronomer's in sentences of form "The location of Halley's comet at time t will be **x**" generally correlate pretty well with the location of Halley's comet at time t, and in certain circumstances the beliefs of physicists in sentences of form "a particle has recently tunnelled through the potential barrier" will correlate with whether a particle has indeed done so.

These observations might make one think that a deflationist is bound to recognize (a non-disquotational version of) the relation "S has truth conditions p", in fact if not in name, since these indication relations constitute the truth-conditions relation. But this overlooks the fact that the project of giving anything close to a believable reduction of talk of truth conditions to talk of indication relations is at best a gleam in the eye of some theorists. A way to see the point is to notice that there are plenty of examples where the indication relations don't reflect what we would intuitively regard as truth conditions. Maybe I systematically exaggerate, so that my believing a sentence of the form "It is n feet high" is strongly correlated with the object before me being f(n) feet high, where f(x) starts dropping off rapidly from x after about 6 feet or so. Or worse, maybe my beliefs of the form "In Bosnia, p" don't stand in any interesting correlations with the actual facts about what's happening in Bosnia, but just reflect what appears in the newspapers I read. The deflationist can recognize the facts about indication, and attribute explanatory importance to them; he can even use the disquotation schema to formulate the distinction between one of his belief states indicating its own truth conditions and its indicating something else (as in the exaggeration example and the Bosnia example).[8] What he *can't* do, it seems to me, is say that *this distinction* is of much explanatory importance: for that would give truth conditions (rather than just indication relations in general) a central role in the theory of mind; and the claim that truth conditions have a central role in the theory of mind is the defining characteristic of inflationism.[9] That the distinction between a belief state reliably indicating its own truth conditions and its reliably indicating something else is of little explanatory importance is a consequence of deflationism that seems at first quite implausible. But it can grow on one, after one has spent some time trying to say just what its explanatory importance is!

Anyway, the deflationist can include indication relations in content; this is enough to make content externalist, but not enough to make it social. However, since we are regarding many of our most important beliefs as in effect attitudes toward sentences in our language, the means to make content social is at hand. That is, it seems reasonable to decree that the content of these belief states is to be influenced by the meaning these sentences have for us; that meaning is of course partly influenced by the content of our intentional states, but since language is social it will be influenced by the contents of the states of other members of our community as well. In particular—and removing the appearance of circularity—we can understand "content" in such a way that *the conceptual roles and indication relations of other people's states of believing a certain sentence are counted as relevant to the content of my state of believing that sentence*;[10] such a way of understanding "content" is not only possible, it is natural when one thinks of the ways that which sentences I believe influence and are influenced by which sentences others believe. Again, construing content as social in this way is quite compatible with deflationism, that is with keeping truth conditions (and hence "that" clauses) out of the fundamental characterization of content.

3 The semantics of logical operators

"Deflationism" and "inflationism" are broad labels, each encompassing many different views. I think it would help to make the contrast between the deflationist and inflationist traditions clearer if I focussed on several problems in the theory of content, and showed how they looked from each of the two broad perspectives.

The first problem I will discuss is the problem of saying what determines the "referent" of a logical operator like "or" or "not" or "all"; or to put it less Fregeanly, the problem of saying what determines the contributions that such a logical operator makes to the truth conditions of sentences that contain it.

I think it is clear in broad outline what an inflationist's best strategy is for answering this question. The answer will have two stages. The first stage involves spelling out the "conceptual role" that "or" has (for a given person, or for the linguistic community generally): in this case, it would largely be a matter of role in deductive inference and perhaps inductive and practical inference as well. For instance, among the relevant facts about my use of the word "or" is that I tend to accept inferences to a disjunction "A or B" from either disjunct, and to the negation of the disjunction from the negations of both disjuncts, but not to the disjuncts from the disjunction; and when I do occasionally slip and infer according to the latter rule, I can be brought to correct myself. Also relevant perhaps is that I tend to assign to a disjunction a degree of belief higher than the degrees of belief of each disjunct but no higher than the sum of the degrees of belief of the disjuncts. (Indeed my degree of belief in a disjunction "A or B" tends to be about equal to the sum of my degrees of belief in the disjuncts minus my degree of belief in A times my conditional degree of belief in B given A.) And so on.

But what does the word's having this conceptual role have to do with its standing for the usual truth function (that is, with its contributing to truth conditions by means of the usual truth table)? Perhaps the conceptual role of "or" determines that it stands for that truth function *in this sense*: any word in any linguistic community that had that conceptual role would stand for that truth function. But that doesn't seem very helpful, for it doesn't tell you why that conceptual role should be associated with that truth function.

There is though a rather natural story to try to tell. The idea is that if we assign truth conditions to our sentences (and hence our belief states) according to this rule of truth for "or" (and the standard rules of truth for "not"), it will make our deductive inferences involving "or" truth-preserving, and presumably will make our inductive inferences involving "or" highly reliable;[11] whereas if we used any other truth table, the deductive and inductive inferences would come out totally unreliable. Reliability considerations seem to give just the sort of link between conceptual role and reference that we want in this case.

There are of course some holes here. One hole is that though it is true that no alternative *truth function* makes our inferences involving "or" at all reliable, this just shows that reliability considerations make the usual truth table for "or" more satisfactory *than alternative truth functions*; but maybe there is an alternative to a truth functional account that would make us equally reliable? A second hole is that in explaining the contribution of "or" to truth conditions, we can't legitimately assume the contribution that "not" makes to truth conditions unless that can be independently established; so unless it can be independently established (which is doubtful), or unless we can avoid mentioning it in our account of what determines the truth table for "or", then we really need an account of how reliability considerations give us the rules of truth for "or" and "not" together. (Using another operator like "if...then" or "implies" instead of "not" would give rise to similar problems.) This deepens the first hole: for now we need to compare the package containing the usual truth functional accounts of "or" and "not" to alternative packages in which both truth rules are varied, and where there is no constraint that either truth rule be truth functional.

Even if the second hole can be avoided, the problem with the first hole is greater for more complicated operators, like quantifiers: for instance, in the case of "some" our usual deductive inferences turn out truth preserving if we suppose that its contribution to truth conditions is that of the unrestricted objectual existential quantifier, but making it a restricted quantifier or substitutional quantifier of a certain sort would also make the inferences truth preserving, and (depending on the details of the restriction) might make us at least equally reliable—even with the truth rules for the truth functional connectives and "implies" unchanged.

So what determines that our word "or" or "not" or "some" makes the contribution to truth conditions that we assume it makes? An inflationist has three choices. Either she can find some sort of naturalistic facts that could be cited in answer to this question (facts involving reliability considerations might work in the end, despite the questions above); or she can say that there is simply no fact of the matter, that we have a surprising example of referential indeterminacy here; or she can say that it is a non-naturalistic fact about us that our word "some" contributes to truth conditions according to the rules of the unrestricted objectual quantifier and that "not" and "or" contribute according to the usual truth tables. But this third option strikes me as rather repellent; the first may be hard to carry out; and the second may not be altogether free of philosophical difficulties.

The same sort of problem arises in the case of the predicate "is identical to" (and the numerical quantifiers such as "there are exactly two" that are definable from it). The axioms that we accept as governing this predicate determine (given a reliability assumption) that it stands for a congruence relation, that is, an equivalence relation for which substitutivity holds; but this is not enough to determine that it stands for genuine identity, that is, for the relation that everything bears to itself and to nothing else. It is especially not enough if the extensions of the other predicates in the language are up for grabs: as Quine has famously pointed out, it isn't so easy to say what facts about us make "identical to" stand for identity and "rabbit" for rabbits, rather than "rabbit" for rabbit stages and "is identical to" for the relation of being stages of the same object. And even if we can find facts about usage that would rule out this example as violating a plausible reliability requirement, it is a tall order to find facts about usage which would rule out *all* choices of nonstandard congruence relations. Again, an inflationist is apparently faced with the three options of finding such facts, or accepting it as simply a brute fact that our word stands for genuine identity, or accepting a surprising level of referential indeterminacy in our basic logical vocabulary. This is a choice that not everyone would be happy to have to make.

A main motivation for deflationism is that it apparently avoids having to make this sort of choice.[12] According to the simplest version of deflationism—that relying on the pure disquotational truth predicate mentioned earlier—it is an entirely trivial matter to explain why one's own word "or" obeys the truth table it does: this follows from truth functional logic together with the logic of the disquotational truth predicate, with no mention of any facts at all about our usage of "or". Recall that if "true" is used purely disquotationally, then "'p' is true" is cognitively equivalent to "p", for any sentence "p" that we understand. As a result, we get that each instance of the "disquotation schema"

(T) "p" is true if and only if p

holds of conceptual necessity, that is, by virtue of the cognitive equivalence of the left and right hand sides. But for any sentences q and r, instances of the following schemas are also instances of (T), and hence conceptually necessary:

"q or r" is true if and only if q or r
"q" is true if and only if q
"r" is true if and only if r.

And now you can use the latter two to substitute into the right hand side of the first, so as to get the conceptual necessity of each instance of the following:

(TF) "q or r" is true if and only if "q" is true or "r" is true.

The conceptual necessity of the instances really isn't enough to justify the claim that "or" obeys the usual truth table: we need the conceptual necessity of the generalization

(TFG) For all sentences S_1 and S_2 of our language, $\langle\!\langle S_1 \text{ or } S_2 \rangle\!\rangle$ is true iff S_1 is true or S_2 is true.

But it is easy to get that if we start not from (T) but from some generalized form of (T). One such generalized form of (T) employs a universal substitutional quantifier:

(TG) Πp ["p" is true if and only if p].[13]

(I assume a theory of substitutional quantification that avoids the semantic paradoxes.) There are also ways to get the generalization without substitutional quantifiers. One alternative is to incorporate schematic letters for sentences into the language, reasoning with them as with variables; and then to employ two rules of inference governing them: (i) a rule that allows replacement of all instances of a schematic letter by a sentence; (ii) a rule that allows inference of ∀x(Sentence(x) ⊃ A(x)) from the schema A("p"), where A("p") is a schema in which all occurrences of the schematic letter p are surrounded by quotes. Such a formalism corresponds to a very weak fragment of a substitutional quantifier language, and is probably preferable to using the full substitutional quantifier. In such a formalism, (T) and (TF) themselves are part of the language, rather than merely having instances that are part of the language; and from (T) we can derive (TF) and thence (by rule (ii) and a bit of syntax) (TFG).

Note that on any of these versions of the pure deflationary account, facts about the meaning of our word "or"—e.g., its conceptual role—need not be explicitly referred to in explaining why our word "or" obeys the usual truth table. Of course, we do need to use logical reasoning, and in particular, the deductive inferential rules that are in fact associated with the word "or". But we needn't mention in the explanation *that these rules are associated with "or"*; in that sense, the meaning of "or" plays no role in the explanation.

Does this mean that a deflationist can't make sense of the idea that "or" obeys the truth table it does *because of* its conceptual role? Not really: the fact that *the deductive inferential rules for "or"* are used in the explanation of "or" having the truth table it has is enough to give one quite natural sense to the claim that it obeys that truth table *because* it obeys those deductive inferential rules. However, the sense of "because" here does not support counterfactuals. That is, because *the fact that these rules are associated with "or"* plays no role in the explanation of "or" having this truth table, we don't get the conclusion that if different rules had been associated with "or", its contributions to truth conditions would have been different. (At least, we don't get this conclusion on the most straightforward reading of the counterfactual.) Indeed, it is clear that this counterfactual (on its straightforward construal anyway) is unacceptable if "truth conditions" is understood in a purely disquotational sense. (This may seem an objection to the purely disquotational notion of truth, but later on I will argue that it is not. I will also consider whether a deflationist can make sense of a modified notion of truth conditions according to which such a counterfactual would be straightforwardly true; if so, the conceptual role of "or" might have to be explicitly referred to in explaining why "or"'s truth conditions in this modified sense of truth conditions are those of the usual truth table.)

What I've said here about the explanation of the truth-theoretic properties of the logical connectives goes for other words as well. Consider "rabbit": an inflationist presumably thinks that the set or property that my term "rabbit" stands for is determined from the facts about this word's conceptual role for me, together with its conceptual role for other members of my community, together with the facts about what my believing various "rabbit" sentences tends to be correlated with, together with the same sort of facts for other members of my community, and so on. This raises the question of precisely how it is determined; and it seems to me that if inflationism is to be believable then the inflationist needs to have some story to tell here. Of course, Quine's well-known difficulty about rabbits v. rabbit-stages would be solved if we solved the problem for identity: reliability with respect to sentences like "For all x and y, if x and y are nearby rabbits then x=y" ties the extension of "rabbit" to that of "identical" in such a way as to handle such individuation problems. But there are further problems: what makes "rabbit" stand for the rabbits rather than the rabbits-or-realistic-imitations, for instance. I don't say that the inflationist can't tell a reasonable story about this, only that there is a story to be told, and perhaps there is room for skepticism about the possibility of telling it adequately. If so, that provides a motivation for deflationism. For the deflationist view is that there is nothing here to explain: it is simply part of the logic of "refers" (or "is true of") that "rabbit" refers to (is true of) rabbits and to nothing else.

The deflationary view of truth and reference as I've presented it here applies only to words and sentences that we understand. This may well seem worrisome, and it is important to ask both whether it should seem worrisome and whether it could be avoided. I'll return to these matters in later sections, but first I want to further explore the contrast between the deflationist and inflationist viewpoints.

4 Inverting the theory of reference

One qualm that one might reasonably have about the deflationist perspective is that a lot of work that has gone into the theory of reference in recent years seems to be onto something, and it seems at first hard to explain just what it could be onto if truth conditions play no central role in the theory of meaning. After all, if truth conditions play no central role, reference can hardly play a central role: whatever importance reference has surely derives from its contribution to truth conditions.

Let's consider first Kripke's observation (Kripke 1980) that description theories of the reference of our proper names[14] are incorrect. If truth conditions play no central role in meaning, and truth is fully explained by the disquotation schema (and of value only as a logical device, in a manner soon to be explained), then the same is true of reference: for the reference of singular terms, the relevant schema is

(R) If b exists then "b" refers to b and nothing else; if b doesn't exist then "b" doesn't refer to anything.

But if this tells us everything we need to know about the reference for our own words, what could Kripke's critique of description theories be telling us?

We need a concrete example before us. Consider Kripke's case against a version of the description theory according to which the referent of our term "Godel" is determined by the associated description "prover of the incompleteness theorem": the referent of the name (if it has one) is to be whatever uniquely fits the description. Kripke's case against this view is a thought experiment, in which we discover the following fact:

(F) The incompleteness theorem was proved by a man baptized "Schmidt" and who never called himself anything other than "Schmidt"; a certain person who called himself "Godel" and got a job under that name at the Institute for Advanced Study stole the proof from him.

In this situation, Kripke asks, who is it natural to say we have been referring to when we used the name "Godel", the guy who called himself "Schmidt" and proved the incompleteness theorem, or the guy who called himself "Godel"? Nearly everyone says the latter, so the description theory (or this version of it) is wrong. Surely there is something important in this critique, and if the deflationist can't make sense of it then something is wrong with deflationism.

I think that the deflationist can make sense of Kripke's observations. On the deflationist viewpoint, though, *the observations aren't at the most basic level about reference but about our inferential practice.* That is, what Kripke's example really shows is that we would regard the claim F as *grounds for inferring* "Godel didn"t prove the incompleteness theorem" rather than as grounds for inferring "Godel was baptized as 'Schmidt' and never called himself 'Godel'". Reference is just disquotational. It does comes in indirectly: from F I can indirectly infer

"Godel" doesn't refer to the guy that proved the incompleteness theorem.

But that isn't because of a causal theory of reference over a description theory, but only because I can infer

Godel isn't the guy that proved the incompleteness theorem,

and then "semantically ascend".

This does seem to me a fairly plausible account of what the Kripke point shows. We see that at least in this case, the deflationist picture leads to a reasonably plausible inversion of standard views, and tends to demote the importance of theories of reference and truth conditions from accounts of language use and cognitive functioning.

But how about the positive view of reference that emerges from the writings of Kripke, Putnam etc.? The positive view is that a typical name of mine refers to what it does because of a causal network of beliefs and utterances involving that name: in the simplest cases, some people acquired beliefs involving a name as a result of direct causal interaction with the thing named; these beliefs led to their using the name in utterances, which led other people to have beliefs involving the name; these in turn passed beliefs on to others, and so forth. And it is because my uses of (say) "Hume" stand in a causal network of roughly this sort, a network whose dominant causal source is Hume, that my uses of the name refer to Hume. The previous discussion shows how a deflationist can partially capture the force of this: he can say that it is just part of our inferential procedure to regard claims of roughly the form "The dominant causal source of our beliefs involving 'b' is b" as pretty much indefeasible. But this doesn't seem to fully capture the importance of the causal theory of reference. It has seemed to many that the causal network emanating from Hume to my uses of the name "Hume" explains what is otherwise mysterious, namely, how my name could be *about* Hume. Obviously a deflationist can't say this: the whole point of deflationism is that the only explanation we need of why my word is about Hume is given by the disquotation schema.

Nonetheless, the deflationist can agree that this causal network story is explanatory of something: what it explains is the otherwise mysterious correlation between a knowledgeable person's beliefs involving the name "Hume" and the facts about Hume. You probably believe quite a few sentences that involve the name "Hume", and a large proportion of them are probably disquotationally true: that is, the conditional probability that Hume was Φ given that you believe "Hume was Φ" is quite high. Surely this correlation between your "Hume" beliefs and the Hume-facts cries out for explanation.[15] And the general lines of the explanation are clearly suggested in the Kripke-Putnam account: you acquired your "Hume" beliefs largely through interactions with others, who in turn acquired theirs from others, and so on until we reach believers with a fairly immediate causal access to Hume or his writings or whatever. Moreover, the causal network has multiple independent chains, and contains historical experts who have investigated these independent chains systematically, so the chance of large errors surviving isn't that high. The role of "experts" that figures heavily in Putnam's account of reference thus also has its analog when focus is put instead on explaining our reliability—indeed, when the focus is put on reliability it is obvious *why* the reliance on "experts" should have such a central place.

Earlier I pointed out that the reliability of my beliefs under the disquotation schema is simply an objective fact about me, stateable without semantic terms, which a deflationist can hardly be debarred from taking note of in his account of meaning. Here I am expanding the point, to observe that he can hardly be debarred from wanting an explanation of it; and the explanation is bound to involve some of the ingredients that inflationists tend to put into their theories of reference.

This of course reraises the possibility mentioned earlier, that by the time the deflationist is finished explaining this and similar facts, he will have reconstructed the inflationist's relation "S has the truth conditions p", in fact if not in name. My guess is that this will turn out not to be the case, but to assert that conclusion with confidence requires a more thorough investigation than I will be able to undertake in this paper. All I really hope to motivate here is that we should be "methodological deflationists": that is, we should start out assuming deflationism as a working hypothesis; we should adhere to it unless and until we find ourselves reconstructing what amounts to the inflationist's relation "S has the truth conditions p". So methodological deflationism is simply a methodological policy, which if pursued could lead to the discovery that deflationism in the original sense ("metaphysical deflationism") is workable or could lead to the discovery that inflationism is inevitable. It could also turn out that we end up constructing something that *might or might not* be regarded as the inflationist's relation "S has the truth conditions p"; in that case, the line between inflationism and metaphysical deflationism will turn out to have blurred.[16]

5 More on disquotational truth

It is time now to be a bit more precise about what exactly deflationism involves. In order to do this, it will help to ask what a deflationist should say about why we need a truth predicate. If truth conditions aren't central to meaning, why not drop talk of truth altogether? As is well known, the deflationist's answer is that the word "true" has an important logical role: it allows us to formulate certain infinite conjunctions and disjunctions that can't be formulated otherwise.[17]

There are some very mundane examples of this, for instance, where we remember that someone said something false yesterday but can't remember what it was. What we are remembering is equivalent to the infinite disjunction of all sentences of form "She said 'p', but not-p".

A more important example of this which has been widely noted arises in discussions of realism. "Realism" has been used to mean many things, but one version of it is the view that there might be (and almost certainly are) sentences of our language that are true that we will never have reason to believe, in contrast to "anti-realist" doctrines that identify truth with long-run justifiability or whatever. To assert realism in this sense one needs a notion of truth. But the reason for this is purely logical: that is, if only finitely many sentences could be formulated in our language, we could put the realist doctrine without use of a predicate of truth: we could say:

> It might be the case that either the number of brontosauruses that ever lived is precisely 75,278 but we will never have reason to believe that; or the amount that Michael Jackson spent on underwear in his lifetime is exactly $1,078,852.72 but we will never have reason to believe that; or ....

where in place of the "..." goes similar clauses for every sentence of the language. It is because we can't complete the disjunction that we need a notion of truth. Or perhaps I should say, because we can't *otherwise* complete the disjunction: for the claim that it might be the case that some sentence of our language is true but that we will never have reason to believe it can be viewed as simply a way of formulating the disjunction.[18]

Another example of "true" as a device of infinite conjunction and disjunction is the desire to utter only true sentences or to have only true beliefs: what we desire is the infinite conjunction of all claims of the form "I utter 'p' only if p" or "I believe 'p' only if p". It is sometimes claimed that a deflationist cannot grant that there is any "substantial norm" of assertion beyond warranted assertibility.[19] This seems to me a serious mistake: any sane deflationist will hold that truth and warranted assertibility (even long run warranted assertibility) can and do diverge: as the previous paragraph should make clear, their divergence is a consequence of the truth schema together with quite uncontroversial facts. Consequently, a norm of asserting the truth is a norm that goes beyond warranted assertibility. But there is no difficulty in desiring that all one's beliefs be disquotationally true; and not only can each of us desire such things, there can be a general practice of badgering others into having such desires. Isn't this enough for there being a "norm" of asserting and believing the truth? Admittedly, this account of norms in terms of badgering is a bit crude, but I see no reason to think that on a more sophisticated account of what a norm is, norms of striving for the truth won't be just as available to the deflationist as they are on the crude account.

I'll give a fourth example of the utility of a device of infinite conjunction and disjunction, since it clearly brings out some points I want to stress. Consider some theory about the physical world, formulated with finitely many separate axioms and finitely many axiom schemas (each schema having infinitely many axioms as instances). For an example of such a theory, one can take a typical first order version of the Euclidean theory of space (which is not finitely axiomatizable). Suppose that one rejects this theory without knowing which specific part of it to reject; or alternatively, suppose that one accepts it but regards it as contingent. In the first case one will put the rejection by saying "Not every axiom of this theory is true"; in the second case, by saying "It might have been the case that not every axiom of the theory was true". But the intended purpose in the first case is of course to deny the infinite conjunction of the axioms, and in the second case to assert the *possibility* of the negation of this infinite conjunction.

My reason for focussing on this example is that it shows clearly the importance of what I earlier called pure disquotational truth. Pure disquotational truth involves two important features that certain other truth concepts lack. The first is that I can understand "Utterance u is true" only to the extent that I can understand utterance u; the second is that for me, the claim that utterance u is true in the pure disquotational sense is cognitively equivalent to u itself as I understand it. (The first pretty much follows from the second: if I can't understand u, and if an attribution of truth to u is cognitively equivalent to u, then I can't understand an attribution of truth to u.)[20] The second feature of the pure disquotational notion of truth means that this notion is of a *use-independent* property: to call "Snow is white" disquotationally true is simply to call snow white; hence it is *not* to attribute it a property that it wouldn't have had if I and other English speakers had used words differently.

In ordinary English we seem to use a truth predicate that does not share these two features. It is not entirely obvious, though, that what we say can't be understood indirectly in terms of disquotational truth. (More on this in Sections 8 and 9.) In any case, these two features of pure disquotational truth make it ideally suited to serve the logical need for a device of infinite conjunction and disjunction illustrated in the examples above, particularly the Euclidean geometry example. In the first place, the only sentences we ever literally conjoin or disjoin are sentences we understand, so it is clear that a notion that is inapplicable to utterances we don't understand will serve our needs for truth as a device of conjunction and disjunction. Second and more important, the use-independence of disquotational truth is *required* for the purposes just reviewed. For if "All sentences of type Q are true" is to serve as an infinite conjunction of all sentences of type Q, then we want it to entail each such sentence, and be entailed by all of them together. This would fail to be so unless "S is true" entailed and was entailed by S. But the only way that can be so is if "true" doesn't ascribe a use-dependent feature to S. Suppose for instance that Euclidean geometry is true, and that we try to express its contingency by saying that the axioms together might have been false. Surely what we wanted to say wasn't simply that speakers might have used their words in such a way that the axioms weren't true, it is that space itself might have differed so as to make the axioms *as we understand them* not true. A use-independent notion of truth is precisely what we require.

Of course, there is another use-independent notion of truth besides disquotational truth that would be usable for these purposes: truth as applied to *propositions*, where propositions are construed as language-independent (rather than, say, as equivalence classes of utterances). But I think that pure disquotational truth is better for these purposes, for two reasons. The first and less important is ontological: it is better to avoid postulating strange entities unnecessarily. The more important reason is that unless one is very careful to limit the use made of the notion of expressing a proposition, the introduction of such a notion of proposition would beg the question in favor of inflationism.[21] There may be good arguments for inflationism, but the need to express infinite conjunctions and disjunctions can be handled with the more minimal apparatus of purely disquotational truth, and it is best to use only the more minimal apparatus as long as the need of the more powerful apparatus is unargued.

I have been arguing that inflationists as well as deflationists need some useindependent notion of truth as a device of infinite conjunction and disjunction, and that such a notion is needed only for sentences that one understands. Pure disquotational truth serves the need admirably; and I think that a deflationist should take pure disquotational truth as the fundamental truth concept. This is not to say that it is the only notion of truth available to the deflationist: in Section 9 I will consider the possibility of introducing a modified kind of disquotational truth, which both applies to sentences in languages we can't understand and is not use-independent. But I have argued that a deflationist needs a notion of pure disquotational truth, and I think that he should regard it as the basic notion of truth in terms of which others are to be explained.

6 Disquotational truth versus Tarskian truth

In this Section I consider the relation between Tarskian truth definitions and disquotational truth. To facilitate the discussion I will pretend that English is a language without indexicals or demonstratives or ambiguous sentences, so that we can apply talk of truth to sentence types. (I will consider what the deflationist should say about indexicality, ambiguity and the like in Section 10.)

As I have explained disquotational truth, axiomatic status is given to some generalized version of the truth schema

(T) "p" is true if and only if p.

The generalized version might be the result of prefixing the schema with a universal substitutional quantifier; alternatively, we might prefer the weaker approach involving schematic variables, mentioned earlier. (Again, I assume sufficient restrictions on the schema to avoid semantic paradoxes.) Actually, if our language contains a modal operator we need something a bit stronger, as the Euclidean geometry example of the previous section indicates: the schema (T) should be replaced by:

(NT) $\Box$["p" is true if and only if p].

But even when the language doesn't have a modal operator, the left hand side of (T) is to be understood as cognitively equivalent to the right hand side. (Any view, no matter how inflationist, accepts the instances of (T) as material biconditionals.)

Tarskian approaches are somewhat different. First I should remind the reader that though Tarski was interested in explicitly defined truth predicates, he also proved a severe limitation of such explicitly defined predicates: they are available only for fragments of one's language. If we explicitly define a truth predicate in a language, not only must we exclude its application to some or all sentences of that language that contain semantic terms, we must also exclude its application to a substantial body of other sentences of the language without semantic terms but with unrestricted quantifiers. And this of course limits the use of the truth predicate as a device of infinite conjunction and disjunction: for instance, we can't use it to form infinite conjunctions and disjunctions of sentences with unrestricted quantifiers, at least if arbitrarily large numbers of alternations of those quantifiers appear among the conjuncts or disjuncts. If we want to avoid such limitations on formulating infinite conjunctions and disjunctions, we should give up on the idea that our truth predicate must be explicitly defined.

Even if a Tarskian were to give up the insistence on *defining* truth, there would still be an important difference between the Tarskian approach and the full-fledged deflationary approach that takes a generalized version of the truth schema as an axiom. For central to what is usually thought of as the Tarskian approach (though perhaps it owes more to Davidson than to Tarski himself) is that truth[22] is characterized (inductively if not explicitly) in terms of compositional structure.[23] This gives compositional principles of truth a much more central role than they have on the full-fledged deflationary account. Recall the deflationist story I gave about why the word "or" obeys the usual truth table: the principle

If S_1 and S_2 are sentences of our language then ⟪S_1 or S_2⟫ is true iff S_1 is true or S_2 is true

is built directly into the inductive characterization of truth on the Tarskian approach, whereas on the deflationary approach it is simply a consequence of the generalized truth schema (together with the principle "∀S(S is a sentence ⊃ Σp(S='p')", on the substitutional quantifier version of the generalized schema). Something similar holds for other compositional principles, such as that a sentence consisting of a 1-place predicate and a referring name is true iff the predicate is true of what the name denotes: on a deflationist account this is simply a consequence of generalized disquotational schemas for "true", "true of" and "refers" (together with principles like the one just given parenthetically, together with some obvious syntactic principles and laws of concatenation and quotation marks).[24]

Why does it matter whether such principles are built into an inductive characterization of truth or viewed as consequences of generalized disquotational schemas? One reason why it matters is that there is no guarantee that for all regions of discourse there will be such compositional principles that follow from the generalized disquotation schemas. The compositional principles for "or" and other truth functional operators simply fall out of the logical rules of inference that govern those operators (together with the disquotational principles for "true"); the same is basically true of other standard compositional principles (except that we sometimes need subsidiary semantic notions such as satisfaction, and disquotational principles governing them). But there is no obvious reason to think that in the case of all operators, e.g. non-extensional ones, there will be subsidiary semantic notions that yield compositional principles.

This shouldn't upset the full-fledged deflationist: for the full-fledged deflationist, such compositional principles have no particular interest in their own right; we can explain why we have them when we do, since they follow from the basic disquotational schemas whenever a substitutivity principle is part of the logic, but they are not of foundational importance. For the Tarskian they are of much more fundamental importance: they are needed in order to have a satisfactory notion of truth. This is one important way in which a Tarskian approach isn't *fully* deflationist.

A Tarskian approach may or may not be *partially* deflationist: whether it is depends on the status that is accorded the Tarskian "truth definitions". In particular, what (if anything) makes such a definition *correct* for a given population? For a view to count as in any serious sense deflationist, it must say either that there is no sense at all to be made of speaking of one Tarski-predicate for a population as "correct", or that the only sense that can be made of it is based on stipulating that the *homophonic* truth predicate counts as correct *for us*.

To elaborate: it is easy to use Tarski-predicates in a theory that is in no way deflationist. One view of the significance of a Tarskian truth definition (whether inductive or explicit) is as partially characterizing an *abstract language*, that is, a language viewed as an abstract entity that exists whether or not anyone actually speaks it: the language is defined by the rules governing it, including Tarskian truth rules. (See Lewis 1975; Soames 1984; Stalnaker 1984.) So in addition to English there is an abstract language English*, with the same rules of grammar but different truth rules: e.g. in English* "or" might obey the truth table for conjunction and "rabbit" true of all and only the dinosaurs. Then questions about the truth conditions of a person's sentences are relocated as questions about which abstract language she speaks. An inflationist thinks that there are facts about a person's employment of her sentences by virtue of which it is one abstract language rather than another that she is speaking; such facts determine that Aristotle spoke in abstract Greek, and in the same way determine that we are speaking abstract English. The problem is to say what these facts are, and how they do the determining. But a deflationist thinks that a homophony condition guarantees that we are speaking English rather than English*, without the need of any such facts about our employment of the language.[25]

There is of course a strong suggestion of the deflationist viewpoint in Tarski himself, stemming from his famous adequacy condition on truth definitions, "Convention T". (I should actually say, a strong suggestion of the *partial* deflationist view, because of the points earlier in this section.) My point is only that if you deemphasize these and focus on the truth definitions themselves, and think it is a straightforwardly factual question which truth definition is correct for a given population, then there is nothing in the least deflationist about the resulting view.

7 Objections to deflationism

There are many different sorts of worries that one might have about deflationism. Some seem to me to be based on misunderstandings. Under this heading I would include the commonly-voiced worry that deflationism cuts language off from the world. The worry is that if I simply accept "T-sentences" like

"There are gravitational waves" is true iff there are gravitational waves,

then unless the sentence on the right hand side already has truth conditions of a more-than-disquotational sort, it has nothing to do with gravitational waves, and so the sentence doesn't really supply truth conditions to "There are gravitational waves". The response is that we do indeed need to establish a connection between the use of "There are gravitational waves" and gravitational waves, independent of the truth schema. But deflationism allows for this (at least in the version I have sketched): it admits that among the important facts about the use of "There are gravitational waves" are facts, stateable quite independent of disquotational truth, that relate the sentence to gravitational waves. For instance, the laws of physics are such that gravitational waves, if they exist, will cause pulses in a quadrupole antenna, and such pulses are one of the things that would increase our confidence in the sentence "There are gravitational waves". The objection tacitly assumed that the only kind of connection between gravitational waves and the use of "There are gravitational waves" (other than the derivative connection that arises simply from the use of "true" in accordance with the disquotation schema) comes in the nondisquotational assignment of truth conditions to that sentence; but this is simply false.

In contrast, many of the worries that one might have about deflationism raise deep issues. In my view the most serious worry about deflationism is that it can't make sense of the explanatory role of truth conditions: e.g. their role in explaining behavior, or their role in explaining the extent to which behavior is successful. Unfortunately it is a big job even to state the worry clearly, and a bigger job to answer it; I must save this for another occasion.[26] Another kind of worry about deflationism that is too big to discuss here is that it can't make the distinction between vague and non-vague discourse, or between discourse that is thoroughly factual and discourse that falls short of this in various ways. I discuss this worry in Field 1994.

But there remain some less serious objections that I can discuss here; discussing them will help clarify what I am taking deflationism to involve. The objections to be discussed are

1 That deflationism can't handle the attribution of truth to utterances in other languages.
2 That deflationism gives the wrong modal properties to "true".
3 That deflationism can't handle ambiguous utterances, indexicals, demonstratives, and the like.

and

4 That it can't make sense of how we learn from others.

I think all of these can be easily answered, but it is worth spelling out how this is to be done, for my treatment will separate my version of deflationism from certain other less radical versions. I will treat these objections in order in the final four Sections.

8 Applying "true" to sentences in other languages

I have emphasized that a person can meaningfully apply a pure disquotational truth predicate only to utterances that he understands. This raises the question of what we are doing when we talk of the truth or falsity of sentences in other languages.

There are at least three different approaches that a deflationist might take toward talk of truth for sentences in other languages. Perhaps the most obvious—but to my mind the least satisfactory—would be to use a notion of interlinguistic synonymy: regard "S is true" (where "S" stands for a foreign sentence) as equivalent to "S is synonymous with a sentence of ours that is true in the purely disquotational sense". This option brings the semantic notion of synonymy into the characterization of truth for foreign sentences. I will call truth as so defined "*extended* disquotational truth".

Some may object that extended disquotational truth is not a notion that a deflationist can allow himself, since it involves interlinguistic synonymy, which must be understood as involving sameness of truth conditions. I hesitate to say anything so strong; I say only that a deflationist who wants to employ a notion of interlinguistic synonymy faces a serious challenge, the challenge of showing how to make sense of it without relying on a prior notion of truth conditions. (Recall that the deflationist/inflationist contrast was explained in terms of whether truth conditions play a role in semantics and the theory of content.) But perhaps this challenge can be met. If for instance one were to adopt a crude verificationism, synonymy would be just interpersonal sameness of verification conditions—assuming of course that *that* can be spelled out. On a more reasonable deflationist view, meaning will involve a variety of components: as discussed earlier, the meaning of a sentence of mine will depend on its inferential role for me, its inferential role for my fellow speakers, and its indication relations for me and my fellow speakers. So whether one of my sentences is synonymous with a sentence used by someone else (e.g., a foreign speaker) will depend on a variety of disparate facts. In that case there is no obvious way to get a useful and well-behaved synonymy relation.[27] Still, it isn't idiotic to suppose that there is an *unobvious* way to do it; so it isn't initially clear that a deflationist can't admit a useful and well-behaved notion of extended disquotational truth.

But extended disquotational truth isn't the only option the deflationist has available for talking about truth conditions for foreign sentences. A second option is more flexible: simply define what it is for a foreign sentence to be *true relative to a correlation* of it to one of our sentences: a sentence is true relative to the correlation if the sentence of ours correlated with it is true in the purely disquotational sense. This approach differs from the previous in that no claim is made that the correlated sentences are synonymous. Of course, if we accept the notion of interpersonal synonymy, we can use it to get the effect of the first option: we can say that a foreign sentence S is true in the extended disquotational sense iff there is a correlation c of S to a *synonymous* English sentence such that S is true relative to this correlation. But the second option can be applied by those like Quine who reject a notion of interpersonal synonymy, or by those who accept it but want to consider truth relative to correlations that violate it, or by those who want to keep track of where notions like synonymy are being used and where they aren't.

I should note that even those like Quine who reject a notion of interpersonal synonymy grant that there are standards of translation: it is beyond controversy that some translations of a foreign sentence are *better than* others, at least for certain purposes. If someone hears an utterance of "Comment ca va?" and translates it as "You have just passed your French exam", then that grossly violates any reasonable standard of good translation. The skeptic about interpersonal synonymy holds that though we of course have standards of translation, they are a matter of being better or worse, not of right and wrong, and also are highly context-dependent (since the purposes for which they are better or worse vary from one context to the next); and that these features together keep them from generating any useful notion of synonymy. I don't want to discuss whether this rejection of interpersonal synonymy is a reasonable position. But note that even if it is, standards of better and worse translation can be employed to partly capture the import of claims about extended disquotational truth: what we are doing when we conjecture whether some utterance we don't understand is true is conjecturing whether a good translation of the utterance will map it into a disquotationally true sentence we do understand. If "good translation" is a highly context-sensitive and interest-relative notion that doesn't reflect an objective synonymy relation, then there is a certain non-objectivity to the question of whether the utterance we don't understand is true, but that consequence is not obviously undesirable.

(Even a deflationist who thinks there is an objective notion of synonymy for good translations to reflect will have a similar consequence to swallow. For presumably if there is an objective synonymy relation, then there could be utterances that we know don't bear this relation to any utterances we understand, and yet presumably it could still sometimes make a certain amount of sense to discuss whether such an utterance was true. An inflationist can take such a discussion at face value; but as far as I can see, the only way for a deflationist to deal with this, even if he accepts a notion of "objective synonymy", is to appeal to context-sensitive and interest-relative standards of translation that do not reflect objective synonymy.)

In addition to extended disquotational truth and truth relative to a correlation, there is a third option for a deflationist who wants to apply "true" to foreign utterances, and that is simply to use the concept of pure disquotational truth as originally defined in connection with the foreign utterance, without relativization. This may seem odd: didn't I say that my concept of pure disquotational truth applied only to utterances in my own language? No: I said that it was defined only for utterances that I understand. I understand the sentence "Der Schnee ist weiss". Following Quine (1953, p. 135), I hold that I can apply schema (T) to it, getting

"Der Schnee ist weiss" is true iff der Schnee ist weiss,

which I can perfectly well understand despite its not conforming to the grammatical rules of any standard language. (If it is objected that there would be a problem had I picked a sentence with a different meaning in German than in English, my response is that in that case "Der Schnee ist weiss" would be ambiguous for me, and there would be no problems in this case that don't arise equally for ordinary ambiguity within a language. I will discuss whether ambiguity creates a problem for deflationism in Section 10.)

I don't see any reason to choose between the second and third options: the deflationist can use whichever one suits his purposes of the moment. For some purposes the third option is better than the second. For instance, if I understand a foreign sentence that has no exact equivalent in English, the third option can be used to give more adequate disquotational truth conditions than the second. The third option is also more useful in certain explanatory contexts, when we want to explain a foreigner's behavior without bringing the English language into the explanation. But the second option is often more useful than the third, in that it can in principle be used even for sentences we don't understand. Sometimes that broader application can come in handy: for instance, in trying to *come* to understand a foreign sentence we may try out several different correlations to our own sentences to see which makes most sense. And in some contexts we want to use the second option in connection with semantic or quasi-semantic notions like synonymy or acceptable translation: for instance, in a perjury trial we might want to know whether there is any acceptable translation of an utterance that makes it come out true. Finally, there are contexts in which the second option is useful even in connection with our own utterances: if we are considering a counterfactual situation in which my use of words is very different, I may be interested in the truth conditions of my sentences relative to a mapping of my language into itself that is not the identity mapping. So a deflationist should not dispense with the second option. In many contexts though I think that the third option is the most natural. It is the one that accords with my original gloss on disquotational truth: a sentence is disquotationally true iff it is true-as-I-understand-it.

I think then that the notion of extended disquotational truth should be avoided if possible: it is not obvious that a deflationist can make sense of it, it is less obvious that he needs it, and it seems better to keep the logical aspects of truth cleanly separated from any semantic and quasi-semantic elements.

9 The modal properties of "true"

A further point about extended disquotational truth as I have defined it is that it is a concept of little theoretical utility. That is because it is a curiously hybrid notion: whether a foreign utterance is true in this sense depends on semantic facts, but whether one of our own sentences is true in this sense doesn't (since as applied to our own sentences, extended disquotational truth is equivalent to pure disquotational truth, which is use independent). Recall that certain logical uses of the pure disquotational truth predicate "$true_{pd}$" (for instance, the modal version of the Euclidean geometry example) require that □("Snow is white" is $true_{pd}$ iff snow is white). So even if "snow is white" had been used in English in pretty much the way that "Grass is red" is actually used, "snow is white" would still have been true in the purely disquotational sense, and hence in the extended disquotational sense as well. Moreover, if in addition grass and the German language had been as they actually are, then "Der Gras ist rot" would have been synonymous with "Snow is white", and hence would have been true in the extended disquotational sense too. The counterfactual supposition of a drastic change in the use of English sentences leaves their extended disquotational truth conditions the same but alters the extended disquotational truth conditions of foreign sentences! This, surely, is not a theoretically useful way to make truth conditions use-dependent.

Obviously what we would need to do, if we wanted a more useful notion of truth conditions that has semantic features built into it, is to build in such features for our own sentences as well as for the sentences of others. And of course inflationary theories of truth conditions do precisely this. The question is, can one do this on a theory of truth conditions with any claims to being deflationary?

There is an obvious modification of the extended disquotational approach: I don't know if a view of this sort should be called deflationary or inflationary, so I'll call it *quasi*-deflationary. It requires that we have not only a notion of synonymy, but a prior notion of meaning such that two sentences are synonymous if they have the same meaning; but meaning is to be defined independently of truth conditions. (The crude illustration would be that meanings are just verification conditions; slightly less crudely, perhaps meanings are some sort of equivalence classes of pairs of conceptual roles and indication relations; the point of using equivalence classes being of course to allow that small differences of conceptual role don't make for a difference of meaning.) Then we define quasi-disquotational truth ($truth_{qd}$) and quasi-disquotational truth conditions by:

□(S is $true_{qd}$ iff Σp[∃m(m is the meaning of S and @(m is the meaning of "p")) and p],

and analogously,

□[S has the quasi-disquotational truth conditions that p iff ∃m(m is the meaning of S and @(m is the meaning of "p"))];

where "@" is an "actually operator" which "temporarily undoes the effects of" the modal operator.[28] This seems to have the modal properties we desire if we want to mimic an inflationary truth predicate in making the truth of sentences use-dependent.

Indeed, it mimics it well enough so that it is natural to wonder whether it shouldn't count as an inflationary notion of truth and truth conditions. For note that according to it, a sufficient condition for having the truth conditions that snow is white is having a certain "meaning" m: perhaps a certain combination of such things as conceptual role, indication relations, and the like. Why then shouldn't this count as an explication of truth conditions in terms of such things as conceptual role and indication relations?

It does nonetheless seem to me that there may be something to be said for counting a view like this as somewhat deflationary, if the idea of a meaning is explained in a sufficiently "un-truth-theoretic" way. After all, it is compatible with this view that there be no very systematic connection between "meanings" and truth conditions: for instance, it is compatible with this way of defining truth conditions, albeit not very plausible, that the "meaning" of "Snow is white or grass is green" have few systematic links to the "meanings" of "Snow is white", "Grass is green", and "or". Note further that this view assigns truth conditions only to sentences that are synonymous with English sentences (or anyway, sentences that we understand). This points up the fact that there need be no "natural connection" between the "meanings" it assigns and truth conditions: the connection between the meanings it invokes and truth is supplied entirely by the disquotation schema for sentences we understand. So the view is somewhat deflationary, though just how deflationary it is will depend very much on the details of what it says about "meanings".

One kind of worry about views of this sort concerns whether any acceptable notion of "a meaning" and of "having a meaning" will do the job required. Putting aside purely ontological concerns, the main worry concerns the notion of synonymy (having the same meaning) that would be generated by any such view of meaning and the "having" of meanings. Long ago Quine observed that it is an open question whether interpersonal synonymy and intrapersonal synonymy can be viewed as two aspects of the same general equivalence relation. (Quine 1953, p. 56; see also Quine 1960, sections 9 and 11.) Obviously we employ different criteria in the two cases—for instance, in the intrapersonal case we use a speaker's willingness to substitute one expression for the other, and this criterion is unavailable in the interpersonal case—and reflection on the criteria we do use in the two cases can lead to skepticism as to how well they cohere. I won't try to elaborate this skepticism here, I simply want to note that such skepticism is possible, and that it would make it impossible to regard intrapersonal synonymy and interpersonal synonymy as both cases of the general relation of "having the same meaning". (In addition, the explanation of synonymy as having the same meaning requires synonymy to be an equivalence relation; this is another assumption about synonymy that has been questioned.)

I'm not sure how seriously to take these worries, but as I said in connection with extended disquotational truth, I think it advantageous to cleanly separate the semantic assumptions one is employing from the logical aspects of truth: failing to do so can easily lead to obscuring the role to which one is putting one's semantic assumptions. (I think in fact there is a serious danger of this in the case of quasi-disquotational truth conditions: it is easy to fall into trying to give them a kind of explanatory role that in fact is precluded given the peculiar way they are defined. But this and other issues about explanation are beyond the scope of this paper.) In any case, I think a full-fledged deflationist should make no commitment to a notion of interpersonal synonymy, let alone to interpersonally ascribable meanings.

Let us return now to counterfactuals like

(1) If we had used "Snow is white" in certain very different ways it would have had the truth conditions that grass is red.

Presumably the average person would call such a sentence true. Doesn't this show that the average person is clearly not using the word "true" in its purely disquotational sense? And doesn't that in turn show that a version of deflationism that puts purely disquotational truth at the center of things, and which refrains from endorsing intersubjective meanings and hence quasi-disquotational truth, is gratuitously departing from common sense? I don't think so. We could after all say that the "cash value" of (1) is

(1*) in considering counterfactual circumstances under which we used "Snow is white" in certain very different ways, it is reasonable to translate it in such a way that its disquotational truth conditions relative to the translation are that grass is red;

and that this is all the ordinary person really means to assert. However, I am suspicious of this and all other claims about what the ordinary person means in making assertions involving "true": I rather doubt that there is a consistent way to make sense of all ordinary uses of this notion. I am rather inclined to think that *many* ordinary uses of "true" do fit the purely disquotational mold, though I regard the question of whether this is so is of only sociological interest. If, as may well be true, there is an ordinary meaning of (1) that (1*) fails to capture, then that would show that ordinary speakers are committed to a notion of truth that goes beyond the purely disquotational. But if we can lessen those commitments in a way that is adequate to all practical and theoretical purposes, and if in doing so we can still capture the "cash value" of ordinary utterances as well as (1*) captures the cash value of (1), then the charge that we are "gratuitously departing from common sense" is quite unfounded.

10 Ambiguity and indexicals

So far I have been a bit cavalier about whether a disquotational notion of truth applies to sentence-types or to utterances. I want it to apply to utterances, so that if an ambiguous sentence or a sentence containing an indexical or demonstrative is uttered on different occasions, we can regard some utterances of it as true and others as false.[29] One substantial worry about deflationism is whether it can accommodate this.

In dealing with this worry it is important to bear clearly in mind that talk of truth conditions as I am construing it is thoroughly non-semantic. "True" in the purely disquotational sense means "true as I understand it": it doesn't mean "true on the correct understanding of it", because the idea of a "correct understanding" of a sentence or utterance is a semantic notion that has no place when we are discussing purely disquotational truth. If on my understanding of "Der Schnee ist weiss" it is equivalent to "$E=mc^2$", then for me this sentence is disquotationally true iff $E=mc^2$.[30] Anyone in the grip of the Frege-Russell tradition will think that this shows that we need a notion of truth conditions very different from the disquotational one; but I don't think it at all obvious that they are right. (As I observed in Section 8, a deflationist can argue that there are standards of adequacy of translation that do not presuppose truth conditions, and can grant the legitimacy of saying that relative to a translation manual that meets those standards the sentence will have different truth conditions.) In any case, this *is* a feature of the purely disquotational notion, and the present question is, can this purely disquotational notion be applied to ambiguous utterances and indexical utterances?

Let's start with ambiguity. I believe that it poses little problem for the deflationist. There is a rather common-sensical story of how we process ambiguous sentences, which I assume the deflationist can help himself to: the story has it that when we come upon a two-way ambiguous sentence like "Visiting relatives can be boring" or "I met my lover at the bank", there are two alternative ways of processing it and using it in inferences, one corresponding to each of the interpretations; indeed, interpreting it one way rather than the other just is processing it in one way rather than the other (for instance, storing it in memory in such a way that it will be used in inferences of one kind rather than the other). When we are undecided as to how to interpret an ambiguous sentence, what we are undecided about is how to process and store it and which of the two sorts of inference to make with it. The fact that we can process and store a sentence in two different ways can be put metaphorically by saying that we attach "inner subscripts" to lexically ambiguous elements and "inner syntactic markers" to mark different ways of resolving the syntactic ambiguities. This metaphor allows us to talk, if we like, as if each person thinks in an ambiguity-free language. On this way of talking, to say that an utterance is disquotationally true is to say in effect that the sentence in my ambiguity-free inner language which I associate with the utterance is disquotationally true. Of course, if I am undecided how to interpret the utterance, there is no unique ambiguity-free inner sentence to use and hence no unique disquotational truth conditions will be generated. We can regard that as a case where we don't understand the utterance, so that the notion of disquotational truth doesn't apply—though of course we can also ascribe it truth conditions relative to each of the ways of understanding it. The metaphor of the ambiguity-free language is not really playing an essential role here: I could equally well have said that I accept all instances of "That utterance of 'Visiting relatives can be boring' is true iff visiting relatives can be boring", but may process the right hand side in either of two ways on different occasions. (I disallow inference from the right hand side processed one way to the right hand side processed the other way.)

Now let's turn to sentences containing indexicals and demonstratives. Here it is natural to divide up the account of truth into two stages. The first stage concerns sentence types: here of course there is no hope of defining an unrelativized truth predicate, since sentence-types like "I don't like her" don't have a truth value, but we can associate a truth value to this type relative to a pair of objects <b,c>; to say that "I don't like her" is true relative to <b,c> is simply to say that b doesn't like c. (I suppose that this isn't strictly "disquotational" in that it involves a grammatical adjustment from "don't" to "doesn't", but surely we can allow the disquotationalist the machinery required for this grammatical adjustment.)

The second stage is to provide an account of unrelativized truth for sentence-tokens. Given the first stage, this simply amounts to associating objects with each of the indexical elements in the sentence, for then we can declare the token true iff it is true relative to the sequence of associated objects. How are we to do the association? If we focus only on indexicals like "I" and "now", there is a simple rule that would work pretty well: always relativize "I" to the producer of the token and "now" to the time of production. But this rule isn't invariably such a good one: consider the subway advertisement "Stop smoking now". At any rate, there seems to be no such simple rule for "she", or "that": the "correct" object to assign, if it makes sense to talk of correctness here, depends in very complex ways on the intentions of the producer. In these cases anyway, and probably even in the cases of "I" and "now", we must regard all talk of the "correct assignment" as a semantic matter which cannot appear in a deflationary account of truth conditions.

Still, nothing stops us from applying talk of disquotational truth conditions to tokens: once we remember that "disquotationally true" means "true-as-I-interpret-it", the obvious thing to say is that an utterance of "p(i_1, ..., i_n)" is disquotationally true (for me, that is, as I understand it) iff the sentence is true relative to the values of a_1,...,a_n I regard as appropriate to associate with the indexicals.[31] When I say that I "associate values" with an indexical, of course, what I do is associate a mental occurrence of one of my own expressions (possibly itself indexical) with it. If I can't associate a term with an indexical in a sentence, then I can't attach disquotational truth conditions to the sentence. This is just an extension of a point made earlier for non-indexical utterances: sentences that I don't understand have no disquotational truth conditions for me.

I've said that the expression I associate with an indexical may itself be indexical: I may assign disquotational truth conditions to an utterance of "She is here now" by thinking "She is here now". As with ambiguity, the deflationist needs to say something about how thoughts involving indexicals are processed, but the story is very similar to the story for ambiguity. When I think a thought involving "she" to myself on a given occasion, that thought will typically hook up causally to a certain "internal file drawer" of thoughts involving other singular terms, perhaps "Sheila" and/or "that woman I saw at the beach last Friday". (It is possible that all the singular terms in the "file drawer" are indexical: you can use an indexical to "open a new file drawer". Even when there are other terms in the "file drawer", nothing need pick out any one person uniquely: the function of these associated terms isn't to explain how we can be referring to a certain person, if indeed we are; the function is simply to tell an obvious story of what it is for me to *regard* a given occurrence of "she" as "about Sheila" or "about that woman I saw at the beach".) Again, you could if you like say that the internal occurrences of indexicals are "subscripted" so as to remove their indexicality; I take this to be just a dispensable manner of speaking for something better stated in terms of the internal processing.

We see that there is no special difficulty in explaining disquotational truth conditions for indexical tokens. If indexicals raise any special difficulty for deflationism, it is that for indexicals it is less believable that we don't need a more inflationist notion of truth conditions. Surely, it may be said, there will typically be a *correct answer* to the question of who another person was referring to with a particular application of "she"; and the deflationist seems unable to accommodate this.

It seems to me though that the internal processing story does a lot to accommodate it. In a typical case where we misinterpret a token of "she"—where we incorrectly interpret the speaker as meaning Mary when in fact she meant Sheila—we do so because of false beliefs about the speaker's internal processing: we think that her token was connected up to an internal file drawer of thoughts involving terms like "Mary" when in fact it was connected up to a file drawer involving terms like "Sheila". Standards of appropriate translation are going to rule that in that case, "Mary" is a bad translation of "she". The sort of facts that this brings into the standards of good translation are not in themselves semantic, so it seems hard to argue that the deflationist isn't entitled to appeal to them. Of course, it may be possible to argue that when we describe the standards of acceptable translation for indexicals in detail we will have to bring in machinery that is powerful enough to provide a reduction of the semantic notion of reference to nonsemantic terms; if this is so, then the would-be deflationist is in fact turning himself into a reductionist inflationist. As I remarked earlier, the distinction between deflationism and reductionist inflationism may not in the end be altogether clear. At any rate, it certainly isn't obvious without argument that the standards of acceptable translation for indexicals give the machinery necessary to reduce the semantic notion of reference to non-semantic terms.

11 Learning from others

The final objection that I will consider is that you need an inflationist view of truth conditions to make sense of how we learn from others. Much of our information about the world is acquired from others—in particular, from their utterances, and from the beliefs we infer them to have. The notion of truth figures in this process: typically, what we do is assume that certain things the other person tells us are probably true—or that certain things we can see that she believes are probably true. It might be thought that an understanding of this process requires a non-deflationary notion of truth; or at least, that it requires more than purely disquotational truth. There are actually two distinct lines of argument that might be given for this conclusion.

The first is that since we learn from other people, including people who speak different languages, translation must somehow be involved, so that some notion of interpersonal synonymy is presupposed in the inference. If this were right it would show that pure disquotational truth, without a synonymy relation, was inadequate for these purposes: you'd need at least extended disquotational or quasi-disquotational truth, and maybe a more thoroughgoing inflationary notion, for the purpose. I'll get back to this after discussing the other line of argument.

The second line of argument purports to show that even pure disquotational truth plus synonymy isn't enough. Let's slur over the possible need for a synonymy relation, by imagining that I am learning from Charley, a speaker of my idiolect. Charley says: "You know, on one day in 1936 there was over a foot of snow on the ground in Mobile Alabama". Do I infer that one day in 1936 there was over a foot of snow in Alabama? For most Charleys and most circumstances, surely not. But suppose that in the past Charley has asserted each of the following: "You know, there are parts of Virginia that are north of parts of New Jersey"; "You know, in 1928 the Soviet government secretly supplied arms to Chang Kai-Shek to be used against Mao"; "You know, Leon Russell was one of the studio musicians for the Fleetwoods". Each time I've found the claim almost unbelievable, but on checking it has turned out true. If he has never said "You know, p" for a p that has turned out false, then I think I might well believe his claim about Mobile.

A crude way to formalize my inference is as an enumerative induction: all the sentences of a certain sort that Charley has uttered under certain circumstances that have been independently checked have been true; "There was a foot of snow in Mobile" is a sentence of that sort uttered under those circumstances; so (in the absence of defeating evidence) probably that sentence is true. In addition to the inductive inference, we need an instance of the disquotation schema, to get from the claim about truth to the object level claim. Obviously the disquotationalist has no trouble with the last step. But the inductive part of the inference might seem more questionable. For suppose we were to try to formalize the inductive inference without use of the word "true". What we would get is this:

1. There are parts of Virginia that are north of parts of New Jersey.

.

.

.

n. In 1928 the Soviet government secretly supplied arms to Chang Kai-Shek to be used against Mao.

n+1. Charley said "You know, there are parts of Virginia that are north of parts of New Jersey."

.

.

.

2n. Charley said "You know, in 1928 the Soviet government secretly supplied arms to Chang Kai-Shek to be used against Mao."

2n+1. Charley said "You know, on one day in 1936 there was over a foot of snow in Mobile Alabama."

Therefore (probably): On one day in 1936 there was over a foot of snow in Mobile Alabama.

And a possible reaction to this inference so formulated is that it has no inductive force whatever: none of the premises, have anything to do with snow or Mobile; the first n have to do with diverse topics, and the last n+1 have to do only with noises that Charley uttered. So, it might be argued, when we reformulate the premises and conclusion of the inference in terms of truth, this can't be the innocent reformulation that the disquotationalist says it is: for the displayed inference has no inductive force, but the reformulation in terms of truth does have inductive force. So the reformulated inference works by attributing a more substantive property than disquotational truth to Charley's utterances, a substantive property on which it is legitimate to enumeratively induce.

I have tried to set out this line of argument persuasively, but in my view it rests on a very naive theory of induction. (I'm not talking about its use of enumerative induction: I take the assumption that learning from Charley is based on an enumerative induction to be a simplifying assumption on which nothing important is likely to turn.) I grant that to someone who had no concept of truth whatever, the displayed inference would probably have no inductive force. But that doesn't imply that we who do have a concept of disquotational truth should attach no inductive force to the very same inference (or equivalently, to the inference as reformulated in terms of disquotational truth). To be sure, our attaching force to this inference does not inevitably follow from our having a disquotational truth predicate; in principle, someone could perfectly well have a disquotational truth predicate and regard it as "unprojectable". But the fact that we aren't like that, that we do regard it as "projectable", doesn't seem to me to have much to do with whether the predicate is "substantive" in the sense employed in the objection: it doesn't show that "true" isn't just a logical predicate defined by its role as a device of infinite conjunction. (It's worth noting that someone could equally well introduce a more theoretically loaded truth predicate and find it "unprojectable": "grue" after all is a "substantive" predicate in the sense in question here, that is, it is not a mere logical device in the way that disquotational truth is.) Our acceptance of enumerative inductions on "true" is presumably due to having discovered that we get useful results by doing so,[32] and such a discovery does not require that truth be anything more than what the disquotation schemas tell us.

If this is right then the second argument that learning from others is incompatible with deflationism has no force. How about the first argument, that learning from others requires an interpersonal notion of synonymy, so that pure disquotational truth by itself is inadequate to the job? This too seems wrong. Suppose Charley speaks another language, which I think I understand: anyway, I have a translation manual that I use for it. Suppose I have found out in the past than when Charley utters sentences, they usually turn out to be true as I understand them—that is, their translations turn out true, on the translation manual I use. Then we have an inductive argument that the next one will be true, on the manual I use: in this way, we can inductively argue to the snow in Mobile, as before. As far as I can see it doesn't matter in the least whether this manual accords with the genuine interpersonal synonymy relation between his sentences and ours, assuming that such talk of the correct interpersonal synonymy relation even makes sense: truth-relative-to-the-manual is the only notion we need in learning from others.

12 Conclusion

I repeat that there are many other arguments to be considered for the need of a more-than-disquotational notion of truth or truth conditions, some much more complicated to deal with than any given here. What I have tried to do here is simply to motivate a fairly strong version of deflationism—strong in that it does not rely even on a semantic notion of synonymy—and to sketch how such a version of deflationism can overcome various objections. I think what I have done here makes some case for what I've called "methodological deflationism", the idea that we should assume full-fledged deflationism as a working hypothesis. That way, if full-fledged deflationism turns out to be inadequate, we will at least have a clearer sense than we have now of just where it is that inflationist assumptions about truth conditions are needed.[33]

Notes

1. Because of the paradoxes, exceptions must be made for certain utterances u that contain 'true'; I won't be concerned here with just how the exceptions are to be carved out.
2. There is more than one acceptable way to understand "cognitively equivalent" here. My own preferred reading, for what it's worth, is that to call two sentences that a person understands "cognitively equivalent" for that person is to say that the person's inferential procedures license a fairly direct inference from any sentence containing an occurrence of one to the corresponding sentence with an occurrence of the other substituted for it; with the stipulation, of course, that the occurrence to be substituted for is not within the context of quotation marks or an intentional attitude construction. (Cognitive equivalence *relative to some other assumption* is the same, except that that assumption is allowed to be used in the inferences.) I would also take the claim of cognitive equivalence to imply that the inferences are more or less indefeasible. (More specifically, that they are empirically indefeasible, and close to indefeasible on conceptual

grounds as well, and that the person is not in possession of defeaters for them. These stipulations are motivated by the assumption that we should describe someone who doesn't know the semantic paradoxes as a person for whom "'p' is true" is cognitively equivalent to "p" across the board; as the person comes to terms with the paradoxes he revises his standards of cognitive equivalence on conceptual grounds.)

3. Certain uses of truth conditional talk in explanations seems to me the most likely target for excision.
4. More radical, I think, than the one advanced in Horwich 1990. While I like much that Horwich says I have substantial disagreements: see Field 1992.
5. Of course, conceptual or computational role can be described at different levels of abstraction, so there is more than one notion of conceptual role that meets this description. I think the notions of meaning and content are too indeterminate for there to be a right answer about which notion of conceptual role to include; one could even include more than one.
6. If the probability of S given E is higher than the probability of S, then (especially if this fact is rather "robust", that is, if except for very special sentences F, P(S|E&F) remains higher than P(S|F)) it is natural to include this fact in the conceptual role of S, even if E is in no sense "observational" and could never be established with enough certainty or whatever to count as evidence for anything. It was central to verificationism to exclude such facts from verification conditions when E was not observational.
7. Part of the idea behind this assumption is that when you read or hear a given unambiguous sentence, there is a type of thought state that you typically undergo in processing it, where this type is identifiable in purely computational terms; and that this type of thought state also typically occurs when you utter such a sentence. This assumption and some other plausible assumptions about the computational processes of the language-user make it possible to define in computational terms a correspondence between many of the person's states of believing and desiring and their unambiguous sentences. A natural computational story about the processing of ambiguous sentences allows us to extend this to such sentences too. I will not attempt to give the details of any of this here.
8. Whether the deflationist can formulate the distinction for *other peoples'* belief states is less clear, and turns on some issues we will discuss.
9. I have heard the objection that a deflationist is free to give truth conditions an explanatory role as long as it is only "deflationary truth conditions" and not "heavy duty truth conditions" that are given that role. This seems to me a confusion. I think it is quite misleading to speak of two kinds of truth conditions, the heavy duty ones and the disquotational ones: this suggests that the advocate of "heavy duty" truth conditions thinks that we should ascribe to "Snow is white" some truth conditions other than that snow is white, and that of course is absurd. It would be better to say that there are two kinds of relation between truth conditions on the one hand and utterances and mental states on the other, the disquotational relation and the heavy duty relation. But the only ways I can see to make sense of the distinction between these relations directly or indirectly preclude giving the disquotational relation certain kinds of explanatory role. (In my view, the preclusion is indirect, and stems from the deflationist's account of how truth conditions attach to sentences and mental states.)
10. This last way of putting things gives a way to make content social without relying on an independent notion of meaning. It thus leaves room for explaining meaning in terms of content if so desired.

11. I mention "not" because the deductive inference rules I listed include the rule that we can infer "not (A or B)" from "not A" and "not B" together. It is possible to replace this by a rule involving "if...then" instead of "not"; or (as in natural deduction systems and sequent calculi) by a rule involving a notion of implication.
12. It may not avoid the threat of indeterminacy in the end: I discuss this in Field 1994. Even so, the account to follow offers an attractive alternative to the inflationist's approach to the determination of the way that our logical symbols contribute to truth conditions; and I will generalize it in Section 6.
13. The argument from (T) to (TF) generalizes as an argument from (TG) to

    ∏p∏q["p or q" is true if and only if "p" is true or "q" is true].

    By use of the additional axiom

    ∀x[x is a sentence of our language ⊃ Σp(x="p")],

    we get (TFG).
14. Or at the very least, description theories that use only non-metalinguistic descriptions.
15. This incidentally is why the Benacerraf problem about mathematical knowledge (Benacerraf 1973) isn't dissolved by a disquotational theory of truth.
16. Methodological deflationism doesn't even end up precluding that we might in the end come to accept an *unreduced* inflationist relation *S has the truth conditions that p*: we might conceivably see the need for introducing non-physical relations as explanatory. I think it does put the burden of proof against such a position, but I think that doing so is appropriate.
17. This needs two small qualifications. The first is that the generalizations can be formulated otherwise if the language contains certain devices of infinite conjunction such as substitutional quantifiers. However, this qualification is not a terribly severe one, since the presence of such substitutional quantifiers would allow you to define "true": S is true iff ∏p(S="p" ⊃ p). (Again, I assume a theory of substitutional quantification that avoids the paradoxes.)

    Note that the use of schematic letters as an alternative to substitutional quantification, mentioned in Section 3, does not allow us to formulate infinite disjunctions without "true", and therefore does not allow us to explicitly define "true".

    The second qualification is that what I've given (in either the substitutional quantifier version or the free schematic variable version) allows statements that are really a bit stronger than infinite conjunctions, in the same way that first order quantifications are stronger than the totality of their instances even when every object has a name: see the discussion in Section 3 of how to get the generalization (TFG).
18. For present purposes I am regarding sentence types as "necessary existents", so that the fact that the disjuncts don't all entail the existence of sentence types doesn't debar a sentence that does entail this from counting as their "infinite disjunction".
19. Both Hilary Putnam (1983, pp. xiv-xv and 279-80) and Crispin Wright (1992, pp. 12-24) object to deflationism on this ground. However, their discussions are directed at a version of deflationism which says that truth is not a property (Putnam) or not a "substantial property" (Wright), and I'm not clear enough as to what that is supposed to mean to know whether the authors would have intended to be arguing against deflationism as I have defined it. (In a long footnote, Wright does say that he thinks his objection applies to the version of deflationism in Horwich 1990, despite the fact that Horwich disavows the "no property" claim.)

20. Opponents of deflationism sometimes try to pin on it the claim that when we come to understand new sentences, or when new words and hence new sentences are added to our language, our concept of truth changes. But a deflationist can agree that on the most natural ways to individuate concepts over time, adding new sentences to the language (or to our domain of understanding) leaves the concept of truth unchanged: after all, once we have come to understand the new sentences, the truth schema dictates how the word "true" is to be applied to them. This doesn't conflict with what is said in the text: the point there was that we don't now understand attributions of disquotational truth to sentences containing future words. (Also, there is no reasonable sense in which such attributions now have disquotational truth conditions, since what truth conditions they may come to have will depend on how the future words will be used.)
21. We can introduce a purely disquotational notion of what it is to express a proposition, with the property that claims of the form "'p' expresses the proposition that p" are necessary truths. We can also introduce certain impurely disquotational notions of what it is to express a proposition; these are analogous to the impure disquotational views of truth that we will consider later. Deflationists about meaning that and believing that think that such disquotational notions of expressing are the only legitimate ones; inflationists disagree. This distinction between inflationist and deflationist notions of expressing a proposition obviously needs to be clarified, if one is going to talk in terms of propositions; I think that some of the rest of the paper suggests a way to clarify it, but I will obviate the need to discuss this by avoiding talk of propositions.
22. Or a more basic notion like satisfaction from which truth is defined.
23. Actually even the demand of a compositional *inductive definition* must be relaxed, if we want to both get a notion of truth that applies to sufficiently many sentences that contain semantic terms and simultaneously avoid limiting the truth predicate to sentences containing no unrestricted quantifiers: the usual methods like Kripke's for defining a notion of truth that applies to sufficiently many sentences that contain "true" require a restriction of quantifiers *even in the inductive definition* (not just in turning it into an explicit definition); that is, what is being defined isn't truth but only "comes out true under such and such a restriction of the quantifiers". I think that a lesson of the paradoxes is that we must go to an axiomatized truth theory rather than defining "true", even inductively.

    But this doesn't undermine the point intended in the text: for one might well demand (more or less in the spirit of Tarski or at least Davidson) that an axiomatized truth theory be built around explicit compositional axioms like "A disjunction is true if and only if at least one disjunct is true". A more full-fledged deflationist view would be that such compositionality has no intrinsic importance.
24. Let P be a one place predicate and N a name. By the assumptions indicated, ΣF(P="F") and Σa(N="a"). By laws of concatenation and quotation marks, it follows that ΣFΣa(P^N="Fa").

    By syntax, ΠFΠa["Fa" is a sentence], so by the truth schema, ΠFΠa["Fa" is true iff Fa]. By first order logic, we can rewrite this as ΠFΠa["Fa" is true iff ∃x(Fx and x=a)]. But then the appropriate schemas for truth of and reference will allow us to rewrite this as ΠFΠa["Fa" is true iff ∃x("F" is true of x and "a" refers to x)]. Combining with the previous paragraph, we get that P^N is true iff ∃x(P is true of x and N refers to x).

    The step labelled "by first order logic" implicitly assumes that N denotes, that is, that Σa[n="a" and ∃x(x=a)]. If this supposition is abandoned, some form of free logic must be used; the details of the free logic affect the details of the compositional principle that is derived.

25. At least, this is so for what I've called a "pure deflationist". The idea of "impure deflationism" will be considered in Section 9.
26. I made a rather confusing attempt to state the problem in Field 1986, Sections IV and V. I now think there is a way around the problem there raised. (Stephen Leeds helped set me straight on this: see Leeds 1995, a draft of which I received just as this paper was being completed.)
27. I'm inclined to think that the problem isn't just that interpersonal synonymy ("is a good translation of") is a highly vague notion, but that it isn't a fully factual notion at all; rather, it is an evaluative notion. This is compatible with many claims of interpersonal synonymy being factual relative to the goals of the translator; but not all interpersonal synonymy claims need be factual even relative to the goals.
28. See for instance Crossley and Humberstone 1977.

    Quantification over meanings seems necessary in this definition: certainly you can't replace the right hand side by "Σp[@(S is synonymous with 'p')) and p]", since this makes only the actual meaning of S relevant to whether S would be true in a non-actual context, contrary to intentions. And you can't simply take meanings to be equivalence classes of expressions under the (actual) synonymy relation: for then the proposed definition would collapse into the inadequate one just mentioned. In these remarks I'm assuming that you don't quantify over possible worlds: if you do, then you can use the relation *expression e as used in world w is synonymous with e' as used in w',* and take meanings to be equivalence classes of pairs of expressions and possible worlds under this equivalence relation.
29. Incidentally, I remind the reader that I am counting it as an example of ambiguity if someone understands the same sentence as meaning one thing in German and something else in English: this was required by my adopting the "third option" for dealing with sentences in other languages, discussed in Section 8.
30. Since it is disquotationally true iff der Schnee ist weiss, and hence, by the equivalence hypothesis, iff $E=mc^2$.
31. Typically these will be the ones I take the producer of the utterance to have intended, but not always: e.g., "now" on the sign intended to be read by various readers at different times. And since we're talking disquotational truth, the actual intentions of the producer don't matter, what matters is the reading the hearer gives.
32. We may well also have an innate predisposition to believe other people, barring evidence to the contrary; this does not affect my point.
33. I've had helpful conversations with many people about these issues in recent years. Among those whose comments have influenced my presentation are Marian David, Michael Devitt, Paul Horwich, Barry Loewer, and Stephen Schiffer. I have also incorporated some useful suggestions by the editors.

References

Benacerraf, Paul 1973: "Mathematical Truth". *Journal of Philosophy*, 70, 19, pp. 661–79.

Crossley, J. and L. Humberstone 1977: "The Logic of 'Actually'", *Reports on Mathematical Logic*, 8, pp. 11–29.

Field, Hartry 1986: "The Deflationary Conception of Truth". In G. McDonald and C. Wright, *Fact, Science and Value*. Oxford: Basil Blackwell, pp. 55–117.

Field, Hartry 1992: "Critical Notice: Paul Horwich's *Truth*". *Philosophy of Science* 59, 2, pp. 321–330.

Field, Hartry 1994: "Disquotational Truth and Factually Defective Discourse". *Philosophical Review*, 103, 3.

Horwich, Paul, 1990: *Truth*. Oxford: Basil Blackwell.

Kripke, Saul 1980: *Naming and Necessity*. Cambridge, Mass.: Harvard University Press.

Lewis, David 1975: "Languages and Language". In K. Gunderson, ed., *Minnesota Studies in Philosophy of Science* vol VII. Minneapolis: University of Minnesota Press, pp. 3–35.

Putnam, Hilary 1983: *Philosophical Papers* vol. 3. Cambridge, Eng.: Cambridge University Press.

Quine, Willard V. 1953: *From a Logical Point of View*. Cambridge, Mass.: Harvard University Press.

Quine, Willard V. 1960: *Word and Object*. Cambridge, Mass.: M.I.T. Press.

Soames, Scott 1984: "What is a Theory of Truth?", *Journal of Philosophy* 81,8, pp. 411–29.

Stalnaker, Robert 1984: *Inquiry*. Cambridge, Mass.: M.I.T. Press.

Wright, Crispin 1992: *Truth and Objectivity*. Cambridge, Mass.: Harvard University Press.

12 On two deflationary truth theories

DOROTHY GROVER

At one time, debates about truth centered on questions concerning the "nature of truth." Then Ramsey (1927) observed that "'it is true that Caesar was murdered' means no more than that Caesar was murdered, and 'It is false that Caesar was murdered' means that Caesar was not murdered." Such observations have led philosophers to question the assumption that truth has a nature that must be theorized about. So there are now two schools of thought concerning truth: Some philosophers argue that truth is to be analysed in terms of either epistemic or metaphysical concepts (as in "Truth is a relational property connecting language with the world");[1] and other philosophers argue that truth is not a substantive relational property. The former are said to advocate a *substantive* analysis of truth, and the latter a *deflationary* analysis. The development of deflationary theories has meant that substantive theorists must not only give an account of the nature of truth but also show that a substantive truth property is needed. On the other side, deflationists (who claim the truth predicate need not have an explanatory role) must either provide some other account of the role of the truth predicate or show the truth predicate is redundant. My project is to provide a comparison of two deflationary theories that claim a role for the truth predicate: the *disquotational theory of truth*[2] and the theory of which Nuel Belnap was a co-founder, the *prosentential theory of truth.*

A preview

The disquotational and prosentential theories are similar in that both claim the truth predicate has utility in providing us with certain kinds of expressibility. There is some agreement about the expressibility provided, because both claim the truth predicate makes available generalization with respect to sentence positions. However, there are differences in their "formal" analyses of this role of the truth predicate. Disquotational theorists utilize first-order quantifiers and an explicit truth predicate in their analyses, while prosentential theorists appeal only to propositional quantifiers. This suggests a difference in the "level" of the truth predicate, for the disquotational analysis of generalization seems to treat 'true' syntactically as a metalinguistic predicate, while the prosentential analysis seems to have 'true' operating at the level of the object language. I argue these differences are not as significant as they might first appear.

I will also address some questions that disquotational theorists have left open. Rather than speculating as to how the theory's proponents might answer these questions, I will show that an available option for disquotational theorists is offered by the prosentential theory.

1 The disquotational theory

The disquotational theory seems to have been inspired by Quine's (1970) remarks about the truth predicate. The account of truth provided by the theory is also said to connect in some way with Tarski's work. I do not know whether Quine subscribes to what is now being recognized as the disquotational theory. But because his brief remarks (pp. 10-13) provide insight others do not provide, I will often rely on Quine's remarks in describing the theory. The key claims of the disquotational theory seem to be the following:

1.1 The truth predicate is a device of disquotation, of semantic ascent and semantic descent. For example,

> Truth is useful, we may say, as a device of (what Quine calls) *disquotation.* (Leeds, 1978)
>
> It is helpful... to focus on something that the truth predicate is good for—namely, what W. V. Quine has called "semantic ascent." (Soames 1984, p. 412)

Soames gives as an example of semantic ascent, the move from 'Snow is white' to "The sentence 'Snow is white' is true."

1.2 The truth predicate is said to have utility in providing a way of generalizing with respect to sentence positions. For generalization with respect to sentence positions can be achieved via quantifiers binding variables in nominal positions. The truth predicate and semantic ascent facilitate this. Soames illustrates the necessary moves in the following passage:

> The importance of semantic ascent is illustrated by cases like (3), in which we want to generalize.
>
> (3) a. Snow is white → (Grass is blue → Snow is white)
>
> b. The earth moves → (The sun is cold → The earth moves)
>
> ...
>
> ... if one wanted to get the effect of asserting all of them, one would have to quantify, replacing sentences with variables. In English such quantification is most naturally, though not inevitably construed as first order and objectual. Thus, if the variables are taken to range over sentences we need a metalinguistic truth predicate. Semantic ascent gives us
>
> (4) For all sentences *x*, *y* (*x* is true → (*y* is true → *x* is true)). (Soames 1984, p. 413)

1.3 Disquotational theorists connect their theory in various ways with either Tarski-style truth definitions or the so-called *T*-sentences of Tarski. Soames thinks that Tarski-style truth definitions legitimize our use of the truth predicate; so defined, "the resulting truth predicate is just what is needed for metatheoretical studies of the nature, structure, and scope of a wide variety of theories." (Soames 1984, p. 425) And Williams (1986) says, "We can agree that the "disquotation" schema '*x* is true in *L* iff *p*' captures something important about truth.

Perhaps in conjunction with some additional conventions to cover cases like 'Everything he told you was true,' where 'true' is used in connection with statements not directly quoted, it fixes the extension of the truth predicate for language *L*."

1.4 Soames's talk of "a metalinguistic truth predicate" and the fact that " 'Snow is white' is true" is assumed paradigmatic, both suggest that disquotational theorists think of the truth predicate as functioning syntactically like a metalinguistic predicate.

1.5 The disquotational treatment of the relevant generalizations seems to suggest that the truth predicate also functions semantically as a metalinguistic predicate. However, *the* disquotational view on this point is not clear, for consider Quine's explanation of the truth predicate's role in semantic ascent: "The truth predicate is a reminder that, despite a technical ascent to talk of sentences, our eye is on the world. By calling the sentence ['Snow is white'] true, we call snow white." (Quine 1970, p. 12) There is a suggestion here, and in other places, that sentences containing the truth predicate are *really* about extralinguistic things. If that is the case, the truth predicate would function in a way different from (other?) metalinguistic predicates.

1.6 According to disquotational theorists, the concept of truth does not have an explanatory role; it does not require analysis in terms of either substantive metaphysical or epistemic relations. This view is expressed in claims like the following:

> Truth is a useful notion, but it is not the key to what there is, or how we represent the world to ourselves through language. (Soames 1984)
>
> To explain the utility of disquotation, we need say nothing about the relations between language and the world. (Leeds 1978)

2 The prosentential theory

Because I can provide only a brief review of the prosentential theory, I will give special emphasis to those parts of the theory that are most relevant to this discussion.[3] The principal claim of the prosentential theory is that the predicates 'true' and 'false' provide prosentential constructions. Prosentences are like pronouns (and other proforms[4]) in that they can be used anaphorically; however, whereas pro*nouns* are atomic and occupy positions nouns occupy, pro*sentences* tend to be nonatomic and occupy the positions that sentences occupy.

My review of the theory will show that the prosentential analysis of sentences containing the truth predicate carries implications regarding both the utility of the truth predicate and how this utility is to be explained.

2.1 A key claim of the prosentential theory is that 'That is true' and 'It is true' function as prosentences. I will illustrate what this can mean in a particular case. When Alan says, 'If that is true, then,...' in

> MARY: Chicago is large.
> ALAN: If that is true, then it probably has a large airport.

Alan says, in effect, "If Chicago is large, then ..." For in the simple cases, part of the role of a proform ('that is true') is to "stand in" for its antecedent sentence (Marys 'Chicago is large').[5] A reason for using the anaphoric 'that is true' (rather than "Chicago is large') is to make clear that Alan is entertaining what Mary has said, rather than saying something on his own initiative. Anaphoric devices establish such connections. More generally, prosentences (and other proforms) are useful when we need to establish connections between different parts of a discourse. Such facts also explain how it is that 'that is true' can be used to express agreement.

2.2 Prosentences can be modified, as in 'That is false' and 'That may be true'. Because 'That is false', in a given context, can be used to assert the contradiction of an antecedent sentence, it can be used to express disagreement. Thus, in

MARY: Chicago is large.
ALAN: That's false.

Alan utilizes the anaphoric overtones of 'That is false' in expressing his disagreement with Mary.

2.3 The prosentential account of the role of the truth predicate in generalization goes roughly as follows: Suppose we want to generalize with respect to the component sentences in

(1) If Eva says that the reactor is unsafe, the reactor is unsafe.

If Eva says the guidelines have been satisfied, the guidelines have been satisfied.

In English we would normally say something like

(2) Everything Eva says (about the safety of the reactor) is true.

Our claim that 'true' has a prosentential role in (2) is based partly on the observation that there are paraphrases of sentences like (2) in which 'true' occurs in a prosentence. In (3), for example, 'true' occurs in the bound prosentence 'it is true'.

(3) For everything Eva says (about the safety of the reactor), it is true.

This bound use of 'it is true' has an analogue in formal languages. Consider, for example,

(4) For any *p* (if Eva says that *p* then *p*)

(3) and (4) say roughly the same thing. In fact, this pair of sentences illustrates our point that bound prosentences function much as bound propositional variables function in formal languages;[6] what this means, among other things, is that the truth predicate provides the expressibility that propositional variables provide us with in formal languages.

I have ignored, in (4), the suggested qualifying clause "about the safety of the reactor." On the assumption that the quantifiers are interpreted substitutionally and we have a quotation functor,[7] I could incorporate the qualification, as follows:

(5) $\forall p$(If (Eva says that *p* & *Qp* is about the reactor's safety) then *p*)

where '*Qp*' stands for "'*p*'".

2.4 It can be seen that the *syntax* of the prosentential truth predicate is a little different from the syntax of those predicates we typically classify as metalinguistic predicates; for we usually think of metalinguistic predicates as combining with terms to form closed sentences. By contrast, in the case of primitive sentences, the pro- sentential truth predicate combines with terms to form prosentences; furthermore, prosentences might reasonably be said to be "bound" by their antecedents.

2.5 There are also *semantic* differences between the prosentential truth predicate and predicates we typically classify as metalinguistic. One difference is that the prosentential truth predicate is only a part of a prosentential construction—so it is, in a sense, an "incomplete symbol." Another difference is that the prosentential truth predicate seems to function at the level of the object language. This is something I need to say a bit more about.

What is in question is the semantic content of sentences containing the truth predicate. Many other truth theories assume that a sentence containing a truth predication, e.g., 'That is true', is about its antecedent sentence ('Chicago is large') or an antecedent proposition. By contrast, the prosentential account is that 'That is true' does not say anything about its antecedent sentence (e.g., 'Chicago is large') but says something about an extralinguistic subject (e.g., Chicago).

In order to see how the sentence 'Chicago is large', itself, need not feature in what is said, it will be helpful to consider the way pronouns function. Consider

(6) The balloon rises when it is filled with helium.

If we are to understand what is said, we must understand that the words 'the balloon' and 'it' are linked. (In this case, syntactical considerations lead us to the linkage.) However, the fact that we must see that there is a link between two expressions does not mean that when we use 'it' we actually *refer* to the words 'the balloon'. Nothing is said in (6) about either the words 'the balloon' or the linking. Similarly, even though a prosentence may be linked with an antecedent expression, we speak only of extralinguistic objects (e.g., snow or Chicago) when we use 'That is true'.

Because we usually talk of such things as balloons and snow at the level of the object language, it seems appropriate to characterize truth predications and modified truth predications as also functioning, so to speak, at the level of the object language.

2.6 The prosentential theory has assumed that truth does not have an explanatory role[8] and that truth does not thereby need to be analysed in terms of either substantive epistemic or metaphysical concepts. What the prosentential theory does require is a theory of anaphora. Such a theory is needed to explain the linguistic and logical aspects of anaphora in order to explain the semantic and pragmatic features of the utility of prosentences more adequately. A formal theory of the logic of prosentences may also reveal possible options regarding the syntax, semantics, and role in inference of prosentential constructions in potentially useful formal languages.

3 Generalization – A comparison

The quantifiers used by the two deflationary theories, in their analyses of generalization, are clearly different. In the one case the bound variables occupy the positions nouns occupy, and in the other the variables occupy the positions sentences occupy. Quine's followers may hold this difference to be critical, for Quine has argued that quantification that involves bound propositional variables is incoherent if a domain-and-values interpretation is given. Such a response by 'Quine's followers' would be too hasty, however. For even if Quine were right about such propositional quantifiers, it has not been shown that the propositional quantifiers employed by the prosentential theory must be given a domain-and-values interpretation. Indeed, I will be discussing a version of the prosentential theory according to which the propositional quantifiers are interpreted substitutionally. For it is this version of the prosentential theory that is most similar to the disquotational theory. Let us look at some of the details.

3.1 Soames's example (in §1.2, above) suggests the following as a disquotational analysis of (3):[9]

(7) For every *x,* if Eva says *x,* then *x* is true.

if we ignore the qualifying clause '"about the safety of the reactor."[10] The quantifiers are interpreted objectually with the variables ranging over a domain of closed sentences. (So that there is no confusion between the prosentential and disquotational analyses, I am using '*x*', '*y*', etc. as variables occupying nominal positions; I reserve '*p*', '*q*', etc. for use as variables that occupy sentential positions.) Because (7) has instances like

(8) If Eva says "the reactor is unsafe" then "the reactor is unsafe" is true.

"semantic descent" is needed to return such instances to direct speech versions of the instances in (2) above. That is, to restore an instance such as (8) to

If Eva says "the reactor is unsafe," then the reactor is unsafe.

Note that the disquotational evaluation of sentences like (7) and (8) requires a domain of sentences, *D,* and an extension for the truth predicate.[11] In the event that the truth predicate can occur in sentences in *D,* we might suppose that a Tarski-style truth definition[12] is used to determine an appropriate extension for 'true' in a given context.

By contrast, for the prosentential theory, I assume the propositional quantifiers are interpreted substitutionally. So, associated with each quantifier will be a set of closed sentences that I call its *substitution range, SR.* We must suppose the sentences of SR mapped into {*1,0*}. In the event that bound propositional variables occur in the sentences of *SR*, we should use a "propositional Tarski-style truth construction" to determine an appropriate mapping for a given use of a quantifier. By a *propositional Tarski-style truth construction* I mean a construction similar to a Tarski-style truth construction, except that propositional quantifiers (substitutionally interpreted) and quantification in and out of quotes are featured, rather than the truth predicate and first-order quantifiers (interpreted with a domain of sentences).

We know that propositional Tarski-style constructions are possible, because it can be shown that sentences of the form

For any *x* (... *x* ... *Tx* ...)

(hereafter, '$\forall xA(x, Tx)$') are provable, just in case sentences of the form

For any *p* (... *Qp* ... *p* ...)

(hereafter, '$\forall pA(Qp, p)$') are provable.[13] Methods of evaluation, similar to those used in Tarski-style constructions to determine the extension of the truth predicate, would be used to assign values to the sentences occurring in the appropriate substitution ranges of the bound propositional variables. The value of a sentence like

(9) For any *p*, if Eva says that *p* then *p.*

could then be determined. For (9) will be assigned the value *1,* just in case all instances obtained by substituting the members of the appropriate *SR* for *'p',* in 'if Eva says that *p* then *p',* have the value *1.*

It is clear that if we view the role of the truth predicate in (8) as similar to that of the bound propositional variable in (9), then even when used for generalizing, the truth predicate functions semantically at the level of the object language—such universal statements are in effect equivalent to a possibly infinite conjunction of sentences of the *object language.*

3.2 These are the two deflationist accounts of the truth predicate's role in generalization. What are we to make of their differences? The first point to be noted is that, if we compare only the assumptions of the quantifiers used in the two analyzing languages, the differences are trivial. For in the examples considered above, the disquotational theory assumes a domain of closed sentences, while the prosentential theory assumes a substitution range of closed sentences. In each case an acceptable evaluation derives from an appropriate Tarski-style truth construction.

In the one case, values of the sentences in the domain are determined by a Tarski-style construction, and in the other, values of the sentences in the substitution range are determined by a propositional Tarski-style construction. It follows that *for roughly the same expressibility the two deflationary theories make the same assumptions.*

There are differences, of course, in the underlying explanations of the role of the truth predicate. For example, one theory talks of semantic ascent and T-sentences, and the other theory of proforms and prosentences. I discuss these differences in the next section. Later, I will say more about my supposition that deflationists can appeal to Tarski-style truth constructions in their analyses of the role of the truth predicate in generalization.

4 Metalinguistic uses of the truth predicate

In our early discussions of the prosentential theory, Belnap was initially concerned that the prosentential theory may not provide an account of 'true' compatible with supposedly metalinguistic uses in model theoretic contexts. Because this is a concern other logicians may share, I will say something about my response.[14] The issue is relevant because it concerns another apparent difference between the two deflationary theories that I have already mentioned: the "level" at which the truth predicate functions.

4.1 I begin with the disquotational theory because the disquotational truth theorists seem to have had their eyes on the logician's employment of the truth predicate.

I have already noted that the truth predicate of the disquotational theory appears to have the syntax of a metalinguistic predicate—the disquotational truth predicate combines with names of sentences to form sentences, and first-order quantifiers are used. Given the effective intersubstitutability of '$\forall x(A(x, Tx))$' and '$\forall p(A(Qp, p))$' in Tarski-style constructions, one wonders whether the disquotational truth predicate really behaves like a metalinguistic predicate. What account do disquotational theorists give of the instances of their universal sentences? In particular, what account do they give of primitive sentences containing the truth predicate? Quine (1970) is the only person who says anything about what is said when truth is predicated of a sentence. He remarks (p. 12): "The truth predicate is a reminder that, despite a technical ascent to talk of sentences, our eye is on the world. ... By calling a sentence true, we call snow white." Unfortunately, Quine does not unpack the metaphors. I read Quine as saying that the truth predicate is not used to say anything about sentences. My reason is that his qualification of the "ascent to talk of sentences" as "technical" shows hesitancy; and the ascent seems canceled when he says that "by calling a sentence true, we call snow white." But then we might ask, if a logician only says something about snow when she says " 'Snow is white' is true," why does she not simply use 'Snow is white'? One reason offered for mentioning sentences is that semantic ascent is required for generalization with respect to sentence positions.[15] However, even if this were true, this explanation does not tell us *what is said* when there is "technical ascent to talk of sentences." Are sentences being talked about, or are they not? Some may claim we do not need to worry about such questions, because all we need know about the truth predicate, beyond its syntax, is its logic. Perhaps this is what those who claim T-sentences play a central role in the disquotational theory have in mind. Williams may be one such philosopher, for he says that the "disquotational schema ... captures something important about truth." It is difficult to figure out what Williams's point is, for it is unclear what he thinks is captured. For a start, we need to be told which sentences count as instances of Williams's schema.[16] Can the sentence within quotes contain indexicals, or the Liar sentence, and on what grounds should we make these decisions? Note also that T-sentences alone do not tell us much about the logic of the truth predicate. For, as Sellars (1963) has noted, " 'Snow is white' (in our language) is true iff snow is white." is viewed with the greatest equanimity by pragmatist and coherentist [and deflationist] alike. Others may claim that Tarski-style constructions capture the logic of the truth predicate. But this view also does not distinguish among truth constructions. I believe we need to unpack Quine's metaphors so that we know how the truth predicate interacts with semantic ascent.

In sum, though disquotational theorists focus on a predicate that seems to have the syntax of a metalinguistic predicate, many questions concerning logicians' uses of the truth predicate presently remain unanswered. Only when these questions are answered will we be clearer about the level of the disquotational truth predicate.

4.2 For the prosentential account of the truth predicate as used by logicians, I need to talk about inheritors. The concept of an inheritor is a generic concept that includes within its domain expressions (including proforms) that function much as proforms function.

4.2.1 In my discussion of the Liar, I pointed out that proforms do not always suffice for the anaphoric tasks that we need accomplished.[17] This is true because proforms are effective only when they occur in close proximity to their antecedents. For example, we cannot normally use 'she' on page 60 to refer unambiguously to May, if we have not mentioned May since page 1. In such a circumstance, we must establish connections with what was said on page 1 in some other way. We can say, for example,

(10) The person I referred to on page 1 can pay her own way.

I claim that when 'the person that I referred to on page 1' is used in place of a pronoun, it is used in much the same way that a pronoun is used. So in (10), 'the person I referred to on page 1' is used to refer directly to May. The definite description functions as an inheritor. In calling such expressions inheritors, my point is that neither the speaker's words nor the speaker's speech act feature in the content of what is said in (10), just as neither the links between the words 'it' and 'the balloon', nor the words 'the balloon', feature in the content of

The balloon will rise when it is filled with helium.

We can think of the work done by the various parts of 'the person I referred to on page 1', in identifying the co-referential term on page 1, as being done, so to speak, in a working column off to the side.

There are also sentential inheritors. Prosentences are included, but there are other kinds of sentential inheritors. For certain combinations of definite descriptions and the truth predicate can stand in for antecedent sentences. For example, there are circumstances where something like

(11) If the last indented sentence is true, ….

must be used, because

If that is true, then …

will not suffice for the task on hand. Let us suppose the speaker wants to acknowledge the antecedent sentence, and 'that is true' cannot be used because the antecedent sentence is not in close proximity. In such a case (11) can function as an inheritor. (Note that in the event the speaker does not know what the last indented sentence is, it might be more appropriate to use quantifiers in analyzing (11).)

According to the prosentential theory, sentences like

(12) 'Snow is white' is true.

are also inheritors. Construed as an inheritor, (12) says something about snow. In this case the antecedent sentence, 'Snow is white', rather than being picked out with a definite description, is explicitly displayed. Either way, the "semantic ascent" involved would not feature in what is said. In Chapter 3 [of Grover 1992 – Ed.] we were grappling with the same issue when we suggested that the display format

Consider: Snow is white. That is true.

can be used to capture a sentence like (12).

4.2.2 It might bo objected that "logicians do not have any use for inheritors, for they talk about languages and sentences, not balloons and snow." I agree that logicians do talk about languages. However, there is usually little point in talking about languages if there is no connection with the object languages in use. Inheritors facilitate connections between mention and "use."[18] For example, in a context where we have been talking about our proof theory, or the syntactical structure of a sentence, we often want to talk about a sentence or the structural form of a set of sentences of the object language. One reason is that tasks are often made easier if they are reduced to symbol-pushing maneuvers. It is in establishing connections between theory and/or symbol-pushing maneuvers and language in use that inheritors can be useful. For inheritors provide us with a way of displaying a sentence while in effect *using* it. Consider, again,

'Snow is white' is true

This inheritor provides us with a way of saying that snow is white, while at the same time displaying the sentence. The antecedent sentence of the inheritor

Snow is white

alone would not do as well. When 'Snow is white' is used alone, our attention is not usually drawn to the structure of the sentence used. One place where explicit display is useful is in an explanation of the logical connectives. For example, we customarily explain disjunction using the following format:[19]

(13) For any sentences *x* and *y*, $(x \vee y)$ is true just in case *x* is true or *y* is true or both *x* is true and y is true.

Why use this format? Given the prosentential account of the truth predicate, and possible intersubstitutability of '$\forall x\ (A(x, Tx))$' and '$\forall p\ (A(Qp, p))$', it might seem for the prosentential theorist that

(14) For any *p* and *q*, $(p \vee q)$ just in case either *p* or *q* or both *p* and *q*.

should do just as well. Because (14) does not contain an explicit truth predicate, it seems more in the spirit of the prosentential theory. Why do we choose the format of (13) over the format of (14)?[20] A reason (13) is more useful is that the structure of the sentences is explicitly displayed: Implicit messages about the structure of the sentences of the object language can be conveyed through such explicit display. (14) is less effective in this regard.

Readers may wonder whether this talk of implicit messages does not ascribe a substantive role to the truth predicate in (13). It should be noted that if propositional quantification and quotation are available in the metalanguage, the implicit messages of (13) could have been conveyed without the use of an explicit truth predicate. For consider

(15) For any *p*, *q*, and *r*, if *Qr* is a disjunction such that *Qp* is its first disjunct and *Qq* its second disjunct, then *r* just in case either *p* or *q*, or both *p* and *q*.

(15) makes explicit the information implicitly conveyed by (13); yet it has the format of '$\forall p(A(Qp, p))$'. The use of propositional quantifiers in (15) suggests only a prosentential role for the truth predicate (in inheritors) in (13). Accordingly, the truth predicate does not seem to have a substantive role in (13)—for it can be "hidden" in prosentential constructions.

Further checking has convinced me that similar accounts can be given of other uses of the truth predicate by logicians.[21] If I am right about all of this, the truth predicate of logicians can be construed as occurring only in prosentential constructions. It functions, so to speak, at the level of the object language. Furthermore, though logicians invariably "mention" sentences in the context of using the truth predicate, the truth predicate does not seem to have a substantive role in what is said about object language sentences. There seems to be little in common, semantically, between the truth predicate in prosentential constructions and those predicates (like 'is a proof') we usually think of as metalinguistic.

5 Disquotation with prosentences

It may now be clear why I think a disquotational theorist has the option of adopting a prosentential explanation of the role of the truth predicate.

5.1 Quine's remark that "by calling the sentence true, we call snow white" agrees with the inheritor account of the content of sentences containing 'true'. Furthermore, my account of the way inheritors function provides one reading of what one might mean by "a technical ascent to talk of sentences." The ascent is "technical" and temporary, because its purpose is to pick out the antecedent sentence of the inheritor in question; and this work is done "off to the side" and does not feature in the content of the inheritor. Hence there is no conflict with Quine's claim that a sentence containing 'true' may be about snow. Also, the intersubstitutability of Tarski-style truth constructions that highlight an explicit truth predicate (as in '$\forall x(A(x, Tx))$') and propositional Tarski-style truth constructions that highlight the prosentential role of the truth predicate (as in '$\forall p(A(Qp, p))$') is consistent with my claim that the disquotational account of generalization can derive from the prosentential account.

It should be noted that acceptance of prosentential explanations would amount to acknowledging that semantic ascent is *not required* for generalization with respect to sentence positions because prosentences provide a way of generalizing without semantic ascent. This is not to deny, however, that semantic ascent may be required for other reasons. Note, also, acceptance of prosentential explanations by disquotational theorists would bring explanations of the utility of the truth predicate in those cases where generalization is not an issue, for example, cases where the truth predicate is used to establish connections between parts of discourse in expressing agreement, etc.

The version of the prosentential theory that I have argued a disquotational theorist could endorse, is that version according to which propositional quantifiers are interpreted substitutionally. It would be another matter for a disquotational theorist to adopt a version of the prosentential theory according to which a domain of propositions is assumed. The question as to whether a substitutional interpretation suffices I leave open until we know more about the rest of language.

5.2 Without saying how such choices would be made, I assumed in §3 that deflationists can choose among alternative Tarski-style constructions for a formal account of the logical role of the truth predicate in generalization. However, deflationists cannot make such a choice without saying something about such issues as falsity, the Liar sentence (for though inconsistency is clearly a problem for substantive theories of truth, it is not so obviously a problem for deflationary truth theories), and "neither true nor false." Because disquotational theorists have not yet addressed these issues, I will make good on my claim that some understanding of the interaction of the truth predicate and "semantic ascent" can provide at least an intuitive basis upon which to choose among Tarski-style constructions.

For suppose the disquotational theorist accepted a prosentential explanation of the truth predicate. Then the prosentential account of the role of 'false' in modified prosentences would follow. So also would the following prosentential account of Liar sentences.[22] Proforms are parasitic in the sense that they must be appropriately connected to antecedent expressions that can supply content. When a proform is so connected, it is *grounded.* In the simplest cases, an occurrence of a proform will be *ungrounded* if it has only another proform as its antecedent. The truth teller ('This is true') is an example of an ungrounded prosentence; and the Liar, an example of an ungrounded modified prosentence. Note that an ungrounded proform will not have content when its antecedent is not of a kind that can initially supply content. Ungrounded proforms can be problematic for this reason—we sometimes need to know whether we run the risk of uttering sentences without content. Accordingly, a disquotational theorist would find useful those Tarski-style truth constructions that show us how to utilize inheritors that may in some circumstances be ungrounded.

On the other hand, a prosentential account of the truth predicate does not require that Tarski-style constructions say anything about philosophers' uses of "neither true nor false". My reasons for this claim have to do with the role of 'not' in "neither true nor false" as rejecting what is said.

We use 'not' or 'no' when we want to reject something. Often the role of 'not' is that of a sentence modifier, as captured in our truth tables – 'not A' is the contradictory of 'A' – but 'not' does not always modify. When 'not' is used as a modifier, 'That is not true' will be a modified prosentence. Suppose 'Snow is white' is our antecedent sentence; then 'That is not true' would be equivalent to 'Snow is not white' and 'That is neither true nor false' would be equivalent to the contradictory 'Snow is not white and snow is white'.

This reading of 'neither true nor false' does not capture most philosophical uses of the phrase, however. We need to consider another way in which 'not' can be used to reject something we find problematic. One reason we need another way of rejecting what someone says is that we cannot always reject something by asserting the contradictory, because the contradictory form may be problematic also.[23] For suppose the antecedent is 'The King of France is bald'; we get nowhere by responding with 'The King of France is not bald'. A better response might be (as Strawson 1950, p. 183 points out)

(16) There's a problem with what you say, for there is no King of France.

Or one might say, 'I reject both!' or 'Neither!' and use display to direct attention to that which one is rejecting.

(17) Neither! The King of France is bald. The King of France is not bald.

If it is important that parts of the discourse are connected, prosentences may be used, as in

(18) Neither! That is true. That is false.

Because the prosentences are displayed/mentioned rather than used, the truth predicate is only mentioned in such uses of 'neither true nor false'. And this is why I think Tarski-style constructions need not be required to explain philosophers' uses of 'neither true nor false'.

6 Summary

We have seen that the disquotational and prosentential truth predicates provide for generalization with respect to sentence positions from roughly the same conservative resources. In the one case a domain of sentences is assumed, and in the other a substitution range consisting of the same set of sentences.

The disquotational explanation of the truth predicate's role in generalization is that the truth predicate facilitates semantic ascent. Semantic ascent, in its turn, is said to facilitate generalization with respect to sentence positions. However, until Quine's metaphors relating the truth predicate and semantic ascent are explained, the disquotational truth predicate's role is not adequately explained.

The prosentential explanation of the role of the truth predicate is that it is used in prosentential constructions. A detour through semantic ascent is not required for generalization. However, inheritors may sometimes be used to draw attention to the syntax of the language under consideration; in this case, a prosentential theorist can with equanimity exploit the inter-substitutability of '$\forall pA(Qp, p)$', '$\forall xA(x, Tx)$'.[24]

In conclusion, I have argued that the disquotational theory can be supplemented with prosentential explanations of the underlying role of the truth predicate; I have also demonstrated some advantages of doing this.[25]

Notes

1. For example, Field 1972 [This volume, Ch. 3 – Ed.]. For other suggestions see Dummett 1976, especially pp. 115–26 and Putnam 1981, pp. 49–56.
2. This is the theory that has been generally ascribed to Leeds (1978), Horwich (1982), Soames (1984), and Williams (1986).
3. The reader is referred to Chapters 3, 4, 6, and 7 [Of Grover 1992– Ed.] for further introductory details.
4. Included among *proforms* are pronouns, proverbs, proadjectives, and prosentences.
5. Though I call the sentence (or noun) with which a proform is connected its antecedent, this does not mean that the antecedent has to occur before the proform.
6. I refer to variables that occupy sentential positions as *propositional variables.* This is only a grammatical categorization, based on the sentential position of the variables.
7. See Chapter 10 [Of Grover 1992 – Ed.] for one suggestion regarding the consistent use of propositional quantifiers and quotation, and quantification in and out of quotes; also Kripke 1976 for further suggestions.
8. This is not to deny that the truth predicate may be utilized in our explanations. We frequently need the expressibility that the truth predicate provides.
9. Though disquotational theorists make much of the utility of 'true' for generalizing, they give few examples. Note also that though both Quine and Soames give examples, their analyses are different.

10. Another possibility is 'For every *x*, if Eva says that *x* is true then *x* is true'.
11. The disquotational theorist will need an operator that produces a that-clause ('that the reactor is unsafe') from the name of a sentence 'The reactor is unsafe' if the actual instances in (2) are to be recovered, unless that-clauses are treated as names of sentences. An alternative approach would be to adopt

    For any *x*, if Eva says that *x* is true, then *x* is true.

    as the disquotational analysis of (3), which has instances like

    If Eva says that 'the reactor is unsafe' is true, then 'the reactor is unsafe' is true.

    Semantic descent returns this instance to the original

    If Eva says that the reactor is unsafe, then the reactor is unsafe.

12. When I refer to Tarski-style constructions, I mean to include not only those of Tarski, but also Kripke's (1975), Gupta's (1982), etc.
13. Anil Gupta confirms that it would be a relatively simple matter to systematically replace occurrences of *'x'*, say, by '*Qp*', and *'Tx'* by '*p*', in his construction.
14. My response persuaded Belnap at the time. I do not know whether he is still persuaded.
15. Quine seems to say this, though I think only in a context where he is not considering the possibility of utilizing a substitutional interpretation. Both Leeds and Soames allow that first-order objectually interpreted quantifiers are not the only alternative.
16. Williams does not explain *'x'* and *'P'*.
17. See Chapter 4 [of Grover 1992 – Ed.] and Brandom 1988, §VI.
18. For more details see Chapters 6 and 7 [Of Grover 1992 – Ed.].
19. I assume first-order objectually interpreted quantifiers, and in the interests of simplicity, an autonomous system of naming expressions in the object language.
20. Note that, without argument, I cannot assume '$\forall x(A(x, Tx))$' and '$\forall p(A(Qp, p))$' are intersubstitutable in all contexts. Propositional attitude contexts may be an exception. For, whereas 'Everything Mary believes is true" might reasonably be represented by 'For every *p*, if Mary believes that *p*, then *p*,' this may not be equivalent to 'For every *x*, if Mary believes *x*, then *x* is true.'
21. Consider, for example, our use of 'true' in "There are true sentences that are not provable." This does not have to be represented formally as "There are *x*'s such that *x* is true and *x* is not provable. We can say 'There are *p*'s, such that *p* and *Qp* is not provable'.
22. See Chapter 4 [Of Grover 1992 – Ed.].
23. I have discussed this issue in greater detail in Chapter 7 [Of Grover 1992 – Ed.].
24. At the time of writing this article I believed providing an explanation of the Liar sentence constituted a challenge for anyone offering an account of the role of the truth predicate and could even provide basic motivation for truth theories. More recently I have taken the position that the Liar is not in this way significant. I have argued (Grover (2005)) that just as division is a coherent and useful arithmetic operation, even though syntactically well-formed terms like '10÷0' are not defined/semantically significant; so, also, the truth and falsity predicates can have a coherent role even if we have no use for 'This is false' and its strengthened versions. For those seeking to explain the role of the truth predicate there is then only the need to explain cases where we *use* the predicate. So I was wrong to talk of inconsistency threatening in this paragraph. If we had good reason, we could in theory add piecemeal, a property-ascribing role to a prosentential truth predicate.
25. I thank Jerry Kapus and Anil Gupta for helpful comments on an early draft of this paper.

References

Brandom, R. 1988. Pragmatism, Phenomenalism, and Truth Talk. *Midwest Studies in Philosophy*, 12 (1): 75–93.

Dummett, M. 1976. What is a Theory of Meaning? (II). In G. Evans and J. McDowell (eds.), *Truth and Meaning*. Oxford: Clarendon Press: 67–137.

Field, H. 1972. Tarski's Theory of Truth. *The Journal of Philosophy*, 69: 347–75. [Ch. 3 of this volume – Ed.]

Grover, D. 1992. *A Prosentential Theory of Truth*. Princeton: Princeton University Press.

Grover, D. 2005. How Significant is the Liar? In JC Beall and Bradley Armour-Garb (eds.), *Deflationism and Paradox*. Oxford: Oxford Univ. Press: 177–202.

Gupta, A. 1982. Truth and Paradox. *Journal of Philosophical Logic*, 11: 1–60.

Horwich, P. 1982. Three Forms of Realism. *Synthese*, 51: 181–201.

Kripke, S. 1975. Outline of a Theory of Truth. *The Journal of Philosophy*, 72: 690–716.

Kripke, S. 1976. Is There a Problem about Substitutional Quantification? In G. Evans and J. McDowell (eds.), *Truth and Meaning*. Oxford: Clarendon Press: 325–419.

Leeds, S. 1978. Theories of Reference and Truth. *Erkenntnis*, 13: 111–29.

Putnam, H. 1981. *Reason, Truth and History*. Cambridge: Cambridge University Press.

Quine, W.V. 1970. *The Philosophy of Logic*. Englewood Cliffs, NJ: Prentice Hall.

Ramsey, F.P. 1927. Facts and Propositions. *Proceedings of the Aristotelian Society*, supp. Vol. 24: 153–70.

Sellars, W. 1963. *Science, Perception, and Reality*. London: Routledge and Kegan Paul.

Soames, S. 1984. What Is a Theory of Truth? *The Journal of Philosophy*, 81: 411–29.

Strawson, P. 1950. On Referring. *Mind*, 59: 320–44.

Williams, M. 1986. Do We (Epistemologists) Need a Theory of Truth? *Philosophical Topics*, 4: 223–42.

13 What is deflationism about truth?

MATTI EKLUND

1 Introduction

In this paper I will be concerned with a certain cluster of questions regarding how best to understand deflationism about truth.

First some relevant background. Deflationism about truth is a kind of reaction to classical theories of truth. Among classical theories of truth are the correspondence theory, according to which truth is correspondence with reality, the coherence theory, according to which truth somehow consists in coherence, and pragmatist and verificationist theories according to which truth somehow consists in ideal verifiability.[1] These theories are all naturally seen as attempting to uncover the nature of truth: and the deflationist retort is that truth has no nature of this kind to uncover.

Sometimes deflationism has been undergirded by a general anti-metaphysical stance. In the *Stanford Encyclopedia of Philosophy* entry on deflationism (2010), Daniel Stoljar and Nic Damnjanovic remark that "One reason for the popularity of deflationism is its anti-metaphysical stance. Deflationism seems to deflate a grand metaphysical puzzle, a puzzle about the nature of truth, and much of modern philosophy is marked by a profound scepticism of metaphysics". Not all deflationists are animated by a general disdain for metaphysics, especially not today, after metaphysics has had a renaissance. Even the ones that are not think that because of something about truth, certain traditional metaphysical questions do not arise in the case of truth. If truth has no nature to uncover, there is no metaphysical project of uncovering the nature of truth.

More specifically, deflationists typically make the following three kinds of claims:

(i) *Exhaustion*. What truth is, is exhausted by some schema like

(ES) (The proposition) that p is true iff p

or

(DS) "p" is true iff p,

or perhaps some suitably universally quantified version thereof. ("ES" for Equivalence Schema and "DS" for Disquotation Schema. "True" as used in (ES) applies to propositions; "true" as used in (DS) applies to sentences.) Much of the discussion of deflationism is concerned with the exact formulation and status of these schemata, or the corresponding variants. What are the appropriate instances? What is the modal status? What about the language-relativization that would appear to be needed in the case of (DS)? Also in the case of (DS), how does one deal with different forms of context-sensitivity? If one operates instead with a universally quantified version, how should one understand the kind of quantification at issue? Does the deflationist's characterization of truth offer everything that one can reasonably expect from a characterization of truth, for example for logical purposes? Even though I will be centrally concerned with how exactly to understand deflationism, I will not be at all concerned with the issues just mentioned. I will sweep all this under the rug, simply *assuming* that the issues just brought up all can be resolved in some satisfactory way. I will speak of the deflationist as thinking that truth is characterized by "the relevant schema", but that should not be understood as my taking a stand on whether a schema or some quantified formulation is best.

In recent years it has become more common to speak of inference rules somehow governing truth. The deflationist might appeal to the rules *from it is true that p to: p* and *from p to: it is true that p*, and say that truth is somehow exhausted by those rules. I do not mean to beg the question against a rule-based characterization although my formulations will concern schema-based ones. The points I make will carry over. (As I will remark on, the problem I will be centrally concerned with is more serious for rule-based approaches.)

Other questions regarding the proper formulation of deflationism about truth concern whether the deflationist can consistently with her overall outlook take truth to be defined in terms of reference and satisfaction, à la Tarski, appealing to deflationary theories of reference and satisfaction in turn. A deflationary thesis about reference analogous to the schema-based characterization of truth would be that a schema like

't' refers to t if t exists, and to nothing otherwise

in some sense exhausts the nature of reference.[2]

(ii) *Expressive device*. A second claim is that truth is just an expressive device, of use for mimicking infinite disjunctions and conjunctions, and for saying things like "Everything the pope says is true" (said by someone who trusts the infallibility of the pope but does not know exactly what the pope has ever said), but without any deeper explanatory use. Sometimes—in connection with truth predicates of sentences—it is said that truth is a device for disquotation. Again some good questions can be asked, for example about what constitutes explanatory uses of the truth predicate. Again that will not be my topic.

(iii) *No genuine property*. Truth is a not a property—or, more cautiously, truth is not a *genuine* property, or truth is not a *substantive* property, or truth is just a property in a "logical" sense. It does not have a "nature" of the kind that other, ordinary properties have. This again stands in some need of clarification, for example because qualifiers like "genuine" and "substantive" as used in the context are not fully clear, and because "property" is used differently by different theorists. Let me first pause on the latter issue. Some theorists use "property" in such a way that they hold that all expressions that semantically function like predicates "ascribe properties". If such a theorist says "truth is not a property", she conveys that the truth predicate (or perhaps so-called truth predicate) does not function semantically like a predicate. Some deflationists—prominently prosententialists—have made this sort of claim.[3] It is an interesting claim, but evaluating it is beyond the scope of this article. I will restrict attention to forms of deflationism which are *moderate* in that they do not deny that the truth predicate functions semantically as a predicate. Other theorists use "property" in such a way that there only are "properties" corresponding to predicates that, as it is often put, carve nature at its joints. If a theorist says that "true" does not ascribe a property in this sense, then while what she says is no doubt of some significance, she only claims about the truth predicate what goes for many predicates, of different kinds. It is not a very distinctive claim.[4] As for "genuine", "substantive" etc., these are somewhat unclear bits of jargon. Some authors—for example Damnjanovic (2010), Edwards (2013) and Wyatt (2016)—have recently done more than has previously been done to elucidate what these pieces of jargon mean. I will later in the discussion have occasion to bring up some suggestions they make.

Thesis (i) is the basic claim, as it is this thesis that constitutes a positive claim about what truth is. It is natural to see theses (ii) and (iii)—making claims about the uses of truth, and about what the property of truth is not, respectively—as carried in the wake of (i). If they do not actually follow from (i), they are at least supposed to be very well motivated given (i). If truth is exhausted by one of the schemata, it is just an expressive device. If truth is exhausted by one of the schemata, then truth is not a property—or at least not a substantive one. There are other respects in which theses like (ii) or (iii) might be more basic. They might speak more directly to the motivation behind deflationism. Or they might be more nearly definitional of what makes a view deflationary. But those are different matters.

My main focus will be thesis (i). I will discuss some basic questions regarding what this thesis means. Specifically, I will ask whether it is supposed to concern only the *concept* TRUTH or also the *property* of being true, argue that it must be the latter, and then make critical remarks regarding what (i), understood as concerning the property, might mean. Questions about whether the property of being true is a "substantive" property will not be my main focus, but issues in that vicinity will come up. One question I will be concerned with is whether (i) can serve as a characterization of the property of being true which serves deflationist purposes and rules out traditional views on truth. One question there is whether (i) can lend support to (iii), and then the interpretation of (iii) becomes relevant.

2 Concepts and properties

As indicated, what I will be centrally concerned with is the distinction between *concepts* and *properties*, and how attention to this distinction matters to the discussion of deflationism. Properties are had by their bearers; concepts represent. There can be different concepts of the same property. Even if the property of being water = the property of being H_2O, arguably the concept WATER ≠ the concept H_2O. To illustrate the concept/property distinction, compare a famous use of the concept/property distinction in metaethics. G.E. Moore (1903) apparently sought to establish something about the nature of the property of being good from the fact that for any analysis of the concept good, it is an open question whether something which satisfies the analysans is thereby good. This is the famous *open question argument*. The argument is also famously problematic. While this argument is often held to establish that the *concept* GOOD is not identical to any naturalistic concept, many theorists resist the further conclusion that the *property* of being good therefore cannot be identical with any naturalistic property, and Moore is criticized for not properly heeding the concept/property distinction.

Although I will for the most part be focusing on the distinction between concepts and properties, more generally the relevant distinction is between representational devices on the one hand—whether words or concepts—and properties on the other. I will sometimes talk about the predicate "true" instead of the concept TRUTH.

Some may have philosophical objections to the distinction between properties and concepts. They may for example be skeptical that concepts, understood as described, are usefully postulated. I have two remarks on this sort of skepticism. First, much of what I say under the heading of the concept/property distinction can equally well be presented under the heading of the distinction between a word and the property it stands for. Second, what I will eventually be mainly concerned with is how deflationism about the property of being true is best construed. For many purposes, the discussion of concepts is there only as a foil, warning against a conflation between different things. If we should simply renounce concepts, so be it.

We can ask concerning any philosophical account of X whether it works (or is supposed to work) as an account of the concept X or as an account of the property X. This applies also in the case of truth. For example, one possibility is that the *concept* TRUTH is unanalyzable but one of the classical theories of truth is correct regarding the *property* of being true. The correspondence theory of truth can fail as an analysis of the concept TRUTH, but still provide a correct account of the property of being true. One can generally be skeptical of the project of providing conceptual analyses but be more optimistic about the corresponding project of giving a correct and informative account of the nature of some property.[5]

With the concept/property distinction on the table, return to (i). When stating (i) above, I was deliberately cagey. I said that on the deflationist view, (i) states "what truth is". But is a characterization along the lines of (i) best understood as an account of the concept TRUTH, the property truth, or both?

Note incidentally that the two other theses, (ii) and (iii), speak to different sorts of things. Someone who affirms thesis (ii), that truth is just an expressive device, must be speaking of a representational device—the truth predicate, or the concept TRUTH. It is representational devices that are the sort of thing that can be expressive devices. *Properties* are hardly the sort of thing that can be expressive devices. One can perhaps posit a property for the expressive gains that doing so offers, but that is different. Someone who affirms thesis (iii), that truth is not a genuine property, must mean that what the concept TRUTH stands for is not a genuine property. That the concept TRUTH is not a property is trivial.

Suppose first that (i) only purports to characterize the *concept* TRUTH. What this would mean is, I take it, something like that the concept TRUTH is exhausted by one of the schemata in the sense that it is necessary and sufficient for competence with the concept to be disposed to accept the instances of these schemata.[6]

There are complications here. Quine was a prominent deflationist, and many more recent deflationists are clearly inspired by Quine. And Quine very prominently and centrally disavowed claims about what is necessary and sufficient for competence—this is part and parcel of his attack on analyticity. So there are deflationists for whom there arise problems regarding how to understand (i) when the thesis is conceived of as concerning the concept

TRUTH. But let me anyway for now set this aside. One may simply think: so much the worse for the coherence of the Quinean package of views.

If thesis (i) only concerns the concept, then thesis (i) is fully compatible with the correspondence theorist being right about the property of being true.[7] This is not to say that (i) thus understood is uninteresting: but deflationism about the concept does not by itself have the metaphysical import that deflationism is often taken to have.

Suppose then that (i) (also) concerns the *property*. (Recall yet again that I am setting aside versions of deflationism which deny that truth grammatically is a predicate, as well as quibbles about which genuinepredicates stand for properties.) This raises a question: what does the exhaustion claim come to there? Since one cannot reasonably talk about competence with a property as opposed to competence with a concept, one cannot simply adapt what was suggested in the case of the exhaustion claim regarding the concept.

Early on I mentioned that some who defend deflationary theses in the style of (i) take what characterizes truth not to be the instances of some schema but instead to be corresponding rules of inference. But if the characterization of truth alluded to under (i) essentially appeals to rules of inference, it is hard to see how it could be the *property* that is characterized, since inference rules govern expressions and concepts, not properties. A property can certainly in some sense validate the rules, but that is different. What are governed by rules are not properties but representations thereof, and if one spoke of properties couching things in terms of rules would at best be misleading. So for the characterization to pertain to the property, it will have to be of a different kind, and in discussion of the property of being true that follows I will presume that it is.

Here is a first stab at what the characterization claim might come to:

(E1) (The instances of) the schema state all the facts about truth.

But claiming this would be silly. There will certainly be other facts about truth besides facts stated by (instances of) the schema. Second stab:

(E2) (The instances of) the schema state all the *necessary* facts about truth.

But there will certainly be other necessary facts besides facts stated by (instances of) the schema. For example, that it is necessarily true that 7+5=12. If one focuses on (DS) rather than (ES) and conceives of the truth predicate as a predicate of sentences, it is somewhat more tricky to come up with counterexamples to (E2), for it is natural to think that it is not necessarily the case that "7+5=12" is true—the sentence could have meant something else. But first, deflationists focusing on (DS) tend to take the instances of (DS) as necessary; and then, given that it is necessary that 7+5=12, it will be necessary that "7+5=12" is true. Second, even if the instances of (DS) are not taken as necessary, there are other necessary facts about truth in the vicinity, for example that it is necessarily the case that *actually*, "7+5=12" is true.

A better suggestion is:

(E3) (The instances of) the schema state all the facts pertaining to the *essence* or *nature* of truth.

But (E3) too faces problems. First, if the deflationist's claim is (E3), what happened with the supposed anti-metaphysical stance? Positive claims about what is part of the essence or nature of what are part and parcel of hardcore metaphysics. (This first point only concerns the compatibility of reliance on (E3) with the anti-metaphysical stance that often goes together with deflationism. The friend of deflationism could in principle just respond by eschewing the anti-metaphysical stance.) Second, even if (E3) does yield a characterization of the property of being true incompatible with all the traditional inflationary views, the question remains of why what is characterized is a properly deflationary view given which truth is somehow not as much of a genuine property as other properties. Why isn't this an alternative form of inflationism? Truth too has a nature; it is just that its nature is different from what traditional theories of truth have taken it to be. How does the truth of (E3) lend support to (iii), on any reasonable interpretation of the latter thesis?

Apart from these problems, note that even given (E3), it could be that when something is true it corresponds with reality—and even that this is so as a matter of metaphysical necessity. (E3) is incompatible with a claim to the effect that truth's *nature* is correspondence, but that is another matter. Similar points hold for other inflationary theories. Of course, this need not bother the deflationist: she can still say that she disputes the inflationist claims about truth's nature. But so long as truth necessitates correspondence, all the familiar supposed problems regarding correspondence remain.

It may be tempting for the deflationist who is worried about the use of ideology like "essence" or "nature" to try to avoid the talk of essences or natures by appeal to how all the facts about the property of truth are *explained* by the instances of the relevant schema together with independent facts. The other problem regarding (E3) still remains, but it may still be useful to pause on this appeal to explanation. What does "explanation" mean here? One can distinguish two different ways of talking about explanation. On a pragmatic way of talking about explanations, explanations are simply answers to "why"-questions, and since interests and background knowledge can vary with context so does what is an acceptable explanation in this sense. Second, sometimes in philosophy a more metaphysical notion of explanation is employed, and what is considered is what genuinely explains what in the nature of things. I take it that the deflationist claim we are now considering would have to concern explanation in the second sense: it is about what truth is like in itself. But then while "explanation" is not as overtly steeped in metaphysics as "essence" and "nature" are, the brand of explanation we are dealing with here is metaphysical explanation. We're talking about what really, in the nature of things, constitutively depends on what. We're not using a pragmatically infused notion of explanation simply relating to "why"-questions whose import vary from context to context. Once it is emphasized that it is properly metaphysical explanation we are talking about, the talk of explanation in this context should seem no less hardcore metaphysical than talk of natures or essences. Moreover, the other problems with appeal to essences or natures remain. (Similar remarks apply to suggestions according to which the instances of the schema state the *fundamental* facts about truth.)

It may be suggested that explanation means deductive explanation. I am not sure that there is a separate species of explanation deserving of the name deductive explanations. Not all deductions are explanatory. (Most obviously, deductions like $A \vdash A$.) But maybe the appeal to explanation is a red herring in the suggestion anyway. Maybe the core idea is to appeal neither to the essence or nature of truth nor to the order of metaphysical explanation, but to say that (the instances of) the relevant schema exhaust the property of truth precisely in that all facts about truth *can be deduced* from them together with facts not involving truth—nothing more and nothing less. It is natural to want to object that this disguises the problem rather than solves it. Is it not surreptitiously assumed that these deduction relations track some metaphysical relation: why else accord this significance to them? However, suppose the friend of appeal to deduction insists that her talk of deduction is not disguised talk of natures: instead of embracing the nature ideology she simply talks about what can be deduced from what. Doing this she embraces the view that no collection of claims from which all facts about truth follow is privileged; all such collections of claims are on a par. Adopting this package of views, she does get around the first of the problems for (E3) that were mentioned. The second problem concerned why what was being proposed was not a form of inflationism. To this it can now be responded that where the inflationist talks about truth's nature, the form of deflationism we are now exploring eschews the nature talk in favor of merely talking about what can be deduced from what. Something like what has been suggested strikes me as more promising than any of the earlier suggestions. But the cost is that it (pardon the pun) deflates the import of appeal to a schema. The schema now provides nothing more than a starting point for deductions; it is not claimed to be in any other way especially fundamental or central to the property of being true.[8]

The above considerations conclude the main negative argument of the present paper. It is not sufficient for the deflationist to think of (i) as a thesis concerning the concept TRUTH: for thus conceived (i) is compatible with traditional views on the property of being true. She must then think of (i) as (also) characterizing the property. But there are serious problems regarding how to understand the claim that one of the deflationist's schemata fully characterizes the property, as opposed to the concept.

In the sections to follow, I will discuss some suggestions from the recent literature on how to explicate the claim that truth is not a "substantial" property. It may be thought that these suggestions also might help elucidate in what sense in which the property of truth is supposed to be exhausted by some schema. However, my conclusions will be negative.

3 Transparency

One discussion that is in some ways unusually careful about the issues I have sought to highlight regarding the concept/property distinction and its relevance for discussions of deflationism is Michael Lynch's (2009) discussion of these matters (though Lynch is himself no deflationist). Lynch is explicit that the deflationist schema-based characterization of truth is a characterization of the concept, and he explicitly brings up the question of how this characterization of the concept relates to what to say about the property:

> ...deflationists share a metaphysical view: truth has no nature... [Contemporary deflationists] allow that the truth concept does express a property—in the sense that the concepts of existence of identity express either a property or a relation. Such properties, we might say, are *metaphysically transparent* or *pleonastic* properties. Metaphysically transparent properties have no underlying nature that isn't revealed in our grasp of the concept; grasping the relevant concept tells us the whole essence of the property.[9]

Note first that the transparency of the property is presented as something additional to the concept TRUTH's being fully characterized by the relevant schema. Wisely, Lynch does not claim the former to follow from the latter.

Lynch's notion of transparency might be thought helpful when it comes to some different issues relating to deflationism. It might be thought to help explicate what it means for the property of truth to fail to be substantive: the thought being that the substantive properties are exactly the non-transparent properties. The points I will go on to make show that this thought is mistaken. But the issue of what it means for truth not to be a substantive property is not my main topic. I am instead primarily concerned with the issue of how to make sense of (i), understood as being about the property of being true. I will return to this issue at the end of the discussion of transparency.

But what exactly is it for a property to be "metaphysically transparent"?[10] Lynch seems to say

(MT1) A property F is transparent iff F has no nature that isn't revealed in our grasp of the concept.

But *which* concept is meant here? Lynch's statement seems to be elliptical for:

(MT2) A property F is transparent iff F has no nature that isn't revealed in our grasp of *the concept of F*.

But there is an immediate problem: there are different possible concepts ascribing the same property. So one can't really speak of *the* concept. How can this be remedied? Here is one suggestion:

(MT3) A property F is transparent iff F has no nature that isn't revealed in our grasp of *every concept of F*.

But the condition for transparency stated by (MT3) is so strong that even the friend of deflationism should find it implausible that the property of being true satisfies the condition. Even if the nature of the property of being true is as the deflationist says it is (however exactly this is to be construed), can there not be some concept of the property that fails to fully reveal its nature?[11] Avoiding this one may turn to:

(MT4) A property F is transparent iff F has no nature that isn't revealed in our grasp of *some concept of F*.

But this condition is so weak that many properties (perhaps every property?) turns out to be transparent. For a given property, consider a concept of the property that fully spells out its nature—even if our ordinary concept of the property fails to do so. (Compare perhaps: given that the property of being water = the property of being H_2O, one can say that while the concept WATER fails to reveal the nature of this property, the concept H_2O manages to do so.)

Instead one may then propose:

(MT5) A property F is transparent iff F has no nature that isn't revealed in our grasp of *the ordinary* concept of F.

The condition stated by (MT5) arguably avoids the problems afflicting (MT3) and (MT4), and it marks some sort of perhaps not uninteresting distinction between properties. But it does not directly mark a distinction between properties as they are in themselves, but only via the way we think and talk about them. Even if our ordinary concept TRUTH is fully revealing, the ordinary concept WATER is not—but that is in the first instance just a point about how we ordinarily conceptualize truth and water, respectively. While it may perhaps be suggested that the way we think and talk about properties is evidence of real distinctions between the properties themselves, that would need to be made out.[12] Lynch attempts to say something about what (on the deflationist view) is distinctive about the nature of the property of being true but only via the relationship between the concept TRUTH and the property it ascribes.

Having discussed characterizations of transparency, let me now explicitly return to different purposes to which the notion of transparency may be put. First, it could, as mentioned, be suggested that a property is substantive iff it is non-transparent, and thus that the appeal to transparency elucidates what it means to call truth non-substantive. But if, as per (MT5), transparency does not characterize a property per se but only the relation between a property and the ordinary concept thereof, this does not work. Second, could appeal to transparency help with the problems we have encountered in making sense of the deflationist's thesis (i), understood as concerning the property of being true? It could be of help here even if by itself it does not help elucidate non-substantivity. It could be suggested that the ordinary concept TRUTH is amenable to a schema-based characterization and if moreover, the property is transparent in the sense of (MT5), the schema also characterizes the property. But it is not hard to see that we have failed to make any progress at all: we have not made any further progress on the question—to which (E1)–(E3) were failed answers—of what it is for (the instances of) the schema to fully characterize the property to begin with.

Damnjanovic (2010) holds that while, for reasons similar to those I have rehearsed, a transparency claim by itself does not suffice to characterize deflationism, a transparency claim together with the further claim that truth is a logical concept characterizes an interesting form of deflationism. The claim of Damnjanovic's deflationist is that the concept TRUTH is a *logical concept*, and that since this special kind of concept moreover fully reveals the property it ascribes, that property is of a special kind—it is a *logical property*. But first, one immediate worry is that this amounts to punting. What is it for some concept or property to be logical? Damnjanovic simply remarks that the distinction is intuitive, even if it is hard to give a precise characterization of it.[13] But even if the distinction is intuitive and should be taken on board, concerns remain. On some characterizations of logic, logic is characterized by formality and lack of content. On others, what characterizes logic is simply its absolute generality. Only given the first kind of characterization of logic does saying that truth is logical go any way toward vindicating the claim that it is somehow insubstantial or lacking a nature. Second, Damnjanovic's suggestion arguably runs into the same problems as those discussed in the last section. He wants to draw a significant conclusion about the nature of the property of being true from the concept TRUTH being a logical concept together with a transparency claim. The claim is then apparently that whichever features of the concept TRUTH renders it logical are also features of the property. Relating this to a schema-based characterization of deflationism, suppose that the concept TRUTH qualifies as a logical concept because it is, say, exhausted by (ES). Then the property of being true is a logical property because it is exhausted by (ES). But the topic of the previous section concerned what the exhaustion claim comes to in the case of properties and the conclusions were negative.

Wyatt (2016) discusses what claims about the metaphysics of the property of being true those deflationists who take truth to be a property are committed to, and he suggests that there are two such claims. First,

(Unconstituted) There is a property *truth*, but it is insusceptible to an opaque constitution theory.[14]

Opacity is here non-transparency. But where other theorists have discussed whether the property truth is itself transparent, Wyatt argues that what is at issue is really the constitution theory for the property, where a constitution theory for a property is a theory stating in what the property's being instantiated by something consists. I will not get into the details of this argument. Second,

(Non-Explanatory) There is a property *truth*, but *truth* lacks explanatory power in that there are no facts that are explained by facts about *truth*'s essence.[15]

It is actually unclear to me why Wyatt focuses on essence here. Why not instead say "…in that there are no facts that are explained *by facts about what is true*"? (Non-Explanatory) might seem too weak, leaving open the possibility that facts about what is true are explanatory, saying only that truth's essence is explanatorily powerless. I will not press the point. Maybe Wyatt relies on some bridge principle given which facts about what is true are explanatory only if truth's essence is.

As Wyatt rightly stresses, (Unconstituted) and (Non-Explanatory) are independent. One can perfectly well affirm one without affirming the other.

I like the idea of focusing on (Non-Explanatory), and I will return to this in the concluding section. But clearly—and this is no criticism of Wyatt—(Non-Explanatory) is not in any way a claim about what truth is, but only a claim about what truth can and cannot do. (Unconstituted), while only giving an indirect and partial characterization of what truth is like, at least speaks to the question of what truth is.

Earlier complaints about appeals to transparency apply also to (Unconstituted). Wyatt says "A constitution theory for *truth* is transparent iff one who possesses the ordinary concept TRUTH is ipso facto in a position to know that its axioms are true solely on the basis of conceptual argumentation".[16] This explicitly adverts to the ordinary concept TRUTH. Saying that the property *truth* has a transparent constitution theory is only to say something about the relation between the ordinary concept TRUTH and the property of being true. Again to stress, all sorts of properties (and their constitution theories) can be opaquely presented by some concepts and transparently presented by others. That some property is presented some way by the ordinary concept of the property says more about our conceptual scheme than anything else.[17]

4 Explanatory role

It is common to associate deflationism with the idea that truth lacks an explanatory role—this is for example part of the point of the slogan that truth is merely an expressive device. A number of different authors have tried to explicate the supposed insubstantiality of the property of truth in terms of its not having any explanatory role. In this last section I will discuss some deflationary views in this spirit, and how they relate to schema-based characterizations of the kind problematized here.

I have already mentioned Wyatt's appeal to (Non-Explanatory). Edwards (2013) and Asay (2013, ch. 4, 2014) appeal to the notion of there being natural, or, as I will say, elite, properties, and says that if one operates with a notion of eliteness that admits of degrees, deflationism's characteristic claim about the property of being true is that it is relatively non-elite, whereas deflationism's opponents claim that it is relatively elite. While being elite is not the same as being explanatory, explanatoriness is one central aspect of eliteness.

As against both proposals, which are similar in spirit, it can be pointed out that even paradigmatic non-deflationary theories, like the correspondence theory, are perfectly compatible with truth being non-explanatory and non-elite. To state the obvious, moreover, appeal to truth's lack of explanatory role does not even promise to help elucidate how a schema-based characterization can be thought to exhaust the property truth. And intuitively, non-explanatoriness does not have anything to do with insubstantiality. Insubstantiality is intuitively a matter of not having very much by way of nature. But something can be quite substantial in this sense, but still be quite useless.[18] Of course, none of these points militates against a revisionary proposal regarding the debate about truth, according to which one should shift the focus from the question of whether truth is substantial—whatever that means exactly – to the question of to what extent truth is explanatory, or elite.

Louis deRosset (manuscript) proposes a metaphysics of truth that he thinks captures important deflationist motivations. According to this metaphysics of truth, individual truth facts of the form *that p is true* are grounded in the corresponding facts *p*, and these truth facts do not themselves in turn ground or metaphysically explain anything else. This may be an attractive view, and one that indeed does capture important deflationist motivations. But the connection between this form of deflationism and a deflationism that accords pride of place to one of the schemata remains unclear; nor does deRosset claim anything else.

In other work—Eklund (2010)—I myself have distinguished between the deflationist's positive claim about truth, as in some sense being fully characterized by (DS) or (ES), and the negative claim that truth does not have any useful explanatory or theoretical role, but insofar as the truth predicate has a use at all it is as an expressive device. What I stressed there was that the negative claim could in principle be plausible even if the positive claim turns out to be problematic. Even if no characterization of truth of the supposedly thin kind that deflationists strive for is correct, that is by itself no obstacle to the negative claim. I introduced the label *rejectionism* for the negative claim alone. Of course, rejectionism does not promise to deliver everything deflationism delivers. The point is precisely to focus on the negative claim only.

A theory I would now like to bring up—and which I will call *indeterminism*—is a bit closer to deflationism in saying something about what truth is (as opposed to merely what it doesn't do). According to indeterminism, all that is determined regarding the truth predicate, and the concept TRUTH, is that their meaning/content is exhausted by the relevant schema, in the sense that competence with the predicate or concept consists in being disposed to accept all instances of the schema. This is just what was suggested when it was discussed above what it might mean for the schema to exhaust the concept. But when it comes to the property of being true, what the indeterminist goes on to say is that there are many different properties that all could be ascribed by the concept TRUTH for all that this characterization determines. The conditions associated with the concept do not uniquely pick out one property as being what the concept stands for. For example, the indeterminist might say that any property satisfying the relevant schema would do. The concept TRUTH is semantically indeterminate as between all these properties. None of these individual properties need be in any reasonable sense exhausted by the schema. But the schema captures everything that these different properties that the concept TRUTH is indeterminate between have in common.[19]

Indeterminism comes closer than rejectionism does to capturing what one would associate with deflationism. It accords pride of place to (ES) or (DS) in a way that rejectionism does not. (The flip side of this is that while rejectionism can be accepted by orthodox Quineans, indeterminism's claim about the concept TRUTH incorporates a view on content alien to Quine.) While indeterminism cannot strictly say that there is a property truth whose nature is thin or insubstantial, it can say that what the candidates for being the property that "true" ascribes *have in common* is something fairly meagre.

There are objections that can be raised against the indeterminist proposal. For example, can't there be properties that satisfy the relevant schema but aren't plausibly candidate referents of "true"? But these are general concerns about how the truth predicate can have its semantic value fully determined by the relevant schema, and do not arise only for indeterminism.

Let me close by briefly returning to deflationist theses (i)–(iii). Thesis (i) can be understood to be about the concept TRUTH or the property of being true. Thesis (iii) can amount to different things, for example depending on how the substantiveness talk is understood. There is also unclarity I haven't yet paused on in thesis (ii). One type of claim is simply that a truth predicate's theoretical usefulness is exhausted by its use as an expressive device. A more ambitious claim is that somehow, due to the kind of meaning it has, it is guaranteed already by the semantics of the truth predicate that it is so.

The only one of these deflationist theses that the rejectionist embraces is thesis (ii), in its less ambitious form. The indeterminist also adheres to thesis (i), understood as a claim about the concept TRUTH as opposed to the property of being true. Rejectionism and indeterminism may be attractive for a would-be deflationist, and there is a clear intuitive sense in which they deflate truth, there is much in what (i)–(iii) say that they do not vindicate.[20]

Notes

1. For a helpful overview of theories of truth, see Glanzberg (2013).
2. See e.g. Båve (2009), Field (1994), Horwich (1998, ch. 5), Leeds (1978) and McGee (1993, 2016) on deflationism about reference.
3. On prosententialism, see primarily Grover (1992) [Ch. 12 of this volume - Ed.].
4. Burgess and Burgess (2011), p. 47f, also complain, and along similar lines, that slogans of this kind are not very helpful.
5. See the discussion in the early pages of Wright (1998). Someone may object to the suggestion in the text that any reasonable argument in favor of some theory of the property of being true would have to be a priori in character, and that any good a priori reasoning would have to be conceptual in character. But both assumptions relied upon are eminently questionable.
6. Or perhaps to be committed to so accepting them. The details regarding the account of competence do not matter for present purposes. The important point is that the exhaustion claim, understood as being about the concept, can be taken to be about what competence with the concept involves.
7. See here also Alston (1996).

8. Not that it should be surprising that this is where we end up. This is the expected consequence of consistently avoiding the ideology of nature or essence, or anything similar.
9. Lynch (2009, p. 106f); my emphasis.
10. The discussion to follow parallels earlier discussions by Damnjanovic (2010), Edwards (2013), and Eklund (2012).
11. What about, e.g., the concept *has that property which Paul Horwich made distinctive claims about in his 1990 book*? Well, the example arguably does not work in that form: the italicized expression does not ascribe the property truth but the second-order property of having the property that Horwich made distinctive claims about. A more convincing example illustrating the point is this. Suppose one introduces "schmuth" simply as a predicate ascribing whichever property that Horwich made distinctive claims about. Then arguably the concept SCHMUTH stands for the property of truth but fails to fully reveal the nature of the property it stands for. The possession conditions of the concept SCHMUTH are different from those associated with the concept TRUTH.
12. It may incidentally be noted that (MT5) by itself is quite compatible with the correspondence theory. A correspondence theorist might well hold that the ordinary concept TRUTH is a correspondence concept, and grasping it puts one in a position to know that the property of being true is the property of corresponding with reality. She can then hold that truth's nature is correspondence, so truth has no nature that isn't revealed by the ordinary concept TRUTH. By (MT5) she then holds that the property of being true is transparent. (Thanks here to Panu Raatikainen.)
13. Damnjanovic (2010, p. 46).
14. Wyatt (2016, p. 371).
15. Wyatt (2016, p. 372).
16. Wyatt (2016, p. 371).
17. In his statement of (Unconstituted), Wyatt uses "insusceptible", suggesting that there is a modal element in the characterization. But given his characterization of what a constitution theory for truth is, and his tying transparency to the ordinary concept TRUTH, I don't see that his "insusceptible to an opaque constitution theory" cannot be replaced without loss by "does not have an opaque constitution theory".
18. Think perhaps of what are often called "gerrymandered" properties, grue and its ilk. Their natures can be quite complex; still they are explanatorily pretty useless.
19. There are some structural similarities to truth pluralism. There are now different, sophisticated varieties of truth pluralism but let me here give a simple characterization, lacking all sophistication. [For more sophistication see e.g. Lynch (2009) and the essays collected in Pedersen and Wright (2013).] According to this simple truth pluralism any predicate or property that meets certain general conditions qualifies as a truth predicate or truth property, and different predicates and properties are truth predicates and truth properties for different discourses. The structural similarites are the focus on satisfaction of general conditions [though truth pluralists add more than (DS) or (ES)], and the emphasis on a plurality of predicates and properties that in some sense can be seen as truth predicates and truth properties. But the indeterminist says that occurrences of "true" are semantically indeterminate as between different properties, whereas the pluralist needn't commit to any such indeterminacy claim and can hold that an occurrence of "true" in, say, physics discourse *determinately* ascribes one property whereas an occurrence of "true" in, say, moral discourse *determinately* ascribes another. Conversely, it is no part of indeterminism to say that what "true" ascribes depends on the discourse. (Sophisticated

pluralists might say not that "true" ascribes different properties depending on the discourse, but that the functionalist property truth is realized by different properties. The differences with indeterminism remain, mutatis mutandis.)

20. Many thanks to Jeremy Wyatt and to two anonymous referees for helpful comments on earlier versions. Thanks also to audiences at the University of Tampere and Umeå University for helpful feedback.

References

Alston, William: 1996, *A Realist Conception of Truth*, Cornell University Press, Ithaca, New York.

Asay, Jamin: 2013, *The Primitivist Theory of Truth*, Cambridge University Press, Cambridge.

Asay, Jamin: 2014, 'Against *Truth*', *Erkenntnis* 79: 147–64.

Båve, Arvid: 2009, 'A Deflationary Theory of Reference', *Synthese* 169: 51–73.

Burgess, Alexis and John Burgess: 2011, *Truth*, Princeton University Press, Princeton.

Damnjanovic, Nic: 2010, 'New Wave Deflationism', in Wright and Pedersen (2010), pp. 45–58.

deRosset, Louis: manuscript, 'The Metaphysical Transparency of Truth'.

Edwards, Douglas: 2013, 'Truth as a Substantive Property', *Australasian Journal of Philosophy* 91: 279–94.

Eklund, Matti: 2010, 'Rejectionism About Truth', in Wright and Pedersen (2010), pp. 30–44.

Eklund, Matti: 2012, 'Theories of Truth', in Gillian Russell and Delia Graff Fara (eds.), *Routledge Companion to the Philosophy of Language*, Routledge, New York, pp. 199–208.

Field, Hartry: 1994, 'Deflationist Views of Meaning and Content', *Mind* 103: 249–84.

Glanzberg, Michael: 2013, 'Truth', in Ed Zalta (ed.), *Stanford Encyclopedia of Philosophy*, http://plato.stanford.edu/entries/truth/.

Grover, Dorothy: 1992, *A Prosentential Theory of Truth*, Princeton University Press, Princeton.

Horwich, Paul: 1998, *Meaning*, Oxford University Press, Oxford.

Leeds, Stephen: 1978, 'Theories of Truth and Reference', *Erkenntnis* 13: 111–129.

Lynch, Michael: 2009, *Truth as One and Many*, Oxford University Press, Oxford.

McGee, Vann: 1993, 'A Semantic Conception of Truth?', *Philosophical Topics* 21 (2): 83–111.

McGee, Vann: 2016, 'Thought, Thoughts, and Deflationism', *Philosophical Studies* 173: 3153–68.

Moore, G. E.: 1903, *Principia Ethica*, Cambridge University Press, Cambridge.

Pedersen, Nikolaj J.L.L. and Cory D. Wright (eds.): 2013, *Truth and Pluralism: Current Debates*, Oxford University Press, Oxford.

Stoljar, Daniel and Nic Damnjanovic: 2010, 'The Deflationary Theory of Truth', *Stanford Encyclopedia of Philosophy*, http://plato.stanford.edu/entries/truth-deflationary/.

Wright, Cory D. and Nikolaj J.L.L. Pedersen (eds.): 2010, *New Waves in Truth*, Palgrave Macmillan.

Wright, Crispin: 1998, 'Truth: A Traditional Debate Reviewed', *Canadian Journal of Philosophy* 28: 31–74.

Wyatt, Jeremy: 2016: 'The Many (Yet Few) Faces of Deflationism', *Philosophical Quarterly* 66: 362–382.

Section 4 Primitivist theories of truth

Editor's introduction

DOUGLAS EDWARDS

Primitivist theories of truth disagree with all the views we have considered so far, and thus aim to stake out a unique position on the analysis of truth. Unlike the traditional views they think that there is no interesting analysis of truth to be had; but, unlike the deflationists, they do not think that truth has no nature. The claim instead is that truth has a substantive nature, but it is not a nature that can be specified. Truth, the thought is, is so basic that it cannot be given a substantive analysis in terms of other things, so it must be taken as a primitive thing.

Primitivism can be held at different levels, and the two theories outlined in the papers in this section are examples of the two main forms. We can see the view as the view that the *concept* of truth is a primitive concept, or we can see the view as the view that the *property* of being true is a primitive property. Donald Davidson's paper gives us an example of the former view; Trenton Merricks's paper gives us an example of the latter. Of course, the two views are not mutually exclusive, and one could hold that both the concept of truth and the property of being true are primitive.

As we have seen, attempts to analyse truth frequently run into difficulties. Davidson's thought is that this is no accident, for we should not expect every philosophically interesting concept to be neatly analysable in terms of other concepts. This is particularly so, Davidson thinks, when we consider truth, for, he thinks, truth is one of the most basic concepts we have. As such, it is a fool's errand to try to define truth in terms of more basic concepts, as there are none!

However, for Davidson, taking truth as a primitive concept does not mean that we can say nothing about it. On the contrary, Davidson holds that liberating ourselves from the constraint of thinking that we have to find a reductive analysis of truth opens the door to a different form of conceptual illumination. On Davidson's view we should look to the connections we can make between truth and other concepts, such as meaning, belief, knowledge and successful action. In doing so we can learn some things about truth, even if we cannot give a reductive analysis of the nature of truth. This method advocates the development of a 'network' of concepts, where each has specific ties to others. For instance, truth and belief are related in a number of ways: beliefs are things that can be true, and truth is the norm of belief.

This is one dimension upon which primitivism can be distinguished from deflationism, as deflationists do not think that there are constitutive connections between truth and other concepts. Davidson also discusses his influential contributions to the theory of meaning, and the connection between truth and meaning. This is another key dimension of the difference between deflationism and primitivism, as Davidson is keen to point out. Davidson is a central proponent of a truth-conditional theory of meaning, which holds that the meaning of a sentence is given by the conditions under which it is true. This gives truth a key theoretical role to play, and truth must be substantial enough to play that role. Deflationary theories of truth, on the other hand, typically reject truth-conditional theories of meaning in favour of theories of which attempt to explain meaning in terms of use. Deflationists are generally barred from holding truth-conditional theories of meaning on the grounds that, on their view, truth is not substantial enough to play any significant theoretical roles.

Trenton Merricks proposes a theory of truth where truth is explicitly thought of as a primitive *property*. Merricks rejects all the traditional views which attempt to analyse truth as a relation, instead proposing that we should think of truth as a 'monadic' property. However, this is not to imply that truth should be thought of as 'lightweight' in anything like the deflationist's sense, rather Merricks takes Davidson's thought about the concept of truth and applies them explicitly to the property: truth is a primitive property, that we can understand in terms of its connections to other properties, but which is incapable of analysis in virtue of its fundamental status.

The chapter by Merricks is an excerpt from his book *Truth and Ontology*, originally published in 2007, which is a detailed study of the metaphysics of truthmaking, and part of the motivation for Merricks's primitivism about truth comes from these findings. Truthmaker theory holds that every truth is made true by some existing entity. Merricks argues this view by saying that it is a mistake to think that all truths are made true by some existing entity. A central set of examples are negative existential claims, such as the proposition that there are no hobbits. Merricks claims that propositions like this are true, but they are not made true by any existing entity. Indeed, negative existential claims seem to be the exact kind of claims that cannot be made true by any existing entity, for if there were a relevant existing entity they would not be true in the first place. If Merricks is correct, examples like 'there are no hobbits' serve as counterexamples to the idea that all truths are made true by some existing thing. He also argues that these sorts of concerns are sufficient to cause significant problems for the correspondence theory of truth. This is because the correspondence theory of truth holds that all truths correspond to facts, but, if this is so, it also seems to struggle with the truth of negative existentials like the proposition that there are no hobbits. This is because it seems as though there cannot be a fact that there are no hobbits without the existence of hobbits, but if there is no fact that there are no hobbits, on the correspondence theory of truth the proposition that there are no hobbits cannot be true, as there is no fact for it to correspond to. After arguing that the correspondence theory of truth is incorrect, Merricks also rejects coherence, pragmatist and deflationist views, which leaves little option but the idea that truth is unanalysable.

Further reading

Other versions of primitivism can be found in Frege (1918/1956) and Moore (1910). More recent developments of the view in terms of primitivism about the concept of truth can be found in Sosa (2001), Patterson (2010) and Asay (2013). In terms of introductory volumes on truth, discussion of primitivism can be found in Künne (2003, Ch. 1).

References

Asay, J. 2013. *The Primitivist Theory of Truth*. Cambridge: Cambridge University Press.

Frege, G. 1918/1956. Der Gedanke. Published in English as '*The Thought*: A Logical Inquiry'. *Mind* 65 (259): 289–311.

Künne, W. 2003. *Conceptions of Truth*. Oxford: Oxford University Press.

Moore, G. E. 1910. *Some Main Problems in Philosophy*. London: Allen & Unwin.

Patterson, D. 2010. Truth as Conceptually Primitive. In C. D. Wright and N. Pedersen (eds), *New Waves in Truth*, New York: Palgrave Macmillan.

Sosa, E. 2001. Epistemology and Primitive Truth. In M. P. Lynch (ed.), *The Nature of Truth*, Cambridge: MIT Press.

14 The folly of trying to define truth

DONALD DAVIDSON

In the *Euthyphro,* Socrates asks what holiness is, what "makes" holy things holy. It is clear that he seeks a definition, a definition with special properties. He spurns the mere provision of examples or lists, asking in each case what makes the examples examples, or puts an item on the list. He rejects merely coextensive concepts ("something is holy if and only if it is dear to the gods"): what makes something dear to the gods is that it is holy, but not vice versa. The dialogue ends when Socrates begs Euthyphro to enlighten him by coming up with a satisfactory answer; Euthyphro decides he has another appointment.

The pattern of attempted definition, counterexample, amended definition, further counterexample, ending with a whimper of failure, is repeated with variations throughout the Socratic and middle Platonic dialogues. Beauty, courage, virtue, friendship, love, temperance are put under the microscope, but no convincing definitions emerge. The only definitions Plato seems happy with are tendentious characterizations of what it is to be a sophist. He also gives a few trivial samples of correct definitions: of a triangle; of mud (earth and water).

In the *Theaetetus,* Plato attempts to define empirical knowledge. Like many philosophers since, he takes knowledge to be true belief plus something more—an account that justifies or warrants the belief. It is the last feature which stumps him (again foreshadowing the subsequent history of the subject). It seems no more to occur to Plato than it has to most others that the combination of causal and rational elements that must enter into an analysis of justified belief (as it must into accounts of memory, perception, and intentional action) may in the nature of the case not be amenable to sharp formulation in a clearer, more basic, vocabulary.

What is important in the present context, however, is the fact that in attempting to define knowledge, it is only with the concept of warrant that Plato concedes defeat. He does not worry much about the equal involvement of knowledge with truth and belief.

Again, though, Plato was simply blazing a trail that other philosophers over the ages have followed: you follow his lead if you worry about the concept of truth when it is the focus of your attention, but you pretend you understand it when trying to cope with knowledge (or belief, memory, perception, and the like). We come across the same puzzling strategy in David Hume and others, who forget their skepticism about the external world when they formulate their doubts concerning knowledge of other minds. When a philosopher is troubled by the idea of an intentional action, he would be happy if he could analyze it correctly in terms of the concepts of belief, desire, and causality, and he does not for the moment worry too much about those (at least equally difficult) concepts. If memory is up for analysis, the connections with belief, truth, causality, and perhaps perception, constitute the problem, but these further concepts are pro tem taken to be clear enough to be used to clarify memory, if only the connections could be got right. It is all right to assume you have an adequate handle on intention and convention if your target is meaning. I could easily go on.

There is a lesson to be learned from these familiar, though odd, shifts in the focus of philosophical puzzlement. The lesson I take to heart is this: however feeble or faulty our attempts to relate these various basic concepts to each other, these attempts fare better, and teach us more, than our efforts to produce correct and revealing definitions of basic concepts in terms of clearer or even more fundamental concepts.

This is, after all, what we should expect. For the most part, the concepts philosophers single out for attention, like truth, knowledge, belief, action, cause, the good and the right, are the most elementary concepts we have, concepts without which (I am inclined to say) we would have no concepts at all. Why then should we expect to be able to reduce these concepts definitionally to other concepts that are simpler, clearer, and more basic? We should accept the fact that what makes these concepts so important must also foreclose on the possibility of finding a foundation for them which reaches deeper into bedrock.

We should apply this obvious observation to the concept of truth: we cannot hope to underpin it with something more transparent or easier to grasp. Truth is, as G. E. Moore, Bertrand Russell, and Gottlob Frege maintained, and Alfred Tarski proved, an indefinable concept. This does not mean we can say nothing revealing about it: we can, by relating it to other concepts like belief, desire, cause, and action. Nor does the indefinability of truth imply that the concept is mysterious, ambiguous, or untrustworthy.

Even if we are persuaded that the concept of truth cannot be defined, the intuition or hope remains that we can characterize truth using some fairly simple formula. What distinguishes much of the contemporary philosophical discussion of truth is that though there are many such formulas on the market, none of them seems to keep clear of fairly obvious counterexamples. One result has been the increasing popularity of minimalist or deflationary theories of truth—theories that hold that truth is a relatively trivial concept with no "important connections with other concepts such as meaning and reality."[1]

I sympathize with the deflationists; the attempts to pump more content into the concept of truth are not, for the most part, appealing. But I think the deflationists are wrong in their conclusion, even if mostly right in what they reject. I shall not pause here to give my reasons for refusing to accept correspondence theories, coherence theories, pragmatic theories, theories that limit truth to what could be ascertained under ideal conditions or justifiably asserted, and so on.[2] But since I am with the deflationists in being dissatisfied with all such characterizations of truth, I shall say why deflationism seems to me equally unacceptable.

Aristotle, as we all know, contended that

(1) To say of what is that it is not, or of what is not that it is, is false, while to say of what is that it is, or of what is not that it is not, is true.

When Tarski[3] mentions this formulation in 1944, he complains that it is "not sufficiently precise and clear," though he prefers it to two others:

(2) The truth of a sentence consists in its agreement with (or correspondence to) reality.

(3) A sentence is true if it designates an existing state of affairs (ibid., p. 343).

In 1969, Tarski[4] again quotes (1), and adds,

> [T]he formulation leaves much to be desired from the point of view of precision and formal correctness. For one thing, it is not general enough; it refers only to sentences that "say" about something "that it is" or "that it is not"; in most cases it would hardly be possible to cast a sentence in this mold without slanting the sense of the sentence and forcing the spirit of the language (ibid., p. 63).

He adds that this may be the reason for such "modern substitutes" for Aristotle's formulations as (2) and (3).

In the *Wahrheitsbegriff,* however, Tarski[5] prefers the following informal statement:

> **(4)** A true sentence is one which says that the state of affairs is so and so, and the state of affairs indeed is so and so (ibid., p. 155).

It seems to me that Aristotle's formulation is clearly superior to (2), (3), and (4); it is more in accord with Tarski's own work on truth; and Tarski's comment that (1) is "not general enough" is strangely out of keeping with the spirit of his own truth definitions.

(1) is superior to (2) – (4) for three reasons. First, (3) and (4) mention states of affairs, thus suggesting that postulating entities to correspond to sentences might be a useful way of characterizing truth. ("A true sentence is one that corresponds to the facts," or "If a sentence is true, there is a state of affairs to which it corresponds.") But facts or states of affairs have never been shown to play a useful role in semantics, and one of the strongest arguments for Tarski's definitions is that in them nothing plays the role of facts or states of affairs. This is not surprising, since there is a persuasive argument, usually traced to Frege (in one form) or Kurt Gödel (in another), to the effect that there can be at most one fact or state of affairs. (This is why Frege said all true sentences name the True.) Tarski's truth definitions make no use of the idea that a sentence "corresponds" to anything at all. We should not take seriously the mention of "states of affairs" in such remarks of Tarski's[6] as this: "[S]emantical concepts express certain relations between objects (and states of affairs) referred to in the language discussed and expressions of the language referring to those objects" (ibid., p. 403).

A second reason for preferring Aristotle's characterization of truth is that it avoids the awkward blanks marked by the words 'so and so' in Tarski's version (4); one is hard pressed to see how the blanks are to be filled in. Aristotle's formula, on the other hand, sounds much like a generalization of Tarski's convention-T.

The third reason for preferring Aristotle's characterization is that it makes clear, what the other formulations do not, that the truth of a sentence depends on the inner structure of the sentence, that is, on the semantic features of the parts. In this it is once again closer to Tarski's approach to the concept of truth.

Tarski's convention-T, which he understandably substitutes for the rough formulas I have been discussing, stipulates that a satisfactory definition of a truth predicate 'is true' for a language *L* must be such as to entail as theorems all sentences of the form

s is true-in-*L* if and only if *p*

where 's' is replaced by the description of a sentence, and '*p*' is replaced by that sentence, or a translation of the sentence into the metalanguage. Since it is assumed that there is an infinity of sentences in *L*, it is obvious that, if the definition of the truth predicate is to be finite

(Tarski insisted on this), the definition must take advantage of the fact that sentences, though potentially infinite in number, are constructed from a finite vocabulary. For the languages Tarski considered, and for which he showed how to define truth, all sentences can be put into the form of an existential quantification, or the negation of an existential quantification, or a truth-functional compound of such sentences. So how "incomplete," from Tarski's point of view, is Aristotle's formulation (1)? It deals with four cases. There are the sentences that "say of what is that it is not": in modern terms it is a false sentence that begins 'It is not the case that there exists an *x* such that…'. An example might be: 'There does not exist an *x* such that $x = 4$'. Then there are sentences that "say of what is not that it is"; for example: 'There exists an *x* such that $x = 4$ & $x = 5$'. There are sentences that "say of what is that it is"; for example: 'There exists an *x* such that $x = 4$'. And, finally, there are sentences that "say of what is not that it is not"; for example, 'It is not the case that there exists an *x* such that $x \neq x$'. According to the classical formulation, sentences of the first two kinds are false and of the second two kinds are true. Tarski is so far in agreement. What would Tarski add? Just the truth-functional compounds (beyond those involving negation) of the types of sentences already mentioned; these are true or false on the basis of the truth or falsity of the kinds of sentences already provided for. Of course, Tarski also showed in detail how the truth or falsity of the first four types of sentences depended in turn on their structure.

Thus, the classical formulation regarded as an informal characterization is "incomplete" in only a minimal way compared to Tarski's own work, and is better than Tarski's informal attempts to state the intuitive idea. Needless to say, someone might question the extent to which natural languages can be adequately characterized using such limited resources; but this is a comment equally applicable to Tarski.

Despite his nod in the direction of a correspondence theory, in which sentences are said to correspond to facts, Tarski ought not to be considered as giving comfort to serious partisans of correspondence theories, nor should Aristotle. For neither Aristotle's formula nor Tarski's truth definitions introduce entities like facts or states of affairs for sentences to correspond to. Tarski does define truth on the basis of the concept of satisfaction, which relates expressions to objects, but the sequences that satisfy sentences are nothing like the "facts' or "states of affairs" of correspondence theorists, since if one of Tarski's sequences satisfies a closed sentence, thus making it true, then that same sequence also satisfies every other true sentence, and thus also makes it true, and if any sequence satisfies a closed sentence, every sequence does.[7]

If Tarski is not a correspondence theorist (and he certainly does not hold a coherence theory or a pragmatic theory or a theory that bases truth on warranted assertibility), is he a deflationist? Here opinions differ widely: W. V. Quine thinks he is, and so does Scott Soames. John Etchemendy thinks Tarski simply says nothing about truth as a semantic concept, and Hilary Putnam, though for somewhat different reasons, agrees.[8]

If Tarski has said "all there is to say" about truth, as Stephen Leeds, Paul Horwich, and Soames all contend, and Quine has strongly hinted, then a sort of deflationary attitude is justified; this is not quite the same as the "redundancy" view, but close to it. The redundancy view, taken literally, is the same as the disquotational view taken literally: we can always substitute without loss a sentence for that same sentence quoted, and followed by the words 'is true'. What Tarski added, as Michael Williams and others have pointed out, is a way of predicating truth of whole classes of sentences, or of sentences to which we do not know how to refer; you may think of this as an elaboration of the redundancy theory in that it allows the elimination of the truth predicate when applied to sentences of a language for which that predicate has been defined.

At the same time that we credit Tarski with having shown how to make sense of remarks like 'The English sentence Joan uttered about Abbot was true' or 'Everything Aristotle said (in Greek) was false' or 'The usual truth table for the conditional makes any conditional true that has a false antecedent', we have to recognize that this accomplishment was accompanied by a proof that truth cannot (given various plausible assumptions) be defined in general; there can be no definition of 'For all languages *L*, and all sentences *s* in *L*, *s* is true in *L* if and only if ... *s* ... *L* ...'. In other words, Tarski justified the application of a truth predicate to the sentences of a particular language only by restricting its application to the sentences of that language. (It is ironic that in much recent writing on deflationary theories, Tarski has been taken to have lent support to the idea that there is a single, simple, even trivial, concept of truth.)

A deflationary attitude to the concept of truth is not, then, encouraged by reflection on Tarski's work. One can adopt the line advanced by Putnam and Etchemendy that Tarski was not even doing semantics, despite his insistence that he was; but this construal of Tarski does not support a deflationary theory: it simply denies the relevance of Tarski's results to the ordinary concept of truth. If, on the other hand, one takes Tarski's truth definitions to say something about the relations of specific languages to the world, one cannot at the same time claim that he has told us all there is to know about the concept of truth, since he has not told us what the concept is that his truth definitions for particular languages have in common.

I think that Tarski was not trying to define *the* concept of truth—so much is obvious—but that he was *employing* that concept to characterize the semantic structures of specific languages. But Tarski did not indicate how we can in general reduce the concept of truth to other more basic concepts, nor how to eliminate the English predicate 'is true' from all contexts in which it is intelligibly applied to sentences. Convention-T is not a rough substitute for a general definition: it is part of a successful attempt to persuade us that his formal definitions apply our single pretheoretical concept of truth to certain languages. Deflationists cannot, then, appeal to Tarski simply because he demonstrated how to handle the semantics of quantification for individual languages. Leeds, Horwich, Williams, and others who have contended that all Tarski did was reveal the usefulness of an otherwise dispensable concept are wrong. They are right that we need a truth predicate for the purposes they, along with Tarski, mention; but they fail to note the obvious fact that at the same time Tarski solved one problem he emphasized another: that he had not, and could not, given the constraints he accepted, define or fully characterize truth.

Over the years, Quine has said a number of things about truth, but there has been, from early days until the most recent, what seems a consistent embrace of a deflationary attitude. Thus, Quine has made much of the "disquotational" aspect of the truth predicate, the fact that we can get rid of the predicate 'is true' after the quotation of an English sentence simply by removing the quotation marks as we erase the truth predicate. As Quine put it in *From a Logical Point of View,*[9] we have a general paradigm, namely,

(T) '—' is true-in-*L* if and only if —

which, though not a definition of truth, serves to endow 'true-in-*L*' with

> every bit as much clarity, in any particular application, as is enjoyed by the particular expressions of *L* to which we apply [it]. Attribution of truth in particular to 'Snow is white' ... is every bit as clear to us as attribution of whiteness to snow (ibid., p. 138).

In *Word and Object,* Quine[10] remarks that "To say that the statement 'Brutus killed Caesar' is true, or that 'The atomic weight of sodium is 23' is true, is in effect simply to say that Brutus killed Caesar, or that the atomic weight of sodium is 23" (ibid., p. 24). The theme is repeated thirty years later in *Pursuit of Truth:*[11]

> there is surely no impugning the disquotation account; no disputing that "Snow is white" is true if and only if snow is white. Moreover, it is a full account; it explicates clearly the truth or falsity of every clear sentence. (ibid., p. 93).

"Truth," he summarizes, "is disquotation" (ibid., p. 80). On this matter, Quine has not changed his mind.

It is the disquotational feature of truth, in Quine's opinion, which makes truth so much clearer a concept than meaning. Comparing theory of meaning and theory of reference, Quine says that they constitute "two provinces so fundamentally distinct as not to deserve a joint appellation at all."[12] The former deals with such tainted topics as synonymy, meaning, and analyticity. The concepts treated by the latter, which include truth, are by contrast "very much less foggy and mysterious...." For although 'true-in-*L*' for variable '*L*' is not definable, "what we do have suffices to endow 'true-in-*L*', even for variable '*L*', with a high enough degree of intelligibility so that we are not likely to be averse to using the idiom" (ibid., pp. 137–38). "What we do have" is, of course, the paradigm (T) and the "expedient general routine" due to Tarski for defining 'true-in-*L*' for particular languages.

The disquotational feature of truth, wedded to the thought that this may exhaust the content of the concept of truth, encourages the idea that truth and meaning can be kept quite separate. But can they in general? Scattered remarks in Quine's work suggest otherwise. In 1936, Quine published the brilliant and prescient "Truth by Convention."[13] In it he remarks that "in point of meaning ... a word may be said to be determined to whatever extent the truth or falsehood of its contexts is determined" (ibid., p. 89). It is hard to see how truth could have this power of determining meaning if the disquotational account were all there were to say about truth. Other passages in Quine suggest the same idea: "First and last, in learning language, we are learning how to distribute truth values. I am with Davidson here; we are learning truth conditions."[14] Or again, "Tarski's theory of truth [is] the very structure of a theory of meaning."[15]

Up to a point it may seem easy to keep questions of truth and questions of meaning segregated. Truth we may think of as disquotational (in the extended Tarski sense) and therefore trivial; meaning is then another matter, to be taken care of in terms of warranted assertability, function, or the criteria for translation. This is the line followed, for example, by Horwich in his recent book *Truth* (op. cit.), by Soames,[16] and by Lewis.[17] It may, at least at one time, have been Quine's view. In *Word and Object,* in a passage that immediately precedes the remark that to say that the sentence 'Brutus killed Caesar' is true is in effect simply to say that Brutus killed Caesar, Quine despairs of a substantive concept of truth, and concludes that we make sense of a truth predicate only when we apply it to a sentence "in the terms of a given theory, and seen from within the theory" (op. cit., p. 24). This is, I think, what Quine means when he says that truth is "immanent." The point is not merely that the truth of a sentence is relative to a language; it is that there is no transcendent, single concept to be relativized.[18]

Most recently, however, Quine muses that truth "is felt to harbor something of the sublime. Its pursuit is a noble pursuit, and unending"; he seems to agree: "Science is seen as pursuing and discovering truth rather than as decreeing it. Such is the idiom of realism, and it is integral to the semantics of the predicate 'true'."[19]

I turn now to Horwich's version of deflationism [See Ch. 10 of this volume – Ed.], for he seems to me to have accepted the challenge other deflationists have evaded, that of saying something more about an unrelativized concept of truth than we can learn from Tarski's definitions. Horwich's brave and striking move is to make the primary bearers of truth propositions—not exactly a new idea in itself, but new in the context of a serious attempt to defend deflationism. He is clear that he cannot provide an explicit definition of a truth predicate applying to propositions, but he urges that we really have said all there is to know about such a predicate (and hence the predicate it expresses) when we grasp the fact that the "uncontroversial instances" of the schema:

The proposition that *p* is true if and only if *p*

exhaust its content. (The limitation to "uncontroversial instances" is to exclude whatever leads to paradox.) The schema is taken as an axiom schema: the totality of its instances constitute the axioms of his theory.

This theory is, of course, incomplete until the controversial instances are specified in a non-question-begging way; and since the set of axioms is infinite, it does not meet one of Tarski's requirements for a satisfactory theory of truth. But perhaps the first difficulty can be overcome, and the second may be viewed as the price of having an unrelativized concept of truth. There are, further, the doubts many of us have about the existence of propositions, or at least of the principles for individuating them.

All these considerations give me pause, but I plan to ignore them here. I want to give deflationism its best chance, since it seems to me to be the only alternative to a more substantive view of truth, and most substantive views are in my opinion, as in Horwich's, clear failures. But although I enthusiastically endorse his arguments against correspondence, coherence, pragmatic, and epistemic theories, I cannot bring myself to accept Horwich's "minimal" theory.

I have two fundamental problems with Horwich's theory, either of which alone is reason to reject it if it cannot be resolved; and I do not myself see how to resolve them.

The first problem is easy to state: I do not understand the basic axiom schema or its instances. It will help me formulate my difficulty to compare Horwich's axiom schema with Tarski's informal (and ultimately supplanted) schema:

'—' is true if and only if —

Tarski's objection (among others) is that you cannot turn this into a definition except by quantifying into a position inside quotation marks. The complaint ends up with a question about the clarity of quotations: How does what they refer to depend on the semantic properties of their constituents? It has sometimes been proposed to appeal to substitutional quantification, and one may wonder why Horwich cannot generalize his schema:

(*p*) (the proposition that *p* is true if and only if *p*)

by employing substitutional quantification. But here Horwich quite rightly explains that he cannot appeal to substitutional quantification to explain truth, since substitutional quantification must be explained by appeal to truth.

Why, though, does Horwich not try generalizing his schema by quantifying over propositions? The answer should be: because then we would have to view ordinary sentences as singular terms *referring* to propositions, not as *expressing* propositions. This brings me to the crux: How are we to understand phrases like 'the proposition that Socrates is wise'? In giving a standard account of the semantics of the sentence 'Socrates is wise', we make use of what the name 'Socrates' names, and of the entities of which the predicate 'is wise' is true. But how can we use these semantic features of the sentence 'Socrates is wise' to yield the reference of 'the proposition that Socrates is wise'? Horwich does not give us any guidance here. Could we say that expressions like 'the proposition that Socrates is wise' are semantically unstructured, or at least that after the words 'the proposition that' (taken as a functional expression) a sentence becomes a semantically unstructured name of the proposition it expresses? Taking this course would leave us with an infinite primitive vocabulary, and the appearance of the words 'Socrates is wise' in two places in the schema would be of no help in understanding the schema or its instances. A further proposal might be to modify our instance of the schema to read:

The proposition expressed by the sentence 'Socrates is wise' is true if and only if Socrates is wise.

But following this idea would require relativizing the quoted sentence to a language, a need that Horwich must circumvent.

So let me put my objection briefly as follows: the same sentence appears twice in instances of Horwich's schema, once after the words 'the proposition that', in a context that requires the result to be a singular term, the subject of a predicate, and once as an ordinary sentence. We cannot eliminate this iteration of the same sentence without destroying all appearance of a theory. But we cannot *understand* the result of the iteration unless we can see how to make use of the same semantic features of the repeated sentence in both of its appearances—make use of them in giving the semantics of the schema instances. I do not see how this can be done.

My second difficulty with Horwich's theory is more dependent on my own further convictions and commitments. Horwich recognizes that to maintain that truth has, as he says, "a certain purity," he must show that we can understand it fully in isolation from other ideas, and we can understand other ideas in isolation from it. He does not say there are no relations between the concept of truth and other concepts; only that we can understand these concepts independently. There are several crucial cases so far as I am concerned, since I do not think we can understand meaning or any of the propositional attitudes without the concept of truth. Let me pick one of these: meaning.

Since Horwich thinks of truth as primarily attributable to propositions, he must explain how we can also predicate it of sentences and utterances, and he sees that to explain this without compromising the independence of truth, we must understand meaning without direct appeal to the concept of truth. On this critical matter, Horwich is brief, even laconic. Understanding a sentence, he says, does not *consist* in knowing its truth conditions, though if we understand a sentence we usually *know* its truth conditions. Understanding a sentence, he maintains, consists in knowing its "assertability conditions" (or "proper use"). He grants that these conditions may include that the sentence (or utterance) be true. I confess I do not see how, if truth is an assertability condition, and knowing the assertability conditions *is* understanding, we can understand a sentence without having the concept of truth.

I realize, however, that this is disputed territory, and that heavy thinkers like Michael Dummett, Putnam, and Soames, following various leads suggested by Ludwig Wittgenstein and H. P. Grice, believe that an account of meaning can be made to depend on a notion of assertability or use which does not in turn appeal to the concept of truth.

My hopes lie in the opposite direction: I think the sort of assertion that is linked to understanding already incorporates the concept of truth: we are *justified* in asserting a sentence in the required sense only if we believe the sentence we use to make the assertion is true; and what ultimately ties language to the world is that the conditions that typically cause us to hold sentences true *constitute* the truth conditions, and hence the meanings, of our sentences. This is not the place to argue this. For now I must simply remark that it would be a shame if we had to develop a theory of meaning for a speaker or a language independently of a theory of truth for that speaker or language, since we have at least *some* idea how to formulate a theory of truth, but no serious idea how to formulate a theory of meaning based on a concept of assertability or use.

I conclude that the prospects for a deflationary theory of truth are dim. Its attractions seem to me entirely negative: it avoids, or at least tries to avoid, well-marked dead ends and recognizable pitfalls.

Let me suggest a diagnosis of our aporia about truth. We are still under the spell of the Socratic idea that we must keep asking for the *essence* of an idea, a significant *analysis* in other terms, an answer to the question what *makes* this an act of piety, what *makes* this, or any, utterance, sentence, belief, or proposition true. We still fall for the freshman fallacy that demands that we *define* our terms as a prelude to saying anything further with or about them.

It may seem pointless to make so much of the drive to define truth when it is unclear who is trying to do it: not Tarski, who proves it cannot be done; not Horwich, who disclaims the attempt. Who, then, *admits* to wanting to define the concept of truth? Well, that is right. But. But the same ugly urge to define shows up in the guise of trying to provide a brief criterion, schema, partial but leading hint, in place of a strict definition. Since Tarski, we are leery of the word 'definition' when we are thinking of a concept of truth not relativized to a language, but we have not given up the definitional urge. Thus, I see Horwich's schema on a par *in this regard* with Dummett's notion of justified assertability, Putnam's ideally justified assertability, and the various formulations of correspondence and coherence theories. I see all of them as, if not attempts at definitions in the strict sense, attempts at *substitutes* for definitions. In the case of truth, there is no short substitute.

Now I want to describe what I take to be a fairly radical alternative to the theories I have been discussing and (with unseemly haste) dismissing. What I stress here is the *methodology* I think is required rather than the more detailed account I have given elsewhere. The methodology can be characterized on the negative side by saying it offers no definition of the concept of truth, nor any quasi-definitional clause, axiom schema, or other brief substitute for a definition. The positive proposal is to attempt to trace the connections between the concept of truth and the human attitudes and acts that give it body.

My methodological inspiration comes from finitely axiomatized theories of measurement, or of various sciences, theories that put clear constraints on one or more undefined concepts, and then prove that any model of such a theory has intuitively desired properties—that it is adequate to its designed purpose. Since among the models will be all sorts of configurations of abstract entities, and endless unwanted patterns of empirical events and objects, the theory can be applied to, or tested against, such specific phenomena as mass or temperature only by indicating how the theory is to be applied to the appropriate objects or events. We cannot demand a precise indication of how to do this; finding a useful method for applying the theory is an enterprise that goes along with tampering with the formal theory, and testing its correctness as interpreted.

We are interested in the concept of truth only because there are actual objects and states of the world to which to apply it: utterances, states of belief, inscriptions. If we did not understand what it was for such entities to be true, we would not be able to characterize the contents of these states, objects, and events. So in addition to the formal theory of truth, we must indicate how truth is to be predicated of these empirical phenomena.

Tarski's definitions make no mention of empirical matters, but we are free to ask of such a definition whether it fits the actual practice of some speaker or group of speakers—we may ask whether they speak the language for which truth has been defined. There is nothing about Tarski's definitions that prevents us from treating them in this way except the prejudice that, if something is called a definition, the question of its "correctness" is moot. To put this prejudice to rest, I suggest that we omit the final step in Tarski's definitions, the step that turns his axiomatizations into explicit definitions. We can then in good conscience call the emasculated definition a theory, and accept the truth predicate as undefined. This undefined predicate expresses the *general,* intuitive, concept, applicable to any language, the concept against which we have always surreptitiously tested Tarski's definitions (as he invited us to do, of course).

We know a great deal about how this concept applies to the speech and beliefs and actions of human agents. We use it to interpret their utterances and beliefs by assigning truth conditions to them, and we judge those actions and attitudes by evaluating the likelihood of their truth. The empirical question is how to determine, by observation and induction, what the truth conditions of empirical truth vehicles are. It bears emphasizing: absent this empirical connection, the concept of truth has no application to, or interest for, our mundane concerns, nor, so far as I can see, does it have any content at all.

Consider this analogy: I think of truth as Frank Ramsey thought of probability. He convinced himself, not irrationally, that the concept of probability applies in the first instance to propositional attitudes; it is a measure of degree of belief. He went on to ask himself: How can we make sense of the concept of degree of belief (subjective probability)? Subjective probability is not observable, either by the agent who entertains some proposition with less than total conviction and more than total disbelief, or by others who see and question him. So Ramsey axiomatized the pattern of preferences of an idealized agent who, more or less like the rest of us, adjusts his preferences for the truth of propositions (or states of affairs or events) to accord with his values and beliefs. He stated the conditions on which a pattern of such preferences would be "rational," and in effect proved that, if these conditions were satisfied, one could reconstruct from the agent's preferences the relative strengths of that agent's desires and subjective probabilities. Ramsey did not suppose everyone is perfectly rational in the postulated sense, but he did assume that people are nearly enough so, in the long run, for his theory to give a content to the concept of subjective probability—or probability, as he thought of it.

A brilliant *strategy*! (Whether or not it gives a correct analysis of probability.) The concept of probability—or at least degree of belief— unobservable by the agent who has it and by his watchers, linked to an equally theoretical concept of cardinal utility, or subjective evaluation, and both tied to simple preference by the axiomatic structure. Simple preference in turn provides the crucial empirical basis through its manifestations in actual choice behavior.

We should think of a theory of truth for a speaker in the same way we think of a theory of rational decision: both describe structures we can find, with an allowable degree of fitting and fudging, in the behavior of more or less rational creatures gifted with speech. It is in the fitting and fudging that we give content to the undefined concepts of subjective probability and subjective values—belief and desire, as we briefly call them; and, by way of theories like Tarski's, to the undefined concept of truth.

A final remark. I have deliberately made the problem of giving empirical content to the concept of truth seem simpler than it is. It would be *relatively* simple if we could directly observe—take as basic evidence— what people *mean* by what they say. But meaning not only is a more obscure concept than that of truth; it clearly involves it: if you know what an utterance means, you know its truth conditions. The problem is to give *any* propositional attitude a propositional content: belief, desire, intention, meaning.

I therefore see the problem of connecting truth with observable human behavior as inseparable from the problem of assigning contents to all the attitudes, and this seems to me to require a theory that embeds a theory of truth in a larger theory that includes decision theory itself. The result will incorporate the major norms of rationality whose partial realization in the thought and behavior of agents makes those agents intelligible, more or less, to others. If this normative structure is formidably complex, we should take comfort in the fact that the more complex it is, the better our chance of interpreting its manifestations as thought and meaningful speech and intentional action, given only scattered bits of weakly interpreted evidence.

Notes

1. These words are quoted from Michael Dummett's jacket blurb for Paul Horwich's *Truth* (Oxford: Oxford University Press, 1990). This is not, of course, Dummett's view.
2. I spell out my reasons for rejecting such views in "The Structure and Content of Truth," *Journal of Philosophy,* LXXXVII, 6 (June 1990): 279–328.
3. "The Semantic Conception of Truth," *Philosophy and Phenomenological Research,* IV (1944): 342–360.
4. "Truth and Proof," *The Scientific American,* CCXX (1969): 63–77.
5. "The Concept of Truth in Formalized Languages," in *Logic, Semantics, Metamathematics* (New York: Oxford, 1956), pp. 152–278 (originally published in German in 1936).

6. "The Establishment of Scientific Semantics," in *Logic, Semantics, Metamathematics,* pp. 401–408.
7. At one time I suggested calling Tarski's concept of truth a correspondence theory on the strength of the role of sequences in satisfying closed sentences, but I subsequently withdrew the suggestion as misleading. For the suggestion, see "True to the Facts," in *Inquiries into Truth and Interpretation* (New York: Oxford, 1984). For the retraction, see "Afterthoughts, 1987," in A. Malichowski, ed., *Reading Rorty* (Cambridge: Blackwell, 1990), pp. 120–138.
8. For references, and further discussion, see my "The Structure and Content of Truth."
9. Cambridge: Harvard, 1961.
10. Cambridge: MIT, 1960.
11. Cambridge: Harvard, 1990. [Reprinted as chap. 20.—Ed.]
12. *From a Logical Point of View,* p. 130.
13. Reprinted in *The Ways of Paradox* (Cambridge: Harvard, 1976).
14. *The Roots of Reference* (La Salle, IL: Open Court, 1974), p. 65.
15. "On the Very Idea of a Third Dogma," in *Theories and Things* (Cambridge: Harvard, 1981), p. 38.
16. "What Is a Theory of Truth?" *Journal of Philosophy,* LXXXI, 8 (August 1984): 411–429.
17. "Languages and Language," *Minnesota Studies in the Philosophy of Science,* volume VII (Minneapolis: Minnesota UP, 1975).
18. The preceding paragraphs on Quine are partly quoted and partly adapted from a longer and more detailed study of Quine on truth: "Pursuit of the Concept of Truth," in P. Leondardi and M. Santambrogio, eds., *On Quine: New Essays* (New York: Cambridge, 1995). The relevant pages are 7–10.
19. *From Stimulus to Science* (Cambridge: Harvard, 1995), p. 67.

15 Truth as a primitive

TRENTON MERRICKS

The correspondence theory, the coherence theory, and the identity theory all purport to analyze truth as a relation between a truth-bearer and some existing entity or entities, whether those entities be states of affairs or beliefs or something else. (The hypothetical version of the coherence theory endorses such an analysis only in the ideal case.) As we saw above, one reason that all three of these theories fail is that some truths—those that lack truthmakers—are not true in virtue of how they are related to any positively existing entity or entities.

Some truths are not true in virtue of how they are related to any existing entity or entities. So we should reject any theory of truth that implies that every truth is true in virtue of how it is related to some existing entity or entities. And so we should reject any theory that implies that *what it is* to be true is to be appropriately related to some existing entity or entities. And so we should reject any theory of truth that takes *being true* to be a relation between each true (primary) truth-bearer and some entity or entities. Therefore, we should conclude that *being true* is not a relation between a truth and some entity.

Being true is not a relation. One might react to this by denying that there is any property, relational or otherwise, of *being true*. I shall consider this denial in the next section. But for now, let us assume that there is a property of *being true*. Assuming this, and given that *being true* is not a relation, we have a single option. *Being true* is a monadic property.[1]

Being true is monadic. But it is not intrinsic. For whether a proposition exemplifies *being true* is often a matter of how things are around it. For example, whether *that dogs bark* is true is not only a matter of what that proposition is like, but also a matter of whether there are any dogs and what those dogs do.

Non-intrinsic monadic properties should be familiar. Both Truthmaker and TSB[2] require (something relevantly like) the property of *being such that there is nothing more in the universe* (Merricks 2007: Ch. 3; Ch. 4, §VII). Suppose that that property were exemplified by something without proper parts. Then that property could not be a relation between what exemplifies it and something else, since, *ex hypothesi*, there is nothing else. So it would be monadic. So—if there is such a property at all—it is monadic. But it is not intrinsic, since whether something has that property is a matter of what (if anything) else there is.

Truthmaker and TSB imply (something like) a 'nothing more' property. Similarly, I think that every account of *being true* as a relation needs (something like) a 'nothing more' property. For every such account must deliver, for each negative existential, some entity such that that negative existential is true in virtue of how it is related to that entity. Thus any relational account of *being true*, no less than an account of *being true* as a monadic property, is committed to some non-intrinsic monadic property or other.[3]

But *being true* is monadic. Because it is monadic, if *being true* has an analysis, that analysis must be in terms of monadic properties had by each and every truth-bearer. But—here is the weak step in this argument—I do not think any monadic properties of truths deliver an analysis of *being true*.[4] So I conclude that *being true* has no analysis. That is, *being true* is a primitive property.[5]

Perhaps you have doubts about the weak step in the argument. Perhaps you think there is, or at least might be, a genuine analysis of *being true* in terms of the other monadic properties of truth-bearers. I do not want to argue about it. For the monadicity of *being true* is the main point here. Its primitivity is not essential to the other claims about truth made in this chapter or, indeed, in this book.[6]

Nevertheless, I do think that *being true* is primitive. And others have drawn more or less the same conclusion. Here is Donald Davidson:

> For the most part, the concepts philosophers single out for attention...are the most elementary concepts we have... Why then should we expect to be able to reduce these concepts definitionally to other concepts that are simpler, clearer, and more basic? We should accept the fact that what makes these concepts so important must also foreclose on the possibility of finding a foundation for them which reaches deeper into bedrock.
>
> We should apply this obvious observation to the concept of truth: we cannot hope to underpin it with something more transparent or easier to grasp. Truth is, as G. E. Moore, Bertrand Russell, and Gottlob Frege maintained...an indefinable concept. (1996, 264–265) [This volume, Ch. 14, pp. 228 – Ed.]

When he mentions Moore and Russell, Davidson cannot have in mind their correspondence theories discussed above. Instead, he must be thinking of an earlier position of theirs, defended in Moore (1899) and Russell (1904, 521–524; see also 1907).[7] And with his reference to Frege, Davidson must be thinking of 'Der Gedanke', where Frege says: 'So it seems likely that the content of the word 'true' is *sui generis* and indefinable' (1997b, 327).[8]

Paul Horwich objects to the idea that *being true* is a primitive property:

> ...there is the one-time thesis of Moore (1899...) and Russell (1904) that truth is an indefinable, inexplicable quality that some propositions simply have and others simply lack—a fundamental property of which no account can be provided. This gives a sense of impenetrable mysteriousness to the notion of truth and can be the resort only of those who feel that the decent alternatives have been exhausted. (1998, 9–10)

Horwich objects that if truth were not analyzable, it would be mysterious.

My reply to this objection begins by noting that, even if we set *being true* aside, there are some primitive and non-analyzable properties. And surely some of these are not mysterious. Moreover, if they were all mysterious, analyzable properties would be equally occult, themselves ultimately analyzed in terms of the inscrutable primitive properties.

Some might reply that the analysis of non-primitive properties never bottoms out in primitive properties, but rather descends through other analyzable properties *ad infinitum*. Taking this option into account—and assuming that not every property is mysterious—we must say at least one of two things. First, some non-mysterious properties have no analysis. Second, some non-mysterious properties have an infinitely complex analysis.

I endorse the first: among the non-mysterious properties are some that are primitive. This is partly because if a property had an infinitely complex analysis, an analysis that we could not possibly grasp, that property would seem to be mysterious. And it is partly because we obviously do grasp certain primitive properties. Among these are *identity*, *existence*, and—as was suggested at the end of Chapter Five [of Merricks 2007 – Ed.]—some modal properties.[9]

Focus on *identity*. The received view about *identity* is that it is primitive and cannot be analyzed into more fundamental relations or properties (see Merricks, 1998, 110; Hawthorne, 2003, 99). The received view does not monger mystery. For even if identity is primitive, we know a lot about it. We know, for example, that it is transitive, reflexive, and symmetric and also that it implies indiscernibility. And we can even make claims of identity in English without using the word 'identity'. For example, we can say that *x* is one and the same as *y*.

Similarly, the primitive nature of *being true* is consistent with our knowing a lot about truth. It is consistent with our knowing that, necessarily, *that hobbits do not exist* has the property of *being true* if and only if there are no hobbits; more generally, it is consistent with our knowing that realism about truth is correct. Similarly, it is consistent with truth's depending on being in a trivial and uncontroversial way. That is, even if *being true* is primitive, *that hobbits do not exist* is true because hobbits do not exist. More generally, the many claims about truth defended throughout this book, along with the arguments in support of them, are consistent with *being true*'s being primitive. And we can, while speaking English, assert that a statement is true without using the word 'true'. For example, we can say that a particular statement tells it like it is.

Being true is primitive. This does not render truth mysterious. Moreover, I think that a primitive property of *being true* is preferable to the primitive properties implied by Truthmaker, TSB, and relational theories of *being true*. That is, a primitive (and monadic and non-intrinsic) *being true* is preferable to primitive (and monadic and non-intrinsic) properties like *being such that there is nothing more in the universe*.

Notes

1. More carefully, the argument just given shows that *being true* is both monadic and, moreover, is not had by a truth-bearer in virtue of that truth-bearer's standing in a relation to something else. (In this regard *being true* differs from, for example, *being married*, which is monadic but which one has in virtue of standing in the *being married to* relation to someone else.) In what follows, when I speak of 'monadic but non-intrinsic properties', I shall mean only those properties that are not only monadic, but also not had by something in virtue of standing in a relation to something else.

   My argument for the monadicity of *being true* does not rule out the possibility that *being true* is not a monadic property, but is instead a relation that holds between a proposition and itself. (The same goes for *being such that there is nothing more in the universe*, discussed below.) But I shall ignore this possibility, since I think that it makes no significant difference to the points at issue here.
2. [Editor's note: 'Truthmaker' refers to the claim that, for each true claim, there exists some entity which makes that claim true. 'TSB' refers to the thesis that truth supervenes on being. For more details, see the introduction to Merricks 2007.]

3. Truthmaker, TSB, and relational accounts of *being true* can also make do with a *totaling* or *alling* relation, which is a relation that holds between entities if and only if there are no other entities in existence—and so only if what is happening 'outside' those entities is a certain way. Any such relation is relevantly like a monadic but non-intrinsic property.
4. Russell considers—just to slap away—the idea that truth could be analyzed as the intrinsic 'vividness' of a belief (1912, 70) [This volume, Ch. 1, p. 8.]
5. That is, the truth of primary truth-bearers is not analyzable. But the truth of a derivative truth-bearer is analyzed in terms of its expressing a primary truth-bearer that has the primitive property of *being true*. (And while I think that *being true* and *being false* can be 'interdefined', I deny that this gives us a genuine analysis of either.)
6. [Editor's note: 'this book' here refers to Merricks (2007).
7. Russell and Moore's position also has elements of an identity theory of truth (see Cartwright, 1987; Candlish, 1989). Like the identity theorist, Russell (1904) takes true propositions to be events. Unlike the identity theorist, however, Russell thinks only those events that have the primitive property of *being true* are true (these are 'facts', in the parlance of Russell (1904)). And Russell (1904) says that false propositions are events with the primitive property of *being false* (these are 'objective falsehoods').

   Moore (1899, 180) takes a proposition to be a 'synthesis of concepts'. He then goes on to tell us:

   > It seems necessary, then, to regard the world as formed of concepts. These are the only objects of knowledge. They cannot be regarded fundamentally as abstractions either from things or from ideas; since both alike can, if anything is to be true of them, be composed of nothing but concepts. (1899, 182) (See also Moore, 1901–02)

   I defend Russell and Moore's view that *being true* is primitive, but of course I deny that the bearers of *being true* are events or states of affairs. Nor can I make good sense of the events that are supposed by Russell and Moore to have the property of *being false*.
8. But note: 'The *Bedeutung* of the word 'true' seems altogether *sui generis*. May we not be dealing here with something which cannot be called a property in the ordinary sense at all? In spite of this doubt, I will begin by expressing myself in accordance with ordinary usage, as if truth were a property, until some more appropriate way of speaking is found' (Frege, 1997b, 328–9). It is hard to square these claims with Frege's earlier and better known discussion of truth in 'Über Sinn und Bedeutung', in which Frege claims that truth, or at least the True, is the referent of each and every true sentence (see Frege, 1997a, 157–8).
9. Grasping primitive properties is more problematic than grasping properties generally only if the only way to grasp a property is by grasping its analysis. (Obviously, we do not grasp primitive properties by grasping their analyses; they have no analyses.) But it is false that the only way to grasp a property is by grasping its analysis. To see this, consider that either some of the properties we grasp are analyzed in terms of primitive properties or none are. If some are, then to grasp their analysis requires grasping primitive properties—but that cannot be done if the only way to grasp a property is to grasp its analysis. If none are, then to grasp the analysis of a property requires grasping an infinitely complex and unending analysis—but that is not something we can do. So I conclude that at least some properties can be grasped even if we do not grasp their analyses. Further support for this conclusion comes from the observation that few properties have uncontroversial analyses, and so if to grasp a property always required grasping its analysis, we would grasp far fewer properties than we actually do grasp.

References

Candlish, S. 1989. The Truth about F.H. Bradley. *Mind* 98: 331–48.

Cartwright, R. 1987. A Neglected Theory of Truth. In his *Philosophical Essays*, Cambridge: MIT Press.

Davidson, D. 1996. The Folly of Trying to Define Truth. *Journal of Philosophy* 93: 263–78. [This volume, Ch. 14 – Ed.]

Frege, G. 1997a. On *Sinn* and *Bedeuntung*. In M. Beaney (ed.), *The Frege Reader*, Oxford: Blackwell: 151–172. Originally published in *Zeitschrift für Philosophie und philosophische Kritik*, 100 (1892): 25–50.

Frege, G. 1997b. Thought [*Der Gedanke*]. In M. Beaney (ed.), *The Frege Reader*, Oxford: Blackwell: 325–346. Originally published in *Beiträge zur Philosophie des deutschen Idealismus*, I (1918–19): 58–77.

Hawthorne, J. 2003. Identity. In M.J. Loux and D. Zimmerman (eds.), *The Oxford Handbook of Metaphysics*, Oxford: Oxford University Press.

Horwich, P. 1998. *Truth*. Oxford: Oxford University Press.

Merricks, T. 1998. There Are No Criteria of Identity over Time. *Noûs*, 32: 106–24.

Merricks, T. 2007. *Truth and Ontology*. Oxford: Oxford University Press.

Moore, G.E. 1899. The Nature of Judgment. *Mind* 8: 176–93.

Moore, G.E. 1901–02. Truth. In J. Baldwin (ed.), *Dictionary of Philosophy and Psychology*. London: MacMillan.

Russell, B. 1904. Meinong's Theory of Complexes and Assumptions. *Mind* 13: 204–19, 336–54, and 509–24.

Russell, B. 1912. *The Problems of Philosophy*. London: Williams & Holgate.

Section 5 Pluralist theories of truth

Editor's introduction

DOUGLAS EDWARDS

Introduction

Pluralist theories of truth hold that there is a nature to truth – that truth is capable of analysis – but that this nature may not always be the same. Pluralists are keen to emphasize the variety of different subject matters we think and talk about, and they relate this to the idea that different theories of truth seem better placed to account for different kinds of subject matters. For example, the correspondence theory of truth may seem well-suited for propositions about the physical world, at least if we take it to involve causal relations, but it seems poorly suited to account for the truth of mathematical claims, particularly if numbers and the like are treated as abstract objects. Likewise, it does not seem particularly well-suited to serve as a theory of truth for moral or aesthetic claims, as it is hard to make sense of these as being about completely mind-independent things. On the other hand, theories like coherence and pragmatism seem well-suited to account for the truth of mathematical claims, as well as perhaps moral and aesthetic claims, but they struggle to account for the truth of claims about the mind-independent physical world.

While the deflationist and primitivist take these problems for these theories as evidence that there either is no nature to truth or that its nature cannot be analysed, the pluralist takes this as evidence that there is reason to think that the nature of truth might not be uniform across subject matters. The pluralist thus proposes that there are multiple natures of truth, captured by different theories in different cases. Truth in physics might be different from truth in mathematics, which might in turn be different from truth in ethics.

Beyond this point there are a number of different ways to develop the basic pluralist proposal, and the distinctions we made at the beginning of the book between the concept of truth and the property of being true are important here.

Crispin Wright, 'Truth: A traditional debate reviewed'

In Crispin Wright's chapter 'Truth: A Traditional Debate Reviewed', he examines various theories of truth before proposing the idea that different theories may be applicable in different areas. Before we discuss Wright's positive view, we should say a few words about his influential 'inflationary argument' against deflationism.

Wright's 'inflationary argument'

As we have seen, deflationists hold that there is no nature to truth. One consequence of this is that they think that truth is not a distinctive norm of inquiry (for more on norms see the introduction to Section 6). Wright argues that the deflationist cannot consistently hold this position alongside their key endorsement of the equivalence schema, and thus that view is unstable. We have already seen that deflationism holds that instances of (ES) are central:

> (ES) It is true that p if and only if p.

Wright will argue that this alone (plus some uncontroversial claims about warranted assertibility) show that deflationism *is* committed to truth being a distinctive norm of inquiry. The argument, in its simplest form, goes as follows.

> (ES) can be proved to entail instances of 'Negation Equivalence' (NE):[1]

> (NE) It is true that not-p if and only if it is not true that p.

This is a schema about truth, on the deflationary view. Now consider a way that we can evaluate a proposition, namely whether or not a proposition is warrantedly assertible. We can show that warranted assertibility and truth come apart because the equivalent claim of (NE) for warranted assertibility (WNE) is false:

> (WNE) It is warrantedly assertible that not-p if and only if it is not warrantedly assertible that p.

(WNE) is false because warranted assertibility allows for *neutral* states of information: a lack of warrant for p does not entail that we have warrant for p's negation. For example, we do not have warrant to assert that it snowed on the spot where St Paul's Cathedral is located 300,000 years ago today. However, the fact that we lack warrant for asserting that it snowed on that spot 300,000 years ago *does not* mean that we have warrant for asserting that it *did not* snow on that spot 300,000 years ago today: the absence of evidence in favour of the claim does not translate into evidence against it.

(Note that the notion of truth governed by (ES) does *not* allow for such neutrality: if it is not true that p, then it is true that not-p, and vice versa.)

So, Wright argues, this shows that a proposition's truth is a *different* matter from whether that proposition is warrantedly assertible. He thinks that this shows – contra deflationism – that there must be *something in which being true consists* which marks how being true is different from being warrantedly assertible.

The argument, then, is that deflationism is unstable: it denies that there is anything in which truth consists, yet its basic principles entail that there is something in which truth consists.

Wright's pluralism

Having argued that, contra deflationism, there is a substantial nature to truth, Wright explores the idea that this nature might vary according to subject matter. Wright's key thought is that, while the concept of truth might be uniform, the property that satisfies this concept may change from one domain of discourse to the next. On this view, we have consistency in the meaning of the predicate 'is true', as this is always expressing the same concept, but divergence in what this concept picks out, as different properties will correspond to the concept of truth in different domains. One way to think of this model is to draw an analogy with pain. On some views of pain, pain is something which is 'multiply realizable'. While we have a common understanding of pain, captured by such thoughts as 'pain is something that is avoided', and 'pain is caused by tissue damage', what it actually is that being in pain consists in might vary across different organisms. For example, what pain is for humans (perhaps c-fibres firing) might be different for what pain is in octopodes (perhaps d-fibres firing, say). The idea here is that we have one single concept of pain, which describes the role that the state of being in pain plays, but that different physical states might play, or 'realize', that role in different organisms.

The idea in relation to truth is that we have a single concept of truth, which describes the role that truth plays in our thought and talk, but that different properties might play that role in different domains of discourse. Wright explores the idea that coherence and a property he calls 'superassertibility' might be serviceable as truth properties in different domains.

On Wright's view in this chapter, we have a single concept of truth, but many properties of being true. The permissibility of this model has been challenged by a pair of 'mixing' problems presented by Christine Tappolet (1997, 2000). Consider first the 'problem of mixed inferences'. This asks us to consider the inferences like the following:

1. Torture causes pain.
2. If something causes pain, then it is wrong.
3. Therefore, torture is wrong.

This is an argument that includes premises from different domains of discourse: (1) is a physical claim, and (2) and (3) are moral claims. Now, a common understanding of the validity of an argument is that it preserves truth across the inference, but if different premises are subject to a different truth property, how is a single thing – truth – preserved across the inference? To illustrate, consider the argument again with the truth properties explicitly noted:

1. Torture causes pain is TRUE 1
2. If something causes pain, then it is wrong is TRUE 2
3. Therefore, torture is wrong is TRUE 2

Here it is clear that there is not a single property of being true which is preserved from the premises to the conclusion, for premise one has a different truth property to premise two. The concern thus is that if we would like to think of validity as truth preservation, Wright's view has a problem.

The second concern is the 'problem of mixed compounds'. Consider the following proposition:

(C) Torture is wrong and 2+2=4.

This is a compound proposition, a conjunction, which contains conjuncts from different domains of discourse: moral and mathematical. Intuitively, such a conjunction can be true, but in what way can it be true on Wright's account? It seemingly cannot be just true in the moral sense, as that ignores the mathematical component, and vice versa. Is it true in both ways, neither ways?

These problems, while perhaps not irresolvable, do suggest some pressure on the structure of Wright's view. It is undeniable that we often mix up propositions from different domains, whether in making inferences or making new propositions, and this is something that pluralism cannot ignore. They also suggest that it might be very useful for a pluralist to have access to not only a single concept of truth but also a single property of being true, which is shared by all true propositions.

Douglas Edwards, 'Simplifying alethic pluralism'

Douglas Edwards,[2] drawing upon work by Wright and Michael Lynch, develops a pluralist theory which is able to maintain a single property of being true, applicable to all true propositions. Edwards develops the analogy between truth and winning, originally emphasized by Michael Dummett (1959). There is an affinity between truth and winning to the extent that, just as winning is the aim of playing a competitive game, truth is the aim of belief. Moreover, Edwards suggests, just as winning is a single thing that can be attained in different ways depending on the game being played, truth is a single property that can be possessed in different ways depending on the domain of discourse in question.

Edwards holds that there is a general property of being true, which is described by the platitudes about truth that Wright describes, and that this property is related to properties like correspondence and superassertibility in virtue of truth being determined by those properties. The basic idea behind determination is that a property F determines another property G when possession of F entails possession of G. For example, in the games example, amassing a majority of the allotted sets is the winning-determining property for playing tennis, as possession of the property of having amassed the majority of the allotted sets entails possession of the property of being the winner of that game. Likewise, the idea is that, in the moral domain, for example, superassertibility determines truth as possession of the property of being superassertible entails possession of the property of being true.

Edwards's view has some advantages over Wright's in relation to the problems discussed earlier. In the case of mixed inferences, for example, there is a single property – truth – which is preserved across a valid inference, as all true propositions share the same property of being true, with the difference between them being that this property is determined by different properties in different domains.

Gila Sher, 'In search of a substantive theory of truth'

Gila Sher presents an important alternative to the ways of thinking about pluralism discussed earlier. One challenge all of the previous proposals face is how to explain how we have a unified theory of truth in the face of the apparent diversity between the ways that truth is understood in different areas. Sher takes up this issue of unity and diversity in extensive detail in her chapter, and provides a powerful framework for accommodating these demands, which is very different from the views given earlier. Sher proposes thinking not that there are radically different truth properties, but rather that the different truth properties are all variations of one particular kind of truth property, namely correspondence.

One reason for this is that Sher thinks that the unifying principles of truth need to be more substantive than the unifying principles Wright and Edwards offer. Both Wright and Edwards take the basic 'truisms' about truth which capture the heart of the concept of truth (and, for Edwards, the property of being true as well) as minimal principles which are acceptable to all. Sher questions whether this provides the level of unity required by the unity challenge, and instead explores the idea that the unifying principles must carry more weight. This is done by holding that a substantial principle about truth holds across the board, namely the principle that truth consists in correspondence to the facts. This is more than a mere platitude for Sher, and is an explicit commitment to a substantial theory of truth which involves the relation of correspondence and the existence of facts as key components.

In holding that the unity of truth consists in a substantial commitment to the idea that truth is correspondence to fact, Sher faces a challenge when it comes to explaining the diversity of truth, which is a key feature from a pluralist's perspective. Her proposal is to understand correspondence to fact as something which comes in various forms. As truth is identified with correspondence to fact, it follows that truth comes in various forms. Sher suggests that, while truth is always correspondence to fact, the way in which the correspondence relation works, and perhaps also the way facts are understood, can vary from one domain of discourse to the next. Accordingly, we might have one form of correspondence for physical truths, a different form for moral truths, and a different form for mathematical truths, to take just three examples. Sher explores the example of logical truth to demonstrate one such correspondence relation, where she holds that the correspondence relation for logic is one which connects the logical structure of a sentence with a specific law governing the activity of the properties denoted by the predicates contained in the sentence.

In addition to advancing her view, Sher also provides an argument against deflationism on the grounds that it does not live up to the demands of a theory of truth, and addresses the mixed inferences problem for pluralism noted earlier. Her solution utilizes the notion of logical truth mentioned earlier, allowing us to understand validity in terms of truth as formal correspondence.

Sher's view has the advantage over Wright and Edwards's proposals in that the problem of the unity of truth is less pronounced: truth is always and everywhere correspondence, as opposed to being associated with correspondence in one domain, and superassertibility in another. The differences, for Sher, lie in the forms that correspondence can take. However, the flip side of this is that Sher's view may have more problems accommodating the diversity of truth if there are domains where correspondence does not seem appropriate in any of its forms. For example, some have proposed (Lynch 2009; Cotnoir and Edwards 2015; Edwards 2018) that in some domains it makes sense to understand truth in terms of reference, and in other domains it makes sense to understand reference in terms of truth. Views like Wright's and Edwards's can accommodate this, as they are open to understanding truth non-referentially in some domains. Sher, however, given her commitment to global correspondence, is always committed to understanding truth in terms of reference, and not the other way around. This is not necessarily a problem, as it depends on the viability of understanding truth non-referentially, but it does limit the use of the view to a would-be pluralist.

Notes

1. (1) It is not true that p iff not-p
   (2) It is true that not-p iff not-p
   (NE) It is true that not-p iff it is not true that p (1,2, Transitivity of the Biconditional).
2. Please excuse the reference to myself in the third person here!

Further reading

For general introductions to truth pluralism, see Pedersen and Wright (2013a) and Edwards (2012). Three central books in the field are Wright (1992), Lynch (2009) and Edwards (2018). Wright's most recent contribution to the debate is Wright (2013), and for more on other views, see Lynch (2013), Edwards (2013) and Pedersen and Wright (2013c). Recent work on truth pluralism is collected in Pedersen and Wright (2013b). For alternative views in the spirit of Sher's view, see Horgan (2001). Sher's most recent contributions to the debate can be found in Sher (2013) and Sher (2016). For more on the problems of mixed inferences and mixed compounds, see Tappolet (1997, 2000), Beall (2000), Pedersen (2006), Edwards (2008, 2009), Cotnoir (2009, 2013) and Cook (2011). In terms of introductory volumes on truth, discussion of truth pluralism can be found in Wrenn (2015, Ch. 7) and Burgess and Burgess (2011, Ch. 6.6).

References

Beall, J. C. 2000. On Mixed Inferences and Pluralism about Truth Predicates. *The Philosophical Quarterly* 50 (200): 380–2.

Burgess, P. and Burgess, A. 2011. *Truth*. Princeton: Princeton University Press.

Cook, R. T. 2011. Alethic Pluralism, Generic Truth and Mixed Conjunctions. *The Philosophical Quarterly* 61 (Issue 244): 624–9.

Cotnoir, A. J. 2009. Generic Truth and Mixed Conjunctions: Some Alternatives. *Analysis* 69(2): 473–9.

Cotnoir, A. J. 2013. Validity for Strong Pluralists. *Philosophy and Phenomenological Research* 86 (Issue 3): 563–79.

Cotnoir, A. J. and Edwards, D. 2015. From Truth Pluralism to Ontological Pluralism and Back. *The Journal of Philosophy* 112 (Issue 3): 113–40.

Dummett, M. 1959. Truth. *Proceedings of the Aristotelian Society* 59 (1): 141–62.

Edwards, D. 2008. How to Solve the Problem of Mixed Conjunctions. *Analysis* 68, (2): 143–9.

Edwards, D. 2009. Truth-conditions and the Nature of Truth: Re-solving Mixed Conjunctions. *Analysis* 69 (4): 684–8.

Edwards, D. 2012. Truth, Pluralist Theories of, *Internet Encyclopedia of Philosophy* (eds. J. Fieser and B. Dowden), URL = <http://www.iep.utm.edu/plur-tru/>.

Edwards, D. 2013. Truth, Winning, and Simple Determination Pluralism. In N. J. L. L. Pedersen and C. D. Wright (eds), *Truth and Pluralism: Current Debates*. Oxford: Oxford University Press, 113–22.

Edwards, D. 2018. *The Metaphysics of Truth*. Oxford: Oxford University Press.

Horgan, T. 2001. Contextual Semantics and Metaphysical Realism: Truth as Indirect Correspondence. In M. P. Lynch (ed.), *The Nature of Truth*. Cambridge: MIT Press.

Lynch, M. P. 2009. *Truth as One and Many*. Oxford: Oxford University Press.

Lynch, M. P. 2013. Three Questions about Truth Pluralism. In N. J. L. L. Pedersen and C. D. Wright (eds), *Truth and Pluralism: Current Debates*. New York: Oxford University Press.

Pedersen, N. J. L. L. 2006. What can the Problem of Mixed Inferences Teach us about Alethic Pluralism? *The Monist* 89 (1): 102–17.

Pedersen, N. J. L. L. and Wright, C. D. 2013a. Pluralist Theories of Truth. In Edward N. Zalta (ed.), *The Stanford Encyclopedia of Philosophy*, URL = http://plato.stanford.edu/archives/spr2013/entries/truth-pluralist/

Pedersen, N. J. L. L. and Wright, C. D. (eds) 2013b. *Truth and Pluralism: Current Debates*. New York: Oxford University Press.

Pedersen, N. J. L. L. and Wright, C. D. 2013c. Pluralism about Truth as Alethic Disjunctivism. In N. J. L. L. Pedersen and C. D. Wright (eds), *Truth and Pluralism: Current Debates*. New York: Oxford University Press, 87–112.

Sher, G. 2013. Forms of Correspondence: The Intricate Route from Thought to Reality. In N. J. L. L. Pedersen and C. D. Wright (eds), *Truth and Pluralism: Current Debates*. New York: Oxford University Press, 157–79.

Sher, G. 2016. *Epistemic Friction*. Oxford: Oxford University Press.

Tappolet, C. 1997. Mixed Inferences: A Problem for Pluralism about Truth Predicates. *Analysis* 57 (3): 209–10.

Tappolet, C. 2000. Truth, Pluralism and Many-Valued Logics. *The Philosophical Quarterly* 50 (200): 382–3.

Wrenn, C. 2015. *Truth*. Cambridge Polity Press.

Wright, C. J. G. 1992. *Truth and Objectivity*. Cambridge: Harvard University Press.

Wright, C. J. G. 2013. A Plurality of Pluralisms. In N. J. L. L. Pedersen and C. D. Wright (eds), *Truth and Pluralism: Current Debates*. New York: Oxford University Press, 123–53.

16 Truth: A traditional debate reviewed

CRISPIN WRIGHT

I

Every student of English-speaking analytical metaphysics is taught that the early twentieth century philosophical debate about truth confronted the Correspondence theory, supported by Russell, Moore, the early Wittgenstein and, later, J.L. Austin, with the Coherence theory advocated by the British Idealists.[1] Sometimes the Pragmatist conception of truth deriving from Dewey, William James and C.S. Peirce is regarded as a third player. And as befits a debate at the dawn of analytical philosophy, the matter in dispute is normally taken to have been the proper analysis of the concept.

No doubt this conception nicely explains some of the characteristic turns taken in the debate. Analysis, as traditionally conceived, has to consist in the provision of illuminating conceptual equivalences; and illumination will depend, according to the standard rules of play, on the *analysans*' utilising only concepts which, in the best case, are in some way prior to and independent of the notion being analysed—or, if that's too much to ask, then concepts which at least permit of some form of explication which does not in turn take one straight back to that notion. Thus if it is proposed, in this spirit, that truth is correspondence to external fact, it will be possible for a critic both to grant the *correctness* of the proposal and to reject it nevertheless—because, it may be contended, it fails to comply with the conditions on an illuminating *analysis*. In particular, it will be an obligation on an analysis of truth in terms of correspondence that it be possible to supply appropriate independent explications of the notions of "correspondence" and "fact", and it is exactly here, of course, that many of the traditional difficulties for the correspondence proposal have been located. Likewise, if we propose to analyse truth in terms of coherence, or on broadly pragmatist lines, we must be prepared to allow that any and every occurrence of "true" as applied to what the analysis recognises to be its primary bearers—sentences, or propositions, or whatever—may be replaced, without change of meaning,[2] by an expression of the preferred analysans. And, again, many of the knots into which critics have tied proposals of these kinds depend upon exploitation of this constraint. As recently as 1982, for instance, Alvin Plantinga observed that if "true" just means: *would be believed by cognitively ideal subjects operating under cognitively ideal conditions*, then there seems to be no prospect of recovering, without paradox, an account of the content of the thought: it is true that conditions are not cognitively ideal.[3]

When the debate is all about the analysis of the concept of truth, then at least two other kinds of position have to be possible—and, historically, they have indeed been occupied.

One is the Indefinabilist view adopted by Frege: that truth allows of *no* analysis, because it is too simple, or primitive, or because any notions involved in a formulation which is at least correct will rapidly bring one back to truth, so compromising illumination. Frege held this view for reasons whose cogency is a matter of dispute[4] but the apparent paucity of successful analyses of *anything* in analytical philosophy, and the inchoate and uneasy state of the methodology of analysis itself, must encourage the thought that this negative stance will not easily be dismissed. Quite different—and rather more interesting—is the proposal that correspondence, coherentist, pragmatist and even indefinabilist conceptions of truth all err in their common conviction that "true" presents a substantial concept at all. This is the Deflationist tradition, which is usually thought to have originated in Ramsey, was defended in rather different ways by Ayer and Strawson, and which survives in contemporary writers such as Paul Horwich and Hartry Field.[5] According to deflationism, there simply isn't anything which truth, in general, *is*. It's a misconstrual of the role of the adjective, "true" to see it as expressing the concept of a substantial characteristic of which one of the traditional accounts might provide a correct analysis, or which might allow of no correct analysis. Those who think otherwise are missing the point that the role of a significant adjective doesn't have to be to ascribe a genuine property.

My first principal point is that, notwithstanding the fact that it rationalises many of the moves made, and doubtless reflects therefore the intentions of many of the protagonists, the conception of the traditional debate about truth as centred upon reductive analysis of the concept is not best fitted to generate the most fruitful interpretation of it. To see this, suppose for the sake of argument that the indefinabilists are right: that "true", like—say—"red", admits of no illuminating conceptual breakdown. It is striking that philosophical discussion of colour has hardly been silenced by the corresponding point about the concept *red* or basic colour concepts generally. The contention that there is, as Locke thought, an interesting distinction between primary and secondary qualities of objects and that red is a secondary quality; the contention that whether an object is red is, in some way, a 'response-dependent' matter, or more generally that there is some form of implicit relativity in the idea of an object's being red; the contention that red is, on the contrary, a non-relational property of objects or, more specifically, that red things form a natural kind; even the "error-theoretic" view that a complete inventory of characteristics found in the real world would contain no mention of the colours—all these views, and an acknowledgement of the interest of the debates to which they contribute, are consistent with recognition of the indefinability of colour concepts. So, consistently with its indefinability—if it is indefinable—a similar range of issues can be expected to arise in connection with truth. "True"—even when taken, in the broad sense which interests us, as a predicate of content-bearing things—is predicated of a variety of items: beliefs, thoughts, propositions, token utterances of type sentences. But whatever such items we have in mind, we can ask whether one of them being true is in any way an *implicitly relational* matter—and if so, what are the terms of the relation; whether it is a *response-dependent* matter, or in any other way dependent on subjectivity or a point of view; whether there is indeed nothing generally in which the truth of such an item consists—whether an inventory of all the properties to be found in the world would include mention of *no such thing as truth*.

Indeed, such issues arise for any putative characteristic, Φ. Should we (ontologists) take Φ seriously at all, or is some sort of error-theoretic or deflationary view appropriate? If we do take it seriously, should we think of the situation of an item's being Φ as purely a matter of how it is intrinsically with that item, or are we rather dealing with some form of relation? Is an item's being Φ an objective matter (and what does it mean to say so?). These are analytic-philosophical issues *par excellence*, but their resolution need not await—and might not be settled by—the provision of a correct conceptual analysis.

II

Suppose we discard the analysis-centred conception of the traditional debate and look at it instead in the way suggested by the foregoing reflections. Clearly the deflationary option remains in play, holding that truth is not a genuine characteristic of anything—that it would find no place in an inventory of what is real. The other views all allow the reality of truth but differ about its *structure*, or in respects relevant to the broad question of objectivity. Correspondence theory holds that truth is a relational characteristic whose terms are respectively propositions—to pick one among the possibilities[6]—and *non-propositional items*—facts, or states of affairs—in an independent world.[7] The proposal thus bears both on structure and, so proposers of correspondence intend, on objectivity too. Coherence theory agrees about the relationality of truth, but disagrees about the terms of the relation: on this type of view, the truth of a proposition consists not in a relation to something non-propositional but in its participation in a system, meeting certain conditions, whose other participants are likewise propositions—so ultimately in relations to those other propositions. This is again, in the first instance, a view about the structure of truth, but it was intended by its original proponents to provide a vehicle for their Idealism. And Pragmatism—the view that truth is, broadly, a matter of operational success of some kind—while making no clear suggestion about structure (though there may be commitments in this direction once the relevant dimensions of success are clarified), stands in opposition to the correspondence theorists' thoughts about objectivity without—intentionally anyway—implying anything like such Idealism.

Let's focus for the time being on the question of structure, and return later to some of the issues connected with pragmatism. We may chart the possibilities in a tree as follows:

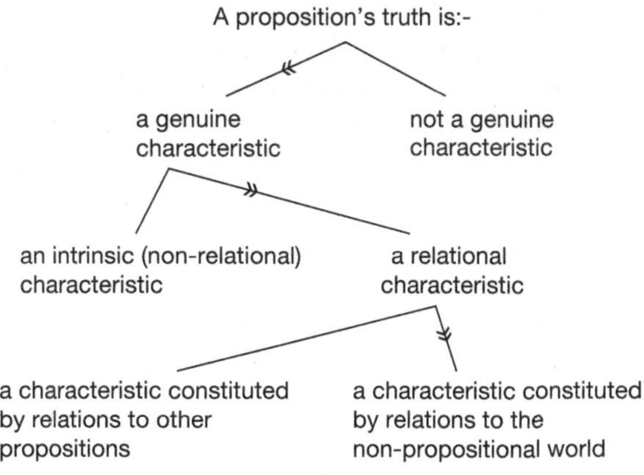

Essentially, then, just four structural proposals are possible: deflationism, intrinsicism, and the two forms of relationalism, coherentism, and correspondence. I think it's fair to say that this conception of correspondence, shorn of any further analytical or explanatory obligations, comes across as highly commonsensical. In general, we'd want to think both that there's a real distinction marked by the classification of some propositions as true and others as false, and that it is a distinction which cannot generally be understood without reference to things which are not themselves propositions, so cannot be understood in intrinsicist or coherentist terms.

This piece of commonsense is not to be confused with the idea that, understood one way, Correspondence is nothing more than a platitude. The platitude is that predications of "true" may always harmlessly be glossed in terms of correspondence to fact, telling it like it is, etc. These paraphrases incorporate no substantial commitment about the structure of truth—any more than the paraphrasability of "she did it for John" by "she did it on John's behalf" involves a commitment to the view that altruistic action is really a three term relation. By contrast, the ordinary, commonsensical conception of the kind of thing a proposition's truth is involves exactly the structural commitments associated with the path that leads to correspondence on the above tree.

It will be a second main contention of this paper that there is no stable alternative to allowing at least some scope to this commonsensical conception.

III

In order to make good that contention, we need to see that each of the three alternatives gives rise to intractable problems.

Intrinsicism is the easiest case to deal with. Fix attention on the case of contingent truths. If its truth-value were an intrinsic—but contingent—property of a particular proposition, then no contingent change in any other object should entail change in the proposition in that particular respect. That's an instance of a quite general principle. The mass, for instance, of a given body is a contingent but intrinsic property of that body only if no contingent change in any other object would entail change in that object's mass. By contrast, a property—for instance, being a grandfather—is essentially relational, even if expressed by what looks like a semantically simple predicate, if change in other objects may entail that a particular object sheds, or acquires that property. By this simple test, truth is, manifestly, not an intrinsic property. For the truth-value of any contingent proposition must co-vary with hypothetical changes in the characteristics of things it concerns—so that a hypothetical change, for instance, in the location of my coffee cup may entail an alteration in the truth value of the proposition that there is no coffee cup on my desk, even though that proposition and the particular coffee cup in question are quite distinct existences. To be sure, this line of thought creates no difficulty for the idea that the truth value of a *necessary* proposition might be an intrinsic property. So, indeed, it may be. But clearly intrinsicism cannot handle the general run of contingent cases.[8]

It might be rejoined that the canvassed account of the contrast between intrinsic and relational properties is incorrect or circular. For a property F may be an intrinsic characteristic of an object and yet it's loss, say, may still be entailed by change in another object provided that latter change is permitted to be in *non-intrinsic respects*. For instance, if G is a ("Cambridge") property possessed by any object just in case *a* has intrinsic characteristic F, then any other object's losing G will entail that *a* has lost F. This observation is, however, beside the point. All the objection to intrinsicism needs is that the account be correct, not that it be explanatory. If it is at least granted that F is an intrinsic property of *a* just in case no *intrinsic* change in any other object can entail change in *a* in that respect, it will follow as before that truth cannot be an intrinsic property of any proposition whose content is that another object has some particular intrinsic but contingent property.

IV

It is a rather more complicated business to elicit what is fundamentally unsatisfactory about the deflationary conception of truth. The difficulties here are owing partly to the point that deflationism is more of a "tendency" than a definite philosophical position, and different deflationists display differences of formulation and emphasis which make it hard to see what may be essential and what optional in their views. There are, however, a number of characteristic, interrelated claims: first

(i) that there is no property of truth which is an appropriate object of philosophical attention: something which we might try to analyse, or in whose structure we might be interested, or which might give rise to issues about objectivity. Contrary to the presupposition both of the traditional debate and of its revision canvassed above, there is *nothing* in which the truth of a proposition, e.g., consists. "True" expresses no real property.[9]

That negative contention is then characteristically augmented by a variety of considerations about the meaning or positive function of the word "true"; for instance

(ii) that, as applied to sentences, "true" is just the device of *disquotation*—a device for affirming at the metalinguistic level (by locutions of the form: "p" is true) exactly what can be affirmed at the object-language level by an assertoric use of "p";

(iii) that the Disquotational Scheme

"p" is true if and only if p,

(or if the primary grammar of "true" is considered to be that of an operator on (or predicable of) propositions, the Equivalence Schema

It is true that p/that p is true if and only if p)

is (all but) a complete explanation of the meaning of "true";

(iv) that "true" is just a device of endorsement—we only have any use for such a term because we sometimes choose to endorse propositions indirectly, without specifying their content ("The sixth sentence of *Remarks on the Foundations of Mathematics* IV, §3 is true" or "Fermat's Last Theorem has turned out to be true") and sometimes want to endorse whole batches of propositions at once ("Almost everything Chancellor Kohl says is true"). In other kinds of case we can dispense with the word altogether.

Deflationism has been subjected to a variety of criticisms: for instance, that its characteristic lionisation of the Disquotational Scheme is in tension with the manifest unacceptability of that principle when vagueness or other phenomena leading to failures of Bivalence are operative;[10] that it is inconsistent with a truth-conditional conception of meaning or more generally with the semantic role of truth;[11] that it cannot accommodate the idea of scientific progress; most generally, that it violates our intuitions about correspondence, about truth as bestowed by fit with an external, objective world.[12] Here I shall rehearse an argument I have given elsewhere to the effect that deflationism is internally unstable.[13] Specifically, there is a contradiction between the kind of account of the function of "true" which deflationists broadly want to give and the contention of the concept of truth, properly understood, is not the concept of a genuine, substantial property.

Let us focus, for ease of exposition, on "true" as predicable of propositions, and on the positive deflationist contention that, in its most basic use, the word is essentially a device of endorsement which, except in cases where the content of the proposition endorsed is not explicitly given, or where quantification over propositions is involved, may be dispensed with altogether in favour of a simple assertion of the proposition characterised as "true".

It is hardly deniable that "true" does have this kind of function and that its uses may often be paraphrased away without materially affecting the content of what is said. The issue is rather whether the point can carry the intended deflationary implications. And the crucial question for that issue is, what is it to *endorse* a proposition? Endorsement generally involves an element of recommendation, or approval of an item as meeting a certain standard. That's what I'm doing when, for example, in helping my child choose an ice cream I point at the pistachio and say "That's a nice one". What kind of commendation is involved in the case of "true"? Plausibly, that if I affirm a proposition's truth, I'm recommending its acceptance, commending it as meeting a certain doxastic standard, as it were. In this way, affirmations of truth—and likewise denials of truth—are normative claims. To endorse a proposition as true is to affirm that it is acceptable as a belief or statement; to deny that a proposition is true is to affirm that it's correspondingly unacceptable.

To be sure, nothing in that should impress as immediately uncomfortable for deflationism. No deflationist has wanted, or ought to have wanted, to deny that believing and statement-making are normatively constrained activities—activities governed by standards, non-compliance with which opens a thinker to criticism. However once that is accepted, the question has to be confronted of what the relevant standards are. In particular, if "true" is essentially just a device of endorsement, then in using it, I'm saying that a proposition is in good shape as far as certain relevant norms are concerned. What, for deflationism, are those norms?—what does "good shape" here consist in?

Believing and stating are, naturally, subject to rather different norms. In very many contexts, justification for a belief is insufficient to confer justification for its public expression, partly because assertion is socially constrained—the public expression of a fully justified belief may give offence, or bore people, etc.—and partly because complex principles of conversational implication make it possible to encourage false beliefs in an audience by the judicious selection and assertion of fully justified ones.[14] However, if one wanted to criticise an assertion on this type of broadly social or pragmatic ground, one wouldn't do so by denying its truth. So, as a first approximation, it seems the deflationist should say that the use of "true" in the basic kind of case is to endorse a proposition as *epistemically justified*, or to endorse an utterance as acceptable just insofar as the epistemic justification of the proposition it expresses is concerned.

In any case, what the deflationist clearly *cannot* allow is that "true", when used to endorse, has the function of commending a proposition for its satisfaction of *some distinctive norm* which contrasts with epistemic justification and which only "true" and equivalents serve to mark. For if there were a distinctive such norm, it could hardly fail to be reckoned a genuine property of a proposition that it did, or did not comply with it. And if the norm in question were uniquely associated with "true" and its cognates, that would be as much as to allow that there was a special property of *truth*—at which point the deflationary game would have been given away. So for the deflationist, it appears, the basic use of "true" has to be to signal a proposition's compliance with norms whose proper characterisation will not proceed in terms of equivalents of "true". If it is propositions, rather than utterances, that we are concerned with, epistemic justification would then seem to be the only plausible candidate.[15]

It would follow that the basic use of "not true" should be to signal a proposition's *non*-compliance with relevant norms of epistemic justification. But if that were so, there should in general be nothing to choose between the denial that a proposition is true and the denial that it is justified. And not only does that misrepresent the ordinary usage of the terms: it is inconsistent with principles to which deflationism itself is committed, and which are, indeed, at the heart of the deflationary account: the Disquotational Scheme and, its analogue for propositions, the Equivalence Schema.

I'll illustrate the relevant point as it flows from the latter. The schema provides that, for an arbitrary proposition p,

It is true that p $\longleftrightarrow$ p.

If we substitute 'not-p' for 'p' at both occurrences, we have

It is true that not-p $\longleftrightarrow$ not-p,

while if we negate both sides, we derive

It is not true that p $\longleftrightarrow$ not-p.

And from the latter two principles, via transitivity of the biconditional, we have

It is not true that p if and only if it is true that not-p.

In brief: the Equivalence Schema entails, given only the most basic assumptions about its scope and about the logic of negation, that truth and negation commute as prefixes. Manifestly, this is not true in general of warrant and negation: there is, in general, no sound inference from

It is not the case that p is warranted,

to

It is the case that not-p is warranted.

This pattern of inference cannot be sustained in any case where the correctness of its premise is owing to the *neutrality* of our state of information—to the fact that we have no evidence bearing either on p or its negation.

The Equivalence Schema itself, then, is a commitment to repudiating the idea that "... is not true" is a device for denying that a proposition complies with norms of warrant/justification—for if it were such a device, it ought not to commute with negation. But what other account can deflationism offer of what the denial of truth amounts to, given its express contention that "... is true" is merely a device of endorsement, so a device for affirming a proposition's compliance with some norm or other, and given that the only norms on the board—in a context in which the existence of any self-standing norm of truth has been rejected—are justificatory ones?[16]

In fact, it's intuitively perfectly evident that the use of "true" *is* tied to a norm—to a way in which acceptance of a proposition may be in good, or bad standing—quite separate from the question of its justification in the light of the acceptor's state of information. An acceptance that grass is green, that is, may open to censure if there is no warrant for accepting that grass is green; but it is in bad standing in quite another way if, warranted or not, it is actually not the case that grass is green. Correspondingly it is in good standing, in one way, just if accepted on the basis of sufficient justification, whether or not grass is green; but it is in good standing in another way if, irrespective of what justification may be possessed by the acceptor, grass is actually green. The concept of truth is a concept of a way a proposition may or may not be in good standing which precisely *contrasts* with its justificatory status at any particular time. That's the point which we've elicited from the Equivalence Schema. But it is independently evident, and any satisfactory philosophy of truth has to respect it.

There is no hope, then, for a deflationary account of truth which allows, or is anyway committed to the idea that "true", in its most basic use, is a device for endorsing propositions as complying with other norms. A device of endorsement it may be, at least in the basic case. But the concept of the associated norm is of something *sui generis*.

Can the deflationist regroup? What the foregoing forces is an admission that, for each particular proposition, we have the concept of a norm which is distinct from warrant and is flagged by the word, "true". And once it's allowed that the role of "true" is to mark a particular kind of achievement, or failing, on the part of a proposition, contrasting with its being warranted or not, there will have to be decent sense in the question, what does such an achievement, or failing, amount to? To be sure, that is a question which may turn out to admit of no very illuminating or non-trivial answer—but if so, that would tend to be a point in favour of Frege's indefinabilism, rather than deflationism. If a term registers a distinctive norm over a practice, the presumption ought to be that there will be something in which a move's compliance or non-compliance with that norm will consist. And whichever status it has, that will then be a real characteristic of the move. So what room does deflationism have for manoeuvre?

There are two possibilities. First, it might be contended that all, strictly, that has been noted—has been shown to follow from the Equivalence Schema—is that "true" is so used as to *call for*—express—a norm over the acceptance of propositions which is distinct from warrant. It's quite another matter whether there *really is* such a norm—whether there really is such a way for a proposition to be in, or out of good standing. It's one thing for an expression to be used in the making of a certain distinctive kind of normative claim; quite another matter for there to be such a thing as a bearer's *really qualifying for* a judgement of that kind. An error-theorist about morals, for example, like John Mackie,[17] would presumably readily grant that moral language is *used* normatively—is used to applaud, or censure, particular actions, for instance. What he will deny, nevertheless, is that there are any real characteristics which respond to this use—any real characteristics by possessing which an action may qualify for a deserved such appraisal.

It is easily seen that deflationism cannot avail itself of any counterpart of this first line of defence. For the deflationist must surely be quite content to allow that all manner of statements *really are true*—when the right circumstances obtain: that grass is green, for instance, really is true just when grass is green; that snow is white really is true just when snow is white, that the earth's orbit is an ellipse is true just in case the earth's orbit really is an ellipse, and so on. For deflationism, there has to be, for each proposition—or at least for those of an objective subject matter—*an objective condition*, viz. the very one specified by the appropriate instance of the Equivalence Schema, under which it qualifies as true. So there is no possibility of refuge in error theory in this context. The Equivalence Schema itself determines what the conditions of rightful application of "true" to a particular proposition, p, are; if as a matter of fact they obtain, then this, coupled with the distinctive normativity of the predicate, enforces the recognition that there really is such a thing as p's complying, or failing to comply with the distinctive norm of truth. It is not merely that our concept of truth calls for such a norm; the call is answered.[18]

We should conclude that two characteristic claims of deflationism are lost. It is not true, first, that "true" *only* functions as a device of (indirect, or compendious) endorsement—it also functions, for each proposition, to advert to the satisfaction of a distinctive norm, whose satisfaction is—at least for a proposition with an objective subject matter—a real matter of fact. Second, it is hard to hear a distinction between that last point and the admission that truth, for each such proposition, is a real property. But there is still a final line of defence—one last characteristic deflationary claim which a proponent might try to salvage. The question remains so far open whether the property in question should be regarded as *the same* in all cases. Perhaps the deflationist can dig a last ditch here. For if the property were not the same, we might yet have the resources to undercut the classical debates about the *general* constitution of truth; and that those debates were bad was one major point that deflationism wanted to make.

A line of thought with that tendency is nicely expressed by Simon Blackburn as follows:

> "... compare 'is true', ... with a genuine target of philosophical analysis: 'is conscious', or 'has rights', for example. We investigate these by looking for the principles which determine whether something is conscious, or has rights. These principles are intended to govern any such judgement, so that we get a unified class: the class of conscious things, or things that have rights. Each item in such a class is there because it satisfies the same condition, which the analysis has uncovered. Or, if this is slightly idealised, we find only a 'family' of related conditions or 'criteria' for the application of the term. Still, there is then a family relationship between the members of the class. But now contrast 'is true'. We know *individually* what makes this predicate applicable to the judgements or sentences of an understood language. 'Penguins waddle' is a sentence true, in English, if and only if penguins waddle. It is true that snow is white if and only if snow is white. The reason the first sentence deserves the predicate is that penguins waddle, and the reason why the judgement that snow is white deserves the predicate is that snow *is* white. But these reasons are entirely different. There is no single account, or even little family of

accounts, in virtue of which each deserves the predicate, for deciding whether penguins waddle has nothing much in common with deciding whether snow is white. There are *as* many different things to do, to decide whether the predicate applies, as there are judgements to make. So how *can* there be a unified, common account of the 'property' which these quite different decision procedures supposedly determine? We might say: give us any sentence about whose truth you are interested, and simply by 'disquoting' and removing the reference to truth, we can tell you what you have to judge in order to determine its truth. Since we can do this without any analysis or understanding of a common property of truth, the idea that there is such a thing is an illusion."[19]

Blackburn here captures with characteristic felicity a thought which has unquestionably influenced many deflationists—(though he does not himself explicitly endorse it.) However it surely provides no very good reason for the intended conclusion—that truth is no single property. For the pattern it calls attention to is a commonplace, exemplified by a host of properties which we should not scruple to regard as unitary, or as potentially open to philosophical account. *Many* properties, that is, are such that their satisfaction conditions vary as a function of the character of a potential bearer. Consider the property of having fulfilled one's educational potential. What it takes to instantiate this will depend naturally on other characteristics of the individual concerned; but that ought to be quite consistent with the substantiality and commonality of the property in question since there is a clear sense in which anyone who has fulfilled his educational potential has done the same thing as anyone else who has done so, and what they have both done may be expected straightforwardly to allow of a uniform account. In general, how x has to be in order to be F can depend in part on how things stand in other respects with x, and vary accordingly, without any motive thereby being provided for regarding it as an error to suppose, or to try to characterise, a general condition which being F involves satisfying. Otherwise you might just as well say that there is no single thing in which being twice as old as one's oldest child consists (being a *doubletenarian*) since for me it would involve being twice as old as Geoffrey, for Prince Charles being twice as old as William and for Blackburn being twice as old as Gwen.

The general pattern, it should be evident, is that of properties whose satisfaction consists in an individual's meeting a condition implicitly involving existential quantification over the right field of a relation. To fulfil one's educational potential is for there to be certain levels of academic attainment such that under certain normal educational conditions it is possible for one to meet them, and such that one has met them. To be twice as old as one's oldest child is for there to be some individual of whom one is a father or mother and whose actual age is half one's own. In general, to be the bearer of such a property will be to stand in a relation of a certain kind to an appropriate instance or instances of this implicit quantifier, and the identity of that instance or instances may vary depending on the identity and character in other respects of the bearer in question. It is in the *nature* of properties of this general character to admit such variation, and it compromises their unity not at all.

There is accordingly no comfort for a deflationist in the platitude that how things have to be in order for particular propositions to be true varies. Propositions vary in *how they claim matters to stand*—as parents vary in how old their children are, or people vary in what their educational potential is—and propositions' truth values will naturally be a function of the specific such claims they make. To impose the rubric explicitly: for any proposition p, it is true that p just in case *there is a way things could be* such that anyone who believed, doubted, etc. that p would believe, doubt, etc. that things were that way, and things are that way.[20] This paraphrase is doubtless wholly unilluminating—it offers little more than a long-hand version of the Correspondence Platitude. It's merit is to serve as a reminder how truth is naturally conceived to share a conceptual shape with e.g. doubletenarianship, or fulfilment of educational potential, and thus to bring out why no conclusions follow about its integrity from the line of thought outlined in Blackburn's remarks.

A sympathiser with deflationism may essay a final throw. It may be contended that the position at which we have arrived, although inconsistent with the traditional formulations of deflationism, is still nothing terribly at odds with its spirit. Maybe it has to be recognised that truth is a property after all, contrasting with justification, and normative over assertion and belief. But the conviction of the traditional debate is that it is a *metaphysically deep* property, whose essence is unobvious and controversial. By contrast, the characterisation of it now offered by way of rebuttal of the tendency of Blackburn's remarks is nothing if not obvious and *trivial*; and this triviality surely just as effectively cuts the ground from under the traditional debate as would the findings that truth is no unified property, or no property at all. The victory over deflationism is therefore Pyrrhic: the skirmishing has led us to say what truth in general is in such a way as to drain all metaphysical interest from the question in the process.[21]

Someone inclined to resist this would not be prudent to stake all on the possibility of a less trivial account of truth. Where the rejoinder goes astray is in its oversight, rather, of the contrast, drawn at the start, between the project of analysis of the concept of truth and the debate about the structure and objectivity of the property of truth. One meritorious claim in the deflationist portfolio—though not its exclusive possession—may well be that the success of any purported analysis of the concept must pay a price in terms of triviality. But the above account of truth for propositions, trivial as it may be, simply does not engage the structural alternatives charted earlier nor the debate they delimit. Anyone who has mastered the concept of truth and does not scruple to quantify over "ways things could be" can accept it as necessary and sufficient for the truth of a proposition that there be a way things could be which anyone who believes that proposition will suppose realised, and which is indeed realised. To accept that much enjoins so far no commitment on the matter of what kind of characteristic—intrinsic, relational (if so, what are the terms of the relation?), etc.—the truth of a proposition is, nor on whether or to what extent its possession may be viewed as objective. Exactly those are the metaphysically substantial matters.

V

The third and last alternative to a correspondence account of the structure of truth is coherentism. Here is an expression of an old and sometime very influential objection to the coherence theory:

> "... the objection to the coherence theory lies in this, that it presupposes a more usual meaning of truth and falsehood in constructing its coherent whole, and that this more usual meaning, though indispensable to the theory, cannot be explained by means of the theory. The proposition 'Bishop Stubbs was hanged for murder' is, we are told, not coherent with the whole of truth or with experience. But that means, when we examine

it, that something is *known* which is inconsistent with this proposition. Thus what is inconsistent with the proposition must be something *true*: it may be perfectly possible to construct a coherent whole of *false* propositions in which 'Bishop Stubbs was hanged for murder' would find a place. In a word, the partial truths of which the whole of truth is composed must be such propositions as would commonly be called true, not such as would commonly be called false; there is no explanation, on the coherence theory, of the distinction commonly expressed by the words *true* and *false*, and no evidence that a system of false propositions might not, as in a good novel, be just as coherent as the system which is the whole of truth."[22]

The Right Reverend W. Stubbs died of natural causes. Russell's point is that we may nevertheless envisage a comprehensive *fiction* part of which is that he was hanged for murder, and that in point of coherence such a fiction may very well stand comparison with what we take to be the truth. In order, then, to recover the idea that such a fiction *is* fiction, we need recourse to a notion of truth which the coherence account is powerless to explicate. Whatever "coherence" is taken to involve in detail, it seems likely that mutually incompatible, equally comprehensive, internally coherent systems of beliefs will be possible; more, *any* self-consistent proposition is likely to participate in *some* coherent system of belief with whatever degree of comprehensiveness you want. So the coherence theory cannot discriminate truth from falsehood—and it cannot justify principles like (Non-Contradiction):

if p is true, not-p is not true.

Yet surely any correct account of truth has to sustain such principles.

Notice that this objection in no way depends upon the detail of any particular proposed conception of coherence, and thus does not presuppose that the coherence account is being offered as an *analysis* of truth. The objection is purely structural. The driving thought is that whatever coherence is taken to consist in, the suggestion that the truth of a proposition consists in its participation in a coherent system in effect falls foul of a dilemma: if *fiction* can constitute such a system, then participation in such a system is clearly insufficient for truth. If it cannot, then it appears that truth is not constituted purely in inter-propositional relations—the propositions in question have to meet some other condition, so far unexplicated, and Russell's hostile suggestion is that the only available such condition is: truth as ordinarily understood.

There are two possible lines of response. First, the coherentist may go relativist, conceding that there is indeed no *absolute* truth, and embracing the contention that, to the contrary, truth is relative to the system. Thus the proposition that Bishop Stubbs was hanged for murder can indeed be true, relevant to a sufficiently coherent and comprehensive body of propositions which includes it. What we are pleased to regard as *the* truth merely reflects the actually entrenched such system. Principles, like Non-Contradiction, which seem to require that the truth cannot extend to every conceivable coherent system of propositions, are misconstrued when taken to have that implication. Sure, they are valid *within* systems: no proposition can participate in a coherent system for which its negation is already a member. But they have no valid application *across* systems.

Alternatively, a coherentist might try to avoid this extreme and rather unappealing form of relativism by earmarking certain propositions as in some way *privileged*, and construing truth not as participation in any old sufficiently comprehensive, coherent system of propositions, but as participation in such a system which is required in addition to include the privileged propositions. To be sure, thinking of truth as having such a structure does not by itself guarantee its uniqueness. But the resources may be available to do so if the theorist chooses the privileged base class cannily and interprets the relation of coherence in some correspondingly suitable way. For instance, the base class might consist of a large sample of our most basic beliefs. Then what might ultimately defeat the truth, conceived as by Coherence, of the proposition that Bishop Stubbs was hanged for murder would be its inability to participate in a maximally coherent and comprehensive system of belief incorporating that particular membership.

This manoeuvre, however, appears open to an extremely powerful objection. The objection does, admittedly, make an assumption about the general character of the inter-propositional relationships which coherence, conceived as a structural proposal, might regard as important—albeit an assumption suggested by the very term, "coherence", and validated by all the actual proposals which have been made under its head. That assumption is that the relations in question are *internal* relations: that the coherence, or otherwise, of a system of propositions is grounded *purely in their content*. The salient question is then: how can any proposal of this kind handle *contingency*? The general form of account proposed is that p's truth consists in its participation in a coherent system based on a specified base class, i.e. its coherence with the other propositions in that system. But that situation, when it obtains, should be a matter of relations of a purely internal character holding between p and the other propositions in the system. If p coheres with those propositions, it will therefore do so in *all possible worlds*. So how could the truth of p, when it is true, ever be a contingent matter?

There is only one possible line of response. If p, although true, could be false, and if its truth consists in its sustaining internal—necessary—relations to a system of propositions, then what contingency needs is the possibility of a switch in the system—a change in which are the propositions coherence with which determines truth—and the possibility that p may fail to cohere with the new system. If we say that a system is *dominant* if it is coherence with *it* that constitutes truth, then what contingency demands is flexibility in the matter of dominance. (Dominance might be interpreted just as a matter of incorporating lots of what we actually believe, and its flexibility would then be secured by the flexibility in the identity of our beliefs.)

Now, though, interestingly, we find we have come full circle with the re-emergence of a version of the Bishop Stubbs objection. All contingency is now being construed as turning on contingencies of dominance. So the obvious next question is: what properly coherentist account is to be given of the truth of a proposition of the form,

(K) S is dominant?

Naturally, the Coherentist has to view the truth of an instance of K, like that of any true proposition, as a matter of its coherence with a system—but which system? Presumably any coherent system S will be such that it will cohere with S to suppose it is dominant even if it is not in fact so—if, for example, dominance is construed as a matter of what is actually believed, it ought in general to cohere perfectly with a system of beliefs that we do not in fact hold to suppose that we do hold them. So in general, for each comprehensive, coherent system S, whether dominant or not, the relevant instance of K will cohere with S with the consequence, first, that the fact of dominance—the actual truth value of that instance—goes unrecovered; and second, that we remain powerless to explicate the contingency of a system's dominance, since the coherence of the relevant instance of K with the system in question will be a matter of necessity.

There is thus no prospect of explicating what it is for a proposition of the form, S is dominant, to be true in terms purely of relations of coherence if the truth in question is conceived as contingent—as it has to be, if contingency in general is to be recovered in terms of a coherentist account. What has to be said, it seems, is that for that proposition, like any other, truth is a matter of relations with *what is in fact* the dominant system. But then exactly the move has been made that Russell triumphantly anticipated: for this appeal to the notion of *what is in fact so* has not been, and apparently cannot be explicated in terms of coherence.

The upshot is that coherentism, taken as a proposal about the general nature of truth-constituting relations, has no means—provided the relations in question are all internal—to recover the notion of contingent truth except that the cost of, one way or another, an appeal to a notion of what is in fact true of particular belief systems (that they are based on what we mostly believe, or otherwise dominant in some sense to be supplied) whose contingency is taken for granted and whose obtaining cannot be construed in terms of coherence. In brief, coherentism demands exceptions to its own account.[23] It thus has nothing to offer as a general account of the structure of truth.[24]

VI

We have now reviewed each of the three possible structural alternatives to a correspondence conception of truth, and found that each is subject to seemingly decisive difficulties. It may seem to have been established, accordingly, that among the four paths on the original tree, only the path to the correspondence conception is viable—that, contra deflationism, our ordinary concept of truth requires us to think of a proposition's being true as, so to speak, a distinctive accomplishment, and that, contra intrinsicism and coherentism, we may not satisfactorily conceive of this accomplishment as an intrinsic property of a proposition or a characteristic conferred upon it by dint of its relation to other propositions. It would follow that even if no satisfactory *analysis* of truth in terms of correspondence can be given, we are nevertheless squarely committed to a correspondence *conception* of truth—that there is no alternative but to thinking of the truth of a proposition as conferred upon it, in the general case, by its relations to non-propositional reality.

That is, in effect, the second main contention of the paper earlier advertised. But two very important qualifications are needed here. First, in the traditional debate, as we remarked, the correspondence theory was conceived as expressing a form of metaphysical *realism*, standing opposed to the idealism which kept company with the coherence theory. It merits emphasis that even if the effect of the foregoing arguments is indeed to impose a conception of truth as conferred on a proposition by aspects of non-propositional reality,[25] that conclusion certainly carries no direct implications for the realism debate in its modern conception. For example, nothing is yet implied about the *nature* of the relations in question, so there is consequently no immediate implication of the idea that the truth of a proposition consists in its successfully *representing* an aspect of reality, in any distinctively realist sense of "represent". There may in general be no alternative to thinking of propositions as made true when they are true, by, inter alia, non-propositional matters. But there is so far no commitment to any specific general conception of the kind of relations that may be involved in truth, or of the nature of the non-propositional items in their fields. Any broad view which assigns a role in the constitution of truth to a domain outside the bearers of truth would be consistent with our findings; and that much most modern anti-realisms, for example those canvassed by Dummett and Putnam, certainly do. In particular, nothing is implied about *cognitivism*—about whether the factors involved in appraising truth are invariably wholly cognitive—nor about *evidential constraint*: about whether it is possible for truth to outrun all evidence available in principle. Someone who thought, for example, of moral truth as broadly a matter of what *we* find acceptable in the light of a full appreciation of the non-moral facts and certain non-cognitive dispositions to moral sentiment would be making no demands on the notion to take him off the correspondence path; on such a view, moral truth would be a complex matter, but one essentially implicating certain relations to aspects of the non-propositional world. Likewise, a proponent of a broadly Peircian conception of truth, that truth is what would be agreed upon by thinkers operating under epistemically ideal conditions, would be quite at liberty to think of the status of such propositions as owing in part to the impingements of a non-propositional world which such thinkers would feel. In sum: our findings at this point have almost no impact on the second of the great issues associated with the classical debate about truth: the issues of realism and objectivity.

However—this is the second necessary qualification—there ought in any case, I believe, to be no presumption in favour of a *monistic* view of truth.[26] If the difficulties which we have been exploring are to dispose of all the alternatives to correspondence once and for all, then it needs to be assumed that truth everywhere must possess a *uniform constitution*: that the truth of any true proposition always consists in the same sort of thing. Yet why should that be so? For instance, both intrinsicist and coherentist conceptions of truth fell into difficulty over the construal of contingent truth, but a proponent of either view could conceivably retrench if it could be argued that truth is only *sometimes* to be conceived as an intrinsic property of a proposition, or a property bestowed upon it by its relations of coherence with certain other propositions, while in other cases the structure of truth is best conceived as by correspondence. The upshot of the argument is that if truth has a single uniform constitution, then that constitution must be conceived along broadly correspondence lines. But what enforces the assumption of uniformity?

I think the answer is: nothing. In fact, an opposed pluralistic outlook is intuitively quite attractive. It is quite appealing, for instance, to think of the true propositions of number theory as those which sustain certain internal relations—an appropriate kind of semantic consequence—to a certain base class of propositions—the Dedekind-Peano axioms, for instance. Such an account, it should be noted, would extend to the axioms themselves (assuming the reflexivity of the relevant internal relation.) What it would not comfortably extend to would be truths of the form: p is a Dedekind-Peano axiom (more generally, p is a member of the relevant base class.) But once coherentism forswears the ambition to a *comprehensive* account of the structure of truth, that limitation need not be a difficulty. An account along broadly similar lines might also be attractive for truth as it applies to general moral principles (as opposed to their applications).

A pluralistic conception of truth is also philosophically attractive insofar as an account which allows us to think of truth as constituted differently in different areas of thought might contribute to a sharp explanation of the differential appeal of realist and anti-realist intuitions about them. But I acknowledge, of course, that more detail and a sharper theoretical setting is required for the proposal before it can really be clear that it makes genuine sense, let alone possesses merit. In particular, an account is owing of what would make it *truth* that allowed of variable forms of instantiation in different areas—what would make for the relevant *unity*. (This is not work that one might excuse oneself by pleading that truth is a "family resemblance" concept, or whatever. Even that suggestion would at least require that there be a network of marks of truth, any true proposition qualifying as such by its exemplification of some sufficiently substantial set of them; and the task of characterising these marks would remain.)

In order to clarify the cast which a defensible alethic pluralism might assume, it will help to revisit the conception, dominating the traditional debate, that the winning position would be the provision of a satisfactory necessary-and-sufficient-conditions analysis of the concept. Earlier, I was concerned to point out that scepticism about that project remained consistent with the interest of many of the questions, about structure and objectivity in particular, which provided the driving force of the traditional debate, and that these questions could survive in a setting in which the idea of analysis of the notion of truth had been abandoned altogether. Now though it is time to reconsider and qualify that scepticism. For misgivings about the project are driven by the particular conception we had in play of what a successful analysis—of truth, or anything—would have to accomplish. And on that score there is clearly some scope for relaxation. Such a necessary-and-sufficient-conditions analysis, after all, even if it could be provided, would only culminate in one particular a priori—presumably, conceptually necessary—claim. Why should not other such claims—even if not biconditional-, or identity-claims—not provide illumination of essentially the same kind? To be sure, if one wants conceptual clarity about what truth—or beauty, or goodness, etc.—is, then the natural target is an identity, (or a biconditional). But perhaps the point of the enquiry can be equally if less directly served by the assembly of a body of conceptual truths which, without providing any reductive account, nevertheless collectively constrain and locate the target concept and sufficiently characterise some of its relations with other concepts and its role and purposes to provide the sought-for reflective illumination.

Faced, then, with the manifest improbability of an illuminating necessary-and-sufficient-conditions analysis of truth, there is still a different, more relaxed programme of analysis which we might undertake before despairing of the whole business and falling back on the issues to do with structure. This more relaxed project will see us trying to build an overall picture of the concept of truth—of its contents and purposes—by the assembly and integration of as wide a variety as possible of basic a priori principles about it—"platitudes", as I've elsewhere termed them.[27] What would such principles be for the case of truth?

The method here should be initially to compile a list, including anything that chimes with ordinary thinking about truth, and later to scrutinise more rigorously for deductive articulation and for whether candidates do indeed have the right kind of conceptual plausibility. So we might begin by including, for instance, the transparency of truth—that to assert is to present as true and, more generally, that any attitude to a proposition is an attitude to its truth—that to believe, doubt or fear, for example, that p is to believe, doubt or fear that p is true. (*Transparency*)

the opacity of truth—incorporating a variety of weaker and stronger principles: that a thinker may be so situated that a particular truth is beyond her ken, that some truths may never be known, that some truths may be unknowable in principle, etc. (*Opacity*)

the conservation of truth-aptitude under embedding: aptitude for truth is preserved under a variety of operations—in particular, truth-apt propositions have negations, conjunctions, disjunctions, etc. which are likewise truth-apt. (*Embedding*)

the Correspondence Platitude—for a proposition to be true is for it to correspond to reality, accurately reflect how matters stand, 'tell it like it is', etc. (*Correspondence*)

the contrast of truth with justification—a proposition may be true without being justified, and vice-versa. (*Contrast*)

the timelessness of truth—if a proposition is ever true, then it always is, so that whatever may, at any particular time, be truly asserted may—perhaps by appropriate transformations of mood, or tense—be truly asserted at any time. (*Timelessness*)

that truth is absolute—there is, strictly, no such thing as a proposition's being more or less true; propositions are completely true if true at all. (*Absoluteness*)

The list might be enlarged,[28] and some of these principles may anyway seem controversial. Moreover it can be argued that the Equivalence Schema underlies not merely the first of the platitudes listed—Transparency—but the Correspondence Platitude[29] and, as we have seen in discussion of deflationism, the Contrast Platitude as well.

There's much to be said about this general approach, and many hard and interesting questions arise, not least, of course, about the epistemological provenance of the platitudes. But such questions arise on *any* conception of philosophical analysis, which must always take for granted our ability to recognise truths holding a priori of concepts in which we are interested.

Let us call an analysis based on the accumulation and theoretical organisation of a set of platitudes concerning a particular concept an *analytical theory* of the concept in question.[30] Then the provision of an analytical theory of truth in particular opens up possibilities for a principled pluralism in the following specific way: that in different regions of thought and discourse *the theory may hold good, a priori, of - may be satisfied by - different concepts*. If this is so, then always provided the network of platitudes integrated into the theory were sufficiently comprehensive, we should not scruple to say that truth may consist in different things in different such areas: in the instantiation of one concept in one area, and in that of a different concept in another. For there will be nothing in the idea of truth that is not accommodated by the analytical theory, and thus no more to a concept's being a concept of truth than its furnishing a model of the ingredient platitudes. In brief: the *unity* in the concept of truth will be supplied by the analytical theory; and the *pluralism* will be underwritten by the fact that the principles composing that theory admit of collective variable realisation.

One important question is whether any unmistakably coherentist conception of truth is indeed such a truth-realiser for a particular region of thought.[31] Another candidate I have explored elsewhere[32] is the notion of *superassertibility*. A proposition is superassertible just in case someone investigating it could, in the world as it actually is, arrive at a state of information in which its acceptance was justified, which justification would then persist no matter how much more relevant information was acquired. Clearly a notion of this kind must make sense wherever the corresponding notion of justification makes sense—wherever we have a concept of what it would be to justify a particular proposition, it will be intelligible to hypothesise the attainment of such a justification and its stability through arbitrarily extensive further investigation. It turns out that in any region of discourse meeting certain constraints, superassertibility will satisfy each of the platitudes listed above, so a prima facie case can be made that, with respect to those regions, the concept of superassertibility is a truth concept.[33] In these areas, it is consequently open to us to regard truth as consisting in superassertibility. In other areas, by contrast, where the relevant background conditions arguably fail,—in particular, if we can see that there is no essential connection between truth and the availability of evidence,—then the concept of truth will not allow of interpretation in terms of superassertibility, and the constitution of truth must accordingly be viewed differently. It is perhaps superfluous to remark that a superassertibilist conception of truth chimes very nicely with the semantic anti-realism which Michael Dummett has presented as a generalisation of mathematical Intuitionism, whose cardinal thesis may indeed be taken to be that truth is *everywhere* best construed in terms of superassertibility.

To be sure, the method of analysis incorporated in the analytic-theoretical approach is, as far as it goes, consistent with a monistic view of the target concept—but the approach cautions against prejudice in that respect since such an account, may, in any particular case, prove to allow of multiple realisation. That's a matter which will depend on the detail of the account, on whether it includes all relevant platitudes, and on whether the concept in question may justifiably be taken to have further components which are necessarily omitted by such an account (for instance, a component fixed by ostensive definition.) Here, I have meant only to sketch how a principled pluralism about truth might conceivably emerge.

VII

I conclude by noting a different potential corollary of the analytic-theoretical approach to truth. If its satisfaction of the platitudes suffices for a concept to be a concept of truth, then wherever we can introduce a concept which is such a satisfier with respect to a particular class of contents, that fact on its own will justify us in regarding the contents in question as *apt for truth*. Or put another way: wherever the word "true" operates in a fashion agreeable to each of the theorems of a satisfactory analytical theory, then we should think of it as expressing a genuine concept of truth, and of the contents being expressed as genuinely truth-apt accordingly. And this will always be so just when we are dealing with contents which meet certain constraints of syntax and discipline. Roughly: the contents in question must allow for combination and recombination under the connectives—negation, the conditional, conjunction, disjunction—of ordinary sentential inference; they must allow of embedding within expressions of ordinary propositional attitudes; and their affirmation must be subject to recognised standards of warrant.[34] If that is right, then it falls out of the very analysis of the notion of truth that the aptitude for truth is a comparatively promiscuous property. Comic, moral, aesthetic and legal discourses, for instance, all exhibit the requisite syntax and discipline and so presumably pass the test. The upshot is thus a tension with one traditional form of anti-realism about such discourses: the idea, typified by "expressivism" in ethics, that a target discourse whose surface exhibition of these features is not questioned may nevertheless not really be dealing in truth-apt contents—in "genuine" propositions—at all.

However some recent critics[35] have objected that this upshot depends on focusing only on a selection of the platitudes which constrain the notions of truth and assertion, and ignoring in particular equally platitudinous connections of those notions with *belief*. Their thought is that one may be forced to look below the propositional surface of e.g. ethical discourse if one takes it as a platitude that an assertion is a profession of belief[36] but also accepts, with Hume, that no belief can be, in and of itself, a *motivational* state and regards it as clear that whatever is professed by an ethical "assertion", it *is* such a motivational state.

One who advances this line of thought need not, it merits emphasis, be offering any criticism of the analytic-theoretical approach to truth as such. Moreover the general point being made is obviously perfectly fair: conclusions drawn from a proposed analytic theory of a concept are, of course, liable to be vitiated if that theory omits to recognise what are in fact valid conceptual ties between the target concept and others. But what of the specific objection?

It might seem that the only clean way to dispose of it would be to controvert one of its two auxiliary premises; that is, to argue directly that certain kinds of belief *are* intrinsically motivational after all[37] or to make a case that the attitudes expressed by sincere ethical claims are, appearances notwithstanding, not *intrinsically* motivational.[38] However it is not, on reflection, evident that it is necessary to take on either of those projects (even if either might very well succeed.) Rather, the anti-expressivist may respond that, insofar as the questions, whether a belief can be, in and of itself, a motivational state, and whether the states professed by ethical utterances are indeed intrinsically motivational, are taken to be open, philosophically substantial questions, to that extent it is simply *not* a platitude that the assertion of any truth-apt content is a profession of belief. Or better: for one who accepts that those issues are open, *belief* is not the notion in terms of which to articulate the platitude which lurks in the vicinity. Instead, an alternative expression can be found by taking over for the purpose a term which Simon Blackburn conveniently introduces in his writings on these issues: *commitment*.[39] Blackburn's 'commitments' are typically expressed by indicative sentences; they may be argued for and against, reasoned to and from, accepted, doubted and entertained. So the notion ought to provide everything here required: the relevant platitude is, in effect, that the assertion of any truth-apt content is the profession of a commitment. Since the two auxiliary premises are not simultaneously good for commitments, the objection accordingly lapses.

Someone who sympathises with the view that only some commitments are pukka *beliefs* owes an account of what is distinctive of the narrower class. I know of no reason to reject out of hand the suggestion that a worthwhile such distinction may exist; and if it exists, the annexure of the term, "belief", to the narrower class might conceivably be a well-motivated linguistic *reform*. Until then, the fact remains that our ordinary practice does not scruple to use 'belief' across the range of cases where the expressivist would have us worry about it; and the anti-expressivist is free to respond to the objection by charging that it is only with this more generous notion that there is a platitudinous connection with assertion, and that the two auxiliary premises which the objection exploits cannot both be acceptable if it is the more generous notion of belief that is in play.

Appendix: Two illustrative satisfiers of the platitudes for truth

We shall reckon with just the seven platitudes proposed above: Transparency, Opacity, Embedding, Correspondence, Contrast, Timelessness, and Absoluteness. First, we note the following dependencies:

(i) *Transparency* is tantamount to the validity of the Equivalence Schema,

It is true that P if and only if P,

for all propositional contents, P, which in turn ensures that of the Disquotational Scheme,

"P" is true if and only if P,

assuming only the validity of the corresponding instance of

"P" says that P,

and the stipulation that the truth of a sentence is to enjoin and be enjoined by that of the proposition it expresses.

(ii) *Correspondence* is a platitude, whether for propositions or for sentences, only if suitably neutrally interpreted—that is interpreted so as to be neutral on the status of the Correspondence *theory*. As a platitude it thus carries no commitment to a real ontology of facts—"sentence-shaped" worldly truth-conferrers—nor to any seriously representational construal of "correspondence", but merely claims that talk of truth may be paraphrased by any of a variety of kinds of correspondence idiom. We may thus take the correspondence platitude for propositions to be, for example, this:

(CPP) It is true that P if and only if matter stand in conformity with the proposition that P.

CPP is an immediate consequence of the Equivalence Schema, together with the analogous equivalence controlling correspondence idiom itself:

Matters stand in conformity with the proposition that P if and only if P

Likewise the Correspondence platitude for sentences may suitably neutrally be taken to be:

(CPS) "P" is true if and only if matters stand as "P" says they do.

Now wherever we have that

"P" says that P,

it follows that

Matters stand as "P" says they do if and only if P.

CPS is immediate from the last together with the Disquotational Scheme.[40]

(iii) *Contrast*—the contrast between truth and justification—is straightforwardly derived from the Equivalence Schema (or Disquotational Scheme) together with Embedding (specifically, its instance that every truth-apt content has a negation which is likewise truth-apt) and a very basic proof theory for negation. For propositions, the derivation runs as follows. Negation of both halves of the Equivalence Schema provides that

> It is not true that P if and only if not P,

while substitution of 'not P' for 'P' at each of its occurrences in the Equivalence Schema provides that

> It is true that not P if and only if not P.

Transitivity of the biconditional then yields what I termed the Negation Equivalence,

> It is not true that P if and only if it is true that not P,

- the commutativity of truth and negation. It then suffices for Contrast to reflect that, for any range of propositions for which neutral states of information are a possibility, negation does *not* commute with justification. For in such a neutral state, a lack of justification for P precisely does not convert into justification for its negation.

The upshot, then, is that our illustrations need address only the following: the Equivalence Schema, Opacity, Embedding, Timelessness, and Absoluteness.

Illustration I: Pure arithmetical truth conceived as coherence

Assume a language, L, containing just the usual resources of first-order logic with identity plus the non-logical constants: Nx ("x is a natural number"), Sx ("the immediate successor of x") and the decimal numerals, '0', '1', '2', '3'.........etc. Take as the coherence-base, **B**, the Peano axioms suitably formulated in this language, say as:

(i) N(0)

: Zero is a number

(ii) $(\forall x)(Nx \longrightarrow NSx))$

: Every number is immediately succeeded by a number

(iii) $(\forall x)(\forall y)(\forall z)(\forall w)(Nx \ \& \ Ny \longrightarrow (Sx = Sy \longrightarrow x = y))$

: Numbers are the same if their successors are the same.

(iv) $(\forall x)\ (Nx \longrightarrow \neg 0 = Sx)$

: Zero is not a successor

(v) $(F0 \ \& \ (\forall x)((Nx \ \& \ Fx) \longrightarrow FSx))) \longrightarrow (\forall x)(Nx \longrightarrow Fx)$

: Any characteristic possessed by zero and by the successor of any number which possesses it is possessed by all numbers

plus the standard recursive clauses for '+' and '±':

(vi) $(\forall x)\ x + 0 = x$

(vi) $(\forall x)(\forall y)\ x + Sy = S\ (x + y)$

(vii) $(\forall x)\ x \pm 0 = 0$

(viii) $(\forall x)(\forall y)\ x \pm Sy = (x \pm y) + x$

and axioms to govern the definition of the regular decimal numerals from '1' onwards in terms of iterations of 'S' on '0'.

The proposal, then, is that a statement's being a *pure arithmetical truth of first-order* may be identified with its *cohering with* **B**. How is coherence here to be understood? Intuitively all the significant statements of first-order number theory fall into one of two classes: a *simple-arithmetical* base class whose members draw on no expressive resources save the numerals, the expressions for addition, multiplication and identity, and expressions for other operations which may be (recursively) defined in terms of those notions; and a remainder, each of which can be formed by (iterated) introductions of the logical constants into sentences of the base class in accordance with the standard first-order formation rules. From a classical point of view, it is quite intuitive that the truth-value of every first-order pure arithmetical sentence *supervenes upon* the truth-values of sentences in the base class: specifically, determine the truth-value of each of the latter and you have implicitly settled the truth value of every pure arithmetical thought which may be expressed at first-order. (The crucial point, of course, is that simple arithmetic has the resources to name every element in the domain of quantification of full first-order arithmetic.) A natural version of truth as coherence, which should be attractive to those of broadly formalist disposition, simply follows through on this intuition, characterising the coherence of simple-arithmetical sentences in terms of their syntactic derivability from ingredients in **B**, and that of the remainder in accordance with the sort of recursive clauses familiar from standard truth-theories. It could run like this:

(i) If A is a simple-arithmetical sentence of L, then A coheres with **B** just if A may be derived from elements of **B** in standard (classical) first-order logic with identity.

(ii) If *A* x is any open sentence of L in one free variable, x, and A is $(\forall x)Ax$, then A coheres with **B** just if each of *A*0, *A*1, *A*2, ..., coheres with **B**.

(iii) If *A* x is any open sentence of L in one free variable, x, and A is $(\exists y)(Ay)$, then A coheres with B just if at least one of *A*0, *A*1, *A*2, ..., coheres with **B**.

(iv) If A is B & C, then A coheres with **B** just if both B and C cohere with **B**.

(v) If A is B v C, then A coheres with **B** just if either B coheres with **B** or C coheres with **B**.

(vi) If A is B ⟶ C, then A coheres with **B** just if it is not the case that A coheres with **B** and C does not.

(vii) If A is ¬B, then A coheres with **B** just if B does not.

To the platitudes, then. First does this proposal validate the Equivalence Schema? Can it be affirmed, for all first-order expressible pure arithmetical statements, P, that

(E^C) P coheres with **B** if and only if P?

Dialectically, the status of a positive answer is somewhat akin to that of Church's thesis, that all effectively calculable arithmetical functions are general recursive. A formal proof of Church's Thesis would demand some independent formal characterisation of the effectively calculable functions - the very thing that Church's thesis purports to provide. Likewise a proof of (E^C) would demand some independent characterisation of the first-order arithmetical truths. So, as with Church's Thesis, it seems it cannot be definitely excluded that *intuitive* counterexamples to (E^C) might be forthcoming: sentences of the relevant kind which intuitively ought to rank as true yet which there is no reason to regard as cohering with **B** in the light of the stated clauses; or conversely, sentences which intuitively ought *not* to count as true, yet which do apparently so cohere. What can be said to make it plausible that there are no such cases?

Well, if (E^C) did have counterexamples, then - assuming the consistency of **B** - they could not come from within simple arithmetic, which comprises a complete and consistent system which is axiomatised within **B**. So their provenance would have to be of one of two kinds. *Either* truth in first-order arithmetic does not supervene upon simple-arithmetical truth—so that some arithmetical truths are determined by factors beyond the truth-value assignments in simple arithmetic and the semantics of the constants. That is surely excluded by the fact that '0'. '1' and their suite collectively name everything in the domain. *Or* conversely, coherence as characterised outruns arithmetical truth (as it would if **B** were inconsistent or if, say, some quite different - perhaps Intuitionistic - account of the truth-conditions of universally quantified arithmetical sentences was thought appropriate than that which informs clause (ii)) Prescinding from the scenario of inconsistency, then, it does seem reasonable to doubt—or at least that one of realist inclination should doubt —that intuitive counterexamples of either kind will be forthcoming.

Of course, some kinds of arithmetical realist will doubtless regard truth, so characterised, as at best merely *extensionally equivalent* with the real thing. But even for such a realist, the coincidence in extension would be necessary. What, if anything, is wrong with the coherentist account would not be its extensional inaccuracy.

(ii) How much Opacity should be required of a truth predicate is controversial but the arithmetical coherentist proposal is generous on this score. Matters of syntactic derivability, even though effectively decidable, can be mistaken or unknown by any single competent judge, or group of judges, in practice. And the presence of clause (ii) ensures that coherence in effect follows the Omega Rule, so that the proposal is hospitable to the idea that some arithmetical truths may be unknowable in principle.

(iii) Embedding: any statement couched purely in first-order arithmetical vocabulary can be regarded as in the relevant sense apt to cohere with the Peano axioms. Since the logical constants are part of that vocabulary, aptitude for coherence with the Peano axioms is thus conserved under the usual logical operations.

(iv) Timelessness: relations of coherence as defined are eternal.

(v) Absoluteness: relations of coherence as defined do not admit of degree.

Illustration II: Truth conceived as superassertibility

Recall that a statement is superassertible just in case it is justified by some accessible state of information and will continue to be so justified no matter how that state of information is improved. (When *I* is such a state of information with respect to a statement, S, I shall say that *I* is S-stable.) Superassertibility models the truth-platitudes under three assumptions concerning the region of discourse, D, with which we are concerned:

(I) that it is a priori that all truths of D are *knowable*;

(II) that the states of information which specifically bear on the characteristic claims of D are of a timelessly accessible kind;

(III) that it is a necessary condition of knowledge (at least of the subject matter of D, if not in general) that it exists only where a claimant does not thereby lay themselves open to a charge of irrationality.

(I) is a repudiation of evidence-transcendent truth for D. (II) has the effect that the opportunity for justification of a particular claim within D is never ephemeral but remains eternally open in principle for any suitable enquirer, no matter what her circumstances. (Note however the qualification: *suitable* enquirer. Suitability may demand, in particular, a certain innocence. It may be impossible for one who *knows too much* to justify a certain statement, even though evidence speaking defeasibly on its behalf is timelessly available.) (II) also implies that states of information may be conceived as *additive*—accessing one such state never costs you in principle the opportunity to access another (though again, since warrant is a function of one's *total* state of information, the import of a body of information under addition may naturally be different to what it would have been in isolation.) (III) imposes a boundary on externalist conceptions of knowledge: let it be that, at least with respect to certain subject matters, knowledge should be viewed as grounded purely in the exercise of what are in fact reliable cognitive powers and stands in no need of further internal qualification—still, it should not be open to internal *dis*qualification. There is no knowledge, even of such subject matters, in any case where persistence in a knowledge claim would commit a subject to disregarding the balance of the available evidence and so convict her of irrationality.

Pure mathematics and issues of moral and aesthetic principle may arguably be thought to supply examples of discourses meeting these conditions under only relatively modest idealisations of the powers of their practitioners. Discourse concerning the spatially and/or temporally remote would do so, if at all, only under more elaborate idealisations—maybe of dubious coherence, like the possibility of time-travel.

The platitudes of Opacity, Embedding, Timelessness and Absoluteness are all straightforward under these assumptions. To take them in that order:

First, it is clear that the superassertibility of a statement can *in practice* elude any single competent judge, or group of judges. On the other hand it cannot be undetectable *in principle*: if a statement is superassertible, then that fact will show in the S-stability of the relevant—superassertibility-conferring—state of information and hence will be detectable, albeit inconclusively, in just the same way that such S-stability is detectable. But that is no objection under the assumption (I) that we are operating in a region where it is a priori that all truths are knowable. For that is to suppose that the truths are detectable in any case.

Second, any statement is apt to be superassertible which is apt to be warranted in the first place, since its superassertibility is merely a matter of the S-stability of some warrant-conferring state of information. But aptitude for warrant itself is, of course, inherited under embedding within the standard logical operators. So such embeddings conserve aptitude for superassertibility.

Next, since one of our assumptions is exactly that states of information are accessible timelessly, it follows that superassertibility is, likewise, an eternal characteristic of any statement that has it.

Last, the definition of superassertibility—though the notion must inherit any vagueness in the notion of (all things considered) warrant—manifestly makes no provision for degrees: one statement may be more warranted than another, but if both are nevertheless all-things-considered warranted, and if their warrants are respectively stable, then they are equally and absolutely superassertible.

The key issue is accordingly the status of the Equivalence Schema with "true" interpreted as: superassertible,

(E^S) It is superassertible that P if and only if P.

There are some subtleties here[41] but our discussion is simplified by the announced assumption (I), that we are working in a region where the schema,

P ⟶ It is knowable that P,

holds good a priori.

We consider each direction of (E^S) in turn. First, suppose that it is superassertible that P but that it is not the case that P. Then, by (I), it can be known that it is not the case that P. But that is absurd. For whatever state of information was possessed by one who had that knowledge, it would have—by the implication of additivity in (II)—to be able to co-exist with the enduring all-things-considered warrant for P ensured by its superassertibility. And no-one could be said to know that not P whose total state of information warranted, to the contrary, a belief in P unless—contrary to (III)—the belief that not P can be an example of knowledge even when irrationally held.

Now suppose that P but that it is not superassertible that P. Since P is not superassertible, we have it that there is no P-stable state of information—that any warrant for P can be defeated. So any subject who claims to know that P is nevertheless destined to lose a debate with a sufficiently resourceful agnostic; for—by additivity—the agnostic will always be able to come up with some consideration which will spoil whatever case the believer advances for P. It follows that it will not be possible rationally to sustain a belief in P. So, by (III), P cannot be known; whence by (I) it cannot be that P, contrary to hypothesis.[42]

Notes

1. Two *loci classici* of coherentism are H. H. Joachim, *The Nature of Truth* (Oxford: Oxford University Press 1906) and F.H Bradley, *Essays on Truth and Reality* (Oxford: Oxford University Press 1914). Ralph Walker has argued that coherentism is implicit also in the forms of anti-realism canvassed by Michael Dummett and Hilary Putnam (at least, the Hilary Putnam of *Reason, Truth and History*). See Ralph Walker, *The Coherence Theory of Truth: Realism, Anti-Realism, Idealism*, (London and New York: Routledge 1989). Myself I doubt this—for further discussion, see my critical study of Walker's book, "Truth and Coherence", in *Synthese* 103 (1995), pp. 279–302.

2. How this constraint may be made to consist with the requirement that analysis be illuminating is, of course, the heart of Moore's Paradox of Analysis. But the sort of objection about to be noted need read no more into sameness of content than sameness of truth-conditions.
3. Alvin Plantinga, "How to be an Anti-Realist", *Proceedings and Addresses of the American Philosophical Association*, 56 (1982), pp. 47–70. Plantinga's point also engages certain formulations of the Coherence Theory. For instance to suppose that "true" means: *would be believed by a subject who had arrived at a maximally coherent and comprehensive set of beliefs*, is again implicitly to surrender the means to construe the truth of the thought: no-one holds a maximally coherent and comprehensive set of beliefs. The problem is a special case of the so-called Conditional Fallacy: any analysis in terms of subjunctive conditionals is potentially in trouble if its intended range comprises statements which are incompatible with the protases of the relevant conditionals.
4. For discussion, see Peter Carruthers, "Frege's Regress", *Proceedings of the Aristotelian Society* LXXXII (1981), pp. 17–32. See also the useful account in Ralph C.S. Walker's survey article, "Theories of Truth" in the Blackwell *Companion to the Philosophy of Language* edited by Bob Hale and Crispin Wright (Oxford: Blackwell 1997), especially §6.
5. Paul Horwich's *Truth* (Oxford: Blackwell 1990) provides a detailed defence of the deflationary tradition and a useful bibliography of its literature. While Field's "The Deflationary Conception of Truth" (in *Fact, Science and Morality*, ed. G. Macdonald and C. Wright, Oxford: Blackwell 1986, pp. 55–117) eventually suggests that there are purposes for which a correspondence conception is needed; his more recent "Deflationist Views of Meaning and Content" (*Mind* CIII, 1994, pp. 249–85) takes a more committed deflationary line.
6. Sentences, token utterances, statements, beliefs and thoughts are some among the other content-bearing items which we ordinarily think of as apt for truth.
7. Excepting, of course, the case where a proposition is itself about propositions.
8. I do not know that anyone has ever seriously proposed an intrinsicist conception of truth quite generally.
9. Horwich is more guarded on this than many writers in the deflationist tradition. But although he seems unwilling expressly to deny that truth is a property, it is not, he contends, a "complex property" -not "an ingredient of reality whose underlying essence will, it is hoped, one day be revealed by philosophical or scientific analysis." (*Truth*, p. 2). Thus there is, for Horwich, nothing to say about what truth really consists in; no real question for e.g. Correspondence and Coherence accounts to address themselves to.
10. This criticism is first lodged, I believe, in Michael Dummett's early paper, "Truth", *Proceedings of the Aristotelian Society* LIX (1959), pp. 141–62.
11. This claim too is advanced in Dummett's "Truth".
12. All these directions of criticism are usefully referenced and reviewed in Horwich's *Truth*.
13. See chapter 1 of my *Truth And Objectivity* (Cambridge, Mass.: Harvard University Press 1992).
14. The classic treatment of the phenomenon is, of course, H. P Grice's "Logic and Conversation" reprinted in his *Studies in the Way of Words* (Cambridge, Mass.: Harvard University Press 1989).
15. This would be less than a commitment to the idea that "true" *means*: epistemically justified. There is a distinction between holding that a word expresses no property but is used to commend items for their possession of a certain property and holding that it expresses that very property.

16. There is scope for some skirmishing. Ian Rumfitt has responded (in "Truth Wronged", *Ratio* VIII (New Series), 1995, 100–107) that the divergence in the behaviour of "true" and "assertible" just noted may straightforwardly be accommodated in a fashion entirely consonant with the purposes of deflationism, without admission of a distinctive norm of truth, provided the deflationist is prepared to allow primitive norms of *warranted denial* to operate alongside those of warranted assertion. Rather, that is, than restrict his distinctive deflationary claims to the word, "true", the deflationist should contend

> .....that 'is true' and 'is not true' function purely as devices for endorsing *and rejecting* assertions, beliefs and so on ... and which therefore register no norms distinct from justified assertibility *and justified deniability* ("Truth Wronged", p. 103; compare *Truth and Objectivity*, p. 30.))

How would this help to explain the commutativity of truth and negation? Rumfitt is not entirely explicit, but the point may seem clear enough. Since denying a statement is asserting its negation, a primitive warrant—*an anti-warrant* is Rumfitt's term—for the denial of P, registered by a claim of the form, it is not true that p, will be *eo ipso* a warrant for asserting the negation of P, so—via the Disquotational Scheme—for asserting that it is true that not-P. So the problematical direction of commutativity is secured, while the invalidity of the corresponding principle for assertibility is vouchsafed, as before, by the possibility of states of information in which one has neither warrant nor anti-warrant for P.

However the problem recurs. Consider again the problematical equivalence,

It is not true that p if and only if it is true that not-p.

and the result of negating both its sides:

It is not not true that p if and only if it is not true that not-p.

Supposing that the role of "(is) not true" were merely to register the presence of an anti-warrant, there seems no way of shirking the transition to

It is not anti-warranted that p if and only if it is anti-warranted that not-p.

But that, of course, is no less unacceptable when neutral states of information are possible than is

It is not warranted that p if and only if it is warranted that not-p.

In short, for any discourse in which neutral states of information are a possibility, the Equivalence Schema imposes a contrast both between "is true' and "is assertible;" *and* between "is not true" and "is anti-warranted". Rumfitt's proposal that the deflationist should recognise anti-warrant as primitive—whatever its independent interest—is thus of no assistance with her present difficulty.

17. J.L. Mackie, *Ethics – Inventing Right and Wrong*, (Harmondsworth: Penguin 1977).
18. This simple observation is a partial response to a recent tendency of Richard Rorty's, viz. to dismiss those features of our practice with "true" which are recalcitrant to 'pragmatist' interpretation as mere reflections of the concept's absorption of a misguided representationalist metaphysic. See, for instance, his "Is Truth a Goal of Enquiry? Davidson *vs*. Wright" in *The Philosophical Quarterly* 45 (1995) pp. 281-300. But it is to be expected, of course, that he would refuse to hear any but a metaphysically inflated reading of "an objective subject matter".
19. From Simon Blackburn, *Spreading the Word* (Oxford: Oxford University Press 1984), pp. 230–231.

20. For truth as a property of sentences, the rubric might naturally be applied to issue in something along the lines: for any sentence, s, an utterance of s in a particular context is true just in case there is a proposition, that p, which such an utterance would express, and which is true.
21. Compare the remarks of Horwich quoted in note 9.
22. From pp. 33–4 of Bertrand Russell, 'On the Nature of Truth', *Proceedings of the Aristotelian Society* VII (1906–7), pp. 28–49.
23. This moral is repeatedly emphasised in Ralph Walker's excellent study, *The Coherence Theory of Truth* (se note 1 above).
24. The explicit argument has been against a response to the original Bishop Stubbs objection—the privileging manoeuvre—which was canvassed as an alternative to relativism about truth. Briskly, then, to review how a similar difficulty afflicts the relativistic move. The relativist proposal has it that truth is always coherence with a system, but that there are thus as many versions of the truth as there are coherent comprehensive systems. Thus the proposition that Bishop Stubbs was hanged for murder, while unfit to participate in any comprehensive coherent system which is controlled by what we actually believe, may—presumably will—participate in other comprehensive and coherent systems. Well, we should now immediately press the question: what account has this relativism to offer of the truth of contingencies about belief—of propositions of the form, S is believed? Again, it should cohere with any particular coherent comprehensive system to suppose that it is in fact believed—so such a proposition should be true relative to each particular system. So now the fact of actual belief seems fugitive. Suppose there is a single comprehensive and coherent system, S, incorporating (most of) what we actually believe, and that the proposition that Bishop Stubbs was hanged for murder is not a participant. Consider by contrast such a system, S', in which that proposition is a participant. Add to each the proposition that it is believed by most human beings. Clearly a Martian, presented only with axiomatisations of each system, would have no way of telling, just on the basis of facts about coherence, which, if either, we *did* believe. So the truth of the proposition, that it is S we believe, if constituted just in facts about coherence, must reside in other such facts. The relativist-coherentist will offer, presumably, that it will be a matter of coherence with the Martian's own beliefs. But that is to appeal to a non-reconstructed notion of *what is in fact believed* by the Martian—and it was exactly the counterpart fact about us that the proposal seems to have no means to construe. So there is no progress.
25. Except in cases, naturally, where the proposition is actually about other propositions.
26. - that is, in favour of the view that truth everywhere consists in the same thing. (This kind of 'monism' about truth contrasts of course with that of Bradley and Joachim, for whom the thesis of monism is rather that reality is an intrinsically unified whole which is distorted when conceived as a totality of individual states of affairs, each apt to confer truth on a single proposition considered in isolation.)
27. The limitation to a priori cases effects, of course, a restriction on the standard lay use of "platitude", which applies to anything which no-one would dispute, (and also carries an unwanted connotation of tedium.)
28. One possible addition is reviewed in section VII below.
29. For elaboration of this claim, see *Truth and Objectivity* pp. 24–7.
30. Readers familiar with Michael Smith's work will note a point of contact here with the conception of a *network analysis* which he derives from Ramsey and Lewis; (see in particular chapter 2, section 10 of Smith's *The Moral Problem*, Oxford: Basil Blackwell 1994.) The principal contrast

with the approach to truth here canvassed is that a network analysis has to be based on a comprehensive set of platitudes whose conjunction so constrains the target concept that the replacement within them of all expressions for that concept by a variable and its binding by the description operator results in a definite description which is at the service of an analytically true identity,

Φ–ness is the property, F, such that {.....F.... & ....F...... & .....}

which thus effectively supplies a reductive analysis of the concept Φ. An analytical theory, by contrast, need not - though it may - subserve the construction of such an analytically true identity.

31. For exploration of one local case - arithmetic - see the Appendix.
32. *Truth and Objectivity*; an earlier discussion is in Ch. 14, "Can a Davidsonian Meaning-Theory be Construed in terms of Assertibility" of the 2nd. edition of my *Realism, Meaning and Truth* (Oxford: Blackwell 1993.)
33. For relevant details see the Appendix.
34. How does it follow that a satisfier of the platitudes will be definable on such contents? Very straightforwardly. First, if we are dealing with a range of genuine contents - to the extent ensured by the hypothesis of discipline - for which we have the conditional construction, then nothing can stand in the way of the definitional introduction of a predicate, or operator which is subject to the Equivalence Schema:

    That P is Φ if and only if P.

    As noted, that will then suffice for versions of Transparency, Contrast, the minimal degree of Opacity that attends Contrast, and a Correspondence platitude for Φ. It will further be open to us to insist that Φ be defined for all combinations of specified kinds of the contents in question and thereby secure Embedding. Assuming that the contents in question allow of tensed expression, Timelessness - effectively the principle that whatever may truly be thought or expressed at any particular time may, by appropriate variations of tense, be truly thought or expressed at every time - may be secured by stipulating that Φ is to be governed by analogues of the usual truth-value links between differently tensed counterparts. (If the contents in question are tenseless, then Timelessness will hold by default.) Absoluteness, for its part, will hold by default in any case unless we explicitly fix the use of a comparative.
35. For instance, Frank Jackson, Graham Oppy and Michael Smith, in their "Minimalism and Truth Aptness" *Mind* CIII (1994), pp. 287–302.
36. Of course, an assertion may be insincere. For an utterance to be a *profession* of a certain state means that one who accepts its sincerity must be prepared to ascribe that state to the utterer.
37. This is a view often taken to be defended by John McDowell; see his "Are Moral Requirements Hypothetical Imperatives?", *Proceedings of the Aristotelian Society*, Supp. Vol. 52 (1978), pp. 13–29.
38. Michael Smith himself eventually takes such a view in *The Moral Problem*.
39. See *Spreading the Word*, passim but especially Chapters 5 and 6.
40. For parallel discussion, see *Truth and Objectivity*, pp. 25–7.
41. See *Truth and Objectivity*, chapter 2, section V.
42. A version of this paper was originally written for delivery as a lecture in the series, "Unsere Welt - gegeben oder gemacht? Wissensproduktion zwischen sozialer Konstruktion und Entdeck-

ung" held at the Johann Wolfgang Goethe-Universitat in Frankfurt in the Spring of 1996. It is published in German in Matthias Vogel and Lutz Wingert (eds.), *Unsere Welt gegeben oder gemacht? Menschliches Erkennen zwischen Entdeckung und Konstruktion*, Frankfurt/M.: Suhrkamp 1999. Thanks to the discussants on that occasion and also to participants at colloquia at University College, Dublin, the University of Kent at Canterbury, Columbia University, and the 1998 Austin J. Fagothey S.J. Philosophy Conference on Truth at Santa Clara University; and to Bob Hale, Fraser MacBride, Stewart Shapiro and Charles Travis.

17 Simplifying alethic pluralism

DOUGLAS EDWARDS

1 Introduction

What is truth? What precisely is it that truths have that falsehoods lack? Pluralists about truth (or 'alethic pluralists') tend to answer these questions by saying that there is more than one way for a proposition, sentence, belief—or any chosen truth-bearer—to be true. This view is developed in relation to the idea that natural language is composed of various 'domains of discourse'[1], such as moral discourse, mathematical discourse, and discourse about the nature—or state—of the material world. Given the differences between these domains, it is thought that truth may require different treatments accordingly.

This paper is mainly concerned with the proper formulation of alethic pluralism. After briefly examining the general motivations for the view, I argue that two influential forms of alethic pluralism, those of Wright (1992, 2003a) and Lynch (2009), are subject to serious problems. I go on to outline a new approach for alethic pluralism that does not suffer from these problems, what I call 'simple determination pluralism'. This approach offers a new framework for pluralist theories which has the potential to have applications beyond the theory of truth.

2 The motivations for alethic pluralism

Equipped with the traditional notion of truth as correspondence to the facts, acknowledging that statements within a domain are apt to be described as true or false carries with it significant metaphysical baggage: in other words, it can be thought of as implying realism about that domain, or that there are facts of the matter which our statements, thoughts or beliefs map onto. This has posed particular problems about employing the notion of truth in the moral or social domains, for example, where the idea of there being mind-independent facts of the matter causes a degree of uneasiness.[2] It also causes problems in the mathematical domain, where we might be more comfortable thinking that there are mind-independent facts of the matter, but, due to the abstract nature of the facts involved, the notion of 'mapping onto' these facts seems misguided.

Some respond to this uneasiness by giving up on the applicability of truth in these problematic domains.[3] But pulling in the other direction is the attractive view of minimal truth-aptness. That is, that a domain can sustain a truth predicate in virtue of meeting very basic standards of syntactic discipline. Briefly, a domain will qualify as being syntactically disciplined if its component sentences can be used as the antecedents of conditionals, be negated, and feature as the targets of propositional attitude statements. In addition, there ought to be a distinction between seeming to be right and being right, along with the intelligibility of speakers saying 'I used to think that *p* but now I realize I was mistaken'. Moral discourse, for example, plausibly meets these standards. It would not be unusual to say things like 'I used to think that eating meat was morally permissible, but now I realize I was mistaken', or 'I wonder whether abortion is morally wrong'. Furthermore, moral sentences such as 'murder is wrong' can feature as the antecedents of conditionals, such as 'if murder is wrong, then those that murder will be punished', or be negated, as in 'it is not the case that murder is right'. It is this feature in particular that pushes us towards the truth-aptness of these sentences. As Geach (1960, 1965) argues, only truth-apt sentences can feature as the antecedents of conditionals, so, given that moral sentences are able to do so, they must be apt for truth.[4]

2.1 Deflationism

Of course, one may well point out that this is not such a problem: there is *already* a plausible, and popular, theory of truth which explains how these kinds of claims are truth-apt, and without any unwanted metaphysical baggage: *deflationism*.[5] Deflationist theories of truth typically hold that the concept of truth is entirely captured by all known instances of the following (ES) schema:

(ES): <*p*> is true iff *p*.[6]

Moreover, deflationists think that there is nothing more to be said about truth. That is, that there is no 'substantive'[7] truth property, such as the property of corresponding to the facts, or of representing reality. At most, a deflationist will allow that all true propositions share an honorific, 'lightweight' property of falling under the concept of truth. Deflationists about truth thus reject that the intuitive thoughts about truth amount to anything substantial about truth. They do not think the nature of truth consists in some relation between linguistic and non-linguistic entities, or between language and the world. The deflationist instead insists that the truth predicate exists just to perform certain logical functions, such as the endorsement of a proposition, or generalization over a potentially infinite number of propositions. One common deflationist claim is that the truth predicate serves an *expressive* function: to say 'the proposition, *p*, is true' is just another way to assert that *p*, or to express one's endorsement of the proposition that *p*. Moreover, deflationism is often paired with the minimal notion of truth-aptness, a natural companion given its deflated view of truth.[8] Consequently, sentences about morals will be apt for truth just as sentences about mathematics, or sentences about the material world will be: there is no deep problem here at all.

However, deflationism may be able to give us the resources to explain how all of the classes of sentences we are considering can be true, but it does so at the expense of being unable to say anything interesting about truth. It also does so at the cost of being unable to account for the idea that truth is valuable, and being unable to use truth as an explanatory resource when attempting to understand other concepts.[9] There are also concerns that deflationism is an *internally* unstable view, expressed in Wright's (1992) 'inflationary argument'.[10] I will not go into these problems in depth here, but suffice to say that, for the sake of the dialectic here, it is fair to say that deflationism does not offer a free solution to the problem under discussion.[11]

3 Alethic pluralism

The alethic pluralist agrees with the deflationist that all of the sentence classes we have considered are capable of being true. However, the alethic pluralist does not think, like the deflationist, that this is the end of the matter. There is a story to tell about the nature of truth, the pluralist thinks, but this story will not always be the same. According to the alethic pluralist, there will be a robust property in virtue of which the propositions expressed by sentences in a particular domain of discourse will be true, but this property will change depending on the domain we are considering. In other words, although the notion of truth as correspondence to the facts might fit our domain of discourse about the material world, a different notion of truth—perhaps one with less metaphysical baggage, constructed out of coherence, or justification or warrant—may fit the domains in which the correspondence notion looks problematic.[12] Consequently, alethic pluralism offers a treatment of truth which allows for a wide range of beliefs, sentences and the like to be true, whilst holding onto the idea that there are interesting things to say about truth.

Before putting forward my view of how alethic pluralism should be formulated, I wish to explain why we ought not to be satisfied with two of the main proposals on the table, those of Wright (1992, 2003b), and Lynch (2009).[13]

3.1 Wright's pluralist theory

The original statement of alethic pluralism is due to Crispin Wright (1992). According to Wright, any domain of discourse that meets certain basic standards of syntactic discipline is able to sustain a truth property; that is, sentences belonging to that domain will be capable of expressing propositions, and will be capable of being true in a 'robust', i.e. not simply deflationary, way.

Wright holds that the concept of truth is exhausted by a number of a priori principles, or 'platitudes'[14] about truth, such as:[15]

Transparency: That to assert a proposition is to present it as true and, more generally, that any attitude to a proposition is an attitude to its truth—that to believe, doubt, or fear, for example, that *p* is to believe, doubt, or fear that *p* is true.

(ES): <*p*> is true iff *p*.[16]

Embedding: A proposition's aptitude for truth is preserved under a variety of operations—in particular, truth-apt propositions have negations, conjunctions, disjunctions, etc., which are likewise truth-apt.

Straight-talking: A true proposition 'tells it like it is', in some way.[17]

Contrast: A proposition may be true but not justified, and vice versa.

Stability: If a proposition is ever true, then it always is, so that whatever may, at any particular time, be truly asserted may—perhaps by appropriate transformations of mood, or tense - be truly asserted at any time.

Absoluteness: Truth is absolute—there is, strictly, no such thing as a proposition's being more or less true; propositions are completely true if true at all.

Wright holds that this concept remains fixed across domains of discourse, but states that the property that satisfies the concept will change depending on the nature of the syntactically disciplined domain we are considering. The thought is that, if a property is to count as a legitimate truth property, it must exhibit the features set out in these platitudes. In other words, a property must behave a certain way if it is to count as a truth property. Descriptions of the property must thus be such that they include descriptions analogous to those of truth in the platitudes. For instance, if correspondence is to count as a truth property, then it must hold of the property of corresponding to the facts that a proposition, *p*, corresponds to the facts iff *p*. Likewise, it must hold that propositions that correspond to the facts can be justified yet not correspond to the facts, and vice versa. The same must hold of all the platitudes in the above list (or at least the set of platitudes that are eventually agreed upon). Note also that these descriptions are not descriptions that must hold at the level of *concept*, rather they are descriptions that must hold at the level of *property*. It is the behaviour of the *properties* in question that we are interested in here, not their corresponding concepts.[18]

Wright's thought thus allows one to hold that, in our talk about the nature or state of the material world, the property that satisfies the truth concept may well be the property of corresponding to the facts, but that, in the moral domain, the truth property may be a property constructed out of justification or warrant. Wright argues that a good candidate for the truth property in such a domain is what he calls 'superassertibility'.[19] Wright also (in the Appendix to Wright 2003b [Ch. 16 of this volume – Ed.]) offers a demonstration of how coherence may be identified with truth in pure arithmetical discourse. According to Wright's view, then, we have different truth properties, each tied to a specific domain of discourse.[20]

3.1.1 A PROBLEM FOR WRIGHT

However, there are significant problems with Wright's proposal. To see them, what we need to do first is distinguish between the *global* satisfaction of platitudes, and *local* satisfaction of platitudes. In other words, we require a distinction between unrestricted and restricted interpretations of the truth platitudes. The unrestricted interpretations of the truth platitudes make no reference to notions of truth that just apply in particular domains. Accordingly, the truth platitudes are taken at face value; no indexing to particular domains is required to identify the property that satisfies them. The restricted interpretation of the truth platitudes, on the other hand, requires that the platitudes be indexed to a particular domain in order to identify the property that satisfies them. The platitudes thus require a revisionary phrasing: instead of an unrestricted platitude like '<*p*> is true iff *p*', we get 'In domain D1 <*p*> is true iff *p*', or - better - <*p*> is true (in D1) iff *p*.

It is interesting to note that Wright's form of pluralism is required to interpret the platitudes *restrictedly*, for the unrestricted readings would come out as false on his account. Here is why. Suppose, with Wright, that we are to *identify* truth with the relevant domain-specific property, and take the properties of corresponding to the facts (as the truth property for the material world domain) and superassertibility (as the truth property for the moral domain), for example. On the unrestricted reading, it seems as though *neither* of these properties will actually be able to be considered truth properties, as none will be able to satisfy the platitudes unrestrictedly, for all propositions. Take a version of the (ES) schema platitude and its interpretation on a view of truth as corresponding to the facts in the domain of discourse about the material world:[21]

(ES): <*p*> is true iff *p*.

(EC): <*p*> corresponds to the facts iff *p*.[22]

The key difference between (ES) and (EC) is that (ES) holds true for *all* propositions, whereas (EC) only holds true for propositions in the domain of discourse concerning the state of the material world. If, for instance, we were to plug a moral proposition into (EC), it would come out as false, as moral propositions are subject instead to the following principle:

(EM): <*p*> is superassertible iff *p*.

(EC), then, cannot globally satisfy (ES), as some propositions will be subject instead to (EM). But, of course, (EM) cannot globally satisfy (ES) either, as some propositions will be subject to (EC). It thus follows that neither correspondence nor superassertibility can satisfy the unrestricted reading of (ES). As, by the lights of Wright's theory, the truth platitudes are supposed to specify features that it is *necessary* that any candidate truth property must satisfy, the failure of these properties to satisfy this platitude means that they are not worthy of being regarded as truth properties.

It thus seems as though we must then read the claim *restrictedly*, and say that truth properties only apply within domains of discourse, and that a truth property for a domain can be identified by its ability to satisfy the platitudes in that domain. In order to do this, we must first restrict all of the truth platitudes, which can no longer be understood in their original unrestricted forms. Accordingly, (ES) becomes:

(ED): <*p*> is true (in D) iff *p*.

The satisfaction of this platitude now requires more than just the substitution of the name of the property for 'true': prior to this, we must plug the domain in question into D position. Working still with the properties of correspondence and superassertibility for domains of material world and moral discourse respectively, consider material world discourse as domain D1, and moral discourse as domain D2. What we will get are the following two models of (ED):

(ED1): <*p*> corresponds to the facts (in D1) iff *p*.

(ED2): <*p*> is superassertible (in D2) iff *p*.

Unlike (EC) and (EM), (ED1) and (ED2) both come out as true, thus rescuing the prospects for correspondence and superassertibility being considered truth properties. It will hold for all propositions in domain D1 that <*p*> corresponds to the facts in D1 iff *p*, just as it will hold for all propositions in domain D2 that <*p*> is superassertible in D2 iff *p*. Provided we restrict the platitudes in question, it looks as though the properties Wright considered do have the pedigree to be considered truth properties.

This restriction, however, brings with it two rather serious problems. The first is that Wright's pluralism is in danger of becoming a far more *revisionary* and controversial view about truth than it originally cast itself to be. One of the main points of the methodological strategy adopted by Wright is to construct an analysis of the concept in question—here truth—by reference to a set of uncontroversial, highly intuitive platitudes. However, by restricting the truth platitudes to specific domains, Wright's view loses most, if not all, of this methodological strategy. Firstly, the original platitudes identified by Wright were, of course, unrestricted: they make no reference to domains, and aim to characterize truth from a theory neutral, and pre-theoretical perspective. Once restricted, however, they certainly do not characterize truth from a theory-neutral, and pre-theoretical, perspective. Even if the theory that truth consists in different properties in different domains is correct, it is certainly not platitudinous: it is a substantial theoretical claim, which is highly contentious, and far from being theory-neutral. Consequently, as soon as domain-specificity is built into the very truth platitudes, these platitudes cease to be platitudes, at least in the sense originally intended. What we have are revisionary, theory-laden interpretations of the original truth platitudes: we do not have the truth platitudes themselves.

The second problem is that the restriction of the platitudes to specific domains has serious implications for the structure of Wright's view as he presents it. His thought is that we have a single truth concept, exhausted by the unrestricted platitudes, which is satisfied by different properties in different domains. However, with the restriction of the platitudes in each domain, what we end up with is a number of distinct truth concepts as well as distinct truth properties. This is because—in this case at least—the content of concepts is given by platitudes, so if the platitudes are restricted, so will the concept be. What we end up with, then, is not a general truth concept satisfied by different properties in different domains, but rather different truth concepts in different domains (e.g. truth-in-ethics, truth-in-mathematics, etc.) which pick out different truth properties. It is important for Wright that, even if the truth properties vary from domain to domain, the general truth concept remains constant across domains.[23] However, if these considerations are correct, it does not seem that it does.

I propose that these considerations leave us with is the idea that the global, unrestricted platitudes are expressive of the concept of *truth itself*, and the restricted, local platitudes are expressive of a concept which, whilst not worthy of being *truth itself*, is certainly worthy of being considered a closely related notion. Later on, I will suggest that this notion is best captured as a truth-*determining* property, but, for now, let us consider the second view on the table: Michael Lynch's 'functionalist' proposal.[24]

3.2 Lynch's functionalist theory

Lynch's functionalist theory, as proposed in Lynch 2009, differs from Wright's view in that it does not identify truth with the domain-specific properties that are taken to satisfy the truth platitudes, or realize the truth role. Lynch holds that we ought to conceive of truth as a single property, that is held distinct from all the domain-specific properties. On the functionalist view, whilst there may be a different story to tell about how, say, mathematical propositions get to be true from the story told about how moral propositions get to be true, these propositions, if they are true, are all in possession of the very same truth property. Lynch does share with Wright the important view that the concept of truth is captured by a set of platitudes about truth, although Lynch prefers a slightly different list composed of:

Objectivity: The belief that *p* is true if, and only if, with respect to the belief that *p*, things are as they are believed to be.

Warrant Independence: Some beliefs can be true but not warranted and some can be warranted without being true.

Norm of Belief: It is prima facie correct to believe that *p* if and only if the proposition that *p* is true.

End of Inquiry: Other things being equal, true beliefs are a worthy goal of inquiry. (Lynch 2009: 8-12)

However, according to Lynch, we ought to take the truth platitudes (or the 'truish features' in his words) to specify the nature of the truth property, as well as the nature of the truth concept:

> the functionalist...can claim that there is a single property and concept of truth. The property *being true* (or the property of truth) is the property that has the truish features essentially or which plays the truth-role *as such*. (Lynch 2009: 74)

Lynch does not want to disregard the 'domain-specific' properties, such as correspondence and superassertibility, that we saw Wright identify truth with. But Lynch does not want to *identify* truth with these properties, rather he wants to say that truth is *manifested* in these properties:

> this approach allows the functionalist to claim that truth is, as it were, *immanent* in ontologically distinct properties. Let us say that where property F is immanent in or *manifested by* property M, it is a priori that F's essential features are a subset of M's features. (Lynch 2009: 74)

Lynch's view thus requires that the truth features—as expressed in the characterization of the truth property—are a subset of the features of the particular domain-specific properties. That is, each of the properties that, in Lynch's terms, 'manifest' truth in a domain, must contain the truth property as a proper part. So, for example, for superassertibility[25] to manifest truth in a domain, it would have to be part of the features of superassertibility that the belief that *p* is superassertible if, and only if, things are as they are believed to be; that some beliefs can be superassertible but not warranted and some can be warranted without being superassertible; that it is prima facie correct to believe that *p* if and only if the proposition that *p* is superassertible; and that, other things being equal, superassertible beliefs are a worthy goal of inquiry.

If the above considerations concerning the restricted and unrestricted interpretations of the truth platitudes are correct, it seems as though Lynch also has a problem. This is because the specification of the truth property requires that the truth platitudes that compose it are read *unrestrictedly*; that is, it is a crucial part of Lynch's view that the truth property *itself* is not annexed to any specific domain. But, in line with what was said above, if the domain-specific truth-manifesting properties exhibit the truth features, they *cannot* exhibit them *unrestrictedly*, because none of the properties manifest truth in *all* domains. Consequently, as they only manifest truth in specific domains, they can only be said to exhibit the truth features for those domains in which they manifest truth.

For example, suppose that superassertibility manifests truth just in the moral domain, and consider the 'Norm of Belief ' platitude. It is not part of the features of superassertibility that it is prima facie correct to believe that *p* iff the proposition that *p* is superassertible. On the view we are supposing, this is only part of the features of superassertibility *in the moral domain*; in other domains, different properties will ground the norm of belief. What we should say instead is that it is part of the features of superassertibility that, *in the moral domain*, it is prima facie correct to believe that *p* iff the proposition that *p* is superassertible. But, of course, this is to restrict this feature of superassertibility to a specific domain, which is to restrict the feature of truth in question to a specific domain. At the very most, then, the 'truth' features which superassertibility, in this case, can manifest *must* be restricted to a specific domain.

Consequently, at most, the property of superassertibility can manifest a restricted truth property (perhaps moral truth, in this case). But this is not the result Lynch needs; he needs superassertibility—and all the domain-specific properties—to manifest the *generic* truth property. That is, he needs them to contain the features of the *domain-free* truth property as a proper part. The generic truth property, however, is composed of the *unrestricted* readings of the truth platitudes, and, thus, to manifest truth, a property must contain *these* features as a proper part. But, it seems, this cannot be done: at most they can manifest a property composed of *restricted* readings of these platitudes which, as we saw above, may constitute a notion *closely related* to truth, but, unfortunately, not truth itself.[26] The problem for Lynch's view, then, is that the claim that truth is *manifested* in the domain-specific properties ends up in tension with the claim that truth is a property independent of any domain-specific annexing.

The problem for Lynch's view, then, is that the claim that truth is manifested in the domain-specific properties ends up in tension with the claim that truth is a property independent of any domain-specific annexing. Both Wright's and Lynch's views suffer because they either try to identify truth with the domain-specific properties (Wright), or maintain that truth is to be considered a part of those properties (Lynch). I will now move on to outline a view—'simple determination pluralism'—which aims to avoid these problems.[27]

4 The structure of simple determination pluralism

4.1 Simple determination pluralism's truth property

The first issue to address is what account simple determination pluralism gives of the truth property. Simple determination pluralism occupies the same ground as Lynch's functionalism on this point, in that it states that the nature of the truth property is captured by the truth platitudes. When questioned about the nature of truth, the simple determination pluralist will thus be able to say things like:

Truth is the property that is the goal of inquiry.
Truth is a property that is distinct from justification.
Truth is a property that is distinct from warranted assertibility.
The proposition that *p* has the property of being true if and only if *p*.
To have the property of being true is to tell it like it is.
To assert *p* is to present *p* as possessing the property of truth.[28]

These features, and others like them, will tell us all that there is to know about the essential features of the truth property. In response to the question of what the truth property is, the simple determination pluralist will be able to give an elucidation of the property by reference to the list of features given by the platitudes about truth, but will have no response to any further questions about what the *nature* of truth is.

Accordingly, we can think of the truth property as a 'simple', non-reducible property. It is just the property that necessarily has the truth features.[29] The truth property thus should not be identified with any of the domain-specific properties (like correspondence, coherence or superassertibility): there is only one property that has the pedigree to be the truth property, and that is just the simple property that necessarily has the truth features. However, as we will see, these domain-specific properties will have an important role in explaining why it is that propositions are true.[30]

4.2 The truth property and domains of discourse

According to simple determination pluralism, then, the truth property is just the property that necessarily has the truth features. Now we must address the question of how it is that propositions get to have this property. The first thing to note is that simple determination pluralism aims to maintain the basic pluralist thought that natural language contains different domains of discourse, but to reconcile this thought with the idea that there is a single truth property that all true propositions share. The thought is that propositions—insofar as they are true—are held to by a pluralist to always be true *in some way*, so there must be an explanation of what way it is - or in virtue of which property it is—that the proposition or belief is true.

An analogy to help explain this is winning.[31] Winning, or the property of being a winner, seems to be a fairly non-reducible property. It is a property that is highly desirable in itself and it is a property that one can get in a variety of different ways, depending on the game being played. What it takes to be a winner in a game of pool (e.g. potting the black before your opponent) is very different from what it takes to be a winner in a race (crossing the finish line first). The property of being a winner plausibly remains the same, though, despite the fact that is determined by the possession of different properties in different games. It is important to note that, despite the relationship between winning and the 'win-making' properties in each game, the property of winning ought not to be identified with those properties, nor considered to be manifested in those properties.

We can minimally define winning as the property that players of all games aim to possess in playing their respective games. We can also say that, for each particular game, there will be a 'win-making' property such that the possessor of that property will automatically possess the property of being the winner in that game. In the case of pool, for example, the 'win-making' property could be defined as potting the black before your opponent (after potting all of your own balls, of course). This property is considered a distinct property from the property of being a winner, and it is not supposed that this property contains the property of being a winner as a proper part.

This is how we ought to think about truth on the simple determination pluralist view. We hold that the achievement of being true is always the same, regardless of the domain of discourse we are considering: it always consists in the possession of the same single truth property. However, what *will* change from one domain to another will be the property which gets the proposition the truth property, just as the property which gets a player to be the winner changes from game to game.[32]

4.3 Determining truth

We must now address the question of how it is that propositions get to have the truth property, and how this changes from domain of discourse to domain of discourse. We can return to our analogy with games to find one way of explaining this. We can hold that, for a particular domain that passes basic tests of syntactic discipline, there will be a 'truth-making' property, the possession of which will bring with it the possession of the property of being true. This ought to maintain the separation between the truth property and the domain-specific properties, whilst staying true to the idea that our analysis of the truth of propositions ought to be different from one domain of discourse to the next. This is the basic idea, but—in order to avoid confusion with other theories,[33] and for reasons to be discussed below—I propose to call the domain-specific properties 'truth determining' properties, as opposed to 'truth-making' properties.

Possession of the truth-determining property in a domain must be both necessary and sufficient for the possession of the truth property in a domain. In other words, in, say, the material world domain, we want possession of the correspondence property to be both necessary and sufficient for the possession of the truth property.[34] We can demonstrate this as follows. Take the (ES) platitude once more:

(ES): <*p*> is true iff *p*.

We then take its restricted version:

(ED1): <*p*> is true (in D1) iff *p*.

Supposing that D1 is a correspondence domain, we get the following model:

(ED1C): <*p*> corresponds to the facts (in D1) iff *p*.

Then, using transitivity of the biconditional, from (ED1) and (ED1C) we can get the following:

(TC): <*p*> is true (in D1) iff <*p*> corresponds to the facts (in D1).

(TC) gives us the desired result: a property the possession of which is both necessary and sufficient for the possession of the truth property in domain D1.

We can note that (TC) should not be taken as a statement of identity. We should read it in much the same way as we would read the following biconditional:

(WR): In a race: X is the winner (in that race) iff X crosses the finish line first (in that race).

In other words, we ought to think of the right-hand side of the biconditional as specifying the conditions under which the left-hand side is satisfied. In the case of (WR), the right-hand side specifies the property an individual, x, must have in order to have the property of being the winner. Likewise, in the case of (TC), the right-hand side specifies the property a proposition, *p*, must have in order to have the property of being true. We can say, then, that there is an *order of determination* in the biconditionals in question. A plausible case of a biconditional with an order of determination is the following:

(C) <*p* & *q*> is true iff <*p*> is true and <*q*> is true.[35]

(C) specifies the truth conditions for conjunction, in the form of a biconditional. There is an order of determination in the biconditional, as what explains the truth of <*p* & *q*> is the truth of the components, <*p*> and <*q*>. To put the point slightly differently, the truth of the right-hand side *determines* the truth of the left-hand side, but not vice-versa: the fact that <*p* & *q*> is true does not explain why <*p*> is true, and why <*q*> is true.

We should read biconditionals like (TC) in a similar fashion. What (TC) essentially says is that the truth of a proposition in domain D1 is dependent on that proposition's having the property of corresponding to the facts: a proposition will be true in domain D1 just in case it has the property of corresponding to the facts. In addition, possession of the property of corresponding to the facts *determines* the truth of a proposition, and also plays a significant role in *explaining why* that proposition is true.

With this account in hand, we can see why we should refer to these domain-specific properties as truth-determining properties; the properties that determine the possession of the truth property.

4.4 Identifying the truth-determining properties

We have a distinction, then, between the truth property (captured by the unrestricted truth platitudes) and the truth-determining properties (the properties that are responsible for establishing the propositions in a domain which possess the truth property). We must now address the question of how we identify the truth-determining properties within each of the domains.

We can get some guidance by looking at what was said earlier in relation to Wright and Lynch's views. If we are operating within the framework of alethic pluralism, we are comfortable with the idea that properties like correspondence and superassertibility have important roles to play when it comes to accounting for the truth of propositions in certain domains. The problem—as we have seen with Wright and Lynch—is to explain just how they are able to do so. Using notions like identity and manifestation did not seem to work, as those notions required satisfaction of the unrestricted truth platitudes, whereas properties like correspondence and superassertibility could only satisfy the restricted versions. However, it is interesting to note that—in both those cases—there was taken to be no problem establishing that properties like correspondence and superassertibility were able to satisfy the *restricted* versions of the truth platitudes. What simple determination pluralism does is embrace this fact already established—that these properties satisfy the restricted platitudes—and say that they need do nothing more.

The thought thus is that the domain-specific truth-determining properties are identified by their ability to satisfy the restricted interpretations of the truth platitudes, and thus, whilst they do not count as properties of *truth*, globally conceived, they still have the status of being the properties in virtue of which propositions in those domains get to be true. In other words, they explain how propositions in the domains in question get to be true—they are true because they possess the relevant *truth-determining* property for their domain. These properties have this status due to their ability to satisfy the localized truth platitudes, which essentially give the job description for the property that any proposition in the domain in question must have in order to be true. However, as we have noted, these properties should not be identified as *truth* properties, as they only satisfy the restricted platitudes, not the unrestricted platitudes. Whilst, according to simple determination pluralism, these properties are essential in the story told about why a proposition is true, they are not identical to the truth property itself, and nor do they manifest the truth property.

Here, then, is the picture. The truth-determining property in a domain is identified by its ability to satisfy the restricted truth platitudes (restricted to that domain). Possession of this property will bring with it possession of the truth property (just as possessing the property of crossing the finish line first in a race brings with it the property of being the winner in that race). The truth-determining properties, which must satisfy the restricted, localised versions of the truth platitudes, are contrasted with the truth property itself, which is identified by its ability to satisfy the unrestricted, global interpretations of the truth platitudes. As has been proposed above, according to simple determination pluralism, the only property that has the pedigree to be considered a truth property, so conceived, is the simple property that necessarily has the truth features. This property—truth—is not tied to any story about domains of discourse, and requires no revision of the folk platitudes about truth in order to satisfy them. Consequently, it should be worthy of the title of a truth property on *any* theory of truth, whether pluralist or not.

4.5 Simple determination pluralism, Wright's view, and functionalism

By maintaining the distinction between the truth property and the truth-determining properties, simple determination pluralism is able to avoid the problems we noted for Wright and Lynch's views. In fact, it uses the criticism of those views—that the domain-specific properties are only able to satisfy the restricted truth platitudes - as a strength. It takes this on board and specifies these properties as truth-determining properties, held distinct from the truth property, which does not participate in any restriction to domains. This preserves the ability of truth to be preserved as a notion characterized by the unrestricted platitudes, thus avoiding the pitfalls of Wright's view and functionalism.

5 Summary

Using the notion of truth-determination gives us the sketch of a pluralist theory of truth which does not suffer from the problems of Wright's view or Lynch's functionalism. This model of determination also provides us with a new model for pluralist theories in general, one which is recognisably distinct from the standard functionalist proposals.

A key concern for pluralist theories for any subject matter is the reconciliation of unity and diversity: unity in the sense that the different ways of being Z must recognizably *be* ways of being Z, and diversity in the sense that the different ways of being Z must all be *different* ways of being Z. The determination model offered by simple determination pluralism gives a clear account of both unity and diversity. Unity is given by the simple account of the property of being Z—which is possessed by all things that are Z—and diversity is provided by the different properties that determine Z in the various circumstances (whatever they are required to be). Whether or not the benefits simple determination pluralism gives us in the truth debate can cross over to other areas is a matter for further discussion. However, the model is adaptable, and if it offers a solution to the general need to reconcile unity and diversity in the case of truth, there is perhaps reason to be optimistic about its utility elsewhere.[36]

Notes

1. For more on the notion of a domain, see Edwards (2018, Ch. 4).
2. For an extended discussion of truth in the social domain, see Edwards (2018, Chs.4 and 5).
3. Such as expressivists (e.g. Ayer 1936, Blackburn 1998) about the moral domain, and fictionalists about mathematics (e.g. Field 1980, 1989).
4. There are, of course, a lot of contentious issues surrounding this claim. Expressivists, for example, who think that moral sentences express attitudes, and not beliefs, maintain that although such sentences appear truth-apt, they are not. There is much debate about whether they can maintain this claim in the face of the intuitive discipline exhibited by the moral domain, and, indeed, whether or not there is anything more to a domain's dealing in truth-apt contents over and above it's appearing to do so. For a small sample, see Wright 1992, Smith 1994 and 1994a, Divers and Miller 1994 and 1995, Boghossian 1990 and Jackson, Oppy and Smith 1994.
5. One type of deflationism is Horwich's (1998) 'minimalist' view [See Ch. 10 of this volume – Ed.]. See Field 1994 [Ch. 11 of this volume – Ed.] for an alternative type of deflationism, and Grover and Eklund's works in this volume (Chs. 12 and 13) for further kinds.
6. (ES) is the form of Tarski's (1944) T-schema adopted if we take propositions to be the primary truth bearers in a language – the angles brackets < > stand for 'the proposition that'. I use (ES) as much of the discussion has Horwich's view in mind, which does take propositions to be the primary truth bearers, but this should not be taken to be distinctive of deflationary views in general.
7. For more on the notion of a 'substantive' property, see Edwards 2013 and 2018, Ch. 2. See also Eklund's Ch. 13 of this volume.
8. Though whether deflationism entails minimal truth-aptness this is controversial - see, for example, Jackson, Oppy and Smith 1994.
9. See, for example, Lynch 2004a, Davidson 1999, Field 1986.
10. See also Ch. 16 of this volume. The inflationary argument is also discussed in Horwich 1996 and 1998, Rumfitt 1995, van Cleve 1996, Kölbel 1997 and Miller 2001.
11. See Edwards 2018, Ch. 3 for an extended critique of deflationism.
12. These alternative notions of truth ought not to be too surprising, given that many have sponsored full-blown versions of these views in the past. Coherence theory, for instance, is often set up as the traditional competitor to correspondence theory - see, for example, Walker 1989. We also have theories that identify truth with what would be justified under ideal epistemic circumstances (e.g. Putnam 1981).

    It is not my purpose in this paper to argue for any particular notions of truth for each domain, rather to set up the general structure a pluralist view ought to take. Consequently, I shall not go into the nature of these properties in too much detail.
13. There is also a previous version of the view put forward by Lynch in Lynch 2001, 2004, and discussed in detail in C.D. Wright (2010). But as Lynch rejects this view in Lynch 2009, for reasons with which I am sympathetic, I will not discuss this view here.
14. For more on the use of platitudes in philosophical methodology, see Nolan 2009. Broadly speaking, platitudes are designed to reflect highly intuitive, pre-theoretical, and perhaps even theory-neutral thoughts about a concept.
15. This list is adapted from Wright 2003b: 271-272 [This volume, Ch. 16, pp. 269 – Ed.].

16. Whilst Wright does not include (ES) in his list of platitudes referenced here, he and Lynch (2009: 9) take it to be derivable from other platitudes given some minimal assumptions (Wright 1992, 2003b). For more on whether (ES) is fundamental or derived, see Edwards 2018, Ch. 3.
17. Wright's original platitudes in this area are phrased directly in terms of true propositions 'corresponding to the facts'. Wright, however, claims that this seemingly loaded terminology is in fact equivalent to a more neutral phrasing like that which I use here. See, e.g. Wright 1992: 24-27.
18. In other words, we are not looking for identity of concepts—the concept of corresponding to facts or superassertibility need not be identical to the concept of truth - rather looking for a property (or properties) that exhibit the features set out in the truth concept. These descriptions must thus hold at the level of property. See Alston 2002, Wright 2003b and Lynch 2009 for more on the concept/property distinction in this context.
19. Roughly, a proposition is superassertible when it is warrantedly assertible at a stage of inquiry, and would remain warrantedly assertible at any future stages of inquiry. See Wright 1993.
20. It is worth pointing out that some theories of truth along pluralist lines take it that there is not such a radical difference in the nature of the truth property across domains. For instance, Horgan 2001 and Sher 2004 [This volume, Ch. 18 – Ed.] take it that truth always consists in correspondence to the facts, but that the nature of the correspondence relation changes according to the conception of the subject matter. I will not discuss this type of view here, but see Edwards 2018, Ch. 5 for an assessment of this type of pluralism.
21. See Wright 1992 and 2003b [This volume, Ch. 16 – Ed] for more details on the process of modelling the platitudes in this way.
22. One way to derive (EC) is to use (ES) along with the claim (F) <p> is true iff <p> corresponds to the facts. Transitivity of the biconditional would yield (EC) from (ES) and (F). Note that (F) would presumably have to hold if corresponding to the facts is to be identified with truth.
23. This is to stop the view from slipping into the view that 'true' has a number of distinct meanings, a view which neither Wright nor Lynch think is promising. See, e.g. Lynch 2009: Ch. 3.
24. There are other problems noted for Wright's view in the literature, some more serious than others. For objections see Tappolet 1997, 2000 and Lynch 2006. For rejoinders and discussion see Beall 2000, Pedersen 2006, Edwards 2008 and 2009 and Cotnoir 2009.
25. Note that Lynch prefers the term 'superwarrant' to 'superassertibility', but, for ease of use, I will continue to use 'superassertibility'.
26. One could, of course, reject the platitudes altogether—a strategy hinted at by Pedersen (2010: 100), particularly in response to the debate between C.D. Wright (2005) and Lynch (2005). But this leaves the pluralist with the hard problem of how to identify the domain-specific properties *without* the platitudes—the platitude strategy being a strategy prominent in a number of cases, see, e.g. Lynch 2001a and 2004, Jackson 1998, Lewis 1979.
27. I should note that the view I will present is not the only other option on the table. For example, Pedersen (2010) explores taking the truth property to be a disjunction of all the domain-specific properties—i.e. a proposition is true iff it corresponds, or is superassertible, or coheres, etc. For discussion of proposals of this sort see Lynch 2009: Ch.3, and Edwards 2018: Ch. 7.
28. These are all taken to be consistent with the truth platitudes discussed so far.
29. As the truth features are expressive of the unique aspects of truth, it is part of the view that there is just one property that necessarily has the truth features—at least as they are phrased in the truth platitudes (i.e. unrestrictedly). In other words, any property which has these features is necessarily the very same property as the simple determination theorist's truth property.

30. One might worry that this property is dangerously close to the lightweight property proposed by deflationism. It is worth noting that Lynch's functionalism faces this concern too. Lynch claims that the robustness of the truth property, on his view, lies in the fact that it is manifested in other properties - a fact that is not simply read off from the truth platitudes (Lynch 2009: 83–4). If this approach is satisfactory, presumably the simple determination pluralist can offer a similar response by holding (as we will see) that, according to simple determination pluralism, the truth property is determined by other properties—also a fact that cannot be read off from the truth platitudes. Note also that the fact that truth is determined by other properties gives us a substantial explanatory story to tell about the properties in virtue of which propositions are true, something which is not offered on a deflationary account, and which ought to assist the simple determination pluralist in avoiding the pitfalls of deflationism briefly noted above. Of course, these issues require fuller consideration in a separate study—see Edwards 2018.
31. An analogy between truth and winning was originally emphasized by Dummett (1978). The analogy is useful given the similarity between the normativity of the property of winning (in that the aim of a game is (usually) to win), and the normativity of truth (in that the aim of belief or assertion is (usually) truth).
32. It is important to note that simple determination pluralism is not second-order functionalism (the view of truth of which is expressed by Lynch 2001a, 2004, 2005, 2006). For one thing, the simple truth property is not a second-order property: it is the property that exhibits the truth features, not the property of having a property that exhibits the truth features. Accordingly, simple determination pluralism is not open to the main objections to second-order functionalism. Lynch (2009) demonstrates that the main problem for the view is that the second-order truth property (the property of having a property that realizes truth) does not itself satisfy the truth platitudes, thus leaving it unfit to be considered a truth property. As, according to simple determination pluralism, the truth property is defined as the property that necessarily has the truth features, this problem is avoided.
33. I refer here to the independent discussion of truthmakers, see, e.g. Beebee and Dodd 2005. In truthmaker theory, every true proposition is taken to have a truthmaker (usually construed as a fact) which grounds the truth of that proposition. Simple determination pluralism is not incompatible with such a view—at least in certain domains—but it would hold that the truthmaker for a proposition (as a fact) would be the ground of the proposition possessing the truth-making property (or, in my terms, the truth-determining property) for its domain, and hence the truth property.
34. If the possession of correspondence is only necessary for truth in the material world domain, we might get propositions which correspond to the facts, but that are not true. If it is only sufficient, we might get propositions that are true but that do not correspond to the facts. Neither of these situations looks favourable, as the role of the correspondence property in accounting for the truth of propositions looks decidedly confused.
35. The order of determination in biconditionals like (C) is also discussed in Edwards 2008.
36. This is a lightly updated version of a paper originally published in *The Southern Journal of Philosophy* in 2011. My edits have mostly been made to include updated details for further discussion in the references. I would like to thank Patrick Greenough, Michael Lynch and Crispin Wright for very helpful discussions and comments on the original paper. I would also like to thank two anonymous referees for the *The Southern Journal of Philosophy* for their comments. Earlier versions of this paper were presented at research seminars at the University of St Andrews, University College Dublin, and the University of Connecticut, and also at conferences

at Jagiellonian University, the University of Sydney, and the University of Padua. I would like to thank audiences at all these presentations for their comments. The originally published paper was completed with the support of a postdoctoral award from the Irish Research Council for the Humanities and Social Sciences, which I gratefully acknowledge.

References

Alston, W.P. 2002. Truth: Concept and Property. In *What is Truth?* ed. R. Shantz. Berlin and New York: Walter de Gruyter: 11–26.

Ayer, A.J. 1936. *Language, Truth and Logic*. Camelot Press, London.

Beall, J.C. 2000. On Mixed Inferences and Pluralism about Truth Predicates. *The Philosophical Quarterly* Vol. 50, No. 200: 380–382.

Beebee, H. and Dodd, J. 2005. *Truthmakers: the Contemporary Debate*. Oxford: Clarendon Press.

Blackburn, S. 1998. *Ruling Passions*. Oxford University Press.

Boghossian, P.A. 1990. The Status of Content. *The Philosophical Review*, Vol. 99, No. 2, pp. 157–184.

Cotnoir, A.J. 2009. Generic truth and mixed conjunctions: some alternatives. *Analysis*, Vol. 69, No.2: 473–479.

Davidson, D. 1999. The Folly of Trying to Define Truth. *Journal of Philosophy* 93, no. 6: 263–279.

Divers, J. and Miller, A. 1994. Why Expressivists about Value Should Not Love Minimalism about Truth. *Analysis*, Vol. 54, No. 1: 12–19.

Divers, J. and Miller, A. 1995. Platitudes and Attitudes: A Minimalist Conception of Belief. *Analysis*, Vol. 55, No.1: 37–44.

Dummett, M. 1978. Truth. In his *Truth and Other Enigmas*. Oxford University Press.

Edwards, D. 2008. How to solve the problem of mixed conjunctions. *Analysis*, Vol. 68, No. 2: 143–149.

Edwards, D. 2009. Truth-conditions and the nature of truth: re-solving mixed conjunctions. *Analysis*, Vol. 69, No. 4: 684–688.

Edwards, D. 2013. Truth as a Substantive Property. *Australasian Journal of Philosophy*, 91 (2): 279–294.

Edwards, D. 2018. *The Metaphysics of Truth*. Oxford: Oxford University Press.

Field, H. 1980. *Science Without Numbers*. Blackwell, Oxford.

Field, H. 1986. The Deflationary Conception of Truth. In C. Wright and G. Macdonald (eds.) *Fact, Science and Morality*. Blackwell, Oxford: 55–119.

Field, H. 1989. *Realism, Mathematics and Modality*. Blackwell, Oxford.

Field, H. 1994. Deflationist views of meaning and content. *Mind*, 103: 247–285. [This volume, Ch. 11 – Ed.]

Geach, P.T. 1960. Ascriptivism. *Philosophical Review*, 69: 221–5.

Geach, P.T. 1965. Assertion. *Philosophical Review*, 74: 449–465.

Horgan, T. 2001. Contextual Semantics and Metaphysical Realism: Truth as Indirect Correspondence. In Lynch 2001: 67–96.

Horwich, P. 1996. Realism minus Truth. *Philosophy and Phenomenological Research* 56: 877–881.

Horwich, P. 1998. *Truth: Second Edition*. Blackwell.

Jackson, F. 1998. *From Metaphysics to Ethics*. Oxford University Press.

Jackson, F., Oppy, G. and Smith, M. 1994. Minimalism and Truth Aptness. *Mind*, New Series, Vol. 103, No. 411: 287–302.

Kölbel, M. 1997. Wright's Argument from Neutrality. *Ratio* NS 10: 35–47.

Lewis, D. 1979. How to Define Theoretical Terms. *Journal of Philosophy*, 67: 427–446.

Lynch, M.P. 2001. *The Nature of Truth*. MIT Press.
Lynch, M.P. 2001a. A Functionalist Theory of Truth. In Lynch 2001.
Lynch, M.P. 2004. Truth and Multiple Realizibility. *Australasian Journal of Philosophy*, Volume 82, Number 3: 384–408.
Lynch, M.P. 2005. Alethic Functionalism and our Folk Theory of Truth. *Synthese* Vol. 145, No. 1: 29–43.
Lynch, M.P. 2006. ReWrighting Pluralism. *The Monist*, Vol. 89, No. 1: 63–84.
Lynch, M.P. 2009. *Truth as One and Many*. Oxford University Press.
Miller, A. 2001. On Wright's Argument against Deflationism. *The Philosophical Quarterly*, Vol. 51, No. 205: 527–531.
Nolan, D. 2009. Platitudes and Metaphysics. In D. Braddon-Mitchell and R. Nola (eds.) *Conceptual Analysis and Philosophical Naturalism*. MIT Press.
Pedersen, N. 2006. What can the problem of mixed inferences teach us about alethic pluralism? *The Monist*, Vol. 89, No. 1: 102–117.
Pedersen, N. 2010. Stabilizing Alethic Pluralism. *The Philosophical Quarterly*, Vol. 60, No. 238: 92–108.
Putnam, H. 1981. *Reason, Truth and History*. Cambridge University Press.
Rumfitt, I. 1995. Truth Wronged. *Ratio*, NS 8: 100–7.
Sher, G. 2004. In Search of a Substantive Theory of Truth. *Journal of Philosophy*, 101: 5–36. [This volume, Ch. 18 – Ed.]
Smith, M. 1994. Why Expressivists about Value Should Love Minimalism about Truth. *Analysis*, Vol. 54, No. 1: 1–11.
Smith, M. 1994a. Minimalism, Truth-Aptitude and Belief. *Analysis*, Vol. 54, No. 1: 21–26.
Tappolet, C. 1997. Mixed inferences: a problem for pluralism about truth predicates. *Analysis* 57: 209–10
Tappolet, C. 2000. Truth, Pluralism and Many-Valued Logics. *The Philosophical Quarterly*, Vol. 50, No. 200: 382–383.
Tarksi, A. 1944. The Semantic Conception of Truth and the Foundations of Semantics. Reprinted in A.P. Martinich (ed.) *The Philosophy of Language*. Oxford University Press. 2001.
Van Cleve, J. 1996. Minimal Truth is Realist Truth. *Philosophy and Phenomenological Research* 56: 869–75.
Walker, R.C.S. 1989. *The Coherence Theory of Truth*. Routledge, London.
Wright, C.D. 2005. On the Functionalization of Pluralist Approaches to Truth. *Synthese* Vol. 145, No. 1: 128.
Wright, C.D. 2010. Truth, Ramsification, and the Pluralist's Revenge. *Australasian Journal of Philosophy* , Vol. 88, No. 2, pp. 265–283.
Wright, C.J.G. 1992. *Truth and Objectivity*. Harvard University Press.
Wright, C.J.G. 1993. *Realism, Meaning and Truth, Second Edition*. Oxford University Press.
Wright, C.J.G. 2003a. *Saving the Differences*. Harvard University Press.
Wright, C.J.G. 2003b. Truth: A Traditional Debate Reviewed. In Wright 2003a. [This volume, Ch. 16 – Ed.]

18 In search of a substantive theory of truth

GILA SHER

> The layman ... expects philosophers to answer deep questions of great import for an understanding of the world .... And the layman is quite right .... Yet he finds most writings by philosophers of the analytical school disconcertingly remote from these concerns .... The complaint ... is understandable .... [A]nalytical philosophy passed, comparatively recently, through a destructive phase .... During that phase, it appeared as though demolition was the principal legitimate task of philosophy. Now most of us believe once more that philosophy has a constructive task; but, so thoroughly was the demolition accomplished, that the rebuilding is of necessity slow.
>
> **—Michael Dummett**[1]

Is a substantive theory of truth feasible? What would be the scope, structure and content of such a theory? My idea of "a substantive theory" has the everyday connotation of "a theory that provides an explanatory, constructive, and systematic account of a rich, significant, and fundamental subject-matter." "A substantive theory of truth" in this sense contrasts with "a deflationist theory of truth." Where deflationists say that "truth is entirely captured by the ... triviality ... that each proposition specifies its own condition for being true"[2], advocates of a substantive theory of truth (henceforth, *substantivists*) say that truth is not entirely captured by this triviality; where deflationists say that "the truth predicate exists solely for the sake of a certain logical need"[3] (that is, indirect reference to, and generalization over, propositions), substantivists say that it exists for other needs as well; where deflationists say that truth is not a deep notion, substantivists say it is; and where deflationists say that a theory of truth cannot be, or need not be, genuinely explanatory, substantivists say it can and should be. Substantivists accept the deflationist claim that truth is not mysterious, but they believe truth yields itself to substantive inquiry. My notion of a substantive theory of truth is close to what some call an "inflationary theory,"[4] but "substantive," in its everyday usage, better captures the ordinary, common-sense considerations that motivate me. Like Michael Dummett, I believe that philosophy should take on important "questions ... for ... understanding ... the world", and like the early Hartry Field I think that "we'd be crazy to give ... up in [philosophy] ... a methodology [of substantive theorizing] that has proved extremely fruitful in science."[5]

The attempts to construct a substantive theory of truth, however, have come upon great difficulties, and many philosophers have given up hope of ever producing such a theory. Field, for example, has renounced his plan for a substantive theory of truth (based on a causal account of reference), and today he, along with many adherents of his original plan, is an avid champion of deflationism. Not all contemporary philosophers, however, are satisfied with the prevalent trend. Donald Davidson, Michael Devitt, Anil Gupta, Michael Lynch, Hilary Putnam, Crispin Wright, and others (including me in an earlier article) have dissented, to a greater or lesser extent, from main-stream deflationism.[6]

Here I will further pursue the attempt to construct a substantive theory of truth by investigating some of the challenges facing it and offering a few ideas about how to meet them. In particular, I will connect the methodological challenges facing the theorist of truth with those facing the natural (and social) scientist. This will enable me to place the debate on truth in a new, broader perspective, and point to new ways of approaching the issues. I will concentrate on two complementary challenges: the challenge of *disunity,* and the challenge of *unity*. In the case of truth, these are the challenges of (i) recognizing the diversity, complexity and multidimensionality of truth, and (ii) uncovering its unifying principles.

The article is divided into two sections: (I) Disunity, and (II) Unity. Section I presents two disunity challenges: a radical challenge, conducive to deflationism, and a moderate challenge, compatible with a substantive theory. I argue that the radical challenge is unsound but the moderate challenge is a genuine challenge, confronting any theory of a broad and diverse subject matter. To meet this challenge, I propose a few commonsensical guidelines, and I note a few similarities and differences between my approach and that of earlier philosophers (specifically Kant, James, and Wittgenstein).

One ramification of the disunity challenge is moderate pluralism. Moderate pluralism with respect to truth has recently been advanced by Wright and Lynch. Wright, for example, raises the possibility that truth in physics is based on correspondence while truth in mathematics is based on coherence. My own analysis suggests a different kind of pluralism: pluralism within the bounds of correspondence. The idea is that truth both in physics and in mathematics is based on correspondence, but since physics and mathematics involve different aspects of language and the world, their correspondence principles differ. This kind of pluralism brings us closer to the ideal of a balanced theory: a theory balancing the demands of unity with those of diversity. Two problems for any pluralist conception of truth are: (i) In what sense are diverse principles of truth principles of the same thing, namely, truth? and (ii) How can logical inference transmit truth from sentences governed by one type of truth to sentences governed by another? Solutions to both problems are offered in section II.

Section II: The debate on unity and diversity in science sometimes gives the impression that recognition of diversity and a search for unity are incompatible. Like many philosophers, I believe that unity and diversity complement rather than exclude each other, and neither has priority over the other. Wright, too, accepts this view, but his conception of the unifying principles differs from mine. While Wright's conception is minimalistic (the unifying principles are mere "platitudes"), I believe the unifying principles can and should be substantive. Unity is linked to substantiveness through its role in explanation, and the question is not whether substantive unification is possible, but what kind(s) of substantive unifiers are available in our field. I point out two types of such unifiers, *core unifier* and *specialized unifier,* and I formulate two theses exemplifying these types of unifier, the *Immanence Thesis* and the *Logicality Thesis*. The first thesis has implications for correspondence and skepticism; the second yields a new solution to the problem of logical inference across types of truth.

1 The disunity of truth[7]

I.A. Radical Disunity Challenge. A well-known argument against the feasibility of a substantive theory of truth says that since every thought (proposition, belief, cognition, judgment, sentence of a given language) has its own unique truth condition, a general and substantive account of truth is impossible. I will call this argument "the radical disunity argument". One formulation of this argument is:

> [C]ompare 'is true' ... with a genuine target of philosophical analysis .... We know *individually* what makes ['is true'] applicable to the judgements or sentences of an understood language. 'Penguins waddle' is a sentence true, in English, if and only if penguins waddle. It is true that snow is white if and only if snow is white. The reason the first sentence deserves the predicate is that penguins waddle, and the reason why the judgement that snow is white deserves the predicate is that snow *is* white. But these reasons are entirely different. There is no single account, or even little family of accounts, in virtue of which each deserves the predicate, for deciding whether penguins waddle has nothing much in common with deciding whether snow is white. There are *as* many different things to do, to decide whether the predicate applies, as there are judgements to make. So how *can* there be a unified, common account of the "property" which these quite different decision procedures supposedly determine?[8]

The theoretical principle underlying the radical disunity argument is clearly expressed by Kant in the introduction to "Transcendental Logic" of the *Critique of Pure Reason.* Inquiring whether it is possible to go beyond a minimalist characterization (literally, name clarification) of truth as agreement of a cognition with its object and provide a criterion that determines the precise conditions under which each cognition is true, Kant reasons:

> If truth consists in the agreement of a cognition with its object, then this object must thereby be distinguished from others; for a cognition is false if it does not agree with the object to which it is related even if it contains something that could well be valid of other objects. Now a general criterion of truth would be that which was valid of all cognitions without any distinction among their objects. But it is clear that since with such a criterion one abstracts from all content of cognition (relation to its object), yet truth concerns precisely this content, it would be completely impossible and absurd to ask for a mark of the truth of this content of cognition, and thus it is clear that a sufficient and yet at the same time general sign [Kennzeichen] of truth cannot possibly be provided. Since above we have called the content of cognition its matter, one must therefore say that no general sign of the truth of the matter of cognition can be demanded, because it is self-contradictory.[9]

A somewhat different formulation of this line of reasoning appears in Kant's logic lectures:

> A universal material criterion of truth is not possible; it is even self-contradictory. For as a *universal* criterion, valid for all objects in general, it would have to abstract fully from all difference among objects, and yet at the same time, as a material criterion, it would have to deal with just this difference, in order to be able to determine whether a cognition agrees with just that object to which it is related and not just with any object in general, in which case nothing would really be said. ... [I]t is absurd to demand a universal material criterion of truth, which should abstract and at the same time not abstract from all difference among objects.[10]

The point is that a general and substantive criterion of truth would give rise to an irresoluble conflict between generality and particularity. Using 'theory of truth' for 'theory that provides a criterion of truth', we may express the radical disunity argument as follows:

(a) Truth consists in the particular agreement of a thought with its unique object.

(b) A general theory of truth must, in order to be general, abstract from the particularity of this relation.

(c) But a substantive theory of truth cannot (if it is to be substantive) abstract fromits particularity. Hence:

(d) A general and substantive theory of truth is impossible.[11]

Now, on some level, this argument is persuasive. Not only is it formally valid, but its conclusion is, in some sense, correct: It is absurd to think that the theorist of truth could come up with a general and substantive criterion (or necessary and sufficient condition) that would determine, all by itself, the truth value of each and every truth bearer. But in a deeper and more important way the radical disunity argument is unsound. The argument assumes an altogether unreasonable conception of a substantive theory of truth as consisting of, or offering, a Kantian criterion of truth. There is no reason that a theory aiming at a philosophical explanation of truth be interested in, or be required to provide, such a criterion. Achieving a genuine understanding of truth does not mean detecting all the minute differences between any distinct truths, or determining what exactly has to be done in order to find out whether such sentences as 'Penguins waddle' and 'Snow is white' are true. There is a whole array of intermediate projects between the minimalist (deflationist) project of name clarification of truth and the maximalist project of providing a Kantian criterion of truth. And a substantive theory of truth aims at (some of) the intermediate projects. A comparison with the theory of knowledge might help. No one, least of all Kant, would require a substantive theory of knowledge to provide a full and detailed criterion of knowledge - a criterion determining, all by itself, with respect to each and every judgment, whether it should be included in our corpus of knowledge. Why should the theory of truth be required to provide such a detailed criterion of truth? One might answer that truth is special: the truth of a thought *is* dependent on its specific content and object. But does not the same hold for knowledge? (Are not the knowledge conditions of 'Penguins waddle' and 'Snow is white' just as particular and just as diverse as their truth conditions?) Should we conclude, then, that a substantive theory of knowledge is also impossible?[12]

The radical disunity argument is, in my view, best interpreted as a *reductio ad absurdum* of the criterial, maximalist view of a substantive theory of truth. Substantive theories are, in general, selective; they abstract from, that is, overlook, some aspects, features and differences of objects in their domain.[13] The choice is not between a deflationist theory and a criterion of truth; the choice is between the former and a substantive account of the *major principles* and *facets* of truth.

It is not clear whether Kant himself drew a false dilemma between (what we call today) a deflationist theory and a criterion of truth. On the one hand, in introducing his argument he does appear to contrast the mere "name clarification" of truth (his conception of a deflationist theory) with a criterion of truth.[14] On the other hand, elsewhere he repeatedly affirms the existence of substantive accounts of various facets of truth and makes substantive claims about truth. For example, he declares that general logic provides a universal negative criterion of truth; he characterizes Transcendental Analytic as "a logic of truth" (saying it sets negative but not narrowly logical conditions on the possibility of truth); He claims that "transcendental truth, which precedes all empirical truth and makes it possible, consists in the general relation [of cognitions to the entirety of all possible experience]"; he suggests that an account of "the formal conditions of empirical truth" is possible; he proclaims that the principle of causality is a condition of empirical truth; he argues that the possibility of experience is a necessary condition for truth; he implies that a "sufficient mark of empirical truth" is possible; and he contends that his own theory, unlike Berkeley's, is capable of providing a "certain criterion for distinguishing truth from illusion" (in a more reasonable sense of 'criterion' than in the introduction to "Transcendental Logic").[15] Be that as it may, the dilemma raised by the radical disunity argument is a false dilemma. The radical disunity argument rejects the possibility of a substantive theory of truth by arguing against an absurd conception of such a theory.

Furthermore, the radical disunity argument assumes that the theory of truth has only one goal: account for the truth conditions of sentences (cognitions, and so forth). But the theory of truth has other goals as well: explain the normativity of truth, determine its applicability to various fields of discourse, adjudicate between different conceptions of truth (correspondence, coherence, and so forth), elucidate the relation between truth and other topics of philosophical investigation, and so on. The radical disunity argument does not question the feasibility of any of these goals.[16]

But while the radical disunity challenge is a false challenge, the tensions between generality and particularity, unity and diversity, abstraction and detailed investigation, to which it directs our attention, do pose a genuine, if not insurmountable, challenge to knowledge. This challenge was taken up by Kant (in another section of the *Critique of Pure Reason*), James, and Wittgenstein, but I prefer to approach it through a more contemporary venue - the ongoing debate on disunity in science. It seems to me that many of the issues raised in this debate pertain to substantive theories in general, and the challenge facing the theorist of truth would be better understood by a judicious comparison with the one facing the scientist.

I.B. Moderate Disunity Challenge. Challenges to substantive theories of truth may be of three kinds: (a) challenges to substantive theories *in general*, (b) challenges to substantive *philosophical* theories, and (c) challenges to substantive theories of *truth*. The moderate disunity challenge falls under the first category, and to discuss it I will turn to the literature on disunity in science.[17]

The disunity of science is commonly conceived either as a disunity of theories or as a disunity of their subject matter, namely, nature. These two types of disunity are interconnected, but the former places a greater emphasis on conceptual differences, the latter on "the disorder of things" (to borrow the title of John Dupré's book). The disunity of theories challenges the unification of science on three levels: (i) total unification (that is, construction of a "theory of everything"), (ii) intertheoretic unification (for example, reduction of psychology to biology), and (iii) intratheoretic unification (for example, elimination of the particle-wave duality in physics). The disunity of nature challenges the ability of science to systematize its subject matter. It is an open question how much order there is in nature and, as a result, whether nature can be subsumed under general laws. Now, it seems to me that both challenges can be generalized to other fields of knowledge, including philosophy with its broad, diverse, and highly complex subject matters - knowledge, ontology, meaning, and truth. Among the more general considerations raised by scientists and philosophers of science are:[18]

(1) *The complexity of the world:*

(a) The world exhibits different complexities and interdependencies on different levels, and at each level of complexity entirely new properties appear (P.W. Anderson).

(b) There are both higher and lower organizing principles, and in the course of investigation we sometimes have to add new levels of basic entities, concepts, and principles (Dupré, R.B. Laughlin and David Pines, Laughlin *et al.*).

(c) The behavior of objects and properties is sensitive to a multiplicity of factors governed by multiple principles (Dupré, Nancy Cartwright).

(2) *The limitations of our cognitive powers:*

The great complexity of the world on the one hand, and our cognitive limitations on the other, limit our ability to comprehend it by a single, unified principle or theory (Comte[19]).

(3) *The partiality of knowledge:*

Human knowledge is, by its nature, partial: (i) universal principles and explanations are, due to their high level of abstraction and idealization, inherently partial, covering certain aspects of the phenomena under discussion while leaving others uncovered; (ii) as concepts and knowledge are extended, universal principles become partial, so that what was thought, at one point, to be complete, turns out, later on, to be unfinished (Patrick Suppes, Noam Chomsky[20], Ian Hacking, Stephen Hawking[21], Laughlin and Pines).

(4) *Richness of interests, multiplicity of perspectives, human creativity*:

There are many legitimate ways of dividing things into units and many advantageous points of view on things; these, given our creativity, give rise to a multiplicity of theories, a multiplicity which enriches our understanding rather than impedes it (Jerry Fodor, Suppes, Dupré).

(5) *Other methodological considerations*:

(a) In any field of knowledge we are continuously confronted with new situations and new problems; as new problems arise, new theories and new methods of investigations are often required (Suppes, Hacking).[22]

(b) There can be many unifiers, of different interest, in any field of knowledge; hence, there may be room for more than one unifying theory (Hacking).

(c) Generality is not always a guide to a better theory. A small collection of simple principles is preferable to a single, highly complex, universal principle (Hacking).

None of these considerations has to do with the specific features of science, and all are either directly applicable or easily extendable to philosophy. In the field of truth, they have the potential of changing our perspective on existent theories, suggesting further developments, and pointing to new solutions to old problems. I will not be able to work out the details of these influences here, but a few examples might indicate the direction of change.

Consider the equivalence schema. Deflationists claim that the equivalence schema (or something like it) exhausts the topic of truth. But from the present perspective the equivalence schema describes only one, high-level, principle of truth, and as such it provides a *partial* account of truth, to be complemented by other accounts, centering on other principles of various levels of generality.

One example of a lower-level account of truth is given by Alfred Tarski's theory.[23] While the equivalence schema treats all sentences on a par, Tarski's theory distinguishes them along a given parameter - logical structure. Sentences exhibiting distinct logical structures have different Tarskian truth conditions, whereas those exhibiting the same logical structure have essentially the same truth condition. From the present perspective, Tarski's theory provides an account of a special factor of truth - the *logical factor* - and as such it is a mid- (or low-) level theory.[24] Most importantly, Tarski's theory, like the equivalence schema, offers a *partial* account of truth (logical structure is not the only thing that determines the truth value of sentences), and a "complete" account of truth must go beyond it.

One way of going beyond Tarski's theory was suggested by Field.[25] While Tarski's theory does not distinguish the truth conditions of atomic sentences in any informative manner, Field envisions an informative account of their truth conditions. The realization of Field's vision has, however, come upon great difficulties, and these are commonly attributed to a special feature of his approach, namely, its physicalistic orientation. (Field wants to base the account of atomic truth on a physicalistic theory of reference, application and fulfillment - in short, satisfaction - for our nonlogical vocabulary.) The disunity perspective points to a different explanation. The problem, from our perspective, lies in an implicit assumption of Field's project, independent of physicalism, namely, that the satisfaction conditions of the entire vocabulary of human thought (minus a small part of this vocabulary - the logical vocabulary) are based on one and the same principle, or kind of principle. From our perspective this assumption is unwarranted: the totality of extralogical expressions exhibits an enormous diversity, and one cannot take it for granted that physical and moral expressions, biological and philosophical expressions, psychological and mathematical expressions, expressions pertaining to religion and expressions pertaining to technology, are all governed by the same satisfaction principle, or the same kind of principle.

Field's reaction to the difficulties faced by his project was a retreat to deflationism. But the right lesson from our perspective is not deflationism, minimalism, or quietism. A more productive lesson is openness and flexibility in devising our methodology. The theorist of truth, like the scientist, must adjust his methodology to the peculiarities of his subject matter, and to do so effectively he should take a cue from his fellow theorists and follow such straightforward, commonsensical, and workable guidelines as:

(A) In constructing a theory of truth, do not legislate in advance the form the theory shall take. Whether the study of truth will lead to the discovery of a single, universal principle (definition, schema, necessary and sufficient condition), or to a number of partial principles, is an open question, the answer to which largely depends on features of our subject matter, that is, on things that will emerge in the course of, not prior to, investigation. The answer also depends on our resources and capacities, but they, too, cannot always be determined at the outset of inquiry.

(B) Do not think of the study of truth as focused on a single problem. Truth is a broad, complex, and diversified topic, and as such it poses a plethora of problems rather than a single problem. Today, it is common to center the study of truth on the subject of truth conditions, but although this undoubtably is a central subject, it does not exhaust, or even come close to exhausting the topic of truth. Other subjects include the normativity of truth, the role of truth in knowledge, the relation between truth and correspondence, skepticism and relativism with respect to truth, the interplay between mind and world in creating a standard of truth, and so on.

(C) In developing a theory of truth, aim at a fruitful balance between universality and particularity, similarity and diversity, abstraction and attention to detail, systematicity and applicability. Freeman Dyson's dictum that "every theory needs for its healthy growth a creative balance between unifiers and disunifiers"[26] applies not only to scientific but also to philosophical theories.

(D) Think of the development of a theory of truth as a dynamic process, in the course of which the theory is likely to expand, contract, undergo revision, change direction, stall, make leaps of progress, yield unexpected results, and so forth. The question is not whether the theory of truth *is* (atemporally or eternally) a unified or a disunified theory; the question is what steps can we take to increase its unity without sacrificing its substantiveness.

These guidelines suggest that we need not conceive the theory of truth as either a Tarski-style definition, or an equivalence-like schema, or a Kantian criterion. Tarski's characterization of truth with its emphasis on logical structure is extremely fruitful in logic, where it is incorporated in the definition of logical consequence and, through it, makes an invaluable contribution to logical semantics. But it is not clear that to understand whether, why, and how truth applies to, say, ethics we need a Tarskian definition of truth for moral discourse. A similar point applies to correspondence. Obviously, if we start with the usual paradigms of correspondence associated with simple observational statements ('Snow is white', 'Grass is green', 'The cat is on the mat'), we are likely to conclude that correspondence is out of question in ethics. But if we investigate the moral domain without prejudice, if we take it by its own measure, we open up the possibility of new insights into correspondence, insights that would liberate us from the naive, simple-minded view of true thought as a *mirror of* (or as *isomorphic to*) reality.

The disunity challenge, as a challenge to knowledge in general and/or to philosophy in particular, was discussed by a number of philosophers. To further clarify my view, I will indicate a few points of similarity and difference with the views of three of these: Kant, James, and Wittgenstein.

Kant. In "On the Regulative Use of the Ideas of Pure Reason" (first *Critique*), Kant says:

> To the logical principle of genera which postulates identity there is opposed another, namely that of **species**, which needs manifoldness and variety in things despite their

agreement under the same genus, and prescribes to the understanding that it be no less attentive to variety than to agreement. This principle (of discrimination, or of the faculty of distinguishing) severely limits the rashness of the first principle (of wit [an innate talent of the mind for comparing and assimilating things that are superficially different]); and here reason shows two interests that conflict with each other: on the one side, an interest in the **domain** (universality) in regard to genera, on the other an interest in **content** (determinacy) in respect of the manifoldness of species.

> Reason thus prepares the field for the understanding: 1. by a principle of **sameness of kind** in the manifold under higher genera, 2. by a principle of the **variety** of what is same in kind under lower species .... We can call these the principles of the **homogeneity** [and] **specification** ... of forms.
>
> The first law ... guards against excess in the manifold variety of original genera, and recommends sameness of kind; the second, on the contrary, limits in turn this inclination to unanimity, and demands that one distinguish subspecies before one turns to the individuals with one's universal concepts.[27]

Like Kant I regard the disunity problem as a problem of balance, but Kant's construal of the problem strikes me as too narrow. Kant tries to fit the disunity problem into a neat and orderly picture of our system of knowledge as a hierarchical, species–genera structure, but the tension between unity and diversity, as I see it, is more complex, intricate, and multidimensional than the species-genera picture suggests. Accordingly, I regard our system of knowledge as a polymorphic structure rather than a regular tree-structure, as envisaged by Kant.

James. In his lectures on Pragmatism, James subsumes the disunity problem under the classical puzzle of "the one and the many":

> If ... we talk in general of our intellect and its needs, we quickly see that unity is only one of them.... What our intellect really aims at is neither variety nor unity taken singly, but *totality*. In this, acquaintance with reality's diversities is as important as understanding their connexion.
>
> The ... point is to notice that the oneness and the manyness are absolutely co-ordinate here. Neither is primordial or more essential or excellent than the other.[28]

While James, too, regards the disunity problem as a problem of balance, his solution to the problem is fundamentally unbalanced. James recommends a shift toward radical pragmatism, a pragmatism that requires, at least in philosophy, rejecting the rational, the abstract, and the theoretical in favor of the experiential, the concrete, and the practical. I agree with James that balancing the demands of unity and diversity requires a certain amount of pragmatic "juggling". But I see no reason why this should conflict with rational, abstract, and theoretical reasoning. The disunity challenge is a challenge to the *design* of theories, not to theorizing itself; it necessitates the introduction of pragmatic considerations into philosophy, not the elimination of theoretical, rational, and abstract considerations from philosophy.[29]

Wittgenstein. Wittgenstein's disunity challenge is expressed in his "family resemblance" remarks. Wittgenstein objects to what I have elsewhere called "the myth of the common denominator", namely, the view that to understand a concept is to identify the common denominator of all objects falling under it, or to formulate a necessary and sufficient condition for falling under it (*op. cit.*). Many concepts, according to Wittgenstein, have no single defining characteristic (or a small set of such characteristics); instead, they exhibit "a complicated network of similarities overlapping and criss-crossing: sometimes overall similarities, sometimes similarities of detail."[30] This is the case, in particular, with concepts representing the traditional subject matters of philosophy: language, thought, number, and, significantly, truth.[31]

I share many of Wittgenstein's views: that philosophy tends to produce "network" rather than "one characteristic" concepts, that its theories face a serious disunity challenge, that its vulnerability to disunity is due to the breadth, complexity, and multidimensionality of the problems it seeks to resolve, and so forth. I also support Wittgenstein's conclusion that philosophers should increase the element of "looking" in their investigations: "Do not say: 'There *must* be something common, or they would not be called ['truths']' – but *look and see* whether there is anything common to all." "[D]o not think, but look!" (*op. cit.*, §66). Wittgenstein, however, goes too far. Like James he concludes that philosophy "may not advance any kind of theory", that it "must do away with all *explanation*" (*op. cit.*, §109)[32], and that it should abandon any aspirations to systematicity. These conclusions, I believe, are *nonsequitur.* It is an open question how much disunity there is in various branches of philosophy; whether this disunity rules out the existence of structure, hence of theory and explanation; and how resourceful philosophers will be in facing this disunity.[33] The tensions between unity and plurality, generality and particularity, abstraction and attention to detail challenge philosophy but need not stifle it. In fact, they create a fertile ground for theory construction, since what is it to construct a theory but to systematically connect elements that, prior to the construction, are disparate, varied, disorderly, and disconnected? Just as important, there is no real conflict between looking and thinking. Much of thinking is looking, and in many fields (for example, meta-logic) looking is abstract (for example, looking at a proof system to see whether it is complete). Philosophers ought to increase the element of "looking" in their methodology: carefully examine the objects of their inquiry, be open-minded and nondogmatic, aim at correctness, provide justification, be mindful of counter-evidence, and so forth. But this does not conflict with theory and explanation.

The idea that truth might be based on multiple principles suggests a *moderate pluralism* with respect to truth. The idea is that the theory of truth may profitably be constructed as a *family* of theories, rather than a single theory. Each theory in the family would investigate some area, aspect, or factor of truth, and together these theories would produce (in the ideal limit) a comprehensive account of truth. This pluralism is moderate since, on the one hand, it does not rule out the possibility that a single, exhaustive, and substantive theory of truth can, in principle, be constructed; on the other hand, it holds that such a theory (though desirable) is not a *sine qua non* for a thorough and genuine (that is, substantive) understanding of truth.

Moderate pluralism has recently been advocated by a number of philosophers, for example, Wright and Lynch.[34] Wright, like me, argues that universal principles might not exhaust the topic of truth and if they do not, they may be complemented by other, more specific, principles. But for Wright this means that different fields of discourse (physics, mathematics, ethics, the comic, and so forth) might be governed by altogether different types of truth, say, physical discourse by correspondence truth and mathematical discourse by coherence truth. This is a rather radical division, and it is important to note that pluralism may come in more moderate versions. First, the plurality of truth may lie within the bounds of a single type of truth, say, correspondence. In that case, truth in all areas of discourse would be based on correspondence, but the principles underlying correspondence in physics would differ from those underlying correspondence in, say, mathematics. (Later on I will argue that truth is in fact based on correspondence, and the potential multiplicity of principles of truth is indeed a multiplicity of correspondence principles). Second, the plurality of truth need not center on "fields" of truth; it might center on "factors" of truth. The point is that truth might be based on a multiplicity of factors, but the same factor may operate in diverse fields of truth. Thus consider the "moral" sentence 'All humans are good', and the "biological" sentence 'All humans are two-legged'. The truth values of these sentences are determined by (at least) three factors - the logical factor (which is reflected in the satisfaction conditions of the universal quantifier and the conditional), the biological or physical factor (which is reflected in the satisfaction conditions of 'is human' and 'is two-legged'), and the moral factor (which is reflected in the satisfaction conditions of 'is (morally) good'). Two of these factors are relevant to the truth value of both the moral and the biological sentence, and only one distinguishes between them. A pluralism based on factors of truth is finer and more nuanced than one based on fields of truth, yet it recognizes (and can account for) differences among truths in different areas of discourse.

Two objections to pluralist conceptions of truth naturally arise:

(1) If truth is based on multiple principles, in what sense are these principles principles of the same thing, namely, truth?

(2) If two statements are governed by different types of truth (or their truth is determined by different factors) how can logical inference transmit truth from one to the other? For example, how can a comical conclusion follow logically from a physical premise (or from a set of premises which essentially contains a physical premise)?[35]

Solutions to both problems will be offered in section II.

2 The unity of truth

II.A. Unity Challenge. The unity challenge is the challenge of finding as significant, as comprehensive, as informative, and as enlightening unities as possible. Unity, as many philosophers have pointed out, is a condition as well as a goal of knowledge. One aspect of unity, namely, its contribution to the explanatory power of theories (a major mark of substantive theories), is especially relevant to the present inquiry. The connection between unity and explanation has been emphasized by several philosophers of science (Carl Hempel, Michael Friedman, Philip Kitcher, and others[36]), and much of what they say about the role, forms, and problems of unity applies to philosophy is well: Philosophical unification, like scientific unification, may be local or global (unification of disparate elements of a single philosophical field, unification of hitherto distinct philosophical fields, unification of all fields of philosophy, and unification of philosophy with other fields of knowledge). It may center on elements of different kinds: laws and principles, theories, arguments, concepts, methods of inquiry, justification procedures, and so forth. Its goals, like those of scientific unification, may vary: decreasing the overall number of tenets and principles, creating reliable styles (patterns) of argumentation, harmoniously integrating disparate elements, and so forth. Philosophical unification may be stricter or looser: reduction versus supervenience, supervenience versus (mere) integration, hierarchical integration versus holistic integration, and so forth. Among the reductionist projects in philosophy are idealism, materialism, physicalism, logicism, the *Aufbau* project, the "linguistic turn," and extreme naturalism; all major philosophical systems and movements – rationalism, empiricism, transcendental idealism, moderate naturalism, and so on – aim at harmonious integration of some issues, principles, problems, and/or methods.

Two well-known pitfalls of scientific unification are *spurious* unification and *exclusionary* unification. Spurious unification trivially reduces multiple laws to fewer laws without gain in understanding. One example (due to Hempel and Paul Oppenheim[37]) is conjunction: unifying A and B by constructing their conjunction, A&B. In the field of truth, deflationists often define truth by an infinite list, or an infinite conjunction, of T-sentences (instances of the disquotational schema). Such a definition arguably provides a spurious unification of diverse truth conditions. Field's criticism of Tarski's theory is also one of spurious unification, directed at Tarski's list-like specification of the truth conditions of atomic sentences.

Exclusionary unification is a flaw in attitude: to think that the success of, say, string theory would leave no worthwhile scientific questions unanswered, or would rule out the usefulness of all other unifiers, is to yield to this pitfall. Disquotationalism arguably suffers from this flaw as well. It is not uncommon for a disquotationalist to say that *all* there is to truth is disquotation, meaning *all* worthwhile philosophical questions about truth are answerable by the disquotational schema, and the *only* genuine unifier of truth is this schema.

The connection between unity and explanation in science has been recently challenged by Margaret Morrison.[38] Morrison argues that the highest degree of unification is achieved by structural explanations, but the best scientific explanations are causal rather than structural. I will not get into the issue of structural versus causal explanation here. The claims that structural explanations are not the only unifying explanations, that different kinds of explanation are unifying in different ways, and that the most general explanations do not automatically impart the greatest degree of understanding, I find congenial. But the implicit suggestion that science admits only one type of effective explanation (namely, causal explanation), and the sweeping declaration that "general principles fail to be explanatory in any substantive sense" (*ibid.,* p. 33), I regard as unfounded. The latter, in fact, is refuted by Morrison herself, since many of her causal principles are in fact highly general. The search for a substantive theory, as I understand it, is first and foremost a search for explanatory unifiers, on various levels of generality.

The view that in spite of its diversity truth can be unified by general principles is supported by Wright.[39] Wright proposes a series of universal principles of truth, including:

(P1) To assert is to present as true.

(P2) Any truth-apt content has a significant negation which is likewise truth apt.

(P3) To be true is to correspond to the facts.

(P4) A statement may be justified without being true, and vice versa.[40]

My own conception of the universal principles differs from Wright's in one respect. While Wright regards the universal principles as "platitudes," and as such as minimalistic, that is, deflationist, I see no reason why the universal principles could not be substantive (informative, explanatory, and so forth). The key to a balance between unity and diversity is, in my view, not platitudiness (with its implication of triviality), but *partiality*. The universal principles are partial in the sense of not exhausting the topic of truth, that is, leaving room for other principles, on various levels of generality.[41] Below I will propose two substantive and universal principles of truth: *Immanence* and *Logicality*. The former is related to Wright's (P1) and (P3), the latter is somewhat related to his (P2).

II.B. Substantive Unifiers of Truth. 1. Two types of universal and substantive unifiers. Consider a broad and multidimensional concept, *C*, that (due to its breadth and multidimensionality) cannot be fully captured by either a single definition or a necessary-and-sufficient condition. This situation leaves open at least two possibilities for (substantive) universal unifiers of *C*: (i) a "core" unifier - a unifier that traces the roots of *C* to some general principle(s) of human thought and/or the world (without purporting to exhaust *C*), and (ii) a "specialized" unifier - a unifier centering on a particular factor of *C* (one among many) that, due to its special features, applies to all instances of *C* (or to many instances of *C* in every area to which *C* applies). Below I will delineate two universal and substantive unifiers of truth: a core unifier, *Immanence*, described by the "Immanence Thesis", and a specialized unifier, *Logicality*, described by the "Logicality Thesis."

2. Immanence Thesis. The Immanence Thesis (upper-case 'I') traces the roots of our concept of truth to three basic principles of human thought: *immanence* (lower-case 'i'), *transcendence,* and *normativity*.

A. Immanence. The immanence principle says that one basic mode of human thought is the *immanent* mode. By 'immanence' I understand something akin to, but more general than, W.V. Quine's notion of immanence.[42] Quine says that to speak immanently is to speak from within a theory, where speaking from within a theory is speaking literally and assertively, that is, declaring that a certain object or *n*-tuple of objects (mentioned in a sentence) possesses a certain property (also mentioned in it), or more generally that things are (literally) thus and so. For me, an immanent thought is not necessarily assertive or literal. A thought is immanent if it attributes some property to some object(s) or says (assertively or unassertively) that things are one way or another. In other words, any thought attachable to Frege's content stroke is immanent in my sense.

The Immanence Thesis says that truth is immanent in three ways: (i) truth is a property of immanent thoughts, (ii) the question of truth arises for all immanent thoughts, and (iii) truth statements - that is, statements of the form '*X* is true/false' (or 'It is true/false that *X*') - are immanent. Thus: (i) If truth is a property of *X*, *X* is a thought that attributes some property to some object, or says how things are. ('Snow is white', for example, of which truth is a property, is a thought - a sentence - and it attributes some property (the property of being white) to some object (the stuff snow).) (ii) If *X* is an immanent thought, the question of truth, that is, the question 'Is *X* true?', arises with respect to *X*. (The question 'Is it true?' arises with respect to 'Snow is white', 'Coal is green', and so forth.) (iii) If *X* is a truth statement (for example, the statement '"Snow is white" is true'), then *X* attributes some property (namely, the property of being true) to some object (in our example, the sentence 'Snow is white').

The range of immanent thoughts is vast and diverse: immanent thoughts may take the form of a sentence or a theory, they may be realistic or fictional, contingent or law-like, directed at objects and properties of one kind or another (physical, mathematical, philosophical, moral), syntactically simple or syntactically complex (logical compounds, modal compounds, subjunctive conditionals), and so on. The vastness, diversity, and inner complexity of the immanent domain partly explain the breadth, complexity, and diversity of our concept of truth.

B. Transcendence. The principle of transcendence is a generalization of Tarski's principle of meta-linguistic predication. This principle says that a second basic mode of human thought is the transcendent mode: We transcend a given thought, or domain of thoughts, in order to *reflect* upon it. "Transcendence" has fallen into disrepute lately. To say that truth is transcendent is (so it is claimed) tantamount to saying that we have a "God's eye view" on the world, that we have access to "things in themselves", and so forth. *Transcendence, as I use this term here, has neither of these connotations.* What I mean by 'transcending' is casting a reflective look at a thought, or at a region of thought, from a standpoint external to it, yet within the domain of (human) thought. Transcendence does not rule out immanence. On the contrary, most transcendent thoughts are immanent: they attribute properties to thoughts, draw relations between thoughts, say this is how things are with respect to thoughts.[43] The Immanence Thesis says that truth is a transcendent property of thoughts and that truth statements are (immanent) transcendent statements.

C. Normativity. The principle of normativity says that a third basic mode of human thought is the normative mode, a mode closely related to the human proclivity for critical reflection. This is how Christine Korsgaard (who studies normativity in the moral domain, but draws analogies to other domains as well) explains it:

> Normative concepts exist because human beings have normative problems. And we have normative problems because we are self-conscious rational animals, capable of reflection about what we ought to believe and do. That is why the normative question can be raised in the first place: because even when we are inclined to believe that something is right and to some extent feel ourselves moved to do it we can still *always* ask: But is this really true? And must I really do this? ... It is ... because we are normative animals who can question our experience, that normative concepts exists.... [I]t is always possible for us to call our beliefs and motives into question.[44]

In the present case, it is our disposition to question whether things are as our thoughts say they are, that leads to the concept of truth. The critical question is: 'Is it so as a given thought says it is?' and truth is a *standard* for a positive answer to this question. The question 'Is it so?' is an especially broad and basic question: it applies to any immanent thought, and is included in other critical questions (for example, critical questions concerning knowledge). The Immanence Thesis says that the concept of truth is a normative concept, and its breadth is associated with the universality of the critical question 'Is it so?' in the (vast) domain of immanent thought.

D. Immanence Thesis. Truth, according to the Immanence Thesis, lies at the juncture of three basic principles of human thought: immanence, transcendence, and normativity. Given an immanent thought, *t*, the critical, transcendent question 'Is it so as *t* says it is?' arises with respect to *t*, and truth is a standard for a positive answer to this question, a standard for *it being so as t says it is*: object *o* has the property *P*, objects $o_1,\ldots,o_n$ stand in the relation *R*, and so forth. Truth, of course, is not the only standard for immanent thoughts; other standards (associated with other critical questions) include coherence, justification, empirical verification, explanatory value, utility, and so forth. But the critical question 'Is it so?' is one of the more basic questions of human thought, and truth, therefore, is a fundamental standard of thought. A theory of truth explains this standard, specifies its principles, and works out its connections to other standards of human thought.

In developing a theory of truth it is important to recognize that the domain of Immanent thought is an ever expanding, ever changing domain. The dynamic nature of this domain is connected to our tendency to create new concepts, acquire new interests, develop new perspectives, raise new problems, revise our concepts and theories, devise new cognitive tools, and so on. One task of the theory of truth is to study how changes in the domain of immanent thought affect our concept of truth. Other tasks are to determine whether the concept of truth actually applies to a given domain of thought, how it applies to it (for example, directly or indirectly), and so forth. Expressivists, for example, argue that truth does not apply to ethics; Russell argues that truth applies to sentences containing definite descriptions indirectly, through sentences that do not contain such descriptions; physicalists argue that truth conditions for any statements must be reformulated in physicalistic terms; and so on. Much more remains to be said about the Immanence of truth and the three principles underlying it, but the main idea should be clear: Truth is a transcendent standard, or a family of standards, for immanent thoughts - a standard for a positive answer to the critical question 'Is it so?' directed at such thoughts.

The Immanence Thesis is rich in consequences. Two of its consequences concern (a) correspondence, and (b) skepticism and relativism with respect to truth.

(a) *Correspondence.* Truth, according to the Immanence Thesis, is a standard for a positive answer to the question 'Is it so, as a given immanent thought says it is?' Given the content of this question, a positive answer carries us outside the given thought into things external to it, things it is about – "the world" in a broad sense of the word. The question is whether the objects the thought is about have the properties it attributes to them or, more generally, whether the world is as it says it is. This, of course, is a correspondence question, and in this way the Immanence Thesis implies a correspondence view of truth – the view that for an immanent thought to be true there must be some positive correlation between what it says (literally or nonliterally) and how things are. But while the Immanence Thesis affirms correspondence, the view it affirms does not suffer from the rigidity, simplism, and dogmatism that correspondence views are often charged with. The reason is that, as we have seen above, the thesis is sensitive to expansions, changes, and variations in the domain of thought, both internal and transcendent, and this sensitivity protects it from commitment to an overly simplistic, one-dimensional view of correspondence.

Correspondence, from the standpoint of the Immanence Thesis, is a *research program* rather than a *dogma.* Among the questions raised by this program are: What correspondence principles govern truth in logic? Mathematics? Physics? Psychology? (or what are the logical, mathematical, physical, and psychological factors of correspondence?) What are their similarities and differences? Is there correspondence in ethics? What kind of correspondence? (Are we misled by the surface structure of ethical thoughts?) All these are open questions, and a judicious response to them requires an understanding not just of correspondence per se, but of the specific field of knowledge in which it is realized (to which its various factors belong). Below I will offer an account, or rather an outline of an account, of one type (aspect, factor) of correspondence, the *logical* one, based on prior investigations of logic.[45]

(b) *Skepticism with respect to truth.* Skepticism is often divided into two kinds: *local skepticism*, and *global skepticism*. Local skepticism with respect to truth questions the existence of a standard of truth in a specific area; global skepticism questions the existence of a standard of truth in any area. Local skeptical challenges are part and parcel of a critical approach to knowledge; global skepticism is a barrier to knowledge. The Immanence Thesis affirms the legitimacy of skepticism, leaving the success of local skepticism (in particular cases) an open question, and posing counterchallenges to global skepticism.

Skepticism is sanctioned by the same principles that sanction truth itself: immanence, transcendence, and normativity. Given a "truth thought", *t*, that is, a thought that attributes truth/falsity to some thought (or truth aptness to some domain of thought), the critical transcendent question 'Is it so?' arises with respect to *t*, and one possible answer to this question is the skeptical answer: there is no way to determine whether things are as *t* says they are; there is no standard of truth for *t*.

Local skepticism. Consider the following local skeptical statements, expressing three degrees of skepticism with respect to *moral* truth:[46]

(1) Moral statements have a standard of truth, but this standard is a standard of psychological truth, not of *sui generis* moral truth. Explanation: although the surface structure of moral statements is '*X* has moral property *Y*', their deep structure is 'Speaker *Z* has attitude *Y** toward *X*', where '*Y**' stands for a psychological attitude, mental state, or feeling correlated with *Y* (for example, 'Y' stands for 'good' and '*Y**' for 'approbation'). The standard by which the truth of moral statements is measured is, therefore, a standard of psychological truth.

(2) Moral statements have a standard of truth (either a standard of *sui generis* moral truth or a standard of some other kind of truth), but this standard is not their primary standard of success. Explanation: While moral statements do attribute properties to objects (actions, intentions, and so forth), their main goal is to express, support, or arouse feelings or attitudes. Their primary success standard is therefore a standard of persuasiveness or expressivity, not a standard of truth.

(3) Moral statements have no standard of truth whatsoever, either primary or secondary. Explanation: Moral statements are not immanent. They do not attribute any properties to any objects or purport to say how things are. They *merely* express attitudes or feelings, and expressions of feelings are not subject to a standard of truth.

The Immanence Thesis is compatible with all three degrees of moral skepticism, leaving their correctness an open question. That is, from the point of view of the Immanence Thesis it is an open question whether moral statements are literal, whether truth is their main standard of success, and whether they are immanent.

Global skepticism. Global skepticism says that there is no standard of truth for any thought whatsoever. The Immanence Thesis challenges the global skeptic to defend his view by showing either (1) that there are no immanent thoughts, or (2) that the critical transcendent question 'Is it so as *t* says it is?' does not apply to any immanent thought *t*, or (3) that there are no standards for a positive answer to this question with respect to any *t*.

These challenges are not easy to meet. All of them involve negative existential claims which, especially in philosophy, are notoriously difficult to establish. Furthermore, each of them poses a special difficulty: to meet (1) the skeptic has to show that the skeptical statement itself is not immanent, and do so without using any other immanent statement - a self-defeating task according to many philosophers, for example, Thomas Nagel.[47] To meet (2) the skeptic has to explain how the question 'Is it so?' cannot apply to a thought that says that things *are* thus and so - something that goes against both grammar and semantics. And to meet (3) the skeptic has to establish not just that a certain truth standard does not apply to any thought, but that no truth standard at all (either one that has already been considered or one that might some day be considered) does - a formidable task indeed.

While the Immanence Thesis answers the first critical question posed at the end of Section I - What makes the (potentially) diverse principles of truth principles of the same thing, namely truth? - in a traditional manner, that is, by pointing to a *core* principle underlying all truths, the Logicality Thesis offers a nontraditional answer to this question. The Logicality Thesis identifies a *highly specialized* factor of truth and shows that it is due to its specialty that it is universally applicable in the domain of truth. (Its specialty renders it so abstract that it overlooks all, or most, differences between fields of truth.)

3. Logicality Thesis. The Logicality Thesis says that one central factor of truth is *the logical factor*, a factor having to do with the role played by *logical structure* in rendering sentences true (false). The logical factor applies to truths and falsehoods in all areas of discourse and all fields of knowledge; at the same time, it is just one among a whole array of factors of truth, and its contribution to truth is specific and sharply delimited. The logical factor is, thus, an example of a factor of truth that, while substantive and universal, is partial and highly specialized - an example, in fact, of a factor whose substantiveness and universality are closely related to its partiality and specialization.

A comprehensive discussion of the logical factor in truth is beyond the scope of the present article.[48] Briefly, however, and without going into detail, my conception of the logical factor is the following:

The distinctive characteristic of the logical factor is its *formality*, which is most clearly expressed in the semantics of the logical constants. Logical constants are *formal* in the sense of *not distinguishing between objects (properties, relations) that are structurally the same,* or more precisely, not distinguishing between *argument structures* (see below) that are structurally the same. To see what this amounts to, consider three logical constants: identity ('='), the universal quantifier ('∀'), and conjunction ('&'). An argument structure for '=' is a pair, <*A*, <*b,c*>>, where *A* is a universe (that is, a nonempty set of individuals, either actual or possible) and *b,c* are individuals in *A*; an argument structure for '∀' is a pair, <*A,B*>, where *A* is as above, and *B* is a subset of *A*; and an argument structure for '&' is a pair <*A*, <*X,Y*>>, where either *A* is as above and *X,Y* are subsets of *A*, or *A* is a universe of propositions (with a truth value) and *X,Y* are members of *A*. (The former is the case when & functions as an operator on predicates (open formulas); the latter is the case when & functions as an operator on propositions.) Let us call an argument structure whose universe is a set of individuals 'an objectual argument structure' and an argument structure whose universe is a set of propositions 'a propositional argument structure'. Say that (i) two objectual argument structures for a given constant are *structurally the same* if and only if they are *isomorphic,* that is, if and only if each is obtainable from the other by a 1-1 replacement of the members of their universes[49]; (ii) two propositional argument structures for a given constant are structurally the same iff they are "*T-isomorphic*", that is, their corresponding elements have the same truth values.[50] Now, '=' does not distinguish between isomorphic argument structures in the sense that if $<A_1,<b_1,c_1>>$ and $<A_2,<b_2,c_2>>$ are isomorphic, $<b_1,c_1>$ satisfies '=' in A_1 if and only if $<b_2,c_2>$ satisfies it in A_2. '∀' does not distinguish between isomorphic argument structures in the sense that if $<A_1,B_1>$ and $<A_2,B_2>$ are isomorphic, B_1 satisfies '∀' in A_1 if and only if B_2 satisfies it in A_2. And similarly for '&'. Since formality is preserved under combinations of logical constants, logical structures in general are formal.

The formality of the logical constants explains their universality, that is, their applicability in any field of discourse. If a logical constant, *C*, applies to an argument structure $<A,\alpha>$, where *A* is a universe of objects/propositions of any type (physical, psychological, cultural, mathematical, and so forth), then it applies to any isomorphic image, $<B,\beta>$, of $<A,\alpha>$, no matter what type the objects/propositions in *B* are. That is, if *C* applies to one type of object/proposition, it applies to all types of object/proposition. Moreover, the satisfaction conditions of *C* do not change from one type of object/proposition to another; that is, if $<A,\alpha>$ is isomorphic to $<B,\beta>$, the conditions under which α satisfies *C* in *A* are exactly the same as those under which β satisfies it in *B*. In short, *C* abstracts from all (nonformal) differences between domains of objects/propositions.

Now, generally the logical factor does not determine, all by itself, the truth value of sentences, but it combines with other factors to determine their truth value. For example, the truth value of 'Wet cats are funny',[51] formulated (in order to display its logical structure) as:

(1) $(\forall x)[(\text{Wet } x \ \& \ \text{Cat } x) \supset \text{Funny } x]$,

is determined by three factors - the physical factor, *P*, reflected in the satisfaction conditions of 'Wet' and 'Cat', the comical factor, *C*, reflected in the satisfaction conditions of 'Funny', and the logical factor, *L*, reflected in the satisfaction conditions of '∀', '&', and '⊃'.[52]

While the *L*-factor plays only a partial role in determining the truth value of (1), it determines, all by itself, the truth value of

(2) $(\forall x)(\text{Cat } x \lor {\sim}\text{Cat } x)$.

And in general, the *L*-factor is the only relevant factor in the truth (falsity) of logical truths (falsehoods). When we turn to logical inferences, the *L*-factor is the only relevant factor for their *validity* but not for their *soundness*. Consider, for example, the logically valid and, let us assume, sound inference,

(I)
(1) $(\forall x)\,[(\text{Wet } x \,\&\, \text{Cat } x) \supset \text{Funny } x]$
(3) $(\exists x)\,(\text{Wet } x \,\&\, \text{Cat } x)$
———————————————
(4) $(\exists x)\,(\text{Cat } x \,\&\, \text{Funny } x)$.

The validity of (I) is guaranteed by the *L*-factor alone, but the soundness of (I) is guaranteed by the *L*-factor *together with* the *P*- and *C*-factors.

We can now answer the second critical question raised at the end of section I: How can logical inference transmit truth across fields of discourse? For example: How can logical inference transmit truth from the physical domain to the domain of the comic?.

The answer is: The logical factor plays a role in determining the truth value of sentences in all areas of discourse, including the physical and the comical, and this common role enables it to transmit truth from sentences in one area to sentences in another. More specifically:

(a) The truth value of sentences is generally determined by a multiplicity of factors, including factors that are not distinctive of the field of discourse to which these sentences belong.

(b) Due to its strong invariance property the logical factor can operate in all areas of discourse, that is, combine with all sorts of other factors in determining the truth conditions of sentences.

(c) The logical factor sets formal conditions on the truth of logically-structured sentences, and these conditions interact with other conditions, set by other factors, in determining the truth conditions of these sentences. For example, (3) is true if and only if the formal condition of nonemptiness is satisfied by the formal structure of intersection, applied to two collections of objects satisfying the physical conditions of being a cat and being wet, respectively.

(d) Due to connections between the formal elements of the truth conditions of sentences, the satisfaction of one constellation of formal conditions - that applicable to the premises of a given argument - may guarantee the satisfaction of another constellation of formal conditions - that applicable to the conclusion of this argument and, in so doing, tie the truth of the premises to that of the conclusion.

(e) In the case of (I), the logical factor guarantees that for any predicates, Φ,Ψ,Ω, and any factors, X, Y, Z, dominant in their satisfaction, the occurrence of the formal patterns

All objects which X-satisfy Φ and Y-satisfy Ψ also Z-satisfy Ω

and

Some object X-satisfies Φ and Y-satisfies Ψ

is always accompanied by occurrence of the formal pattern

Some object Y-satisfies Ψ and Z-satisfies Ω.

And it is this guarantee that enables us to infer the truth of the comic (yet logically structured) sentence (4) from the truth of the comic and physical (yet also logically structured) sentences (1) and (3).

Logical Correspondence. The Immanence Thesis implies that truth, in general, is based on correspondence. In what sense is logical truth (and logical consequence) based on correspon- dence? Our analysis suggests the following explanation: Truth has to do with how things are in the world, and things in the world have formal properties in addition to physical, comical, and other kinds of properties. The two main principles of logical correspondence are: (i) Logical constants are denoting constants: they denote formal objects (properties, relations, functions) in the sense of formality explained above. (For example, '=' denotes the identity relation in any universe, '∃' denotes the second level property of nonemptiness (of 1st-level properties) in any universe, and '&', applied to predicates, denotes the operation of intersection, or more generally Cartesian product, in any universe.) (ii) Logical truth and consequence are based on formal laws governing and connecting structures of objects, the structures of objects (properties, relations) delineated by the sentences involved.[53] We can represent the workings of logical correspondence in the logical truth (2) and the logical inference (I) by the following diagrams:

Language: *Logically True* '$(\forall x)[Cx \vee \sim Cx]$'

(2*) $\Uparrow$ $\downarrow$

World (*formal law*): *Universal* $\boldsymbol{C} \cup \overline{\boldsymbol{C}}$

Language: *True* '$(\forall x)[(Wx \& Cx) \supset Fx]$'; *True* '$(\exists x)[Wx \& Cx]$'- - -> *True* '$(\exists x)[Cx \& Fx]$'

(I*) $\downarrow$ $\downarrow$ $\Uparrow$ $\uparrow$

World (*formal law*): $\boldsymbol{W} \cap \boldsymbol{C} \subseteq \boldsymbol{F}$; *Non-empty* $\boldsymbol{W} \cap \boldsymbol{C} \rightarrow \rightarrow \rightarrow \rightarrow$ *Non-empty* $\boldsymbol{C} \cap \boldsymbol{F}$

The truth of (2) is based on correspondence in the following way: (2) is true because (a) it attributes the property of being universal to the union of the set of cats and its complement (in the given universe of discourse), and (b) the union of these sets is in fact universal (in that universe). But (2) is not simply true, it is logically true. And its logical truth is due to the fact that the correspondence responsible for its truth is of a special kind, connecting the *logical structure* of (2) with a *law* governing the *formal* behavior of the properties denoted by its predicates.

The transmission of truth in (I) - assuming the premises to be true - is based on correspondence in the following way:

(A) Materially, the transmission of truth is due to the fact that : (a) the truth of (1) guarantees that the intersection of the set of cats and the set of wet things is (in fact) included in the set of funny things; (b) the truth of (3) guarantees that the intersection of the set of cats and the set of wet things is (in fact) not empty; (c) it is a regularity (that holds in the actual world) that whenever a nonempty intersection of a set of cats and a set of wet things is included in a set of funny things, the intersection of the set of cats and the set of funny things is not empty; (d) the nonemptiness of the intersection of the set of cats and the set of funny things (materially) guarantees the truth of (4).

(B) But the transmission of truth in (I) is not just materially, but also logically guaranteed. And its logical guarantee is due to the fact that the regularity mentioned in (c) is not accidental, but an instance of a *formal law*: the law that whenever a nonempty intersection of two sets is included in a third set, the intersection of the second and third sets is not empty.

In this way that the truth of (2) and the validity of (I) are based on correspondence, not physical or comical correspondence, but logical, or formal, correspondence: a systematic connection between the logical structure of linguistic entities on the one hand and patterns of objects-possessing-properties-and-standing-in-relations that constitute formal laws on the other.[54]

3 Conclusion

In this article I have examined the prospects of a substantive theory of truth and some of its challenges. Those who deny the feasibility of such a theory tend to construe its problems as relatively narrow, that is, as problems specific to the theory of truth (or at least to philosophy). My countersuggestion is that the problems facing the theory of truth are, in the first place, general methodological problems, problems arising for any theory of a broad, complex, and multi-faceted subject matter in any field of knowledge, and that it is important to realize the universality of these problems in order to deal with them effectively.

I have concentrated on two interrelated problems facing the theorist of truth: unity and disunity. The challenge facing the theorist of truth, like that facing the scientist, is finding a fruitful balance between the unity and diversity of his subject matter - truth. That is, the theorist of truth must balance recognition of the multiplicity of principles of truth (the variety of ways truth is realized in different fields of knowledge) with a search for order, common principles, and systematic interconnections. The key to a balanced theory is, I suggested, partiality. We may think of the theory of truth as a family of theories, each investigating one central aspect or factor of truth, and all being connected by a network of unifying principles, on various levels of generality. The theory of truth, on this conception, is not a deflationist theory. Like other theories in other branches of knowledge it aims at a genuine and deep understanding of its subject matter, and this it tries to achieve by renouncing unhelpful preconceptions (for example, that of capturing the whole topic of truth by a single definition or schema) and by committing itself to an open-minded and undogmatic investigation. My approach to a substantive theory of truth involves a new, moderate version of pluralism. This pluralism subsumes all truths under the correspondence principle, but correspondence itself it construes as a network of interconnected (sub-)principles.

Turning to unity, I have emphasized the importance of unity for substantiveness (through explanation) and I distinguished two types of substantive unifiers: "core unifiers", and "specialized unifiers." The first type is exemplified by the Immanence Thesis, the second by the Logicality Thesis. The Immanence Thesis identifies a common source of our concept of truth in a combination of three basic principles of human thought: immanence, transcendence, and normativity. The Logicality Thesis identifies a special unifying factor of truth - the logical factor - a factor that, due to its unique features, partakes in the determination of truth in all areas of discourse regardless of their differences. Together, the Immanence and Logicality theses provide an answer to the two critical questions: (i) What is common to all truths? (ii) How is logical inference across diverse fields of truth possible?

Much work remains, of course, to be done. But I hope the general lessons from science, the idea of a moderate pluralism of correspondence principles, and the steps toward unraveling the substantive unifiers of truth, demonstrate (or make some progress toward demonstrating) the feasibility of a substantive philosophical theory of truth.[55]

Notes

1. *The Logical Basis of Metaphysics* (Cambridge: Harvard, 1991), p. 1.
2. Paul Horwich, *Truth* (Cambridge: Blackwell, 1990), p. xi.
3. Horwich, p. 2. (A compilation of two sentences in inverted order.)
4. See, for example, Hartry Field, "Deflationist Views of Meaning and Content," *Mind* CIII (1994): 249-84.
5. Field, "Tarski's Theory of Truth," *The Journal of Philosophy*, LXIX, 13 (July 13, 1972): 347-75, here p. 363. [This volume, Ch. 3, p. 43 – Ed.] The full sentence is: "This is a methodology that has proved extremely fruitful in science, and I think we'd be crazy to give it up in linguistics." Field treats the theory of truth as part of linguistics, but what he says is directed to whatever

discipline the theory of truth belongs to, that is, on our demarcation, philosophy. He specifically refers to reductionist theories which, he says, are pointless unless substantive. I think it is reasonable to presume that he extends this point to scientific theories in general. Note: some philosophers identify "substantive theory of truth" with "correspondence theory of truth"; I prefer to distinguish between the two. Although I will eventually advocate a substantive correspondence theory of truth, I do not want to rule out in advance the possibility of either a substantive noncorrespondence theory of truth or a nonsubstantive correspondence theory.

6. See Davidson, "The Structure and Content of Truth," *The Journal of Philosophy*, LXXXVII, 6 (June 1990): 279-328, and "The Folly of Trying to Define Truth," *The Journal of Philosophy*, XCIII, 6 (June 1996): 263-78 [This volume, Ch. 14, – Ed.]; Devitt, *Realism and Truth,* 1st/2nd edition (Cambridge: Blackwell, 1984/91); Gupta, "Minimalism," *Philosophical Perspectives*, VII (1993): 359-69, and "A Critique of Deflationism," *Philosophical Topics*, XXI, 2 (1993): 57-81; Lynch, *Truth in Context* (Cambridge: MIT, 1998); Putnam, *Reason, Truth and History* (New York: Cambridge, 1981), and *The Many Faces of Realism* (La Salle, IL: Open Court, 1987); Wright, *Truth and Objectivity* (Cambridge: Harvard, 1992), and "Truth: A Traditional Debate Reviewed," in Simon Blackburn and Keith Simmons, eds., *Truth* (New York: Oxford, 1999): 203-38; and Gila Sher, "On the Possibility of a Substantive Theory of Truth," *Synthese* CXVII (1998-99): 133-72.
7. This part of the article continues my earlier discussion of the disunity of truth in "On the Possibility of a Substantive Theory of Truth." It is, however, self-sufficient.
8. Simon Blackburn, *Spreading the Word* (New York: Oxford, 1984), p. 230. This argument may also be interpreted as an argument against the existence of a *property* of truth, but here I am interested in it as an argument against the possibility of a substantive account of truth. Blackburn, it should be noted, does not endorse this argument.
9. *Critique of Pure Reason,* 1st/2nd ed., 1781/87 (New York: Cambridge, 1998): A58-9/B83.
10. *Lectures on Logic,* "The Jäsche Logic", 1800 (New York: Cambridge, 1992), p. 558.
11. My reading of Kant's argument is different from James Van Cleve's in his *Problems from Kant* (New York: Oxford, 1999), chapter 13. Van Cleve regards Kant's argument as a version of the *diallelon,* an ancient argument which, based on circularity considerations, says that one cannot determine whether a cognition agrees with its object; one can only determine whether it agrees with another cognition of that object. While Kant's argument does appear in a section whose opening sentence mentions circularity - "The old and famous question with which the logicians were to be driven into a corner and brought to such a pass that they must either fall into a miserable circle [in the second edition, *Dialexis*; in the first, *Dialele*, that is, reasoning in a circle (editor's note)] or else confess their ignorance, hence the vanity of their entire art, is this: **What is truth?**" [A57-8/B82] - attention to the *content* of his argument shows that it makes an altogether different point from the *diallelon*. I should indicate that I agree with other aspects of Van Cleve's analysis, for example, his claim (contra Putnam and Kemp Smith) that this argument does not signal Kant's withdrawal from the correspondence view of truth.
12. Note that for a while analytic philosophers did expect the theory of knowledge to provide something akin to a full and detailed definition, namely a necessary and sufficient condition of 'x knows that P'. But this is no longer the goal of (most) current epistemologists, nor was it Kant's goal. Note, too, that the chaotic results of the search for a necessary and sufficient condition of knowledge (reflected in the incessant stream of counter- and counter-counterexamples) undermined many philosophers' confidence in the possibility of a substantive analytic epistemology.

13. One exception might be mathematics, whose objects are already abstract and incomplete (in Alexius Meinong's sense).
14. See *Critique of Pure* Reason, A58/B82.
15. See *Critique of Pure Reason*, A59-60/B83-84 and *Lectures on Logic,* 280-01, 455-56, 558-60; *Critique,* A62/B87 and A131/B170; A146/B185; A191/B236; A202/B247; A489/B517; A651/B679; and *Prolegomena to Any Future Metaphysics,* 1783 (New York: Macmillan, 1950), p. 124.
16. For further criticisms of the radical disunity argument see Wright, "Truth: A Traditional Debate Reviewed," [This volume, Ch. 16 – Ed.] and Sher.
17. See, for example, P.W. Anderson, "More Is Different," *Science*, CLXXVII (1972): 393-96; Jerry Fodor, "Special Sciences," *Synthese*, XXVIII (1974): 77-115; Patrick Suppes, "The Plurality of Science," *Philosophy of Science*, II (1978): 3-16; John Dupré, *The Disorder of Things* (Cambridge: Harvard, 1993); Ian Hacking, "The Disunities of the Sciences," in Peter Galison and David Stump, eds., *The Disunity of Science* (Stanford: University Press, 1996), pp. 37-74; Nancy Cartwright, *The Dappled World* (New York: Cambridge, 1999); R.B. Laughlin and David Pines, "The Theory of Everything," *Proceedings of the National Academy of Sciences of the USA*, XCVII (2000): 28-31; and Laughlin, *et al.*, "The Middle Way," pp. 32-37.
18. The points listed below constitute a pastiche of multiple ideas by multiple authors. At the end of each point I will indicate some of its sources. For fuller references see last footnote and the following footnotes.
19. See Hacking, pp. 38-39.
20. "Language and Interpretation: Philosophical Reflections and Empirical Inquiry" (1988), in John Earman, ed., *Inference, Explanation, and Other Frustrations* (Berkeley: California UP, 1992), pp. 99-128.
21. See Hacking, p. 54.
22. Partly a citation from Suppes, pp. 14-15.
23. "The Concept of Truth in Formalized Languages" (1933), in *Logic, Semantics, Metamathematics* (Indianapolis: Hackett, 1983), pp. 152-278.
24. For a relevant discussion of Tarski's theory see Sher, "What is Tarski's Theory of Truth?", *Topoi* 18 (2): 149–66.
25. "Tarski's Theory of Truth". [This volume, Ch. 3 – Ed.]
26. *Infinite in All Directions* (New York: Harper & Row, 1988), p. 47.
27. A654/B682 (explanation in square brackets based on editors' footnote 117, p. 749), A657-58/B685-86, A660/B688.
28. "Pragmatism" (1907), in *Pragmatism and Other Writings* (New York: Penguin, 2000), pp. 1-132. Citations from pp. 59 and 62. [See also Ch. 8 of this volume – Ed.]
29. A similar point was made by Robert Brandom with respect to Putnam's pragmatism - "Hilary Putnam: *Renewing Philosophy*", *The Journal of Philosophy*, XCI, 3 (March 1994): 140-43. It should be noted that not all interpreters view James's pragmatism as constricting in the way I described (see, for example, Yemima Ben Menachem, "Pragmatism and Revisionism: James's Conception of Truth", *International Journal of Philosophical Studies*, III (1995): 270-89). But the tendency to associate pragmatism with a negative attitude towards abstract, rational theorizing is sufficiently prevalent to make it worthwhile to point out that an adequate solution to the disunity problem does not require such an attitude.
30. Ludwig Wittgenstein, *Philosophical Investigations,* 3rd ed. (Oxford: Blackwell, 1953), §66.

31. See Juliet Floyd, "On Saying What You Really Want to Say: Wittgenstein, Gödel, and the Trisection of the Angle", in *Essays on the Development of the Foundations of Mathematics,* Jaakko Hintikka, ed. (Dordrecht: Kluwer, 1995), pp. 373-425.
32. See also §126: "Philosophy simply puts everything before us, and neither explains nor deduces anything."
33. This point was also made by G.P. Baker and P.M.S. Hacker, *Wittgenstein: Understanding and Meaning* (New York: Blackwell, 1980), p. 327.
34. Other contemporary philosophers who consider pluralism with respect to truth (or cognate subject matters) are Davidson, Dummett, Resnik, Devitt and Putnam, to name but a few. See Davidson, "Reality Without Reference," *Dialectica* XXXI (1977): 247-53; Dummett, "Realism," in *Truth and Other Enigmas* (Cambridge: Harvard, 1978), pp. 146-65; Michael Resnik, "Immanent Truth," *Mind*, XCIX (1990): 405-24; Devitt; and Putnam, "Sense, Nonsense, and the Senses: An Inquiry Into the Powers of the Human Mind," *The Journal of Philosophy*, XCI, 9 (September 1994): 445-517.
35. See, for example, Christine Tappolet, "Mixed Inferences: A Problem for Pluralism about Truth Predicates," *Analysis*, LVII (1997): 209-10, and "Truth Pluralism and Many-Valued Logics: A Reply to Beall," *Philosophical Quarterly*, L (2000): 382-85. A similar question was raised by Cora Diamond ("Unfolding Truth and Reading Wittgenstein", Manuscript, 1999) with respect to the view that truth is relative to language games.
36. Hempel, *Aspects of Scientific Explanation* (New York: Free Press, 1965) and *Philosophy of Natural Science* (Englewood Cliffs, NJ: Prentice Hall, 1966); Friedman, "Explanation and Scientific Understanding", *The Journal of Philosophy*, LXXI, 1 (January 17, 1974):5-19; and Philip Kitcher, "Explanatory Unification", *Philosophy of Science*, XLVIII (1981): 507-31, and "Explanatory Unification and the Causal Structure of the World", in Kitcher & Wesley Salmon, eds., *Scientific Explanation* (Minneapolis: Minnesota UP, 1989), pp. 410-505.
37. "Studies in the Logic of Explanation", *Philosophy of Science*, XV (1948): 98-115.
38. *Unifying Scientific Theories* (New York: Cambridge, 2000).
39. *Truth and Objectivity*, and "Truth: A Traditional Debate Reviewed." [This volume, Ch. 16 – Ed.]
40. *Truth and Objectivity*, p.34 (almost verbatim).
41. It should be noted that Wright's claim that the unifying principles are minimal is made in a particular context, namely that of showing that truth aptness does not carry a commitment to a full-fledged realism. Construing the unifying principles as minimalistic is one way of showing this. It should also be noted that Wright does not rule out the possibility of substantive unifying principles. Thus he says, concerning the assertibility platitude: "On reflection, ... [i]t is not necessary to insist that there is *no* suitable notion of deep assertoric content. It suffices that there is, at any rate, at least a more superficial one, carried by surface syntactic features; and that a minimal truth predicate is definable on any surface-assertoric discourse" - *Truth and Objectivity*, p. 29.
42. "Ontological Relativity", in *Ontological Relativity and Other Essays* (New York: Columbia, 1969), pp. 26-68.
43. For an earlier articulation of the notion of immanent transcendence, see Sher, "Is There a Place for Philosophy in Quine's Theory?" *The Journal of Philosophy*, XCVI, 10 (October 1999): 491-524, p. 523.
44. *The Sources of Normativity* (New York: Cambridge, 1996), pp. 46-49.

45. See Sher, *The Bounds of Logic* (Cambridge: MIT, 1991); "Semantics and Logic", in Shalom Lappin, ed., *Handbook of Contemporary Semantic Theory*, (Cambridge: Blackwell, 1996), pp. 509-35; "Did Tarski Commit 'Tarski's Fallacy'?" *Journal of Symbolic Logic,* LXI (1996): 653-86; "Is Logic a Theory of the Obvious?" *European Review of Philosophy,* IV (1999): 207-38; "The Formal-Structural View of Logical Consequence", *Philosophical Review,* CX (2001): 242-61; and "Logical Consequence: An Epistemic Outlook", *Monist,* LXXXV (2002): 555-79.
46. These statements are loosely based on discussions of moral expressivism in contemporary literature - see, for example, Allan Gibbard, *Wise Choices, Apt Feelings* (Cambridge: Harvard, 1990).
47. *The Last Word* (New York: Oxford, 1997).
48. For further discussion see Sher, "On the Possibility of a Substantive Theory of Truth".
49. Formally, the structures $<A,\alpha>$ and $<B,\beta>$ are isomorphic if and only if there is a bijection f from A onto B such that β is the image of α under f. For the origins of this criterion, see *The Bounds of Logic,* pp. 61-65.
50. Formally, the propositional structures $<A,\alpha>$ and $<B,\beta>$ are T-isomorphic if and only if β is the image of α some truth-preserving bijection f from A onto B (that is, a bijection f that assigns to every a in A a proposition b in B with the same truth value).
51. Tappolet, "Mixed Inferences: A Problem for Pluralism about Truth Predicates," p. 209.
52. I use 'satisfaction' here as a generic term for 'application' and 'fulfilment', which apply to predicates, including quantifiers (2nd-level predicates) and functions, respectively.
53. As I use the term 'law' here, laws contrast with accidental generalizations: a biological law holds in all biologically-possible structures of objects, a physical law holds in all physically-possible structures of objects, ..., and a formal law holds in all formally-possible structures of objects. Formal laws apply to all structures of objects, regardless of their nonformal properties.
54. For further discussion see the works mentioned in note 45.
55. I would like to thank Roberta Ballarin, Yemima Ben Menachem, Charles Parsons, Carl Posy, Oron Shagrir, Peter Sher, Mark Steiner, Cory Wright, and the participants in my recent graduate seminar on truth for very helpful comments and conversation.

Section 6 The value and normativity of truth

Editor's introduction

DOUGLAS EDWARDS

We saw in the section on pragmatism earlier that many make a connection between truth and what it is good to believe. This connects to some ideas with which we began, such as that it is good to tell the truth, and that truth is something valuable and worth striving for. In the remaining two sections of the book we will examine these ideas in more detail, aiming to discern the extent to which truth is valuable or normative, and how truth connects with other epistemic values.

Norms and values

The chapters in this section are directed at slightly different aspects of truth. Zagzebski and Lynch are interested in the value of truth – whether and how truth is a good; whereas Price is interested in the normative features of truth – how (if at all) truth functions as norm or standard for assertion. These aspects of truth are closely related, but they are slightly different. We can think of norms in terms of the rules of a game: the offside rule, for example, is a norm governing the game of football. It regulates the way that the game is played, and sets a standard for players playing the game. It also gives players of the game reasons for doing and not doing certain things in order to comply with the rule. Work on the normativity of truth is work on the issue of whether and how truth functions as a norm of belief and assertion. We can think of the process of forming beliefs or making assertions as moves in a certain conversational game, where the forming of some beliefs or the making of some assertions is justified, whereas others are not. One question is whether truth has a role in determining which beliefs or assertions are justified, and which are not. If it does, then truth has a role as a norm governing the formation of beliefs or the making of assertions. Discussion of these issues is discussion of the *norm* of truth.

Discussion of the value of truth is slightly different. To return to our football analogy, we can recognize that the offside law is a rule governing the playing of football, but we can also recognize that it is possible to discuss whether the offside law is something that is *good*. For example, some may argue that the offside law is a bad rule as it is too open to interpretation; whereas others may argue that it is a good rule as it prevents goalhanging. In other words, the recognition that something is a norm is a separate issue from whether or not that thing is good or valuable. Often there are connections between values and norms, in that norms are established in light of what we take to be valuable. In the offside case, it might be because we value fair play and defensive strategy that we establish the norm of the offside law. Likewise, it is because we value justice that we set up the norms governing free trials by jury. To return to truth, we can (if we choose) recognize that truth is a norm governing assertion and belief and still ask the question of whether truth is a good. We can also ask questions about how exactly truth is good, and what sort of value truth has, and these are questions that can be asked independently of truth's status as a norm.

Linda Zagzebski, 'Intellectual motivation and the good of truth'

Linda Zagzebski aims to examine in detail the way in which we take truth to be a good, and the sense in which we should say that our beliefs aim at the truth. She is particularly concerned with thinking about belief in terms of a cognitive act. She holds that it is useful to think of forming a belief as a form of action, and consider the values by which we evaluate such actions. Specifically, she is interested in how the value of true belief affects the way in which these cognitive acts should be carried out.

Zagzebski surveys four different ways in which true beliefs can contribute to the value of cognitive activity: as being things of consequentialist value; as being things of teleological value as natural ends; as being things of teleological value as intentional ends; and as being motives. To hold that our cognitive activities have just consequential value is to hold that we should evaluate our cognitive activities merely in terms of whether or not they yield true beliefs. A process of belief-formation on this view is good just in case it ends in true belief, and bad if it ends in falsehood. One problem with this proposal is that it sets no intrinsic limits on the kinds of behaviour that count as good cognitive activities. For example, if I guess the answer to a question and get it right, I have done just as well as you even if you got it right because you carefully studied for the question. Of course, this is an isolated case, and we may say that careful study generally leads to more true beliefs than guessing, but this is not necessarily so. There are possible scenarios where guessing is a more reliable method than careful study, and this opens up a disconnect between what we take to be responsible cognitive activity and its value. Perhaps this shows that the consequentialist value is too crude, and we need something more nuanced.

Zagzebski then considers two teleological options, the first being that true belief is a natural end, and the second being that true belief is an intentional end. True beliefs are a natural end if they are part of what is naturally good for us as creatures. Cognitive activities that get us to this end are thus good as they help us get what is naturally good for us. However, Zagzebski suggests that the idea that true belief is a natural end is in danger of collapsing into the consequentialist position: if we value certain cognitive activities because they get us what is naturally good for us (true beliefs), is this any different from valuing them for their consequences? The idea of true beliefs being an intentional end is the idea that cognitive activity is of value if it intentionally aims at true belief. This allows us to avoid the problem with the consequentialist view discussed earlier: the problem with the guesser is not that they don't get the truth, but rather that their activity is not directed towards it. Zagzebski defends this proposal from some criticisms from Sosa before suggesting that it still might not be quite right, as it requires the idea that one consciously entertains that one is aiming at the truth, and she does not think that this adequately represents the psychological features of the situation.

Zagzebski then turns to her fourth option, the idea that truth features in the evaluation of cognitive acts as part of a person's motivation. She proposes that we consider the love of truth as a motivation which prompts certain cognitive activities, and that these activities will be virtuous if they flow from this motive of loving truth. She uses compassion as an example here, holding that compassion is an aversion to the suffering of others. One can be prompted to act by this motive, as one does if one helps someone in need. Moreover, Zagzebski claims, acts motivated by compassion are better than acts that simply minimize suffering. For instance, if I accidentally drop my sandwich without noticing, and it helps a hungry person, then this act has minimized suffering, but it seems to carry less value than my giving the person my sandwich out of compassion. Correspondingly, Zagzebski thinks, cognitive acts motivated by a love of truth will be better than cognitive acts which simply get to the truth without the associated motive.

This is a striking proposal, and is one that ties seeking the truth closely with other virtues, such as integrity, courage and fairness. Someone who properly values truth is someone who acts from a motive of loving the truth, and this will stand them in good stead in cases where finding the truth is difficult, dangerous or harmful.

Lynch, 'Minimalism and the value of truth'

Michael Lynch is particularly interested in how we understand the idea that it is good to believe what is true. He aims to disentangle the various threads of this idea in the context of examining whether a deflationary view of truth, such as Horwich's minimalism, is able to account for it. Lynch begins by specifying his interest in the following principle:

(TN) Other things being equal, it is good to believe a proposition if and only if it is true.

He goes on to examine in what ways it is good to believe what's true, considering both the idea that truth is instrumentally good and the idea that truth is more than instrumentally good. Lynch argues that we should consider truth to be good in both of these senses. Not only is truth instrumentally good in that it having true beliefs helps us navigate the world around us but it is also preferable to have true beliefs rather than false ones even if there is no practical advantage to be gained in doing so. This latter claim is controversial and moves Lynch's view on the value of truth beyond the thoughts the pragmatists gave us earlier on. Pragmatists famously tie the value of a thing to its utility, and take the value of true beliefs to be connected to their usefulness. Lynch, however, takes a stronger stance here, holding that true beliefs have value in and of themselves, regardless of the potential benefits or utility they might have.

Having argued for these claims, Lynch moves on to the main focus of his chapter, which is whether deflationist views can account for these features of truth. He uses Paul Horwich's minimalist view as the central case, but also offers considerations in regard to disquotationalism in the appendix. Of particular interest to Lynch is whether the minimalist can account for the principle (TN) above. This seems to express a fact about truth, so the minimalist needs to explain it away. Lynch suggests that, given that the minimalist only has the instances of (ES)

It is true that p if and only if p

available to them, the only option that seems available is to use the instance of (ES) to change (TN) into:

(MN) Other things being equal, it is good to believe that p if and only if p.

The minimalist can then claim that the apparently truth-involving principle (TN) is explainable in terms of the non-truth-involving principle (MN), and the occurrence of truth in (TN) is only there due to the substitution using the relevant instance of (ES). However, as Lynch points out, it is important to note that Horwich cannot help himself to (MN) as a general principle. This is because, as noted in the introduction to Section 3, he cannot express general principles of this sort. At most he can have a long list of independent, yet identically structured, propositions, such as:

(MP1) Other things being equal, it is good to believe that snow is white if and only if snow is white.
(MP2) Other things being equal, it is good to believe that grass is green if and only if grass is green.
(MP3) Other things being equal, it is good to believe that roses are red if and only if roses are red.

These independent 'mini-principles' are the foundational principles for Horwich, specifying, for each proposition, the conditions under which it is good to believe it. The move from these mini-principles to (TN) exhibits the minimalist's use of the truth predicate as a device of generalization, for once we use (ES) to change

Other things being equal, it is good to believe that snow is white if and only if snow is white
to
Other things being equal, it is good to believe *that snow is white* if and only if it is true *that snow is white*

we have singular terms on both sides of the biconditional (indicated by the italicized phrases), which can be removed and replaced with a bound variable to get:

(∀x) (Other things being equal, it is good to believe *x* if and only if *x* is true)

This is the formal analogue of (TN), so it seems as though the minimalist has an explanation of (TN) which appeals to basic non-truth-involving principles, with the introduction of the truth predicate just being necessary as a device of generalization.

The debate between Lynch and Horwich subsequently turns on whether this is a satisfactory account of (TN). Lynch claims it is not, as he thinks that we cannot take the individual principles (MP1) to (MP3) to be more basic than (TN), for we need a unified explanation of why they all hold. The fact that we have a bunch of different principles with the very same form is a fact that Lynch thinks needs explaining, and the best way to explain it, he thinks, is to take (TN) as the basic general rule from which the individual principles can be derived. Horwich, on the other hand, endorses a form of particularism, where the individual principles are basic, and, if there is a general rule to be found, it is dependent on the basic principles.

Price, 'Truth as convenient friction'

In his chapter Huw Price is interested in specifying what the norm that truth provides is, and the essential role it plays in our language. He sets up his discussion as a response to those, such as Richard Rorty, who deny that there is any norm of truth at all. Rorty thinks that the only relevant norm governing assertion is that a person is justified in making the assertions they make, and that there is no role for a separate norm of truth to play. Price aims to argue against this, identifying a unique truth norm and showing how it has a distinctive role to play.

Price identifies three distinct norms of assertion: sincerity, justification and truth. The sincerity norm he characterizes as 'subjective assertibility' as follows:

> A speaker is incorrect to assert that p if she does not believe that p; to assert that p in these circumstances provides *prima facie* grounds for censure, or disapprobation.

This norm essentially tells us not to assert what we do not believe, hence the connection to sincerity. If one says something they do not believe, then they are liable to censure as a result.

The second norm concerns not whether a person believes the thing that they assert, but instead whether they have appropriate reason to assert the thing they do. Price calls this the norm of 'warranted assertibility':

> A speaker is incorrect to assert that p if she does not have adequate (personal) grounds for believing that p; to assert that p in these circumstances provides *prima facie* reasons for censure.

This norm counsels us to make sure that we have adequate reason to assert the things that we do. For example, if I tell you that the bus comes at 4.50pm but have not checked the timetable, then I have violated this norm of assertion. It does not matter if I am being sincere – perhaps I believe this to be the case because of a dream I had about catching the bus – my failure to have proper reasons to make my assertion render me in violation of the norm.

These two norms of subjective assertibility and warranted assertibility evidently play large roles in how we communicate with others. We can all recognize times when we have violated one or other of these norms, and probably suffered some sort of negative consequence as a result. The key issue for Price is whether a third norm – a truth norm – is needed in addition to these two norms. To examine this Price imagines a community of speakers, which he calls the 'Mo'ans', so-called because their speech acts are limited to 'merely-opinionated assertions' ('MOA'). MOA are speech acts governed just by these two norms discussed above. I must make sure to assert what I believe, and that I have reason to assert what I do, but that is all: if I have done both of these things then I am beyond reproach. It is important to note that if two Mo'ans disagree on an issue, then the only grounds for resolving their disagreement are violations of the two norms above. For example, think about a debate about climate change in the Mo'an community. Consider a case where A asserts that climate change is real, and B asserts that climate change is not real. A asserts what she believes, and has reason for doing so: she has read the views of a number of scientists. B also asserts what she believes, and has reason for doing so: she has read extensively on the history of the Earth's geological features. In the Mo'an community there is no apparent way to resolve this disagreement, as both sides – by stipulation – have satisfied both norms of assertion.

Price considers this community and holds that, whatever its merits may be, it is not an accurate description of our community. In our speech community, according to Price, we do not just let such disagreements lie, we hold that there *is* some further norm by which to adjudicate this dispute, namely, *the truth*. We do not simply let such disagreements rest, we are determined to find out who is really correct; whose view is true, and whose is false. Price holds that this is initial evidence to think that there is a third norm – a truth norm – governing our assertoric practice, which he expresses as:

> If not-p, then it is *incorrect* to assert that p; if not-p, there are *prima facie* grounds for censure of an assertion that p.

Due to the differences between our linguistic practice and the Mo'an linguistic practice, Price holds that we have reason to think that we do treat truth as if it supplies a norm of assertion. Price then considers what this means about truth itself. In his discussion of the Mo'ans he allows that there be a truth predicate that performs the sort of functions deflationists think the truth predicate performs, as this is not substantial enough to provide a norm of truth. If this is correct, then the identification of the truth norm seems to give reason to think that there is an aspect of truth that deflationism cannot account for (readers are encouraged to compare Price's argument here with Wright's inflationary argument against deflationism in Chapter 16). Price also rejects the idea that this norm of truth can be supplied by the Peircean idea that truth is what would be believed at the end of inquiry. This may suggest an inevitable path to some form of the correspondence theory of truth, but towards the end of the paper Price floats an intriguing alternative: that we do not need to consider *truth* itself to supply this norm; rather all that we need is to treat truth *as if* it supplies such a norm. This suggests a 'fictionalist' account of truth, which is quite unlike any other view available. It suggests that truth is a fiction, a creation, which nevertheless does an essential job which requires us to treat it as if it is not something fictitious.

Catherine Elgin, 'True enough'

We have seen that many philosophers take truth to be something of value. We should aim to have true beliefs as we navigate the world around us, and we should expect our scientific theories to aim at truth: the best theories are the true theories. In her chapter Catherine Elgin examines this idea carefully, exploring the idea that many scientific theories are not true, and do not aim to be true at all. Rather, what we expect from a good theory is an ability to make a phenomenon intelligible and understandable. Elgin examines many such successful theories and suggests that they are not actually true at all, rather they are useful fictions. For instance, consider the model of an atom that we are all familiar with, with coloured balls on wires representing the various component particles. This enables us to understand what an atom is, and how it is structured. However, strictly speaking, as a model of an atom it is a poor representation, and should be considered a false account of what an atom is. It is not *completely* misguided, of course, and bears closer resemblance to what it aims to represent than it does to a horse, for example, but it is not an exact representation of an atom. Perhaps this means that we should reject these models on the grounds that they are not true models of atoms, but Elgin thinks that this would be to essentially abandon all scientific theories. Scientific theories are often not exactly true, and they often involve useful fictions which make certain complex things intelligible where they would not otherwise be. We can, and should, of course, note where the useful fiction begins and ends, and how exactly its aspects connect to the way things really are, but this does not affect the essential role that the fiction plays in helping someone to understand a key idea.

If Elgin is right, then it suggests that there are cases where, strictly speaking, *truth* is not the only value in play. What also matters is *understanding*, and if there are cases where the strict truth is an obstacle to understanding, then the value of understanding may trump the value of truth. Indeed, Elgin thinks that this is exactly what happens in many areas where complex ideas are in need of clear and competent explanation. One key question for Elgin is whether this picture retains a need for the value of truth at all. If understanding matters more than truth, then perhaps theories need not be hostage to the truth at all, and we should just look to give the clearest and most accessible theories, without concerning ourselves with whether they are true. Elgin is sensitive to this concern, and aims to develop a framework in which the value of truth is retained to avoid a complete disregard for the value of truth.

Further reading

The issue of whether and how truth is a norm of belief has received much attention in recent work. See Glüer and Wikforss (2016) for an overview, and particular attention has been given to Bykvist and Hattiangadi (2013), Engel (2001), Gibbard (2005), Shah (2003) and Wedgwood (2002). In terms of issues concerning the value of truth, extensive treatments are given in Lynch (2004) and Williams (2002). On the issue of whether deflationism can respond to the concerns expressed by Lynch and Price in Ch. 20 and Ch. 21, see Horwich (2010, 2013), this volume Ch. 10, and McGrath (2003). See also the articles by, Davidson (Ch. 14) and Wright (Ch. 16) in this volume. In terms of introductory volumes on truth, discussion of the value and normativity of truth can be found in Wrenn (2015, Ch. 3). Further discussion of the issue of the value of understanding can be found in Kvanvig (2003), Elgin (1996) and Brogaard (2007). The issue of whether understanding is more valuable than knowing is taken up in the context of technological developments in Lynch (2016).

References

Brogaard, B. 2007. Can Virtue Reliabilism Explain the Value of Knowledge? *Canadian Journal of Philosophy* 36: 335–54.

Bykvist, K. and Hattiangadi, A. 2013. Belief, Truth, and Blindspots. In T. Chan (ed.), *The Aim of Belief*, Oxford: Oxford University Press, 100–22.

Elgin, C. 1996. *Considered Judgement*. Princeton: Princeton University Press.

Engel, P. 2001. Is Truth a Norm? In P. Kotatko, P. Pagin and G. Segal (eds), *Interpreting Davidson*. Stanford: CSLI Publications.

Gibbard, A. 2005. Truth and Correct Belief. *Philosophical Issues* 15 (1): 338–50.

Glüer, K. and Wikforss, Å. Spring 2016 Edition. The Normativity of Meaning and Content. In Edward N. Zalta (ed.), *The Stanford Encyclopedia of Philosophy*, URL = http://plato.stanford.edu/archives/spr2016/entries/meaning-normativity/

Horwich, P. 2010. The Value of Truth. In his *Truth-Meaning-Reality*. Oxford: Oxford University Press.

Horwich, P. 2013. Belief-Truth Norms. In T. Chan (ed.), *The Aim of Belief*. Oxford: Oxford University Press, 17–31.

Kvanvig, J. 2003. *The Value of Knowledge and the Pursuit of Understanding*. Cambridge: Cambridge University Press.

Lynch, M. P. 2004. *True to Life*. Cambridge: MIT Press.

Lynch, M. P. 2016. *The Internet of Us: Knowing More and Understanding Less in the Age of Big Data*. New York: W.W. Norton & Company.

McGrath, M. 2003. Deflationism and the Normativity of Truth. *Philosophical Studies* 112 (Issue 1): 47–67.

Shah, N. 2003. How Truth Governs Belief. *The Philosophical Review* 112: 447–82.

Wedgwood, R. 2002. The Aim of Belief. *Philosophical Perspectives* 16: 276–97.

Williams, B. 2002. *Truth and Truthfulness*. Princeton: Princeton University Press.

Wrenn, C. 2015. *Truth*. Princeton: Polity Press.

19 Intellectual motivation and the good of truth

LINDA ZAGZEBSKI

1 Introduction

According to the medieval doctrine of the Transcendentals there is a fundamental unity between the good and the true. We still think of truth as good, but we use the concept of truth differently than our predecessors did. To us truth is not a property of a belief. At best, it is a property of the object of belief—a proposition. In a deflationary theory truth does not even get the status of a property at all. Either way, truth is not a form of good. A true proposition is not like a good person or a good state of affairs. It is not even like a good thief since a true proposition is not better *as* a proposition than a false one. So when we speak of the good of true belief, we do not mean that truth is a good property for something to have. What we mean is that the relation that obtains between the believer and the proposition believed in a case of true belief is a good one. We can put the point another way without mentioning truth at all: roughly, what is good about a true belief is that the mind fits reality. Slightly less roughly, the agent's propositional representation of reality is accurate. Not all mental representations are propositional in form and not all representations aim to be accurate. Believing aims at accurately representing some part of reality propositionally.[1] When a belief is true it *is* accurate.[2]

To the medieval philosophers truth was identified as the property a *judgment* has when it is accurate; it is not a property of a proposition. So if accuracy in one's intentional aim is a form of good, they were right to speak of truth as a good. We continue to speak of the value of truth because of this history, but even though we are right to think that beliefs are good when they have true objects, the goodness of a true belief is not in the truth. The thing we think is good—the state of belief—is not true. The thing that is true—the proposition—is not good. But as long as we are clear about this distinction, I doubt that there is anything wrong with speaking about the good of truth.

We have made another change in traditional terminology that hopefully does not unduly complicate the issue of the value of true belief. Our category of belief is broader than the medieval category of judgement. When we speak of true beliefs we usually include dispositional states as well as judgements, where a judgement is a mental act but a belief may not be. True beliefs include dispositions to have accurate propositional representations, where being accurate is the aim of the representation. A true belief is therefore good because it is successful in its representational aim or is a disposition to be successful.

One part of the world we represent is ourselves representing the world. We represent ourselves representing accurately or inaccurately. We are therefore able to ask about the truth of our beliefs at the second order level while simultaneously believing them at the first. Beliefs aim at truth just because they are beliefs, but our ability to represent ourselves having false beliefs makes it possible for us to raise the question of whether our beliefs are true and hence good. We would not have an idea of good and bad believing if we did not have the second order capacity to represent ourselves representing and to think that we could do it accurately or inaccurately. Nor would we have the idea of knowledge, which is the form of good believing that has most captivated the imaginations of Western philosophers since Plato. Nor would there be an issue of responsibility for beliefs which, like responsibility for acts, requires the ability to examine our beliefs as objects. To have a belief is to think it is true; otherwise it would not be a belief. But even though we think every one of our beliefs is true, it can still be the case that we should not have thought so and we are quite capable of wondering if we should think so even while thinking so. We wouldn't be responsible for our beliefs if we couldn't wonder in this way.

The situation is similar but not identical in the evaluation of our acts. Aquinas thought that we always do an act 'under the aspect of good'.[3] But thinking that our acts are good does not in itself relieve us of responsibility if they are not good. We are responsible for our acts because we can reflect upon them. Similarly, when we have a belief we *ipso facto* think the belief is true, but it does not follow that we have no responsibility for believing what is true. Even while having a belief and thereby thinking it is true, we can, and sometimes should, ask ourselves whether it is true. Our responsibility for that portion of our cognitive activity that leads to belief arises out of the fact that we have this ability.

Our responsibility for our belief states suggests that there is a parallel between beliefs and acts. The degree to which beliefs *are* acts is an important issue in the philosophy of the mind and I do not insist that beliefs are literally acts. Nonetheless, I think it aids our understanding of the evaluative status of beliefs to see them as at least analogous to acts. As I mentioned, we tend to include dispositions in the category of beliefs, in which case beliefs ought to be considered acts and dispositions to perform acts of a cognitive nature. The focus of this chapter is on the evaluation of such acts and the cognitive activity that generates them. In particular, I am interested in the kind of evaluation that can function as useful advice in the way we conduct ourselves cognitively.[4] Since cognitive acts of this kind aim at true belief and since true belief is good, the good of true belief is bound to play a significant role in the evaluation of cognitive acts. Similarly, the production of good states of affairs is the aim of much of our overt activity. But since there are many ways in which the good of acts is related to the good of the outcomes of acts, there are also many ways in which the good of acts of belief can be related to the good of true belief. In the next four sections I will discuss four ways in which the value of cognitive acts can be related to the value of true belief. I will raise the issue of knowledge briefly when we get to section VI, but it is not the primary focus of this chapter.

2 Consequentialist value

One way our cognitive activity could be evaluated is in terms of its consequences. We could take accuracy of propositional representations, or to return to the terminology of truth, true belief to be the basic epistemic good and false belief the basic epistemic bad. We could then say that cognitive activity is good just in case it is successful in its aim of reaching truth and avoiding falsehood. This is parallel to the evaluation of acts in consequentialist moral theories, in particular, hedonistic utilitarianism. Mill acknowledges that hedonist value is more complex than it appears, however, because pursuing pleasure and avoiding pain are different strategies. Mill does not find this problematic, but concludes that there are two kinds of happy lives:

> The main constituents of a satisfied life appear to be two, either of which is often found sufficient for the purpose: tranquillity and excitement. With much tranquillity, many find that they can be content with very little pleasure: with much excitement, many can reconcile themselves to a considerable quantity of pain.[5]

There is an epistemic parallel to Mill's tranquil life and exciting life, as William James pointed out.[6] A person who successfully avoids false beliefs may be content with few true beliefs, whereas with many true beliefs she may be able to reconcile herself to a number of false ones.

Simple reliabilism is epistemic consequentialism. Reliabilists say we want to maximize the ratio of true to false beliefs, but we also want lots of the former. One problem with this approach is that it is not at all obvious how we are to weigh the two values against each other. Is 85 per cent accuracy with many beliefs better or worse than 87 per cent accuracy with somewhat fewer beliefs? We could, I suppose, say that a preference for safety from falsehood over acquiring truth is just a matter of personal taste and epistemic temperament. Perhaps, like Mill, we could just agree that it doesn't matter. If Mill is right that there are two kinds of happy lives, perhaps there are two kinds of epistemically happy lives too—two ways of being epistemically good. Could we get away with the epistemic position parallel to Mill's—that quantity and a high accuracy ratio are both ways of being epistemically good and favouring one over the other is up to the individual?

It seems to me that in spite of any virtues that position may have in ethics, its epistemic parallel makes epistemic value too much a matter of personal preference. Any set of beliefs that either includes a lot of true beliefs or has a 'high' ratio of true to false beliefs would count as good, and we would be forced to permit an enormous range of variation in recognition of the two values. Epistemologists rarely have been so tolerant. Assuming we are right to find this unacceptable, we need a procedure to adjudicate the two. I will leave that question for others to investigate.

In spite of these difficulties, I think it is tendentious to deny that consequentialist value is a value. The real issue is whether it is the most important or the most interesting value and, as in debates over ethical consequentialism, we need to look at cases of epistemic value conflict to test that. I will mention two.

First, there is the problem that on the consequentialist/reliabilist approach no substantive activity is automatically evaluated positively, whether it be weighing evidence, following established logical procedures, or trusting that most authorities in one's epistemic community are reliable until proven otherwise. It is an empirical question whether any of these activities leads to truth and away from falsehood or furthers the goals of inquiry. None of these behaviours is epistemically valuable unless it is reliable, and it is valuable only because it is reliable. (Elsewhere I call this the alignment problem.[7]) Some utilitarians worry about the parallel problem in ethics and some do not. Is it good to be a kind and generous person? Shouldn't we know that it is in advance of looking at the evidence for the consequences of such behaviour? But a committed utilitarian will be unmoved by this difficulty. One can always remain a consistent utilitarian if one is willing to make some adjustments—sometimes rather serious—in prior intuitions about what is good and bad behaviour, and it is possible to be a consistent reliabilist in the same way. Some people are willing to let it be an open question whether kind behaviour is a good thing. And for the same reason, they can let it be an open question whether it is a good thing to weigh evidence, or be intellectually fair, impartial, thorough, and careful.

A related problem is that what happens and what we try to make happen can come apart on the consequentialist approach. A conscious aim for the good does not necessarily have good consequences; in fact, it has sometimes been suggested that better consequences result from a different aim. As Sidgwick says, 'Happiness is likely to be better attained if the extent to which we set ourselves consciously to aim at it be carefully restricted.'[8] This is another test of how consequentialist a theorist really is. We can evaluate a person's intentions either by the value of their consequences, or by the value of the ends at which she aims. Suppose the epistemic position parallel to Sidgwick's is right—that we are more likely to get true beliefs if we do not consciously aim at truth. What if aiming at falsehood is more truth-conducive than aiming at truth? Here is another way in which maintaining consequentialism consistently comes with a price. If we cannot assume in advance a connection between aiming for truth and getting truth, then reliabilism does not give us any epistemic advice, and so reliabilism does not help us with the kind of evaluation pertinent to our responsibility to have true beliefs whether or not it is a good theory of knowledge. As long as it is an open question whether anything in particular is reliable, the advice can't be to be reliable. It is to do what we independently find out is reliable. So if the reliabilist approach is to be helpful, we need a reason to think there is a connection between reliability and trying to get the truth. Hopefully, there *is* such a connection, as John Greco has argued,[9] but then the latter is doing the work. This leads us away from consequentialism to another way in which the value of cognitive activity can be related to true belief: the teleological approach.

3 Teleological value 1: Natural ends

Instead of evaluating our cognitive activity by the extent to which true belief is a consequence, we could evaluate it in terms of whether true belief is its end. True belief can be a teleological value rather than a consequentialist one. That in turn could mean either a natural end or an intentional end—that is, what we move towards by nature, or what we consciously aim at. An end in either sense and a consequence are not the same thing.

Let us start with the first sense of 'end'—a natural end rather than an intentional aim. Could the value of true belief contribute to the value of cognitive activity as the natural end of that activity? Perhaps we can tell an Aristotelian story supporting this approach. (I do not mean a story from Aristotelian epistemology; I mean Aristotelian ethics.) The shortest version of the story would be something like this: having true beliefs is part of one's natural end, living a life of *eudaimonia*. Good cognitive activity contributes to the natural end of human life in the same way as good moral activity.

Now I have no interest in arguing that this approach won't work. In fact, I hope it does. In spite of the problems with natural teleology, it is hard to deny the sensibleness of the basic value idea of natural teleology, namely, that some things are *good for* us, and they're good for us just because we are the kinds of beings that we are and the world is the way it is.

We have already seen that truth is the intentional object of the state of belief and there is a sense in which we call that end good; it is a natural good in that it is the aim of belief. Of course, that is not sufficient to show that true belief is good *for* us. Nevertheless, it *is* reasonable to think that true beliefs are (in general) good for us. If so, it seems reasonable to evaluate cognitive activity according to how well it gets us what is good for us: true belief. Such activity would then be good for us in a derivative sense—like nutritious food and sufficient sleep. But this threatens to collapse into the first position, the consequentialist one. Is the value of cognitive activity anything over and above its tendency to have a good consequence, something that is good for us in a non-derivative sense? Presumably, Aristotle thought that moral and intellectual virtues are constituents of *eudaimonia*, and since *eudaimonia* is an active state, it includes components of morally and intellectually virtuous acts. So acts of intellectually virtuous true belief may be components of *eudaimonia* in roughly the same way morally virtuous and successful acts are components of *eudaimonia*. But this raises questions about the need for the success component. *Eudaimonia* no doubt includes lots of virtuous acts, both moral and intellectual, but there is no reason to think it is limited to virtuous acts that are successful in their ends—truth in the case of believing, many other ends in the case of moral acts. Do acts of intellectually virtuous true believing have a special place in a life of *eudaimonia*? The intellectually virtuous contemplation of truth does seem to be the central part of the good life as Aristotle describes it in Book X of the *Nicomachean Ethics*, but since the contemporary model of cognitive activity is inquiry rather than contemplation, this approach would probably have to be modified in many ways to fit it comfortably into contemporary discourse. I think, then, that this route has promise, but it is complicated. Let me move on.

4 Teleological value 2: Intentional ends

The second sense in which true belief can be an end of cognitive activity is as an intentional aim. If true belief is good, whether good as a final end or as a means to some other good, cognitive activity might derive value from being intentionally aimed at true belief. This is different from the consequentialist approach for the same reason that evaluating an act according to whether it aims at utility is different from evaluating an act according to whether it leads to utility. It differs from the first teleological approach in that it does not appeal to natural ends or what is good for us. Note that on this approach true belief can either be instrumentally good or good as a final end.

There is reason to think that we do evaluate positively acts that intentionally aim at goods, including the good of true belief. We commend people who make others happy, and we also commend people who try to make others happy. We praise even more the people who do both. And we praise the most people who make others happy in part because they try to do so. It is the same with the value of true belief. We commend people who have true beliefs, and we also commend people who try to have true beliefs. We praise even more people who do both, those who both have true beliefs and try to do so. Most of all we praise people who not only have true beliefs and try to do so, but who have true beliefs in part *because* they try to do so. This is something I've argued before.[10]

Ernest Sosa has recently made some critical comments about aiming for the truth 'as such'.[11] Aiming for the truth as such is not the same as aiming at the truth for its own sake (as a final end), and I think he is right about that. Sosa explains the distinction as follows. Someone could want the truth as such even though she wants it as a means to some other end. For example, Sosa says he may want to open a door as such even though he wants to open it in order to enter a certain room. To do that he may want a key with a certain shape, but he does not want a key with that shape as such. What he wants as such is to open that door. Similarly, he may want to know the number of the winning lottery ticket as such even though knowing that is not something he wants for its own sake, but rather as a means to the end of winning the big money. Now I find Sosa's terminology confusing because he takes himself to be objecting to the idea that getting truth should be an epistemic *motive*, whereas it seems to me that the actual object of his criticism is the view that getting true belief should be an intentional aim. I will therefore take Sosa's objections to apply to the approach of this section and will address the value of motives in the next section.

Could cognitive acts get value from aiming at truth as such? One way the aim of truth could govern our belief-forming activities would be that we resolve to act on a maxim to believe *p* just in case *p* is true. But Sosa objects that if we are in a position to apply the maxim, then we already believe *p*. Such a maxim is useless. We might instead try to adopt a maxim to use practices that are truth-conducive, but that gets us into a vicious regress because we are led into a hierarchy of practices each of which is adopted because of a prior belief that propositions of sort *F* are likely to be true. So if it makes sense intentionally to aim at true beliefs in one's cognitive activity, it cannot be by adopting one of these maxims. I agree with Sosa about that.

Nonetheless, as we saw in the first section, our ability to reflect about the truth of our beliefs at the second order level makes it possible for us to consider the issue of whether our beliefs are true even while believing them. I suggested that one of the reasons we ought to reflect about our beliefs is that we have responsibility for them and for the cognitive activity that leads to them. There are many kinds of responsibility and they have different functions in our ethical practices, but one of the ways in which responsibility for our beliefs arises is from our responsibility to others to be accurate informants. Given the plausible assumption that human beings are naturally garrulous and that we often reveal our beliefs involuntarily, we cannot be accurate informants unless we have mostly true beliefs. Hence, we have a responsibility to others to have accurate beliefs. Assuming that the kind of evaluation relevant to our responsibility for our beliefs is something we can take as advice, something we can act upon, it follows that there must be something we are able to do consciously, i.e. advice we can follow, to satisfy our responsibility to others to have true beliefs. Clearly, the advice 'Have true beliefs' is no advice at all, but the advice 'Try to have true beliefs' is something many of us think we can follow and, vague as it is, it captures the essence of our epistemic responsibility to others. But since Sosa is right that we cannot do that by following the practical syllogisms he describes, we must be able to do it in some other way.[12]

Sosa proposes a case that we can use to test the suggestion of this section that cognitive activity gets extra value from having truth as an intentional end. He asks us to consider his belief that his parents cared for him. It is possible that his desire that the belief be true disposes him to discount or ignore evidence that his parents did not care for him. But since there is no such evidence, his non-virtuous disposition is never engaged. He believes that they cared for him because he has plenty of evidence that they did. Sosa wants to say two things about this case: (1) his belief has epistemic value, even the kind that gives him knowledge (although knowledge is not my topic in this section); (2) he does not believe in a way that aims at truth as such since he might still have believed it had it been false. But it seems to me that Sosa's description of the case is not one in which he does not believe with the aim of getting truth as such; rather, it is a case that shows that aiming to get truth and aiming to avoid falsehood are not the same thing, as James showed us. Let me illustrate with a different example.

Here's what it would be like not to aim at truth as such: suppose I need to buy a new bathroom scale and I announce to my friends that I want to buy a scale that says I have lost 5 lbs. Why do they laugh? Because if we assume that it is reasonable for me to want to lose 5 lbs, then I should want a scale that indicates I have lost the weight because I *have* lost the weight. But if I simply want a scale that says I have lost 5 lbs, I do not want the truth of the belief as such. I want the pleasure of the belief rather than the truth of the matter, and that is silly. But if the scale indicates I have lost the weight, the belief that I have is probably true, assuming most new scales are reasonably accurate, so I probably wouldn't be able to get the belief unless it was true. But I do not want the truth as such because I want a true belief only in so far as such a belief is one I enjoy having. I don't really care about accuracy. What I care about is the enjoyment of having the belief. I want the belief qua enjoyable, not qua true. This is like Sosa's example of wanting a key with a certain shape as one that opens a certain door. He wants the key qua key that opens that door, not qua key with the shape that it has. He doesn't really care that the key has that shape, and I don't really care that my belief is true. But a key with that shape is the one he wants (one that opens the door), and a true belief is the one I want (one I enjoy having).

Now let us return to Sosa's belief that his parents loved him. As he describes the case, it seems to me that he *does* care if it's true, and he does aim at having a true belief as such. It's not that he wants to enjoy having the belief. But he is much more motivated to believe accurately if the belief is true than if it's false. And the same situation could apply to my believing that I've lost 5 lbs. Let's suppose now that I *do* want to know if I've lost 5 lbs—that is, if I've lost the weight, I want to know it. But maybe I do not want to know if I have not lost weight, and I especially do not want to know if I have gained 5 lbs instead. But that does not mean that if I want to know the truth when I've lost 5 lbs I am not motivated by the aim of getting that true belief as such. After all, I do not want to miss the fact that I've lost 5 lbs if I have, and I want that *as such*. It is like wanting there to be a God, and wanting not to miss finding out if there is one, but being much less motivated to find out if there isn't one. So it seems to me that Sosa and I *are* aiming to get at the truth as such in these cases, even though we're much less motivated to get at the truth as such if the negations of our beliefs are true instead. Now we may be epistemically criticizable, of course, but I don't see that either of us can be criticized on the grounds that we are not aiming at truth as such.[13]

The moral is that valuing truly believing some proposition *p* as such is compatible with not putting equal value on truly believing *not p* should *not p* be true instead. And it is compatible with not putting equal disvalue on falsely believing *p*. So I may not disvalue falsehood to the same extent that I value truth about some proposition, but James already alerted us to that possibility. It is rather common to value believing truths about matters of concern to us more than believing their negations should the negations be true, but that does not mean that we do not aim at the truth as such. It just means that we do not value the truth as such and disvalue falsehood as such across the board. Very little of what we value is across the board anyway.

So I can aim for truth as such in my belief formation, although Sosa is right that we cannot form our beliefs as the result of a practical syllogism the major premise of which is either 'Believe what is true' or 'Adopt belief-forming practices that are truth-conducive'. It is highly doubtful that I follow any such syllogism, even implicitly, but this should not be too surprising when we consider that many things at which we aim do not typically appear as a major premise in a practical syllogism, for example, our own happiness. Like true belief, happiness is an aim we have for ourselves. But for the most part, I doubt that we follow a practical syllogism: (1) Be happy. (2) X leads to happiness. (3) Do X. I seriously doubt that we use any such syllogism for most of what we do, even implicitly. But that does not mean that we do not have the intentional end of being happy. More importantly, valuing happiness and truth typically operate in our psychology not as ends in any sense, but as motives. Let us turn, then, to the fourth way in which the value of true belief can contribute to the value of cognitive activity—as a motive.

5 The value of motives

Motives and ends are not the same thing. A motive is not the same thing as the intention to bring about a certain end. More than one motive can have the same end and the same motive can aim at different ends. For example, the end of giving someone a gift could be variously motivated by love, pity, or gratitude. And a motive such as love can cause an agent to aim at different ends, even at the same time. I take a motive to be a certain kind of psychic state in the agent that causes her to act and which can explain or make intelligible the acts it motivates. An end, in the sense discussed in the last section, is a state of affairs the agent tries to bring about through her act. A desire or intention to bring about an end is a psychic state, and these states are commonly associated with particular motives, but neither one is identical with a motive; a motive is not even the same kind of state as either a desire or an intention to bring about a certain end. Nonetheless, knowing that an agent aims at a certain end is often sufficient to identify her motive. So when we say that an agent's motive for her searching behaviour is to find her keys, we understand the typical motivational state associated with the end of finding one's keys, even though there is more *in* the motive than a state directed towards that end.

In my view motives are emotional states that move us because they are ways of representing the world affectively. However, my position on the nature of emotion and the way it motivates us is not important for my points in this chapter. I want to focus on the way motives can add to the value of the acts they motivate. The motives I will use for illustration are non-controversial examples of motives. These are the emotions of compassion and love. Neither is a determinate emotion, but they have many forms arising from the nature of their intentional objects. The love of true belief differs significantly from other forms of love and it is no part of my project to distinguish love of truth from, say, appreciation of truth. My point in this section depends only on the position that love of true belief is a psychic state that includes the valuing of true belief, and that it can motivate cognitive activity. For comparison

I will discuss compassion, which is a disvaluing of the suffering of another person, and which also can motivate action. For brevity I will sometimes speak of the love of truth, but given my remarks at the beginning of this chapter, I will take that to mean love of true belief since truth itself is not a good.

What kind of value does the love of true belief have? Presumably it at least has extrinsic value derived from the value of true belief. This might be due to a general principle that love of something valuable is itself valuable. Love of truth might also be good *for* us. Robert Adams has recently argued that what is good for a person is a life characterized by enjoyment of the excellent.[14] Presumably, he also thinks it is good for us to act in ways motivated by enjoyment of the excellent. If we applied Adams's approach to cognitive activity we could say something like this: (1) True belief is an excellence. (2) It is good for us to appreciate true belief. (3) Cognitive activity motivated by such an appreciation is good for us.

My own preference is for a non-teleological approach, but I do not deny that it is good for us to be motivated by love of truth, nor do I deny that love of truth gets some of its value from the value of true belief. I also think love of truth has intrinsic value, by which I mean value that is not derived from the value of anything else. But what I am particularly interested in here is whether the love of truth has a kind of value that is capable of conferring additional value on the acts it motivates, and I want to argue that it does. Whether it can do that without being intrinsically valuable is an issue in the metaphysics of value that I will discuss only briefly in this chapter.

One way to defend the position that love of truth can confer value on the acts it motivates without going very far into the metaphysics of value is by example. Let me use an analogy between the value of cognitive acts motivated by love of truth and the value of overt acts motivated by compassion. Apart from what compassion motivates a person to do and the ends it aims to accomplish, and apart from the consequences of acting on it, compassion is a good state because it is an accurate emotional fit with its intentional object, a suffering person. It is a disvaluing or aversion to the suffering of others. Acts motivated by compassion are better than acts arising from just any reliable process or faculty for relieving suffering. For example, suppose suffering persons were helped just by being around other people and hearing them talk, that the sound of the human voice eased their pain. And suppose also that people were not aware of that connection. Talking when around a suffering person would have consequential value, but we would not evaluate it the same way we would evaluate an act with the same consequence that is motivated by compassion. An act motivated by compassion is better than an act that merely has the consequence that the suffering of another is relieved.

An act motivated by compassion is also better than an act that aims at alleviating suffering but without the motive of compassion. Suppose I am the sort of person who gets nauseated at the sight of a person suffering, so I aim to eliminate their suffering. I do not really disvalue their suffering as such; I just don't like to be nauseated. I would think that an act with such a motive is not as laudable as an act motivated by compassion. The conclusion is that, other things being equal, an act motivated by compassion is more valuable than an act that has the aim of compassion but without the motive, and is more valuable than an act that has the consequence at which compassion aims but without either the motive or the aim.

Compassion is a disvaluing or aversion to the suffering of others. The most straightforward epistemic parallel is an aversion to false beliefs. I maintain that such an aversion is a good thing quite apart from the fact that it motivates a person to act cognitively in ways that lead away from false beliefs. It is better for the same reason that compassion is better than the propensity to do something that happens to relieve suffering. This makes cognitive acts motivated by an aversion to falsehood better than those that arise from processes that lead away from falsehood but without such a motive. Furthermore, cognitive acts motivated by an aversion to falsehood are better than those acts that aim to avoid falsehood, not because the agent actually disvalues false beliefs as such, but for some other reason. Maybe, as in the compassion case, I get nauseated every time I have a false belief and, realizing the connection, I aim to shun false beliefs. More realistically, I might aim to avoid false beliefs because false beliefs give me a bad reputation. In these cases I would not be motivated by an aversion to false belief as such. I suggest that acts motivated by an aversion to a bad reputation are not as good as acts motivated by an aversion to falsehood as such. It follows that acts motivated by compassion or the aversion to false belief confer value on the acts they motivate in addition to any other value the acts have because of their ends or consequences.

The aversion to falsehood and the aversion to human suffering are negative motives, but positive motives can also confer value on the acts they motivate, in particular love. I propose that love of truth is a motive that confers value on acts of belief in addition to any other value such acts might have. Here we might pause for a moment to take a closer look at the motives of love of truth and aversion to falsehood because I have sometimes heard it said that the motive for truth is so natural and automatic that it is trivially satisfied. We have already seen one reason why that cannot be the case—the aim to get truth and the aim to avoid falsehood are two different aims, and it is unlikely that they arise from the same motive. A love of truth is not the same as a dislike of falsehood any more than a love of comfort is the same as a dislike of discomfort. We will return to the problem of a potential clash of epistemic motives. But first I want to say that neither one of these motives is trivially satisfied. To think so does not do justice to the commonality of wishful thinking. There is a sense in which everyone wants to believe the truth, but there is a difference between someone who wants to believe *p* if *p* is true, and someone who wants *p* to be true and wants to believe it. When we indulge in wishful thinking, we believe *p* because we want *p* to be true, and we want *p* to be true because we want to believe it. The love of truth as such does not operate as a motive for the belief. The typical motive in wishful thinking is closer to love of the possible state of affairs of a certain proposition's being true.

One difficulty mentioned in section II on consequential value is that getting truth and avoiding falsehood are not only distinct values, but they are sometimes in tension. Unless we are willing to settle for a very high degree of personal preference in weighing the two, we need a way to adjudicate between them. This problem arises in all four of the approaches we have considered, including the motivational approach I am supporting. An appreciation for true belief can be at odds with an aversion to false belief. The parallel phenomenon is well known in ethics. The value of autonomy can be at odds with the value of trust in others, and there is similar tension between the values of perseverance and flexibility, open-mindedness and steadfastness, honesty and kindness, and many others. In other work I have suggested that one of the functions of the Aristotelian virtue of *phronesis*, or practical wisdom, is to adjudicate among the competing demands of different virtues and the different values relevant to a given situation. I propose that the *phronimos* not only has good judgement about the extent to which in a given situation autonomy should be balanced against trust in others, or perseverance against flexibility, or honesty against kindness, but he is also the standard of good judgement about the extent to which it is worth risking falsehood in order to get a true belief concerning some proposition.[15] It is very doubtful that there is any rule or decision procedure that captures such good judgement. What ultimately counts as good motives, whether cognitive or moral, are the motives of a practically wise person. The motivational approach I endorse can therefore avoid the need for a third value by adopting this virtue-ethical approach to resolving moral quandaries. A quandary requires practically wise judgement.

6 The value of knowledge

In the last section we looked at the way the value of a motive can add value to the act it motivates. Given two acts, both of which are successful in their ends, the acts can differ in value because of a difference in their motive. In this section I want to address briefly the question of whether the value of the motive can explain the value that knowledge has in addition to the truth of the belief.

Before proceeding, let me say that I have become increasingly sceptical that the question of what constitutes knowledge can be resolved since the concept of knowledge has been made to serve so many different philosophical purposes. Sometimes knowledge is thought to be no more than the minimum state we expect out of a reasonable person with respect to a given proposition, but sometimes it represents the pinnacle of our cognitive aspirations. The value I am talking about in this chapter is unlikely to be the pinnacle, but it is probably more than the minimum we can get away with. I don't know how it could be demonstrated that the value of a cognitive state is of the right sort to convert true belief into knowledge, but for the purposes of this chapter I want to argue only that if we think of knowledge in the way I will describe, we can explain why knowledge is more valuable than true belief.

Many times I have claimed that moral discourse can aid us in understanding the evaluative aspects of our cognitive behaviour, but I used to think that this strategy does not help in the analysis of knowledge since, as far as I could tell, knowledge has no ethical analogue. There are parallels between moral motives and cognitive motives, moral acts and cognitive acts, and morally good outcomes analogous to true beliefs, but how can moral outcomes be converted into something more valuable the way true belief is said to be converted into knowledge? My position now is that I was thinking of knowledge on the wrong analogy. It's true that a good outcome such as relief of suffering cannot be made better by the act that produced it, much less by the motive of the act that produced it, but that's because the outcome is a state of affairs separate from the act. In the case of acts of belief, the intended outcome is a property of the act itself. The closest moral analogy would be an act that aims at having a certain property, a property that is determined by something outside the agent. I don't know if there are acts like that, but I suggest that if there are, they are the closest analogues to the state of knowing. They are good when they are successful in achieving the intended property, but they are even better when they arise from the right motive.

Let us return to the bathroom scale cases to test whether acts of true belief motivated by love for truth have the value that makes knowledge better than mere true belief. Recall that in the first bathroom scale case I believe what the scale says and since the scale is accurate, I am unlikely to have the belief unless it is true, but I don't care whether it is true or not. What I want is to enjoy believing that I have lost 5 lbs. Let us suppose the belief is true, that I have lost 5 lbs. Do I know that I have? The scale is reliable and its reading is good evidence, but I care neither about the reliability of the scale nor its evidential support of my belief. Still, I am not so irrational that I can believe what I want at will, and so there is *some* connection between the fact that there is good evidence for the belief and my belief. After all, I cannot believe a proposition unless I think it is true, and I cannot think it is true if there is no indication of its truth. But I do not care about the indicators of the truth as such. I care only about having whatever it takes to enjoy believing that I've lost weight. I doubt that very many of us are able to manufacture a belief out of thin air; we cannot form a belief without indicators of its truth. But I doubt that that means we are incapable of wishful thinking. In the first scenario I believe I have lost weight because I want to. The evidence for the truth of my belief plays no role except to make it psychologically possible for me to form the belief at all. It thus shields me from the most extreme form of irrationality, but it hardly makes me grasp the truth in a good way. My getting the truth is a matter of luck in a certain sense of luck. In a way, it is not an *accident* that I got the truth since it is not accidental that I believe what the scale says and it is not accidental that the scale is accurate. Still, from a certain point of view it *is* an accident that I got the truth.[16] I don't get *credit* for getting the truth. I suspect that that is sufficient to deprive me of knowing, but I don't know to what extent we can really expect to settle the matter. My point is just that my act of true belief arising in this way is not as good as an act of true belief arising out of the right motive.

In the second bathroom scale case I do value the truth as such with respect to believing that I've lost 5 lbs, but I do not equally value the truth as such with respect to believing that I have not lost weight. And I might not disvalue believing that I've lost weight falsely as much as I value believing that I've lost weight truly. This means that I do not impartially value truth and disvalue falsehood about the matter of my weight. Nonetheless, I do value believing that I've lost weight truly. In fact, I value it highly. My cognitive activity in this case therefore has the following virtues: I value believing that I've lost weight if it's true that I have, I use a reliable process and good evidence in forming the belief because of my valuing the truth in this case, and I get to the truth in part because of my motive and the processes to which it gives rise. From my point of view, the accuracy of the scale is not accidental, as it is in the first case. Granted, I do not get as much credit as I would if I valued truth more impartially and consistently, but it does seem to me that I get credit for believing the truth, and that is probably sufficient to attribute knowledge to me. Sosa's case of believing that his parents cared for him is similar. In both cases we care about the truth of a particular proposition, we care about the evidence *as* evidence, and our believing seems to be knowing, although not unqualifiedly. Again, I'm not sure whether we can settle the matter, but my primary point is that my belief state in the second bathroom scale case is better than in the first.

In *Virtues of the Mind* I defined a category of act I called 'an act of virtue'. An act of virtue V is an act motivated by a V-motive, is an act a person with virtue V would characteristically do in the circumstances, and is successful in reaching the end of virtue V because of these other good-making features of the act. When this schema is applied to intellectual virtue, we can say that an act of intellectual virtue is an act motivated by the motivational component of intellectual virtue, is an act an intellectually virtuous person would characteristically do in these epistemic circumstances, and is successful in reaching the truth because of these other features of the act. I then argued that knowledge can be defined as true belief arising out of acts of intellectual virtue, and showed how this definition avoids Gettier problems.[17] Now I think that this definition can also solve the value problem, but to do so the schema of acts and outcomes needs to be modified. True belief is not an end state analogous to relief of suffering that is the product of intellectual acts. True believing *is* an intellectual act, or at least, it is strongly analogous to an act. Of course, it is an act that is in part generated by a series of previous acts. Nonetheless, it is enough like an act to make a comparison with overt acts illuminating. I propose, then, to modify my definition of knowledge as follows: knowledge is an act of intellectual virtue.

7 Conclusion

Ever since the ancient Greeks Western thinkers have admired those who are relentless in the pursuit of truth. Such people are thought to be noble, certainly beyond the ordinary. I suspect that the source of this idea also comes from the Greeks—the pervasive suspicion that much of what we take to be true isn't really true. When left to our own devices and the conventions of our various cultures, we do not do a very good job of getting at the truth.[18] We are unreliable, both individually and collectively. Of course, we are much more reliable about some things than others. That is why there has been so much emphasis in modern epistemology on clear perception of medium-sized objects. But the wide disagreements in practical, moral, religious, and philosophical beliefs, as well as many categories of scientific beliefs, is evidence that reliability about many important matters is not widely distributed among the general human population. This makes the desire for truth a desire to rise above the common lot. Traditionally, that desire led to a search for one or two inspired people who have the truth and can become one's mentors. Nowadays we are less likely to think that such a search will be successful, and so we rely upon ourselves. And that often means flouting convention. In any case, it takes special effort. John Dewey is probably right that human beings are naturally credulous, which means that all too often learning the truth involves unlearning a falsehood. And that is what is noble about the desire for truth: we often have to give something up. If I'm right about this, the difficulty in getting at truth means that the right way to behave cognitively requires the motives needed when there are internal or external obstacles to overcome, the motives constitutive of autonomy, courage, perseverance, humility, fairness, open-mindedness, and other intellectual virtues. In this chapter I have concentrated only on the motive of valuing truth, which is probably primary, but I suspect that for many categories of truth we are not going to get truth at all unless we have the motives that are constituents of these other virtues. Within some domains the situation is not just that some people get the truth through virtuous activity and others by non-virtuous but reliable processes and we credit the former more than the latter. Rather, it's that the latter don't exist at all. Reliability in getting many of the most valuable truths requires dispositions to have virtuous motives. If so, the criteria given by reliabilism coincide with virtue criteria in these domains. I have argued that virtuous motives give the beliefs they produce a value that mere reliability cannot. What *makes* the thinking agent reliable is what is really valuable.[19] It is also what makes the resulting belief truly her own.

Notes

1. Not every propositional representation is a belief because not every such representation has the aim of representing reality accurately. Wishes, hopes, and fears are in this category. Wishes aim at making reality correspond to the propositional content of the wish. In contrast, beliefs aim at making their propositional content correspond to reality. (If I am right about this, corresponding is not a symmetrical relation. Correspondence has a direction.) This difference in the aim of these intentional states may explain why it is problematic to speak of an accurate wish even when you get what you wish for.
2. Compare David Velleman's claim that a belief is accepting something as true with the aim of getting truth in Velleman (2000: ch. 11).
3. *Summa Theologica* I–II, q. 19, a. 1.
4. This raises the issue of cognitive control. It might be that we are only responsible for our cognitive activity to the extent to which we can control it. If so, this leads to my requirement that the kind of cognitive evaluation relevant to our responsibility to have true beliefs is something we can use in making ourselves better cognizers. I will leave aside the control issue for this chapter, however, relying on the intuition that if we are responsible for our cognitive conduct, then there must be a kind of evaluation of it that we can use in such conduct. That is the sort of evaluation that interests me in the next four sections of this chapter.
5. Mill (1957: 18).
6. James (1979).
7. Zagzebski (1999); revised and reprinted as Zagzebski (2000).
8. Sidgwick (1966: 405).
9. Greco (1990).
10. Zagzebski (1996: p. II, sec. 6).
11. Sosa (2001).
12. Notice that if we think of cognitive evaluation as arising primarily from our responsibility to others, that tends to make our responsibility not to have false beliefs stronger than our responsibility to have true beliefs. I would conjecture that this is related to the fact that we have a greater responsibility not to harm others than to do them good. Social responsibility therefore favours a conservative approach. This is probably a mistake, but it is an understandable one.
13. Sosa's footnote on this starts out right and then goes into an example that does not apply to our case here. He construes the desire that if *p*, I believe *p* as the desire that it not be the case that *p* and I don't believe *p*. His example is one where that is satisfied because I don't want *p* to be true. But the bathroom scale case is not like that. I want *p* to be true and I want to make sure that if it is, I take notice.
14. Adams (1999: 93). Adams's view on excellence seems to blur the distinction between intrinsic goods and final goods. He says an excellence is a non-instrumental good, good as an end, but he also says an excellence is a type of intrinsic good (ibid. 14).
15. See Zagzebski (1996: p. II, sec. 5.2).
16. See Riggs (1998).
17. Zagzebski (1996: 248 and 270–1).
18. Not only philosophers have this suspicion. It is standard among educators to say that they aim to train the young to learn how to learn, implying, of course, that the young won't do it right if they are not trained.

19. I have defended this point in another way in Zagzebski (2001). I argue that reliability is not strictly necessary for knowledge, but it is a good sign of what is necessary: the presence of agency.

References

Adams, R. (1999), *Finite and Infinite Goods* (Oxford: Oxford University Press).
Greco, J. (1990), 'Internalism and Epistemically Responsible Belief ', *Synthese*, 85: 245–7.
James W. (1979), 'The Will to Believe', in F. Burkhardt, F. Bowers and I. Skrupskelis.(eds.), *The Will to Believe and Other Essays in Popular Philosophy* (Cambridge, MA: Harvard University Press).
Mill, J. S. (1957), Utilitarianism, ed. O. Piest (Indianapolis: Bobbs-Merrill).
Riggs, W. (1998), 'What are the "Chances" of Being Justified?', *The Monist*, 81: 452–72.
Sidgwick, H. (1966), Methods of Ethics(New York: Dover Publishing).
Sosa, E. (2001), 'For the Love of Truth?', in A. Fairweather and L. Zagzebski (eds.), *Virtue Epistemology: Essays on Epistemic Virtue and Responsibility* (Oxford: Oxford University Press), ch. 4.
Velleman, D. (2000), *The Possibility of Practical Reason* (Oxford: Oxford University Press).
Zagzebski, L. (1996), *Virtues of the Mind* (Cambridge, Cambridge University Press).
Zagzebski, L. (1999), Phronesis and Christian Belief ', in G. Brüntrup (ed.), *The Rationality of Theism* (Dordrecht: Kluwer), 177–94.
Zagzebski, L. (2000), 'Phronesis and Religious Belief ', in G. Axtell (ed.), *Knowledge, Belief and Character: Readings in Virtue Epistemology* (New York: Rowman and Littlefield Publishers), 205–20.
Zagzebski, L. (2001), 'Must Knowers Be Agents?', in A. Fairweather and L. Zagzebski (eds.),*Virtue Epistemology: Essays on Epistemic Virtue and Responsibility* (Oxford: Oxford University Press), 142–57.

20 Minimalism and the value of truth

MICHAEL P. LYNCH

Minimalists generally see themselves as engaged in a descriptive project. They maintain that they can explain everything we want to say about truth without appealing to anything other than the T-schema, i.e., the idea that the proposition that p is true iff p. I argue that despite recent claims to the contrary, minimalists cannot explain one important belief many people have about truth, namely, that truth is good. If that is so, then minimalism, and possibly deflationism as a whole, must be rejected or recast as a profoundly revisionary project.

1 False idols

It has long been thought that if the good is that towards which all things aim, then the good in the way of belief is truth. Truth is a value. Yet this apparently innocent assumption has come under fire recently. Some believe that truth is not valuable because it is unknowable. Others believe that truth is relative, and therefore what matters is the cultural practices that determine it, not the truth itself. Still others believe that the entire notion, like the chia pet, the lava lamp or the liberal American politician, is simply *passé*.[1]

Philosophers sometimes loftily dismiss these views as incoherent or self-defeating (if the truth about truth is that it does not matter, then why should we care that it does not matter?). But tempting as that reply may be, it is a mistake. Sceptics about the value of truth like Richard Rorty are engaged in conceptual revolution: their aim is not to describe our views about the importance of truth but to change them. Rorty has a penchant for portraying 'us pragmatists' (as he puts it) as early atheists struggling against the tyranny of the inquisition.[2] Like the atheistic martyrs of old, Rorty and his fellow travellers *expect* their views to sound paradoxical. If they do not, the revolutionary committee had better start cranking out some new pamphlets.

Try as I may, I confess I am unable to shake my own sense of natural piety towards the truth. But I am not going to argue here against the above forms of scepticism about truth's value. In this paper I shall consider a different form of sceptic. In terms of Rorty's religious analogy, this is the person who agrees that God does not really exist, or at least does not exist in the robust way the tradition believes, but insists that the concept and the associated ideas of piety, worship, and so on, are still extremely valuable, perhaps even in some sense indispensable, and that their function in thought can be explained without recourse to anything spooky or metaphysical. In terms of truth, the position I have in mind is perhaps best exemplified by Paul Horwich's so-called minimalist theory of truth. Minimalists of the Horwichian stripe see themselves quite differently from the Rortyan sceptic I mentioned earlier. In their own eyes, they are friends of truth, as pious as the rest of us. Their project, they insist, is descriptive, not revisionary. Thus they claim, as Paul Horwich likes to put it, that they can explain, without appeal to any underlying property or metaphysical picture, everything that needs explaining about truth.

Yet as Michael Dummett pointed out over forty years ago, views like minimalism seem to have a difficult time explaining a basic truism about truth, namely that it is normative, or good.[3] Against recent replies by Horwich and others, I am going to argue in this paper that Dummett's thesis is essentially correct.[4] My argument will therefore be similar *in form* to arguments that claim that minimalism cannot account for other central truisms about truth, such as the platitude that truth is a matter of correspondence to reality, or that to know something is to know that it is true. To say that such principles are platitudes or truisms, in my view, is not to say that they are trivial or universally believed or occurrently believed. Revisionary sceptics about truth typically reject all or most of them, after all. Rather, by calling such principles 'truisms' I mean that they are basic elements of a tacitly held 'folk theory' of truth.[5] Accordingly, whether a given form of deflationism can account for a truism about truth is independent from the question of whether that truism is true. In the first two sections, I explain what it means to say that truth is normative, and briefly consider reasons in favour of the status of this claim as a folk truism. I then turn my attention to how this affects Horwichian-style minimalism. In a brief appendix, I speculate about how the normativity of truth may affect two other varieties of deflationism, and whether they too must abandon their project or join ranks with the revisionary sceptics, declare truth to be without deep value, and storm the temple gates.

2 Truth as normative

Nobody likes to be wrong. If anything is a truism, this is. And it suggests that we value believing the truth. Roughly speaking, we think it is good to believe the truth, and not to believe the false. In philosophers' speak, truth is normative.

This thought is a fibre spun from three threads. The first two threads are comparatively easy to unravel. First, and most simply, there is the ordinary language point that the word 'true' has an evaluative use. Part of what you are doing when you say something is true is commending it. (Here I am reserving 'evaluative' as a modifier of a word or a word's use, as opposed to 'normative', which I reserve for describing properties.) And just as we evaluate actions as correct or incorrect, 'true' and 'false' are used to evaluate *beliefs* as correct or incorrect. This reveals the second thread: as William James put it, truth 'is the good in the way of belief'.[6] Others sometimes say that truth is the aim of belief. This is not literally so, of course. Beliefs do not literally aim at anything. But both expressions get at the point that truth is a property that it is good for beliefs to have. Since propositions are the contents of beliefs, and it is the content of a belief, not the act of believing, that is true, we can also say that truth is the property that makes a proposition good to believe, or alternatively, that a belief's being true is good. In short,

TN. Other things being equal, it is good to believe a proposition if and only if it is true.

A property is normative *of* something (in either the superficial or deep sense, see below) when it is good for that something to have it. Being true is the good of belief; therefore being true is a normative property of belief.

Norms guide action. The norm that, other things being equal, it is good to keep my promises implies that I ought, other things being equal, to try to keep my promises. The goodness of keeping one's promises gives me a reason for acting in some ways rather than others. So too with truth: it is good, other things being equal, to believe what is true and only what is true, and this gives me a reason, other things being equal, to *pursue the truth*, and *to avoid error,* or *believing what is not true*. The goodness of believing what is true means that having true beliefs, like repaid debts, or kept promises, is a goal worthy of pursuit.

A few clarifications are needed to stave off some common misunderstandings. First, to say that truth is normative does not mean that it is wholly normative. If truth is a value, it is a *thick* sort of value. Thick normative properties, like being courageous or being a promise, have both nonnormative (or 'descriptive') and normative aspects. For example, when we correctly describe an act as courageous, we are both describing it and evaluating it. We are commending it as something to be emulated, saying it is good and so on, *and* describing it as an action that was done despite the danger of doing it. Similarly, when we say that a belief is true, we are at once evaluating it, saying it is good, *and* describing it as a property that beliefs have when they 'correspond to the facts', or whatever else one might think the descriptive content of truth amounts to.[7]

Some philosophers reject the idea that truth is normative of belief, because sometimes other values should take precedence over the value of truth.[8] This is so, but it is not a reason to reject (TN). A belief's being true is *always prima facie good, good considered by itself, or good other things being equal*. Believing truly is not always good absolutely, or all things considered. Almost everything that is good is *prima facie* good. Keeping your promises is like this. As everyone knows, keeping your promises is not always good without qualification, in all circumstances whatsoever.

Cognitive goods like true belief are no different. Some propositions can be true but not good to believe all things considered. The truth, as we say, can hurt. People often seek the truth about things of which, in some cases at least, they might be better off ignorant: spousal fidelity, the identity of biological as opposed to adoptive parents, even, in some cases, their health. And some true propositions would not be good to believe for more mundane reasons: some are too complicated for any human to believe, while others may be too trivial to be worth the effort. So while being true makes it good to believe something, it may be better, all things considered, not to believe it. Conversely, a false proposition may still be good to believe, all things considered. It may be good, all things considered, to believe something overwhelmingly justified by the evidence and therefore thought to be true, even if turns out later to have been false. And self-deception may sometimes be good all things considered, even though it means believing something that is false. In short, a belief's being true is *prima facie* good, not absolutely good. And that just reminds us of the obvious fact that while truth is a value, it is not the only value.

This brings me finally to the more tangled thread running through the common thought that truth is good. This concerns *why or in what sense* truth is good, in particular whether a belief's being true is only instrumentally good, or whether it is also good in a deeper sense, for instance by being intrinsically good or a constituent part of a whole that is intrinsically good, or both. Something is instrumentally valuable when it is good because it is a means to something else we want. Importantly, any old property can be instrumentally valuable. A particular body-weight can be instrumentally valuable for an athlete as a means towards winning. But while instrumentally good for the athlete, being of that particular weight remains a purely natural 'descriptive' property. I can summarize this by saying that being of the right weight, or being wealthy, or being legible and so on, are only *superficially normative* properties. It is good to be wealthy for example, but there is nothing about being wealthy that is 'good in itself', as it is often put. It is the instrumental *effects* of being wealthy that explain why we might think wealth is worthy of pursuit. Hence a property like this is a dubious candidate for being a thick value or norm in the way we think being courageous is. A property F is *deeply* normative, on the other hand, when being F is essentially more than instrumentally good, and therefore worthy of caring about for its own sake. For such properties, the thought is that there is something about being F that makes being F good. Therefore, to believe that truth is deeply normative – normative to the degree we might think that many of our moral notions are normative – is to think a belief's being true is more than instrumentally good.

3 Truth as more than instrumentally good

I shall assume that having true beliefs is at least instrumentally good, and that we believe this is so. Stephen Stich or no Stephen Stich, I think this is a pretty safe assumption, as assumptions go: life would be nasty, brutish and short if, for example, you lacked true beliefs when crossing a highway.[9] So the question is not whether we value truth as a means: the question is whether we believe that exhausts its value. In point of fact, the philosophers I am concerned with do not tend to think so; they generally *agree* that truth is more than instrumentally good.[10] So I could simply assume this as well, and move on to the question of whether minimalists can account for that fact. But it is worth pausing and briefly thinking about whether everyone shares this view. Do we believe that truth is more than instrumentally good?

I think that many do believe this, or are at any rate rationally committed to believing it by other tacit folk beliefs they have about truth. One way to see this is just to consider that there are times in most of our lives when we simply want to know for no other reason than the knowing itself. Curiosity is not always motivated by practical concerns. For example, with regard to at least some extremely abstract mathematical conjectures, knowing their truth would get us no closer to anything else we want. None the less, if we were forced to choose between believing truly or falsely about the matter, we would surely prefer the former. Even when guessing about such things, we prefer to guess correctly. And we sometimes care about the truth despite extremely impractical consequences. People often wish to know the truth about a spouse's infidelity even when there is an excellent chance that nothing productive will come of it. Finally, unless truth has more than instrumental value, there would be nothing wrong with believing trivial falsehoods, such as the proposition that 100 gazillion trillion is the highest number. But as Bernard Williams puts it, the falsity of a proposition is in fact a terminal objection to believing it.

These initial considerations already provide some grip on how people think folk-theoretically about the value of truth, but there are further 'intuition-pumps' at my disposal. These indicate that (a) many of us have a basic preference for the truth; (b) this is not a mere preference; and (c) many of us therefore think truth is worth caring about for its own sake.

By a 'basic preference' I mean a preference for something that cannot be explained by our preference for other things. Avoidance of pain is perhaps a basic preference; preference for money is not. If truth were *not* a basic preference, then if I had two beliefs b_1 and b_2 with identical instrumental value, I should not prefer to believe b_1 rather than b_2. The considerations above point to the fact that this is not so. Moreover, if people did not have a basic preference for the truth, it would be hard to explain why they find the prospect of being undetectably wrong so disturbing. We do not want to live in a fool's paradise. Given the choice (perhaps via choosing either a blue pill or a red pill, as in the film *The Matrix*) between living in the actual world or the world created for us by Descartes' imaginary evil demon, I would not choose the demon world. But of course there is nothing experientially different about the demon world as compared with the actual world: in particular, beliefs that are false in the demon world have exactly the same experiential consequences as true beliefs in the actual world. Thus in so far as what I want is to have certain experiences, my beliefs in both worlds have the same instrumental value – they are equally good at getting what I want. There is none the less a difference between the two that matters.

You may rightly protest that we want more than mere experiences out of life. If so, then you will reject the assumption that my beliefs in the demon world have the same instrumental value as my beliefs in the actual world, even though they have the same experiential consequences. Indeed; so consider Russell's scenario, that without our knowledge, the world began yesterday (or last month, or two minutes ago). If we really lived in a Russell world, as I shall call it, almost all my beliefs about the past would be false. Yet my beliefs in a Russell world, unlike those in the demon world, have the same causal consequences as my beliefs in the actual world. This is because the present and future of both worlds unfold in exactly the same way. If I believe truly in the actual world that if I open the refrigerator I shall get a beer, then I shall get a beer if I open the refrigerator. Since events in the Russell world are just the same as in the actual world once it begins ticking along, I shall also get that beer in the Russell world if I open the refrigerator, even if (in the Russell world) I believe falsely that I put it there yesterday. In short, whatever future-directed desires I satisfy in the actual world, based on beliefs about what happened in the past, I shall also satisfy in the Russell world, even though those beliefs about the past are simply false. And yet, given the choice between living in the actual world and in a Russell world, I would strongly prefer the actual world. Of course, once 'inside' that world, I would not see any difference between it and the real world; in both, after all, events crank along in the same way. But that is beside the point. For the fact remains that when I *now* think about the worlds in so far as they are identical in instrumental value, there is a difference between the two worlds that matters to me. Even when it has no effect on my other preferences, I, and presumably you as well, prefer true beliefs to false ones.

In preferring not to live in a demon or Russell world, I do not merely prefer that the world should be arranged in a certain way. My actual preference is complex: it involves my beliefs and their proper functioning, so to speak. For not only do I not want to live in a world where I am a brain in a vat, or deceived by a demon, or whatever, *I also do not want to live in a world where I am not thus deceived, but believe that I am*. That is, if such and such is the case, I want to believe that it is, and if I believe that it is, I want it to be the case. I can put this by saying that I want my *beliefs and reality* to be disposed in a certain way – I want my beliefs to track reality, to 'accord with how the world actually is' – which is to say I want them to be true.

Furthermore, my basic preference for truth is not just a *mere* preference, like a preference for chocolate ice cream. It goes deeper than that. This is apparent when I think about my attitudes towards my preference. Like many other people, I not only prefer the truth for its own sake in such cases, I do not want to be the sort of person who does not – who would prefer the life of illusion. In Harry Frankfurt's language, I have a second-order desire for having true beliefs.[11] I not only desire the truth, I desire to desire the truth. I want to be the sort of person, for example, who has intellectual integrity, who, other things being equal, is willing to pursue what is true even when it is dangerous or inconvenient or expensive to do so. This suggests that my desire for the truth is not a mere passing fancy; it is grounded in what matters to me. I do not just prefer the truth, in other words, I *care* about it. And normally, the fact that we care about something is very good evidence that we find it *worthy* of caring about. Accordingly, if I care about truth for its own sake, then I presumably believe that truth is worth caring about for its own sake – it is more than instrumentally good.

This is what I meant by saying we can learn about what we believe from these sorts of scenarios. For many people, our reactions to these cases suggest that (a) we have a basic preference for the truth; (b) this preference matters to us; and thus (c) we believe that truth is more than instrumentally good. In short, we accept that where the belief that *p* and the belief that not-*p* have identical instrumental value, it is better, just on that ground alone, to hold the true belief than the false belief.

It is worth emphasizing that none of this shows that this is all we believe. I believe, for example, that truth is also worth caring about for purely instrumental reasons. And I believe that sometimes the negative consequences of having a true belief will outweigh its *prima facie* non-instrumental goodness. The belief that truth is worth caring about for its own sake does not imply that this worth is paramount or absolute. Nor, again, do these considerations show that we are correct to believe that truth is more than instrumentally good: what they show is that for many people, the idea that truth is good is part of a tacit folk-theoretic conception of truth. This again does not mean that everyone will share this idea, just as not everyone shares the view that truth is a matter of correspondence, or that some propositions could be true but never known to be true, or that truth is absolute, or that it is timeless, or any other folk truism about truth I might name. Some may already be committed to a version of pragmatism about truth that prevents them from even distinguishing demon worlds from the actual world, for example. But others may simply learn, by reflecting on why they do not share these attitudes, that they just do not care about truth for its own sake. That is too bad, on my view. But as I noted earlier, to be a platitude or truism, a proposition need not be universally believed, which is a good thing, because I know of no proposition that is universally believed.

I wish to underline the fact that nothing that I have said so far, all by itself, is an objection to minimalism. I can easily put my position in minimalist terms as well: *where p, and yet the belief that p and the belief that not-p have identical instrumental value, it is better to believe that p*. Indeed, in the present context this is an entirely unobjectionable way of putting the point, since all that is at issue here is whether we believe that truth is more than instrumentally valuable, not what its proper analysis might be. This is not to say that the belief that truth is deeply normative has no metaphysical implications, given certain other facts. Non-deflationary accounts must account for these as well, and it is possible that some will be unable to do so; this is simply a further matter.

Nothing about this conclusion forces us to hold that it is a consequence of the concept of truth. Indeed, whether truth's non-instrumental value is a conceptual matter, or whether it is simply a substantive fact about truth, is a separate issue – just as what the additional value of truth actually is, and how realist anyone wishes to be about this additional value, are separate issues. These questions are important, but for present purposes I can here leave them unanswered.

4 Minimalism and truth's value

According to Paul Horwich, there is no harm in thinking that truth is a property; it is simply not the sort of property we can say much about, metaphysically speaking: it is not a property with a nature. Horwich calls his view minimalism. This is an apt name; like a minimalist painting, a minimalist theory of truth eschews the baroque. What matters are simplicity, clean lines and pure form.

Horwich has developed minimalism in significant detail, and I shall not try to summarize everything one might say about it.[12] But here is a rough sketch. Like any deflationary view of truth, minimalism has a metaphysical part and a semantic/conceptual part. Metaphysically, minimalism, as I have just noted, allows that truth can be a property, of sorts. That is, if you think that any normal predicate expresses a property, then truth is a property. It is just not a *substantive* property. Substantive properties, according to Horwich (p. 143), are properties that admit of a constitution theory. That is, they are properties that can be reductively defined or identified with some more basic property. It is these properties, on this view, that have an explanatory role in our theorizing about the world: we appeal to them in explaining other things of interest. They are properties that have underlying natures that need explaining. Truth, according to the minimalist, has no such role, and no such nature.

Conceptually, the key idea behind minimalism is that our grasp of the concept of truth consists entirely in our disposition to accept instances of the propositional version of the T-schema, or

T. The proposition that *p* is true if and only if *p*.

The function of the truth predicate, on this account, is that it serves as a device of generalization. Purely in virtue of (T), it allows us to summarize open-ended strings of claims. Thus when we say 'Something Alice said was true', we usefully summarize an open-ended disjunction of conjuncts, e.g., 'Either Alice said that roses are red, and roses are red; or Alice said that snow is white, and snow is white'; and so on. The basis for our use and understanding of the truth predicate, and the thin property it expresses, is hence simply our acceptance of the instances of the T-schema. On that ground, minimalism claims to explain both the concept of truth and *all the facts that involve truth* (Horwich, p. 7). No robust metaphysical account, and in particular, no account of a substantive truth property, is needed.

The aspect of minimalism I focus on here is this last point, namely, that the minimal theory can explain all the facts that involve truth. Which facts are these? Obviously, we have no more direct access to the facts about truth than to facts about anything else. So in practice, any evaluation of the minimalist's claim appeals to certain central beliefs or folk truisms about truth. And one of those central beliefs is that truth is good; that is,

TN. Other things being equal, it is good to believe that *p* if and only if it is true that *p*.

The main point I need to press is that (TN) cannot be derived from the purely non-normative (T). Therefore, *contra* minimalism, that schema cannot fully capture everything believed true of truth. Assuming that (TN) is true, (T) cannot capture all the facts about truth.

Horwich, of course, disagrees. According to Horwich, (T) may not entail (TN) directly, but it does do so given the assumption of certain other obvious facts *not* involving truth. On this basis, one might claim that whatever else (TN) might be, it is not a substantive fact about *truth as such*.

According to Horwich, claims about the value of truth are simply one more case where we are using the word 'true' to generalize a more complicated thought. (TN), in other words, is simply shorthand for our disposition to accept every instance of

(B) Other things being equal, it is good to believe that *p* if and only if *p*.

(B) does not mention truth at all. In other words, to say that it is good to believe the truth is simply shorthand for saying we are disposed to accept an open-ended stream of little belief norms, namely,

> It is good to believe that the dog has fleas if and only if the dog has fleas; and it is good to believe that roses are red if and only if roses are red; and it is good to believe that ...; and so on.

The result is that we explain the value of truth in terms that do not explicitly mention truth. The concept of truth is needed only to help us express that infinite collection of commitments. As a result, the value of truth is derivable from the non-normative T-schema, and hence constitutes no threat to minimalism.

This reply does not succeed. If we are to use (B) to help us derive (TN) from (T) then we must be rationally justified in accepting its instances. But if we are willing, *a priori*, to endorse an infinite list of *normative* propositions all of which fit a particular pattern, it is highly likely that there is a general principled reason why we should do so. And my view is that the reason why we accept (B)'s instances is that we accept (TN); therefore (B) cannot be used to deduce (TN) itself from (T). This is what I shall now argue.

What is the reason why one might think that it is good to believe that Socrates was a philosopher if and only if he was, and so on? What, in other words, justifies or rationally explains acceptance of all the instances of (B)? In order to show the force of this demand, I shall first look at why one sort of explanation is *not* going to work. It is not the sort of reply that a minimalist would make, but it will display the difference between the present call for explanation and a similar one in the case of (T). Suppose one asks why one is inclined, *a priori*, to endorse every (non-paradoxical) instance of (T). Here a more traditional deflationist, like a redundancy theorist, will claim that it is true that *p* does not say anything significantly more than saying that *p*. This is how the thought that there is really nothing in common amongst the things that are true that makes them true gets off the ground. At first, it may look as if there must be a general principled explanation, an explanation in terms of some common property shared by all and only true propositions, of why one accepts every instance of (T). The redundancy theorist argues, however, that the need for this explanation is illusory, since the claim that the proposition that snow is white is true is, in some sense or other, telling us nothing more than that snow is white.

Whatever its merits in the case of (T), that answer is definitely implausible when I turn to (B). I am not talking about *snow*, elliptically or otherwise, if I say that it is good to believe that snow is white! I am saying that one *ought* to have a certain *belief*. So, unlike the case of (T), there is no reason to think there is a semantic equivalence between the right- and left-hand sides of (any instance of) either (B) or (TN). So one cannot appeal to any such equivalence in explaining why anyone is rationally disposed to accept every instance of these schemata.

So this leaves the question: what is the reason for accepting the infinite list of little belief norms? Answering this question is crucial, because the non-minimalist has a ready and obvious answer. The reason to accept that it is good to believe that snow is white just when snow is white, and good to believe that Socrates was a philosopher just when he was, is that it is good to have true beliefs. What makes it good to believe a proposition is that proposition's *being true*: (TN) is true. In other words, the non-minimalist can justify acceptance of instances of (B) by pointing to an important fact *about truth*. But obviously the minimalist cannot adopt this simple and obvious explanation. For according to minimalism, there is no fact involving truth that does not derive from (T). In other words, there is nothing about a belief's *being true* that itself could, in the minimalist's view, rationally explain why one thinks it is good to have that belief. As a result, minimalists must either come up with some other explanation, or admit they cannot explain every fact about truth.

Horwich has acknowledged the force of this demand in several places.[13] I now turn to three ways in which the minimalist might try to meet it.

(a) *We can rationally explain why we accept all the instances of (B) solely by appealing to the pragmatic value of having true beliefs*.[14] We ought to pursue all those beliefs we rationally believe will satisfy our desires. So if we want to get to the hotel, and we believe that we shall if we take the train, then it will be good if it really is the case that if we take the train then we shall get to the hotel. More generally, for anything *x* that I might happen to want, I ought to make sure all of my beliefs of the form 'If I do *a*, then I shall get *x*' are true. Further, since such beliefs are always the result of inferences from other beliefs about the world and how its contents behave, I have a solid pragmatic rationale for always seeking the truth of all my beliefs, which is to say, for accepting all the instances of (B). For I can never know what beliefs might be useful in the future for helping me get what I want.

This explanation will not do, for at least two reasons. First, the argument presupposes the truth of (TN), and hence cannot be used to justify (TN)'s being inferred from (T). For the argument just given assumes that we ought to pursue those beliefs that we *rationally* believe will satisfy our desires. This qualification is important. For clearly we should not pursue just those beliefs we just happen *to think* will satisfy our desires. We should pursue those beliefs we have some reason or evidence for thinking will satisfy our desires. But which beliefs do we rationally believe will satisfy our desires? Arguably, the ones we *have reason to think are true*, that is the ones that are epistemically rational. But by invoking what is epistemically rational to believe, (1) necessarily ends up relying on the notion of truth. This is because (TN) is partly constitutive of the facts about epistemically rational belief. One would not count as understanding what it is to believe rationally in the epistemic sense unless one at least implicitly accepted that it is good to have true beliefs. So while it may be true that we seek the truth when we are epistemically rational, this is precisely because being epistemically rational involves seeking the truth. Epistemic rationality is 'truth-conducive', and it is just this that is typically thought to distinguish epistemic rationality (or justification) from prudential or moral rationality (or justification).

Therefore facts about epistemically rational belief themselves involve truth, and cannot be used in any argument that attempts to derive (TN) from (T) and facts that do not involve truth. Yet the main problem with (a) is even simpler: it runs smack up against the point that truth has more than instrumental value. In more recent work, Horwich has noted this, and argued that minimalism can account for this fact as well. Bernard Williams, interestingly, agrees.[15] The point is not difficult. According to Williams, accepting that truth is more than instrumentally good amounts to accepting

BI. It is more than instrumentally good to believe that *p* if and only if *p*.

But here again the minimalist faces the problem of explanation, and this time in spades, for now we are accepting an open-ended list of deep noninstrumental norms. What rationally explains our accepting infinite statements of this form? What makes it more than instrumentally good to believe that Socrates is a philosopher just when he is? Again the answer cannot be in terms of some good-making property of beliefs. The minimalist must explain our acceptance of all the instances of (BI) by appealing to some other reason, such as

(b) *Instances of (B) or (BI) are explanatorily basic in precisely the same sense as that in which the instances of (T) are basic.* That is, we accept them in 'the absence of any supporting argument' and 'we do not arrive at them, or seek to justify our acceptance of them, on the basis of anything more obvious or more immediately known'.[16] If so, then the minimalist may argue that he *can* justify the value of truth as follows: we can deduce (TN) from (i) the equivalence schema (T), and (ii) for each *p*, the explanatorily basic fact that it is good to believe that *p* if and only if *p*. Since facts of this form do not involve truth, it follows that (TN) poses no problem for minimalism.

Again I have two replies. First, to say that instances of (BI) are basic is to say that we do not need to justify our acceptance of them. But many philosophers, the revisionists I spoke of earlier, believe that we do need to justify our acceptance of them. These philosophers do not think it is obvious that we should think that for any *p*, it is more than instrumentally good to believe that *p* if and only *p*. These sceptical views are coherent, even if they are not correct. We need arguments to dispose of them. But it would be hard to see how we would have needed these arguments if instances of (BI) were just explanatorily basic in the sense just described. It is certainly reasonable to ask why anyone should think that it is more than instrumentally good to believe that roses are red if and only if roses are red. It is not a question that necessarily seems to answer itself.

My second point is that by claiming that instances of (BI) are explanatorily fundamental, the minimalist is committed to holding an implausible form of *particularism* about cognitive norms. Particularism is the view that there are no general rules, not even *prima facie* rules, for determining what is good or bad in particular cases. Rather, particular normative judgements are explanatorily basic: they are not justified by any more basic normative rules.

The most familiar form of particularism is moral particularism. Thus, the traditional moral theorist, for example, will justify a particular judgement (you should keep this promise of yours) on the basis of a principle (you should, other things being equal, keep your promises). The moral particularist, on the other hand, takes each situation as different and even unique, and denies that an appeal to principles will help us justify our decisions about what to do. The fact that you have kept this one promise today involves no appeal to any general rule that would justify keeping a different promise tomorrow.

My point is that if we say that instances of (BI) or (B) are basic in the sense that we do not need to justify them, then we are adopting an analogous form of *cognitive* particularism. Moral particularists may agree that it is good to keep this promise, and that one, and so on. What they disagree with is that we need to justify all this promise-keeping by a general norm of the form *If x amounts to keeping your promise then x is good*. Similarly, the minimalist suggests that it is good to believe that snow is white if and only if snow is white, and good to believe that grass is green if and only if grass is green, but denies that we need to justify this by appealing to the cognitive norm that *It is good to believe what is true*.

Particularism is classically very difficult to maintain, for at least two reasons.[17] First, it is difficult for the particularist to explain how we learn from our experience. As Hare notes, 'to learn to do anything is never to learn to do an individual act; it is always to learn to do acts of a certain kind in a certain kind of situation; and this is to learn a principle'.[18] For example, a child learns to say 'Thank you' after receiving something, just when he grasps that the next time someone gives him something, he *should* say 'Thank you'. Learning takes place in particular situations, but it is *learning* just when it involves the adoption of general rules. This in turn uncovers the second point: that normative reasoning always implicitly involves general rules. This is because in making normative judgements, we are required to make similar judgements in similar circumstances.

In the moral case, suppose I advise two friends to keep their promises, even though they are different promises made to different people. If questioned, it would be odd if I did not try appealing to a general principle which explained why I treated the cases alike. And it would be very odd if I instead insisted that there was nothing alike between the cases, and that it was just a basic fact that in each situation the promise should be kept. Similarly, it would be just as odd if I told one friend to keep a promise and the other not to do so but refused to explain why the cases were different. Either way, it would be as if I had opted out of the normative point of view. It is part of normative reasoning to treat like cases alike, and in so doing, we implicitly appeal to principles that pick out the common features of the situations in question. And it is hard to see why the same point will not hold in the case of belief. If I am justified in thinking it is more than instrumentally good to believe that snow is white just when snow is white, and so on for every other instance of (BI), then it seems reasonable, just on the basis of these uncontroversial facts about normative reasoning, that this is because there is something in common between all these instances: namely, in each case, it is good to believe what is true.

This last point is important, because it shows why the debate between minimalists and their opponents over (BI) or other normative principles is different from their debates over other platitudes, such as the correspondence platitude. Unless one is a particularist, normative judgements implicitly commit one to informative normative rules, even if those rules are not without exception.

Non-minimalists can adopt cognitive particularism as well, of course. But if the above reasoning is right, minimalists are committed to it. And that seems a serious problem for minimalism. For even if we allow that the jury is still out on the question of whether cognitive particularism is correct, this means that minimalism is tied to it in a way in which other views are not.

(c) *We can rationally explain our acceptance of the instances of (BI) by appealing to the beneficial practical effects of believing that true beliefs are more than instrumentally good*. Perhaps what justifies our acceptance of the idea that it is more than instrumentally good to have true beliefs is nothing more than the fact that is useful to have that belief. If so, then we have a general explanation for our acceptance of the instances of (BI) without appealing to any fact involving truth.

Minimalists are not the only ones who might feel the pull of this sort of account of truth's more-than-instrumental value. Reductive naturalists like Stich could adopt the same position, as might Rorty. For (c) is completely consistent with the idea that truth is not more than instrumentally good, yet none the less *it pays to think that it is.* Beliefs obviously can have all sorts of practical effects independently of whether they are actually true or false. Wishful thinking can lead to greater success than one could otherwise obtain. Very like the naïve amateur mountain-climber, whose false belief that the summit is attainable helps him get farther up the slope than he might otherwise have been able to, believing falsely that truth is deeply good may help us to obtain other ends, like better scientific theories and more honest societies.

I certainly have no quarrel with the idea that there is a pragmatic pay-off to believing that truth is more than instrumentally good. But this cannot be the whole story. Thinking that it is would be an inherently unstable or even self-undermining position. It reminds one of Pascal's 'argument' for believing in God, according to which it is useful to believe that there is a God even if there is no such thing. Famously, this reasoning itself could never produce sincere belief. One either submits oneself to brainwashing or ends up just pretending. Then there is rule utilitarianism, which endorses, on strictly utilitarian grounds, rules or dispositions to engage in actions that would ordinarily not be chosen by a utilitarian. Like Pascal's view, rule utilitarianism seems impossible to put into practice without engaging in pretence or brainwashing. For when faced with a decision about whether to follow some rule and do something that would result in negative utility, the reflective rule utilitarian only has considerations of utility to fall back on.

So one thing you might say is that the situation is similar in the present debate over the value of truth. The position embodied in (c), that the only reason for believing that truth is more than instrumentally good is that it is useful to do so, becomes a sort of pretence. And like most pretences, this one is bound to erode under reflection.

While I think the 'one thought too many' point is worth making, there is a much simpler point to make against someone who believes something like (c). The real problem is not that the advocate of (c) has 'one thought too many' about the value of truth. The real problem is that the mere fact (if it is a fact) that it is useful to believe that truth is deeply normative does not explain why it is, or even how it can be. And that, surely, is the question at issue. All the noise about what it is useful to believe simply evades the main worry at hand, namely, that if, as minimalists believe, there is nothing more to a belief's being true than what is given in the instances of (T), there are not enough resources to explain why a belief's being true is more than instrumentally good. And that means they have not explained everything their opponents believe is true about truth.

It would be too hasty to say that the arguments given above prove that minimalism, or deflationism in general, is mistaken. The right lesson to draw is subtler, if just as interesting. What the above considerations show is that if minimalism is to be maintained, it must cast its lot with the revisionists. For a key assumption of the above argument, one Horwich himself grants, is that truth is, at least to some extent, more than instrumentally valuable. Again, one might reject this claim, or even, as Stich and Rorty do, reject the idea that truth has any value at all. But if minimalists reject these assumptions, they must admit that they are no longer trying simply to capture all the things people normally want to say about truth, all the facts about truth, as one might say. Rather, like Rorty and Stich, they must admit they are trying to make converts, to change people's minds about truth and its value, to cast down, once and for all, false idols.

5 Expressivism, pure disquotationalism and normativity

Minimalism is only one type of deflationism. In this final section, I shall briefly consider two other forms of deflationism in the light of truth's normativity. The issues raised by these theories are complicated; the considerations raised here therefore remain unsettled pending further investigation.

Expressivism. The first view I shall consider is actually a family of views, distinguished as a group by their endorsement of a thoroughly nondescriptive account of truth, or more accurately of 'true'. The expressivist about truth, in other words, holds that in ascribing 'true' to our beliefs and assertions, we are not describing those beliefs or assertions, or saying that they possess some property, but 'manifesting a stance towards them'[19] or 'undertaking a commitment'[20] or 'paying them a compliment'.[21] In short, while expressivist theories may differ considerably on other details, all agree that to say that your belief that snow is white is true does not describe that belief: it expresses a pro-attitude towards it.

Expressivists about truth, far from dismissing or otherwise playing down the normativity of truth, see it as the central feature of the concept. On the surface, then, they may appear to have no problem explaining the value of truth.

Boghossian has famously pointed out that views of this sort threaten to be self-undermining.[22] If ascriptions of truth are non-descriptive, then how can we make a principled distinction between those utterances/statements and so on that are descriptive and those that are not? The traditional way of making this distinction is by saying that descriptive or factual claims are those that are capable of being true or false; non-descriptive or non-factual claims are those that are not so capable. But if we then say that claims involving 'true' and 'false' are themselves non-descriptive, it seems we have said that the very distinction between descriptive and non-descriptive claims falls on the non-descriptive side of the line. We begin to lose all sense of the distinction. But to this initial objection there is a now familiar response: there are attitudes, and then there are attitudes, so to speak. That is: the objection just mounted presupposes that we cannot distinguish descriptive claims from non-descriptive claims in any way other than by appealing to some robust theory of truth, but this is not so. For normative stances, expressions of attitude and so on come in different types; and one could presumably appeal to the differences between these types to distinguish descriptive from non-descriptive claims at the outset.[23]

This may be so, but it seems to me that another threat remains. Suppose we grant that truth ascriptions are entirely non-descriptive. What would a claim like *It is good to believe what is true and only what is true* mean on this view? It will not mean that it is good for a belief to have the property of being true. Rather, to say that it is good to believe what is true on the expressivist account will presumably amount to holding that it is good to adopt a particular stance, or express a particular attitude towards those beliefs we call 'true'. (And if we are expressivists all the way down, then to think it is good to do so means to express a particular attitude towards the expressing of that sort of attitude.) Fine. But why is it good to express pro-attitudes towards 'true' beliefs and negative attitudes towards 'false' ones? What makes one sort of response appropriate in the case of a belief like the belief that snow is white and not towards the belief that grass is white? This sort of question cannot just be dismissed. As expressivists themselves emphasize, attitudes and stances do not just appear out of thin air.[24] They are appropriate reactions to certain phenomena in the environment around the person adopting that stance or expressing that attitude. As such, they can be apt or not, reasonable or not, and so on. So what makes it apt to use 'true' to express a pro-attitude in some situations and not others?

I am not saying that this question cannot be answered. Far from it; expressivists typically give quite sophisticated answers (Kraut, for example, holds that a speaker holds claims true when they are 'ineliminable relative to his explanatory agenda'). But it is hard to see how any answer to this question can appeal to anything more than the practical or instrumental value of holding some beliefs as opposed to others. For the account itself, at least as it is typically understood, rules out anything in common to the 'true' beliefs which would make them good to have – which would make it apt for expressions of pro-attitudes. Accordingly, it is hard to see how the expressivist has the resources to explain what it is about true propositions that make them more than instrumentally good to believe. There simply is nothing about a belief's being true that could help us explain why this is so.

This, I suspect, will not come as news to most expressivists. Such philosophers typically see themselves as advocating a revisionary pragmatist view of truth in the first place. They would simply reject the idea that truth is more than instrumentally good. They do not see this as a problem. I do.

Pure Disquotationalism. The other theory I shall reflect on briefly is Hartry Field's pure disquotationalism. On this theory, 'the claim that utterance *u* is true in the pure disquotational sense is cognitively equivalent to *u* itself as I understand it'.[25] There are a variety of interesting and distinguishing features of Field's view, but for present purposes, the most important is that unlike Horwich, Field allows that a schema like

DS. '*p*' is true if and only if *p*

is itself part of the language, 'rather than merely having instances that are part of the language'.[26] Assuming this move is permitted, Field seems well situated to account for the truism that truth is normative. As he says (pp. 120–1),

> Another example of 'true' as a device of infinite conjunction and disjunction is the desire to utter only true sentences or to have only true beliefs: what we desire is the infinite

conjunction of all claims of the form 'I utter "*p*" only if *p*' or 'I believe "*p*" only if *p*'.... There is no difficulty in desiring that all one's beliefs be disquotationally true; and not only can each of us desire such things, there can be a practice of badgering others into having such a desire. Is not this enough for there being a 'norm' of asserting and believing?

Frankly, I do not think it is enough: for a start, the fact that we desire something does not mean it is good (even by our own lights); for another, 'badgering others' does not do justice to our practice of giving and asking for *reasons* in relation to our normative stances. But putting that aside for the moment, I shall unpack Field's suggestion a bit more, in the terms used in this paper. Field can be seen, like Horwich, as holding that (TN) is clearly derivable from (DS), or a similar principle involving belief, together with

(B) It is good to believe that *p* if and only if *p*.

Again (B) says nothing about truth. The difference is that on Field's account, because it permits schemata, there is no further question of why we accept all the instances of (B), since (B) itself, together with the rules governing such schemata, can be used to derive (TN). This avoids the danger of cognitive particularism, for we now have a general rule (or at least a rule schema). To think it is good to have all and only true beliefs in the purely disquotational sense is to think it is good to believe *p* when and only when *p*.

What is lacking on this account? Apart from worries about the view as a whole, there is another worry, one which, interestingly enough, is similar to the one just raised about expressivism. The worry is simple: why is it good to have true beliefs in the purely disquotational view? What makes it good to believe that *p* if and only if *p*?

Again the worry is not that the pure disquotationalist cannot give an answer to this question. The worry is that no answer will be adequate to account for beliefs about the way in which truth is good. Of course, the nondeflationist will also have to answer the question of why truth is good, or what makes it good, both instrumentally and non-instrumentally, to have true beliefs. But here the thought is that what makes truth more than instrumentally good is something about a belief's being true. That is, it is something about the property of truth that makes it good to believe that which has the property. But this is not the sort of answer that a pure disquotationalist is in any position to give.[27]

Notes

1. See, for example, numerous articles by Richard Rorty, including 'Is Truth a Goal of Inquiry? Donald Davidson *vs* Crispin Wright', repr. in M.P. Lynch (ed.), *The Nature of Truth* (MIT Press, 2001), pp. 259–87, and 'Universality and Truth', in R. Brandom (ed.), *Rorty and his Critics* (Oxford: Blackwell, 2000), pp. 1–30; B. Allen, *Truth in Philosophy* (Harvard UP, 1993). Davidson has also recently argued that truth is not a goal of enquiry: see his 'Truth Rehabilitated', in *Rorty and his Critics*, pp. 65–74.
2. See, e.g., Rorty, 'Is Truth a Goal of Inquiry?', p. 279.
3. See M. Dummett, 'Truth', *Proceedings of the Aristotelian Society*, 59 (1958), pp. 141–62. A number of other philosophers, especially Crispin Wright, have also made this point vigorously, e.g., Wright, *Truth and Objectivity* (Harvard UP, 1992); and H. Putnam, 'Does the Disquotational Theory of Truth Solve All Philosophical Problems?', repr. in his *Words and Life* (Harvard UP, 1995), pp. 264–78.

4. See, e.g., Horwich, 'Norms of Truth and Meaning', in R. Schantz (ed.), *What is Truth?* (Berlin: De Gruyter, 2001), pp. 133–45; B. Williams, *Truth and Truthfulness* (Princeton UP, 2002); S. Blackburn, 'Reason, Virtue and Knowledge', in A. Fairweather and L. Zagzebski (eds), *Virtue Epistemology: Essays on Epistemic Virtue and Responsibility* (Oxford UP, 2001), pp. 15–29, at p. 23.
5. See my 'Truth and Multiple Realizability', forthcoming in *Australasian Journal of Philosophy*.
6. W. James, *Pragmatism and the Meaning of Truth* (Harvard UP, 1975), p. 42. [See also Ch. 8 of this volume – Ed.]
7. The distinction between thick and thin values stems from Bernard Williams: see, e.g., his *Ethics and the Limits of Philosophy* (Harvard UP, 1985), p. 128. Williams applies the distinction to concepts, as opposed to properties as I do here. Adam Kovach claims that truth is a thick value-*concept*, 'Truth as a Value Concept', in A. Chapuis and A. Gupta (eds), *Circularity, Definition and Truth* (New Delhi: Indian Council of Philosophical Research, 2000), pp. 199–215.
8. See for example, P. Engel, 'Is Truth a Norm?', in P. Kotatko *et al.* (eds), *Interpreting Davidson* (CSLI Publications, 2001), pp. 37–50. For an understanding of (TN) closer to the one presented in the text, see Blackburn, 'Reason, Virtue and Knowledge', p. 23.
9. I refer to Stich's infamous argument for the conclusion that having true beliefs is no more instrumentally valuable than having true* or true** beliefs: see his *The Fragmentation of Reason* (MIT Press, 1990).
10. See Horwich, 'Norms of Truth and Meaning', p. 143; Williams, *Truth and Truthfulness*, pp. 65–6.
11. Frankfurt, 'Freedom of the Will and the Concept of a Person', repr. in *The Importance of What We Care About* (Cambridge UP, 1988), pp. 11–25.
12. Horwich, *Truth*, 2nd edn (Oxford UP, 1998).
13. Horwich, *Truth*, 2nd edn; *Meaning* (Oxford UP, 1998), p. 190–1; and 'Norms of Truth and Meaning', in Schantz (ed.), *What is Truth?*, pp. 133–45.
14. Horwich, *Truth*, 2nd edn, pp. 44–5; 'Norms of Truth and Meaning', pp. 140–1.
15. Williams, *Truth and Truthfulness*, p. 65.
16. Horwich, *Meaning*, p. 104, and 'A Defense of Minimalism', in Lynch (ed.), *The Nature of Truth*, pp. 559–78, at p. 560 [Ch. 10 of this volume, p. 152 – Ed.].
17. For detailed discussions of particularism, see B. Hooker and M. Little (eds), *Moral Particularism* (Oxford UP, 2000).
18. R.M. Hare, *The Language of Morals* (Oxford: Clarendon Press, 1952), p. 60.
19. R. Kraut, 'Robust Deflationism', *Philosophical Review*, 102 (1993), pp. 247–63. The first advocate of an expressivist view, as I understand him, was P.F. Strawson: see his 'Truth', *Proceedings of the Aristotelian Society*, Supp. Vol. 24 (1950), pp. 129–56.
20. Brandom, 'Pragmatism, Phenomenalism and Truth-Talk', in P. French *et al.* (eds), *Midwest Studies in Philosophy*, Vol. XII: *Realism and Anti-Realism* (Minnesota UP, 1988), pp. 75–94, at p. 83.
21. Rorty sometimes makes remarks tending in this direction: see, e.g., his *Philosophy and the Mirror of Nature* (Princeton UP, 1978), pp. 307–8.
22. P. Boghossian, 'The Status of Content', *Philosophical Review*, 99 (1990), pp. 157–84.
23. This is the sort of response given by Kraut in his 'Robust Deflationism'.
24. Blackburn, for example, often emphasizes this point with regard to moral expressivism: see his *Ruling Passions* (Oxford UP, 1998).

25. Field, *Truth in the Absence of Fact* (Oxford UP, 2001), p. 121. [Ch. 11 of this volume, p. 161 – Ed.]
26. Field, p. 115. He suggests that inferences involving schematic letters are governed by two rules: one that permits us to replace all instances of a schematic letter with a sentence and another that allows us to infer that for any *x*, if *x* is a sentence then *x* is F from the schema F('*p*'). As he notes, this amounts to using what is essentially a fragment of substitutional quantifier language.
27. Earlier versions of this paper benefited from comments received at the Moral Sciences Club, the University of St Andrews, the University of Wales, the University of Connecticut, the University of Cincinnati, the Mississippi Philosophical Association and the Eastern Pennsylvania Philosophical Association. Thanks also to Paul Bloomfield, JC Beall, Simon Blackburn, Patrick Greenough, Paul Horwich, Alessandra Tanesini, Chase Wrenn, Crispin Wright and two anonymous referees for their comments.

21 Truth as convenient friction

HUW PRICE

1 Introduction

In a recent paper, Richard Rorty begins by telling us why pragmatists such as himself are inclined to identify truth with justification:

> Pragmatists think that if something makes no difference to practice, it should make no difference to philosophy. This conviction makes them suspicious of the distinction between justification and truth, for that distinction makes no difference to my decisions about what to do.[1]

Rorty goes on to discuss the claim, defended by Crispin Wright, that truth is a normative constraint on assertion. He argues that this claim runs foul of this principle of no difference without a practical difference:

> The need to justify our beliefs to ourselves and our fellow agents subjects us to norms, and obedience to these norms produces a behavioral pattern that we must detect in others before confidently attributing beliefs to them. But there seems to be no occasion to look for obedience to an *additional* norm – the commandment to seek the truth. For – to return to the pragmatist doubt with which I began – obedience to that commandment will produce no behavior not produced by the need to offer justification.[2]

Again, then, Rorty appeals to the claim that a commitment to a norm of truth rather than a norm of justification makes no behavioral difference.

This is an empirical claim, testable in principle by comparing the behavior of a community of realists (in Rorty's sense) to that of a community of pragmatists. In my view, the experiment would show that the claim is unjustified, indeed false. I think that there is an important and widespread behavioral pattern that depends on the fact that speakers do take themselves to be subject to such an additional norm. Moreover, it is a behavioral pattern so central to what we presently regard as a worthwhile human life that no reasonable person would knowingly condone the experiment. Ironically, it is also a pattern that Rorty of all people cannot afford to dismiss as a pathological and dispensable by-product of bad philosophy. For it is conversation itself, or at any rate a central and indispensable part of conversation as we know it—roughly, interpersonal dialogue about "factual" matters.[3]

In other words, I want to maintain that in order to account for a core part of ordinary conversational practice, we must allow that speakers take themselves and their fellows to be governed by a norm stronger than that of justification. Not only is this a norm which speakers acknowledge they may fail to meet, even if their claims are well-justified—this much is true of what Rorty calls the cautionary use of truth[4]—but also, more significantly, it is a norm which speakers immediately assume to be breached by someone with whom they disagree, *independently of any diagnosis of the source of the disagreement*. Indeed, this is the very essence of the norm of truth, in my view. It gives disagreement its immediate normative character, a character on which dialogue depends, and a character which no lesser norm could provide.

This fact about truth has been overlooked, I think, because the norm in question is *so* familiar, so much a given of ordinary linguistic practice, that it is very hard to see. Ordinarily we look through it, rather than at it. In order to make it visible, we need a sense of how things would be different without it. Hence, in part, my reason for beginning with Rorty. Though I disagree with Rorty about the behavioral consequences of a commitment to "a distinction between justification and truth," I think that the issue of the behavioral consequences of such a commitment embodies precisely the perspective we need, in order to bring into focus this fundamental aspect of the normative structure of dialogue.

In sharing Rorty's concern with the role of truth in linguistic practice, I share one key element of his pragmatism. But my kind of pragmatism about truth is not well marked on contemporary maps, and hence my second reason for beginning with Rorty. Rorty has explored the landscape of pragmatist approaches to truth more extensively than most pragmatist writers, past or present, and at different times has been inclined to settle in different parts of it. By locating my own kind of pragmatism with respect to views that Rorty has visited or canvassed, I hope to show that there is a promising position that he and others pragmatists have overlooked.

As noted, my view rests on the claim that a norm of truth plays an essential and little-recognized role in assertoric dialogue. In pursuit of this conclusion, it will turn out to be helpful to distinguish three norms, in order of increasing strength: roughly, sincerity, justification and truth itself. Though somewhat crudely drawn, these distinctions will suffice to throw into relief the crucial role of the third norm in linguistic practice. My strategy will be to contrast assertion as we know it with some non-assertoric uses of language. In these latter cases, I'll argue, the two weaker norms still apply. Moreover, it turns out that some of the basic functions of assertoric discourse could be fulfilled in an analogous way, by a practice which lacked the third norm. But it will be clear, I hope, that that practice would not support dialogue as we know it. What is missing—what the third norm provides—is the automatic and quite unconscious sense of engagement in common purpose that distinguishes assertoric dialogue from a mere roll call of individual opinion. Truth is the grit that makes our individual opinions engage with one another. Truth puts the cogs in cognition, at least in its public manifestations.[5]

To use a Rylean metaphor, my view is thus that truth supplies factual dialogue with its essential esprit de corps. As the metaphor is meant to suggest, what matters is that speakers think that there is such a norm—that they take themselves to be governed by it—not that their view be somehow confirmed by science or metaphysics. Science has already done its work, in pointing out the function of the thought in the lives of creatures like us. This may suggest that a commitment to truth is like a commitment to theism, an analogy which Rorty himself draws, against Wright, in the paper with which I began. In effect, Rorty's point is that it is one thing to establish that we do employ a realist notion of truth, a normative notion stronger than justification; quite another to establish that we ought to do so. As in the case of theism, we might do better to wean ourselves of bad realist habits.

However, there are several important differences between the two cases. First, the behavioral consequences of giving up theism are significant but hardly devastating.[6] But if I am right about the behavioral role of truth, the consequences of giving up truth would be very serious indeed, reducing the conversation of mankind to a chatter of disengaged monologues.[7]

Second, it is doubtful whether giving up truth is really an option open to us. I suspect that people who think it is an option haven't realized how deeply embedded the idea of truth is in linguistic practice, and therefore underestimate the extent of the required change, in two ways. They fail to see how radically different from current practice a linguistic practice without truth would have to be, and they overestimate our capacity to change our practices in general to move from here to there (underestimating the practical inflexibility of admittedly contingent practices[8]).

Third, and most interestingly of all, the issue of the status of truth is enmeshed with the terms of the problem, in a way which is quite uncharacteristic of the theism case. Metaphysical conclusions tend to be cast in semantic vocabulary. Theism is said to be in error in virtue of the fact that its claims are not *true,* that its terms fail to *refer.* For this reason, it is uniquely difficult to formulate a meaningful antirealism about the semantic terms themselves. In my view the right response to this is not to think (with Paul Boghossian[9]) that we thereby have a transcendental argument for semantic realism. Without an intelligible denial, realism is no more intelligible than antirealism. The right response—as Rorty himself in any case urges—is to be suspicious of the realist–antirealist debate itself.[10] However, Rorty ties rejection of the realist–antirealist debate to rejection of a notion of truth distinct from justification, and of the idea of representation. I think this is the wrong path to the right conclusion. We should reject the metaphysical stance not by rejecting truth and representation, but by recognizing that in virtue of the most plausible story about the function and origins of these notions, they simply don't sustain that sort of metaphysical weight.

Concerning his own view of truth, Rorty describes himself as oscillating between Jamesian pragmatism, on the one hand, and deflationism, on the other: "swing[ing] back and forth between trying to reduce truth to justification and propounding some sort of minimalism about truth."[11] My own view is neither of these alternatives, but has something in common with each. On the one hand, it is certainly some sort of minimalism about truth, but not the familiar sort that Rorty has in mind—not "Tarski's breezy disquotationalism," as he calls it.[12] I agree with familiar disquotationalist minimalists such as Quine[13] and Paul Horwich[14] that truth is not a substantial property, about the nature of which there is an interesting philosophical issue. Like them, I think that the right approach to truth is to investigate its function in human discourse—to ask what difference it makes to us to have such a concept. Unlike such minimalists, however, I don't think the right answer to this question is that truth is merely a grammatical device for disquotation. I think that it has a far more important function, which requires that it be the expression of a norm. But like other minimalists, again, I think that there is no further question of interest to philosophy, once the question about function has been answered.

On the other hand, my view of truth is also pragmatist, for it explicates truth in terms of its role in practice. (This is also true of standard disquotational views, of course, although they ascribe the truth predicate a different role in practice.) In another sense, it conflicts with pragmatism, for it opposes the proposal that we identify truth with justification. This contrast reflects a deep tension within pragmatism. From Peirce and James on, pragmatists have often been unable to resist the urge to join their opponents in asking "What is truth?" (Indeed, the pragmatist position as a whole is often characterized in terms of its answer to this question.) Pragmatism thus turns its back on alternative paths to philosophical illumination about truth, even though these alternative paths—explanatory and genealogical approaches—are at least compatible with, if not mandated by, the pragmatist doctrine that we understand problematic notions in terms of their practical significance.

Rorty himself is well aware of this tension within pragmatism. In "Pragmatism, Davidson and Truth," for example, he notes that James is less prone than Peirce to try to answer the "ontological" or reductive question about truth, and suggests that Davidson may be thought of as a pragmatist in the preferable non-reductive sense.[15] As he swings between pragmatism and deflationism, then, Rorty himself is at worst only intermittently subject to this craving for an *analysis* of truth. All the same, it seems to me that he is never properly aware of the range of possibilities for non-reductive pragmatism about truth. In particular, he is not properly aware of the possibility that such a pragmatism might find itself explaining the fact that the notion of truth in ordinary use is (and perhaps ought to be, in whatever sense we might make of this) one that conflicts with the identification of truth with justification: a normative goal of inquiry, stronger than any norm of justification, of the very kind that realists about truth—opponents both of pragmatism and of minimalism—mistakenly sought to analyze. In other words, Rorty seems to miss the possibility that the right thing for the explanatory pragmatist to say might be that truth is a goal of inquiry distinct from norms of justification, and that the realist's mistake is to try to *analyze* this normative notion, rather than simply to investigate its function and genealogy. It is this latter possibility that I want to defend.

2 Falsity and lesser evils

As I have said, I want to argue that truth plays a crucial role as a norm of assertoric discourse. It is not the only such norm, however, and a good way to highlight the distinctive role of truth is to distinguish certain weaker norms, and to imagine a linguistic practice which had those norms but not truth.[16] By seeing what such a practice lacks, we see what truth adds.

There are at least two weaker norms of assertion, in addition to any distinctive norm of truth.[17] The weakest relevant norm seems to be that embodied in the principle that it is prima facie appropriate to assert that p only when one believes that p—prima facie, because of course many other factors may come into play, in determining the appropriateness of a particular assertion in a particular context. Let's call this the norm of *subjective assertibility*.[18] The norm is perhaps best characterized in negative form—that is, in terms of the conditions under which a speaker may be censured for failing to meet it:

> (Subjective assertibility)
>
> A speaker is incorrect to assert that p if she does not believe that p; to assert that p in these circumstances provides prima facie grounds for censure, or disapprobation.

The easiest way to see that this norm has very little to do with truth is to note that it is analogous to norms which operate with respect to utterances which we don't take to be truth-apt. Prima facie, it is inappropriate to request a cup of coffee when one doesn't want a cup of coffee, but this doesn't show that requests or expressions of desires are subject to a norm of truth. In effect, this norm is simply that of sincerity, and some such norm seems to govern much conventional behavior. Conventions often depend on the fact that communities censure those who break them in this specific sense, by acting in bad faith.

The second norm is that of (personal) *warranted assertibility*. Roughly, 'p' is warrantedly assertible by a speaker who not only believes that p, but is *justified* in doing so. The qualification 'personal' recognizes the fact that there are different kinds and degrees of warrant or justification, some of them more subjective than others. For example, is justification to be assessed with reference to a speaker's actual evidence as she (presently?) sees it, or by some less subjective lights? For the moment, for a degree of definiteness, let us think of it in terms of subjective coherence—a belief is justified if supported by a speaker's other current beliefs. This is what I shall mean by *personal* warranted assertibility.

Again, this second norm is usefully characterized in negative or censure form:

> (Personal warranted assertibility)
>
> A speaker is incorrect to assert that p if she does not have adequate (personal) grounds for believing that p; to assert that p in these circumstances provides prima facie grounds for censure.

A person who meets both the norms just identified may be said to have done as much as possible, *by her own current lights*, to ensure that her assertion that p is in order. Obviously, realists will say that her assertion may nevertheless be incorrect. Subjective assertibility and (personal) warranted assertibility do not guarantee truth. To an extent, moreover, most pragmatists are likely to agree. Few people who advocate reducing truth to (or replacing truth by) a notion of warranted assertibility have personal warranted assertibility in mind. Rather, they imagine some more objective, community-based variant, according to which a belief is justified if it coheres appropriately with the other beliefs of one's community. If we call this *communal* warranted assertibility, then the point is that we can make sense of a gap between the personal and communal notions. A belief may be justified in one sense but not the other.

Pragmatists and realists may thus agree that there is a normative dimension distinct from subjective assertibility and personal warranted assertibility—an assertion may be *wrong*, despite meeting these norms. This does not yet establish that the normative standard in question need be marked in ordinary discourse. In principle, it might be a privileged or theoretical notion, useful in expert second-order reflection on linguistic practice but unnecessary in folk talk about other matters. In practice, however, there seems a very good reason why it should not remain restricted in this way. Unless individual speakers recognize such a norm, the idea that they might *improve* their views by consultation with the wider community is simply incoherent to them. (It would be as if we gave a student full marks in an exam, and then told him that he would have done better if his answers had agreed with those of other students.)

It may seem that as yet, this argument doesn't favor realism over pragmatism. If the normative standard an individual speaker needs to acknowledge is that of the community as a whole, there is as yet no pressure to a notion of truth beyond community-wide warranted assertibility. But what constitutes the relevant community? At any given stage, isn't the relation of a given community to its possible present and future extensions just like that of the individual to her community? If so, then the same argument applies at this level. At each stage, the actual community needs to recognize that it may be wrong by the standards of some broader community.[19]

The pragmatist might now seem obliged to follow Peirce, in identifying truth with warranted assertibility in the ideal limit of inquiry. The useful thing about this limit, in this context, is that it transcends any actual community. But in my view, as I'll explain below (and as Rorty in some moods already case agrees), a better move for a pragmatist is to resist the pressure to *identify* truth with anything—in other words, simply to reject the assumption that an adequate philosophical account of truth needs to answer the question "What is truth?" Better questions for a pragmatist to ask are the explanatory ones: Why do we have such a notion? What job does it do in language? What features does it need to have to play this role? And how would things be different if we didn't have it?

For the moment, we have the beginnings of an answer to the last question. If we didn't have a normative notion in addition to the norms of subjective assertibility and personal warranted assertibility, the idea that we might improve our commitments by seeking to align them with those of our community would be simply incoherent. I'll call this the passive account of the role of the third norm—passive, because it doesn't yet provide an active or causal role for a commitment to truth. Later, I'll argue that the third norm not only creates the conceptual space for argument, in this passive sense, but actively encourages speakers to participate.[20]

3 The third norm in focus

The best way to bring the third norm into focus is again to consider its negative or censure form:

(Truth)

If not-p, then it is *incorrect* to assert that p; if not-p, there are prima facie grounds for censure of an assertion that p.

The important point is that this provides a norm of assertion which we take it that a speaker may fail to meet, even if she does meet the norms of subjective assertibility and (personal) warranted assertibility. We are prepared to make the judgment that a speaker is *incorrect*, or *mistaken*, in this sense, simply on the basis that we are prepared to make a contrary assertion; in advance, in other words, of any judgment that she fails to meet one or other of the two weaker norms.[21]

One of the reasons why this third norm is hard to distinguish from the two weaker norms of assertibility is that when we apply it in judging a fellow speaker right or wrong, the basis for our judgment lies in our own beliefs and evidence. It is not as though we are in a position to make the judgment from the stance of reality itself, as it were. I think this can make it seem as if application of this norm involves nothing more than re-assertion of the original claim (in the case in which we judge it correct), or assertion of the negation of the original claim (in the case in which we judge it incorrect). Construed in these terms, our response contains nothing problematic for orthodox disquotational versions of the deflationary view, of course. Re-assertion of this sort is precisely one of the linguistic activities which disquotational truth facilitates. Construed in these terms, then, there is no need for truth to be a distinct *norm*.

However, our response is not merely re-assertion, or assertion of the negation of the original claim. If it were, it would involve no commendation or criticism of the original utterance. This non-normative alternative is hard to see, I think, because the norm in question is so familiar and so basic. As a result, it is difficult to see the immense difference the norm makes to the character of disagreements. But it comes into focus, I think, if we allow ourselves to imagine a linguistic practice which allowed re-assertion and contrary assertion, but without this third normative dimension. What we need to imagine, in other words, is a linguistic community who use sentences to express their beliefs, and have a purely disquotational truth predicate, but for whom disagreements have no normative significance, except in so far as it is related to the weaker norms of assertibility.

This imaginative project is not straightforward, of course. Indeed, it isn't clear that it is entirely coherent. If there is a third norm of the kind in question, isn't it likely to be constitutive of the very notions of assertion and belief? If so, what sense is there in trying to imagine an assertoric practice which lacked this norm?

Well, let's see. What we need is the idea of a community who take an assertion—or rather the closest thing they have to what we call an assertion—to be *merely* an expression of the speaker's opinion. The relevant idea is familiar in the case of expressions of desires and preferences. It is easy to imagine a community—we are at least close to it ourselves—who have a language in which they give voice to psychological states of these kinds, not by *reporting* that they hold them (which would depend on assertion), but directly, in conventional linguistic forms tailored specifically for this purpose.

Think of a community who use language primarily for expressing preferences in restaurants, for example. (Perhaps the development of such a restricted language from scratch is incoherent, but surely we might approach it from the other direction. Imagine a community of dedicated lunchers, whose language atrophies to the bare essentials.) In this community we would expect a norm analogous to subjective assertibility: essentially, a normative requirement that speakers use these conventional expressions sincerely. Less obviously, such a practice might also involve a norm analogous to personal warranted assertibility. In other words, expressed preferences might be censured on the grounds that they were not well-founded, by the speaker's own lights (for example, on the grounds they did not cohere with the speaker's other preferences and desires). However, in this practice there need be no place for a norm analogous to truth—no idea of an objective standard, over and above personal warranted assertibility, which preferences properly aim to meet.

At least to a first approximation, we can imagine a community who treat expressions of beliefs in the same way. They express their beliefs—that is, let us say, the kind of behavioral dispositions which we would characterize as beliefs—by means of a speech act we might call the *merely-opinionated assertion* (*MOA,* for short). These speakers—"Mo'ans," as I called them in another paper[22]—criticize each other for insincerity and for lack of coherence, or personal warranted assertibility. But they go no further than this. In particular, they do not treat a disagreement between two speakers as an indication that, necessarily, one speaker or other is mistaken—in violation of some norm. On the contrary, they allow that in such a case it may turn out that both speakers have spoken correctly, by the only two standards the community takes to be operable. Both may be sincere, and both, in their own terms, may have good grounds for their assertion.[23]

A speech community of this imagined kind could make use of a disquotational truth predicate, as a device to facilitate agreement with an expression of opinion made by another speaker. 'That's true' would function much like 'Same again', or 'Ditto', used in a bar or restaurant. Just as 'Same again' serves to indicate that one has the same preference as a previous speaker, 'That's true' would serve to indicate that one holds the same opinion as the previous speaker. The crucial point is that if the only norms in play are subjective assertibility and personal warranted assertibility, introducing disquotational truth leaves everything as it is. It doesn't import a third norm.

The difficulty we have in holding on to the idea of such a community stems from our almost irresistible urge to see the situation in terms of our own normative standards. There really is a third norm, we are inclined to think, even if these simple creatures don't know it. If two of them make incompatible assertions then one of them must be objectively incorrect, even if by their lights they both meet the only norms they themselves recognize. (I think even pragmatists will be inclined to say this, even though they want to equate the relevant kind of incorrectness not with falsity but with lack of some kind of justification more objective than that of personal warrant.) But the point of the story is precisely to bring this third norm into sharp relief, and hence I am quite happy to allow challenges to the story on these grounds, which rely on the very conclusion I want to draw. *For us*, there is a third norm. But why is that so? Where does the third norm come from? What job does it do—what difference does it make to our lives? And what features must it have in order to do this job?

4 What difference does the third norm make?

Let's return to the Mo'ans, and their merely-opinionated assertions. Recall that Mo'ans use linguistic utterances to express their "beliefs," as well as other psychological states, such as preferences and desires. Where they differ from us is in the fact that they do not take a disagreement between two speakers in this belief-expressing linguistic dimension to indicate that one or other speaker must be at fault. They recognize the possibility of fault consisting in failure to observe one of the two norms of subjective assertibility or personal warranted assertibility, but lack the idea of the third norm, that of truth itself. This shows up in the fact that by default, disagreements are of a no-fault kind, in the way that expression of different preferences often are for us.

What does it take to add the third norm to such a practice? Do the Mo'ans need to come to believe that there is a substantial property that the attitudes they use MOAs to express may have or lack—perhaps the property of corresponding to how things are in the world, perhaps that of being what their opinions are fated to converge on in the long run? Does adoption of the third norm depend on a piece of folk metaphysics of this kind? Not at all, in my view. The practice the Mo'ans need to adopt is simply that whenever they are prepared to assert (in the old MOA sense) that p, they also be prepared to ascribe fault to anyone who asserts not-p, independently of any grounds for thinking that that person fails one of the first two norms of assertibility. Perhaps they also need to be prepared to commend anyone who asserts that p, or perhaps failure-to-find-fault is motivation enough in this case. At any rate, what matters is that disagreement itself be treated as grounds for disapproval, as grounds for thinking that one's interlocutor has fallen short of some normative standard.

At this point it is worth noting what may seem a serious difficulty. If the Mo'ans don't *already* care about disagreements, why should they care about disagreements about normative matters? Suppose that we two are Mo'ans, that you assert that p, and that I assert that not-p. If this initial disagreement doesn't bother me, why should it bother me when—trying to implement the third norm—you go on to assert that I am "at fault," or "incorrect"? Again, I simply disagree; and if the former disagreement doesn't bite then nor will the latter. And if what was needed to motivate me to resolve our disagreement was *my* acceptance that I am "at fault," then motivation would always come too late. If I accept this at all, it is only after the fact—after the disagreement has been resolved in your favor.

To get the sequence right, then, I must be motivated by your disapproval itself. This is an important point. It shows that if there could be an assertoric practice which lacked the third norm, we couldn't add that norm simply by adding a normative predicate. In so far—so very far, in my view—as terms such as 'true' and 'false' carry this normative force in natural languages, they must be giving voice to something more basic: a fundamental practice of expressions of attitudes of approval and disapproval, in response to perceptions of agreement and disagreement between expressed commitments. I'll return to this point, for it is the basis of an important objection to certain other accounts of truth.

Imagine for the moment that the Mo'ans could add the third norm by adding a normative predicate, or pair of predicates ('correct' and 'incorrect', say). What would be the usage rule for these predicates? Simply that one be prepared to assert that p is correct if and only if one is prepared to assert that p; and to assert that p is incorrect if and only if one is prepared to assert that not-p. In other words, the usage rule is something very close to the disquotational schema ('p' is true if and only if p). As a result, the present proposal, that the truth predicate is an explicit expression of the third norm, already seems well on the way to an explanation of the disquotational functions of truth. We have already noted that the converse argument does not go through. A practice which lacked the third norm could still make use of a disquotational truth predicate.[24]

For the moment, we are interested in the function of the third norm. Why might the invention of such a norm be useful? What distinctive job does it do? We already have one answer to the latter question, and hence possibly to the former, in the passive account. Without a norm stronger than that of warranted assertibility *for me*, or *for us*, the idea of improving *my*, or *our*, current commitments would be incoherent. The third norm functions to create the conceptual space for the idea of further improvement. To do this job, we need a norm stronger than that of warranted assertibility for any *actual* community. (Of course, this doesn't yet show that we need something more than Peircean ideal assertibility, but one thing at a time.)

However, we can do better than the passive account. The third norm doesn't just hold open the conceptual space for the idea of improvement. It positively encourages such improvement, by motivating speakers who disagree to try to resolve their disagreement. Without the third norm, differences of opinion would simply slide past one another. Differences of opinion would seem as inconsequential as differences of preference. With the third norm, however, disagreement automatically becomes normatively loaded. The third norm makes what would otherwise be no-fault disagreements into unstable social situations, whose instability is only resolved by argument and consequent agreement—and it provides an immediate incentive for argument, in that it holds out to the successful arguer the reward consisting in her community's positive evaluation of her dialectical position. If reasoned argument is generally beneficial—beneficial in some long-run sense—then a community of Mo'ans who adopt this practice will tend to prosper, compared to a community who do not.

I'll call this the active account of the role of the third norm. In effect, it contends that the fact that speakers take their belief-expressing utterances to be subject to the third norm plays a causal, carrot-and-stick role in encouraging them to settle their differences, in cases in which initially they disagree. The force of these carrots and sticks should not be over-stated, however. In any given case, we are free not to give voice to our third-norm-grounded disapproval. If we do express it, the speakers with whom we disagree are free not to rise to the bait. Many factors may determine what happens in any particular case. My claim is simply that the third norm adds something new to the preferential mix. In particular, it gives rise to a new preferential pressure towards resolution of the disagreement in question—a pressure which would not exist in its absence, which does not exist for the Mo'ans, and which could not exist for us, if we did not care in general about the approval and disapproval of our fellows. The third norm depends on the fact that (to varying extents in varying circumstances) we do care about these things. It exploits this fact about us to make disagreements matter, in a way in which they would not otherwise matter. But the third norm does not come for free, with a general disposition to seek the approval of our fellows. What we have but the Mo'ans lack is an additional, special purpose, disposition: the disposition to disapprove of speakers with whom we disagree. This disposition is the mark of the third norm.

As in the case of the passive account of the role of the third norm, we need to be careful that this active account does not viciously presuppose the very notions for which it seeks to account. The notion of disagreement requires particular care. For one thing, recognition that one differs from a previous speaker must take some form more basic than the belief that he or she has said something "false," for otherwise there could not be a convention of applying this normative predicate when one perceives that one differs. For another, there is an important sense in which on the proposed account, it is the practice of applying the third norm which creates the disagreement, where initially there was mere difference. Properly developed, the view seems likely to be something like this. There is a primitive incompatibility between certain behavioral commitments[25] of a single individual, which turns on the impossibility of both doing and not doing any given action A—both having and not having a cup of coffee, for example. All else—both the public perceived incompatibility of "conflicting" assertions by different speakers, and the private perceived incompatibility essential to reasoning—is by convention, and depends on the third norm.

Obviously, much more needs to be said about this. At another level, much also needs to be said about possible advantages of such a mechanism for resolving differences—about its long-run advantages, for example, both compared to the case in which there is no such mechanism and compared to the case in which there is some different mechanism, such as deference to social rank. For immediate purposes, however, my claim does not depend on this latter work. For the present, my claim is simply that truth does play the role of this third norm, in providing the friction characteristic of factual dialogue as we know it. (I also claim, roughly, that this is perhaps the most interesting fact about truth, from a philosophical perspective.) In principle, this claim could be true, even though the practice in question was not advantageous. In principle, truth, and with it dialogue, could turn out to be a bad thing for the species, biologically considered.[26] No matter. It would still be true that we wouldn't have understood truth until we understood its role in this debilitating practice.

Is talk of dialogue really essential here? Couldn't we say simply that the third norm is what distinguishes a genuinely assertoric linguistic practice from the "merely opinionated" assertoric practice of the Mo'ans? The distinguishing the mark of genuine assertion is thus that by default, difference is taken as a sign of *fault,* of breach of a normative standard.

It would not strictly be incorrect to say this, in my view, but it ought to seem unsatisfying, by pragmatist lights. A pragmatist is interested in the practical significance of the notions of truth and falsity, in the issue of what difference possession of these notions makes to our lives. According to the view just suggested, the answer will be something like this. The difference that truth and falsity make is that they make our linguistic practice genuinely assertoric, rather than Mo'an. "I see that," the pragmatist will then say, "But what practical difference does *that* difference make, over and above the obvious difference—that is, over and above the fact that we approve and disapprove of some of our fellow speakers on occasions on which we wouldn't otherwise do so?"

My own answer to the new question is that these habits of approval and disapproval tend to encourage dialogue, by providing speakers with an incentive to resolve disagreements. It is true that at this point the pragmatist's question—"What difference does *that* make?"—can be (indeed, should be) asked all over again. The importance I have here attached to dialogue rests in part on the gamble that this question will turn out to have an interesting answer, in terms of the long-run advantages of pooled cognitive resources, agreement on shared projects, and so on. But not entirely. Dialogue seems such a central part of our linguistic and social lives, that the difference between a world without dialogue and our world is much greater than *merely* the difference between MOAs and genuine assertions. So even if were to turn out that the development of dialogue had been an historical accident, of no great value to the species biologically considered, it would still be true that the most interesting behavioral consequence of the third norm would be dialogue, and not merely the more-than-merely-Mo'an assertion which makes dialogue possible.[27]

Recall that I began by challenging Rorty's claim that no behavioral consequences flow from a distinction between justification and truth. In one sense, my challenge does indeed amount to pointing out that the third norm—a notion of truth stronger than justification—brings with it the following behavioral difference: a disposition to criticize, or at least disapprove of, those with whom one disagrees. But if this were all the challenge amounted to, Rorty would be entitled to reply that of course there is this difference, but that this difference makes no interesting further difference. Hence the importance of dialogue, in my view, which turns a small difference in normative practice into a big difference in the way in which speakers engage with one another (and thereby ensures that Rorty's claim fails in an interesting rather than an insignificant way).

5 Peirce regained?

Now to the question deferred above. Does the third norm need to be other than a more-than-merely-personal notion of justification? In particular, couldn't it be a Peircean flavor of ideal warranted assertibility? I have several responses to this suggestion.

First, I think that the proposal is mistakenly motivated. As I said in the introduction, I think it stems from the tendency, still too strong in Peirce, to ask the wrong question about truth. If we think that the philosophical issue is "What is truth?," then naturally we'll want to find an answer—something with which we may identify truth. Then, given standard objections to metaphysical answers, it is understandable that Peirce's alternative should seem attractive. But the attraction is that of methadone compared to heroin. Far better, surely, from a pragmatist's point of view, to rid ourselves of the craving for analysis altogether. To do this, we need to see that the basic philosophical needs that analysis seemed to serve can be met in another mode altogether: by explanation of the practices, rather than reduction of their objects. (Moreover, the explanatory project has the potential to allow us realist truth without the metaphysical disadvantages. The apparent disadvantages of realist truth emerge in the light of the reductive project, for it is from this perspective that it seems mysterious what truth could be. If we no longer feel obliged to ask the question, we won't be troubled by the fact that it is so hard to answer. We lose the motivation for seeking something else—something less "mysterious" than correspondence—with which to identify truth.)

"I accept all that," the pragmatist might say. "Nevertheless, perhaps it is true of the notion of truth (as we find it in practice), that it is identical (in some interesting sense) to ideal warranted assertibility. Shouldn't you therefore allow, at least, the possibility that a Peircean account is the correct one?"

Two points in response to this. The first, an old objection, is that it is very unclear what the notion of the ideal limit might amount to, or even that it is coherent. For example, couldn't actual practice be improved or idealized in several dimensions, not necessarily consistent with one another. In this sense, then, the Peircean pragmatist seems a long way from offering us a concrete proposal.[28]

The second point—also an old point, for as Putnam observes, it is essentially the naturalistic fallacy[29]—concerns the nature of the proposed identification of truth with ideal warranted assertibility. Truth is essentially a normative notion. Its role in making disagreements matter depends on its immediate motivational character. Why should ideal warranted assertibility have this character? If someone tells me that my beliefs are not those of our infinitely refined future inquirers, why should that bother me? My manners are not those of the palace, but so what? In other words, it is hard to see how such an identification could generate the immediate normativity of truth.[30] (It seems more plausible that we begin with truth and define the notion of the ideal limit in terms of it: what makes the limit ideal is that is reaches truth. This doesn't tell us how and why we get into this particular normative circle in the first place.)

I haven't yet mentioned what seems to me to be the most telling argument against the pragmatist identification of truth with warranted assertibility (in Peircean form or otherwise). It often seems to be suggested (by Rorty himself, among others—see the quotes with which I began), that instead of arguing about truth, we could argue about warranted assertibility. This seems to me to miss a crucial point. Without truth, the wheels of argument do not engage; disagreements slide past one another. This is true of disagreements about any matter whatsoever. In particular, it is true of disagreements about warranted assertibility. If we didn't already have truth, in other words, we simply couldn't argue about warranted assertibility. For we could be aware that we have different opinions about what is warrantedly assertible, without that difference of opinion seeming to matter. What makes it matter is the fact that we subscribe to a practice according to which disagreement is an indication of culpable error, on one side or other; in another words, that we already take ourselves to be subject to the norms of truth and falsity.[31]

The crucial point is thus that assertoric dialogue requires an intolerance of disagreement. This needs to be present already in the background, a pragmatic presupposition of judgment itself. I am not a maker of assertions, a judger, at all, unless I am already playing the game to win, in the sense defined by the third norm. Since winning is already characterized in terms of truth, the idea of a conversational game with some alternative point is incoherent. It is like the idea of a game in which the primary aim is to compete—this idea is incoherent, because the notion of competition already presupposes a different goal.[32]

There is a connection here with an old objection to relativism, which tries to corner the relativist by asking her whether she takes her own relativistic doctrine to be true, and if so in what sense. The best option for the relativist is to say that she takes the doctrine to be true in the only sense she allows, namely, the relativistic one. When her opponent replies, "Well, in that case you shouldn't be troubled by the fact that I disagree, because you recognize that what is true for me need not be true for you, and vice versa," the relativist has a reply. She can argue that truth is relative to communities, not to individual speakers, and hence that disagreements don't necessarily dissolve in this way.

My pragmatist opponents fare less well against an analogous argument, I think. The basic objection to their position is that in engaging with me in argument about the nature of truth (as about anything else), they reveal that they take themselves to be subject to the norm whose existence they are denying. If they didn't take themselves to be subject to it, they would be in the same boat as the Mo'ans, with no reason to treat the disagreement between us as a cause for concern. They affirm p, I affirm not-p; but by their lights, this should be like the case in which they say 'Yes' and I say 'No', in answer to the question 'Would you like coffee?' (This is what it should be like even if p is of the form 'q is warrantedly assertible'.) The disagreement simply wouldn't bite.

6 Truth as convenient fiction?

The third norm thus requires a notion of truth that differs from justification, even of a Peircean ideal variety. In this sense, then, the present account is realist rather than pragmatist about truth. In another sense, however, the view surely seems antirealist. After all, I have argued that what matters is that speakers take there to be a norm of truth, not that there actually be such a norm, in some speaker-independent sense. Isn't this antirealism, or more precisely, in the current jargon, a form of *fictionalism* about truth?

If so, could this be a satisfactory outcome? If truth does play the role I have claimed for it in dialogue, wouldn't the realization that it is a fiction undermine that linguistic practice, by making it the case that we could no longer consistently feel bound by the relevant norms?

Let's call this objection the threat of dialogical nihilism. In my view, it isn't a practical threat. I think that in practice we find it impossible to stop caring about truth. This isn't an argument for realism, of course. The discovery that our biological appetites are not driven by perception of pre-existing properties—the properties of being tasty, sexually attractive, or whatever—does not lessen the force of those appetites, but no one thinks that this requires a realist view the properties concerned. Even if nihilism were a practical threat, this wouldn't be reason for thinking that the claim that truth is a fiction is *false,* by the lights of the game as currently played. It might be a pragmatic reason for keeping the conclusion quiet, but that is a different matter altogether (especially according to my realist opponents).

So even if the present view is correctly characterized as a form of fictionalism about truth, the nihilism objection is far from conclusive. But are the labels 'fictionalism' or 'antirealism' really appropriate? The need for caution stems from the fact that this approach to truth threatens to deprive both sides of the realism–antirealism debate of conceptual resources on which the debate seems to depend. As I noted earlier, the relevant metaphysical issues tend themselves to be framed in terms of truth, and related notions. A theory is said to be in error if its claims are not *true*, or if its terms fail to *refer*, for example. So the issue of the status of truth is here enmeshed with the terms of the problem, in a way which is quite uncharacteristic of metaphysical issues about other notions. As a result, it may be impossible to formulate a meaningful antirealism or fictionalism about the semantic terms themselves. This doesn't mean that we have to be realists about semantic notions, but only that if we are not realists we should be cautious about calling ourselves antirealists (or fictionalists), if these categories presuppose the very notions we want to avoid being realist about.

This may sound like an impossible trick, but in fact the kind of distinction we need is familiar elsewhere. It is the distinction between someone who "talks god talk" and espouses atheism, and someone who rejects the theological language game altogether (on Carnapian pragmatic grounds, say). These are two very different ways of rejecting theism. In the present case, the point is that we may consistently reject semantically-grounded realism about the semantic notions themselves, so long as we do so by avoiding theoretical use of semantic notions altogether, rather than by relying on those notions to characterize our departure from realism. (Why "theoretical use"? Because there is nothing to stop us continuing to use these semantic notions in a deflationary or disquotational sense.)

It might be suggested that we can sidestep this difficulty altogether by casting the relevant metaphysical issues in ontological rather than semantic terms. On this view, the relevant issue is whether truth exists, not whether (some) truth-ascriptions are true. Against this suggestion, however, it is arguable that the relevant metaphysical issues arise initially from data concerning human linguistic usage, and only become metaphysical in the light of substantial semantic assumptions about the functions of the language concerned—for example, that it is truth-conditional, or referential, in function. If so, then truth is once again enmeshed with the terms of the problem. And even if we concede the possibility of the ontological shift, the authority of Quine, Carnap and others may perhaps be invoked in support of a deflationary attitude to ontology, with the result that the realist–antirealist issue still dissolves.[33]

These issues are complex, and deserve a much more detailed examination than I can give them here. For present purposes, I simply flag the following as a possible outcome (of considerable plausibility, in my view). In common with other deflationary approaches to truth, the present account not only rejects the idea that there is a substantial metaphysical issue about truth (a substantial issue about the truthmakers of claims about truth, for example). Because it is about truth, it also positively prevents "reinflation." In other words, it seems to support a general deflationary attitude to issues of realism and antirealism. If so, then deflationism about truth is not only not to be equated with fictionalism, but tends to undermine the fictional–nonfictional distinction, as applied in the metaphysical realm.[34]

As I noted at the beginning, the present account of truth is hard to find on contemporary maps. In part, as should now be clear, this is because it combines elements not normally thought to be compatible. In one sense it is impeccably pragmatist, for example, for it appeals to nothing more than the role of truth in linguistic practice. Yet it rejects the pragmatist's *ur*-urge, to try to identify truth with justification. Again, it defends a kind of truth commonly seen as realist, but does so from a pragmatist starting point, without the metaphysics that typically accompanies such a realist view of truth. So in thinking about how to characterize this account of truth, we should be sensitive to the possibility that our existing categories—fictionalism, realism, and perhaps pragmatism itself—may need to be reconfigured. If so, then putting the position on the map is not like noticing a small country (Lichtenstein, perhaps) that previously we'd overlooked. It is more like discovering a geographical analog of the platypus, a region which our pre-existing cartographical conventions seemed a priori to disallow.

I began with Rorty's claim that the distinction between justification and truth makes no difference in practical life, no difference to our "decisions about what to do." Rorty regards a commitment to a notion of truth stronger than justification as a relic of a kind of religious deference to external authority. He recommends that just as we have begun to rid ourselves of theism, we should rid ourselves of the "representationalist" dogma that our beliefs are answerable to standards beyond ourselves. For Rorty, then, realist truth is a quasi-religious myth, which we'd do better without.

Despite my reservations about the fictionalist label, I have agreed that truth is in some sense a myth, or at least a human creation.[35] But I have denied that in providing a norm stronger than justification, a commitment to truth makes no behavioral difference. On the contrary, I've argued, it plays an essential role in a linguistic practice of great importance to us, *as we currently are*. It is not clear whether we could coherently be otherwise, whether we could get by without the third norm. If so, however, then the result would be a very different language game. My main claim is that we haven't understood truth until we understand its role in the game we currently play.[36]

Notes

1. "Is Truth a Goal of Enquiry? Donald Davidson versus Crispin Wright," in *Truth and Progress: Philosophical Papers Vol. 3* (New York: Cambridge University Press, 1998), pp. 19–42, at p. 19.
2. Ibid., p. 26.
3. Irony aside, nothing here turns on whether by 'conversation' I mean the same as Rorty. For me, what matters is the role of truth in the kind of interpersonal linguistic interaction I'll call factual or assertoric dialogue, or simply dialogue. I don't claim that dialogue exhausts conversation, in Rorty's sense or any other. I used scare quotes on 'factual' above in anticipation of the sug-

gestion that the notion of factuality in play might depend on that of truth, in a way which would create problems for my own account of the role of truth in dialogue. There is no such difficulty, in my view. On the contrary, I take the perceived "factuality" or "truth-aptness" of the utterances in question to be part of the explanandum of the kind of account here proposed; cf. fn. 25.

4. "Pragmatism, Davidson and Truth," in *Objectivity, Relativism and Truth: Philosophical Papers Vol. 1* (New York: Cambridge University Press, 1991), pp. 126–150, at p. 128.
5. If private cognition depends on the norms of public dialogue then truth plays the same role, at second hand, in the private sphere. This is a plausible extension of the present claim, in my view, but I won't try to defend it here.
6. At least compared to the alternative.
7. "Global *Waiting for Godot,*" as a member of an audience in Dundee suggested I put it. Even more seriously, as noted above, giving up truth might silence our own "internal" rational dialogues.
8. Jonathan Rée makes a point of this kind against Rorty: "[C]ontingencies can last a very long time. Our preoccupations with love and death may not be absolute necessities, but they are not a passing fad either, and it is a safe bet that they will last as long as we do." "Strenuous Unbelief," *London Review of Books* XX, No. 20, 15 October 1998.
9. Paul Boghossian, "The Status of Content," *Philosophical Review* XCIX, No. 2, 157–184.
10. A realist could object that a commitment to the third norm might be useful and yet in error, but Rorty can't. It is fair for him to object against Wright that this commitment might be like theism, because Wright takes metaphysics seriously. By Wright's professed standards, then, the theism objection poses a real threat.
11. "Is Truth a Goal of Enquiry? Donald Davidson versus Crispin Wright," in *Truth and Progress: Philosophical Papers Vol. 3* (New York: Cambridge University Press, 1998), pp. 19–42, at p. 21.
12. Ibid., p. 21.
13. *Philosophy of Logic* (Englewood Cliffs: Prentice-Hall, 1970).
14. *Truth* (New York: Basil Blackwell, 1990).
15. Robert Brandom makes a similar point in "Pragmatism, Phenomenalism, and Truth Talk," *Midwest Studies in Philosophy* XXII, 75–93 (1988).
16. For present purposes I can remain open-minded on the question as to whether such a practice is really possible. Perhaps a truth-like norm is essential to any practice which deserves to be called linguistic. At any rate, my use of the following linguistic thought experiment does not depend on denying this possibility.
17. In what sense "weaker"? In the sense, at least, that they apply to a wider range of linguistic behaviors. 'Less specialized' might be a better term.
18. This corresponds to a common use of the term 'assertibility condition', as for example when it is said that the subjective assertibility condition for the indicative conditional 'If p then q' is a high conditional credence in q given p.
19. Cf. Rorty's remark that "[f]or any audience, one can imagine a better-informed audience." ("Is Truth a Goal of Enquiry? Donald Davidson versus Crispin Wright," in *Truth and Progress: Philosophical Papers Vol. 3* (New York: Cambridge University Press, 1998), pp. 19–42, at p. 22.)
20. This account has prescriptive and non-prescriptive readings. The former uses the notion of improvement full-voice, saying that if speakers are to improve their commitments, they need the idea of the third norm. But as N. J. J. Smith pointed out to me, it could well be objected that the relevant notion of improvement simply presupposes the third norm, and therefore can't provide

any independent rationale for adopting it. However, no such circularity undermines the non-prescriptive reading, whose point is that because our existing conversational practice does take for granted such a notion of improvement, it thereby reveals its commitment to a third norm.

21. Note the contrast with Rorty's cautionary use of true. In that use we say of a claim that we take to be well-justified that it might not be true. In the present use we say of a claim that we might even allow to be well-justified by its speaker's own lights that it is not true. It is the difference between mere caution and actual censure.
22. "Three Norms of Assertibility, or How the MOA Became Extinct," *Philosophical Perspectives* XII, 241–54 (1988). The present section and the next draw significantly on that paper.
23. As I noted earlier, my use of this example does not depend on the claim that such a linguistic practice be possible. It is doubtful whether notions such as belief, assertion and opinion are really load-bearing, in the imagined context. However, much of the effect of the example could be achieved in another way, by imposing suitable restrictions on real linguistic practices—by imagining self-imposed restrictions on what we are allowed to say. One way to approach the Mo'an predicament from our own current practice would be to adopt the convention that whenever we would ordinarily assert 'p', we express ourselves instead by saying 'My own opinion is that p'.
24. A defender of the disquotational view might argue that although there is a third norm, it is not the function of the truth predicate to express it. This will be a difficult position to defend, however. If any predicate—'correct', for example—expresses the third norm, then that predicate will function as a disquotational predicate, for the reason just mentioned. Hence it will have been pointless to maintain that true itself is not normative. So the disquotationalist needs to claim that the third norm is not expressed at all in this predicative form, and that seems implausible.
25. This is another place where circularity threatens. We need to be sure that the psychological states mentioned at this point are not thought of as already "factual" or "representational" in character, in a way which presupposes truth. In so far as it is truth-involving, the "factual" character of the domain in question needs to be part of the explanandum—something that emerges from, rather than being presupposed by, the pragmatic account of the origins and consequences of "truth talk." In my view, one of the attractive features of this approach is that it offers the prospect that the uniformity of "factual," truth-involving talk might be compatible with considerable plurality in the nature and functions of the underlying psychological states. It thus offers an attractive new form for expressivist intuitions. Cf. my *Facts and the Function of Truth*, (New York: Basil Blackwell, 1988), Ch. 8, "Metaphysical Pluralism," *The Journal of Philosophy*, LXXXIX, 387-409 (1992), §IV, and "Immodesty Without Mirrors—Making Sense of Wittgenstein's Linguistic Pluralism," in Max Kölbel and Bernhard Weiss (eds), *Wittgenstein's Lasting Significance* (Boston: Routledge & Kegan Paul, forthcoming).
26. Even if not dangerous on its own, the third norm might become so in combination with some particularly deadly source of intractable disagreements, such as religion commitment. More generally, the thought that argument is sometimes dangerous suggests a link between the concerns of this paper and the motivations of the Pyrrhonian skeptics. On the present view of truth, the question whether we could get by without truth seems closely related to that as to whether we could live as thoroughgoing Pyrrhonian skeptics.
27. This point would acquire new and even stronger force, if it were to be established that private cognition rests on the norms of public dialogue, in the way suggested in fn. 5.

28. As Rorty notes (in "Pragmatism, Davidson and Truth," in *Objectivity, Relativism and Truth: Philosophical Papers Vol. 1* (New York: Cambridge University Press, 1991), pp. 126–150, at p. 130), Michael Williams makes a point of this kind: "[W]e have no idea what it would be for a theory to be ideally complete and comprehensive ... or of what it would be for inquiry to have an end." (M. Williams, "Coherence, Justification and Truth," *Review of Metaphysics* XXXIV, 243–272, at p. 269)
29. *Meaning and the Moral Sciences* (Boston: Routledge & Kegan Paul, 1978), p. 108.
30. It may seem that this argument begs the question against the pragmatist, by assuming that there is an epistemologically relevant gap between ideal warranted assertibility and truth. (I am grateful to a referee at this point.) But the issue is not whether we need some norm in addition to ideal warranted assertibility, but whether ideal warranted assertibility itself could be immediately normative, in the way in which truth is. No one disputes that the manners of the palace are normative for those who live there—that's what it is to be manners—but it is an open question whether they are or should be normative for the rest of us. Similarly for ideal assertibility, except that in this case no one lives at the limit, so that there is no one for whom the question is not open.
31. I noted above that the same point applies to the normative predicates themselves. If we weren't already disposed to take disagreement to matter, we couldn't do so simply by adding normative predicates, for disagreement about the application of those predicates would be as frictionless as disagreement about anything else. My claim is thus that the notions of truth and falsity give voice to more primitive implicit norms, which themselves underpin the very possibility of "giving voice" at all. In effect, the above argument rests on the observation that this genealogy cannot be reversed: if we start with a predicate—warrantedly assertible or any other—then we have started too late. (I suspect that by "giving voice," I mean something close to "making explicit," in Brandom's sense.)
32. Here, incidentally, we see the essential flaw in the pious sentiments of Grantland Rice (1880–1954):

    For when the One Great Scorer comes,
    To write against your name,
    He marks—not that you won or lost—
    But how you played the game.

    The One Great Scorer might assign marks on this basis, for divine purposes. *Pace* Rice, however, we couldn't play the game in question with such marks as our primary goal, for then it would be a different game altogether.
33. I defend the first of these two options in "Naturalism Without Representationalism," in Mario de Caro and David Macarthur (eds), *Naturalism in Question* (Cambridge, Mass.: Harvard University Press, 2003); and the second in "Metaphysical Pluralism," *The Journal of Philosophy*, LXXXIX, 387–409 (1992) and "Naturalism and the Fate of the M-worlds," *Proceedings of the Aristotelian Society, Supp. Vol.*, LXXI, 247–267 (1997).
34. Rorty often says that he wants to walk away from realist–antirealist disputes. In other words, he doesn't think that there is an interesting philosophical question as to whether our commitments "mirror" reality. The above argument suggests that like other deflationists about truth, I have reason to follow Rorty in walking away from these issues. (In particular, my defence of truth over justification does not force me to stay.)

35. In the light of the argument above, this is a point more about the genealogy than about the reality of truth.
36. The first version of this paper was written for a conference in honour of Richard Rorty at ANU in 1999. I am grateful to participants at that conference and to many subsequent audiences for much insightful discussion of these ideas; and also to an anonymous referee for helpful comments on an earlier version.

22 True enough

CATHERINE Z. ELGIN

Epistemology valorizes truth. Sometimes practical, or prudential, or political reasons convince us to accept a known falsehood, but most epistemologists deny that we can have cognitively good reasons to do so. Our overriding cognitive objective, they maintain, is the truth, preferably the whole truth, and definitely nothing but the truth (Goldman 1999, p. 5; Lehrer 1986, p. 6; Bonjour 1985, p. 9). If they are right, then at least insofar as our ends are cognitive, we should accept only what we consider true, take pains to insure that the claims we accept are in fact true, and promptly repudiate any previously accepted claims upon learning that they are false. I suggest, however, that the relation between truth and epistemic acceptability is both more tenuous and more circuitous than is standardly supposed. Sometimes, I contend, it is epistemically responsible to prescind from truth to achieve more global cognitive ends.

At first blush, this looks mad. To retain a falsehood merely because it has epistemologically attractive features seems the height of cognitive irresponsibility. Allegations of intellectual dishonesty, wishful thinking, false consciousness, or worse immediately leap to mind. But science routinely transgresses the boundary between truth and falsehood. It smoothes curves and ignores outliers. It develops and deploys simplified models that diverge, sometimes considerably, from the phenomena they purport to represent. Even the best scientific theories are not true. Not only are they plagued with anomalies and outstanding problems, but where they are successful, they rely on laws, models, idealizations and approximations that diverge from the truth. Truth-centered epistemology, or *veritism,* as Alvin Goldman calls it, easily accommodates anomalies and outstanding problems, since they are readily construed as defects. The problem comes with the laws, models, idealizations, and approximations which are acknowledged not to be true, but which are nonetheless critical to, indeed constitutive of, the understanding that science delivers. Far from being defects, they figure ineliminably in the success of science. If truth is mandatory, much of our best science turns out to be epistemologically unacceptable and perhaps intellectually dishonest. Our predicament is this: We can retain the truth requirement and construe science either as cognitively defective or as non-cognitive, or we can reject, revise, or relax the truth requirement and remain cognitivists about, and fans of science.

I take it that science provides an understanding of the natural order. By this I do not mean merely that an ideal science *would* provide such an understanding or that in the end of inquiry science *will* provide one, but that much actual science has done so and continues to do so. I take it then that much actual science is cognitively reputable. So an adequate epistemology should explain what makes good science cognitively good. Too strict a commitment to truth stands in the way. Nor is science the only casualty. In other disciplines such as philosophy, and in everyday discourse, we often convey information and advance understanding by means of sentences that are not literally true. An adequate epistemology should account for this as well. A tenable theory is a tapestry of interconnected sentences that together constitute an understanding of a domain.[1] My thesis is that some sentences that figure ineliminably in tenable theories make no pretence of being true, but are not defective on that account. If I am right, theories and the understandings they embed have a more intricate symbolic structure than we standardly suppose. Nevertheless, I do not think that we should jettison concern for truth completely. The question is what role a truth commitment should play in a holism that recognizes a multiplicity of sometimes conflicting epistemological desiderata.

Consensus has it that epistemic acceptability requires something like justified and/or reliable, true belief. The justification, reliability, and belief requirements involve thresholds. '[O]ne may need to be confident enough and well enough justified and one's belief must perhaps derive from a reliable enough source, and be little enough liable to be false.'(Sosa 2000, p. 2) But truth, unlike the other requirements, is supposed to be an absolute matter. Either the belief is true or it is not. I suggest, however, that the truth requirement on epistemic acceptability involves a threshold too. I am not saying that truth itself is a threshold concept. Perhaps such a construal of truth would facilitate treatments of vagueness, but that is not my concern. My point is rather that epistemic acceptability turns not on whether a sentence is true, but on whether it is true enough – that is, on whether it is close enough to the truth. 'True enough' obviously has a threshold.

I should begin by attempting to block some misunderstandings. I do not deny that (unqualified) truth is an intelligible concept or a realizable ideal. We readily understand instances of the (T) schema:

'Snow is white' is true ≡ snow is white
'Power corrupts' is true ≡ power corrupts
'Neutrinos have mass' is true ≡ neutrinos have mass

and so on. A disquotational theory of truth suffices to show that the criterion expressed in Convention (T) can be satisfied. One might of course, want more from a theory of truth than satisfaction of Convention (T), but to make the case that the concept of truth is unobjectionable, a minimalist theory that evades the paradoxes suffices. Moreover, not only does it make sense to call a sentence true, we can often tell whether it is true. We are well aware not only that 'Snow is white' is true ≡ snow is white, but also that 'Newly fallen snow is white' is true. The intelligibility and realizability of truth, of course, show nothing about which sentences are true or which truths we can discover. Nevertheless, as far as I can see, nothing about the concept of truth discredits veritism. Since truth is an intelligible concept, epistemology can insist that only truths are epistemically acceptable. Since truth is a realizable objective, such a stance does not lead inexorably to skepticism. I do not deny that veritism is an available epistemic stance. But I think it is an unduly limiting one. It prevents epistemology from accounting for the full range of our cognitive achievements.

If epistemic acceptance is construed as belief, and epistemic acceptability as knowledge, the truth requirement seems reasonable. For cognizers like ourselves, there does not seem to be an epistemically significant gap between believing that *p*, and believing that *p* is true.

Ordinarily, upon learning that our belief that *p* is false, we cease to believe that *p*. Moreover, we consider it cognitively obligatory to do so. One ought to believe only what is true. Perhaps a creature without a conception of truth can harbor beliefs. A cat, for example, might believe that there is a mouse in the wainscoting without believing that 'There is a mouse in the wainscoting' is true.[2] In that case, the connection between believing that *p* and believing that *p* is true is not exceptionless. But whatever we should say about cats, it does not seem feasible for any creature that has a conception of truth to believe that *p* without believing that *p* is true. If epistemic acceptance is a matter of belief, acceptance is closely linked to truth. Assertion is too. Although asserting that *p* is not the same as asserting that *p* is true, it seems plain that one ought not to assert that *p* if one is prepared to deny that *p* is true or to suspend judgment about whether *p* is true; nor ought one assert that *p* is true if one is prepared to deny that *p* or to suspend judgment about whether *p*. Assertion and belief, then, seem committed to truth. So does knowledge. Whether or not we take knowledge to be equivalent to justified or reliably generated true belief, once we discover the falsity of something we took ourselves to know, we withdraw the claim to knowledge. We say, 'I thought I knew it, but I was wrong,' not 'I knew it, but I was wrong'.

Being skeptical about analyticity, I do not contend that a truth commitment is part of the meanings of 'belief,' 'assertion,' and 'knowledge'. But whatever the explanation, because the truth commitment tightly intertwines with our views about belief, assertion, and knowledge, it seems best to retain that connection and revise epistemology by making compensatory adjustments elsewhere. Once those adjustments are made, knowledge and belief turn out to be less central to epistemology than we standardly think. I do not then claim that it is epistemically acceptable to *believe* what is false or that it is linguistically acceptable to *assert* what is false. Rather, I suggest that epistemic acceptance is not restricted to belief (Cohen, 1992). Analogously, uttering or inscribing seriously and sincerely for cognitive purposes – call it 'professing' – is not limited to asserting. Understanding is often couched in and conveyed by symbols that are not, and do not purport to be, true. Where such symbols are sentential, I call them felicitous falsehoods. I contend that we cannot understand the cognitive contributions of science, philosophy, or even our ordinary take on things, if we fail to account for such symbols. Let's look at some cases:

Curve smoothing: Ordinarily, each data point is supposed to represent an independently ascertained truth. (The temperature at t_1, the temperature at t_2, …) By interpolating between and extrapolating beyond these truths, we expect to discern the pattern they instantiate. If the curve we draw connects the data points, this is reasonable. But the data rarely fall precisely on the curve adduced to account for them. The curve then reveals a pattern that the data do not instantiate. Veritism would seem to require accepting the data only if we are convinced that they are true, and connecting these truths to adduce more general truths. Unwavering commitment to truth would seem then to require connecting all the data points no matter how convoluted the resulting curve turned out to be. This is not done. To accommodate every point would be to abandon hope of finding order in most data sets, for jagged lines and complicated curves mask underlying regularities. Nevertheless, it seems cognitively disreputable simply to let hope triumph over experience. Surely we need a better reason to skirt the data and ignore the outliers than the fact that otherwise we will not get the kind of theory we want. Nobody, after all, promised that the phenomena would accommodate themselves to the kind of theory we want.

There are often quite good reasons for thinking that the data ought not, or at least need not be taken as entirely accurate. Sometimes we recognize that our measurements are relatively crude compared with the level of precision we are looking for. Then any curve that is within some δ of the evidence counts as accommodating the evidence. Sometimes we suspect that some sort of interference throws our measurements off. Then in plotting the curve, we compensate for the alleged interference. Sometimes the measurements are in fact accurate, but the phenomena measured are complexes only some of whose aspects concern us. Then in curve smoothing we, as it were, factor out the irrelevant aspects. Sometimes we have no explanation for the data's divergence from the smooth curve. But we may be rightly convinced that what matters is the smooth curve the data indicate, not the jagged curve they actually instantiate. Whatever the explanation, we accept the curve, taking its proximity to the data points as our justification. We understand the phenomena as displaying the pattern the curve marks out. We thus dismiss the data's deviation from the smooth curve as negligible.

Ceteris paribus claims: Many lawlike claims in science obtain only ceteris paribus.[3] The familiar law of gravity

$$F=Gm_1m_2/r^2$$

is not universally true, for other forces may be in play. The force between charged bodies, for example, is a resultant of electrical and gravitational forces. Nevertheless, we are not inclined to jettison the law of gravity. The complication that charge introduces just shows that the law obtains only ceteris paribus, and when bodies are charged, ceteris are not paribus. This is no news. 'Ceteris paribus' is Latin for 'other things being equal', but it is not obvious what makes for equality in a case like this. Sklar glosses it as 'other things being normal' (Sklar 1999, p. 702), where 'normal' seems to cash out as 'typical' or 'usual'. Then a 'ceteris paribus law' states what usually happens. In that case, to construe the law of gravity as a ceteris paribus law is to contend that although there are exceptions, bodies usually attract each other in direct proportion to the product of their masses and in inverse proportion to the square of the distance between them.

This construal does not always work. Some laws do not even usually hold. The law of gravity is one. Snell's law

$$n_1 \sin i = n_2 \sin r$$

which expresses the relation between the angle of incidence and the angle of refraction of a light ray passing from one medium to a second, is another.[4] As standardly stated, the law is perfectly general, ranging over every case of refraction. It is not true of every case, though; it obtains only where both media are optically isotropic. The law then is a ceteris paribus law. But it is not even usually true, since most media are optically anisotropic (Cartwright 1983, pp. 46–47). One might wonder why physicists don't simply restrict the scope of the law: 'For any two optically isotropic media, $n_1\sin i=n_2\sin r$'. The reason is Gricean: expressly restricting the scope of the law implicates that it affords no insight into cases where the restriction does not obtain. Snell's law is more helpful. Even though the law is usually false, it is often not far from the truth. Most media are anisotropic, but lots of them – and lots of the ones physicists are interested in – are nearly isotropic. The law supplies good approximations for nearly isotropic cases. So although explanations and calculations that rely on Snell's law do not yield truths, they are often not off by much.

The law is valuable for another reason as well. Sometimes it is useful to first represent a light ray as conforming to Snell's law, and later introduce 'corrections' to accommodate anisotropic media. If we were interested only in the path of a particular light ray, such a circuitous approach would be unattractive. But if we are interested in optical refraction in general, it might make sense to start with a prototypical case, and then show how anisotropy perturbs. By portraying anisotropic cases as perturbations, we point up affinities that direct comparisons would not reveal. The issue then is what sort of understanding we want. Showing how a variety of cases diverge from the prototypical case contributes valuable insights into the phenomenon we are interested in. And what makes the case prototypical is not that it usually obtains, but that it cleanly exemplifies the features we deem important.

Idealizations: Some laws never obtain. They characterize ideal cases that do not, perhaps cannot, occur in nature. The ideal gas law represents gas molecules as perfectly elastic spheres that occupy negligible space and exhibit no mutual attraction. There are no such molecules. Explanations that adduce the ideal gas law would be epistemically unacceptable if abject fidelity to truth were required. Since helium molecules are not dimensionless, mutually indifferent, elastic spheres, an account that represents them as such is false. If veritism is correct, it is epistemically unacceptable. But, at least if the explanation concerns the behavior of helium in circumstances where divergence from the ideal gas law is negligible (roughly, where temperature is high and pressure is low), scientists are apt to find it unexceptionable.

Stylized facts are close kin of ceteris paribus claims. They are 'broad generalizations, true in essence, though perhaps not in detail' (Bannock, et al. 1998, pp. 396–7). They play a major role in economics, constituting explananda that economic models are required to explain. Models of economic growth, for example, are supposed to explain the (stylized) fact that the profit rate is constant.[5] The unvarnished fact of course is that profit rates are not constant. All sorts of non-economic factors – such as war, pestilence, drought, and political chicanery – interfere. Manifestly, stylized facts are not (what philosophers would call) facts, for the simple reason that they do not obtain. It might seem then that economics takes itself to be required to explain why known falsehoods are true. (Voodoo economics, indeed!) This cannot be correct. Rather, economics is committed to the view that the claims it recognizes as stylized facts are in the right neighborhood, and that their being in the right neighborhood is something economic models need to account for. The models may show them to be good approximations in all cases, or where deviations from the economically ideal are slight, or where economic factors dominate non-economic ones. Or the models might afford some other account of their often being nearly right. The models may differ over what is actually true, or as to where, to what degree, and why the stylized facts are as good as they are. But to fail to acknowledge the stylized facts would be to lose valuable economic information (for example, the fact that if we control for the effects of non-economic interference such as wars, epidemics, and the president for life absconding with the national treasury, the profit rate is constant). Stylized facts figure in other social sciences as well. I suspect that under a less alarming description, they occur in the natural sciences too. The standard characterization of the pendulum, for example, strikes me as a stylized fact of physics. The motion of the pendulum that physics is supposed to explain is a motion that no actual pendulum exhibits. What such cases point to is this: The fact that a strictly false description is in the right neighborhood is sometimes integral to our understanding of a domain.

A fortiori arguments from limiting cases: Some accounts focus on a single, carefully chosen case and argue that what holds in that case holds in general. If so, it does no harm to represent the phenomena as having the features that characterize the exemplary case. Astronomy sometimes represents planets as point masses. Manifestly, they are not. But because the distance between planets is vastly greater than their size, their spatial dimensions can safely be neglected. Given the size and distribution of planets in the solar system, what holds for properly characterized point masses also holds for the planets. Another familiar example comes from Rawls. *A Theory of Justice* represents people as mutually disinterested. Rawls is under no illusion that this representation is accurate. He recognizes that people are bound to one another by ties of affection of varying degrees of strength, length, and resiliency. But, he believes, if political agents have reason to cooperate even under conditions of mutual disinterest, they will have all the more reason to cooperate when ties of affection are present. I do not want to discuss whether Rawls is right. I just want to highlight the form of his argument. If what holds for the one case holds for the others, then it does no harm to represent people as mutually disinterested. That people are mutually disinterested is far from the truth. Conceivably, no one on Earth is wholly indifferent to the fates of every other person. But if Rawls is right, the characterization's being far from the truth does not impede its function in his argument.

The foregoing examples show that in some cognitive endeavors we accept claims that we do not consider true. But we do not indiscriminately endorse falsehoods either. The question then is, what makes a claim acceptable? Evidently, to accept a claim is not to take it to be true, but to take it that the claim's divergence from truth, if any, is negligible. The divergence need not be small, but whatever its magnitude, it can be safely neglected. We accept a claim, I suggest, when we consider it true enough. The success of our cognitive endeavors indicates that we are often right to do so. If so, a claim is acceptable when its divergence from truth is negligible. In that case it is true enough.

In practical, political, or prudential contexts, both the acceptance and the acceptability of falsehoods are widely recognized. One can accept, and be right to accept, the dean's latest dictum, if what matters is that the dean hath said it, not that it is true. But epistemic contexts are supposed to be different. Many epistemologists contend that when our concerns are cognitive we should accept only what we consider true. I disagree. I suggest that *to accept* that *p* is to take it that *p*'s divergence from truth, if any, does not matter. *To cognitively accept* that *p*, is to take it that *p*'s divergence from truth, if any, does not matter cognitively. The falsehood is 'as close as one needs for the purposes at hand' (Stalnaker 1987, p. 93). In what follows, I take 'acceptance' to mean 'cognitive acceptance'.

This raises a host of issues. Perhaps the most pressing is to say something about what I mean by 'cognitive'. A familiar line is that for a consideration to be cognitive is for it to aim at truth or to be truth conducive. Plainly, I can say no such thing. I suggest rather that a consideration is cognitive to the extent that it figures in an understanding of how things are. This is admittedly vague, but I am not sure that it is any worse than untethered remarks about truth-conduciveness and the like.

It might seem that my characterization just postpones the evil day (and not for long enough!), since 'an understanding of how things are' must itself be explicated in terms of truth or truth-conduciveness. To see the problem, compare three concepts – belief, thought, and understanding. Belief aims at truth. Roughly, a belief fulfills its goal in life only if it is true (Wedgwood, 2002; Adler, 2002). Thought, however, can be aimless. Musings, fantasies, and imaginings can be fully in order whether or not they are true. Understanding, the argument goes, is more like belief than like thought. Since there is such a thing as misunderstanding, understanding is subject to a standard of rightness. It has an aim. Misunderstanding evidently involves representing things as they are not. This suggests that the aim of understanding is truth. If so, it may seem, divergences from truth, even if unavoidable, are always cognitive defects.

The argument goes too fast. That misunderstanding involves representing things as they are not does not entail that whenever we represent things as they are not, we misunderstand them. At most it indicates that understanding is not indifferent to truth. But it does not follow that every sentence – or for that matter, any sentence – that figure in an understanding of how things are has its own truth as an objective. Understanding involves a network of commitments. It is not obvious that an aim of the network must be an aim of every, or indeed any, sentential node in the network. A goal of the whole need not be a goal of each of its parts. 'Understanding' is a cognitive success term but, in my view, not a factive. I do not expect these sketchy remarks to persuade anyone that I am right to loosen the tie between understanding and truth. My hope is that they are enough to persuade you that the jig is not yet up, that a willing suspension of disbelief is still in order.

Let us turn then to acceptance. To accept that *p*, I said, is to take it that *p*'s divergence from truth, if any, is negligible. In that case, *p* is true enough. Whether this is so is manifestly a contextual matter. A sentence can be true enough in some contexts but not in others. A variety of factors contribute constraints. Background assumptions play a role. 'A freely falling body falls at a rate of 32 ft/sec.^{2}' is true enough, assuming that the body is within the Earth's gravitational field, that nothing except the Earth exerts a significant gravitational force on the body, that the effects of non-gravitational forces are insignificant, and so on. But even when these assumptions are satisfied, the formula is not always true enough, since gravity varies slightly with longitude. Sometimes it matters where in the gravitational field the freely falling body is. Whether 'G=32ft./sec.^{2}' is true enough depends on what we want the formula for, what level of precision is needed for the calculation or explanation or account it figures in. There is no saying whether a given contention is true enough independently of answering, or presupposing an answer to the question 'True enough for what?' So purposes contribute constraints as well. Whether a given sentence is true enough depends on what ends its acceptance is supposed to serve.

Function is critical too. If to accept that *p* is simply to take it that *p*'s divergence from truth does not matter, it might seem that we accept all irrelevant propositions. None of my projects, cognitive or otherwise, is affected by the truth or falsity of the claim that Ethelred the Unready was a wise leader. So, its divergence from truth, if any, does not matter to me. Since acceptance can be tacit, the fact that I have never considered the issue is not decisive. Nevertheless it seems wrong to say that my indifference makes the claim true enough. The reason is that the contention is idle. It performs no function in my cognitive economy. Owing to my indifference, there is no answer to the question 'True enough for what?'

Context provides the framework. Purposes fix the ends. Function is a matter of means. The sentences that concern us tend not to have purposes or functions in isolation. Rather, they belong to and perform functions in larger bodies of discourse, such as arguments, explanations, or theories that have purposes. In accepting a sentence then we treat it in a given context as performing a function in a body of discourse which seeks to achieve some end. Whether 'G=32 ft./sec.^{2}' is acceptable depends on whether the body of discourse it figures in serves its cognitive purpose – whether, that is, it yields the understanding of the domain that we seek.

A statement's divergence from truth is negligible only if that divergence does not hinder its performing its cognitive function. Hence whether a contention is true enough depends not just on its having a function, but on what its function is – on what role it plays in the account it belongs to. To determine whether a statement is true enough, we thus need to identify its function. It might seem that for cognitive purposes only one function matters. If the criterion for felicity is being true enough, one might think, the function of all felicitous falsehoods is to approximate. There is, as it were, a tacit 'more or less' in front of all such claims. This will not do.

One reason is that the proposal is not sufficiently sensitive. Not all approximations perform the same function. Some are accepted simply because they are the best we can currently do. They are temporary expedients which we hope and expect eventually to replace with truths. We improve upon them by bringing them closer to the truth. Such approximations are, in Sellars's terms, promissory notes that remain to be discharged. The closer we get to the truth, the more of the debt is paid. They are, and are known to be, unsatisfactory. But not all approximations have this character. Some are preferable to the truths they approximate. For example, it is possible to derive a second-order partial differential equation that exactly describes fluid flow in a boundary layer. The equation, being non-linear, does not admit of an analytic solution. We can state the equation, but cannot solve it. This is highly inconvenient. To incorporate the truth into the theory would bring a line of inquiry to a halt, saying in effect: 'Here's the equation; it is impossible to solve.' Fluid dynamicists prefer a first-order partial differential equation, which approximates the truth, but admits of an analytical solution (Morrison, 1999, pp. 56–60). The solvable equation advances understanding by providing a close enough approximation that yields numerical values that can serve as evidence for or constraints on future theorizing. The approximation then is more fruitful than the truth. There is no hope that future inquiry will remedy the situation, for it is demonstrable that the second-order equation cannot be solved numerically, while the first-order equation can.[6] That reality forces such a choice upon us may be disappointing, but under the circumstances it does not seem intellectually disreputable to accept and prefer the tractable first-order equation. One might say that acceptance of the first-order approximation is only practical. It is preferable merely because it is more useful. This may be so, but the practice is a cognitive one. Its goal is to understand fluid flow in boundary layers. In cases like this, the practical and the theoretical inextricably intertwine. The practical value of the approximation is that it advances understanding of a domain. A felicitous falsehood thus is not always accepted only in default of the truth. Nor is its acceptance always 'second best'. It may make cognitive contributions that the unvarnished truth cannot match.

Moreover, not all felicitous falsehoods are approximations. Idealizations may be far from the truth, without thereby being epistemically inadequate. Political agents are not mutually disinterested. They are not nearly mutually disinterested. Nor is it the case that most political agents are mutually disinterested. There is no way I can see to construe Rawls's model as approximately true. Nevertheless, for Rawls's purposes, the characterization of political agents as mutually disinterested is felicitous if the features it highlights are constitutive of fair terms of cooperation underlying the basic structure of a democratic regime. There is no reason to think that in general the closer it is to the truth, the more felicitous a falsehood.

I suggest that felicitous falsehoods figure in cognitive discourse not as mistaken or inaccurate statements of fact, but as fictions. We are familiar with fictions and with reasoning about fictions. We regularly reason within the constraints dictated by a fiction, inferring for example, that Hamlet may not have been mad, but Ophelia surely was. We also reason (with more trepidation) from a fiction to matters of fact. We may come to see a pattern in the facts through the lens that a fiction supplies. For example, we might understand the contemporary youth gang conception of being 'dissed' by reference to the wrath of Achilles at Agamemnon's affront.[7] What is needed then is an account of how fictions can advance understanding.

David Lewis (1983) interprets fictional statements as descriptions of other possible worlds. We understand them in the same way that we understand ordinary statements of fact. For example, we understand the Sherlock Holmes stories in the same way we understand histories of Victorian England, the crucial difference being that the histories pertain to the actual world, while the stories pertain to other possible worlds. Lewis's realism about possible worlds is hard to countenance, but we need not enter into debates about it here. For even if we accept his metaphysics, a problem remains. It is puzzling how knowing what happens in another possible world can afford any insight into what happens in this world. Lewis measures the proximity of possible worlds in terms of similarity (Lewis 1973). The closest possible worlds are the ones most similar to the actual world. But even if one thinks that there is a non-question-begging way to assess the relative similarity of different possible worlds, the gap remains. It hard to see how the knowledge that a nearby world is populated by rational economic agents should contribute to our understanding of the economic behavior of actual human agents.

Kendall Walton (1990) construes fiction as make-believe. To understand a fiction is to make believe or pretend that it is true. Stephen Yablo uses Walton's account to underwrite fictionalism in the philosophy of mathematics (1998, 2002). We can, Yablo maintains, avoid ontological commitment to mathematical entities by construing mathematics as an elaborate, highly systematic fiction. Then in doing mathematics, we make believe that there are such entities and make believe that they are related to one another in the ways the theorems say. Although at first glance this seems promising, it faces two serious problems. First, what it is to pretend is by no means clear. Exactly how one can pretend that power sets or cube roots exist if they do not, is not obvious. Second, the problem we saw with Lewis's theory also plagues Walton and Yablo. It is not at all clear how a pretence illuminates reality – how, for example, pretending that human beings are rational economic agents provides any insight into actual human economic behavior.

Philip Kitcher (1993) suggests that scientific idealizations are stories whose referents are fixed by stipulation. The scientific statements involving the idealizations are true by convention. The gap remains. If a story is to advance scientific understanding we need to know the connection between the story and the facts. Otherwise, the realization that certain relations among pressure, temperature, and volume are true by stipulation in the story of the ideal gas leaves us in the dark about the relations among pressure, temperature, and volume in actual gases.

The gap can be bridged by appeal to exemplification, the device by which samples and examples highlight, exhibit, display, or otherwise make manifest some of their features (Goodman 1968, pp. 45–67). To make this out requires a brief discussion of the device. A commercial paint sample consists of a patch of color on a card. The patch is not merely an instance of the color, but a telling instance – an instance that exemplifies the color. By so doing, the sample equips us to recognize the color, to differentiate it from similar shades. The sample then affords epistemic access to the color. Although the patch on the sample card has a host of other features – size, shape, location, and so on – it standardly does not exemplify them. Exemplification is selective. It brings out some features of an exemplar by overshadowing, downplaying, or marginalizing others. Nothing in the nature of things dictates that the patch's color is worthy of selection, but its shape is not. What, if anything, an item exemplifies depends on its function. The very same item might perform any of a variety of functions. The patch on the sample card could be used to teach children what a rectangle is. In that case, it would exemplify its shape, not its color. The sample card could be used as a fan. Then the patch would not exemplify at all. Exemplification is not restricted to commercial and pedagogical contexts. Whatever an item exhibits, highlights, or displays, it exemplifies. A poem might exemplify its rhyme scheme, its imagery, or its style. A water sample might exemplify its mineral content, its flavor, or its impurities. Exemplification, I have argued elsewhere, is ubiquitous in art and science (Elgin 1996, pp. 171–183).

Treating paint samples as paradigmatic exemplars may encourage the idea that exemplified features are all like expanses of color – homogeneous qualities spread out before us, lacking depth and complexity, hence able to be taken in at a glance. Many are not like that. Pick up a rock containing iron ore. It might serve as a sample of iron, or of hematite, or of something that bears a striking resemblance to your high school algebra teacher. It can exemplify such features only where certain background assumptions are in place. Not just anyone looking at the rock could tell that it exemplified these features.

Moreover, although in principle any item can serve as an exemplar and any feature can be exemplified, a good deal of effort may be required to bring about the exemplification of a recondite feature. Some of that effort is mental. Just as we ignore the shape of the paint sample and focus on the color, we can ignore the fact that the rock looks like your algebra teacher and focus on its hardness. This is a start. But some irrelevant features so intricately intertwine with relevant ones that more drastic measures are called for. If we seek to exemplify recondite features of iron, mental agility alone may not be enough to bracket the effects of other minerals in the rock. So we refine the ore and filter out the impurities. The result of our efforts is pure iron. It is a product of a good deal of processing[8] which eliminates complicating factors and brings to the fore characteristics that are hard to detect and difficult to measure in nature. To facilitate the exemplification of the feature of interest, we do not just mentally sideline features we consider irrelevant, we physically remove some of them.

Even then, we do not just contemplate the bit of iron as we might a paint sample. We subject it to a variety of tests. We seek to produce circumstances where the features of interest stand out. We not only investigate the iron's behavior in standard conditions, we study what happens in extreme conditions – very high or low pressure or temperature, in a vacuum, under intense radiation, and so forth. Although we recognize that the test conditions do not ordinarily (or perhaps ever) obtain in nature, we take it that the behavior of the refined metal in the test conditions discloses something about the natural order. If so, by understanding what happens in the lab, we can understand something of what happens in the world. The connection is, of course, indirect. It involves a complicated extrapolation from situations and materials that are highly artificial and carefully contrived. One might argue that the lab itself is a fictional setting and the conclusions we draw about nature on the basis of our laboratory findings are projections from fiction to fact. I don't quite want to say that (although I suspect that Nancy Cartwright does). But I do want to point out that experimentation involves a lot of stage setting.

There is a tendency to think of experiments as processes that generate information, hence as ways to find things out. This of course is true. But it is worth noting that an experiment is not like an oracle,[9] or an anchorman, or a fortune cookie. It does not just issue a report stating its results. It displays them. It shows what happens to the magnetic properties of iron in conditions near the melting point. The experiment exemplifies its results.

No matter how carefully we set the stage, irrelevancies remain. We do not and ought not read every aspect of the experimental result back onto the world. Not only are there irrelevant features, there are issues about the appropriate vocabulary and level of precision for characterizing what occurs. The fact that the experiment occurred in Cleveland is unimportant. The fact that the sample has a certain mass or lattice structure may or may not be significant. The fact that the temperature is above 770° C may matter, while the fact that it was above 790° C does not. Some features of the iron in the experimental situation are telling features. Others are not. The telling features are the ones that the experiment discloses or makes manifest. By exemplifying certain features, the experiment brings them to light and affords epistemic access to them. That is its cognitive contribution. Other features, though equally real, are not exemplified. The experiment embodies an understanding of the phenomenon in question through its exemplification of telling features. By making these features manifest, it affords an understanding of the phenomenon.

If the cognitive contribution of an exemplar consists in the exemplification of select features, then anything that exemplifies exactly those features can, in a suitable context, make the same contribution. Return for a moment to the paint sample. I spoke of it as though it is a sample *of paint*, a telling instance of the stuff you might use to paint the porch. This is not true. The sample on the card does not consist of paint, but of an ink or dye of the same color as the paint whose color it exemplifies. If the sample were supposed to exemplify the paint itself, or the chemical features of the paint, the fact that it is not paint or has a different chemical composition would be objectionable. But since it exemplifies only the color, all that is needed is something that is the same color as the paint. The exemplar need not itself be paint. Similarly in scientific cases. Consider a DNA molecule that exemplifies its molecular structure. Anything that exemplifies the same structure has the capacity to perform the same function in our understanding of DNA. No more than the paint sample needs to consist of paint, does the exemplar of DNA's molecular structure need to consist of DNA. A schematic model that exemplifies the same features but has a different material (or even immaterial) substrate could to the job.

Here is where felicitous falsehoods enter the picture. Something other than paint can serve as a paint sample, affording epistemic access to a color also instantiated by the paint. Something other than a molecule can exemplify molecular structure, thereby affording epistemic access to a structure also instantiated by the molecule. A felicitous falsehood then is a fiction that exemplifies a feature in a context where the exemplification of that feature contributes to understanding. The utility of such a falsehood is plain. It is sometimes inconvenient, difficult, or even impossible to bring it about that the phenomena exemplify all and only the features that interest us. (DNA molecules are very small, charged pions are short lived.) If we introduce a falsehood that exemplifies those features – a bigger, longer-lasting model, for example – we can highlight them and display their significance for the understanding of the phenomenon in question. By exemplifying features it shares with the phenomena, a felicitous falsehood affords epistemic access to how things actually are. The camel's nose is now officially inside the tent.

There is more than one role that such fictions can play. Some serve as points of reference. We understand things in terms of them. In the simplest cases, like the model displaying the helical structure of the DNA molecule, they are simply schemata that exemplify factors they share with the phenomena they concern. They qualify as fictions because they diverge from the phenomena in unexemplified properties. (DNA molecules are not made of tinker toys.) In other cases, the connection to the facts is less direct. No real gas has the properties of the ideal gas. The model is illuminating though, because we understand the properties of real gases in terms of their deviation from the ideal. In such cases, understanding involves a pattern of schema and correction. We represent the phenomena with a schematic model, and introduce corrections as needed to closer accord with the facts. Different corrections are needed to accord with the behavior of different gases. The fictional ideal then serves as a sort of least common denominator that facilitates reasoning about and comparison of actual gases. We 'solve for' the simple case first, then introduce complications as needed.

Acknowledging the role of corrections might seem to suggest that the detour through fictions is just a circuitous route to the truth. Rather than a simple true description of the behavior of neon, we get a complicated truth that makes reference to deviations from some ideal. But the full cognitive contribution of the exercise resides in the truth, not the fiction. I don't think this is right for several reasons. The first is that sometimes the corrections that would be needed to yield a truth are unnecessary or even counterproductive. A fortiori arguments from limiting cases succeed because the corrections are unnecessary. If a consideration holds for one case, even if that case is a fiction, it holds for all. The multiple and complicate ways actual cases diverge from the fictive ideal make no difference. If Rawls's argument is sound, 'correcting for' ties of affection just muddies the waters. Nor is this the only case where fidelity to the facts can prove a hindrance. It follows from the ideal gas law that as volume goes to zero, pressure becomes infinite. This would not happen. Given a fixed number of molecules, pressure increases as volume decreases – not to infinity, but only to the point where the container explodes. No one of course denies this. But to understand what would happen in the limit, we need to prescind from such material inconveniences and pretend that the walls of the container are infinitely strong. We need then to introduce not corrections that bring us back to the facts, but further idealizations. A second reason is that the requisite corrections often yield not truths, but more refined models. They supplant one falsehood with another. A third reason is that even where corrections yield truths, the fiction may be more than a *façon de parler*. It can structure our understanding in a way that makes available information we would not otherwise have access to. If, e.g., we draw a smooth curve that skirts the data and construe the data as a complex of relevant and irrelevant factors (signal and noise), or construe a transaction in terms of an economic model overlaid with non-economic factors which skew the outcome, we impose an order on things, highlight certain aspects of the phenomena, reveal connections, patterns and discrepancies, and make possible insights that we could not otherwise obtain (Dennett 1991). We put ourselves in a position to see affinities between disparate occurrences by recognizing them as variations on a common theme.

Still, to say that felicitous falsehoods figure ineliminably in our understanding of certain phenomena is not to say that without them we would have no understanding whatsoever of those phenomena. Even without Snell's law, inspection and instantial induction would provide some insight into what happens when light passes between air and water, or between any other two specified media. What we would lack is a systematic understanding of how the several cases are alike. Felicitous falsehoods configure a domain, enabling us to characterize the phenomena in ways that would otherwise be unavailable. When, for example, we can construe seemingly divergent phenomena as variants of a common scheme, or as perturbations of a regular pattern, or as deviations from a simple norm, we see them and their relations to one another in a new light. We can discern systematic interconnections that direct inspection of the facts would not reveal. The fictions and the configurations of the domains that they engender provide conceptual resources for representing and reasoning about the phenomena in new and sometimes fruitful ways.

If I am right, not every theory is a conjunction of sentences, all of which are supposed to be true. Rather, a theory may be composed of both factual and fictional sentences, and the fictional sentences may play any of several different roles. This means that to understand what a theory conveys, and to understand the phenomena in terms of the theory requires sensitivity to the different roles the different sentences play. And to assess a theory requires determining whether the component sentences are true enough for the parts they are assigned to play. Yablo is investigating the metaphysical implications of the idea that fictions infuse even our must fundamental theories (Yablo 1998; 2002). I want to underscore the epistemological implications. One obvious consequence is that it is not plausible to think of an acceptable theory as a mirror of nature. Even if the goal of a theory is to afford an understanding of a range of facts, it need not approach or achieve that goal by providing a direct reflection of those facts.

I have argued that a variety of components of cognitively acceptable theories neither are nor purport to be true. Rather, they are fictions that shed light on the phenomena they concern. They thereby contribute to our understanding of those phenomena. Even if my account makes sense of models and idealizations in science, a worry remains. My position threatens to make the world safe for postmodernist claptrap. If truth is not required for epistemic acceptability, why isn't a flagrantly false account acceptable? What is the objection to claiming that a theory attesting to the healing powers of crystals is as acceptable as the theories constituting mainstream crystallography? We seem to lose a valuable resource if we can't simply say, 'Because it is false!' My seemingly wimpy requirement that an acceptable account must yield an understanding of how things are gives us what we need. An account that yields such an understanding must accommodate the facts in a domain. The accommodation may be indirect. Strictly false idealizations may be deployed. Detours through stylized facts may be made. The justification for the falsehoods is that they figure in accounts that make sense of the facts. A cognitively acceptable account sheds light on its subject. Where felicitous falsehoods are involved, the light may be oblique.

A theory can claim to make sense of a range of facts only if it is factually defeasible – only if, that is, there is some reasonably determinate, epistemically accessible factual arrangement which, if it were found to obtain, would discredit the theory. A felicitous falsehood is acceptable only if the theory or system of thought it belongs to accommodates the epistemically accessible facts. Exactly what this requires needs to be spelled out. The usual considerations about evidence, simplicity, scope, and so forth come into play. Even though some of the sentences in a theory are not supposed to be true, the way the world is constrains the acceptability of the theory they figure in. If, for example, evidence shows that friction plays a major role in collisions between gas molecules, then unless compensating adjustments are made elsewhere, theories that model collisions as perfectly elastic spheres will be discredited. An acceptable theory must be at least as good as any available alternative, when judged in terms of currently available standards of cognitive goodness. So such a theory would also be discredited by a theory that better satisfied those standards. Neither a defeated nor an indefeasible theory is tenable. Because it is indifferent to evidence, claptrap is indefeasible. Hence it is untenable. I said earlier that even in theories that include felicitous falsehoods truth plays a role. We see now what the role is. A factually defeasible theory has epistemically accessible implications which, if found to be false, discredit the theory. So a defeasible theory, by preserving a commitment to testable consequences retains a commitment to truth. My account then does not turn science into a genre of fiction. Quine said that the sentences of a theory face the tribunal of experience as a corporate body (Quine, 1961, p. 41). Although he recognized that not all the members of the corporation could be separately tested against experience, he probably believed that all were supposed to be fine, upstanding truths. I suggest that this is not so. An acceptable theory must make its case before the tribunal of experience. But the members of the corporation are more various and some a bit shadier than Quine suspected.[10]

Notes

1. I use the term 'theory' broadly, to comprehend the ways mature sciences and other disciplines account for the phenomena in their domains. Under my usage, a physical theory would include its models rather than being distinct from them.
2. I do not have strong intuitions about this case, but I do not think it is clearly wrong to say that the cat has such a belief.
3. Whether so-called ceteris paribus laws are really laws is a subject of controversy. See, for example, *Erkenntnis* 57, 2002, for a range of papers on the issue. Although for brevity I speak of them as laws, for my purposes, nothing hangs on whether the generalizations in questions really are laws, at least insofar as this is an ontological question. I am interested in the role such generalizations play in ongoing science. Whether or not they can (in some sense of 'can') be replaced by generalizations where all the caveats and restrictions are spelled out, in practice scientists typically make no effort to do so. Nor, often, do they know (or care) how to do so.
4. *i* and *r* are the angles made by the incident beam to the normal and n_1 and n_2 are the refractive indices of the two media.
5. 'The profit rate is the level of profits in the economy relative to the value of capital stock.' (Bannock et al. 1998, p. 397).

6. Conceivably, of course, the equations in question will be superceded by some other understanding of the subject, but the fact that the equation we consider true does not have an analytical solution provides no reason to think so. Nor does it provide reason to think that the considerations that supersede it will be mathematically more tractable, much less that in the long run science will be free of all such irksome equations.
7. I am indebted to Amelie Rorty for this example.
8. This is why Nancy Cartwright thinks the laws of physics lie. The laws are developed on the basis of, and are strictly true only of the processed samples, not their naturally occurring counterparts.
9. Actually, of course, I don't know how oracles are supposed to operate. I have always assumed that they simply emit true sentences like 'Socrates is the wisest of men.'
10. I would like to thank Jonathan Adler, Nancy Nersessian, Amelie Rorty, Robert Schwartz, Bas van Fraassen, Stephen Yablo, and members of my audiences at Bryn Mawr College, Tufts University, and the 2003 Rutgers Epistemology Conference for helpful comments on earlier drafts of this paper.

References

Adler, Jonathan. (2002) *Belief's Own Ethics*, Cambridge: MIT.

Bannock, Graham, R.E., Baxter, Evan Davis. (1998) *Dictionary of Economics*, New York: John Wiley and Sons.

Bonjour, Laurence. (1985) *The Structure of Empirical Knowledge*, Cambridge, MA: Harvard.

Cartwright, Nancy. (1983) *How the Laws of Physics Lie*, Oxford: Oxford.

Cohen, L. Jonathan. (1992) *An Essay on Belief and Acceptance*, Oxford: Clarendon.

Dennett, Daniel. (1991) 'Real Patterns,' *Journal of Philosophy* 88: 27–51.

Elgin, Catherine Z. (1996) *Considered Judgment*, Princeton: Princeton.

Goldman, Alvin. (1999) *Knowledge in a Social World*, Oxford: Clarendon.

Goodman, Nelson. (1968) *Languages of Art*, Indianapolis: Hackett.

Kitcher, Philip. (1993) *The Advancement of Science*, Oxford: Oxford.

Lehrer, Keith. (1986) 'The Coherence Theory of Knowledge,' *Philosophical Topics* 14: 5–25.

Lewis, David. (1983) 'Truth in Fiction,' *Philosophical Papers I*, Oxford: Oxford, pp. 261–281.

Lewis, David. (1973) *Counterfactuals*, Cambridge: Harvard.

Morrison, Margaret. (1999) 'Models as Autonomous Agents,' *Models as Mediators*, ed. Mary S. Morgan and Margaret Morrison, Cambridge: Cambridge, pp. 38–65.

Quine, W. V. (1961) 'Two Dogmas of Empiricism,' *From a Logical Point of View*, (New York: Harper & Row, pp. 20–46.

Sklar, Lawrence. (1999) 'Philosophy of Science, ' *Cambridge Dictionary of Philosophy*, ed. Robert Audi, Cambridge: Cambridge, pp. 700–704.

Sosa, Ernest. (2000) 'Skepticism and Contextualism, *Skepticism*, ed. Ernest Sosa and Enrique Villanueva, Boston: Blackwell, pp. 1–18.

Stalnaker, Robert. (1987) *Inquiry*, Cambridge: MIT Press.

Wedgwood, Ralph. (2002) 'The Aim of Belief,' *Philosophical Perspectives* 16: 267–297.

Walton, Kendall. (1990) *Mimesis as Make-Believe*, Cambridge, MA: Harvard.

Yablo, Stephen. (2002) 'Abstract Objects,' *Philosophical Issues* 12: 220–240.

Yablo, Stephen. (1998) 'Does Ontology Rest on a Mistake?' *Proceedings of the Aristotelian Society*, Supplementary Volume 72: 229–261.

Index